Art in Germany 1909–1936
From Expressionism to Resistance

The Marvin and Janet Fishman Collection

International Transportation provided by

Lufthansa
German Airlines

Art in Germany 1909–1936

From Expressionism to Resistance

The Marvin and Janet Fishman Collection

Reinhold Heller

with a foreword by Eberhard Roters
and contributions by Stephanie T. D'Alessandro,
Corinne D. Granof, Amy T. Schlegel,
Bessie Tina Yarborough

Prestel

This book was published in conjunction with the exhibition *From Expressionism to Resistance: Art in Germany 1909–1936—The Marvin and Janet Fishman Collection*, organized by the Milwaukee Art Museum and shown there from 6 December 1990 to 3 February 1991.

Also shown at: Berlinische Galerie, Museum für Moderne Kunst, Photographie und Architektur im Martin-Gropius-Bau, Berlin (1 March–28 April 1991); Schirn Kunsthalle, Frankfurt am Main (7 June–18 August 1991); Kunsthalle, Emden (29 August–29 October 1991); The Jewish Museum, New York (21 November 1991–25 January 1992); High Museum, Atlanta (6 June– 30 August 1992).

Milwaukee Art Museum
750 North Lincoln Memorial Drive
Milwaukee, Wisconsin 53202
U.S.A.

Published by Prestel Verlag
Mandlstrasse 26, D-8000 Munich 40
Federal Republic of Germany

Distributed in continental Europa by Prestel Verlag,
Verlegerdienst München GmbH & Co KG,
Gutenbergstrasse 1, D-8031 Gilching, Federal Republic of Germany

Distributed in the USA and Canada by te Neues Publishing Company,
15 East 76th Street,
New York, NY 10021, USA

Distributed in Japan by YOHAN-Western Publications Distribution Agency,
14–9 Okubo 3–chome, Shinjuku-ku, J-Tokyo 169

Distributed in the United Kingdom, Ireland and all other countries by Thames & Hudson Limited,
30–34 Bloomsbury Street, London WC1B 3QP, England

Library of Congress Cataloging-in-Publication Data

Art in Germany 1909–1936: from expressionism to resistance: the Marvin and Janet Fishman collection/Reinhold Heller, with contributions by Stephanie D'Alessandro . . . (et al.).
p. cm.
Catalogue of an exhibition held at the Milwaukee Art Museum, Dec. 6, 1990–Feb. 3, 1991, and at other 5 German and U.S. museums, Mar. 1, 1991–Aug. 30, 1992.
Includes bibliographical references.
ISBN 0-944110-02-9 (pbk.)—ISBN 3-7913-1098-4 (hard)
1. Art, German—Exhibitions. 2. Art, Modern—20th century—German—Exhibitions. 3. Fishman, Marvin—Art collections—Exhibitions. 4. Fishman, Janet—Art collections—Exhibitions. 5. Art—Private collections—Wisconsin—Milwaukee—Exhibitions.
I. Heller, Reinhold. II. Milwaukee Art Museum. III. Title: Art in Germany 1909–1936.
N6868.F74 1990   90-60653
                                                                            CIP
Library of Congress Catalogue Card Number 90-60653

Translations from the German by Reinhold Heller, unless otherwise indicated.
Copy editing: Sue Taylor and Sally Ruth May
Photography: Dedra Walls
Typesetting: Fertigsatz GmbH, Munich
Offset lithography: Karl Dörfel GmbH, Munich
Printing and binding: Passavia GmbH, Passau

Printed in the Federal Republic of Germany
ISBN 0-944110-02-9 (softcover edition, not available to the trade)
ISBN 3-7913-1098-4 (hardcover edition)

Contents

Preface

The Milwaukee Art Museum is pleased to present this exhibition of the collection of Marvin and Janet Fishman. Not only is it a collection with a distinctive focus and many major paintings well known as monuments of German artistic expression, but it is also that most rare of collections—one which brings us new knowledge and insight into a time and a culture. The Fishman Collection, formed over a period of some twenty years, has been organized with a thoroughness of both scholarship and connoisseurship which is seldom encountered. Founded on an in-depth representation of independent German Expressionist Ludwig Meidner, the collection has grown to include works of classic German Expressionism (Erich Heckel, Max Pechstein, Conrad Felixmüller), and an even greater concentration of the so-called *Neue Sachlichkeit* (New Objectivity) movement of the 1920s and 1930s (George Grosz, Otto Dix, Christian Schad, Rudolf Schlichter, and others). Also particularly important for American audiences is the number of relatively unknown figures, such as Karl Hubbuch, Jeanne Mammen, Felix Nussbaum, Bruno Voigt, and Richard Ziegler. These artists add greatly to our understanding of the fabric of a period of great turmoil: the economic and political anarchy of the Weimar Republic and the rise of Nazism. All these artists are artists of protest; the pre-World War I German Expressionists protested against the repressions of bourgeois life, and the artists between the wars against the failures of capitalism, the excesses of militarism, and the growing threat of Nazi prejudice and brutality. Although the date of the latest painting in the exhibition, Max Beckmann's *Bar, Brown* of 1945, coincides with the year of Germany's defeat, the real drama of the collection is the reflection of the years leading up to World War II and the reaction of artists to pressures to conform and to the confusion of a troubled nation. The triumph of the Fishman Collection, and the reason it deserves to be widely seen both in this country and abroad, lies not only in the masterpieces it contains, but also in its presentation of artists participating in a personal and societal battle for life and expression.

My first and most profound expression of appreciation must go to Marvin and Janet Fishman, longtime donors and supporters of the Milwaukee Art Museum. Their collection of works by Ludwig Meidner was shown at the museum in 1976. Janet Fishman served as chairman of the museum's docent program, 1980 through 1982, as Chairman of the Second National Docent Symposium, held at the museum in 1983, and as a member of the Board of Trustees from 1982 to 1985. She continues to teach in the docent training and class programs. The Fishmans responded positively to my suggestion in 1987 that an exhibition originally planned by the Madison Art Center be transferred to the Milwaukee Art Museum. Mr. Fishman's requirement was that the exhibition travel nationally and, if possible, internationally, and that the catalogue provide clear documentation of the collection. Marvin Fishman has stayed exceptionally close to the entire project, and his thoroughness and attention to detail is reflected in the catalogue. He committed countless hours to the confirmation of facts of biography and provenance, and to advising the conservation, framing, design, and photographic staff. It must also be acknowledged that it was through the many national and international friendships the Fishmans have formed that the exhibition tour was made possible. This exhibition, like the collection itself, has been a labor of passion, or perhaps even obsession, both to build a meaningful statement and to share it with the public.

My second debt of extraordinary gratitude is to Reinhold Heller, Professor of Art History at the University of Chicago, who has been involved in this project since its inception in 1986. Dr. Heller, a widely published authority on Edvard Munch, northern Symbolism, and pre-1945 German art, wrote the original prospectus of the exhibition, worked with Mr. Fishman to make the final selection of exhibited works, researched and wrote the majority of entries for the catalogue, and provided both a historical essay and an interview with the collectors. Reinhold Heller's ceaseless dedication to the project gave voice to the personal passions and enthusiasms of the collectors and added a context for their communication to the public and to posterity.

My other thanks will necessarily be more brief, but I would like to acknowledge the staff of Prestel Verlag, Munich, for their dedication to bringing this project to realization. My thanks also go to Professor Dr. Eberhard Roters, former director of the Berlinische Galerie, Berlin, and one of the foremost authorities on German art between the wars, for his foreword reflecting the perception of this collection from a German viewpoint. Sue Taylor of the University of Chicago has capably acted as editor of the initial manuscript and entries, while Sally Ruth May edited the biographies and bibliography.

At the Milwaukee Art Museum, Chief Curator James Mundy managed the early phases of this project, including the initial communications with participating institutions. Executive Director Christopher Goldsmith was instrumental in the processes of budgeting the tour and reviewing contracts. Financial Development Director Lucia Petrie coordinated contracts with various potential supporters, including Lufthansa Airlines. Registrar Leigh Albritton provided invaluable assistance in arranging shipping and budget information. Associate Conservator James De Young reviewed all works for conservation purposes, treated a number of works on paper, and supervised the matting and reframing of more than one hundred works. Coordinator of Media Dedra Walls provided photographs of the majority of the works in the exhibition. A number of other members of staff have given additional support to all phases of this exhibition, from handling and shipping to installation and publicity. Like all major exhibitions, this one could not have been achieved without the commitment of the entire staff.

Finally, I must thank the representatives of the participating institutions: from the Berlinische Galerie, Director Jörn Merkert and Dr. Ursula Prinz; Christoph Vitali, Director of the Schirn Kunsthalle in Frankfurt; Mr. Henri Nannen and Mrs. Eske Ebert of the Kunsthalle in Emden; Joan H. Rosenbaum, Director of The Jewish Museum in New York; Gudmund Vigtel, Director of the High Museum, Atlanta, Georgia, for making the national and international tour a reality. In this regard I would also like to express my deep appreciation for the support of Lufthansa Airlines, which provided the overseas transportation. Charles Croce, Manager, Public Relations, USA East and National Programs; Nic Ilijine, Manager, Public Relations International; and Mary P. Phillips, Public Relations Manager, USA Central Region, were especially helpful in achieving this support.

It is particularly fitting that the Milwaukee Art Museum's first internationally touring exhibition be of German art from a collection in the city. Milwaukee enjoys a rich German heritage and the museum is fortunate in possessing an exceptional collection of German art, ranging from the genre and naturalistic works of the nineteenth century represented in the von Schleinitz Collection, to numerous examples of major German Expressionist works, largely from the collections of Mrs. Harry Lynde Bradley and Mr. and Mrs. William D. Vogel, to recent acquisitions of works by such figures as Joseph Beuys, Georg Baselitz, Gerhard Richter, Sigmar Polke, Anselm Kiefer, and Jörg Immendorff. The promised gift by Mrs. Esther Leah Ritz of her extraordinary collection of German Expressionist art, particularly strong in prints and works on paper, is another reason to celebrate the museum's representation of the German artistic heritage. Marvin and Janet Fishman have followed this heritage into the art of the 1920s and 1930s with an unprecedented degree of scholarship and commitment. The Milwaukee community, and now the world, owes them a great debt for their strength to form, and willingness to share, their vision.

RUSSELL BOWMAN
Director
Milwaukee Art Museum

Collectors' Acknowledgments

Our pleasure and judgment in the pursuit of our collection has been fostered by numerous friendships with collectors and scholars in both the United States and Germany. Among American collectors who first shared their knowledge and enthusiasm for modern German art with us, we wish to remember above all Dr. and Mrs. Gerhard Strauss and D. Thomas Bergen. Professor Charles Haxthausen of the University of Minnesota, formerly Director of the Busch-Reisinger Museum, provided our first important dealer contacts in Germany. Fellow American collectors, such as Granvil and Marcia Specks of Evanston, Illinois, and Robert Rifkind of Los Angeles, whose connoisseurship and world-class collection of German Expressionist art is truly unique, widen the circle of people who have made our endeavors in this area so rewarding.

Among German collectors, our collection has been fostered by friendships with Klaus and Jutta Osterhof of Berlin, Dr. Paul Tauchner of Munich, and Dr. Wolfgang Gawin of Coburg. In Siegfried and Gesche Poppe and Titus and Brigitte Felixmüller of Hamburg we have found particularly gracious friends. Numerous German scholars also deepened our appreciation of this material, especially the legendary Professor Dr. Eberhard Roters, who has kindly written a foreword to this catalogue, Bernhard Schulz and Dr. Dominik Bartmann of Berlin,

Professor Dr. Wieland Schmied of Munich, Max K. Pechstein of Hamburg, Henri Nannen of Emden, Dr. Patricia Rochard and Dr. Francois Lachenal of Ingelheim, as well as Dr. Manfred Meinz, Director, and Dr. Karl Georg Kaster, Curator, of the Kulturgeschichtliches Museum, Osnabrück. As experts in the art they offer, dealers Remmert und Barth in Düsseldorf, the Schlichtenmaiers in Grafenau, Bodo Niemann in Berlin, and Michael Pabst and Dr. Richard Hiepe in Munich have been continually helpful, while Hans Brockstedt has always been a knowledgeable and gracious host in Hamburg.

Lastly, it must be said that, while we made many close "art friends" among collectors, museum professionals, and dealers in both Europe and the United States, our most precious memories are of warm visits to Munich spent with Michael and Celina Hasenclever and their children, Silvia and Bennie. Those many hours over meals in their home and gallery, exploring shows and always discussing art, will forever be treasured. Michael, thank you for all the time you spent teaching us. Without your profound assistance our collection could never have assumed its present quality or scope. This exhibition and its catalogue are "gewidmet" to you.

MARVIN AND JANET FISHMAN

Foreword

I do not recall exactly when I heard the names of Marvin and Janet Fishman for the first time. However, I well remember getting to know the Fishmans personally at a reception held in honor of West German Chancellor Helmut Schmidt on the occasion of the exhibition *Expressionism: A German Intuition*, which the Guggenheim Museum in New York organized in the winter of 1980. By this time, we knew more about each other, for I had sent them some catalogues of exhibitions held at the Berlinische Galerie, of which I was director, and had heard more about their collection. We hit it off immediately, quickly compared notes, and then embraced. But though it was a very warm encounter, it was also a very brief one, taking place as it did amidst the hectic throng that inevitably accompanies such receptions. Marvin Fishman insisted that I pay him and his wife a visit in Milwaukee, and I agreed to do so. Unfortunately, ill health prevented me from going, as my doctor forbade me to fly across the Atlantic. The Fishmans then visited me in Berlin. They generously promised me help in preparing the exhibition *Ich und die Stadt* (*The City and I*), which the Berlinische Galerie was organizing in the Martin Gropius Building to mark Berlin's 750th anniversary. As I was unable to travel myself, Bernhard Schulz, my assistant on this project, went to the United States and, while there, called on the Fishmans in Milwaukee. "So how was it?" I asked him on his return. "Pictures!" he exclaimed, still overwhelmed by it all. "Pictures everywhere. The whole house is full of pictures, from top to bottom. I can hardly recall a single space where there wasn't a picture. The works that Marvin and Janet Fishman own would all do the Berlinische Galerie proud." Schulz brought back with him an impressive list of works that we could borrow. After the exhibition opened, the Fishmans came to Berlin again, and we spent several stimulating hours together viewing the paintings. Marvin Fishman halted in front of one of the most outstanding works from their collection, Meidner's hallucinatory, frantic self-portrait from 1913 (cat. no. 100), considered it for some time, then beamed at me and said: "He looks a little bit *meshuge*." He had hit the nail right on the head.

We were soon linked by a common bond when we discovered that we shared the same tastes. We had a special liking for the world-famous artists of Expressionism and *Neue Sachlichkeit*. But our joint predilection went beyond that to encompass artists about whom people had stopped talking long ago and whose work had sunk into oblivion after World War II. Their works were no longer on show, so no one paid attention to these artists, and only now are they beginning to arouse public interest again. We were glad that we had acquired works by such artists at a time when hardly anyone else was aware of them. Like fellow conspirators, we compared and discussed our acquisitions and congratulated each other on our surreptitious spoils. For example, I had just purchased for the Berlinische Galerie a number of pastel drawings by the painter Richard Ziegler which he did in Berlin in the mid-twenties. But the Fishmans were able to trump that: their collection included Ziegler's principal work, the painting *Young Widow* of 1925 (cat. no. 186), which he loaned to us for our exhibition.

What is so astounding and wonderful about the Fishman Collection is precisely the fact that two Americans one day discovered a love for twentieth-century art and went foraging in pastures where, apart from a handful of insiders, very few had grazed, especially in the marginal regions. They developed a passion for German urban Expressionism, Verism, and *Neue Sachlichkeit*, which they then single-mindedly pursued. With great zeal they plunged themselves into their chosen task and did the rounds of the European exhibitions, art dealers, galleries, and auction houses. In doing so, they trusted their eyes rather than their ears. In other words, they did not set about collecting "names"; instead, they collected what they saw, what they liked, all the while guided only by their personal intuition. In this way, a collection grew, assembled by Americans in the USA, which is German in the best sense of the word, a collection of German art, predominantly of the period from 1910 to the late 1920s, which is both full of social comment and reflective of its time. The wide-ranging Fishman Collection provides us with a varied and highly vital all-round view of the classic era of modern German art. Many a German museum would relish the prospect of possessing such an overview. These collectors have shown us the way, set up a standard, not to teach us or to prove anything to us—nothing could be further from their intention—but simply because it gave them such a thrill. These Americans were not only the frontrunners in rediscovering Meidner, they also led the field in reappraising German art in general of the decades prior to 1933.

The importance and scope of the Meidner works make them the natural centerpiece of the Fishman Collection. Gathered around them are works by Otto Dix, George Grosz, Conrad Felixmüller, Rudolf Schlichter, and Georg Tappert, but not only these: there are also works by artists who are less well known or who have been rediscovered only during the last ten to fifteen years. Among these are Albert Birkle, Heinrich Ehmsen, Jeanne Mammen, Bruno Voigt, and Richard Ziegler.

When I remarked earlier that the Marvin and Janet Fishman collection is the envy of many a German museum, this, of course, includes the Berlinische Galerie. But ours is an envy based on cordial friendship, for we can only be grateful that such a magnificent rival collection exists at all, especially as most of the works owned by the Fishmans were produced in Berlin. We couple our thanks with our congratulations to these avid art collectors for having put together such a fine collection. They have realized a lifelong ambition and, at the same time, have rendered the art world an incalculable service.

EBERHARD ROTERS

Interview with Marvin and Janet Fishman

Reinhold Heller

RH: You have formed a remarkable collection of German art, focused on works created during, and immediately prior to, the Weimar Republic. It was a time of immense political and aesthetic ferment in Germany, which produced some of the most intense images in twentieth-century art, images that addressed such issues of fundamental existential significance as war and violence, human sexuality and its perversions, greed and death. While demonstrating technical and formal mastery, much of this imagery is unpleasant in its associations and connotations. This may, in part, account for the fact that it is unusual for collectors to concern themselves with this field, especially in the United States, where I believe your collection is unique in its focus. Indeed, in its thorough analysis of 1920s German art, the collection is unusual the world over. Its closest parallel is West Berlin's Berlinische Galerie, which functions as a celebratory collection of Berlin's artistic heritage in this century and has a particular focus in the Weimar years. Because your collection is so exceptional, I would like to try to find out what contributed to its very special configuration and also what its precise significance is for you.

I believe neither of you has a formal educational background in art.

MF: Yes, that's true.

RH: Marvin, you were known locally largely as a successful realtor and building contractor and for bringing a professional basketball team, the National Basketball Association's Milwaukee Bucks, to your city in 1968.

MF: Yes.

RH: How and when did you become interested in collecting art?

MF: It was while Janet and I were attending the University of Wisconsin at Madison in the late 1940s. We acquired a taste for art and started visiting exhibitions. After we graduated, we began to buy art, inexpensive art by graduate students. We'd participate in some of their art functions while visiting Madison to attend university sporting events. And that gave us the impetus to pursue collecting.

JF: We really didn't have money to spend on art just after we got married.

MF: We started collecting work by local artists, Wisconsin artists who are of regional importance but don't have a national reputation: Karl Priebe and Aaron Bohrod, the former artist in residence at Madison. Then we visited some art collectors here in Milwaukee—the Gerhard Strausses, the Abraham Melameds, both already possessing large collections.

RH: Can you characterize their collections?

JF: At that time, the Strausses were collecting primarily contemporary art, such as Hans Hofmann, but they also had a marvelous Meidner and a Pechstein. The Melameds, too, had contemporary works, by Sidney Goodman, but also some wonderful Dubuffets and a fine selection of Cubist works, mostly Braque. We enjoyed seeing these collections, and we listened to their owners. We learned from these collectors. They were very generous and kind. They told us which dealers to go to. They let us use their names. We went to New York to Klaus Perls, Pierre Matisse, Alan Frumkin, Richard Feigen, and Terry Din-

tenfass. Those collectors probably saved us from making lots of mistakes.

We bought a lot of different things. We didn't know yet in what direction to go. We bought eclectically and our collection lacked a focus. But everything we purchased was high-quality, so that when we did know where we were going, we were able to sell the works that didn't belong to our field.

MF: Let me tell you what we bought. For example, we purchased two Calders from Perls in New York. Typical Calders. Watercolors or gouaches with squiggly things in the middle. But they were good Calders, very colorful.

JF: And we bought a beautiful Monet pastel, an early Schiele oil of his uncle. Things like that.

MF: We bought from Pierre Matisse one of the Miró *anti-plates*, a fine and rare piece. Earlier, we had bought a Miró *anti-plate* here in Milwaukee, at Irving Gallery. They're really original sculptures, not decorative plates or ceramic pieces. We went back later to Pierre Matisse to buy another, but they'd all gone.

JF: We bought the Feininger watercolor, *Battle Fleet* [Fig. 1], on that same trip to New York.

MF: Yes, a dealer who had sold us a doubtful Courbet made up for it by selling the Feininger to us. It was in 1969 and we paid $ 10,000, which probably set a world record for a Feininger watercolor back then.

JF: So that 1969 trip was our first serious one.

RH: What attracted you to the Feininger? It is unlike other works you were buying then.

MF: Yes, we had heard of Feininger's work and seen it in museums and collections, of course. While he was known at that time, he wasn't appreciated as he is today.

JF: It was just a splendid watercolor, so bright and fresh in appearance, unlike any others we knew by Feininger.

MF: The stylized figures of people of the period intrigued us. Most of the pieces we had seen before then were examples of Feininger's "straight-line" watercolors.

JF: The late Peg Bradley owned about twelve Feiningers, all from the same period. She later donated her large and impressive collection to the Milwaukee Art Museum.

MF: Those were some of our initial purchases. I was a general contractor, and built about 100 houses a year in a set style. And I didn't want to take money out of my business, so I went to the bank. For example, when we bought the Feininger, we borrowed the full purchase price, then paid it back as the opportunity arose. I think we were among the first collectors to avail ourselves of bank lending for our purchases.

RH: When you began focusing your collection during the 1970s, it was in the direction of German Expressionism, with particular emphasis on the work of Ludwig Meidner. Meidner was certainly little known in the United States then, and in Germany, although not unknown, he had not yet been recognized as a major innovator of Expressionism, but rather tended to be considered a minor follower of the *Brücke*

Fig. 1 Lyonel Feininger,
Battle Fleet (Schlachtflotte), 1915.
Watercolor on paper, 21 x 25.5 cm
(8¼ x 10 in.)

painters. As a matter of fact, he was probably best known, not for his Expressionist paintings, but for his essay on the painting of the modern metropolis, which, ironically, was viewed as heralding the concerns of *Neue Sachlichkeit*. Despite this, you began to collect Meidner and formed the largest private collection of his work anywhere, with high-quality paintings and drawings from throughout his career. Your collection also included his prints, most of which you have now donated to various museums, and works of documentary significance. You now have what is surely one of the finest libraries of works on, or related to, Meidner, as well as documents, such as the cover drawing for the first Meidner monograph, published in 1919 in the *Junge Kunst* series by Klinkhardt & Biermann [Fig. 2]. Indeed, I first came to know of your collection as a Meidner collection, and it is with his work that the collection continues to be most frequently identified as you contributed major loans to recent exhibitions devoted to, or including, Meidner. An almost symbiotic relationship appears to exist between Meidner and you. Again, could you tell me how this came about?

JF: We got to know Meidner's work through the Strausses, who owned the 1913 self-portrait *My Nocturnal Visage* [cat. no. 100]. It hung in their bedroom, and Marvin was as if hypnotized by it. We used to visit the Strausses, and Marvin would disappear to stand in front of it, not saying a word, admiring the painting and saying he wished we had it. He would momentarily ignore us while we visited another room.

MF: I don't remember being so rude! But I did admire the painting. It is so powerful and intense. Meidner suffered so when he was painting, often not eating or drinking, just painting all through the night. When the Strausses moved to Florida, they couldn't take along all their collection and decided to sell part of it.

JF: They knew how much Marvin admired and really coveted the painting, and so they offered it to us.

MF: They felt it was a museum piece, but didn't want the painting to end up in a German museum, since Meidner, as a Jew, had been forced to leave Germany. We had already begun buying Meidner by then, and they knew we would appreciate the painting and look after it. The Strausses bought it from Richard Feigen, who, in the late 1950s, was the first American dealer to be interested in Meidner and contacted the artist in an attempt to organize an exhibition of his work. Meidner felt disappointed because Feigen, having assembled some of Meidner's greatest works from private collectors, didn't hold the exhibition after all. So Meidner continued to suffer from lack of exposure.

RH: Meidner wrote a marvelous letter to Feigen in which he complained of contemporary art's focus on abstraction and the resultant neglect of figurative artists such as himself. Feigen's championship, whether we now see it as self-serving or not, was out of character with the art scene of the time, and he would surely have found few buyers for Meidner's work in America then. After all, the Fishmans and Robert Rifkind weren't buying Meidner in the 1950s.

MF: That's true. The Strausses purchased Meidner's self-portrait, but no museums were buying Meidners at that time, and there were hardly any collectors interested in him either. When we started collecting Meidner, his works were available at a few small galleries in Germany and once in a while at auctions, but there was little demand for them and they weren't expensive. There was a large Meidner collection put together by D. Thomas Bergen, which we saw while it was at Notre Dame University. He was very interested in Meidner when we met him. He exhibited his collection at Notre Dame and, along with pieces from our collection, at the University of Michigan. He used to share his knowledge of Meidner with us. When he put his collection up for sale, at Christie's in London in the late seventies, we were able to bid on major pieces from it. The sale set price records for Meidner's work, but it was still cheap, much less expensive than that of other major Expressionists. We bought many Meidners at that London sale, both for us and for Bob Rifkind, who was also quick to recognize the artist's major significance.

Interview with Marvin and Janet Fishman 11

Fig. 2 Ludwig Meidner, *Self-Portrait: Cover Design for Lothar Brieger's Meidner Monograph in the Series "Junge Kunst"* (*Selbstporträt: Umschlagszeichnung zu Lothar Briegers Meidner-Buch in der Reihe "Junge Kunst"*), 1919. Brush and ink over pencil, 28 x 20 cm (11 x 7⁷/₈ in.)

RH: During the seventies, you collected other German Expressionist works, the Heckel and Pechstein paintings, for example [cat. nos. 59, 126]. Your interest in German art, might it have a root in Milwaukee's long history of ties with Germany, as a city originally settled and built largely by Germans and still reflecting major German cultural influences today? The German presence, I'm sure, was even more pronounced before World War II. Today, the Milwaukee Art Museum has one of the finest collections of German Expressionist painting in the country, an enviable collection which more famous American museums cannot match, and which is largely composed of donations from Milwaukee collectors. The Museum also has the von Schleinitz Collection of nineteenth-century German art, which includes works of high quality by major artists, along with wonderfully anecdotal paintings that tell us about the taste of German-Americans prior to World War I. Such an intense concentration of German art in one museum is unequalled elsewhere in the United States.

JF: We became interested in the Expressionists, as we said, through Milwaukee collections, including the works now in the Museum. I was also a docent at the Milwaukee Art Museum, so I came to know these paintings well. I researched them in order to be able to explain them to visitors. We were attracted to German art because it was so powerful and rich in content, not like the French works we had collected previously.

RH: You don't regret no longer having the Monet because it didn't fit in with the direction your collection was taking? Janet, it sounded to me earlier as if you, in particular, liked that pastel and maybe wish it were still in your collection.

JF: As you know, the collection of German works has been Marvin's chief concern. I myself have formed a collection of contemporary studio glass, which has also been in museum exhibitions, and I essentially curate that collection. But we make the decisions together about

what to buy. We bought the Monet when we were simply collecting works that appealed to us, eclectically, without regard to the cohesion of the collection. Once we decided to focus the collection in German Expressionism and art of the 1920s, the Monet no longer contributed to it, so we both decided to trade it. It was a view from Antibes and was a beautiful work. Its colors and manner of execution were truly remarkable, and it was a significant picture. But once you had looked at it and appreciated it, that's all there was. I mean, once you learn about how light reflects on a surface and how colors interact, it seems to me there is nothing more to consider. It didn't engage the mind the way the German paintings do.

MF: French paintings tend to be wonderful to look at, and interesting for how they're painted and composed, but they generally lack the Germans' emphasis on content. And these German works derive from such a troubled time in the country's history. That is what we find so compelling. You can't just simply look at them. You get involved with what they say. The works speak to your mind as well as to your eye, especially those of the Weimar artists who were so involved with the upheavals of the time—the war Germany had lost, the revolution, inflation, Hitler. These paintings and drawings make you think even after you've stopped looking at them. The French just didn't paint like that.

RH: Your interest in German Expressionism in the 1970s was reflected, to some degree, by a growing awareness of that art among American art historians and collectors. At about the time you purchased Egon Schiele's remarkable small *Self-Portrait: Anarchist* [Fig. 3], books on him by Alessandra Comini and others were published here in the United States. And Robert Rifkind was beginning to exhibit his encyclopedic collection of German Expressionist graphics in Los Angeles and elsewhere. Other collectors, such as Granvil and Marcia Specks in Evanston, Illinois, also acquired significant prints and paintings at this time, while American museums joined in with exhibitions devoted to German Expressionism. This was in the late seventies and early eighties, when the contemporary German Neo-Expressionist painters were being discovered. It was precisely at this moment in time, when German Expressionism was achieving greater public recognition, that you turned your attention away from it and towards the art of Weimar Germany. And what you began collecting was not what most people would have turned to—examples of Bauhaus work or Paul Klee—but *Neue Sachlichkeit* and other committed figurative art of the 1920s. It was an unexpected choice in terms of collecting patterns of the period, even if it could be argued that Meidner is a bridge between Expressionism and *Neue Sachlichkeit*.

MF: There was a German Expressionist exhibition in Chicago, at the Museum of Contemporary Art in 1978, to which we lent some pieces and which included some examples of *Neue Sachlichkeit*, and these attracted our attention. Then, a little later, in 1980, the Minneapolis Institute of Art organized the exhibition *German Realism of the Twenties: The Artist as Social Critic*, which we saw there and again at its showing in Chicago. Many of the artists, such as Karl Hubbuch [Fig. 4], we had never heard of before. But the works were so powerful. We were bowled over. The images were tough, but it was a tough time. Then we started to look for other examples of these artists' work in museums and in galleries. Works were available; they'd show up at American auctions, and hardly anybody was buying, so they weren't expensive. We were thus able to form a sizable collection of quality works at relatively little expense.

RH: The tragic history of German-Jewish relations during this century, especially, of course, Nazi persecution and the Holocaust, might

Fig. 3   Egon Schiele, *Self-Portrait: Anarchist* (*Selbstporträt: Anarchist*), c. 1910. Pencil and watercolor on paper, 25.5 x 22.3 cm (10 x 8³/₄ in.)

well have led Jewish collectors like yourselves to reject Germans and their cultural and political concerns. Yet you have formed one of the greatest collections of modern German art. Do you see a contradiction in this? How might you explain it?

MF: The works were powerful and were good art. That's why we collected them. They depicted the problems of the 1920s. It was a violent time, a protest period in art. I don't think being Jewish had anything to do with it. I'm not aware of it.

JF: But it was difficult for us. We never wanted to go to Germany. When we bought German works, we had dealers or other collectors who would go to auctions for us or to German galleries, and we deliberately did not go to Germany because of what had happened under Hitler.

MF: That's true. We've been to Munich at least thirty times now, but I can't bring myself to visit Dachau.

JF: At auctions in London and elsewhere, Marvin became acquainted with collectors and dealers from Germany. They invited us to their homes and galleries. We went eventually, but we resisted for a long time. For us, these people are Germany. We also enjoy the cities and the countryside. But we still can't forget what happened.

MF: The art we have collected makes twentieth-century German history more understandable to us. It helps us to comprehend the rise of Hitler and the terrible increase in anti-Semitism. The protest against conditions in Weimar Germany is a constant factor of the works we possess: they show the history and critique the institutions. We did not

Fig. 4   Karl Hubbuch with his painting *The Waitress* (cat. no. 68)

Fig. 5 Chana Orloff, *The Jewish Painter (Le peintre juif)*, 1920. Bronze, 36 x 18.5 x 30 cm (14¹/₈ x 7¹/₄ x 11³/₄ in.)

JF: But I believe there is something Jewish about Meidner's imagery: the anguish and concern, the compassion, are very Jewish. I think many Jews are raised to be thoughtful and particularly sensitive people. They place themselves in the middle of all tragedies. Other artists of the time dealt with the same existential problems as Meidner, but as reporters. Meidner related himself directly to the problems by reflecting them in his own image.

MF: I don't think there's anything Jewish in Meidner's early work. But it's an interesting thing to think about. Curiously enough, later, when he signed his name in Hebrew letters as a gesture of defiance, the quality of his work declined considerably!

There are some non-German artists we find interesting who were Jewish, but quality remains the paramount consideration. There's Chana Orloff, for example, who was such a remarkable sculptor and a major figure in the Paris art world of the 1920s, a kind of Parisian "Mother Ey." We bought her sculpture *The Jewish Painter* [Fig. 5] because it was such a powerful representation of a Jewish artist.

RH: Recently, you've turned to collecting several other non-German artists. Some of these, such as Armand Bouten, had direct connections to Germany, and the work of others, but not all, relates to contemporary German painting—I'm thinking of Charles Clement's *Marseilles Harbor Street* [Fig. 6] or Bobette Van Gelder's horrifying *Interrupted Rendezvous* [Fig. 7]. Then there's Victor Paladini, an Italian painter of the twenties and thirties who is virtually unknown in this country, but whose *Self-Portrait* [Fig. 8] can be compared to some of the best German work of the time. How was it that you became interested in these artists?

MF: Bouten was Dutch and only very recently has started to gain recognition. His work is unusual. He lived like a gypsy, migrating

shy away from unappealing subject matter, as other collectors often do, because this is how it was—the sick, the crippled, the starving, street battles, desperation, angst.

In Weimar Germany, and especially in Berlin, Jews were major contributors to the society and its culture, which are unthinkable without them. The Jews blossomed in this period before Hitler: fine museum directors, fine musicians, fine writers, political leaders such as Rathenau, fine architects—and fine artists. The Meidners, Ludwig and Else, Steinhardt, Hirsch, Nussbaum, Hoexter, Loewenthal, Scheiber, Citroën, Ronay, Neuschul—all were Jewish. When you think of it, that's a very high percentage of the artists in our collection.

RH: Yes, there is an amazing concentration of Jewish artists at this time. Your collection is a fairly accurate representation of the importance of their contribution to Weimar Germany. Most of them thought of themselves solely as German artists. Nussbaum is indicative of this. His early work hardly refers to Jewish motifs, and it was only as a result of Nazi policies that he turned to Jewish imagery at all. I should ask you in this context whether Meidner's Jewishness was a major factor in your decision to collect his work, whether you see something uniquely Jewish expressed in his images, over and above their subject matter.

MF: We were aware that Meidner was Jewish, of course, and perhaps that made him particularly interesting to us, but it was above all the quality and power of his paintings, the mastery of his drawings, that attracted us. People may not agree with me, but I don't think there's been another German artist since Dürer to equal his drawing technique and its impact. He's a very great artist, especially in his finest works, those done in 1913.

Fig. 6 Charles Clement, *Harbor Street in Marseilles (Rue dans le port de Marseille)*, 1924. Watercolor on paper, 47.2 x 38.4 cm (18⁹/₁₆ x 15¹/₈ in.)

Fig. 7 Bobette Van Gelder,
Interrupted Rendezvous
(*Treffpunkt Unterbrechung*),
c. 1925. Watercolor over charcoal on paper, 45.5 x 60.5 cm
(17⁷/₈ x 23¹³/₁₆ in.)

from country to country, from city to city, often residing in the red-
light district and depicting scenes from it. He sold hardly anything
during his lifetime and exhibited very little, but he belongs to the
German art scene: he worked in Berlin and Herwarth Walden recognized his importance.

Bobette Van Gelder was among the Dutch artists who embraced a
style somewhat akin to *Neue Sachlichkeit*. These artists still have to be
discovered and you can buy their works at low prices. Quality is still
available if you search for it.

JF: But we would have to study a lot before becoming as interested in
the Dutch or Italian artists as we are in the Germans of the Weimar
period. There is good work, but it often does not seem to have the
intensity of the German pieces. Maybe it's the difference in background or the different national developments in the twenties.

RH: Let me return briefly to the Jewish issue. Many American collectors of German art are Jewish, and, bearing the Holocaust in mind, this
does seem to be a remarkable state of affairs. Perhaps it doesn't require
explanation in the case of refugees from Germany, who brought with
them what art they could, especially Expressionist paintings. That art
is a part of what they lost, a relic of their past. But why would younger
Jewish collectors without this background turn to German Expressionism as the art of their choice?

MF: I hadn't thought of that. But you're right, many collectors of
modern German art are Jewish. Perhaps there are historical reasons. As
we said, Jews were able to play a vital part in the cultural life of
Weimar Germany as artists—and as collectors, too, who were willing
to support Expressionist and other modern art. But I'm reluctant to
attribute something to Jewishness alone, even if at first it seems a
plausible explanation. I'm sure that, like us, both older and younger
Jewish collectors are simply interested in art, good art.

Fig. 8 Victor Paladini, *Self-Portrait* (*Autoritratto*), 1932.
Oil on canvas, 110 x 93 cm (43⁵/₁₆ x 36⁵/₈ in.)

Confronting Contradictions:
Artists and their Institutions in Wilhelmine and Weimar Germany

Reinhold Heller

I. Introduction

The history of art and of artists in Germany during the years from Expressionism in the Wilhelmine Empire, via the Weimar Republic's reinstatement of realism, to resistance to Hitler's Reich—the development traced by the works in the Marvin and Janet Fishman Collection—is a history of failures and of ineffective alternatives. It charts desperation, co-opted efforts, doomed hopes, unfulfilled ambitions.

That this record of failure contains within it the possibility of subsequent recognition, does not diminish the insuffiency and impotence of the artworks within the material, temporal context of their production. Indeed, the presence of such works in the Fishman Collection in Milwaukee, while testifying to their effectiveness today as a powerful commentary on an historical moment, reflects their inability to infiltrate the reality that formed them. Protected, though precariously, by private ownership and withdrawn into the realm of personal contemplation, the artworks were denied that role as public critique and comment so determinedly intended for them by their creators. Detached from the historical situation to which they today bear witness, they are remarkable relics of a past they could not successfully engage and of contradictions they could not resolve.

In 1923, the conservative Hanseatic Publishing Institute of Hamburg, controlled by the white-collar *Deutschnationaler Handlungsgehilfenverband* (German National Union of Commercial Employees [DHV]), published Arthur Moeller van den Bruck's polemical tract, *The Third Reich*. Advocating a nationalistically oriented "third way" as alternative to both capitalism and Marxist socialism, Moeller proposed a uniquely German "dialectic" which would be able to subsume the class antitheses and struggles besetting contemporary Germany. In this socially active dialectic, the lower classes would be "de-proletarianized" as they were freed of the illusions of class identity and became conscious, instead, of their role as members of the German *Volk* in a future Third Reich that was to be devoid of political parties and class conflict. Moeller's mystical dialectic juxtaposed the historical "First Reich" of the Middle Ages, with its corporatist social order and distinct local identities, to the Bismarckian "Second Reich," seen as a materialistic age inappropriately imperialistic but bound to a unified Germany, in order to prophesy an "End-Reich" synthesis. Founded in a German "New Socialist" order, this state would be marked by communal harmony and by consciousness of its Germanic *Volkstum*, its national and genetic essence:

> We do not think of today's Europe, which is too contemptible to deserve evalution of any kind. We think of yesterday's Europe and of what might survive from it to see another day. And we think of the Germany of all times, of the Germany with a two-thousand-year past, and of the Germany with an eternal present that is alive in

the spiritual realm, but that wants to be secured in the real world, where it can be secured only politically.[1]

The book, with its nationalistically charged analyses, was a political manifesto, vague but nonetheless idealistic in its reactionary solutions.

While Moeller's tract proposed an alternative dialectic according to his perceptions of fundamental German characteristics and historical functions, an extension and partial revision of Marxist dialectics was undertaken in a second book published in 1923, Georg Lukács's *History and Class Consciousness*. Issued in Berlin by Malik Verlag, a publishing house associated with the Communist Party of Germany (KPD), this study by the Hungarian Marxist critic, politician, and theoretician was organized around a central tripartite essay, "Reification and Consciousness of the Proletariat," and aimed at reinstating "Marx's theory *as Marx understood it*."[2] In a project similar in intent to Moeller's, Lukács sought a return to the origins of a principle, in the meantime corrupted, in order to facilitate its implementation in the future. He expounded and applied a dialectic derived from Marx, but submitted it to the control of Hegel's dialectical method, in which it originated, in an attempt to contribute to "efforts to clarify the theoretical problems of the revolutionary movement."[3] The translation of theory into practice, the integration of critical analysis and political struggle, remained Lukács's basic concern, as, expressed less systematically, it was Moeller's on the opposite side of the political spectrum.

Ironically, the two books, linked by a vehement anti-capitalism but otherwise ideologically and methodologically antagonistic, suffered similar fates in their reception by the political groups to which they were addressed. Lukács's attempts to rehabilitate Hegel's Idealist dialectic in the context of Marxist theory were attacked and condemned by Grigori Zinoviev at the Fifth World Congress of the Third International ("Comintern," Moscow, June–July 1924) as utopian and opportunistic. The function of *History and Class Consciousness* as weapon in the ideological struggle of the left, and especially of the KPD during the 1920s, was thereby subverted. Its influence confined

---

1. "Wir denken nicht an das Europa von heute, das zu verächtlich ist, um irgendwie gewertet zu werden. Wir denken an das Europa von gestern, und an das, was sich aus ihm vielleicht noch einmal in ein Morgen hinüberretten wird. Und wir denken an das Deutschland aller Zeiten, an das Deutschland einer zweitausendjährigen Vergangenheit, und an das Deutschland einer ewigen Gegenwart, das im Geistigen lebt, aber im Wirklichen gesichert sein will und hier nur politisch gesichert werden kann." Arthur Moeller van den Bruck, *Das Dritte Reich*, 2d ed. (Hamburg: Hanseatische Verlagsanstalt, 1931), 234–235.

2. "... eine Auslegung der Lehre von Marx *im Sinne von Marx*...." Georg Lukács, *Geschichte und Klassenbewusstsein: Studien über Marxistische Dialektik*, in *Werke*, Vol. 2, *Frühschriften II* (Neuwied and West Berlin: Hermann Luchterhand Verlag, 1968), 164; trans. Rodney Livingstone as *History and Class Consciousness: Studies in Marxist Dialectics* (Cambridge, Mass.: MIT Press, 1971), xlii.

3. "... Versuche, theoretische Fragen der revolutionären Bewegung... zu klären." Ibid., xli.

to a limited philosophical discourse, the book and its author were denied vital interaction with contemporary political practice.[4] Threatened by expulsion from the Party, Lukács recanted and withdrew from active political participation to the realm of book reviews and literary theory.

Two years after publication of his study, Moeller van den Bruck committed suicide. Unlike *History and Class Consciousness*, however, his book remained a notable factor in codifications of conservative political positions in Germany. His formulation of conservative, anti-capitalist fulfillment as a reversal of the socialist November Revolution of 1918, a program for the restoration of anti-republican "German" values and institutions in a future mystical Third Reich, was readily appropriated by the left-wing of the Nazi Party. In 1933, the seductive prophecy of a Third Reich, derived by Moeller from the medieval mystic Joachim of Fiore and identified as "always promised . . . never fulfilled,"[5] furnished Hitler's regime with a powerfully evocative identity, one significantly divorced from the context and conclusions of Moeller's irrationalist, idealist convictions. In the spurious equation drawn between Moeller's book, its title, and the Nazis' millennial Reich, this work, too, was deprived of its capacity to intervene in the political discourse of the time, much as Lukács's study had been.

The reification of the two books after 1923—their limitation to roles other than those intended for them or, indeed, to any appropriate ones —is symptomatic of the structural institutionalization of critical positions, from left to right, within the Weimar Republic and of their appropriation as part of a pragmatically determined strategy of political antagonism and opposition. Class struggle, economic struggle, political struggle were embedded in, and validated by, the structure of Germany's various institutions, rigidly positioned in their mutual animosity. The potential of alternative organizations and modes of thought was strangled either by enforced rejection or by paralyzing appropriation and legitimization. The history of critical opposition to Weimar Germany's dominant alliances of entrenched social and cultural constructs—its institutional elites in politics, the military, the economy, and culture—is necessarily one of persistent failure. Although often attaining an aura of success, even if only through the approbation of later critics, efforts at reform were fundamentally ineffective.

Artistic life in Weimar Germany was marked by artists' efforts to revise, overcome, and transcend the social and institutional structures within which they worked. By means of alternatives they themselves determined, they persistently attempted to supplant the institutions and social structures that defined their interaction with the public. The history of modern art in Germany is a history of attempts to redefine the institutional components of art's communication process.

II. Secession and Prewar Expressionism

Beginning with the Secessions of the 1890s, artists in Germany joined together in formal groups in order to exhibit and propagate their work outside the corporate confines both of *Kunst-* and *Künstlervereine* – the official local associations of artists and patrons that commonly sponsored periodic exhibitions of works by their members and invited guests – and of the academies. These official exhibitions, their juries frequently intolerant of innovative art, were dedicated to the display of extremely large numbers of works as the result of an apparently democratic process. Democracy thus practiced was, however, inimical to the small number of works that broke with established norms; they were repressed by sheer weight of numbers and thereby implicitly proclaimed insignificant or valueless. Yet removed from the pervading context of mediocrity and grouped together in smaller, separate exhibitions, in "secessions" frequently organized to present a shared stylistic approach, the anti-traditional alternatives formed an effective opposition. Secession produced an anti-salon of protest and liberation whose separate, collective voice became a highly distinctive presence in the art world of the time.[6]

Sustained either by alliance with major art galleries, as in the Berlin Secession's association with Bruno and Paul Cassirer, or by rapprochement with state sponsorship, as in Munich, the Secessions vigorously advocated their aesthetic ideologies as they established and defended their share of the contemporary art market. Their stance was therefore necessarily rigid, its cohesive inflexibility effective as a strategy of opposition but also resistant to other alternative artistic approaches. Unwilling to admit younger representatives of stylistic innovation, the Secessions, within a decade of their foundation, appeared repressive, intolerant, and frustrating to artists identifying themselves as the new, revolutionary "youth." Thus, when the artists of Dresden's *Brücke* (Bridge) group wrote in their famous program of 1906, "As youth that is carrying the future, we intend to obtain freedom of movement and of life for ourselves in opposition to older, well-established powers,"[7] they were indicting the Secessions as well as the academies and state-sponsored artists' associations in a challenging rallying call for a new, unified opposition. A few years later, in 1910, when Berlin's New Secession was founded in protest at the Secession's rejection of works by twenty-seven artists (including Emil Nolde, Max Pechstein, and Georg Tappert), the antithesis of the Secession's "Impressionism" —soon to be identified as "Expressionism"—was incorporated in an institutional framework of competition and confrontation that annexed or further coalesced both large artists' groups and local, smaller ones such as *Brücke*.

With a view focused on Secessionist Impressionism, the new secessions founded by the Expressionists accented the contrast in stylistic ideologies by means of a discourse on external and internal nature. As Franz Marc proclaimed:

> Today we search behind the veil of appearances for the hidden aspects of nature, which appear more significant to us than the discoveries of the Impressionists and which they simply passed by. And we seek out and paint this inner, spiritual side of nature not

4. For a richly informative discussion of Lukács's reception during the 1920s, see Paul Breines, "Praxis and its Theorists: The Impact of Lukács and Korsch in the 1920's," *Telos*, no. 11 (Spring 1972): 66–103.

5. Moeller van den Bruck, 320.

6. Modeled on the Salons des Indépendants, which had been held in Paris since 1884, secessionist artists' organizations first appeared in the German Empire in Munich and Karlsruhe in 1893, then in Weimar, Düsseldorf, and Dresden, and finally in Berlin in 1898, the year that also saw the founding of the Vienna Secession.

7. ". . . [A]ls Jugend, die die Zukunft trägt, wollen wir uns Arm- und Lebensfreiheit verschaffen gegenüber den wohlangesessenen älteren Kräften." Ernst Ludwig Kirchner's woodcut of the program has been reproduced frequently, for example by Horst Jähner, *Künstlergruppe Brücke: Geschichte, Leben und Werk ihrer Maler* (East Berlin: Henschelverlag Kunst und Gesellschaft, 1984), 416. For a full translation and further discussion of *Brücke*'s program within the institutional context of German art, see Reinhold Heller, *Brücke: German Expressionist Prints from the Granvil and Marcia Specks Collection* (Evanston, Ill.: Mary and Leigh Block Gallery, Northwestern University, 1988), 5.

because of some whim or desire for novelty, but because we *see* this side, just as previously one "saw" violet shadows and atmosphere around all objects.[8]

Marc's comments, like the organization of Expressionist artists' groups, set off the "young" artists—the distinction between generations employed at the time had little to do with the actual ages of the individuals involved—against the art that preceded theirs in order to define a new attitude towards image, content, and manner of painting that incorporated its precursors in the act of superseding them. "*Es liegt in der Zeit*" (It's a matter of the times), Marc concluded, and thereby emphasized further the new art's place within a temporal progression, linking it to a dependence on the contemporary that developed from, as well as broke with, the past. However, the confrontation thus defined was identified solely in terms of the art of previous generations and previous eras. Opposition was therefore located in, and limited to, a dialectic between the aesthetic and "the spiritual." The material manifestations of the time, social and political, were rejected by being steadfastly ignored.

In the name of the artists exhibiting in Berlin at Herwarth Walden's 1913 *First German Autumn Salon*, this ethos of deliberate self-withdrawal and of purification from "the worldly" was formulated programmatically in the exhibition catalogue:

> Today we do not live in a time when art is the helpmate of life. What true art is created today . . . is the equation drawn from life by abstractly oriented spirits, without desire, without purpose, and without restriction. . . . That is the reason for our self-imposed seclusion from the demands the world makes on us. We do not wish to get mixed up with it.[9]

To establish distinctions and a divorce from the mundane—this was the Expressionist challenge. By 1913, it was being formulated within an expanding number of organizations of varying size that often overlapped in membership. In the meantime, greater support from art galleries and the appearance of periodicals devoted to the new art were testifying to its commercial and critical viability.[10]

The multiplicity of societies and the exhibitions they or their patrons sponsored, presented in juxtaposition with Impressionist Secessions and academy-sponsored traditional art, imposed a process of dialogue on the public. Necessarily viewed in contrast to competing camps of art that the Expressionists identified as temporally superseded, exhi-

bitions of Expressionist works generated a discourse of art movements and images in an attempt to set up new, contemporary criteria of artistic quality. "Among people who are understanding and free of prejudice, the struggle involves only *quality*," Marc wrote. "Here weapons and mode of attack are unrestricted."[11] It was a dialectic of artistic worth and contemporary validity that ensued. For the Expressionists, this entailed the assertion of an artistic vocabulary founded on the principle of opposition, on the rejection of existing vocabularies, and the establishment of a syntax of otherness, of explication in a dialectical process of antithesis and supersession.

III. World War I and Revolution

By 1914, the impact of the Expressionist opposition had become such that yet newer alternative organizations—such as Berlin's Free Secession, with Max Liebermann, the dean of German Impressionists and a founding member of the original Berlin Secession, as honorary president—began to co-opt the membership of dogmatically Expressionist groupings. Former antagonists were melded into improbable alliances that proclaimed further freedom for their art, but at the expense of increasing divisions and re-formations.

World War I interrupted the escalating process of German artists' organization into groups of diverse self-interest. During the war, various formations of "war artists"—ranging from officially sponsored artists recording the military campaigns to those simply serving in the armed forces—came into being, but the "young" artists, insofar as they exhibited and were not prevented from working by their military duties, settled into the organizations they had spawned before the outbreak of war, bowing to the dictates of the time and answering the Kaiser's calls for German cohesion by sponsoring joint exhibitions rather than competitive ones. In an outburst of patriotic fervor, the critic Julius Meier-Graefe, a vehement defender of Impressionism and Neo-Impressionism, observed:

> The war enriches us. We have changed since yesterday. The debate about words and programs is at an end. . . . We had theories. What we lacked was content, and that is being given to us, my brothers, by the times! . . . Unity has been granted us by the war. All parties have joined together to achieve the common goal. Art must follow![12]

As Meier-Graefe's panegyric of belligerent chauvinism makes apparent, the transformations induced by the war were less organizational than attitudinal in nature. Although there had been calls for innovative art to confront life more directly prior to World War I, these remained relatively isolated and inconsistent. Munich's anarchist

8. "Wir suchen heute unter dem Schleier des Scheines verborgene Dinge in der Natur, die uns wichtiger scheinen als die Entdeckungen der Impressionisten und an denen diese einfach vorübergingen. Und zwar suchen und malen wir diese innere, geistige Seite der Natur nicht aus Laune oder Lust am anderen, sondern weil wir diese Seite *sehen*, so wie man früher einmal violette Schatten und den Äther über allen Dingen 'sah.'" Franz Marc, "Die neue Malerei," *Pan* 2, no. 16 (7 March 1912): 469, as reprinted in Marc, *Schriften*, ed. Klaus Lankheit (Cologne: DuMont Buchverlag, 1978), 102.

9. "Wir leben heute nicht in einer Zeit, in der die Kunst die Helferin des Lebens ist. Was heute an echter Kunst entsteht . . . ist die Gleichung, die abstrakt gesinnte Geister aus dem Leben ziehen, wunschlos, zwecklos und ohne Hader . . . . Das ist der Grund unserer selbstgewählten Abschliessung gegen die Anträge, die die Welt uns macht; wir wollen uns nicht mit ihr vermischen." Die Aussteller, "Vorwort," *Erster Deutscher Herbstsalon: Berlin 1913* (Berlin: Der Sturm, 1913), 9.

10. These were important contributory factors in the 1911 "Protest of German Artists," initiated by Carl Vinnen in an attempt to prevent the enchroachment of non-traditional art upon the existing art market.

11. "Unter den Verständigen und Vorurteilsfreien geht der Streit nur um *Qualität*. Hier sind die Waffen und der Angriff frei." Marc, "Neue Malerei," *Schriften*, 103.

12. "Der Krieg beschert uns. Wir sind andere seit gestern. Der Streit um Worte und Programme ist zu Ende. . . . Wir hatten Theorien. Was uns fehlte, der Inhalt, das, meine Brüder, gibt uns die Zeit. . . . Einheit gab uns der Krieg. Alle Parteien gehen mit zum Ziel. Die Kunst folge!" Julius Meier-Graefe, ["Der Krieg beschert uns"], *Kriegszeit: Künstlerflugblätter* 1, no. 1 (31 August 1914): 4. Significantly, this handwritten statement—the form testifies to personal conviction and involvement—is not listed in the "complete" bibliography of Meier-Graefe's writings supplied by Kennworth Moffett, *Meier-Graefe as Art Critic*, Studien zur Kunst des 19. Jahrhunderts, vol. 19 (Munich: Prestel Verlag, 1973), 183 ff.

periodical *Die Revolution* (*The Revolution*), edited by Hans Leybold and Hugo Ball and with Richard Seewald among its artist-contributors, and the Berlin artists associated with Ludwig Meidner as *Die Pathetiker* (The Ones Filled with Pathos) accented critical content oriented towards contemporary life. Most Expressionists, however, generally failed to give expression to their commitment in their imagery. In 1914, the artists of the new secessions, drafted or volunteering for military and military-related service or actively seeking to avoid it, were forcefully removed from the marginal social position to which their professional attitudes and functions had relegated them. Participation in, and general acceptance of, the dominant activities and concerns of the German state and society was now demanded of them. The Expressionists' fundamentally Kantian insistence on an art of disinterestedness was replaced by the recognition that "[o]ur warrior instincts have been aroused and are honed to the countless possibilities offered by victory and resistance."[13]

Substituted for nudes and animals, portraits, landscapes and city scenes in the syntax of Germany's innovative art were scenes from occupied countries, uniforms, and soldiers, the latter bathing, charging into battle, fighting, wounded, dead or dying. During the war's initial years the basic subject matter of works shown in state-sponsored exhibitions was more or less identical to that seen at the new secessions and other organizations that rejected traditional artistic vocabularies. The precise delineation of the subjects, their emphases and configurations, may have differed, and thus reflected some variations in attitude towards the war, but the prewar innovators, previously separatist, now participated in, and complied with, the thematic concerns of their artistic antagonists. In periodicals or periodically issued print portfolios, such as *Kriegszeit* (*Wartime*), *Die Front* (*The Front*), or *Krieg und Kunst* (*War and Art*), they celebrated German victories and nationalistic values with an enthusiasm equal to that of their opponents. Academy exhibitions remained closed to, or were boycotted by, the "young," but nonetheless these artists displayed their work in the company of academicians and Impressionists alike in those privately sponsored exhibitions that were devoted to artists serving in the nation's armed forces. Insistence on otherness was no longer their primary objective. Stationed at such military command centers as Kowno (Kaunas) in Lithuania and Brussels in Belgium, German artists organized exhibitions there of their war-inspired art, presenting it to their comrades as well as to the populace of the occupied areas as a prototype of German cultural achievement, as a corollary of military accomplishments. The previously valued divorce from "the demands the world makes on us" was broken with definitively.

The attitude of acquiescence that eclipsed all others within the Secessions and their offshoots following the outbreak of war was countered only when additional artists' groups were formed that effected a break with Expressionism. In exile in Zurich, where he participated in Swiss anarchist discussions, Hugo Ball inaugurated Dada with an international circle of artists, writers, and musicians at the Cabaret Voltaire, announcing that "[our] total effort is directed, irrespective of the war and the nations, towards recalling the few independent persons who live for other ideals."[14] Expressionism was thus transcended by means of a cooperative attempt to oppose patriotic complicity by a conscious rejection of "*deutsche Mentalität*" (the German mentality) expressed in a communal vocabulary of nihilistic humor.

To translate Expressionism into a tactic of resistance and political opposition within the context of a new organization was likewise the aim of Wieland Herzfelde, John Heartfield, George Grosz, and Franz Jung when they began publishing the journal *Neue Jugend* (*New Youth*)

in Berlin in 1916 and, soon thereafter, founded Malik Verlag. In confronting social issues and presenting them to the public, these ventures signalled a departure from young artists' previous primary concern, which was with exhibitions and their organization. On the model of *Kriegszeit* and similar journals fostering the war effort by means of original prints and reproductions, Malik Verlag sponsored no exhibitions. In this it differed from such prewar publishing concerns as Walden's *Der Sturm*. The innovative exhibitions at Walden's gallery of the same name continued to be accented as the main means of presenting artworks to the public, while his periodical with its prints and essays served to propagandize these efforts. *Neue Jugend* and Malik Verlag concentrated instead on published images as the prime communicators of wide-ranging social critiques in periodicals and almanacs as well as in lithographic portfolios, notably of George Grosz's drawings. There is a significant shift here which reduces and subverts the emphasis on the single original artwork and the unique experience of it. This also effected a move away from the traditional primacy of oil painting to a variety of drawing and duplicative media, as well as to the words (or verbal images) that accompanied them. What was transmitted—the image, its subject matter and its content—not the means of transmission, became the major concern. Prewar artists' priorities had been turned upside down. Art existed less as a confrontation of styles than as a confrontation of the contradictions within society, less as purely aesthetic object than as propaganda, as purveyor of ideologies.

In addition to being published, the works of artists and writers associated with Malik Verlag were presented during readings and performances at I. B. Neumann's gallery in Berlin and at similar commercial galleries in other cities. The emphasis on the transitory in art, rather than the traditional one on permanence, and on the present, rather than on the future, echoed the values of the Zurich Dada artists, whose efforts were linked to those of their Berlin confreres and made more overtly political after Richard Huelsenbeck returned to Berlin from Switzerland in 1917. Together they formed an international coalition of artists that was officially registered as Club Dada. The name selected for the organization significantly distinguished it in type and function from previous artists' groups, associations, and secessions. Implicit in the term "club"—and made explicit in the group's manifesto[15]—is the notion that membership determines identity, rather than vice versa: stylistic conformity did not shape membership. Club Dada's goal was interaction with the events of the present:

> Art in its manifestations and tendencies is dependent on the time in which it lives, and artists are creatures of their epoch. The greatest

13. "Unsere soldatischen Sinne sind wach und sind geschärft für die tausend Möglichkeiten des Sieges und Widerstandes." Franz Marc, "Das geheime Europa," *Das Forum* 1, no. 12 (March 1915), as reprinted in Marc, *Schriften*, 165.

14. ". . . [unsere] ganze Absicht [ist] darauf gerichtet . . . über den Krieg und die Vaterländer hinweg an die wenigen Unabhängigen zu erinnern, die anderen Idealen leben." Hugo Ball, [Programmatic Declaration of 15 May 1916,] *Cabaret Voltaire: Eine Sammlung künstlerischer und literarischer Beiträge*, no. 1 (1916): 5, as reprinted in *Dada in Zürich*, ed. Hand Bolliger, Guido Magnaguagno, and Raymond Meyer (Zurich: Kunsthaus Zürich and Arche Verlag, 1985), 209.

15. "Dada is a CLUB, founded in Berlin, that can be joined without accepting obligations" ("Dada ist ein CLUB, der in Berlin gegründet worden ist, in den man eintreten kann, ohne Verbindlichkeiten zu übernehmen"). *Dadaistisches Manifest* [1918], reprinted in *Dada Berlin: Texte, Manifeste, Aktionen*, ed. Karl Riha with Hanne Bergius, Universal-Bibliothek 9857 (Stuttgart: Philipp Reclam jun., 1977), 25.

art will be that which in its conscious contents presents the thousands of problems of the time. It will be that which can be seen to have let itself be affected by the explosions of the last week, which constantly has to get back on its legs after the shocks imparted to it during the past day.[16]

The activities of Club Dada, founded in a persistently dialectical relationship with the conditions of the present and therefore in perpetual flux in content and style as well as in membership, culminated in 1920 with the *International Dada Fair*, in which the anonymity of montage and collage subsumed individual handwriting and technique. The collective, dialectical approach of Club Dada failed, however, to become the prototype of other artists' organizations during the last years of the war and the time of the revolution. Instead, these reverted to more rigid models, reified according to preordained attitudes or affiliations even as they sought to consort with, and comment on, the dramatic, traumatic present with an emphasis on publicity and publications that was similar to the Dadaists'.

When the chauvinistic fervor of the war's initial years subsided among young German artists they did not abandon their recently acquired concern with contemporary issues, but rather shifted their focus in accordance with their new convictions. The transformation undergone by *Kriegszeit* in 1916, when it was succeeded by *Der Bildermann: Steinzeichnungen fürs deutsche Volk* (The Picture-Board Man: Lithographs for the German People), is symptomatic. Many of the same artists participated in this second wartime venture by Paul Cassirer, but whereas previously the justice of the German cause, the power of German arms, the idealistic self-sacrifice and heroism of Germany's soldiers, and the villainy of Germany's enemies were asserted, now "the German people" were presented with scenes of a longed-for restoration of peace as well as with pleas for this peace and with critiques of war profiteers and of other ill effects of the war on German society and life. During 1917 and 1918, these images were radicalized in Expressionist, activist visions of *Der neue Mensch* (The New Human Being) who was to emerge after the war in a society transformed by its years of bloody sacrifice into a melioristic world-community of fraternal coexistence:

Young painters step forward, heralds of a new world. Hunted, tortured, blessed, and rhapsodic prophets of the wonder of wonders: of this churning world, of humanity raised up to the heavens. . . . Open your eyes! . . . Rise up from your sleep! Rise up from your blindness! School the eye! School the spirit!

You are human, and of you we speak![17]

Messianic Expressionist content, initially apparent largely in literature and in prints by isolated artists—and in other images often not exhibited until later—engendered an avalanche of new periodicals and artists' groups, especially after the collapse of the Empire in 1918. Mixed with vaguely expressed but fervently held beliefs in a new socialism, the sole gain of war and revolution, the gospel of *Der neue Mensch* gathered around it a large number of local artists' organizations, mostly composed of artists just released from military service, in numerous cities, from Barmen and Bielefeld to Stuttgart and Worpswede.[18] Prewar organizations were deemed no longer suitable, and revolutionary alternatives were demanded. Active involvement with the needs of a new society on the part of revolutionary institutions and groups in the cities and regions of the former Empire would generate creative productivity, giving rise to a communal art expressive of the new era's specific requirements in a close linkage of artist, locality, and common people. "The people and art are to form a unity."[19]

In conjunction with revolutionary local councils and groups of artists, nationally oriented organizations—the November Group and the *Arbeitsrat für Kunst* (Work Council for Art)—were formed in Berlin to coordinate regional efforts and to instruct the new state. The "Guiding Principles" of the November Group thus proclaimed:

We demand influence and collaboration:
1. in all architectural projects, as matters of public concern. . . .
2. in the reformation of art schools and their teaching. . . .
3. in the transformation of museums. . . .
4. in the awarding of exhibition space. . . .
5. in the formulation of laws pertaining to art. . . .[20]

The totality of artistic discourse and its institutions was considered and attempts made to reform the institutions in accordance with idealistically revolutionary, republican, and socialist principles in order to forge a bond between artist and people, between art and life.

These renovative organizations were united by reliance on manifestos and programs, questionnaires and pamphlets. With word and image fused, argumentation existed as much in verbal as in pictorial form. New periodicals and newspapers with woodcut imagery accompanied by brief poems, criticism, and political proclamations appeared as mutations of political tracts and of fine art print portfolios in an attempt to overcome the commodity value placed on art by capitalism and to make it available to the masses. The publications were viewed as the first stage in the creation of a people's art that would be expressive of the postwar community and help construct a new society.[21]

16. "Die Kunst ist in ihrer Ausführung und Richtung von der Zeit abhängig, in der sie lebt, und die Künstler sind Kreaturen ihrer Epoche. Die höchste Kunst wird diejenige sein, die in ihren Bewusstseinsinhalten die tausendfachen Probleme der Zeit präsentiert, der man anerkennt, dass sie sich von den Explosionen der letzten Woche werfen liess, die ihre Glieder immer wieder unter dem Stoss des letzten Tages zusammensucht." Ibid., 22.

17. "Junge Maler treten auf, Verkünder einer neuen Welt. Gejagte, gemartete, beglückte und hymnische Propheten des Wunders der Wunder: dieser brausenden Welt, des in die Himmel geworfenen Menschen. . . . Die Augen auf! . . . Auf aus dem Schlaf! Auf aus der Blindheit! Lernt den Blick! Lernt den Geist! Ihr seid Menschen, und von euch ist die Rede!" Walter Rheiner, "Die neue Welt," in *Sezession Gruppe 1919* (Dresden: Galerie Emil Richter, 1919), as reprinted in *Schrei in die Welt: Expressionismus in Dresden*, ed. Peter Ludewig (East Berlin: Buchverlag Der Morgen, 1988), 47–48.

18. For a compilation of the various groups, their programs, and the artists participating in them, see Peter Guenther, "A Survey of Artists' Groups: Their Rise, Rhetoric, and Demise," in *German Expressionism, 1915–1925: The Second Generation*, ed. Stephanie Barron (Los Angeles: Los Angeles County Museum of Art, and Munich: Prestel Verlag, 1988), 99–115.

19. "Volk und Kunst sollen ein Ganzes bilden." Proclamation of the artists' group *Der Wurf* (The Throw), Bielefeld, c. 1919, as reprinted in *Zehn Jahre Novembergruppe*, special issue of *Kunst der Zeit* 3, nos. 1–3 (1928): 24.

20. "Wir fordern Einfluss und Mitarbeit:
1. bei allen Aufgaben der Baukunst als einer öffentlichen Angelegenheit. . . .
2. bei der Neugestaltung der Kunstschulen und ihres Unterrichts. . . .
3. bei der Umwandlung der Museen. . . .
4. bei der Vergebung der Ausstellungsräume. . . .
5. bei der Kunstgesetzgebung. . . ." "Richtlinien der 'Novembergruppe'" (January 1919), as reprinted ibid., 11–12.

21. For extensive reconstruction of the revolutionary activities of German artists, see Joan Weinstein, *Art and the November Revolution in Germany, 1918–1919* (Chicago and London: University of Chicago Press, 1990 [in press]).

IV. The Weimar Republic

The alternative collective forms of public confrontation and communication represented by new artists' groups and publications were short-lived, however, as were the ideals of the revolution itself. The idealistic fervor of 1918 disappeared as a result of pragmatic efforts to shape the Republic and its institutions and to suppress radical alternatives. The institutions of art, while undergoing significant changes in personnel and policy, shared in the national accentuation of pragmatic solutions and of a search for continuity. The desired dialectical relationship between art and public was not achieved. The revolutionary local and national artists' groups were dissolved or were absorbed by the organizations that had been founded during the Empire. Academies and their traditional hierarchies were not replaced according to the principles of a new social order and of reformed artistic practice, as was universally advocated; instead, they appointed prewar Impressionist and Expressionist radicals to their faculties, thereby blunting the effect of opposition while retaining established curricular practice. The few institutions that were reformed and the few new organizations that were created, such as the Bauhaus at Weimar, after plunging into initially enthusiastic activity and proposing idealistic principles of instruction as well as monumental public projects, were forced into positions of resistance, of perpetual self-defense, which condemned them to comparatively modest undertakings and prevented the accomplishment of efforts to reform the interaction of art and society.

A strategy of containment by inclusion dominated the artistic policies of the emergent Weimar Republic. Academies and exhibitions opened themselves up to stylistic innovation but, by doing so, nullified the effectiveness of each style as a separate entity. Otherness was denied and, in a renewed process of apparent democratization, visual statements lost the possibility of forming part of a significant oppositional discourse. From May to July 1920, simultaneous, complementary exhibitions were held in Berlin by the various artists' groups formed prior to the war—the Berlin Secession, the Free Secession, the Jury-Free Art Show—some with overlapping artist participation, none with a predominant stylistic program but rather each mixing Impressionism, Expressionism, and traditional vocabularies. Thus, the *Great Berlin Art Exhibition*, sponsored by the long-established, conservative Association of Berlin Artists, provided the forum for the radical artistic innovation and experimentation of the November Group. Dada provocations by Otto Dix and Hannah Höch, abstract paintings by Vassily Kandinsky, geometricized sculpture by Rudolf Belling, and second-generation Expressionist works by Georg Scholz and Martel Schwichtenberg were afforded equal prominence among themselves and among both idealizing recollections of the war—Richard Bloos's depiction of the marketplace at Kowno, for example, which functioned as testimony to the beneficence of the German occupation there—and monumentalized representations of German peasants that propagated a view of these tillers of the soil as preservers of the homeland's established values. Subsumed within the grand edifice of an apparently liberal, nonpartisan aesthetic, all art products were equalized and the exhibitions served as trade fairs, announcing the availability of an unprecedented variety of wares, all vying for attention.

Symptomatic of the efforts to incorporate extreme diversity in the grandiose unity of art is, again, the *Great Berlin Art Exhibition*. For its 1927 showing, exhibitors were organized into the Cartel of the Unified Associations of Visual Artists of Berlin, Inc., which listed as its components: 1) the All-German Art League: Local Group Berlin; 2) The Architects' Association "The Ring"; 3) The Artists' Association of Berlin Sculptors; 4) "The Abstract": International Association of Expressionists, Futurists, Cubists, and Constructivists; 5) The Women's Art League; 6) The Free Association of Berlin Graphic Artists; 7) The Association of Berlin Women Artists; 8) The Berlin Secession; and 9) the Association of Berlin Artists. The existence of such diverse special-interest groups within the Berlin art community would be worthy of separate analysis and comment. In the present context, the phenomenon testifies to the incongruity of organizations disparately conceived and with a wide variety of purpose being subsumed in a demand for democratizing cohesion.

New periodicals, the most significant being Paul Westheim's *Das Kunstblatt* (*The Art Paper*), founded in 1917, were similarly devoid of partisanship, except in their championing of non-traditional over established art, and thus departed from such prewar models as *Der Sturm*, with its advocacy of Expressionism, and *Kunst und Künstler*, with its propagation of Impressionism. Increasing numbers of art galleries, competing with one another, seconded the democratizing and commercializing efforts of academies and exhibition societies. Arbitrarily devoting exhibitions, now to critical figurative imagery, now to geometric abstraction or neo-traditional works, the galleries further contributed to the denial of difference. Summarizing the dominant art ideology, the introduction that was reprinted annually in the catalogues of the Jury-Free Art Show proclaimed:

> Not the struggle against one particular art movement, nor its exclusive propagation, not reductivism, nor the fostering of cliques, but the aspiration to fairness is the social foundation of the Jury-Free Art Show, Berlin. To keep its doors open to painters and sculptors of all artistic groups—that is the art policy of the Jury-Free Art Show, Berlin. To bring struggling artists to light and to provide a survey of the tendencies of living art—that is the task of the Jury-Free Art Show, Berlin.
>
> To participate in the cultural tasks of the present and to make art accessible to many who have remained distant from it—that is the will and ideal goal of the Jury-Free Art Show, Berlin.
>
> In the struggle for this goal resides its economic significance.[22]

The statement thus demands that all art be granted equal access to the marketplace, with special emphasis on stylistic innovation as deserving greater support. Culture is separated and distinguished from other human concerns, and accorded a privileged but divorced existence through the marketing activities of the exhibitions. Whereas the revolutionary associations had sought direct contact with "the people," the public was now, once again, to be led to art, which was held to inhabit a separate domain. As postulated in the policies of the exhibition organizers, economic effectiveness, not communication, is the "ideal goal."

---

22. "Nicht im Kampf gegen eine Kunstrichtung, noch in ihrer einseitigen Förderung, nicht in der Gleichmacherei oder im Cliquenwesen, sondern im Trachten nach Gerechtigkeit liegt die soziale Grundlage der Juryfreien Kunstschau Berlin. Eine offene Tür zu haben für die Maler und Bildhauer aller Kunstgruppen, das ist die Kunstpolitik der Juryfreien Kunstschau Berlin. Ringende Künstler an das Licht zu bringen und einen Überblick über die Strömungen der lebenden Kunst zu geben, das ist die Aufgabe der Juryfreien Kunstschau Berlin.

"Mitzuarbeiten an den kulturellen Aufgaben der Gegenwart und die Kunst vielen, die ihr noch ferner standen, nahezubringen, das ist der Wille und das ideale Ziel der Juryfreien Kunstschau Berlin.

"Im Kampf für dieses Ziel liegt ihre volkswirtschaftliche Bedeutung." "Geleitwort," Catalogue of the *Juryfreie Kunstschau Berlin*, 1924, n. p.

Absolute commodification or reification of the artwork is the result of this policy as the individual work is deprived of a socially effective role through the stiflingly protective embrace of its exclusively artistic context. In the celebration of their unique power and existence as visual constructs, the artworks themselves became no more than voiceless components of a great aesthetic cross-section.

Efforts to counter the homogenization of art were also mounted, however. The most obvious, perhaps, was the continued fostering of the cult of the artist-individual. The major artist-heroes of the Weimar Republic fall into two general groups: those, such as Lovis Corinth, Liebermann, Nolde, and Pechstein, who survived from the prewar period and were now seen as intrepid pioneers and "front-fighters" of Impressionism, Expressionism, and other forms of modern art, and those—for example, Max Beckmann, Dix, Grosz, Paul Klee, and Kurt Schwitters—whose careers had started before the war but who gained increasing recognition in the early years of the Republic through repeated one-person exhibitions, critical advocacy, and such attention-capturing events as censorship trials. Significantly, not one of the younger artists who began their careers after the war was able to break into this exclusive realm of well-known names, despite the fact that the newcomers were not lacking in opportunities for individual exhibitions or in the publicity associated with controversial attitudes and personalities. Perhaps the historical situation deprived them of sufficient time to attain the status of "art star," but the pervasive homogeneity of the artistic environment, capable of absorbing individuals into the weave of its components, certainly contributed to these artists' failure to acquire exceptional renown.

The achievement of individual distinction was further undermined by the tendency to categorize art and artists in terms of specific movements. As precise characteristics were identified with Impressionism or Expressionism, works could be codified and relegated to a rigidly imposed communal identity, thereby again preventing a process of direct confrontation or statement. El Lissitsky and Hans (Jean) Arp could thus compile a list, with often humorous definitions, of thirteen different, concurrent "art-isms," each distinct from the other.[23] Museum exhibitions, such as the pioneering, epochal *Neue Sachlichkeit* exhibition at the Mannheim Kunsthalle in 1925, similarly accorded collective identities and qualities to new figurative paintings and to their creators, who had not been placed in reifying categories before. Such compartmentalization of artists into movements, the substitution of an identifying label for material confrontation, had existed previously, especially in art criticism, but during the 1920s it was the museums in Germany which became the originators and transmitters of the categories. The term *Neue Sachlichkeit* was thus endowed with the prestige and authority associated with art museums, the revered repositories of the nation's artistic past, and with the formal learning of their curators and directors. Immediately granted book-length studies, such as Franz Roh's *Post-Expressionism, Magic Realism: Problems of Recent European Painting*,[24] "*Neue Sachlichkeit*" attained an unprecedented, apparently scholarly and historical imprimatur as a verifiable means of periodization akin to such accepted historical concepts as "Gothic" or "Renaissance." With such conceptualized group-identification persis-

tently imposed, the individual artist and image were rendered impotent to operate on any level other than that of the stylistic category, and its ideology, that they were considered to represent.

Artists' reputations, the publicity accorded them and their association with a particular contemporary style, were to a large degree dependent on factors outside the artists' direct control. Yet the period of the revolution had been marked by artists' efforts to gain control over the various institutional means of public perception and reception of their work, and these attempts, while no longer a paramount consideration, did not cease after 1919–20. Artists continued to issue manifestos and pamphlets setting out their aesthetic and other concerns, and they published related statements in various periodicals and anthologies.[25] Continuing the practice of Dada, artists also compiled and distributed their own periodicals to propagate their works and ideals, either singly—Schwitters's *Merz* and *i* are notable examples—or in groups, as with *a bis z* (*a to z*), published by Cologne's Group of Progressive Artists, and *Der Wachsbogen* (*The Mimeograph Sheet*), produced by the circle of neo-realist painters in Hanover associated with Erich Wegner and Grethe Jürgens.

Less exclusively motivated in terms of a particular aesthetic was the periodical *Kunst der Zeit* (*Art of the Times*), which began publication in 1929 as official organ of the organization *Künstler-Selbsthilfe* (Artists' Self-Help). Loosely linked to the Socialist Party of Germany (SPD) and to the socialist labor unions, the organization began the first issue with a programmatic appeal:

> The art of the past was the concern of a few persons, in whose hands lay power, ownership, and money.
>
> Today, when the proletarian masses and organizations are more and more becoming the determining power in the processes of life, art should be seen to be at one with them!
>
> Artists and workers must no longer stand in opposition to each other, be a duality, but rather should form an entity: *the productive people*, one in their struggle for a better and more pleasant future.
>
> Even more than the worker, the artist is dependent on the propertied class. It provides him with work—but can dispense with it. Every attempt at rebelling against the existing "order" is punished by not selling his work—by hunger. And no organization can protect him against this disciplinary action.
>
> The working class can gain freedom for art and artists. We will show it the way. . . .[26]

23. El Lissitsky and Hans Arp, *Die Kunst-Ismen* (Erlenbach, Zurich, Munich, and Leipzig: E. Rentsch, 1925), as reprinted in *Manifeste Manifeste 1905–1933*, ed. Diether Schmidt (Dresden: VEB Verlag der Kunst, n. d.), 338 ff.

24. Franz Roh, *Nach-Expressionismus, Magischer Realismus: Probleme der neuesten europäischen Malerei* (Leipzig: Klinkhardt & Bierman, 1925).

25. For recent compilations of German artists' writings of the 1920s, see *Manifeste Manifeste* and *Die Zwanziger Jahre: Manifeste und Dokumente deutscher Künstler*, comp. Uwe M. Schneede (Cologne: DuMont Buchverlag, 1979).

26. "Die Kunst der Vergangenheit war die Angelegenheit für wenige Menschen, die über Macht, Besitz und Geld verfügten."

"Die Kunst der Gegenwart sollte in einer Zeit, wo die proletarischen Massen und Verbände mehr und mehr die bestimmende Kraft im Lebensgetriebe werden, auch in enger Verbindung mit diesen stehen!

"Künstlerschaft und Arbeiterschaft darf keine Gegenüberstellung, keine Zweiheit, sondern soll eine Einheit: *das schaffende Volk* sein, einig in seinem Kampf für eine bessere und schönere Zukunft.

"Schlimmer noch als der Arbeiter ist der Künstler abhängig von der besitzenden Klasse. Sie ist seine Arbeitgeberin, aber—sie kann seine Arbeit entbehren. Jeder Versuch zur Auflehnung gegen die bestehende 'Ordnung' wird bestraft mit Nichtverkauf seiner Werke—mit Hunger. Und keine Organisation kann ihn gegen diese Massregelung schützen.

"Die Arbeiterschaft kann die Freiheit der Kunst und der Künstler erringen. Wir werden ihr den Weg zeigen. . . ." "Aufruf!," *Kunst der Zeit: Zeitschrift der Künstler-Selbsthilfe* 1, no. 1 (October 1929): 1.

In this statement artists are added as a virtually unique class to Marx's analysis of class structure and are allied with the working-class struggle against capitalist exploitation. In addition to the twenty-four-page periodical, which it sent to members of the labor unions, *Künstler-Selbsthilfe* sought other ways of overcoming the gulf that separated the proletariat from the visual arts. Exhibitions of contemporary art and explanatory lectures by the artists represented were organized in labor union meeting halls and, for a monthly subscription and membership fee of sixty pfennigs, workers would receive annually a hand-signed original print "... by Germany's most significant artists ... [in order to furnish] the workers' homes with high-quality decoration."[27]

Close links with formally organized political groups and parties, as in the association of *Künstler-Selbsthilfe* with the SPD and the labor unions, provided artists with additional means, virtually unknown in Germany before 1918, of propagating their unique identity and of exhibiting their work outside the amorphous mass of "high art." What distinguished these efforts from all previous attempts by modern German artists to tie their work to political practice was the favorable attitude of the political parties themselves. Although party newspapers and periodicals before World War I had published art criticism, they seldom sought to forge direct links between their party and particular artistic tendencies. Now, in an active politicization of art and artists, they proposed that specific artistic positions be formally identified with party aims to the exclusion of all others. Most persistent in this was the KPD. A group of artist-members of the Party, many of whom also published drawings in its satirical magazine *Der Knüppel* (*The Cudgel*), formed The Red Group in 1924 in order to submit their "... knowledge and abilities... [as] tools at the service of the class struggle."[28] In 1928, The Red Group, reorganized along the lines of the Association of Visual Artists of Revolutionary Russia (AChRR) and under stricter Party supervision, was formally reconstituted in Berlin as the Association of Revolutionary Visual Artists in Germany (ARBKD or "Asso"), with a membership of several hundred. The organization set up numerous chapters in German cities before its activities were brought to an end by Hitler's accession to power at the end of January 1933.

Political affiliation offered Weimar artists perhaps the most effective alternative to the elitist organizations and exhibition societies that would otherwise have governed the dissemination of their work. However, espousal of this alternative involved submission to another form of external control, to another process of reification. Inextricably bound to a rigid political program, their work possessing only limited appeal for a working class that often remained antagonistic to their efforts, the artists remained subject to the distorting and restrictive effects of institutional commodification.

V. Epilogue

In 1929, in partial emulation of the KPD's artists' groups and organized cultural activities, Adolf Rosenberg founded the National Socialist *Kampfbund für Deutsche Kultur* (Combat Unit for German Culture) with the intent, less of organizing Nazi artists, than of providing a means of controlling artistic production and presentation in general. In 1933, its tenets formed the basis of the Third Reich's campaign against art and artists antipathetic to its ideology, which culminated in 1937 in confiscations of "degenerate art" and in the exhibition of that name.

The insistence on reification and organization that marked artistic activities in the Weimar Republic provided the means with which to terminate them. Readily classified in terms of, and obdurately identified with, an elitist and Republican culture, or with political opposition to the Nazis, artists and artworks were easily compressed further into a single conceptual grouping that disregarded difference or significance. Similarly, the persistent demand for institutional identification and organization was converted into a means of outlawing all artists' organizations other than the official *Reichskulturkammer* (National Chamber of Culture), outside which artists were prevented from working. Like political resistance, artistic resistance to the Third Reich's dictates quickly collapsed or was suppressed: denied a public forum, artists were reduced to working on a small scale in private or were forced into exile.

The discussion of Lukács's and Moeller van den Bruck's books at the beginning of this essay sought to establish a prototype of the process of reification to which artworks were submitted and transformed in their presentation and reception in the Weimar Republic. By their very nature, the institutions and demands that fostered the creation of these artworks, and made the 1920s one of the most diverse and accomplished decades in Germany's recent artistic history, also prepared the way for their violent and ruthless suppression. The efforts to break with the process, to which the individual works in the Fishman Collection testify so eloquently, lacked the capacity to surmount the barriers that separated them from an effective integration in the life of the society that spawned them.

---

27. "... von den bedeutendsten Künstlern Deutschlands... [um] den hochwertigen Schmuck der Arbeiterheime [zu] bilden...." Ibid., 2.

28. "... alle Kenntnisse und Fähigkeiten... nur [als] Werkzeuge... im Dienste des Klassenkampfes...." Rote Gruppe, "Manifest," *Die Rote Fahne*, no. 57 (1924), as reprinted in *Die Zwanziger Jahre*, 106.

Plates

Max Beckmann, *Bar, Brown*, 1944.
Oil on canvas, 89.7 x 42.7 cm
(35⁵/₁₆ x 16¹³/₁₆ in.). Cat. no. 1

Albert Birkle, *Mr. Spindler*, 1921.
Oil on canvas, 48 x 40 cm
(18^{15}/$_{16}$ x 15^{3}/$_{4}$ in.). Cat. no. 3

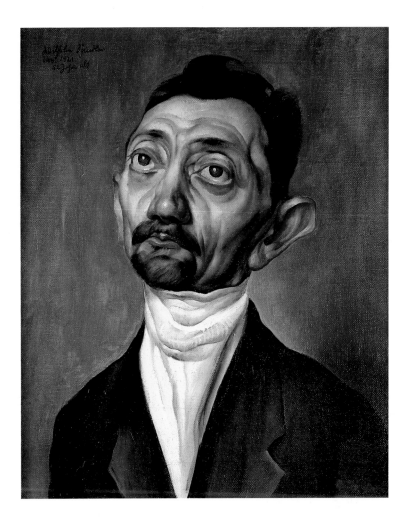

Albert Birkle, *At the Kronprinzenufer, Berlin*, 1924.
Tempera on paper mounted on board,
69 x 94 cm (27^{3}/$_{16}$ x 37 in.). Cat. no. 6

Albert Birkle, *Street with the Butcher's Cart*, 1922.
Oil on artist's board, 60.1 x 92.2 cm
(21⁷/₈ x 36⁵/₁₆ in.). Cat. no. 5

Albert Birkle, *Francis in the Stable*, 1925.
Oil on artist's board, 63 x 101 cm
(24¹³/₁₆ x 39³/₄ in.). Cat. no. 7

Albert Birkle, *My Father, Carl Birkle*, 1928.
Oil on canvas, 98 x 78 cm
(38⅝ x 30¾ in.). Cat. no. 8

Albert Birkle, *Street Scene, Berlin*, c. 1922–23.
Charcoal on canvas, 70.9 x 98.6 cm
(27⁷/₈ x 38³/₄ in.). Cat. no. 4

Albert Birkle, *Blind Man Crossing the Street*, 1921.
Charcoal on paper, 32.7 x 24.9 cm
(12⁷/₈ x 9¹³/₁₆ in.). Cat. no. 2

Volker Böhringer, *Road to Waiblingen*, c.1933.
Tempera on panel, 40.5 x 33 cm
(15^{15}/$_{16}$ x 13 in.). Cat. no. 9

Volker Böhringer, *Untitled (Tile Factory)*, c.1933–34.
Tempera on paper mounted on board, 35 x 24.8 cm
(13^{3}/$_{4}$ x 9^{3}/$_{4}$ in.). Cat. no. 10

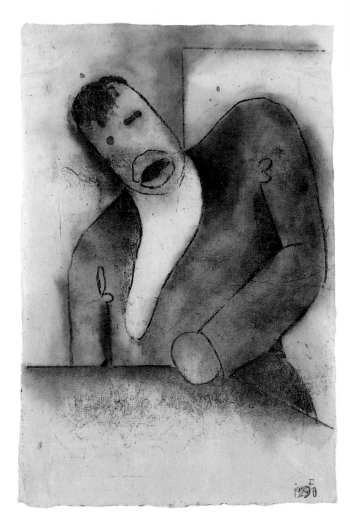

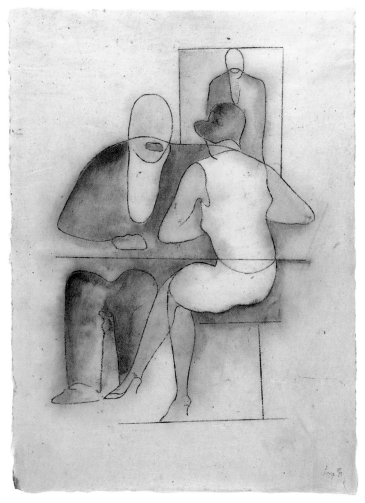

Erich Borchert, *In the Theater Box*, 1929.
Gouache, black chalk, charcoal dust on thin Japan paper,
26.5 x 21.2 cm (10⁷/₁₆ x 8³/₈ in.). Cat. no. 12

Erich Borchert, *Black Singer*, 1929.
Gouache, black chalk, charcoal dust on thin Japan paper,
31 x 21.1 cm (12³/₁₆ x 8⁵/₁₆ in.). Cat. no. 13

Erich Borchert, *Couple in a Café*, 1929.
Black chalk, gouache on paper,
41.5 x 30.9 cm (16³/₈ x 12³/₁₆ in.). Cat. no. 11

Armand Bouten, *Two Lesbian Prostitutes*, c. 1925–30?
Watercolor, brush and ink on paper, 34.6 x 26.3 cm
(13^5/$_8$ x 10^3/$_8$ in.). Cat. no. 15

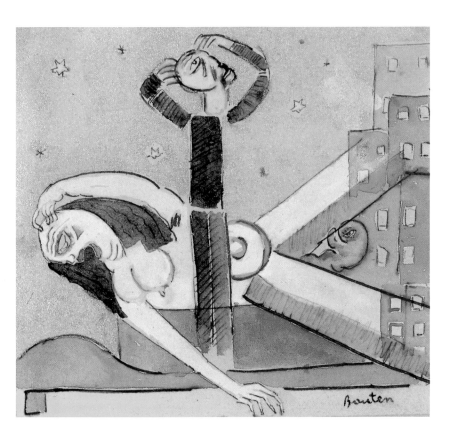

Armand Bouten, *Birth*, c. 1920.
Ink, metallic ink, watercolor on paper,
11.8 x 12.8 cm (4^5/$_8$ x 5^1/$_{16}$ in.). Cat. no. 14

Armand Bouten 33

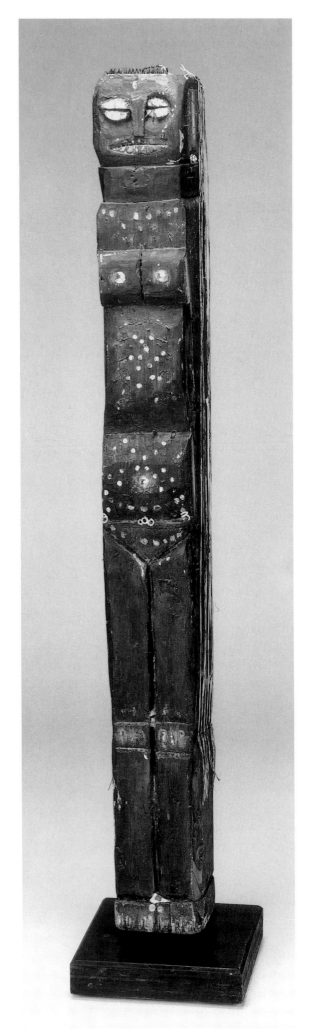

Armand Bouten, *Standing Woman*, c. 1924. Painted wood, glass, straw, wire, string, nails, 129.5 x 13 x 12 cm (51 x 5⅛ x 4¾ in.). Cat. no. 16

Armand Bouten, *Small Standing Woman*, c. 1925–30? Boxwood, colored glaze, glass, beads, metal tacks, h. 28 cm (11 in.). Cat. no. 17

Eduard Braun, *The Possessed*, c. 1930.
Pen and ink on paper, 23.8 x 30.3 cm
(9³/₈ x 11¹⁵/₁₆ in.). Cat. no. 19

Eduard Braun, *Theater Checkroom*, c. 1930.
Pen and ink on paper, 26.5 x 25 cm
(10⁷/₁₆ x 9⁷/₈ in.). Cat. no. 18

Eduard Braun 35

Eduard Braun, *City Bridge*, c. 1930. Watercolor, ink tusche on paper, 18.8 x 14.4 cm (7³/₈ x 5⁵/₈ in.). Cat. no. 20

Fritz Burmann, *Farmer's Children
(Two Children with a Hare)*, 1923.
Oil on canvas, 53.2 x 44.5 cm
(20¹⁵/16 x 17¹/2 in.). Cat. no. 22

Fritz Burmann, *Frau Biene from Worpswede, 87 Years Old*, 1923.
Oil and tempera on canvas, 44.5 x 34.4 cm
(17¹/₂ x 13¹/₂ in.). Cat. no. 21

Pol Cassel, *Cemetery*, c.1925? Oil on canvas, 110 x 129 cm (43⁵/₁₆ x 50³/₄ in.). Cat. no. 23

Pol Cassel, *Forest Interior*, 1921.
Oil. Cat. no. 23 (verso)

Paul Citroën, *Portrait*, 1923. Oil on artist's board, 66.4 x 49 cm (26¹/₈ x 19⁵/₁₆ in.). Cat. no. 24

Otto Dix, *Workers' Children*, 1922.
Pen and ink, watercolor on Japan paper,
52.4 x 37.3 cm (20⁵/₈ x 14¹¹/₁₆ in.). Cat. no. 26

Otto Dix, *Birth*, 1918. Ink, ink wash,
pencil on toned paper, 39.8 x 39.2 cm
(15¹¹/₁₆ x 15⁷/₁₆ in.). Cat. no. 25

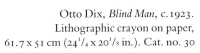

Otto Dix, *Blind Man*, c. 1923.
Lithographic crayon on paper,
61.7 x 51 cm (24^1/$_4$ x 20^1/$_8$ in.). Cat. no. 30

Otto Dix, *Beggar Woman*, 1924.
Brush, tusche, ink on paper, 62.2 x 45.5 cm
(24^1/$_2$ x 17^{15}/$_{16}$ in.). Cat. no. 32

Otto Dix, *From the Catacombs*
(The Catacombs of Palermo), 1923–24.
Watercolor over pencil on paper,
49.5 x 34.5 cm (19¹/₂ x 13⁹/₁₆ in.). Cat. no. 31

Otto Dix, *The Widow*, 1922.
Watercolor, ink over pencil on paper,
44 x 28 cm (17⁵/₁₆ x 11 in.). Cat. no. 29

Otto Dix, *Sunday Outing*, 1922. Oil, tempera on canvas, 75 x 60 cm (29$^{1}/_{2}$ x 23$^{5}/_{8}$ in.). Cat. no. 28

Otto Dix, *Sex Murder*, 1922. Watercolor, brush and ink over pencil on paper, 48.4 x 36.5 cm (19¹/₁₆ x 14³/₈ in.). Cat. no. 27

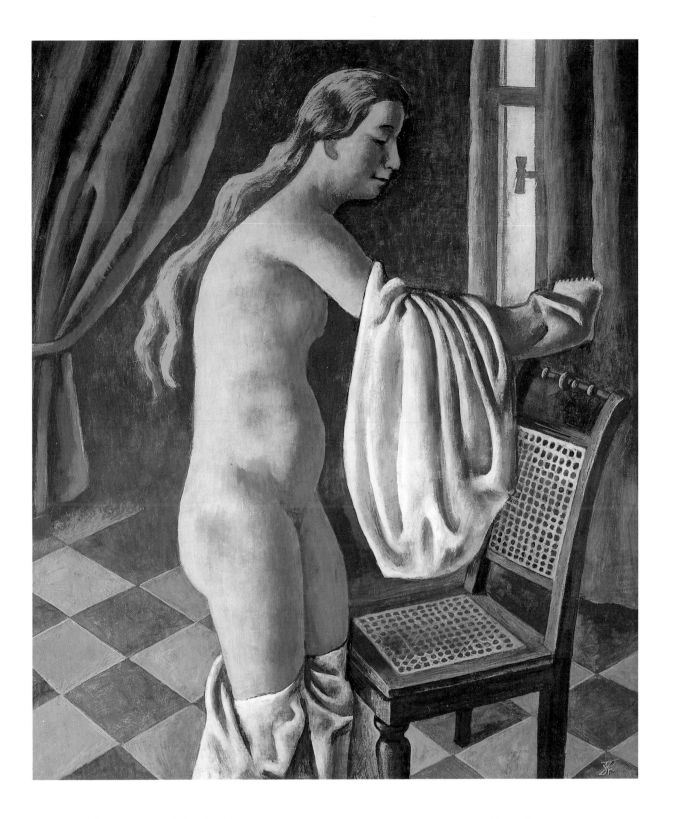

August Wilhelm Dressler, *Nude Standing Near a Chair*, 1925. Oil, tempera on canvas, 70 x 60 cm (27⁹/₁₆ x 23⁵/₈ in.). Cat. no. 33

Heinrich Ehmsen, *Insane Asylum I*, c.1924. Pencil, black chalk on paper, 30.4 x 21.2 cm (12 x 8³/₈ in.). Cat. no. 34

Heinrich Ehmsen, *The Bathing Hut*, 1928. Watercolor over pencil on paper, 47.7 x 33.4 cm (18³/₄ x 13¹/₈ in.). Cat. no. 35

Heinrich Ehmsen, *Invalids*, 1932? Watercolor over pencil on paper, 29.9 x 39.8 cm (11³/₄ x 15¹¹/₁₆ in.). Cat. no. 36

Conrad Felixmüller, *Portrait of Elfriede Hausmann*, c.1917. Oil on canvas, 76.5 x 53.7 cm (30⅛ x 21³/₁₆ in.). Cat. no. 37

Conrad Felixmüller, *Portrait of a Woman from Scotland*, 1927. Oil. Cat. no. 37 (verso)

Conrad Felixmüller, *Portrait of Otto Ritschl (Painter from Wiesbaden)*, 1920. Oil on canvas, 85 x 75 cm (33¹/₂ x 29⁹/₁₆ in.). Cat. no. 38

Ernst Fritsch, *Woman with Babushka*, 1927. Oil on canvas, 84 x 63.5 cm (33^1/$_8$ x 25 in.). Cat. no. 39

"Fuhrmann", *The Suicide*, c. 1936.
Charcoal, pen and ink on paper,
50. 5 x 32. 5 cm (19⁷/₈ x 12¹³/₁₆ in.).
Cat. no. 45

"Fuhrmann", *The Church Controls*, 1936.
Charcoal, pen and ink on paper,
49. 6 x 32. 7 cm (19¹/₂ x 12⁷/₈ in.).
Cat. no. 43

"Fuhrmann", *The Rulers*, 1936.
Charcoal, pen and ink on paper,
49.7 x 33.7 cm (19¹/₂ x 13¹/₄ in.).
Cat. no. 44

"Fuhrmann", *Mardi Gras*, 1936.
Charcoal, pen and ink on paper,
50 x 31.8 cm (19¹¹/₁₆ x 12¹/₂ in.).
Cat. no. 40

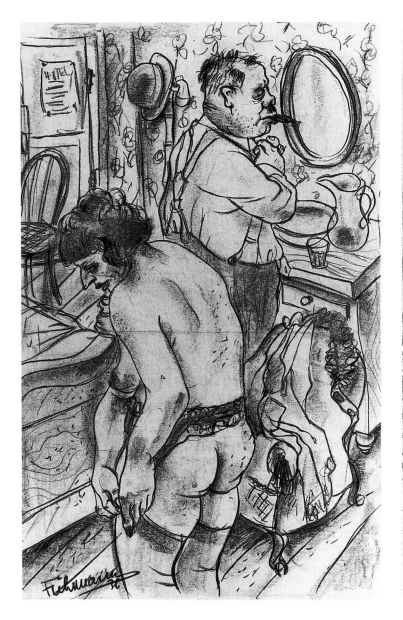

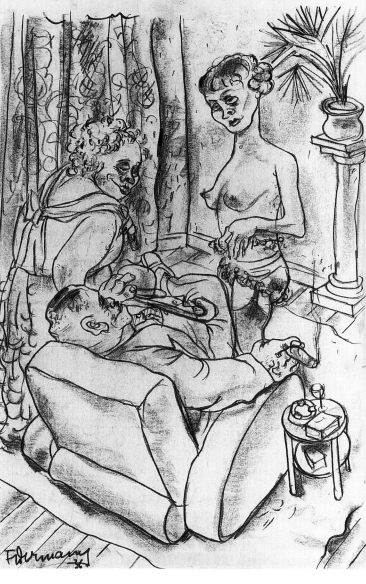

"Fuhrmann", *Lovers Dressing*, 1936.
Charcoal, pen and ink on paper,
50 x 33.5 cm (19¹¹/₁₆ x 13³/₁₆ in.).
Cat. no. 41

"Fuhrmann", *In the Brothel*, 1936.
Charcoal, pen and ink on paper,
50 x 33.7 cm (19¹¹/₁₆ x 13¹/₄ in.).
Cat. no. 42

Otto Gleichmann, *Street Scene*, 1921.
Gouache, tusche, brush and ink on paper,
23 x 31.3 cm (9¹⁄₁₆ x 12⁵⁄₁₆ in.). Cat. no. 46

Otto Griebel, *The Naked Whore*, 1923. Watercolor over pencil on paper, 40.6 x 29.1 cm (16 x 11¹/₂ in.). Cat. no. 47

Rudolf Grossmann, *Portrait of Wolfgang Gurlitt and Frau Tilly Christensen-Agoston*, c. 1930?
Pencil on paper, 34.3 x 47.5 cm (13$^{1}/_{2}$ x 18$^{11}/_{16}$ in.). Cat. no. 48

George Grosz, *The Family*, c.1916. Reed pen, brush and ink on paper, 28.4 x 22 cm (11³/₁₆ x 8¹¹/₁₆ in.). Cat. no. 49

George Grosz, *Dive*, c.1917. Brush and ink on paper, 37.5 x 32 cm (14³/₄ x 12⁹/₁₆ in.). Cat. no. 50

George Grosz, *Seated Woman*, 1923. Brush and ink on paper, 63 x 46 cm (24³/₄ x 18¹/₈ in.). Cat. no. 55

George Grosz, *Pensioners*, c.1923. Brush and ink. Cat. no. 55 (verso)

George Grosz, *To Them Peace is Assured*, 1919. Pen, brush and ink on paper, 47 x 36 cm (18^1/$_2$ x 14^3/$_{16}$ in.). Cat. no. 51

George Grosz, *Orgy*, c. 1922. Watercolor, pen and ink on paper, 50.5 x 49.5 cm (19⁷/₈ x 19⁷/₁₆ in.). Cat. no. 52

George Grosz, *Street Scene, Berlin*, c. 1924. Watercolor, pencil, pen, brush and ink on paper, 58.4 x 46 cm (23 x 18¹/₈ in.). Cat. no. 53

George Grosz, *Street Scene*, c. 1923. Pen and ink on paper, 22.1 x 17.2 cm (8^{11}/$_{16}$ x 6^{3}/$_{4}$ in.). Cat. no. 56

George Grosz, *Funeral*, c. 1927. Pen, brush and ink on paper, 48.3 x 63.3 cm (19 x 24^{7}/$_{8}$ in.). Cat. no. 57

George Grosz, *Sidewalk Café*, c. 1923–24.
Brush and ink on paper, 50 x 39.2 cm
(19^{11}/$_{16}$ x 15^{7}/$_{16}$ in.). Cat. no. 54

John Heartfield (?), *Family (Sunday Walk)*, c. 1919–21. Watercolor, collage, pen and ink over pencil on paper, 28 x 21.3 cm (11 x 8³/₈ in.). Cat. no. 58

Erich Heckel, *Men at a Table*, 1913. Watercolor, gouache, brush and ink on paper, 20.7 x 39.3 cm (8¹/₈ x 15¹/₂ in.). Cat. no. 60

Erich Heckel, *Dangast Village Landscape with Canal*, 1909. Oil on canvas, 69.7 x 80 cm (27⁷/₁₆ x 31¹/₂ in.). Cat. no. 59

Hein Heckroth, *Ada*, c. 1924? Watercolor on paper, 39.7 x 32.2 cm (15⁵/₈ x 12⁵/₈ in.). Cat. no. 61

Otto Herbig, *The Tower*, 1923. Oil on canvas, 74.5 x 56 cm (29³/₈ x 22¹/₁₆ in.). Cat. no. 62

Karl Jakob Hirsch, *Martin Buber
Mourning in a Jewish Cemetery*, c. 1920.
Watercolor over pencil on paper,
35.5 x 28.5 cm (14 x 11¼ in.). Cat. no. 63

John Hoexter, *Clown in Profile*, c. 1920 (c. 1929?).
Gouache on toned paper, 28.1 x 19 cm (11¹/₁₆ x 7½ in.).
Cat. no. 64

Richard Hohly, *Two Unemployed Men*, 1929.
Charcoal, pen and ink on heavy paper,
42.5 x 53 cm (16³/₄ x 20⁷/₈ in.). Cat. no. 65

Karl Holtz, *Farmer's Child*, c. 1921.
Pencil on paper, 28.5 x 19.8 cm
(11¹/₄ x 7¹³/₁₆ in.). Cat. no. 66

Karl Hubbuch, *Detective Story*, 1924. Watercolor, pencil, colored pencil, ink on paper, 54.1 x 41.9 cm (21¼ x 16½ in.). Cat. no. 69

Karl Hubbuch, *Martha with Raincoat*, c. 1926–27.
Pencil with watercolor on heavy paper,
71.2 x 55.2 cm (28 x 21^{11}/$_{16}$ in.). Cat. no. 70

Karl Hubbuch, *Self-Portrait*, 1924.
Lithographic crayon on heavy paper, 52 x 36.4 cm
(20^{7}/$_{16}$ x 14^{5}/$_{16}$ in.). Cat. no. 67

Karl Hubbuch, *The Waitress*, c. 1926. Watercolor, tusche, pencil on paper, 99.5 x 50 cm
(39³/₁₆ x 19¹¹/₁₆ in.). Cat. no. 68

Karl Hubbuch, *In the Theater Loge (Head of a Woman)*, c. 1928–29.
Watercolor over pencil on paper, 80 x 43 cm
(31¹/₂ x 16⁷/₈ in.), sight. Cat. no. 71

Karl Hubbuch, *Head of a Woman*, c. 1928–29.
Watercolor over pencil. Cat. no. 71 (verso)

Karl Hubbuch   73

Willy Jaeckel, *Barges on the Spree*, 1913.
Oil on artist's board, 51 x 71 cm
(20^1/$_{16}$ x 28 in.). Cat. no. 72

Willy Jaeckel, *Hand-to-Hand Combat in a Trench*, 1914.
Pen, ink, ink wash on engraving paper,
43.2 x 41 cm (17 x 16^1/$_8$ in.). Cat. no. 73

Willy Jaeckel, *Thinker*, c. 1916. Gouache on vellum, 33 x 30. 1 cm (13 x 10³/₄ in.). Cat. no. 74

Richard Janthur, *Illustration for Rudyard Kipling's "Jungle Book"*, c. 1920. Watercolor, brush and ink on paper, 42.7 x 33.8 cm (16¹³/₁₆ x 13⁵/₁₆ in.). Cat. no. 75

Grethe Jürgens, *Factory Entrance*, 1923.
Watercolor, gouache, colored pencil on paper,
20.6 x 17.5–17.9 cm (8¹/₈ x 6⁷/₈–7¹/₁₆ in.).
Cat. no. 77

Grethe Jürgens, *Orange Cart*, 1923.
Watercolor, pencil on paper, 26.8 x 23.9 cm
(10¹/₂ x 9⁷/₁₆ in.). Cat. no. 76

Grethe Jürgens   77

Grethe Jürgens, *Spectators at a Traveling Circus*, 1931. Watercolor on paper, 68.6 x 49 cm (26¹⁵/₁₆ x 19¹/₄ in.), sight. Cat. no. 78

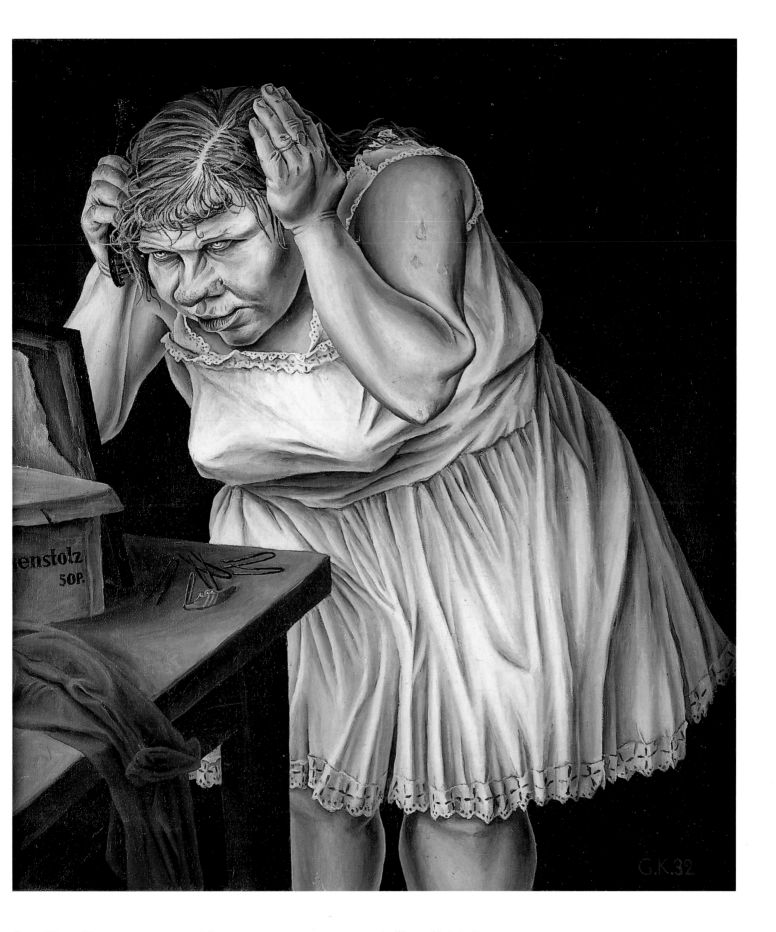

Georg Kinzer, *Woman at a Mirror*, 1932. Oil, tempera on canvas, 73.5 x 64.5 cm ($28^{15}/_{16}$ x $25^{7}/_{16}$ in.). Cat. no. 79

Ernst Ludwig Kirchner, *Small Café Society*, c. 1910. Pen, ink, ink wash on yellow paper, 16.8 x 22.8 cm (6⁵/₈ x 9 in.). Cat. no. 80

Immanuel Knayer, *Locomotive*, c. 1927. Watercolor, brush and ink on paper, 13.6 x 19.5 cm (5³/₈ x 7¹¹/₁₆ in.). Cat. no. 81

D. W. Koeppen (?), *A Woman of 1934*, 1934. Watercolor over pencil, pen and ink on paper, 25.3 x 29.7 cm (10 x 11³/₄ in.). Cat. no. 82

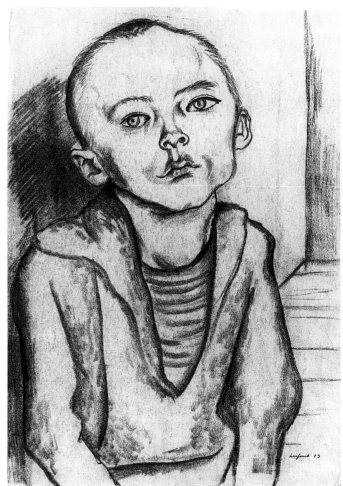

Bernhard Kretzschmar, *Standing Boy*, 1921.
Pencil on paper, 37 x 30.7 cm
(14¹/₂ x 12¹/₈ in.). Cat. no. 83

Wilhelm Lachnit, *Boy in Sailor Suit*, 1923.
Carpenter's pencil on paper, 46–45.7 x 33.4 cm
(18¹/₈–18 x 13¹/₈ in.). Cat. no. 84

Franz Lenk, *Blooming Cactus*, 1931. Watercolor on paper, 40.8 x 29.2 cm (16 x 11¹/₂ in.). Cat. no. 85

Käthe Loewenthal, *Children at the Edge of a Village*,
c. 1924. Pastel on paper, 29.8 x 39.5 cm
(11³/₄ x 15¹/₂ in.). Cat. no. 87

Käthe Loewenthal, *Black Ducks*, c. 1924.
Pastel on paper, 29.4 x 38.4 cm
(11¹/₂ x 15¹/₈ in.), sight. Cat. no. 86

Elfriede Lohse-Wächtler, *Nightclub Balcony*, 1930. Pastel on paper, 72.5 x 55 cm (28¹/₂ x 21⁵/₈ in.). Cat. no. 88

Elfriede Lohse-Wächtler, *Lissy*, 1931. Watercolor over pencil on paper, 68 x 49 cm (19¹/₄ x 26¹³/₁₆ in.). Cat. no. 89

Jeanne Mammen, *The Journey Home*, 1920s. Black chalk on paper, 38.5 x 31.25 cm (15^{1}/$_{8}$ x 12^{1}/$_{4}$ in.). Cat. no. 90

Jeanne Mammen, *Berlin Street Scene*, c. 1927–29. Watercolor over pencil on vellum, 33.8 x 48.4 cm (13^1/$_3$ x 19 in.). Cat. no. 91

Jeanne Mammen, *Boring Dollies*, c. 1927–30. Watercolor over pencil on paper, 38.7 x 28.5 cm (15¼ x 11¼ in.). Cat. no. 92

Herbert Marxen, *The Seamstress*, 1927. Oil on canvas, 51.5 x 47.5 cm (20¹/₄ x 18³/₄ in.). Cat. no. 93

Frans Masereel, *Accordionist in a Tavern*, 1927.
Oil on canvas, 49.8 x 64.9 cm
(19⁹/₁₆ x 25⁹/₁₆ in.). Cat. no. 94

Frans Masereel,
Seaman with a Woman, 1928.
Oil on canvas, 72.5 x 60.1 cm
(28⁹/₁₆ x 23⁵/₈ in.). Cat. no. 95

Frans Masereel, *The Green Smokestack*, 1929. Oil on canvas, 71.5 x 90.5 cm (28¹/₈ x 35⁵/₈ in.). Cat. no. 96

Frans Masereel, *Inner Harbor*, 1932. Oil on canvas, 73 x 60 cm (28³/₄ x 23⁵/₈ in.). Cat. no. 97

Else Meidner, *Double Portrait: Else and Ludwig Meidner*, 1933. Black chalk on paper, 29 x 21.7 cm (11⁷/₁₆ x 8¹/₂ in.). Cat. no. 98

Ludwig Meidner, *Self-Portrait*, 1912. Oil on canvas, 74.9 x 58.3 cm (29$^1/_2$ x 23 in.). Cat. no. 99

Ludwig Meidner, *Apocalyptic Landscape*, 1913. Oil on canvas,
67.3 x 80 cm (26¹/₂ x 31¹/₂ in.). Cat. no. 103

Ludwig Meidner, *Landscape*, c. 1913.
Oil. Cat. no. 103 (verso)

Ludwig Meidner, *My Nocturnal Visage*, 1913. Oil on canvas, 66.7 x 48.9 cm (26^1/$_4$ x 19^1/$_4$ in.). Cat. no. 100

Ludwig Meidner, *Street with Passersby*, 1913.
Pen, brush and Chinese ink over pencil on paper,
53.8 x 46 cm (21³/₁₆ x 18¹/₈ in.). Cat. no. 106

Ludwig Meidner, *Street Scene*, 1913.
Ink, tusche over pencil, with white
highlighting, on paper, 39.8 x 50 cm
(15⁵/₈ x 19⁵/₈ in.). Cat. no. 101

Ludwig Meidner, *Coffeehouse Scene*, 1913.
Pen and ink with white highlighting over pencil,
60 x 40 cm (23⁵/₈ x 15³/₄ in.). Cat. no. 107

Ludwig Meidner, *Grand Café Schöneberg*,
1913. Pen, brush and ink over pencil,
40.6 x 47 cm (15¹⁵/₁₆ x 18¹/₂ in.). Cat. no. 102

Ludwig Meidner, *Street*, 1913. Brush, pen and Chinese ink with white highlighting on paper,
54.6 x 45.1 cm (21¹/₂ x 17³/₄ in.). Cat. no. 105

Ludwig Meidner, *Südwestkorso, Berlin, Five O'Clock in the Morning*, 1913. Carpenter's pencil, pencil on paper, 42.1 x 56.6 cm (16^1/$_2$ x 22^1/$_4$ in.). Cat. no. 104

Ludwig Meidner, *Apocalyptic Vision*, 1913.
Ink over pencil on paper, 54.9 x 43.6 cm
(21⁵/₈ x 17³/₁₆ in.). Cat. no. 108

Ludwig Meidner, *Of the Terrible Doubt of Appearances*, 1914.
Ink over pencil on paper, 47 x 42.5 cm
(18¹/₂ x 16³/₄ in.). Cat. no. 109

Ludwig Meidner   103

Ludwig Meidner, *Battle*, 1914. Pen, brush and ink on paper, 64.9 x 50.6 cm (25^9/$_{16}$ x 19^{13}/$_{16}$ in.). Cat. no. 110

Ludwig Meidner, *Beggar*, 1916.
Pen, brush and ink over pencil on paper,
58.5 x 45.7 cm (23 x 18 in.). Cat. no. 113

Ludwig Meidner, *Prophet*, 1916.
Brush, pen and ink over pencil on paper,
57.7 x 45 cm (22³/₈ x 17¹¹/₁₆ in.). Cat. no. 114

Ludwig Meidner   105

Ludwig Meidner, *Self-Portrait*, 1916.
Brush, pen and ink on paper, 47 x 39 cm
(18$\frac{1}{2}$ x 15$\frac{5}{16}$ in.).
Cat. no. 115

Ludwig Meidner, *Self-Portrait*, 1915.
Carpenter's pencil on paper, 49.5 x 36.5 cm
(19$\frac{1}{2}$ x 14$\frac{3}{8}$ in.). Cat. no. 111

Ludwig Meidner, *Self-Portrait*, 1916. Ink over pencil on paper, 43.5 x 34.9 cm (17^1/$_8$ x 13^{11}/$_{16}$ in.). Cat. no. 112

Ludwig Meidner, *Landscape with Birch*
1919. Oil on canvas, 30 x 34.5 cm
(11³/₄ x 13¹/₂ in.). Cat. no. 116

Ludwig Meidner, *The Call at Daybreak*, 1920.
Gouache, watercolor over pencil on light cardboard,
67.4 x 50.5 cm (26¹/₂ x 19⁷/₈ in.). Cat. no. 117

Ludwig Meidner, *Self-Portrait*, 1923.
Oil on artist's board, 59.1 x 47 cm
(23¹/₄ x 18¹/₂ in.). Cat. no. 118

Ludwig Meidner, *Portrait of a Young Woman from Poland
(Portrait of a Polish Jewish Woman—Domestic Servant)*, 1929.
Oil on artist's board, 70 x 50 cm (27³/₈ x 19⁵/₈ in.). Cat. no. 119

Ludwig Meidner   109

Walter Meyer-Vax, *The Editor*, 1929. Oil and pencil on canvas, 140 x 76 cm (55³/₁₆ x 29¹⁵/₁₆ in.). Cat. no. 120

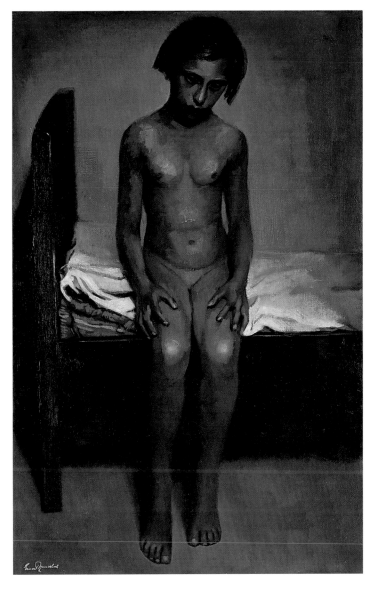

Ernest Neuschul, *Nude Girl*, 1930.
Oil on canvas, 99.8 x 65.2 cm
(29^1/$_4$ x 25^{11}/$_{16}$ in.). Cat. no. 121

Hermann Niehaus, *Prole*, 1924.
Watercolor, gouache, pen and ink on paper,
50.8 x 40.4 cm (20 x 15^7/$_8$ in.). Cat. no. 122

Ernest Neuschul, Hermann Niehaus   111

Felix Nussbaum, *Train Station at Alassio*, 1933.
Gouache on paper, 49.5 x 65.5 cm
(19⁷/₁₆ x 25³/₄ in.). Cat. no. 124

Felix Nussbaum, *Self-Portrait*, 1935.
Gouache on paper, 64.4 x 50.2 cm
(25³/₈ x 19³/₄ in.). Cat. no. 125

Felix Nussbaum, *Park of Antiquities*, 1931. Oil on canvas, 60 x 72 cm (23⁵/₈ x 28⁵/₁₆ in.). Cat. no. 123

Hermann Max Pechstein, *Tempest*, 1911. Oil on canvas, 65.4 x 65.4 cm (25³/₄ x 25³/₄ in.). Cat. no. 126

Max Radler, *Urban Scene with Train*, c. 1930. Oil on canvas, 55.2 x 80.2 cm (21³/₄ x 31⁹/₁₆ in.). Cat. no. 128

Max Radler, *Woman at Her Toilet*, 1931. Pencil on paper, 48.1 x 22.5 cm (18⁷/₈ x 9¹³/₁₆ in.). Cat. no. 129

Max Radler, *Woman in a Doorway*, 1930. Watercolor on heavy paper, 30.7 x 22.6 cm (12¹/₁₆ x 8⁷/₈ in.). Cat. no. 127

Hans Rilke, *Mother and Son*, 1924.
Watercolor, pen and ink, pencil on paper,
46.5 x 30.5 cm (18¹/₄ x 12 in.). Cat. no. 130

Marcel Ronay, *Sailor and Girl*, 1929.
Oil on panel, 54.1 x 42.8 cm
(21¹/₄ x 16¹³/₁₆ in.). Cat. no. 131

Christian Schad, *Narcissus*, 1927. Pencil, pen and ink, watercolor
and tusche with splatter technique on paper,
18.3 x 12.9 cm (7³/₁₆ x 5¹/₁₆ in.). Cat. no. 132

Josef Scharl, *Portrait of a Worker*, 1925. Oil on canvas, 105 x 78.6 cm (41³/₈ x 30⁷/₈ in.). Cat. no. 133

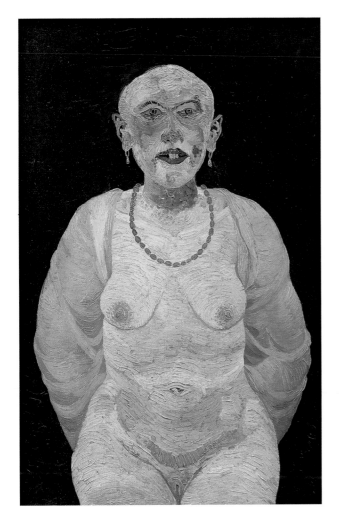

Josef Scharl, *Battered Prostitute*, 1931. Oil on canvas, 87.4 x 56.3 cm (34⁷/₁₆ x 22³/₁₆ in.). Cat. no. 134

Josef Scharl, *Soup Eater*, 1932. Oil on canvas, 115 x 92.5 cm (45⁷/₈ x 36¹/₄ in.). Cat. no. 135

Hugo Scheiber, *Anxiety (Self-Portrait)*, c.1920–22. Oil on cardboard mounted on board, 48 x 48 cm (18⁷/₈ x 18⁷/₈ in.), sight. Cat. no. 136

Rudolf Schlichter, *Circus Children*, c. 1924–25? Pencil on paper, 49.8 x 41.6 cm (19⁹/₁₆ x 16³/₈ in.). Cat. no. 137

Georg Scholz, *Nightly Noise*, 1919. Oil on canvas, 56.8 x 50.9 cm (22³/₈ x 20 in.). Cat. no. 138

Karl Schwesig, *Out to the Demonstration*, 1931.
Watercolor, ink and tusche on paper, 23.9 x 29.8 cm
(9⁷/₁₆ x 11¹³/₁₆ in.). Cat. no. 140

Franz Theodor Schütt, *Young Woman before a Window*, 1929.
Gouache, pencil on paper, 47 x 27.3–32 cm
(18¹/₂ x 10³/₄–12⁵/₈ in.), sight. Cat. no. 139

Karl Schwesig, Franz Theodor Schütt   123

Martel Schwichtenberg, *Girl in Red Striped Skirt*,
c. 1920? Oil on cardboard, 70.8 x 49.8 cm
(27⁷/₈ x 19⁵/₈ in.), sight. Cat. no. 142

Martel Schwichtenberg, *Snowy
Landscape II*, c. 1922. Oil on canvas,
67 x 82.2 cm (26³/₈ x 32³/₈ in.).
Cat. no. 143

Martel Schwichtenberg, *Portrait of a Woman (Seated Woman with Flowers)*, c. 1920–21. Oil on canvas, 94.5 x 78 cm (37^1/$_4$ x 30^3/$_4$ in.). Cat. no. 141

Richard Seewald, *Landscape with Rocky Cliffs and Goats Overlooking the Sea Near Positano*, 1924. Watercolor over pencil on paper, 35 x 28.5 cm (13³/₄ x 11³/₁₆ in.). Cat. no. 144

Friedrich (Fritz) Skade, *Young Woman*, c. 1925? Watercolor over pencil on paper, 47.8 x 32 cm (18¹¹/₁₆ x 12⁹/₁₆ in.). Cat. no. 145

Alice Sommer, *Two Sisters*, 1925. Pencil on toned paper,
64 x 48.2 cm (25³/₁₆ x 19 in.). Cat. no. 146

Alice Sommer, *Portrait: Head of a Woman*, 1925.
Oil on board, 48.5 x 23.9 cm
(19¹/₁₆ x 9¹/₄ in.). Cat. no. 147

Jakob Steinhardt, *Self-Portrait (Drawing for an Exhibition Poster: Die Pathetiker)*, 1912. Pen and ink over charcoal, pencil, with white highlighting, on paper, 43 x 30 cm (16⁷/₈ x 11³/₄ in.). Cat. no. 148

Jakob Steinhardt, *Recollection of the War*, c. 1919. Lithographic chalk on paper, 43 x 40 cm (16¹⁵/₁₆ x 15³/₄ in.). Cat. no. 149

Jakob Steinhardt, *Couple at a Table*, c. 1920?
Pencil, charcoal on toned paper, 29 x 21.8 cm
($11^7/_{16}$ x $8^5/_8$ in.). Cat. no. 150

Jakob Steinhardt, *Plague*, c. 1922–23?
Pen and ink, ink wash on paper,
42 x 50 cm ($16^1/_2$ x $19^{11}/_{16}$ in.). Cat. no. 151

Jakob Steinhardt   129

Georg Tappert, *Woman with Monkey (Reclining Nude with Baboon)*, c. 1913. Oil on canvas, 60 x 67. 5 cm (23⅝ x 26½ in.). Cat. no. 152

Georg Tappert, *Woman in a Café (A Cup of Hot Chocolate)*, c. 1917. Oil on canvas, 82 x 76 cm (32¼ x 29¹⁵/₁₆ in.). Cat. no. 153

Georg Tappert, *Country Street, Evening Mood*, 1936.
Watercolor over pencil on paper, 24.8 x 33.5 cm
(9³/₄ x 13³/₁₆ in.), sight. Cat. no. 156

Georg Tappert, *Waiting*, c. 1927.
Pen and ink on parchment, 31 x 24 cm
(12³/₁₆ x 9¹/₂ in.). Cat. no. 154

Georg Tappert, *Woman's Head with a Red Cap*, c. 1932. Oil on canvas, 45 x 35.5 cm (17³/₄ x 14 in.). Cat. no. 155

Bruno Voigt, *Potter's Lane, Weimar*, 1932.
Pen and ink, splatter technique on blue-gray
paper, 46 x 46 cm (18¹/₄ x 18¹/₄ in.). Cat. no. 160

Bruno Voigt, *The Boss: Thoughts
of a Man Watching an Attractive
Woman in a Café*, 1931.
Pen, brush, ink over pencil on paper,
34.6 x 40.1 cm (13⁵/₈ x 15³/₄ in.).
Cat. no. 157

Bruno Voigt, *The Revolution Will Triumph*, 1933. Watercolor, ink, charcoal on paper, 50.5 x 36 cm (19¼ x 16 in.). Cat. no. 167

Bruno Voigt, *Attack*, 1932. Watercolor, ink on paper, 45.7 x 29.2 cm (18 x 11¹/₂ in.). Cat. no. 164

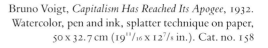

Bruno Voigt, *Capitalism Has Reached Its Apogee*, 1932.
Watercolor, pen and ink, splatter technique on paper,
50 x 32.7 cm (19^{11}/$_{16}$ x 12^{7}/$_{8}$ in.). Cat. no. 158

Bruno Voigt, *Anti-War Demonstration*, 1932.
Watercolor, pen and ink, splatter technique,
over pencil on paper, 50.3 x 35.7 cm (20 x 14^{1}/$_{4}$ in.). Cat. no. 161

Bruno Voigt, *Attack*, 1932. Watercolor, tusche on paper, 50.8 x 35.9 cm (20 x 14¹/₈ in.). Cat. no. 159

Bruno Voigt, *Berlin Street Corner*, 1932.
Black chalk, tusche, watercolor over carpenter's
pencil on paper, 57 x 44.9 cm (22³/₈ x 17³/₄ in.). Cat. no. 162

Bruno Voigt, *In the Brothel*, 1932.
Pen, brush, ink, watercolor on paper, 46.6 x 42.2 cm
(18¹/₄ x 16¹/₂ in.). Cat. no. 165

Bruno Voigt   139

Bruno Voigt, *Solicitation*, 1933.
Pen and ink on paper, 50.6 x 36.3 cm
(19¹⁵/₁₆ x 14¹/₄ in.). Cat. no. 169

Bruno Voigt, *Resignation*, 1932. Black chalk,
brush, pen, ink, and watercolor on paper,
40.4 x 36.2 cm (15¹⁵/₁₆ x 14¹/₄ in.). Cat. no. 163

Bruno Voigt, *Street Fight*, 1932. Watercolor and ink on paper, 50.5 x 36 cm (19⁷/₈ x 14¹/₄ in.). Cat. no. 166

Bruno Voigt, *Cultivate the Music of the German Home*, 1933. Pen and ink, watercolor over pencil on paper, 48.7 x 40.7 cm (19³/₁₆ x 16 in.). Cat. no. 168

Bruno Voigt, *Self-Portrait*, 1935. Oil, tempera on artist's board, 59.5 x 39 cm (23⁷/₁₆ x 15³/₈ in.). Cat. no. 170

Christoph Voll, *Nude near Stove*, c. 1920. Watercolor, pen and ink on paper, 34.8 x 50 cm (13¹¹/₁₆ x 19¹¹/₁₆ in.). Cat. no. 171

Aloys Wach, *Street Scene*, c. 1914.
Brown chalk on brown paper, 43.4 x 31.5 cm
(17^1/$_8$ x 12^7/$_{16}$). Cat. no. 172

Aloys Wach, *Dedicated to Kapp*, c. 1920.
Pen, violet ink, watercolor on toned paper,
30.6 x 23.4 cm (12^1/$_{16}$ x 9^1/$_4$ in.). Cat. no. 173

Aloys Wach   145

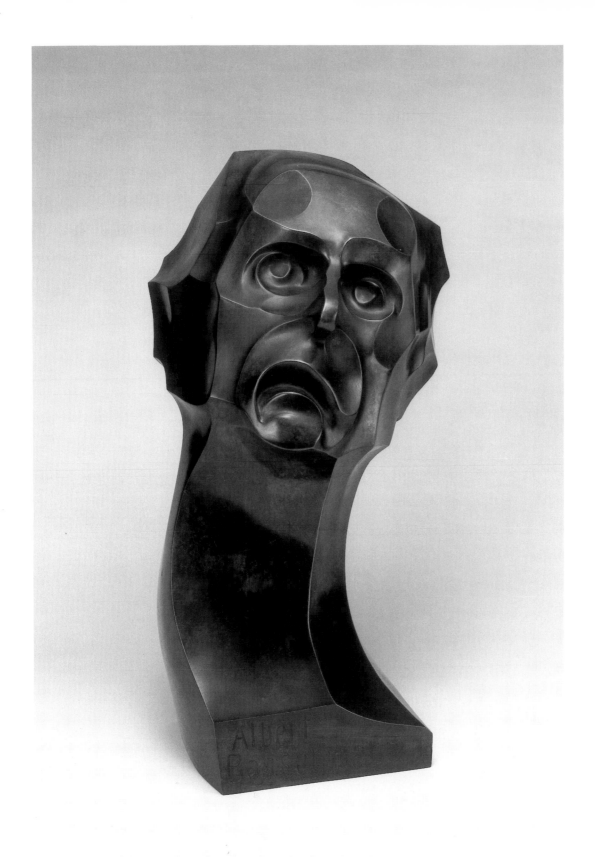

William Wauer, *Portrait of Albert Bassermann*, 1918 (cast 1945).
Bronze, 51 x 20 x 20 cm (20^{1}/$_{16}$ x 7^{7}/$_{8}$ x 7^{7}/$_{8}$ in.). Cat. no. 174

Erich Wegner, *Little Mary*, c. 1920. Oil on canvas, 35.2 x 33.3 cm (13⁷/₈ x 13¹/₈ in.). Cat. no. 175

Erich Wegner, *Woman at a Gate*, 1923.
Gouache on heavy paper, 37.3 x 25.3 cm
(14³/₄ x 10 in.). Cat. no. 178

Erich Wegner, *Sailor in Port*, 1923.
Gouache, brush and ink on heavy brown paper,
32.8 x 24.7 cm (12¹⁵/₁₆ x 9³/₄ in.). Cat. no. 177

Erich Wegner, *Mangling Done Here*, c. 1923.
Watercolor with gouache, brush and ink over
pencil on paper, 30.3 x 26.6–27.1 cm
(11^{15}/$_{16}$ x 10^{1}/$_{2}$–10^{7}/$_{8}$ in.). Cat. no. 176

Erich Wegner, *Couple with a Sailboat*, 1925.
Watercolor over pencil on paper, 35 x 26 cm
(13^{13}/$_{16}$ x 10^{1}/$_{4}$ in.). Cat. no. 179

Erich Wegner   149

Kurt Weinhold, *The New Window Display*, c. 1929–30. Pen and ink on paper, 46 x 59.2 cm (18¹/₈ x 23¹/₄ in.), sight. Cat. no. 180

Gustav Wunderwald, *Underpass (Spandau)*, c. 1927. Oil on canvas, 66.3 x 83.7 cm (26¹/₈ x 33 in.). Cat. no. 181

Magnus Zeller, *Thieves*, 1919.
Watercolor on paper, 29.8 x 36.2 cm
(11³/₄ x 14¹/₄ in.). Cat. no. 183

Magnus Zeller, *In Flight*, 1920.
Watercolor over pencil on paper, 30.4–31.3 x 22.6–23 cm
(12–12⁵/₁₆ x 8⁷/₈–9¹/₁₆ in.). Cat. no. 184

Magnus Zeller, *Macabre Business*, c. 1921–22?
Pencil on heavy Bütten, 18 x 23 cm
(7^{1}/$_{16}$ x 9^{1}/$_{16}$ in.). Cat. no. 185

Magnus Zeller, *In the Insane Asylum*, c. 1919–20.
Pencil on heavy gray paper, 21 x 20.5 cm
(8^{1}/$_{4}$ x 8^{1}/$_{16}$ in.). Cat. no. 182

Magnus Zeller   153

Richard Ziegler, *Young Widow (The New Me)*, 1922. Oil on canvas, 102 x 61 cm (39$^1/_2$ x 24 in.). Cat. no. 186

Richard Ziegler, *Couple at Table*, 1927. Oil on canvas, 100 x 75 cm (39³/₈ x 29⁹/₁₆ in.). Cat. no. 187

Richard Ziegler, *Springtime on Tauentzien Street*, 1927.
Oil pastel, brush and ink on paper, 38 x 28 cm
(15 x 11 in.). Cat. no. 188

Richard Ziegler, *Sylvia von Harden*, 1927.
Oil pastel, pen and ink on rice paper,
29 x 22 cm (11³/₈ x 8¹¹/₁₆ in.). Cat. no. 189

Richard Ziegler, *Judgment of Paris*, 1928.
Oil, ink on canvas, 85.3 x 100.4 cm
(33¹/₂ x 39¹/₂ in.). Cat. no. 193

Richard Ziegler, *On the Way to the Office in the Underground*, 1927.
Oil pastel, brush and ink on rice paper, 35.6 x 25.4 cm
(14 x 10¹/₁₆ in.). Cat. no. 192

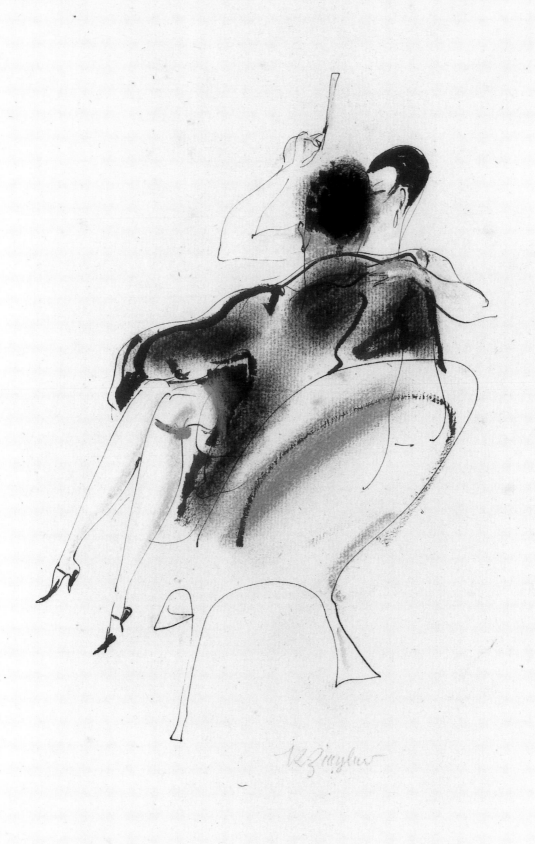

Richard Ziegler, *Lovers in an Armchair*, c. 1928. Oil pastel, pen and ink, ink tusche on rag paper, 23.5 x 16 cm (9¼ x 6¼ in.). Cat. no. 191

158   Richard Ziegler

Richard Ziegler, *In the Café*, c. 1927. Oil pastel, brush and ink on rice paper, 32.4 x 21.7 cm (12³/₄ x 8⁹/₁₆ in.). Cat. no. 190

Catalogue

1 Max Beckmann

Bar, Brown (Bar, braun), 1944

Oil on canvas
89.7 x 42.7 cm (35⁵/₁₆ x 16¹³/₁₆ in.)
Not signed
(Max Beckmann Amsterdam
Inventory, 1944, "11) Bar braun.
August")
Göpel 669

Provenance: Dr. Hildebrand Gurlitt, Dresden and Düsseldorf; Frau Helene Gurlitt, Düsseldorf and Munich; Gurlitt Estate, Munich; Galerie Roman Norbert Ketterer, Campione d'Italia.

Exhibition: Frankfurt a. M., Städelsches Kunstinstitut, June–July 1947, cat. no. 34 (dated 1935).

Among artists active during the Weimar Republic, Max Beckmann was one of the most honored. His works were widely exhibited, and included in international expositions, such as the Venice Biennale of 1930, to represent Germany's artistic culture. Books and articles were devoted to his art, and at Berlin's Kronprinzenpalais, the modern wing of the National Gallery, an entire room was reserved for his work. He served as master teacher at the combined Frankfurt Städel School and School of Applied Arts. This unequaled procession of honors ceased in 1933, however, when Adolf Hitler became Chancellor; Beckmann was then vilified by the Nazis as one of their most despised "degenerate" artists. Following Hitler's speech at the opening of the House of German Art in Munich on 18 July 1937, Beckmann resolved to leave Germany immediately and moved to Amsterdam. There, when efforts to emigrate to the United States failed, he stayed through the German invasion and occupation, and for two more years after the Allied victory in 1945. During this decade of uncertainty, he created nearly three hundred paintings, including five monumental triptychs which are among the most ambitious works of his entire career, and developed the two extensive series of lithographs and drawings devoted to *The Apocalypse* and Goethe's *Faust, Part II*. Faced with persecution and threat of annihilation, Beckmann responded with remarkable activity and production.

In 1944, he was sixty years old. Over Amsterdam, planes engaged in combat; in his diaries, Beckmann entered pessimistic observations on the meaning of life and the relevance and function of art:

> What a gruesome fantasy—constantly waiting to see if the mystery will reveal itself and constantly sitting stupidly before the gray curtain behind which the spirits roam and rumble, or maybe nothing but the void . . . . If you believe the turmoil has meaning, then you shall be happy—but sometime in the distant future—if you believe that it is nothing but chance, then that's your tough luck. —Nevertheless, won't you have to grant me that it is a significant feat to produce a web of images from this nothingness which at least maintains everything in a persisting, extreme state of tension? "It's only possible if you play hide-and-seek with yourself, however."—Anything to amuse

Several ironic confrontations appear in Beckmann's diary entry. As he does frequently elsewhere, he draws an analogy between life and theater, but, unlike earlier texts, this one does not consider the visible action on life's stage, but rather a mystery that remains hidden. A gray curtain and the sounds behind it are the sole evidence of an unknown and unknowable existential theater which impinges upon the artist. He obtains no means from which to manufacture the consistent world-image that his art presents, except the visions within himself. A radical divorce between reality and art is postulated, therefore, as the artist is forced to invent an order and make it visually viable in an act of faith or denial. The artist appears to draw back the curtain to confront the viewer with a personal revelation. In this confrontation, the viewer finds entertainment: "Anything to amuse you," Beckmann ironically declares in his diary. The artist hides behind the illusion he has generated, concealing two realities—the one behind the curtain and the one behind the mask he has adopted—with his amusements. Ego and world are both supplanted by the fiction of the artist's narration and visualization.[2]

Painted in August 1944, after this diary entry, *Bar, Brown* represents five individuals in an interior in a narrow vertical composition. The interior is anonymous, and only the title aids in deciphering the wooden stalls of a bar. Beckmann's practice of submitting the human face to consistent stylization makes identification of the three major figures uncertain, but most likely the woman seen *en face* is his wife, Quappi, and the seated man in profile Dr. Helmuth Lütjens, with whom the Beckmanns lived after the Allied invasion began in June; the upper profile may be Beckmann himself. The scene is one of personal experience, an intimate gathering of friends in a bar or café such as Beckmann had used as a motif repeatedly since the 1920s, now set in wartime Amsterdam.

The cramped and crowded space, in conjunction with the somber brown tonality of the work, grants the scene an uncomfortable, possibly even sinister, quality. The figures, juxtaposed in close physical proximity, seem unaware of each other's presence. Exaggerated disparities of light and shadow, the sharp antithesis of brightly illuminated skin and black clothing, add to the visual drama and tension, as does the jumbled pattern of heavy black lines and limbs crossing and conjoining at pronounced angles in the center of the picture. An underlying chaos, moving in disorder behind the screen of compositional cohesion, permeates *Bar, Brown*, whose minimally categorizing title connotes disinterested, detached description.

Beckmann has soldered together the personae and appearances of his own mature art, the situations and scenes of the 1920s and the style of the 1930s, with a projection of the present.[3] He confronts reality with the product of his ego, professing to have penetrated the gray curtain of existence and to have deciphered the grammar of sounds emerging from behind it. "What I want to show in my work," he had pro-

claimed in 1938, "is the idea which hides itself behind so-called reality."[4] Transcendent order unaffected by transition and time, contained in existential human relationships, suppressed the agony of the present for him. The catastrophe and violence of war, the uncertainties of occupied Amsterdam under attack, the horrors of arbitrary arrests and transportations, the evidence of holocaust were not permitted to enter Beckmann's metaphysics as he wondered at the gray curtain separating him from the imagined world of eternal mysteries. His prolifically produced art became the curtain itself through which Beckmann could exclude the vision of a reality he could not but reject. *Bar, Brown* is a fragment of that curtain which now confronts the mutable world in Beckmann's stead.

C. D. G./R. H.

1. "Welch grausame Fantasie—immer warten, ob sich nun das Geheimnis entschleiern wird und immer mit dummem Gesicht vor dem grauen Vorhang sitzen, hinter dem die Geister rumoren oder auch das Nichts . . . . Glaubst Du an einen Sinn des Rummels, wirst Du selig werden—oh so weit weg—glaubst Du dem Zufall, so ist es Dein Pech.—Du musst mir aber immerhin zugeben, dass es doch eine Leistung ist, aus dem Nichts ein Vorstellungsgeflecht zu schaffen, was immerhin alles in einer stetig gesteigerten Spannung erhält? 'Geht aber nur durch ein Versteck-spiel Deines Selbst.'—Alles um Euch zu unterhalten." Max Beckmann, diary entry, late July 1940, as cited by Doris Schmidt, "Dokumentation zu Leben und Werk," in *Max Beckmann Retrospektive*, ed. Carla Schulz-Hoffmann and Judith C. Weiss (Munich: Prestel Verlag, 1984), 465.

2. See Hans Belting, *Max Beckmann: Die Tradition als Problem in der Kunst der Moderne* (West Berlin and Munich: Deutscher Kunstverlag, 1984), 58ff., for similar observations concerning Beckmann's art.

3. This habit of Beckmann's may account for the frequently incorrect dating of *Bar, Brown*, as in the 1947 Frankfurt exhibition catalogue.

4. Beckmann, "On My Painting," lecture given at New Burlington Gallery, London, 21 July 1938; first published New York: Buchholz Gallery, 1941, reprinted in Herschel B. Chipp, Peter Selz, and Joshua C. Taylor, *Theories of Modern Art* (Berkeley and Los Angeles: University of California Press, 1968), 187.

2 Albert Birkle

Blind Man Crossing the Street (Blinder die Strasse überquerend), 1921

Charcoal on paper
32.7 x 24.9 cm (12⁷/₈ x 9¹³/₁₆ in.)
Signed and dated l. l. "A. Birkle 21"; monogrammed l. r. "A. B."

Provenance: Galerie Bodo Niemann, West Berlin; Galerie Michael Hasenclever, Munich.

Exhibition: West Berlin, Galerie Bodo Niemann, *Arbeiten auf Papier*, 19 March–23 April 1988.

Between January and June of 1921, the German economy improved temporarily, and this drawing may document an optimistic, if short, period of economic growth. Albert Birkle's emphasis,

however, is on one whose burdens are not alleviated by the economic recovery: here a blind war veteran is pitted against a sea of roaring automobiles. Still clad in remnants of an army uniform, he wears the armband with three black circles that identifies him officially as blind. Birkle evokes compassion for the man's predicament primarily by means of contrast. The helpless soldier is articulated in fragile, white, attenuated forms against the massive black machines, the headlights of which oddly echo the dot pattern on the blind man's band. Technology is implicated here, as the veteran, although equipped with "seeing eye" dog and cane, is defenseless against the menacing vehicles. The cars—their grills, headlights, and windshields recalling determined faces —become anthropomorphized, while the man, with his eyes shut, appears to lack both emotion and personality. Birkle sets up an ironic tension, too, between darkness and illumination, between blindness and the artificial "eyes" of the automobiles.

Although each driver is boxed within his own auto, it is the blind man who becomes lonely and estranged against the machinery. Spiritual alienation is intensified by the disparity between the veteran's impoverishment and the prosperity represented by the number of automobiles. Birkle isolated the figure of the pitiful man to emphasize the impersonal forces of technology, affluence, and the modern city. That the handicapped veteran has lost his eyesight for the cause of a country that now neglects his needs stresses the cruelty of his fate and indicts the society of which he is a discarded, powerless victim.

C. D. G.

3 Albert Birkle

Mr. Spindler (Herr Spindler), 1921

Oil on canvas
48 x 40 cm (18¹⁵/₁₆ x 15³/₄ in.)
Signed l. r. "A. Birkle"; signed, dated, and inscribed u. l. "Wilhelm Spindler/November 21/50 Jahre alt"

Provenance: Estate of the artist; Neue Münchner Galerie, Munich.

Exhibitions: Salzburg, Kulturamt der Stadt Salzburg and Museum Carolino Augusteum, *Albert Birkle: Ölmalerei und Pastell*, 11 July–7 September 1980, cat. no. 4; Milwaukee, UWM Art Museum, University of Wisconsin, *Reactions to the War: European Art, 1914–1925*, 2 November–14 December 1986, cat. no. 4 (as *The Actor*).

One of three portraits Albert Birkle painted of the character actor Wilhelm Spindler in the early 1920s, this picture, as indicated in the inscription at the upper left, represents the sitter at age fifty.[1] In each of his portrayals of Spindler, Birkle focuses on the actor's extraordinarily peculiar features: large, bulging dark eyes and long nose, big prominent ears, small mouth and pointed chin partially hidden behind moustache and goatee, long thin neck, and slender drooping shoulders. Against the plain green background, head slightly raised, Spindler is seen as if through a fish-eye lens or in a convex mirror that further distorts his face; his features seem to emanate concentrically from the shiny point of his predominant nose, while his ears virtually explode from the closed globe of his head. Birkle elongates and attenuates aspects of Spindler's already bizarre physiognomy to lend it, through deliberated and systematic exaggeration, a quality of the grotesque.

In response to Birkle's portraits, one critic noted "the psychological aspect, the spiritual immersion and fanciful, yes often fantastic transformation of the sitter," and characterized the artist himself as a "thoroughly unique . . . even willful personality."[2] Less neutrally descriptive was Willy Pastor, who included Birkle, Otto Dix, and George Grosz in a ". . . procession of flagellants who see the world through bloodshot eyes. All of life becomes travesty for them; they see only faults, only the eternal 'however' in every person and every human creation."[3] Carl Meissner, otherwise a committed proponent of Birkle's work, accused these artists of "a moral, intellectual nihilism critical of life and society."[4] Aesthetically and politically conservative, such critics recognized in the image of Spindler, with its disturbing exaggerations cloaked in a drily objective style reminiscent of German Renaissance portraiture, a critique of their own society, an emphasis on misshapen physiognomies suggesting perversion or deprivation. Birkle and his colleagues, they argued in the mid-1920s (and other critics, less tolerant, took up the argument some ten years later), depicted not the robust normalcy of life but the perverse exception, the symptom of disease rather than the glow of health.

In this painting, Spindler, a deformed dandy, recalls the urban *Nervenmensch* of whom Georg Simmel wrote in his essay on the metropolis in 1903,[5] and who responds to the problems of modern life by withdrawing, like J. K. Huysmans's Des Esseintes, into a self-satisfying world of sights, sounds, tastes, and scents. A sensual aesthete, Spindler is all eyes, ears, and nose as he gazes upward in dreamy melancholy, communicating with the spirit. Birkle presents him without context or attribute, except for the high-necked white sweater, a quasi-bohemian or artistic affectation that rejects the shirt, collar, and necktie of the middle class as well as the jacket and collarless blue blouse of the proletariat. He becomes the dialectical counterpart to the revolutionaries, with their loud street demonstrations and brilliant red banners, the signals of public protest and revolt, whom Birkle also painted during the years when he ensnared Spindler's features in the weave of his imagery.

C. D. G./R. H.

1. For the two later portraits, *Spindler mit Zylinder* (*Spindler in Top Hat*) and *Spindler mit Pelzmütze* (*Spindler in Fur Cap*), in private German collections, see Rudolf Pfefferkorn, *Albert Birkle: Leben und Werk* (Hamburg: Christians Verlag, 1983), pls. 48, 49. A charcoal study for the former painting is in the collection of the Museum Sindelfingen.
2. "Das Psychologische, die geistige Durchdringung und phantasievolle, ja oft phantastische Umformung des Gegen-standes. . . . Eine durchaus eigenartige, ja eigenwillige Persönlichkeit. . . ." Unidentified critic discussing the exhibition of Birkle, August Wilhelm Dressler, Conrad Felixmüller, Willy Jaeckel, and Rudolf Schlichter at the Kunsthaus Schaller, Stuttgart, 1925, cited in Pfefferkorn, *Albert Birkle*, 47.
3. ". . . Zug von Geisselbrüdern, die mit blutunterlaufenen Augen in die Welt blicken. Alles Lebendige wird ihnen zum Zerrbild, sie sehen nur Einwände, nur das ewige Aber in jeglichem Menschen und in allem Menschenwerk." Willy Pastor, cited by Carl Meissner, "Stadt und Land in Albert Birkles Kunst," *Westermanns Monatshefte* 146, no. 871 (March 1929): 83.
4. ". . . einem sittlichen, intellektuellen, lebens- und sozial-kritischen Nihilismus." Meissner, "Stadt und Land," 83.
5. Georg Simmel, "Die Grossstadt und das Geistesleben," in *Die Grossstadt: Jahrbuch der Gehe-Stiftung* (Dresden, 1903). For an English translation, see "The Metropolis and Mental Life," in *Georg Simmel, On Individuality and Social Forms: Selected Writings*, ed. Donald N. Levine (Chicago: University of Chicago Press, 1971), 325 ff.

4 Albert Birkle
Street Scene, Berlin (*Strassenszene, Berlin*), c. 1922–23

Charcoal on canvas
70.9 x 98.6 cm (27⁷/₈ x 38³/₄ in.)

Provenance: Neue Münchner Galerie, Munich.

Exhibitions: Milwaukee, UWM Art Museum, University of Wisconsin, *Reactions to the War: European Art, 1914–1925*, 2 November–14 December 1986 (not in cat.); University Art Museum, University of Minnesota, Minneapolis, *Berlin: Art and Metropolis—Works on Paper 1912–1932*, 8 September–11 October 1987; Atlanta, High Museum of Art, *Art in Berlin 1815–1989*, 14 November 1989–14 January 1990, cat. no. 137.

In this study for a painting completed in 1923, Albert Birkle chose a familiar urban setting and familiar social types, assembling them in a disjointed fashion. The pavement, visible in the lower left corner, rakes upward at an impossible angle, while light falls sharply but renders the congested space murky and cavernous. Using incongruities of scale, elongated forms, and exaggerated chiaroscuro, Birkle evokes a sense of spiritual torment. The viewer becomes a participant in this hellish scene by contact with the gaze of the bent old woman in the foreground. Commanding empathy, she stands out from the physical tumult surrounding her, acknowledging the intrusive viewer with a resigned gesture. Thin and ailing, she contrasts with the vigorous cyclist, whose youthful body is revealed by the wind as she rides through the city. Although this athletic figure is almost back to back with the old woman, they exist in separate, impenetrable spaces, and seem to repel one another by dint of the severe angular planes.

Among these desolate wanderers of metropolitan streets is the artist himself. He appears twice, once as the man in suit and hat who gestures in apparent self-addressed conversation in the foreground right, immediately behind the interlocuting old woman. Birkle then emerges again, his own mysterious *Doppelgänger*, as the man rushing into the scene from the right, quickly glancing to his side and nervously quizzing his own duplicate image. Behind them, a newspaper carrier, placed directly above the old woman, flings his arms dramatically upwards. With his face contorted in an urgent cry, he resembles the types Birkle included in images of revolution from the immediate postwar period; but with skeletal, outstretched arms recalling a Crucifixion, the newsboy simultaneously evokes political pathos and Christian suffering. To the left is a bellhop, static and apparently lacking purpose; to his right, a butcher lumbers down the street with a slaughtered pig slung across his shoulders. A common sight on Berlin streets in the 1920s, such carcasses appear frequently in Birkle's oeuvre with a metaphorical significance, introducing death in the very midst of the teeming city.

Birkle repeats the motif in the background, where a butcher's shopwindow is lit up to display a row of flayed carcasses. One of these echoes the impassioned stance of the newspaper carrier, but its inverted posture becomes a statement of impotence as well. In numerous images of the 1920s, such butcher shops and their wares function as symbols of social violence and inhumanity, particularly in the initial years of the Republic, when the butchery of war was extended by the violence of workers' uprisings and their brutal suppression. In the adjacent window, truncated female mannequins echo the theme of violence implicit in the butcher shop.

Naturalistically rendered, the naked mannequins with accentuated breasts constitute an erotic display, by which Birkle draws an analogy between the vending of meat and the peddling of human flesh. With their abbreviated forms, dismembered in a sense, the female busts allude vaguely to Karl Marx's critique of capitalist society as fragmenting and alienating, while the obvious sexual advertisement also recalls his condemnation of capitalist labor relations as fundamentally comparable to prostitution. The theme of prostitution is underscored by two women who appear near the store window. The window display is replicated by their self-display in clinging clothing, and by the acknowledging gaze of the man passing by. Costume, demeanor, and proximity to the innuendo of the naked mannequins suggest that these women are prostitutes, representing the ultimate reduction of human beings to commodities.

Birkle's *Street Scene, Berlin* concludes as an indictment of the Weimar social order which, in the guise of democracy, perpetuated class differences and exploitation, wealth and poverty, and the uneven distribution of goods. Unlike Otto Dix or George Grosz, however, Birkle provides only a broad sense of such contemporary issues, focusing on the general chaos and alienation of urban life in postwar Berlin. His street imagery, impacted and distressed, inspired critic Kurt Wesse's trenchant description of the metropolis as "an anxiety dream." Birkle's city, Wesse wrote, "is an inferno of the possessed, the missing, the damned, who want to get past each other. They grasp at emptiness, and reach out into the surrounding space, with eyes bereft of hope."[1]

C. D. G.

1. ". . . ist ein Inferno von Besessenen, Verschollenen, Verwünschenen, die aneinander vorbei wollen, ins Leere greifen, mit hoffnungslosen Augen in den Raum tasten. Die Stadt ist ein Angsttraum. . . ." Kurt Wesse, catalogue introduction to Birkle's 1928 Berlin Künstlerhaus exhibition, as cited by Carl Meissner, "Stadt und Land in Albert Birkles Kunst," *Westermanns Monatshefte* 146, no. 871 (March 1929): 82.

5 Albert Birkle
Street with the Butcher's Cart (*Strasse mit dem Schlächterwagen*), 1922

Oil on artist's board
60.1 x 92.2 cm (21⁷/₈ x 36⁵/₁₆ in.)
Signed and dated l. r. "A. Birkle 22"; signed on stretcher verso "A. Birkle"

Provenance: Estate of the artist; Neue Münchner Galerie, Munich.

Exhibitions: Salzburg, Kulturamt der Stadt Salzburg and Museum Carolino Augusteum, *Albert Birkle: Ölmalerei und Pastell*, 11 July–7 September 1980, cat. no. 12; Los Angeles County Museum of Art, *German Expressionism 1915–1925: The Second Generation*, 9 October–31 December 1988 (traveled to Fort Worth Art Museum, 2 February–9 April 1989; Kunstmuseum Düsseldorf, 18 May–9 July 1989; Halle, Staatliche Galerie Moritzburg, 9 August–30 September 1989), cat. no. 13.

In this neo-objective variation on earlier paintings of urban multitudes by James Ensor and Edvard Munch, Albert Birkle obscures the setting of the street, so that the view is more of an endless mass of people than of a city thoroughfare. With renewed determination, Birkle restates the Expressionists' anti-urban message, but in terms specific to Berlin after the 1918 Revolution. Birkle's imagery represents a shift from the violence of the revolutionary period to a pervasive sense of doom that accompanied "normalization." The immediate postwar period, characterized by the tumult and chaos of the street scenes depicted by George Grosz and Otto Dix, as well as in Birkle's own earlier works, has given way to an era marked by extreme class contrasts and, especially among the political left with which Birkle identified, a pervasive resignation after the Revolution's failure to forge a meaningful transformation in the social order.

Although all the figures in *Street with the Butcher's Cart* are in motion, an eerie stillness governs the scene. The image is anchored by two coachmen perched motionlessly on their carts in the middle ground, the lanterns on their wagons illuminating the hordes that move towards the picture's edges. The horizontal lengthening of forms creates a sense of trudging slowness or effort-laden movement. Despite the crowd, quiet reigns, as none of the figures engage in contact with one another. A figure at the bottom left meets the viewer's gaze, but all others seem to move thoughtlessly, mechanically, and without communicating, in opposing directions. The glaring inequality of classes is vaguely delineated in the wealthy woman who wears a fur-collared coat, and who does not walk but rides in a carriage. A discrepancy also exists between the individual and the masses: the detailed appearances of the figures at the lower left contrast sharply with the faceless crowds in the background.

Repetition is simultaneously a compositional device and poignant commentary. The butcher's cart with its row of bloody carcasses is the central motif, and the human beings, who also move in unbroken rows, become analogous to the slaughtered animals. This disturbing equation of humans and animals is reinforced by the striking similarity between the neck of the thin man at the bottom left and that of the craning horse in the foreground. The blinders on this horse might then refer to the metaphorical blinders people adopt in their stressful, sometimes tragic urban environment. Individuals figuratively become blind to each others' suffering and to their own miserable fate, as Birkle draws Weimar society together around the butcher's cart, granting that emblem of violence and impersonal death a significance contested only by the carriage of wealth it confronts.   C. D. G.

6 Albert Birkle
At the Kronprinzenufer, Berlin (Am Kronprinzenufer, Berlin), 1924

Tempera on paper mounted on board
69 x 94 cm (27³/₁₆ x 37 in.)
Signed and dated l. l. "Albert Birkle 24"

Provenance: Estate of the artist; Neue Münchner Galerie, Munich.

Exhibition: Salzburg, Kulturamt der Stadt Salzburg and Museum Carolino Augusteum, *Albert Birkle: Ölmalerei und Pastell*, 11 July–7 September 1980 (as *Kronprinzenbrücke*).

Writing for *Die Kunst* in 1928, the critic Bruno Werner discovered the spirit of E. T. A. Hoffmann haunting Albert Birkle's pictures: "The love of the painter belongs to everything eccentric, scurrilous, bogeymannish that can be found in our own times, too. His interest is aroused by something ghostly, frightening, bewitching that even the most banal street corner still possesses, by something infernal, something grotesque in the face of a contemporary."[1] The description is an apt one for the artist's many urban scenes, and readily applies to *At the Kronprinzenufer*. A motif Birkle depicted repeatedly, the Kronprinzenbrücke arching over the River Spree was centrally

located in Berlin, close to the Reichstag, Königsplatz, and Victory Column. Here, however, Birkle neglects those famous structures and, instead, emphasizes the disjointed nature of the architecture, echoed in the relations among the city's inhabitants.

The work is socially critical, but more subtle than the street scenes of Otto Dix, George Grosz, or Rudolf Schlichter. Birkle does not rely on political slogans, nor does he point to any particular factions as the source of social ills. Rather, he creates an elusive sense of estrangement and doom, and achieves an effect of disorientation by various stylistic means. He engages at least two different points of perspective in an essentially illusionistic space: the pedestrians are seen from slightly above, yet the buildings, seen from a lower angle, appear as towering silhouettes in the twilight sky. Looming buildings, streetlamps, and trees dwarf the city dwellers, exaggerating their helplessness. The two barren trees that frame the scene suggest the chill of winter, but are also indicative of the insalubrious, unnatural environment of the metropolis. Various types of architecture, including the prominent modern structures at the center of the canvas, the neoclassical building to the left, and the church steeples, manifest the disparate nature of city life. Relegating the church to the distant background, Birkle might be commenting on the spiritual vacuity he lamented from the mid-twenties on.

Despite the presence of the figures, the scene is a desolate one. Although most of the people are moving in the same direction, there is little connection among the group; nor is the viewer permitted contact with any of the figures. Few faces are visible, save for the profile of one man, whose sunken cheeks and wasted flesh suggest his suffering. There is an unsettling discrepancy between the large head of this single figure and the smaller, full-length figures of the other passersby. While the expanse of sky is unusual in urban scenes for the 1920s, Birkle's use of it is oppressive: the large orb of the moon seems to portend doom rather than emit light. The streetlamps below generate an eerie glow and reinforce the ominous mood of the work, as an impenetrable darkness encroaches upon the scene.

The horse-drawn wagon at the painting's center repeats a motif used so ubiquitously by Birkle as to become symbolic. In conjunction with the neomedieval buildings that enframe it, the covered wagon pulled by a dappled white horse recalls a still-present past within the contemporary urban milieu of Berlin, where automobiles are the expected and more persistently depicted vehicle crowding the streets. With the truncated, leafless trees and the lifeless illumination of moon and streetlamps, the white horse and its mysterious wagon appear as emblems of death, which inexorably draws the city's inhabitants of every age behind it. Werner's "most banal street corner," which here looks at the backs of buildings whose famous façades line the populous and fashionable street of Unter den Linden, thus becomes indeed "ghostly, frightening, bewitching," as

it turns away from the accidentals of contemporaneity and considers the constants of human existence.

C. D. G. / R. H.

1. "Die Liebe des Malers gehört allem Verschrobenen, Skurrilen, Klabautermannhaften, das sich auch in unserer Gegenwart findet. Das Geisterhafte, Beängstigende, Verzauberte, das die banalste Strassenecke noch besitzt, das Infernalistische, Groteske im Antlitz eines Zeitgenossen." Bruno E. Werner, "Albert Birkle," *Die Kunst* 57 (1928): 127.

7 Albert Birkle
Francis in the Stable (Franziskus im Stall), 1925

Oil on artist's board
63 x 101 cm (24¹³/₁₆ x 39³/₄ in.)
Signed and dated l. r. "A. Birkle 25"

Provenance: Estate of the artist; Neue Münchner Galerie, Munich.

Exhibition: Salzburg, Kulturamt der Stadt Salzburg and Museum Carolino Augusteum, *Albert Birkle: Ölmalerei und Pastell*, 11 July–7 September 1980, cat. no. 20.

In this painting, Albert Birkle treats a motif unusual for *Neue Sachlichkeit* artists—St. Francis of Assisi preaching among the animals. Although Christian imagery had informed Expressionist visions of a new age and a new humanity, such iconography became irrelevant for progressive artists when those utopian ideals faded after 1918.[1] Insofar as they were concerned with religious issues at all, artists of the left represented the church as a reactionary institution which joined the judiciary and military to suppress social reform and maintain imperialist capitalism. Traditional religious themes had become the domain of regressive historicist styles and otherworldly ideologies by the mid-1920s. In this context, Birkle was a significant exception.

Around 1925, several prominent intellectuals and artists, including Birkle and George Grosz, began to distance themselves from their previous advocacy of the causes identified with the extreme political left. Lenin had died in 1924, conservative and even moderate leaders were purged from the German Communist Party (KPD), and the KPD-USPD governments in Thuringia and Saxony were suppressed; in the disillusionment that followed, membership in the KPD dropped by nearly two hundred thousand within one year. Birkle departed from such crusades as the International Workers' Aid (IAH) *Eight-Hour Day* brochure and from his celebrations of revolutionary activity. Overtly political subjects largely disappeared from his work, supplanted by landscapes, portraits, and tortured Crucifixions modeled on the sixteenth-century prototypes of Matthias Grünewald.[2] In a Crucifixion of 1929, Birkle's Christ is impaled on a city wall and surrounded by mocking soldiers, bankers, and burghers—as well as a taunting mob waving the red banners of revolution.[3] The artist thus misan-

thropically censures all of society, contrasting its grimacing demonstration with the heroic calm of Christ's accepting figure.[4]

This shift, however, was not as dramatic as it may initially appear. Birkle's identification with extreme-left political and artistic movements was limited even before 1925. Although he signed manifestos supporting KPD and IAH projects, he did not become a member of the Party. His drawings appeared in the IAH's illustrated journal, *Sichel und Hammer (Sickle and Hammer)*, but his contributions to the more moderate socialist humor periodical, *Lachen Links (Laughter on the Left)*, were much more frequent. Instead of radical artists' associations, such as the Red Group, Birkle joined the traditional Association of Berlin Artists, the Berlin Secession, and the liberal Jury-Free Art Show, whose primary goal was to preserve the autonomy of art. He received several awards for his Crucifixion scenes, and by the late 1920s was developing a major reputation for his church murals and projected stained-glass windows. His sympathy for workers and social revolution was closer to the compassion expressed in Jesus's Sermon on the Mount than to the political zeal of Karl Marx's *Communist Manifesto*. Birkle's imagery also indicates, however, that he recognized a kinship between these two proclamations on social injustice and human suffering.[5]

In *Francis in the Stable*, the artist melds his religious and social concerns, depicting the Apostle of the Poor, gaunt and unshaven, in a peasant's or worker's blue blouse rather than the Franciscan habit common in innumerable depictions since Giotto. Birkle thus contemporizes the saint much as, during the 1880s, Fritz von Uhde set biblical scenes in the Bavarian countryside. But where Uhde put an Impressionist style at the service of folklore and anecdote, Birkle fuses precise description with subjective distortion of space and proportions, muted coloration with subtly contrasting areas of light,[6] to extract from the historical religious figure a comment on the human condition in 1925. In physiognomy as well as dress, Francis compares with Birkle's previous depictions of workers, undernourished witnesses to suffering, patient in their determined survival as individual representatives of a class.

Humble and pious, the saint is surrounded by cows, horses, and goats, recalling Rainer Maria Rilke's words in *The Book of Hours*, "poor as in the warm poverty of a stable."[7] Rilke's description of the nobility of poverty, found in Saint Francis, as "a great glow from within" finds a parallel in Birkle's rendering of the nimbus-like flash of light emanating from the saint's head. Francis raises his hand as if speaking, but his audience—except for the viewer—consists only of the animals whose barn he shares. An anonymous, shouting mob stares in through the window in the background; the figures are alien intruders in this world, antagonistic or curious, not listening. A single tear trickles from the saint's left eye, testimony to an overpowering sadness as he points out towards the viewer in a feeble gesture of accusing communication.

In 1925, Birkle's painting offered an alternative to the radical political rhetoric and messages of self-interest that were a consistent aspect of daily life. While ironically questioning its own effectiveness within the cacophony of political diatribes in Weimar Germany, *Francis in the Stable* still glimmers with hope. For the artist, Birkle believed, like the saint who here confronts the viewer, "can guide humanity back to humility and modesty." With the ability to realize the religious wisdom of centuries in a new formal vocabulary, the artist could, Birkle contended, "bring something of the breath of a higher spirituality. It is no more than a very modest contribution, but it seems to me that the artist today is called upon more than anyone else—and I hope that he shall succeed with his meager powers—to preserve the human for humanity."[8]

C. D. G. / R. H.

1. The one major exception was the Crucifixion, since Christ's suffering and martyrdom lent itself to virtually the entire ideological spectrum after Germany's defeat in World War I and during the later years of economic and political disturbance. Birkle was only one of several artists to receive critical acclaim around 1925 for depictions of the violent death of Jesus.
2. Birkle first displayed a Crucifixion at the 1922 *Great Berlin Art Exhibition*. In addition to kinship with Grünewald, his Crucifixion paintings bear comparison with the controversial crucifix carved by Ludwig Gies as a war memorial for the Marienkirche, Lübeck, in 1921, illus. in Stephanie Barron, ed., *German Expressionist Sculpture* (Los Angeles: Los Angeles County Museum of Art, 1983), 38, 39.
3. Rudolf Pfefferkorn , *Albert Birkle: Leben und Werk* (Hamburg: Christians Verlag, 1983), pl. 21.
4. In the foreground of the painting, a soldier grasps Birkle himself violently by the collar, thus distinguishing the artist, like Christ, as a victim of society. This scene was apparently inspired by Birkle's encounter with militiamen of the Kapp Putsch in 1920 as he resisted their efforts to occupy the Berlin Academy. The association of artist and Christ is further accented in that Jesus's features appear to be Birkle's own.
5. Birkle's socio-religious credo corresponded to efforts by German churches to counter the growing influence of extremist political parties: new emphasis was placed on Christian social teachings, new organizations for youth and workers were established and churches built.
6. Birkle's mannerist use of light as an expressive device is even more apparent in a black chalk drawing of this composition in a German private collection, illus. in Rainer Zimmermann, *Die Kunst der verschollenen Generation: Deutsche Malerei des Expressiven Realismus von 1925–1975* (Düsseldorf and Vienna: Econ Verlag, 1980), 114.
7. "Arm wie die warme Armut eines Stalles," Rainer Maria Rilke, *Das Stunden-Buch enthaltend die drei Bücher: Vom menschlichen Leben, Von der Pilgerfahrt, Von der Armut und vom Tode* (Leipzig: Insel Verlag, 1920), 99.
8. "... kann ... [der Künstler] ... die Menschen zu Demut und Bescheidenheit zurückführen .... wenigstens den Suchenden etwas vom Hauch eines höheren Geistigen zu vermitteln. Es ist ein bescheidener Beitrag nur, aber es scheint mir, dass der Künstler heute mehr als jeder andere dazu berufen ist, und ich hoffe, dass es ihm mit seinen schwachen Kräften gelingen möge, den Menschen der Menschheit zu erhalten." Cited by Pfefferkorn, *Albert Birkle*, 97.

8 Albert Birkle
My Father, Carl Birkle (Der Vater, Carl Birkle), 1928

Oil on canvas
98 x 78 cm (38 5/8 x 30 3/4 in.)
Signed and dated l. r. "A. Birkle 28"

Provenance: Estate of the artist; Neue Münchner Galerie, Munich.

Exhibition: Salzburg, Kulturamt der Stadt Salzburg and Museum Carolino Augusteum, *Albert Birkle: Ölmalerei und Pastell*, 11 July–7 September 1980, cat. no. 28.

In 1929, the critic Carl Meissner divided Albert Birkle's portraiture into two phases: the first, skeptical and "abundantly filled with a quality of caricature," included merciless self-portraits; the more recent work, on the other hand, retrieved the reality of each individual sitter. "His new portraits move closer to nature," Meissner wrote, "and thus gain the believability of memorable representations of specific persons, without losing the power of an accented expression of essential character, fundamental to the grotesque."[1] A comparison of Birkle's earlier portrait of Wilhelm Spindler (cat. no. 3) with this painting of the artist's father readily demonstrates the stylistic and conceptual shift Meissner described. Birkle restored a representative ambience to the subject, who is now seated in an interior rather than isolated against an undifferentiated ground. At the same time, he maintained a sober attitude, recording warts, veins, and wrinkled clothing, observing the bulges of belly and genitalia while remaining emotionless, masking empathy and feeling.

Despite its casual appearance, Birkle's spartan composition has been carefully orchestrated. Presented in a traditional, three-quarter-length portrait format, pyramidal and monumental, the sitter is dignified and imposing. Yet, with his limp hands, he assumes a relaxed posture. His head is bracketed precisely by two verticals in the background to lend the composition a subtle sense of balance. There is a tension between illusionistic space and the flat surface of the painting, emphasized by the systematic, architectonic brushwork which is made plainly visible. The juxtaposition of light and dark colors adds a dynamic quality to the otherwise static image. Most striking, however, is the contrast between quasi-geometric forms and the organic volume of the father's corpulent physique and the wicker chair to which it is comfortably welded. The work exhibits the pronounced fusion of informality and rigid organization that characterizes *Neue Sachlichkeit* portraiture in both painting and photography.

Although Birkle's father wears the conventional suit of the middle class, the background elements mostly pertain to art—a sketch pad and stool, and a stretched canvas leaning against the wall. These props indicate an artist's studio, certainly Birkle's own which his father in street clothing—his hat rests on the stool—is visiting. An homage of son to father, a signal of affection and respect, the painting also announces artistic continuity and support. Carl Birkle was himself an interior decorator and painter who maintained a successful workshop in Berlin. The younger Birkle's training at the Stuttgart School of Applied Arts, where his father, too, had studied, prepared him to continue his father's practice, as did a year's apprenticeship in the workshop in 1919.

If Birkle's entrance into the Prussian Academy of Fine Arts in 1920 to study as an independent painter broke with family tradition, he must have had his father's at least tacit support. His matriculation into the academy points, too, to the family's rise from lower-class artisans to middle-class entrepreneurship with the success of the workshop. As a result of this prosperity, Birkle was able to carry on his studies and to enter a profession less financially predictable than many others. In 1928, with mural commissions and a first individual exhibition as testimony to career ambitions fulfilled, Birkle painted this picture documenting paternal approval. The portrait of Carl Birkle, situated in his son's milieu, is an act of filial piety; it is also a proud declaration of a son's achievement.

C. D. G.

1. "... voller Simplizissimusqualität .... Seine neueren Bildnisse rücken näher an die Natur und gewinnen so die Glaubhaftigkeit einprägsamer Menschendarstellung, ohne die Kraft gesteigerten Wesensausdrucks, der im Grotesken liegt, zu verlieren." Carl Meissner, "Stadt und Land in Albert Birkles Kunst," *Westermanns Monatshefte* 146, no. 871 (March 1929): 83.

9 Volker Böhringer
Road to Waiblingen (Strasse nach Waiblingen), c. 1933

Tempera on panel
40.5 x 33 cm (15 15/16 x 13 in.)
Monogrammed l. r. "V. B."; signed and inscribed verso "Volker Böhringer/Strasse nach Waiblingen/Stuttgart S/Neue Weinsteige (b. Berberich)"; stamped "Volker Böhringer, Esslingen-Mettingen" Röttger 224

Provenance: Galleria del Levante, Munich.

Exhibitions: Munich, Galleria del Levante, *Volker Böhringer: Ölbilder und Gouachen aus der Neuen Sachlichkeit*, February–March 1974; Parma, Galleria della Rocchetta, *Volker Böhringer*, 1975; Vienna, Museum im 20. Jahrhundert, *Neue Sachlichkeit und Realismus: Kunst zwischen den Kriegen*, 1977.

In a review of Franz Hessel's *Spazieren in Berlin (Wandering in Berlin)*, Walter Benjamin observed that travelogues are rarely written by natives of the places described. Most commonly, strangers are the ones who consider the picturesque characteristics of a city worthy of commentary. "For the native to turn to representations of the city," Benjamin argued, "requires other, deeper motives—the motives of someone who travels into the past, not into distant lands. City books written by a native always possess something of the quality of a memoir. Not for nothing did their authors experience their childhoods in this place."[1] The city then becomes a "mnemotechnical aid to the lone ambulant," who regards it with "a sovereign attraction towards what is lasting, with an aristocratic revulsion against nuances."[2] Benjamin's revived *flâneur* sees his urban world as a collage of fixed tableaux in harsh projection, each exposing the permanent aspects of the city. His concern is not with the façades of entertainment and representation registered by travelers, but with the structures that shape the actuality of the inhabitant's life.

Volker Böhringer's depictions of the industrial landscape surrounding Stuttgart function in the fashion Benjamin ascribed to Hessel's reflections of Berlin. They represent the "stern home" of the artist's childhood, a muse of memory composed of factories, train tracks, and asphalt roads. Specificity of place combines in his paintings with an airless timelessness to suggest an immutable, somnial hyperreality, landscapes bereft of humanity but comprised of humanity's constructions.[3]

In *Road to Waiblingen*, a road marker indicates the precise location depicted—three kilometers outside the town, near a sharp turn in the macadamized road with metropolitan transit tracks running parallel to the railroad. Shadows fix a late afternoon into frozen permanence. No traffic appears. Ironically, what movement is implied belongs not to plant or animal life, but to the inorganic, manufactured aspects of the landscape. The leafless tree in the foreground is static, emerging from an iron ring; the small white flowers (*Wegerich*, a genus of plantain) appear as repetitive, stenciled fossils of vegetation. But smoke drifts in a graceful pattern from the brick neo-Romanesque factory, lights enliven an industrial façade in the distance, telegraph poles interact in visual dialogue with administrative buildings. In the foreground, the asphalt surface recedes beneath a spreading red stain which threatens to overpower the entire composition. The life of nature is supplanted by the life of industry.

In his stylistic kinship to Italian Metaphysical Painting and his thematic ties to an industrial landscapist such as Carl Grossberg, Böhringer appears late in the context of German *Neue Sachlichkeit*. Essentially, he represents a third wave of the tendency in the early 1930s, retrieving socially critical motifs and themes employed by *Neue Sachlichkeit* artists a decade before. The renewed social and political problems following the brief interval of "normalcy" in Weimar Germany from 1924 to 1928 may be an underlying cause for this resumed representation of malaise in the guise of objectivity. Böhringer, for example, repeats none of the machine romanticism of Grossberg that emanated from the years of prosperity, and focuses instead on a depopulated landscape in which organic life is alien or threatened. Still, the manner has no true parallel among earlier German artists, except perhaps in George Grosz's automaton paintings or Heinrich Hoerle's landscapes of the early twenties, although Böhringer's approach lacks their overt didacticism.

His testimony, moreover, is ultimately more personal than political. Using the style he discovered among his precursors, Böhringer constructed an image of the only world he ever experienced, the area of the Neckar Valley around Esslingen in which he was born. For him, it was a landscape of recollection, turned desperately harsh, offering comfort only in the familiarity of rust stains, train tracks, telegraph wires, and the historicized façades of factories. There is no nuance here, but an unending sameness, witness to the Neckar Valley's industrial identification, its perpetual reality imposed on the memory of one who lived it. R. H.

1. "Als Einheimischer zum Bild einer Stadt zu kommen, erfordert andere, tiefere Motive. Motive dessen, der ins Vergangene statt ins Ferne reist. Immer wird das Stadtbuch des Einheimischen Verwandtschaft mit Memoiren haben, der Schreiber hat nicht umsonst seine Kindheit am Ort verlebt." Walter Benjamin, "Die Wiederkehr des Flaneurs," *Gesammelte Schriften*, vol. 3, ed. H. Tiedemann-Bartels (Frankfurt a. M.: Suhrkamp, 1972), 194.
2. "Die Stadt als mnemotechnischer Behelf des einsam Spazierenden... Eine souveräne Neigung zum Dauernden, ein aristokratischer Widerwille gegen Nuancen...." Ibid., 194, 196.
3. *Road to Waiblingen* is listed in the oeuvre catalogue by Friedhelm Röttger, *Volker Böhringer* (Stuttgart: Clett-Cotta, 1987), 196, no. 224, with no date assigned. The theme of suburban industrial landscapes first appears in Böhringer's work in 1930, and continues with variations throughout his life. In terms of motif, technique, and style, *Road to Waiblingen* fits into a group of works of 1933–34. The setting, near Waiblingen (probably the Neue Rommelshauserstrasse), is unusual in that most Böhringer landscapes represent the area in or immediately adjacent to Mettingen and Esslingen, some fifteen kilometers south of Waiblingen.

10 Volker Böhringer
Untitled (Tile Factory) (Ohne Titel [Ziegelei]), c. 1933–34

Tempera on paper mounted on board
35 x 24.8 cm (13³/₄ x 9³/₄ in.)
Monogrammed l. l. "V. B.";
signed and inscribed verso "Volker Böhringer/Stuttgart S/ Neue Weinsteige 1 (b. Berberich)"; stamped "Volker Böhringer, Esslingen-Mettingen"
Röttger 220

Provenance: Galleria del Levante, Munich.

Exhibitions: Munich, Galleria del Levante, *Volker Böhringer: Ölbilder und Gouachen aus der Neuen Sachlichkeit*, Feb-

ruary–March 1974; Parma, Galleria della Rocchetta, *Volker Böhringer*, 1975; Vienna, Museum des 20. Jahrhunderts, *Neue Sachlichkeit und Realismus: Kunst zwischen den Kriegen*, 1977; Munich, Galleria del Levante, 1980; Munich, Städtische Galerie im Lenbachhaus, *Kunst und Technik in den 20er Jahren*, 1980.

Clearly fascinated by the modern industrial landscape, Volker Böhringer painted four different views of this clay tile factory in the Neckar Valley in the early 1930s.¹ Atop a hillside stands the main plant of the factory; below is the kiln, partially obscured by an amorphous embankment. A tall, slender smokestack looms above the kiln against a bright but overcast sky. The factory is likewise contrasted against a mysterious darkness, which confronts the brightness on a sweeping curve, echoing the abstracted hillside. A small stream, rendered flatly in gray, flows down the hill and off to the right, providing the factory with its water source. One senses that the water irrigating Böhringer's world would taste of sediment, like clay slip, as chalky as the embankment down which it flows. Similarly, the schematized daisy that crops up at the bottom right of the picture seems unnatural, as stiff as the telegraph pole behind it, which in turn balances the rigid vertical of the brick smokestack to the left.

The scene appears devoid of atmosphere, for even the smokestack emits no fumes, yet an eerie haze inexplicably divides the composition in half. A careful, if only slight, articulation of architectural details underscores the vacuous atmosphere and lends the painting an hallucinatory aura. Böhringer distinctly delineates the main elements —chimney, kiln, factory, and telephone pole—but does not provide transitions or modulations among them; the effect is disjointed, alienating, surreal. The precision of his rendering emphasizes surfaces and the reflections of an undisclosed light source on metal and brick. Discrete, individual forms become abstract shapes that interact solely through juxtaposition. The painting thus becomes a kind of mechanized landscape not only in subject but also in technique. A. I. S.

1. For the dating of Böhringer's work, see cat. no. 9, n. 3.

11 Erich Borchert
Couple in a Café (Paar im Café), 1929

Black chalk, gouache on paper
41.5 x 30.9 cm (16³/₈ x 12³/₁₆ in.)
Monogrammed and dated l. r. "1929 EB"
Signed and dated on removed matting "Erich Borchert, Okt. 29"

Provenance: Karl und Faber, Munich.

Café scenes in Weimar German art ranged in intent from George Grosz's social criticism (see cat. no. 54) to Richard Ziegler's renditions filled with

coy sexual innuendo (see cat. no. 190). Erich Borchert's café couple participates in the staid propriety, fashion, and affluence that dominates his depictions of contemporary life. His scenes are transformed into nuanced but simple patterns of soft-edged color blots granted definition by thin, sharp, surely rendered chalk lines modeled on those of Vassily Kandinsky, Paul Klee, and Lyonel Feininger, Borchert's teachers at the Bauhaus.

Evaluating the works of young Bauhaus artists in 1929, the Hungarian Ernst Kállai, who had recently joined the faculty, recognized the influence of Kandinsky, Klee, and Feininger, as well as of Oskar Schlemmer. The doctrine propagated by Walter Gropius that all constructive artistic disciplines should reunify in architecture had been undermined by the presence of such strong painters, despite the efforts of Gropius to resist recognition of painting as a legitimate Bauhaus activity:

> Today there are more young painters at the Bauhaus than one would suspect, and not only in the free painting classes taught by Kandinsky and Klee, but also among the other "faculties." I have been active at the Bauhaus for a year now and still there are "discoveries" for me. Certainly, they are not each one discoveries of extraordinary talent, but they are of Bauhausers who cannot give up painting and more or less secretly indulge in this dangerous and useless vice.¹

In an effort to categorize the works of these young artists, including "...the gentle poetry of Erich Borchert,"² Kállai identified a common search for "the spiritual in art," borrowing Kandinsky's famous title but granting it a far less metaphysical meaning. Mysterious atmospheres and psychological situations provide the contours for Kállai's more limited "spiritual" conceptions.

The minimal means and softly sensual coloration that constitute Borchert's lyricism and that confirm his concern with architectural decoration interact in his café scene to suggest a psychological narrative. The foreground figures of a woman and a man seated at a table are clearly distinguished one from the other. Both color and line shaping their figures remain distinct, but the smaller background figure of a man in a doorway or window, who seems to observe them, shares its contours in continuous lines with those of the woman. A process of linkage or identification between the two is suggested, therefore, which transforms this reductive café scene into a drama of jealousy within a romantic triangle. R. H.

1. "Es gibt heute mehr junge Maler am Bauhaus, als man zunächst vermuten würde, und zwar nicht nur in den freien Malklassen von Kandinsky und Klee, sondern auch unter Angehörigen anderer 'Fakultäten'. Ich bin seit einem Jahr am Bauhaus tätig und noch immer gibt es für mich 'Entdeckungen', wenn auch nicht jedesmal von ungewöhnlichen Begabungen, so doch von solchen Bauhäuslern, die das Malen nicht sein lassen können und mehr oder weniger geheim

diesem gefährlichen und nutzlosen Laster frönen." Ernst Kállai, "Junge Bauhausmaler," *Das Kunstblatt* 13 (1929): 198.
2. "...die zarte Lyrik von Erich Borchert." Ibid., 200.

12 Erich Borchert
In the Theater Box (In der Loge), 1929

Gouache, black chalk, charcoal dust on thin Japan paper
26.5 x 21.2 cm (10⁷/₁₆ x 8³/₈ in.)
Monogrammed and dated l. r. "1929 EB"; signed and inscribed on matting, verso u. l. "Erich Borchert. Dessau Bauhaus"; artist's stamp l. r. "Erich Borchert/Dessau Bauhaus"; inscribed and dated center "In der Loge. 1929"

Provenance: Karl und Faber, Munich.

In an unusual technique, Erich Borchert produced a number of gouaches in which he first stained the paper with the basic configuration and then drew the figures in contour, using black chalk, on both sides of a fine, handmade rice paper. The resultant image could then be viewed from both sides of the sheet. Since unorthodox techniques applied in a modern context was a major aspect of Bauhaus training, it is possible that Borchert conceived these works either as projects for stained-glass windows, as the broad, flat color areas and their stylized curving contours that define the figures suggest, or to be applied in some other aspect of design in which viewing of both sides of an image, subordinating neither, would be a significant factor.

Whatever the purpose of his works, Borchert depended for his motifs on the world of secular entertainment. The broad curves of this charcoal drawing define a fashionably clothed man and woman in a theater box during an intermission or before the performance begins. The single large blue circle of an eye suffices to indicate the man's visual involvement with the woman, whose one visible eye is closed and who seems to turn away demurely from the suitor attracted by the broad *décolleté* of her green dress. Despite the extreme stylized abstraction of the image, Borchert suggests sufficient detail to imply both a minimal narrative and a process of psychological interaction. R. H.

13 Erich Borchert
Black Singer (Schwarzer Sänger), 1929

Gouache, black chalk, charcoal dust on thin Japan paper
31 x 21.1 cm (12³/₁₆ x 8⁵/₁₆ in.)
Dated and monogrammed l. r. "1929 EB"; exhibition stamp on matting verso "Deutsche Kunstgemeinschaft"

Provenance: Karl und Faber, Munich.

Exhibition: Dessau, Deutsche Kunstgemeinschaft, 1929.

Blacks from Africa or the United States received contradictory responses in Germany during the Weimar Republic. The use of black colonial troops, notably by France, in Europe was already controversial during World War I, and was frequently perceived as a racial insult against white German soldiers. Antagonism and fear of blacks were made more severe, however, when France employed Moroccan troops during the occupation of the industrial Ruhr in the 1920s. German propaganda efforts, whether originating with the government or left- or right-wing political groups, concentrated on images of black soldiers—"uncivilized savages" —raping German women and thus complying with a purported systematic French attempt to undermine German racial identity. Feared, despised, and alien, the black found a ready if significantly subordinate place alongside the Jew in German mentality as a despoiler of the nation.

In contrast to this propagandistic manipulation of racial fears and hatred, American black entertainers were celebrated and feted in the major German cities, most notably Berlin. Interest in American jazz, beginning in the early 1920s, and popular dances, such as the foxtrot and black-bottom, were linked to a fascination with the seemingly exotic culture of America, especially black America. In 1926, the black jazz troupe Chocolate Kiddies was the first to tour Germany, and was soon followed by numerous others, while cabarets and nightclubs also sought to hire individual black musicians and singers for their own "Jazzbands" modeled on the Paul Whiteman Orchestra. An even greater sensation was the German premiere in 1925 of the American dancer Josephine Baker as part of the Revue Nègre imported from Paris, to be followed by numerous other nude black dancers. Harry Graf Kessler saw in Baker's performances "an extreme grotesqueness and stylistic purity, like an Egyptian or Greek archaic sculpture that practices acrobatics. . . . This is how women must have danced," he speculated, "for Solomon and Tutankhamen."[1]

Justified in terms of an interest in primeval, pure forms of art, music, and dance, the popularity of black performers also functioned to transfer bourgeois yearnings for sexual freedom without transgressing institutional taboos. The Expressionist poet Iwan Goll thus summed up the triumph of black dancers and musicians as a rediscovery of senses and instincts rooted in an enviable closeness to nature lost to Europeans:

Negroes dance with their senses. (While Europeans can now only dance with their intellects.) They dance with their legs, breasts and belly . . . . We have to envy them, because this is real life, sun, primeval forest, birds singing, leopards roaring, earth.[2]

Typically, the components of racial hatred and exotic admiration meld together here in a perception of sexual prowess and a willingness to equate all blacks, American or African, with the largely imagined, mysterious native inhabitants of unexplored tropical jungles who live out European dreams of primeval innocence and paradise.

Erich Borchert's *Black Singer* derives from this same late-twenties stylish interest in black entertainers and jazz, and manipulates the components of established stereotypes—dark skin, short-cropped black hair, heavy red lips, and impassioned "intuitive" artistic presentation—in the framework of a revived Bauhaus concern with subjectivity in painting. The colors are presented like uncontrolled stains and blots on an absorbent tissue, from which the artist freely elicited his forms, defining them with his elegant black pastel lines. The soft, mixed colors suggest a degree of delicate sensuality recalling, ironically, the Rococo and its supposed decadence. The black singer in this context emerges as a sign of cultural refinement and sensitivity, searching in primeval worlds for new means of stimulation and rejuvenation; but he is also an alien presence, vital and forceful, that intrudes with jutting angles and jarring rhythmic sound into Borchert's ethereal lyricism.

The small gouache presents a subdued, tasteful, and uncritical commentary on contemporary society and its interests, as do Borchert's other images of this time, belying his later radical involvement with Soviet communal architectural projects and city planning. In 1929, he represents the Bauhaus's retreat from its own idealist founding principles and its Constructivist aesthetic, which sought to overcome the limitations of individual artistic production within a grand vision of cooperative, integrative architecture and design. Ernst Kállai, documenting the phenomenon, concluded his brief essay on young Bauhaus painters with a recognition of their links to Romanticism's individualist principles. (In Borchert, he might also have pointed to a kinship between his interior scenes and those of Biedermeier painting, both thematically and compositionally.) Kállai ironically presented the alternatives open to artist and viewer in 1929, incorrectly imagining a period of peaceful prosperity for the immediate future:

The unwavering perseverance with which these young painters pursue their useless handicraft, instead of ceaselessly engraving the sacred commandments of applied architecture into their minds, can be received with contempt or with joyful support by us—depending on whether we perceive humanity as a subaltern product of technology or as a spiritual being possessing the freedom of self-determination.[3]

R. H.

1. ". . . mit äusserster Groteskkunst und Stilreinheit, wie eine ägyptische oder archaische Figur, die Akrobatik treibt . . . . So müssen die Tänzerinnen Salomos und Tut-ench-Ammuns getanzt haben." Harry Graf Kessler, *Tagebücher 1918–1937: Politik, Kunst und Gesellschaft der zwanziger Jahre* (Frankfurt a. M.: Insel-Verlag, 1961), 456.
2. "Die Neger tanzen mit ihren Sinnen. (Während die Europäer nur noch mit dem Intellekt tanzen.) Sie tanzen mit ihren Beinen, Brüsten und Bauch . . . . Man muss sie beneiden, denn das ist das Leben, Sonne, Urwald, Vogelgesang, Leopardengebrüll, Erde." Iwan Goll, "Die Neger erobern Europa," *Literarische Welt*, 1926, as cited in Michael Andritzky and Thomas Rautenberg, eds., *"Wir sind nackt und nennen uns Du": Von Lichtfreunden und Sonnenkämpfern—Eine Geschichte der Freikörperkultur* (Giessen: Anabas, 1989), 174.
3. "Die unbeirrbare Beharrlichkeit, mit der diese jungen Maler ihrem nutzlosen Handwerk nachgehen, anstatt sich restlos den Geboten der heiligen Zweckarchitektur zu ihren Häupten zu fügen, kann unsere Missbilligung oder unsere freudige Zustimmung finden—je nachdem ob wir den Menschen als subalternes Produkt der Technik oder als seelisches Wesen von freier Selbstbestimmung auffassen." Ernst Kállai, "Junge Bauhausmaler," *Das Kunstblatt* 13 (1929): 201.

14 Armand Bouten
Birth (Geburt), c. 1920

Ink, metallic ink, watercolor on paper
11.8 x 12.8 cm (4⅝ x 5¹⁄₁₆ in.)
Signed l. r. "Bouten"

Provenance: Galerie Wending, Amsterdam; Galerie Michael Hasenclever, Munich.

Towards the end of World War I, birth became a frequent motif in German art, an extension of literary and utopian political prophecies of *Der neue Mensch* (The New Human Being) who would emerge after the unprecedented devastation, cruelty, and murder of the war.[1] In rapturous mixtures of chiliastic and cosmological imagery, *Der neue Mensch* was perceived as joining earth and heaven, reaching out for sun and stars, the flames of love bursting wildly from his heart, generating a new community of charitable humanity. The imagery of birth and becoming that German poets and artists propagated in the wake of annihilating war appeared in Dutch art as well, but earlier, in conjunction with the mystical inclinations of artists who had been professing the doctrines of theosophy since the 1890s.[2] Armand Bouten maintained aesthetic ties both with the Netherlands and with Germany—although his apparent lack of interest in commercial success thwarted Herwarth Walden's efforts to exhibit his work at *Der Sturm* gallery in Berlin; in this small work from early in his erratic career, Bouten links elements of Dutch and German art.

The angular and stylized curving elements in *Birth,* for example, derive from the semi-abstract imagery of his Dutch compatriots, mixed with devices borrowed from African sculpture, particularly in the articulation of the woman's body forms. In terms of content, however, Bouten closely approximates German prototypes as he fuses cosmological and erotic elements.[3] The setting of this birth is an expanse of starry nocturnal sky, translating the events depicted from the ordinary to the mythological or archetypal. The vast firmament becomes associated with an implied interior, the appropriate setting for the couch or bed on which the woman reclines. Her body is a pallid white, emblematic of death perhaps or emulative of the white slip frequently found on African sculptures, with green outlines to indicate her stomach and one eye, as well as a mystical triangle, painted on her face. She screams out as her embryonic child emerges from between her spread legs and enters a world, similarly vital red, that consists of the simplified renditions of city houses. An association of the woman with the cosmological forces of night is suggested, while the child is bonded to a constructed reality, manmade but—with its color shared by the child—also implying the life of the future to be built by *Der neue Mensch.* Presiding over the scene is a slender man, significantly smaller than the woman. He looks up towards the sky, and, as the golden yellow of the stars illuminates his face, raises his arms in a gesture of prayer, perhaps of wonder, or despair.

A multiple reading of Bouten's birth scene emerges. That it is a dramatically unconventional depiction of a traditional nativity scene with Joseph, Mary, and the Christ child should certainly be considered; more compelling, however, are its chiliastic associations. Rooted in the mythos of a transformed humanity and its birth, the drawing presents woman as the generative source, delivering her child in pain, but attached to a cosmic past and to recollections of death—not to the structured future of the city that impinges on her form and substitutes its cubic façades for the volumes of her spread legs. The embryonic humanity that emerges between those truncated legs is the future, and possibly it is for this triumph of male over female principles, of logic over intuition, or spirit over matter within this cosmology of futuristic misogyny that the man raises his head and hands in gratitude to the heavens.

R. H.

1. Also see the entry for Otto Dix, *Birth* (cat. no. 25).
2. The Dutch Theosophical Union was founded in 1892. In its efforts to propagate a theosophically oriented art, it sponsored the Vahâna Course of drawing instruction. Dutch artists associated with the movement included Jan Toorop, Jan Thorn-Prikker, Karel P. C. Bazel, Johannes L. M. Lauwericks, Willem van Konijnenburg, and Piet Mondrian. See Centraal Museum, *Het Nieuwe Wereldbeeld: Het begin van de abstrakte kunst in Nederland, 1910–1925* (Utrecht: Centraal Museum, 1972) and Haags Gemeentemuseum, *Kunstenaren der Idee: Symbolistische tendenzen in Nederland, ca. 1880–1930* (The Hague: Haags Gemeentemuseum, 1978).
3. This is not to say that such a synthesis is alien to the Dutch theosophical artists. Indeed, it is a common aspect of their iconography, but more stylized and allegorized than Bouten's blatant representation of birth, which is comparable, for example, to a similar attitude in Otto Dix's contemporary images (although questions of influence here would be misplaced).

15 Armand Bouten
Two Lesbian Prostitutes (Zwei lesbische Dirnen), c. 1925–30?

Watercolor, brush and ink on paper
34.6 x 26.3 cm (13⅝ x 10⅜ in.)
Signed l. l. "Bouten"

Provenance: Galerie Maris, Amsterdam; Galerie Michael Hasenclever, Munich.

Armand Bouten's watercolor is a voyeuristic portrait of two women, nude but for stockings, engaged in mutual erotic stimulation as one straddles the lap of the other. In a style fusing European naïve painting and elements of African and Oceanic sculpture, Bouten transforms the two female lovers, a frequent motif in erotic imagery, into neoprimitive icons of uninhibited sexuality. Heavy black outlines, in a shifting ambience of moist washes, define the women's dark bodies with accented breasts and buttocks. Their faces, turned towards the viewer, are masks rendered in white and dark red respectively, and between them an orchid, emblem of exotic feminine sensuality, echoes the tonality of stockings in white and violet-pink.

Bouten was fascinated by the night life of the cities in which he lived. Harbor cities such as Marseilles and Amsterdam, where the prostitutes' quarters were extensive and famous, particularly attracted him, and with his companion Hanny Korevaar he often lived near the prostitutes' public streets. Since statistical studies of the 1920s purported that some twenty percent of prostitutes were lesbian in their non-professional sexual orientation, it is likely that Bouten would have encountered lesbian couples. However, watching women engage sexually with one another was among the experiences offered customers with voyeuristic inclinations, and the attention Bouten's women pay to the onlooker-artist-viewer, as if their own interaction were a secondary matter, suggests that this watercolor renders such a scene. Their intimacy is not self-determined, then, but responds to the demands of a viewer presumed to be male—whether a viewer of the prostitutes in a brothel or of the work of art. But if the masklike faces and red-tinged orchid visualize a sense of the primitive, they also suggest the demonic and malevolent. The very objects of male desire and domination thus become unknowable forces of female power that could, vampire-like, turn against the men potentially enclosed in their embrace.   B. T. Y.

16 Armand Bouten
Standing Woman (Stehende), c. 1924

Painted wood, glass, straw, wire, string, nails
129.5 x 13 x 12 cm
(51 x 5⅛ x 4¾ in.)

Provenance: Estate of the artist; Galerie Wending, Amsterdam.

Armand Bouten's foray into sculpture in the mid-1920s was the result of di-

verse artistic influences and travels. By this time Bouten had experimented with modernist styles in Amsterdam, Berlin, Hungary, and Paris. In *Standing Woman*, he combines the Africanizing qualities of German Expressionist sculpture with a reverie for African ritual in attached objects as well as the Dada-Constructivist fascination with collage and found objects. Retaining the form of the fence post with which he began, Bouten carved into it details of the female figure and painted it with black enamel; he added nails, bits of glass, straw, wire, and string to render ornamentation or to refer, by means of flax straw, to blond "flaxen hair."

Bouten also clothed the figure with shimmering sequin beads, gluing them to the lower torso of the sculpture. Although many of the actual attachments have since been lost, glued areas allow a general reconstruction of the original effects to be imagined. Over the beads, there are traces of rope or ribbon formerly tied from nail to nail to "draw" the hem of a dancing costume. A zigzag design can be discerned on the lower portion of the figure's body. Intertwining folklike primitive materials, such as the straw and wooden post, with the paint and jewelry of fashionable urban life, Borchert quotes in a playful manner the vocabularies of diverse sources and combines them, Klee-like, into the fantasy world of his own art.   B. T. Y.

17 Armand Bouten
Small Standing Woman (Kleine Stehende), c. 1925–30?

Boxwood, colored glaze, glass, beads, metal tacks
H. 28 cm (11 in.)

Provenance: Estate of the artist; Christie's, Amsterdam.

Armand Bouten's sculptural productions range from large totem-like pieces to small-scale, intimate, and more incidental images. *Small Standing Woman* is one of his intricately designed figurines whose slender dimensions seem almost to prefigure Alberto Giacometti's works of the 1940s, but whose manner otherwise reflects African or Oceanic sculptures, probably as viewed through their earlier emulation by Ernst Ludwig Kirchner, Erich Heckel, and Max Pechstein. There is a willed primitivism in this piece, filtered through prior European reception and adaptation.

In her slim form and muted coloration enlivened by bright-colored beads and glass jewels, *Small Standing Woman* replicates in sculpture Bouten's images of dance hall entertainers, lesbians, and prostitutes. She appears standing in demure pose. Details of clothing—the neckline of a dress, decorative patterns on her short stylish skirt, the hemline, and stockings—are rendered on the metallic base pigment in soft pink glazes. Bouten's sculpture maintains the playful quality of his watercolors and paintings. His accent on fantasy, combined with primitivizing forms and masklike faces, pushes his work close to Surrealism at times, although he always maintains references to both Dutch and German Expressionism, especially their

explicit celebration of female sexuality. The figures are totems of a woman's sexual display.   B. T. Y.

18 Eduard Braun
Theater Checkroom (Theatergarderobe), c. 1930

Pen and ink on paper
26.5 x 25 cm (10⁷⁄₁₆ x 9⅞ in.)
Signed l. c. "Ed. Braun"

Provenance: Estate of the artist; Galerie Nierendorf, West Berlin.

Exhibition: West Berlin, Galerie Nierendorf, *Herbst '87*, 1987 (as *Im Pfandhaus*).

In Eduard Braun's comic ink drawing, people crowd around a checkroom counter attempting to retrieve coats, hats, and canes left there prior to a theater or concert performance. It is a mundane scene which the artist, using a tangled weave of short pen strokes, renders as a commentary on social roles and their reversal as the subservient become dominant, even if only briefly.

The drawing is dominated in the center foreground by the massive, stable form of the checkroom attendant and the pile of clothing she carries. In her demeanor is stability and force, accented by a jowled profile and facial features that bespeak strength and determination, rather than clichés of fragile femininity. Hers is the appearance of the proletariat, akin to the women in Käthe Kollwitz's or Heinrich Zille's drawings and prints, that betrays the test of life under harsh conditions permitting survival only to the very strong and resolutely obstinate.

Like Braun's other drawings for Weimar Germany's illustrated periodicals sponsored by the liberal-to-moderate political left, *Theater Checkroom* presents its satirical commentary in humorous fashion. Exaggerated features press the scene to the edge of caricature, particularly among the milling mob that pushes against the counter. Dainty women with vacuous faces, their bodies compressed uncomfortably by men jostling against them, contrast to bespectacled masks and bearded grins that pop up from the anonymous surging throng. But the comedy of the scene serves to render acceptable and innocuous the juxtaposition of individual and crowd, of determined self-preservation and the mindless rush for fashionable entertainment. Safely behind the barrier of her counter, the attendant attains an illusion of power and a focus of attention which the society pressing towards her normally denies her.   R. H.

19 Eduard Braun
The Possessed (Die Besessenen), c. 1930

Pen and ink on paper
23.8 x 30.3 cm (9⅜ x 11¹⁵⁄₁₆ in.)
Signed l. c. "Ed. Braun";
inscribed l. l. "Die Besessenen"

Provenance: Estate of the artist; Galerie Nierendorf, West Berlin.

Exhibition: West Berlin, Galerie Nierendorf, *Herbst '87*, 1987.

Cafés possess a personality shaped by their clientele. The best-remembered cafés of Weimar Germany are those made famous by their bohemian and artistic patrons, such as the Romanisches Café and Café des Westens frequented by John Hoexter (see cat. no. 64), but innumerable other cafés served less conspicuous groups of customers, neither famous nor infamous. Typically, a mixed clientele of neighborhood types met around small tables crowded together in mirrored rooms filled with cigar and cigarette smoke and the smells of coffee, beer, damp clothing, and human bodies. These were locales of encounter and information, where men met to discuss events of the day, play chess or checkers, read newspapers, and be waited upon by waitresses in black dresses and white aprons.

Eduard Braun's title identifies the frequenters of his café as possessed. Intense gestures accompany conversation here, demoniacal glaring faces hover over a chessboard, and anxious looks accompany a turn away from the ideological lessons of daily newspapers held like shields against the café's encroaching social tumult. But possessed, too, is the recorder of the scene, the artist at the lower right—surely a self-portrait—submitting his models to the imposed measure of his pencil held high. Like the waitress applying her lipstick near him, he does not participate in the games or discussions that surround him but remains resolutely dependent on café life, shaping through it the world of his images, as signifying cosmetic of the society that harbors him.   R. H.

20 Eduard Braun
City Bridge (Grossstadtbrücke), c. 1930

Watercolor, ink and tusche on paper
18.8 x 14.4 cm (7⅜ x 5⅝ in.)
Not signed; estate stamp verso

Provenance: Estate of the artist; Galerie Nierendorf, West Berlin.

Exhibition: West Berlin, Galerie Nierendorf, *370 Werke von 39 Künstlern des zwanzigsten Jahrhunderts*, 24 August–15 November 1988.

With factory smokestacks in the background and workers walking past or lingering in the foreground, Eduard Braun's city bridge cuts through and connects the manufacturing life of a metropolis. A complex weaving of girders and wires links and supports the pedestrian and vehicle traffic that casts the long, deep shadows of early morning onto the bridge's asphalt surfaces. Braun, who sometimes employed the pseudonym "Urban," here illustrates the massive efforts and muscular activity that underlie the city's industrial existence, supplanting all forms of nature with an artificial skeleton of steel, concrete, and iron. In this atmosphere, the color of the sunrise is filtered through grays and dank greens that cover men and surroundings alike, transforming them with its camouflage so that they melt into a single interlocking entity. Precariously supported on tall columns, a black elevated train tracks its illumination along an echoing curve whose rhythms contrast, like the misplaced reminiscence of a Roman aqueduct, with the turmoil and dark spotted shadows of traffic moving along the great city bridge.   R. H.

21   Fritz Burmann
Frau Biene from Worpswede, 87 Years Old (Frau Biene aus Worpswede, 87 Jahre alt), 1923

Oil and tempera on canvas
44.5 x 34.4 cm (17^1/$_2$ x 13^1/$_2$ in.)
Signed and dated u. l. "Fritz Burmann 1923"; inscribed verso "Frau Biene aus Worpswede, 87 Jahre alt"

Provenance: Galerie Nierendorf, West Berlin.

Exhibitions: Mannheim, Städtische Kunsthalle, *"Neue Sachlichkeit": Deutsche Malerei seit dem Expressionismus*, 14 June–13 September 1925, cat. no. 11 (as *Die Arme*, 1924); Berlin, Deutsche Kunstgemeinschaft, Berlin Schloss, *Ostpreussenkunst*, 20 March–24 April 1927, cat. no. 20 (as *Frau Biene*); Milwaukee, Patrick and Beatrice Haggerty Museum of Art, Marquette University, *A Focus on Images: Sense and Form*, 9 November 1984–1 June 1985; Milwaukee, UWM Art Museum, University of Wisconsin, *Reactions to the War: European Art, 1914–1925*, 2 November–14 December 1986, cat. no. 7 (as *Old Woman*); Berlinische Galerie, Museum für Moderne Kunst, Photographie und Architektur in Martin-Gropius-Bau, *Stationen der Moderne: Die bedeutenden Kunstausstellungen des 20. Jahrhunderts in Deutschland*, 25 September 1988–8 January 1989, cat. no. 6/4 (as *Alte Frau*, 1925).

In this disturbing portrait, Fritz Burmann revives the technique and pristine realism of German Renaissance painting, but deliberately subverts it. Whereas subjects were often depicted with symbolic attributes in the older portrait tradition, Frau Biene is shown with the deteriorating remains of a scant meal. Another device borrowed from Northern Renaissance painting is the isolated hand, cropped by the bottom edge of the picture, in this instance without the conventional jewelry, prayer book, or flower, but only the painfully arthritic, knobby fingers conspicuously displayed.

Burmann constructs a deep interior space, and pushes Frau Biene's disproportionately large figure up against the picture plane. With her back hunched, she is cramped into the pictorial space to evoke a sense of her generally oppressed state. Extreme emphasis on hands and face documents her suffering, and the viewer is brutally confronted with her festering eye ailment and cadaverous pallor. The acidic tint of the painting accentuates her malnourished and sickly condition. Her sunken cheeks betray a heavy bone structure, and the gnarled joints of her

hand indicate a life of physical labor, which has not ensured her even basic comforts in her old age.

The sense of hardship is further underscored by the rustic interior, perhaps a barn or storage shed, with ladder, rope, rocks, and wooden-slat door. In this locale, Frau Biene's existence is equated with that of a domestic beast. The meager remnants of her food are already crawling with insects: broken egg shells and the empty pot are indicative of her material deprivation. Her obvious need for food, and the equally obvious lack of any means to meet this need provide the pathos of the scene.

Burmann's portrait represents a form of social commentary. The title reads like a statistician's entry and intensifies the work's detached (*sachlich*) quality, as if it were part of a sociological study. With a clinical scrutiny that gives equal attention to physical deformities and wood grain, Burmann avoids a pathos-laden expression, but evokes compassion by pointing to the woman's tragic destiny. Frau Biene's personality is not the subject of the painting. Rather, by placing her in a specific context and presenting her grotesque condition with almost mechanical precision, the artist produces an image of her social and economic fate.   C. D. G.

22   Fritz Burmann
Farmer's Children (Two Children with a Hare) (Bauernkinder [Zwei Kinder mit Hasen]), 1923

Oil on canvas
53.2 x 44.5 cm (20^{15}/$_{16}$ x 17^1/$_2$ in.)
Signed and dated l. l. "Fritz Burmann/D'dorf. 23."

Provenance: Private collection, Germany; Kunsthaus Lempertz, Cologne.

Exhibition: Milwaukee, UWM Art Museum, University of Wisconsin, *Reactions to the War: European Art, 1914–1925*, 2 November–14 December 1986, cat. no. 6.

Children were discovered as a subject for German art by the Romantics, and the cult of the child they inaugurated extends into the twentieth century. For *Neue Sachlichkeit* artists, the adulation of the child takes on a pessimistic cast; they emphasize, not youthful innocence with its toys and games, but the deleterious effects of modern civilization on the growth, health, and development of children who age beyond their years both physically and psychologically. Fritz Burmann's boy and girl, unlike the urban proletariat who predominate in the iconography of *Neue Sachlichkeit*, are children of the land, seen in a village landscape. The glow of health and happiness, however, popularly attributed to *Bauernkinder* growing up in the open air, is lacking. Their clothing and surroundings, except for a single flowering tree, are drab and somber, their faces pale and frozen in unemotive, resigned expressions.

Burmann, gives the work a distinct tension by eliminating the middle ground, denying a sense of open space. The figures appear aggressively large in

the immediate foreground, and the background converges at an angle immediately behind them in flattened planes that describe hills and meadow, house and white wall. The dry, matte surface reinforces the arid quality in the painting. The children gaze blankly, the boy frowning, either at the viewer or into a vague distance. Central to the painting is the hare cradled gently in the girl's arms. The tender caress of her graceful, elongated hands betrays affection, a normal childhood need for warmth and security. In postwar rural Germany, the girl and boy appear wistful, their mood sober, and their health fragile. The hare now so tenderly protected, we are forced to believe, is doomed to end up on the family's dinner table.   C. D. G.

23   Pol Cassel
Cemetery (Friedhof), c. 1925?

Oil on canvas
110 x 129 cm (43^5/$_{16}$ x 50^3/$_4$ in.)
Not signed
Verso: *Forest Interior (Waldinneres)*, oil, signed and dated l. r. "Cassel/ 21"

Provenance: Galleria del Levante, Munich.

In early nineteenth-century painting, the motif of the cemetery, with its overt references to life, death, and afterlife, well suited the allegorical programs of German Romanticism. It was soon transformed, however, into a sentimental subject evoking a pleasant shudder, an enjoyable sense of the eerie identified in German as *Gruseln*. Cemeteries became the setting for pathetic funerals in realist art and, together with the Romantics' symbolic concerns, were revived as a subject in turn-of-the-century art. Expressionist painters did not continue this interest, but cemetery and mausoleum designs remained a constant aspect of conservative as well as innovative architectural and design exhibitions well into the 1920s. Moreover, during and after World War I, monuments and cemeteries for the millions of "fallen heroes" who died in that suicidal conflict were a persistent and often politically controversial concern of German artists and their public.

In 1924, the architects Thomas Wechs and Eberhard Finsterwalder, assisted by the sculptors Bernhard Bleeker and Karl Knappe, constructed the municipal Warriors' Monument (*Kriegerehrenmal*) at the Army Museum in Munich. Focused on the recumbent figure of a soldier in full uniform modeled on medieval tomb reliefs, the monument takes the form of a crypt situated beneath an abstracted altar, and thereby directly associates the deaths suffered for the German Reich with religious martyrdom and salvation. Erected a decade after the outbreak of World War I—during the year Adolf Hitler was released early from the imprisonment imposed on him after his failed putsch—the monument, with its peacefully sleeping, classically propor-

tioned figure, offers no reflection on the war's violence. Instead, the combined inscriptions—"Unseren Gefallenen" (For Our Fallen) and "Sie werden auferstehen" (They Shall Rise Again)— suggest a sense of revanchism and preparedness for renewed conflict disguised as a religious affirmation of apocalyptic resurrection.

Pol Cassel's *Cemetery* offers an alternative perception of Weimar Germany's social response to, and honoring of, its dead. The subject is neither a monument nor a view of military graves, but a small village cemetery, surrounded by heavy stone walls, in which the graves of "fallen heroes" are interspersed among those of the civilian population. Crosses or other markers locate the individual plots and visitors move among the graves, several of which have been decorated with wreaths. It is All Souls' Day, and the village inhabitants have come to do homage to their deceased. Cassel renders the scene in somber, dark tones in a complexly built-up surface that emulates the weathered stone wall, the mysterious formations of a bordering grove of trees, and the overlapping textures of metallic and marble headstones. The dank coloration is broken by an incongruously bright blue structure—an ossuary or maintenance shed attached to the cemetery wall—which calls attention to the couple about to enter the cemetery gate.

Dressed in refined black, with top hat and white gloves, carrying a cigar along with his cane and a beribboned wreath, the corpulent man walks ahead of his wife; with her aged face disguised by heavy makeup beneath a feathered hat, she ostentatiously displays her fox-fur stole and muff. The day of honoring the dead is transformed into a day of parading one's wealth in conjunction with official public, but insincere, gestures of bereavement and respect. Like Munich's war monument, the cemetery is less a site of solemn mourning than an ironic site of celebration for the established social order. Cassel affects a humorous, quasi-naïve critique of contemporary abuse of tradition and unmasks the rites of bourgeois complacency.

Like Otto Dix and other artists in Dresden and Düsseldorf, Cassel synthesizes Expressionist subjectivity with elements derived from naïve art such as that of Adalbert Trillhaase. Cassel applies Trillhaase's distorted, multiple perspectives to generate an unsystematic recession into depth which reverses the rules of illusionistic perspective that Cassel undoubtedly learned during his academic training. He offers the viewer several views over the wall into a cemetery that seems to twist and shift towards the upper left corner of the canvas. Through his constructed naïveté, Cassel subverts a rational way of looking at the painting; he confuses and obfuscates the path the bourgeois couple at the entrance will take once inside the cemetery. The image projects imbalance and affectation in a formal, stylistic extension of Cassel's commentary on All Souls' Day practiced in a society bereft of grief and remorse, self-satisfied in the hypocrisy of its own false righteousness and virtue.   A. I. S.

24 Paul Citroën
Portrait (Porträt), 1923

Oil on artist's board
66.4 x 49 cm (26¹/₈ x 19⁵/₁₆ in.)
Signed and dated verso
"P. Citroën/1923"

Provenance: Galerie Maris, Amsterdam.

Although born in Berlin, Paul Citroën was a Dutch citizen, as his parents both were Dutch. Trained as a painter in the Training Studios for Painting and Sculpture in Berlin-Charlottenburg, Citroën initially worked in the mode of such German Impressionists as Lovis Corinth and Max Liebermann, but rejected this manner and, indeed, ceased painting altogether after he encountered Herwarth Walden's collection of modern art in 1915. During World War I, Citroën aided Walden with the establishment of a bookstore in Berlin, and then of a branch gallery in neutral and relatively prosperous Holland, potentially a significant source of added income as Germany's economy suffered the effects of war. When Citroën returned to Berlin in 1919, the technique of photomontage mixed with drawing, as practiced by George Grosz and John Heartfield (see cat. no. 58), attracted him and, along with his younger brother Hans, he resumed his activity as an artist in Berlin's Dada milieu. As the Dada movement faded, Citroën turned once more to painting, then entered the Bauhaus to further his training at the encouragement of Georg Muche, who had become one of the Bauhaus masters in 1920.

The preparatory course in which Citroën enrolled was taught by the Swiss artist Johannes Itten with the goal, general to the Bauhaus, of fusing the various art media. Itten's own paintings accented coloristic interactions and a search for color harmony which he also imparted to his students in the training of their "logical thought." "This can occur," he wrote, "in terms of externals, through exercises in construction and through the study of color and form principles, whose pure rationality permits itself to be communicated by means of lines, surfaces, volumes and the colors of the rainbow."[1] Itten's intent was to aid students in achieving a high degree of self-consciousness, an awareness of materials and processes, in order to gain the kind of independence that would guarantee the quality of each work. The artist, then, Itten believed,

... shall not fall as sacrifice to an artistic dogma but, self-reliant, go his own way. With intense determination, today's youth, insofar as it does not sleepily lounge through its days, demands freedom, independence, interiorization—i. e., unification and individual work—and rejects every manifestation of superficial rote learning and of unoriginal, dead knowledge. Because it hates falsehoods, because it loves life and does not wish to lose it.[2]

Painted according to Itten's principles during Citroën's second year as Bauhaus student, the portrait in the Fishman Collection is a deliberate exercise in oil painting. The colors are ap-

plied in clear, interrelated strokes that vary in nature according to whether they compose the fluid black drawing of facial features or the surrounding rectangles. Variation in pigment texture and pattern combine with a willful re-formation of the model into a two-dimensional image that consists, if one applies a musical analogy, of a graceful central melody set off against the steady rhythms of rectangular repetition. Within the portrait, color does not adhere to the predetermined form of the face, but complies with the organizing rectangular scheme, permitting the play of black lines to define likeness. With volume denied, the image is insistently flat, its own rectangular components echoing the rectangle of the artist's board on which it is painted. Truth, in Itten's modernist terms, has been attained in a manipulation of material components and the principles of color harmonies, not in a veristic illusion of the model. With no signature on the front, the painting forms part of the Bauhaus search for collective identity, a personal process of integration within the Bauhaus workshop that corresponded to the ideal integration of all visual arts under the aegis of architecture. R. H.

1. "...des logischen Denkens....Das kann rein äusserlich geschehen durch Konstruktionsübungen und durch das Studium der Form- und Farbgesetze, deren reine Gesetzmässigkeiten sich in den geometrischen Linien, Flächen, Körpern und den Regenbogenfarben kundgeben." Johannes Itten, "Kunst-Hand-Werk," in "Arbeiten von Johannes Itten/Erzeugnisse der Werkstätten des Staatlichen Bauhauses in Weimar," *Wegleitung Nr. 47 des Kunstgewerbemuseums Zürich* (1923), reprinted in Museum für Gestaltung Zürich/Kunstgewerbemuseum, *Bauhaus 1919–1933: Meister- und Schülerarbeiten/Weimar/Dessau/Berlin* (Berne: Bertelli Verlag, 1988), 71.
2. "...wird nicht einem künstlerischen Dogma zum Opfer fallen, sondern in sich selbst ruhend seinen eigenen Weg gehen. Die Jugend von heute, sofern sie nicht verschlafen die Tage hinduselt, verlangt mit grossem Nachdruck nach Freiheit, Selbständigkeit, nach Verinnerlichung, d. i. Vereinheitlichung und individueller Arbeit, und lehnt alles äusserliche Anlernen und unoriginelle, tote Wissen ab. Denn sie hasst die Lüge, weil sie das Leben liebt und es nicht verlieren möchte." Ibid.

25 Otto Dix
Birth (Geburt), 1918

Ink, ink wash, pencil on toned paper
39.8 x 39.2 cm (15¹¹/₁₆ x 15⁷/₁₆ in.)
Signed and dated u. r. "Dix/18"; inscribed verso "dein Blick o Weltraum klirrt wie Erz" ("The view of you, oh cosmos, rings like bronze")

Provenance: Hauswedell and Nolte, Hamburg.

From 1918 to 1920, Otto Dix introduced allegorical representations of women as a major theme in his work, exploring female biological functions in

cosmological terms. Most often these images have an abstract, quasi-erotic quality, heightened by a Futurist-Expressionist vocabulary of force lines and dynamic geometries. *Birth* is one of these severely abstracted compositions, bisected by a diagonal which distinguishes two realms: a stylized mountain landscape with houses, dominated by the floating form of a child on the left; and an even more stylized female torso with four breasts and black pubic triangle on the right. A spiraling vortex indicates the vagina from which the transparent amnion emanates, still enveloping the fetus that hovers over the landscape.[1]

Dix presents the process of birth in universal and mythical terms. The wide-eyed child embryo, just emerged from the womb, remains encased in its amniotic sac as it encounters the external world for the first time.[2] The woman, without head or limbs, is a nebulous, anatomical landscape, her scale matching that of the mountains; her body becomes a vast geographic expanse, a literal Mother Earth. This association of the female body with the earth was a notion familiar from Expressionist art, and one that had currency in literary and popular realms during war and popular realms during the late nineteenth and early twentieth centuries. Women were often compared to, or seen as creatures of, nature, in vivid contrast to civilization, the more familiar territory of men. Dix's fusion of landscape and woman's body carries the analogy to its most radical expressive form.[3]

Also suggested in *Birth* is the emergence of *Der neue Mensch* (The New Human Being), the ideal being embodying an imminent utopian age. In the midst of war, this concept offered hope that a new consciousness would result from what seemed like purely meaningless and destructive bloodletting. The physical birth shown here evokes the figurative birth of *Der neue Mensch*, and the universal, faceless woman becomes a vehicle for this messianic being. In extreme fashion, Dix reifies woman, reducing her to social and cultural insignificance while glorifying her generative power. Deprived of individuality and defined by her reproductive function, however, woman is also recognized as the source of life, as the incarnation of cosmic vitality in a mythical reconstruction of birth as a primeval, archetypal event. C. D. G.

1. The female torso is similarly treated in another ink drawing of 1918, identical in size and technique to *Birth*: *The Divine Triangle (Das göttliche Dreieck)* in the Galerie der Stadt Stuttgart (illus. in *Otto Dix 1891–1969* [Munich: Museum Villa Stuck, 1985], cat. no. 325). The two drawings also relate thematically and appear to be part of a larger series.
2. Dix's bug-eyed newborn has precedents in Egon Schiele's painting *The Dead Mother II (Birth of Genius) (Die tote Mutter II [Geburt des Genies])* (1911) and Max Klinger's engraving *Dead Mother (Tote Mutter)* (1890) from the cycle of prints *On Death II (Der Tod II)*. The association in both of birth and the mother's death should also be noted in relation to Dix's drawing.
3. Antecedents for this melding of female and geographic forms appear in works by

Alfred Weisgerber and Otto Greiner, and in pornographic depictions of gigantic women swarmed upon by (relatively) minuscule men.

26 Otto Dix
Workers' Children (Arbeiterkinder), 1922

Pen and ink, watercolor on Japan paper
52.4 x 37.3 cm (20⁵/₈ x 14¹¹/₁₆ in.)
Signed and dated l. l. "Dix 22" and "Dix"

Provenance: Private collection, New York (?); Alien Custodian Property Auction, New York, 1952; private collection.

Exhibition: Milwaukee, UWM Art Museum, University of Wisconsin, *Reactions to the War: European Art, 1914–1925*, 2 November–14 December 1986, cat. no. 14.

Children were a common theme in German painting and popular illustration throughout the nineteenth and early twentieth centuries. Embodiments of innocence, spontaneity, and freedom, they were presented romantically as foils to the repressed mentality of adulthood, or anecdotally as cloyingly cute, inexperienced actors in pretended adult situations. As naturalist and realist artists focused on the plight of the poor in industrial society, children took on new roles in which their deprivation was demonstrated, often in melodramatic situations intended to arouse the viewer's compassion or social indignation. After World War I, the child caught up in the injustice of modern society was also a frequent motif in the work of Otto Dix, but depicted, perhaps perversely, with an awareness of the sexuality that Expressionists such as Erich Heckel and Ernst Ludwig Kirchner had discovered and celebrated in proletarian and bohemian children.

Dix's *Workers' Children* presents an image of underprivileged youth that emphasizes the pernicious effects of the city environment on their development, while also suggesting incipient adolescent feelings of sexual attraction. The scene concentrates on the foreground figure of a proletarian boy viewed with apparent fascination by the girl accompanying him, in the bleak setting of high stone walls, narrow streets, and factory chimneys. Thematically, the drawing is a variation on the sentimental convention of "spring's awakening," where adolescents in the open air, in poses of mutual admiration and attraction, are equated with springtime blossoms and their promise of summer fruit. But with paved streets instead of flowered meadows, *Workers' Children* offers a statement of physical and psychological constriction, in dominant tones of gray and drab brown.

Dix renders his vision of poverty with a remarkably delicate ink line that defines contours, profiles, and facial features. Counteracting this linear fragility is his broad application of watercolors, which bleed and run together, often regardless of contours, in muddied but somehow translucent hues of urban blight and enduring twilight. Color, rather than drawing, provides details that contribute to the sense of deprivation and abuse, as rust-red blots unmistakably signify the spread of disease in lesions and boils, the effects of malnutrition or inherited syphilis shared by both girl and boy. Perhaps the boy's jutting jaw and clenched mouth suggest determination and pugnacious resistance, but otherwise the image predicts no redemption from the destitution bequeathed to a new generation. The trite sentimentality of scenes of "young love," whose situation and psychology of glances and postures Dix exploits, is invoked in the pathetic context of the proletarian child's world with a calculated irony: the artist employs a highly refined technique to represent its conceptual antithesis, to elicit revulsion through the enticement of his beautiful craft.

C. D. G.

27   Otto Dix

Sex Murder (Lustmord), 1922

Watercolor, brush and ink over
pencil on paper
48.4 x 36,5 cm (19^1/$_{16}$ x 14^3/$_8$ in.)
Signed, dated and inscribed u. l.
"Dix 22/153"

Provenance: Galerie Klihm, Munich;
Marlborough Fine Arts Ltd., London.

Exhibitions: Munich, Galerie Klihm, *Otto Dix*, 1970; Essen, Museum Folkwang, *Otto Dix: Der Krieg (Zeichnungen und Radierungen)* (traveled to Frankfurter Kunstverein and Kunsthalle Bielefeld), 1971–72.

Writing in *Das Kunstblatt* about Otto Dix's controversial painting *The Trench (Der Schützengraben)* in 1923, the Hungarian critic Ernst Kállai observed:

This monumental painting has been much discussed, as the objections of the aesthetically overly sensitive side were countered by pointing to the high ethical pathos of the composition. The entire debate missed the true significance of the painting, which can be understood neither purely aesthetically nor totally in terms of content. Rather, it represents a deeply rooted and spiritually contradictory unity of adulation and revulsion. It is to this unity that the painting owes its uncanny greatness. . . .

Dix's *The Trench* would serve equally well as an object of fervent adoration for a fanatic worshiper of the god of war as it would as a pacifist propaganda image. . . . Dix sinks his teeth into such repulsive themes with a cold cruelty in which revulsion can no longer be distinguished from passionate ecstasy. Ugliness in his compositions attains a sense of great, even celebratory regularity and legitimacy. The most disgusting incidents are called forth with so ceremonial a sense of pathos towards precisely these disgusting scenes that, in the end, the question of whether rejecton or a cult is involved remains totally open.[1]

Even more than to his war scenes, this verdict of ambivalence, in which fascination and horror are inseparable, applies to the representations of rape and sex murders that Dix produced with determined regularity during the early 1920s.[2]

Although sexuality and violence had been linked in his previous imagery, Dix first turned to undisguised motifs of rape and murder in 1920. For three years, he repeatedly depicted women attacked, brutalized, and mutilated. In these scenes, dismembered corpses dominate, their clothes partially ripped off to reveal their sexual organs; in several images, the murderer-rapist is also shown, jubilant in the aftermath of his deed, celebrating or, as in this watercolor, leaving the scene of his crime. In 1922, Dix addressed the subject at least four more times. One of these depictions he presented as a birthday gift to Martha Koch, who had left her husband to live with Dix and would become his wife. Thereafter, Dix ceased to paint the motif.[3]

It is tempting and certainly appropriate to seek out personal, psychological motives to explain this three-year fascination with extreme violence against women. Several of the artist's friends recalled, years later, that Dix approached the works with a macabre, even sadistic humor, and commented that, had he not painted these scenes of sexual aggression, he would have committed murder himself.[4] Such recollections, pieced together, indicate a pattern of conscious sublimation, which Dix himself identified as exorcism, to avoid or conquer aspects of his personality or his world by submitting them to the control of his art:

All art is exorcism. I paint dreams and visions too; the dreams and visions of my time, the dreams and visions of all people! . . . I painted many things, war too, nightmares too, horrible things. . . . Painting is the effort to produce order; order in yourself. There is much chaos in me, much chaos in our time.[5]

Dix voices, and his friends support, an image of the artist as a seer of the essential structures and underlying order of reality, but someone constantly threatened by the unruly forces of genius, so close to insanity. Ironically, the *Neue Sachlichkeit* that Dix professes, whose fundamental principle he identifies as detailed representation of reality's surfaces, is, then, founded on a metaphysical idealism to which is attached an egocentric concern with subjective states and experiences perceived as universal, in which the artist serves as proxy and unique visionary for all humanity. Dix's statements and the self he presented to acquaintances were thus a deliberate acting out of this premeditated artist's role; they may also reveal unguarded elements of his ego, but even if this is so, it is secondary and indeed incidental.

"I shall either become infamous or famous," Dix proclaimed.[6] The subject matter of his work, other than portraits, from 1919 through 1922, when he was a master student at the Dresden Academy, included brutalized soldiers and revolutionaries, disfigured prostitutes, and war cripples, as well as sex

murders. Combined with their unorthodox styles—first Cubist- and Futurist-inspired, then neo-naïve and over-determined in detail—these images of a barbarized reality necessarily provoked a public attached to traditional perceptions of art as "spiritually uplifting," as substituting an idealized, ordered aesthetic reality for the world of a defeated nation. As threats of legal prosecution followed his art, Dix generated extensive publicity for his work such as neither academic recognition nor exhibition prizes would have equaled.

His provocative tactics, characteristic of bohemian artists since the nineteenth century, Dix shared with the Dadaists with whom he exhibited in 1919 and 1920 in Dresden and Berlin. In those exhibitions, rape scenes and sex murders preceded their appearance in his own work, notably in the example of George Grosz, who had begun treating such subjects in 1912.[7] In 1920, as erotic elements increased in Dix's paintings, Conrad Felixmüller complained that "the man is once more a complete Dadaist and 'paints' pornographic pictures of the worst kind; I consider him lost, therefore, since this seems to be a predisposition of his."[8] Felixmüller, concerned with creating an art of social relevance, protested Dix's "Dada" tendency to incite response through sexually explicit imagery in which social issues were subsumed in the process of overt sexual revelation, of provocative display of women's bodies, frequently in postures of submission. Such "Dada" exhibitionism, Felixmüller maintained, prevented Dix's paintings from adequately serving the cause of radical protest and class revolution even as they satisfied his "predisposition."[9]

Felixmüller identified a combination of personal motivation and calculated provocation in Dix; the two remain difficult to separate, as Dix's friends later demonstrated. There is also an economic factor to be considered, for these sexual images appealed to German consumers. Grosz, for example, noted with satisfaction that his drawing *Bourgeois World (Bürgerliche Welt)* (1918), in which *inter alia* women are dismembered, humiliated, and violated, sold well in its lithographic translation.[10] Scholars have traced the sex murder scenes such as pulp novels such as *Jack, der mysteriöse Frauenmörder (Jack the Mysterious Lady Killer)*, which sold millions of copies. Whether or not Grosz and Dix were among their readers, the market for these books points to their effectiveness in meeting a demand for accounts of violent sexual acts. Similarly, newspapers and magazines reported at length and in detail—including photographs of victims, bedrooms, and murder weapons—on the several sex murder cases that became notorious in postwar Germany.[11]

Dix's watercolor confronts the viewer with all the elements of the sex crime: the murderer appears to the right, the body of his victim, with bloodied buttocks and breasts bared, lies splayed on the floor near the bed. The scene is orchestrated to suggest the violent drama that was enacted, but also to distance it from the upper middle-class majority of Dix's admirers: the setting is proletarian, or perhaps an *Absteigequartier*, a cheap hotel room

leased by the hour, without furnishings or decoration other than the bed, curtain, and rug; and the man, with bowler hat shoved back on his head, is a caricatured member of the criminal underclass.

The ability of these images to meet, rather than offend, bourgeois standards finally can be discerned in the resolution of charges brought against Dix for obscenity and pornography, most dramatically in 1922 for depicting a prostitute's pubic hair, vulva, and buttocks in his painting *Girl Before a Mirror (Mädchen am Spiegel)* (1921). Carl Hofer and Max Slevogt came to his defense during the three-month trial, and Dix justified his intention "to put before peoples' eyes where the practice of the condemnable trade of prostitution ultimately leads, and to deter them from frequenting ladies of easy virtue or emulating their way of life." The court concluded:

The possibility that the first full impression of the painting could be one which offends one's sense of shame cannot be . . . ruled out. This impression, however, becomes totally secondary due to the undeniable moralizing tendency recognizable in the painting after a little contemplation, and which the accused seriously sought out in the production of the painting, to which is also to be added the artistic manner of the painting's execution, to which experts in the field have testified.[12]

The sex murder scenes never underwent such legal testing, nor were they condemned. If the court's ruling is used as measure, they presented an "undeniable moralizing tendency," since they demonstrated the possible fate of "women of the street," assuming the victims in Dix's murder images to be prostitutes, which is not apparent even if it is a premise of discussions of them. The moral is in the murder. The murderer acts as instrument of society's retribution. The woman is the criminal. Her sexuality, enacted outside the male-controlled social institution of marriage or other stable heterosexual relationships, was her crime.[13]

If Dix's audience justified its salacious interest in sex murders by condemning the woman, identifying the victim as the instigator of her fate, the mastery of the artist's technique served as additional testimony to the redeeming social value of the works, as the 1922 court verdict indicates. To render this scene of sex and brutality, Dix manipulates his watercolor medium to accent the sense of violence and lack of rational control. Broad, quick brushstrokes move in disparate directions, and colors, unevenly applied, bleed together as if dripping down the surfaces they define. The blue of the killer's suit becomes the blue shadow from which his eyes and teeth emerge white in a grin of sinister, ghoulish satisfaction. For this watercolor, as for *Girl Before a Mirror*, "experts in the field" can testify to the remarkable craft Dix displays: every element within the image contributes to the cohesion of its meaning and form.

In 1922, when Dix produced this image, the German economy suffered its first year of uncontrolled inflation; the mark dropped to roughly .2 percent of its already reduced value of 1919. Dix took up watercolor as his favored medium. It allowed for rapid production in combination with cheap materials, while the comparatively low price assured quick turnover and provided a ready form of investment for progressive middle-class collectors, whose savings inflation was rapidly depleting.[14] With their accentuation of female sexuality, moreover, these works addressed the interests of the predominantly male *Spiesser*, or middle-class philistine, on whom Dix was financially dependent.[15] In a society brutalized by war, revolution, social upheaval, and economic disaster, *Sex Murder* was calculated to be a commercial success for a defined clientele. In this motivation resides the source of the ambivalence between approbation and horror the image contains. R. H./C. D. G.

1. "Dieses Monumentalgemälde ist seinerzeit viel umstritten worden, wobei man den von ästhetisch überempfindlicher Seite erhobenen Einwänden mit dem Hinweis auf das hohe ethische Pathos der Komposition entgegentrat. Der ganze Streit ging an dem eigentlichen Wesen des Bildes vorbei, das weder rein ästhetisch, noch ausschliesslich der Tendenz nach zu erfassen ist. Es stellt vielmehr eine tief verzweigte und innerlich widerspruchsvolle Einheit zwischen Bewunderung und Entsetzen dar. Dieser Einheit hat es seine unheimliche Grösse zu verdanken. . . .

"Das Schützengrabenbild von Dix könnte ebensogut der Gegenstand höchster Anbetung eines fanatischen Kriegsgottverehrers, als pazifistisches Propagandamittel sein. . . . Dix verbeisst sich in solch hässlichen Vorwurf mit einer kalten Grausamkeit, bei der Abscheu nicht mehr von Wollust zu unterscheiden ist. Das Hässliche erhält in seinen Kompositionen den Zug grosser, selbst feierlicher Gesetzmässigkeit. Die Abwehr des Abscheulichen wird mit einem pathetischen Zeremoniell der Heraufbeschwörung eben dieses Abscheulichen ausgeübt, dass schliesslich die Frage ganz und gar offen lässt, ob es sich hier um eine Ablehnung oder um einen Kult handelt." Ernst Kállai, "Dämonie der Satire," *Das Kunstblatt* 11 (1927): 97, 99.

2. For an insightful overview of the sex murder motif in German art of the twenties, see Beth Irwin Lewis, "The View Inside Windows of the Metropolis: *Lustmord*," in Charles Haxthausen and Heidrun Suhr, eds., *Berlin: Culture and Metropolis* (Minneapolis: University of Minnesota Press, forthcoming [1990]).

3. For the most extensive consideration of these scenes, see ibid. Also see Eva Karcher, *Eros und Tod im Werk von Otto Dix*, Studien zur Geschichte des Körpers in den zwanziger Jahren (Münster: Lit Verlag, 1984), 48ff., and Brigid S. Barton, *Otto Dix and Die neue Sachlichkeit, 1918–1925* (Ann Arbor, Mich.: UMI Research Press, 1981), 47–49.

4. See Lothar Fischer, *Otto Dix: Ein Malerleben in Deutschland* (West Berlin: Nikolaische Verlagsbuchhandlung, 1981), 23, and Diether Schmidt, *Otto Dix im Selbstbildnis* (East Berlin: Henschel Verlag, 1978), 58.

5. "Alle Kunst ist Bannung. Ich male auch Träume und Gesichte; die Träume und Gesichte meiner Zeit, die Träume und Gesichte aller Menschen! . . . Ich habe viel gemalt, auch Krieg, auch Alpdruck, auch Scheussliches. . . . Malen ist ein Versuch, Ordnung zu schaffen; Ordnung in sich selbst. Es ist viel Chaos in mir, es ist viel Chaos in unserer Zeit." Dix to O. Wundhammer in *Rheinische Illustrierte*, 1947, as reprinted in Museum Villa Stuck, *Otto Dix 1891–1969* (Munich: Museum Villa Stuck, 1985), 275.

6. "Entweder ich werde berüchtigt oder berühmt." Cited by Schmidt, *Otto Dix im Selbstbildnis*, 280.

7. Lewis, "The View Inside."

8. "Leider ist der Mann wieder vollkommen Dadaist und malt pornographische Bilder übelster Art; ich halte ihn für verloren, deshalb, da dies bei ihm Veranlagung zu sein scheint." Conrad Felixmüller in a letter cited by Gunter Otto and Hans Dickel, *Otto Dix—Bildnis der Eltern—Klassenschicksal und Bildformel* (Frankfurt a. M.: Fischer Taschenbuch Verlag, 1984), 21.

9. It is not Dix's sexual motifs *per se* to which Felixmüller objects, but rather the lack of apparent social signification in their celebration of the sensual. In a review of the Darmstadt exhibition in 1920, Felixmüller praises Dix's depictions of "the human sexual animal" for their ability to visualize the degradation of modern urban life, "the small daily crimes committed against fellow human beings and sex, overheated, exhausted, during the day as well as the night" ("das sexuelle Menschentier. . . . die kleinen täglichen Verbrechen am Mitmenschen und Geschlecht, überhitzt, ermüdet, bei Tag und bei Nacht"). *Das Ey* 3 (1920): 10, as reprinted in Archiv für Bildende Kunst am Germanischen Nationalmuseum Nürnberg, *Conrad Felixmüller: Werke und Dokumente* (Klagenfurt: Ritter Verlag, n. d.), 76.

10. In a 1923 ledger, Grosz recorded that thirty-four impressions had been sold through the Munich art dealer Hans Goltz. Lewis, "The View Inside."

11. See Erich Wulffen, "Die berühmten Sexualprozesse der Nachkriegszeit," in *Zwischen zwei Katastrophen (Sittengeschichte der Nachkriegszeit)*, ed. Magnus Hirschfeld, rev. ed. (Hanau: Karl Schustek, 1966), 469ff.

12. ". . . den Menschen vor Augen zu führen, wohin die Ausübung dieses schimpflichen Gewerbes der Unzucht letzten Endes führe und sie vom Verkehr mit Freudenmädchen bzw. vor einer Nachahmung ihres Lebenswandels abzuschrecken. . . . Die Möglichkeit, dass der erste Gesamteindruck des Bildes ein das Schamgefühl verletzender sein kann, bleibt aber dennoch nicht ausgeschlossen. Dieser Eindruck wird jedoch völlig in den Hintergrund gedrängt durch die bei einiger Versenkung in das Bild unverkennbar moralisierende Tendenz, die der Angeklagte bei Herstellung des Bildes ernstlich verfolgt hat, wozu übrigens noch die von den Sachverständige begutachtete künstlerische Ausführung des Bildes hinzutritt." Cited by Ludwig Leiss, *Kunst im Konflikt: Kunst und Künstler im Widerstreit mit der 'Obrigkeit'* (Berlin and New York: Walter de Gruyter & Co., 1971), 327–329.

13. Compare Frank Wedekind's Lulu plays, *Erdgeist* and *Die Büchse der Pandora* (first published in 1895 and 1904 respectively), which gained their greatest popularity during the 1920s, where Lulu is killed in London by Jack the Ripper after a life of freely expressed, if destructive, sexuality. Also see Atina Grossman, "The New Woman and the Rationalization of Sexuality in Weimar Germany," in *Powers of Desire: The Politics of Sexuality*, eds. Ann Snitow, C. Stansell, and S. Thompson (New York: Monthly Review Press, 1983), 153ff., for discussion of ambiguous approaches to women's sexuality even among the Sex Reform leagues that encouraged female sexuality, but within the context of stable heterosexual couples, especially in marriage.

14. This characterization of Dix's watercolors and motivation largely follows that of the standard Dix monograph, Fritz Löffler, *Otto Dix: Leben und Werk*, 2d ed. (Wiesbaden: Drei Lilien Verlag, 1989), 53.

15. "I am dependent for recognition on neither the bourgeois or the non-bourgeois, but admittedly on the money of the former" ("Ich bin weder auf die Anerkennung durch die Spiesser oder Nichtspiesser angewiesen, wohl aber auf das Geld der ersteren"). Dix in a letter to Felixmüller, 1919, in Archiv für Bildende Kunst, *Conrad Felixmüller*, 76.

28 Otto Dix

Sunday Outing (Sonntagsspaziergang), 1922

Oil, tempera on canvas
75 x 60 cm (29½ x 23⅝ in.)
Signed and dated l. r. "Dix 22"
Löffler 1922/5

Provenance: Neue Kunst Frau Ey, Düsseldorf; Dr. Hans Koch, Düsseldorf; Adalbert Trillhaase, Düsseldorf; Hans Joachim Ziersch, Switzerland.

Exhibition: Munich, Museum Villa Stuck, *Otto Dix 1891–1969*, 23 August–27 October 1987, cat. no. 190.

The bourgeois family was frequently subject to commentary in critical imagery of the Weimar Republic. Essentially defined during the nineteenth century, the small patriarchal family functioned as the basic cell of the social structure, mediating between private and public life and ensuring the orderly propagation and education of the nation. During the Wilhelmine era, the Kaiser with his numerous sons and supportive empress served as a prototype for German families, and this imperial model of supreme male authority ruling over an obedient, unquestioning wife and appropriately emulative offspring remained dominant for the German middle and upper classes through the 1920s, despite efforts of feminists and the political left to define a new family policy for women and children.

Although nineteenth-century attitudes persisted, family issues nevertheless occupied a key position in the political discourse of the 1920s. Article 119 pronounced the family a central concern of the Weimar Constitution, whose self-contradictory ideals set the standard for later considerations:

> As the foundation of family life and the preservation and propagation of the nation, the family stands under the particular protection of the constitution. This rests on the equality of both sexes.
>
> The maintenance of the purity, health, and social promotion of the family is the task of the state and the communities. Families with many children have a right to social services equalizing their burden.
>
> Motherhood has a right to the protection and care of the state.[1]

Despite its insistence that marriage and family be regarded in the context of the constitution's fundamental principle of equality, Article 119 presents the family primarily as a means for producing children, and, within this structure, motherhood is a woman's sole defined role. As Germans looked with alarm at the combined statistics of World War I casualties and a continually declining birthrate, the traditional family was promulgated as the state's basic institution for the procreation and social education of children, with large families officially encouraged by means of subsidies.

Otto Dix painted *Sunday Outing*, his first major commentary on the institution of the family, in Dresden in 1922. It was one of his most productive and inventive years, following his first visit to Düsseldorf, where he had been introduced to the circle of artists and patrons associated with the gallery of Johanna Ey, popularly known as "Mother Ey." Düsseldorf provided Dix with a more extensive audience than Dresden, as well as the companionship of artists more sympathetic to his work than the predominantly late-Expressionist members of the Dresden Secession. Among the patrons Dix found in Düsseldorf was the urologist Hans Koch; this acquaintance would alter both their lives: the doctor's twenty-six-year-old wife, Martha, and Dix fell in love, and Koch decided on a divorce.[2] Martha Koch joined Dix when he returned to Dresden, but over a year would pass before the divorce was final and the two could marry. Hans Koch then married Martha's older sister, with whom he had been having a steady relationship; his and Martha's two children continued to live with him. Throughout this time and later, the sisters, Dix, and Koch remained friendly. Under these circumstances, and having just completed his first large portrait of his own parents, issues of family and personal relationships were newfound concerns for Dix.

Prior to 1922, Dix had already begun to shift from Futurist-inspired, Dadaist images with subjective deformations to a dry verism in which objects appear precisely and volumetrically defined in techniques reminiscent of German Romanticism and Northern Renaissance painting. While in Düsseldorf, Dix added the naïve painting of Adalbert Trillhaase, a retired industrialist and patron of Mother Ey's circle, to this repertoire of artistic prototypes. *Sunday Outing* is one of the first paintings in which Dix applies a neo-naïve stylistic vocabulary; simultaneously he subverts the manner into a parody of itself by accenting satire and contemporaneity rather than the dreams, visions, and memories that Trillhaase and other Sunday painters depicted.[3]

The setting of Dix's bourgeois family outing is the picturesque mountain landscape of the area of Saxony known as Saxon Switzerland, easily reached by rail from Dresden and thus a frequent goal for urbanites seeking the restorative openness of nature. A small railroad station, built to emulate a hunting lodge, announces the site *Zur Wolfsschlucht* (At the Wolf's Glen) with two rocky promontories separated by a deep gorge. What once would have been a life-threatening challenge to mountain climbers has been transformed into a series of railed staircases that lead to a lookout platform, a German flag, and a radio broadcast antenna. The chasm between the two peaks is now spanned by a wooden bridge with signs ostentatiously directing pedestrian traffic. The nature experienced by this family is tamed and constricted, forced into the confines of comfortable paths with distance rigidly marked and newly planted trees blossoming in disciplined rows.

The neo-naïve manner in which Dix represents the landscape poses an ironic illusion of innocence and untutored vision. The lack of aerial perspective, the hyper-detailed focus, flat unmodulated colors, and predilection for profile forms also underscore the pseudo-naturalness of nature transformed for German tourism under the auspices of state-sponsored conservation. The middle-class family enjoying its Sunday excursion continues these commentaries on a landscape characterized by all the orderliness of a bourgeois parlor. The staircases, towers, and evenly spaced tree trunks that appear to lace in the forms of the *Wolfsschlucht* are extensions of the family's sober finery: father's suit and tie; mother's demure skirt and blouse and feathered hat; the little boy's sailor suit, standard attire for children since the days of naval expansion under Kaiser Wilhelm; and the girl's white dress, emblematic of innocence. Old-fashioned in their impractical clothing, prepared for the eventualities of rain and an encounter with wild butterflies, the family hikes through the tidy countryside. Comically in obedient hierarchic formation, father leading and daughter last, they march in step, dutifully enjoying a healthful Sunday walk, a reward of the prosperity and earned leisure of the middle class.

This family is indeed protected by the state, as the constitution proclaims, with its purity, health, and social welfare guaranteed in an environment where even the threats of nature are removed. The order presented may provide little of the equality of the sexes recommended as the "foundation" of family and constitution, but significant shelter and care are implied, as is the demeaning stultification resulting from them. Perhaps not "rich in children," the bourgeois couple has reproduced itself in its offspring while it leaves the vaunted task of enriching the size of the nation's population, to which the father surely subscribes ideologically, to the lower classes conspicuously absent from their Sunday world.   R. H.

1. "Die Ehe steht als Grundlage des Familienlebens und der Erhaltung und Vermehrung der Nation unter dem besonderen Schutz der Verfassung. Diese beruht auf der Gleichberechtigung der beiden Geschlechte.
"Die Reinhaltung, Gesundung und soziale Förderung der Familie ist Aufgabe des Staats und der Gemeinden. Kinderreiche Familien haben Anspruch auf ausgleichende Fürsorge.
"Die Mutterschaft hat Anspruch auf den Schutz und die Fürsorge des Staats." "Die Verfassung des Deutschen Reichs vom 11. August 1919," in *Weimarer Republik 1919-1933*, vol. 3 of *Dokumente der Deutschen Politik und Geschichte von 1848 bis zur*

Gegenwart, ed. Johannes Hohlfeld (Berlin: Dokumenten Verlag Dr. Herbert Wendler & Co., n. d.), 81.
2. Recollections of Martha Dix cited by Lothar Fischer, *Otto Dix: Ein Malerleben in Deutschland* (Berlin: Nikolaische Verlagsbuchhandlung, 1981), 30.
3. As if in testimony to their spiritual patronage of the work, both Koch and Trillhaase came to own *Sunday Outing*. It was among the first group of Dix paintings Mother Ey selected for sale by her gallery; Koch purchased it and then either gave or sold it to Trillhaase.

---

29   Otto Dix
The Widow (*Die Witwe*), 1922

Watercolor, ink over pencil on paper
44 x 28 cm (17⁵/₁₆ x 11 in.)
Signed and dated l. r. "Dix/22"; inscribed verso by Martha Dix, pencil drawing of a comet and dedication: "Für Hans und Maryellchen aus Mutzlis Mäppchen Weihnachen 1922" (For Hans [Koch] and Maryellchen [Martha's sister Maria] from Mutzli's [M. D.'s nickname] little portfolio Christmas 1922); collection stamp, Dr. Hans Koch.

Provenance: Dr. Hans Koch, Düsseldorf; Roswitha Haftmann Modern Art, Zurich; Galerie Nierendorf, West Berlin.

In 1922, Otto Dix occupied himself numerous times with images of widowhood as part of a complex of motifs involving interrelationships between life and death.[1] Consistently, he depicts the widow in black mourning clothing that includes a feathered hat with transparent widow's veil. She appears pale but with robust body, her face a mask of grief which seems to be significantly temporary. In this watercolor, Dix retains these features; the widow walks daintily along a cemetery path while holding a lily, the flower of innocence and afterlife, in her lace-gloved hand.

As in his *Death and Resurrection* etchings of that year, Dix juxtaposes life and death to provide a sardonic commentary. The harsh cynicism that allowed him to set a violated woman's corpse next to a pair of copulating dogs to demonstrate that life continues, uncaring even in face of the most violent and tragic deaths, is lacking from this image. Nevertheless, Dix joins an inventory of trite tristesse—mourning attire, muted colors, fog, and a cemetery setting—to the widow's determination to return to life and to turn away from the morbid preoccupations of the grave.

"Actually, there always was some kind of humorous thought at play whenever he painted," Martha Dix said of her husband.[2] The tone of *The Widow* is ironic but not mocking, as in other Dix images. The widow's face, with its sunken eyes and colorless skin, appears as drained of life as her husband's must have been. Although Dix has rendered it as a comical caricature, the grimaces and disfiguration that can

form part of his vocabulary of vengeful wit are absent. The widow is an object of humor, but also of compassion.
                                               R. H.

1. The most extensive and cohesive result of this is the suite of etchings *Death and Resurrection* (*Tod und Auferstehung*) (Karsch 43-48), published by Dix in 1922.
2. "Eigentlich waren immer irgendwelche humoristischen Hintergründe im Spiel, wenn er etwas gemalt hat." As cited by Lothar Fischer, *Otto Dix: Ein Malerleben in Deutschland* (Berlin: Nikolaische Verlagsbuchhandlung, 1981), 32.

---

30   Otto Dix
Blind Man (*Blinder*), c. 1923

Lithographic crayon on paper
61.7 x 51 cm (24¹/₄ x 20¹/₈ in.)
Signed l. l. "Otto Dix"; verso: unfinished sketch of blind beggar

Provenance: Galerie Nierendorf, West Berlin; Galerie Michael Hasenclever, Munich.

Exhibition: Milwaukee, UWM Art Museum, University of Wisconsin, *Reactions to the War: European Art, 1914-1925*, 2 November-14 December 1986, cat. no. 15.

During the early twenties, Otto Dix commonly focused on individual tragedies, transforming them into typologies of experience that came to represent life in the Weimar Republic. There is an emphatic concern with a single figure in *Blind Man*, yet particular idiosyncrasies, gestural characteristics, and a sense of time and movement are eradicated. The blind beggar loses individuality in this process; despite the details of his situation and malady, he embodies the fate more of a generation or social subclass than his own personal history.

Because of mustard gas and other techniques of modern warfare, World War I produced an inordinate number of blinded victims. Although Germany instituted rehabilatory training for wounded war veterans, the program was often ineffective. Deprived by their handicap of their former means of livelihood and offered few viable substitutes, blind veterans had little alternative but to sell matches on street corners in order to survive. Images of these afflicted beggars, pitifully holding out matchboxes to unseen passersby, abound in the work of early Weimar Republic artists, such as Dix, George Grosz, Rudolf Schlichter, and Heinrich Zille.[1] Most commonly, the beggars in these works wear tattered remnants of the imperial army uniform, a clear indictment of the neglectful fatherland they had served. In other instances, artists make no direct reference to the war, but call attention to the general plight of the displaced, handicapped, or outcast.

Dix's drawing functions on both levels. The blind man wears civilian clothing, a rumpled suit jacket and collarless shirt. But his eyes are tokens of wartime experience: one stares blankly without seeing, the other has been violently plucked out.[2] Not hereditary or

organic, his blindness is characteristic of a shrapnel or bayonet injury. While this physical scar is unavoidably presented, the sociological effect of his disability is also apparent in the veteran's helpless, resigned posture.

His head and torso fill up most of the surface of the drawing, and a sense of the disconnected follows from the truncated body and the lack of context or background. The blind man's head, shown in three-quarter profile against a dark shaded area, contrasts with his relatively fragile body: the prominent, jutting chin and large nose are countered by a weak and sunken upper body, delineated by more tentative contour lines. An uncomfortable imbalance results, as if the head were too heavy to be properly supported by this shrunken torso. His isolation and static posture lend the blind man the quality of an inert object; Dix records him with unremitting detachment, coldness, and dispassion that function, ironically, to increase the pathos of the image.[3]

The man's blindness is made obvious not only by the disfunction of his eyes, but also by the handwritten sign he wears around his neck. Such signs were common in postwar Germany, and they reveal the government's inability to address the needs of the war's victims. The motif becomes especially poignant in Dix's work: the lack of sight segregates this veteran from the mainstream of society and relegates him to the existence of a non-person forced to communicate by means of his identifying placard. In Dix's drawing, as in society at large, the man is reduced to his handicap; blindness becomes his most salient feature. Blindness replaces his name and becomes his identity.

Although Dix's conception seems devoid of compassion on an immediate emotional level, it does not mock or ridicule the blind man. Rather, by looking at him and other unfortunates of Weimar society, by presenting the beggar from the perspective of a passerby looking down on the social detritus seated on the sidewalk, Dix afforded these victims a kind of attention not typically granted to the needy. For Dix, art was not a luxury to entertain, please, or offer an escape from brutal reality into an aestheticized realm. Instead, art was a tool with which to give testimony, most frequently to the underside of contemporary life, the aspects others ignored, slighted, or denied.   C. D. G.

1. The abundance of such imagery may be misleading, however, in projecting the image of a blind match seller on every street corner of major cities. The pathos of such a sight made it a highly effective social commentary, and this, more than the actual number of blind veterans, may explain their frequent depiction by socially critical artists. It also explains why the blind war veteran was a favorite role for professional beggars.
2. The identical eye injury appears in Dix's ink drawing, *Whore and War Cripple* (*Hure und Kriegskrüppel*; alternatively titled *Two Victims of Capitalism* [*Zwei Opfer des Kapitalismus*]) of 1923 (Westfälisches Landesmuseum für Kunst- und Kulturgeschichte, Münster), published in *Die Pleite* (1923) und illus. in *Otto Dix 1891-1969* (Munich: Museum Villa Stuck, 1985), cat. no. 335.

3. The drawing in the Fishman Collection relates to Dix's 1923 lithograph, *Blind Man (Blinder)* (Karsch 52), in theme as well as in the figure's pose and physiognomy. The lithograph, however, indicates blindness largely by means of deep, dark eye sockets and shows no other physical disfiguration. By also showing the seated man holding out a matchbook, with a greater sense of surrounding space, Dix avoided the intense confrontation with the viewer that characterizes the drawing.

31 Otto Dix
From the Catacombs (The Catacombs of Palermo) (Aus den Katakomben [Katakomben von Palermo]), 1923–24

Watercolor over pencil on paper
49.5 x 34.5 cm (19^1/$_2$ x 13^9/$_{16}$ in.)
Signed l. r. "Dix"

Provenance: Galerie Nierendorf, West Berlin.

Exhibition: New York, Solomon R. Guggenheim Museum, *German Realist Drawings of the 1920's*, 15 May–6 July 1986 (traveled to Cambridge, Mass., Busch-Reisinger Museum, Harvard University, 26 July–28 September 1986; Graphische Sammlung, Staatsgalerie Stuttgart, 25 October–28 December 1986), cat. no. 25 (as *Catacombs of Palermo II*).

In 1923, Otto Dix undertook a trip to Italy after ending his studies at the Düsseldorf Academy. *From the Catacombs*, one of a series of ten drawings and watercolors devoted to the mummified corpses he saw in the catacombs of Palermo, documents this trip.[1] Italy had long been a goal of artistic pilgrimage, the fount of European civilization and art, a mecca of artistic creation. Dix's image reveals none of this. Instead, with sharp irony, he depicts the horrid mummy, one of the numerous anonymous corpses stacked below the streets of Roman cities in labyrinthian burial vaults. None of the romantic glory of fervent Christians, heroic in their resistance to pagan persecution, is present in this image, nor the reverence of Christian burial in soil made sacred by saints and martyrs. *From the Catacombs* is, instead, a dispassionate record of the earthly matter of human existence in its final state. Death appears in its most physical, unredeeming terms, without interpretation or redemption.

Dix presents the viewer with a nightmarish closeup view of the cadaver's head. Shown in an upright position, as if seated in a portrait pose, the corpse faces the viewer with its gaping mouth, which seems arrested in an ear-piercing scream. The hollows of the eye sockets echo the black oral cavity. Only a thin membrane of leathery skin covers the skull. Through its very technique, the watercolor suggests decomposition of forms, with colors thinly applied and bleeding into the paper in a wet-on-wet effect. Browns, blues, and reds run together and mix into dirty hues spotted against a dissolved ground.

Dix's preoccupation with death is apparent in many works from the early twenties, but in a manner significantly different from the one seen here. For example, his graphic portfolio *Death and Resurrection (Tod und Auferstehung)* (1922) examines several circumstances of death, but despite the horror there is also regeneration and renewed life. In *From the Catacombs*, no such cycle is indicated. Instead, the work is a raw image of the process of decay, and also lacks the cumulative commentary of Dix's war imagery of these years. Whether in the monumental triptych *The Trench (Schützengraben)* or the fifty intaglio prints of the portfolio *The War (Der Krieg)* (both 1923–24), Dix adapted his technique of reportage to generate an indictment of war's horrors, of its capacity to dehumanize. Such overt didacticism is absent in *From the Catacombs*. With no expression of human grief, nor any suggestion of an afterlife, death alone, uncompromised, is its theme.

The anonymous subject is not shown in the noble state of dying or just having died, nor in the abstracted sign of an unrecognizable skull, but somewhere in between. This state between death and eternity, an unusual choice of subject matter, does not impart any hope of salvation or mystery, martyrdom or sorrow. Dix remains neutral in his candid, clinical record of physical decay, the most gruesome of natural processes. That he treats it with such frankness is a statement in itself. That in Italy he found, not the glory of antiquity or the Renaissance, but death, is another. Death and ugliness were sought out by him, celebrated by him, and presented by him with a compulsion that does not permit any distinction between horror and fascination. C. D. G./R. H.

1. Brigid S. Barton, *Otto Dix and Die neue Sachlichkeit, 1918–1925* (Ann Arbor, Mich.: UMI Research Press, 1981), 150, lists the ten works. She properly questions the Galerie Nierendorf identification of this watercolor drawing as the second of the Palermo catacombs series.

32 Otto Dix
Beggar Woman (Bettlerin), 1924

Brush, tusche, ink on paper
62.2 x 45.5 cm (24^1/$_2$ x 17^{15}/$_{16}$ in.)
Signed l. l. "Otto Dix"; inscribed l. l. "1441"

Provenance: Galerie Nierendorf, West Berlin; Galerie Michael Hasenclever, Munich.

Exhibitions: Munich, Galerie Michael Hasenclever, *Zehn Jahre Galerie Hasenclever*, 1982; Milwaukee, UWM Art Museum, University of Wisconsin, *Reactions to the War: European Art, 1914–1925*, 2 November–14 December 1986, cat. no. 16.

In 1924, the Internationale Arbeiter Hilfe (International Workers' Aid) published the portfolio *Hunger*, consisting of seven lithographs by Otto Dix, George Grosz, Eric Johansson, Käthe Kollwitz, Otto Nagel, Karl Völker, and Heinrich Zille. Organized in 1921 by Willi Münzenberg in response to Lenin's demand for proletarian charitable organizations to complement interna-tional bourgeois charities, the IAH had initially focused its efforts on bringing aid to the hungry in Russia, but soon extended its purview to the needy in Germany. The Komitee Künstlerhilfe (Committee for Artists' Aid), led by Nagel and Erwin Piscator, contributed artworks and organized exhibitions as a means of raising consciousness as well as funds for the kitchens of the IAH. At a meeting of the Committee in Weimar in April 1924, plans for the portfolio *Hunger* and others (not all realized) on the themes of "The Street," "War," "Strike," "Tenement Housing," and "Work" were initiated.

Dix's contribution to *Hunger* was a photolithograph of *Beggar Woman*, which drew from his arsenal of themes of destitution. He reformulated the motif of the beggar to fit the goals of the IAH portfolio, departing from his usual iconography, in which beggars were commonly male war veterans. Here, the beggar is an aged woman, and the direct link of Weimar social ills to the effects of World War I, which can be seen in Dix's previous work, is broken. Unlike a crippled veteran, the emaciated female beggar exposes a more general social problem deriving from the economic collapse, whose hallmarks were inflation, unemployment, poverty, and starvation throughout central and eastern Europe.

The wretched figure in *Beggar Woman* is seated at the edge of a sidewalk, on the cement ledge of an iron fence. The pointed bars of the fence, cage-like in effect, signal an urban, public context. Against the bars' rhythmic repetition, her form is rendered in quick gestural strokes and masses of ink. A deep black characterizes the scarf on her head and shoulders, its oppressiveness precariously supported by the feeble lines of her face and her frail body, depicted by irregular linear patterns lacking rigidity. Despite his placement of the figure in the center of the composition, its anchor as well as its focus, Dix imbues her with a quality of instability, as if she were suffering under an insurmountable burden represented by the scarf and under which her body is deteriorating irreversibly. After persistent neglect, poverty, and malnutrition, she is at the threshold of life and death. Her face has become a skull with catatonic, frozen features and blank, staring eyes; the determined grip on her empty begging bowl is the hopeless grip of death.

By abstracting the figure from all narrative detail, Dix conveys her pitiable isolation from, and rejection by, society. The black clothing identifies her as a widow, in 1924 most likely one of innumerable war widows struggling to exist on state-sponsored pensions. As inflation pushed the value of German currency ever downward, from 4.70 marks to the dollar in 1919 to 4.2 billion marks per dollar in November 1923, the fixed income of a widow's pension, even if adjusted periodically by the government, became worthless. With no marketable skills in an economy where a major segment of the work force was already unemployed, widows without alternative sources of income were forced to depend on charity to supplement their inadequate pensions. Dix's image thus represents not the plight of an individual, but of many women, poor, working-class, and middle-class, who were reduced to beggars in Germany after the war.

C. D. G.

33 August Wilhelm Dressler
Nude Standing Near a Chair (Stehender Akt am Stuhl), 1925

Oil, tempera on canvas
70 x 60 cm (27^9/$_{16}$ x 23^5/$_8$ in.)
Monogrammed l. r. "AuDr"; signed verso "A. W. Dressler"; dated on stretcher "1925"

Provenance: Kunstgalerie Esslingen; Galerie Ralph Jentsch, Munich.

In this painting by the Bohemian-born artist August Wilhelm Dressler, a woman stands near a cane chair and removes her white clothing, letting a portion fall to drape around her knees while she holds the remainder on her outstretched arms. She stands quietly, her motion frozen, her body illuminated from behind by an unknown light, which also shines onto the checkerboard floor of the bare interior, but mysteriously does not emanate from the nearby window. A sense of unreality enters the painting by means of this light, attaching the image not to the experienced world but to its own physiological laws and to the artificial world of art. Light, setting, and figure function, in part, as an homage to Jan Vermeer, who gained renewed admiration during the 1920s, but mood and setting also reflect the intimate world of German late Romantic, Biedermeier painting. The woman, however, in body type, appearance, and surroundings, is clearly modern, so that the picture becomes a complex amalgam of disparate temporal references. The middle classes of seventeenth-century Holland and of nineteenth-century Germany, and classical antiquity, with its semi-draped Venus figures, are simultaneously recalled, echoing within each other while proclaiming the dominance—or, perhaps, the dependence—of the present.

Fusing traditional representations of Venus with Northern European bourgeois interiors in a classicizing image tinged in a silver-gray tonality, Dressler presents a timeless world, unchanging, in sharp contrast to the persistent movement, noise, and impermanence of modernity. The chilled silence and reassuring calm evoked here function as archetypal counterpoint to the normal turmoil of urban life. In Dressler's world, woman practices no commercial trade and does not display the trappings of modern fashion. She is instead an unattainable ideal, perpetually nude, contemplative, and remote.

The intimate scene of her disrobing is revealed by a curtain pulled back to provide the viewer voyeuristic access but also to accent her world's separation from our own, to prevent our entry into hers. Immortalized in her private activity, unselfconscious in her nakedness, she is unaware of us, her audience, as she was, implicitly, of the artist. Just as we do not share her space, but view it surreptitiously as a distanced image of a wished-for world, a reified vision of a timeless past projected into the present, so she does not know our reality. Dressler dramatizes and accentuates the fissure between art and life. He makes no attempt to bridge it except by immersion into a sentimental aesthetic ironically devoid of emotion and passion, striving towards its ideal with nuanced references to art of the past, to times of perceived bourgeois harmony and peace.

Although still associated by critics with *Neue Sachlichkeit*, whose mundane themes his work does reflect, Dressler constructed a self-contained, highly personal art which relates to neoclassical tendencies of the 1920s, but his is a classicism redolent of the pensive comfort of the Biedermeier. "I cannot take leave of what created me," Dressler observed in conversation with the critic Hans Kinkel, who concluded:

This self-willed conservative carries his own world within himself, untouched by isms and programs. For him, memory is a permanent presence that fulfills itself in forms and lines of unpretentious, memorable clarity. There is hardly a painter of his revolutionary generation who so determinedly insisted that the human being, even in this age of anxiety, is the measure of all things. Who, other than Dressler, has delivered a pictorial equivalent to this fundamental insight in which the ordinary appears so poetic and the poetic appears so ordinary?[1]

S. L. D.

1. "Dieser eigensinnig Konservative trägt seine Welt, unberührt von Ismen und Programmen, in sich; für ihn ist Erinnerung permanente Gegenwart, die sich in Formen und Linien von schlichter einprägsamer Klarheit erfüllt. Kaum ein Maler seiner revolutionären Generation hat so unauffällig darauf bestanden, dass der Mensch auch im Zeitalter der Angst das Mass aller Dinge sei. Wer hat, so wie Dressler, dieser fundamentalen Einsicht ein bildnerisches Äquivalent geliefert, in dem das Alltägliche poetisch und das Poetische alltäglich erscheint?" Hans Kinkel, "August Wilhelm Dressler," *Kunstblätter der Galerie Nierendorf* 12 (1967): 5.

34 Heinrich Ehmsen
Insane Asylum I (Irrenhaus I), c. 1924

Pencil, black chalk on paper
30.4 x 21.2 cm (12 x 8³/₈ in.)
Monogrammed l. r. "HE [intertwined]"; inscribed l. l. "Irrenhaus I"; verso, artist's stamp "Professor Heinrich Ehmsen"; inscribed "Irrenhaus 1924–1926"

Provenance: Estate of the artist; Galerie Michael Hasenclever, Munich.

Exhibition: Munich, Galerie Michael Hasenclever, *Heinrich Ehmsen: Druckgraphik und Zeichnungen,* 1983.

Heinrich Ehmsen established his reputation as a critical artist in the 1920s through a series of images of the November Revolution and of the sup-

pression of the Bavarian Soviet Republic. These obsessively varied scenes from 1919 through 1932 depict firing squads, both Revolutionary and Freikorps, executing participants in the Munich uprisings. The compositions derive from Francisco Goya, but Ehmsen apparently witnessed the events first hand.[1] Rejecting art for art's sake, he wrote later of his need "to cry out by means of form and color what it is that rages within me. Compassion for maltreated creatures, anger against the torturers."[2] He developed in these images of executions a mannered style, with activated, undulating contours, elongated figures, and extremes of gesticulation to indicate intense agitation. Physiognomic exaggeration, combined with selected color contrasts, communicated the artist's social and ethical position subjectively in a late manifestation of Expressionism, strangely subdued despite the radical violence of the motifs and the urgency of Ehmsen's testimony.

During the early and mid-1920s, Ehmsen continued to adhere to this subjective, Expressionist approach but applied it to ostensibly mundane motifs, such as bars, circuses, and boxing arenas. He carried on his self-assigned task of serving witness, now portraying a society he viewed as degenerate, approaching an abyss without reflection or remorse. In 1925, to the Vienna exhibition *The Face of the Times (Das Gesicht der Zeit)* he sent a series of scenes, begun in 1923, from an insane asylum—a ready analogue to contemporary society and its anxiety-filled victims. In *Insane Asylum I,* Ehmsen presents a sanatorium's barren interior, with attenuated figures drawn in a wispy, varied line. Overpowering walls, their barred windows offering no view, define spaces reminiscent of Italian Metaphysical Painting: an endless, labyrinthine hallway empties into a large, sterile room in whose center, secluded and imperiled, stands a lone, emaciated man. Feet and legs jammed together, hands pressed to his sides, an old wrinkled suit hanging on his withered frame, his hair in thin tangled strands, he stares forlornly from sunken, unfocused eyes. Compressed against the walls behind and beside him are other men, each existentially isolated, engaged in inexplicable, purposeless activity—kneeling, running, boxing, thrashing convulsively, or gawking without comprehension.

In an extension of Romanticism's perceptions, Expressionists viewed madness as a release from the confinements of bourgeois life; several even put the theory into practice, feigning insanity to escape military conscription during World War I. Thereafter, in works by Otto Dix or Conrad Felixmüller, for example, insanity continued to bring release, but tragically: associated with death, debilitating inertia, and social alienation, it was seen as one of the war's traumatic effects. Among the artists of *Neue Sachlickheit*, Felixmüller lamented those "most valuable people ensnaring themselves in dreary black cages. In despair, strangling their helpless guilt with nerve fibers . . . to consume [themselves] in order then to cry like little children."[3] Isolation and self-destruction are the hallmarks of

this insanity engendered by the experience of modern warfare; it is not the "divine madness" of genius, but a perpetualized state of self-consuming annihilation from which escape becomes impossible.

R. H.

1. For extensive discussion of Ehmsen's Revolution paintings, see Magdalena Droste, "Engagement ohne Gefahr: Heinrich Ehmsen in den zwanziger Jahren," in Neue Gesellschaft für bildende Kunst, *Heinrich Ehmsen, Maler: Leben/Werk/Protokoll* (West Berlin: Elefanten Press, 1986), 50ff.
2. ". . . durch Form und Farbe hinausschreien, was in mir tobt. Mitleid mit der geschundenen Kreatur, Zorn gegen die Peiniger." Heinrich Ehmsen, cited by Adolf Behne, *Heinrich Ehmsen,* Kunst der Gegenwart II (Potsdam: Kiepenheuer, 1946), 9.
3. ". . . wertvollste Menschen in trostlosen schwarzen Gittern sich verfangen. Verzweifelnd ihre hilflose Schuld mit Nervensträngen abwürgen . . . sich selbst verzehren, um darnach wie Kindlein zu weinen." Conrad Felixmüller, "Militär-Krankenwärter Felixmüller XI Arnsdorf," *Menschen* 1, no. 3 (1918), as reprinted in *Schrei in die Welt: Expressionismus in Dresden,* ed. Peter Ludewig (East Berlin: Buchverlag Der Morgen, 1988), 119.

35 Heinrich Ehmsen
The Bathing Hut (Die Badekabine), 1928

Watercolor over pencil on paper
47.7 x 33.4 cm (18³/₄ x 13¹/₈ in.)
Not signed; inscribed on removed matting "Martigues"

Provenance: Ernest Rathenau, Berlin, Hamburg, and New York.

In 1928, with proceeds from his Berlin exhibitions of the preceding year and accompanied by Elisabeth Conradi, Heinrich Ehmsen undertook an extended trip to southern France, to the resort town of Martigues on the Mediterranean Sea. The works he brought back to Germany from this trip, mostly watercolors, demonstrate a new coloristic sense in conjunction with a sensual optimism lacking in his previous imagery. Critics who had enjoined him to cease presenting scenes of revolution, insanity, or prostitution since such social activist concerns were no longer current, now praised the apparently healthy hedonism of the Martigues watercolors.[1]

Searching for evidence that German art was returning to a healthier, more wholesome condition after the tortured imagery of the early 1920s, the critic Richard Bie in 1930 accented Ehmsen's links to his native Holstein soil and sadly inventoried his postwar themes:

In contemporary German painting, scars cover the remaining traces of the war. In a survey of the life's work of the Holstein painter Heinrich Ehmsen, we find the following motifs: attack, barbed wire barriers, acrobats, boxers, ladies of the night, homecoming, insane asylum, paralysis, execution, morphine, dispute,

cemetery, persecution mania, megalomania, bar and end. It is the remnant of the front and the distorted face of the present. It is a passage through the hell of inner visions, of nightmarish dreams, of the lost hope in human dignity. . . . [In the war,] the individual was confronted by a force of nature, by catastrophe, by the threat of a Last Jugdment. If after the war an entire generation loses itself once again in the horrors of recalled memories, then that is no wonder. It is a wonder, however, when this generation survives whole, even in the experience of its art, and when, newly comforted and armored, it finds its way back to a transfigured nature.[2]

Bie's psychology is naïve and postulates that Ehmsen was cured of his anxieties by a virile confrontation with nature beneath the Mediterranean sun:

Ehmsen has possession of the truly Nietzschean, nordic resilience of a manly nature. From a trip . . . to the Mediterranean he suddenly returns with wit and sprightliness, with an entirely new world of forms. Humor brings him salvation and makes him unique. Form is joined by his new sense of color. . . . Suddenly everything takes on meaning, new significance, a new depth. That is the miracle of the artist, that he teaches us to see anew, that he is a prophet of the eye, that he takes what seems probable to him and makes it apparent to us, as if it were a new revelation and recognition of nature. This fundamental ability of the artist, this indepth gaze into nature as the act of creating a new perception of nature and a new world view is possessed by Heinrich Ehmsen.[3]

Ehmsen's *Bathing Hut* is a celebration of life and life's erotic forces, Bie would argue, which has transcended the debilitation suffered in World War I and its revolutionary aftermath. Executions and insanity are replaced by bodies glowing with satisfaction in vibrant, inviting colors. Art, in these terms, presents a new view of a daily existence deprived of care, a perpetually aestheticized bathing hut in which to disrobe in private.

R. H.

1. See Paul Westheim, "Ausstellungen," *Das Kunstblatt* 11, no. 5 (1927): 125, who characterizes Ehmsen's work as "illustration exaggerated into uncontrolled pathos" ("ins masslos Pathetische getriebene Illustration") but nonetheless wishes to encourage him. At the time the Martigues watercolors were exhibited, in contrast, Westheim indicated approval by illustrating two which were purchased by the Städtische Galerie, Munich (*Das Kunstblatt* 13 [1929]: 270–271).
2. "In der deutschen Malerei der Gegenwart ist die Spur des Krieges vernarbt. Bei der Übersicht über das Lebenswerk des holsteinischen Malers Heinrich Ehmsen finden wir folgende Motive: Sturm, Drahtverhau, Artisten, Boxer, Lieblinge des Tages, Heimkehr, Irrenhaus, Paralyse, Erschiessung, Morphium, Disput, Friedhof, Verfolgungswahn, Grössenwahn, Bar und Ende. Das ist ein Nachtrag der Front und das verstörte Antlitz der Gegenwart. Das ist der Durchgang durch die Hölle der inneren Gesichte, der aufgeschreckten Träume, der verlorenen Hoff-

nung auf die Würde der Menschheit . . . . [In diesem Krieg] trat der Einzelne zurück vor der Naturgewalt, vor der Katastrophe, vor der Drohung eines jüngsten Gerichts. Wenn nach dem Kriege ein ganzes Geschlecht sich noch einmal in die Schrecknisse der Rückerinnerung verliert, so ist das kein Wunder. Ein Wunder ist es vielmehr, wenn dieses Geschlecht heil durchkommt, auch im Erlebnis seiner Kunst, und wenn es, aufs neue getröstet und gewappnet, zur verklärten Natur zurückfindet." Richard Bie [Biedrzynski], *Deutsche Malerei der Gegenwart* (Weimar: Alexander Ducker Verlag, 1930), 6.

3. "Ehmsen verfügt über den echten nietzscheanischen, nordischen Widerstand einer männlichen Natur. Von . . . einer Mittelmeerfahrt bringt er auf einmal Witz und Heiterkeit, eine ganze Formwelt mit. Der Humor erlöst ihn und macht ihn eigenartig. Zur Form kommt sein neuer Farbensinn. . . . Alles bekommt auf einmal einen anderen Sinn, eine andere Tiefe. Das ist das Wunder des Künstlers, dass er neu zu sehen lehrt, dass er der Prophet des Auges ist, dass er das, was ihm wahrscheinlich ist, augenscheinlich macht für die Mitwelt, als sei es eine neue Offenbarung und neue Erkenntnis der Natur. Dieses wesentliche Vermögen des Künstlers, diesen Tiefblick in die Natur als Schöpfungsakt einer neuen Naturbetrachtung und Weltanschauung besitzt Heinrich Ehmsen." Ibid., 19–20.

36 Heinrich Ehmsen
Invalids (Invaliden), 1932?

Watercolor over pencil on paper
29.9 x 39.8 cm (11³/₄ x 15¹¹/₁₆ in.)
Signed l. c. "H. Ehmsen";
inscribed, signed, and dated l. l.
"M. lb. Fritz Mosert zu seinem
50. Wiegenfeste!/Ehmsen/Berlin
1932" (To m[y] d[ea]r Fritz
Mosert for his 50th cradle feast!/
Ehmsen/Berlin 1932)

Provenance: Fritz Mosert; Kunsthaus Lempertz, Cologne.

Heinrich Ehmsen's subject in this watercolor, a hospital interior with cripples on crutches or in wheelchairs, enjoyed wide currency early in the 1920s as artists allied with the political left depicted war victims in pitiable conditions, indicting society for its lack of concern or charity. By 1932, however, the probable date of this watercolor,[1] such scenes had lost the critical urgency they possessed in the years immediately following the war; physical wounds healed, and the war invalid became but another invisible component of the urban panorama in a society that had adjusted to his presence.

With balding heads and fringes of gray hair, Ehmsen's invalids lack the ruined youth of the men who returned permanently maimed from the trenches of France, Flanders, or Russia. They are, instead, those young men grown old, locked into institutions that remove them from society's consciousness on the pretense of providing for their medical needs. Comfort is dispensed to them by the fat, self-indulgent priest in the background. He reads his formulas of compassion from booklets of pastoral care that repeat the com-

placent prayers of past wars, prayers applicable as well to future wars and to their crippled survivors. Hobbling red-faced on crutches, or pushed by old women with hunched backs, the cripples pass each other in silent determination. Grimly observed by sullen-faced visitors to their barren environment, the old invalids are transformed by Ehmsen into caricatures of despondent helplessness.   R. H.

1. Although its inscription notes that it was given as a birthday present to Fritz Mosert in 1932, the watercolor may be of an earlier date. Ehmsen's stylistic parameters were limited during the 1920s, so that precise dating on this basis is difficult. However, much of his work of the late twenties and early thirties tends towards a stable form rather than the dissolved vagueness of setting and the active, curvilinear contours characteristic of this work. *Invalids* thus more closely approximates Ehmsen's watercolors of the mid-twenties. This conclusion must be put into the context of Ehmsen's habit of resurrecting this manneristic drawing style at intervals until well into the 1930s.

37 Conrad Felixmüller
*Portrait of Elfriede Hausmann
(Bildnis Frau Elfriede Hausmann),
c. 1917*

Oil on canvas
76.5 x 53.7 cm (30¹/₈ x 21³/₁₆ in.)
Signed l. r. "Felixmüller"
Verso: *Portrait of a Woman from
Scotland (Porträt eines Mädchens aus
Schottland)*, 1927, oil

Provenance: Galerie Brockstedt, Hamburg.

Exhibitions: West Berlin, Berlinische Galerie, Museum für Moderne Kunst, Photographie und Architektur im Martin-Gropius-Bau, *Ich und die Stadt: Mensch und Grosssstadt in der deutschen Kunst des 20. Jahrhunderts*, 15 August–22 November 1987, cat. no. 40; Los Angeles County Museum of Art, *German Expressionism 1915–1925: The Second Generation*, 9 October–31 December 1988 (traveled to Fort Worth Art Museum, 2 February–9 April 1989; Kunstmuseum Düsseldorf, 18 May–9 July 1989; Halle, Staatliche Galerie Moritzburg, 9 August–30 September 1989), cat. no. 47.

A crystallization of form characterizes Conrad Felixmüller's *Portrait of Elfriede Hausmann*, first wife of the Berlin Dadaist Raoul Hausmann. Emulating both French Cubism and Italian Futurism, Felixmüller fractures rounded, organic volumes into geometric planes in an intuitive analysis of his subject's features. The eyes become slits, the nose a vague triangle in this agitated and aggressive reformulation. In a mass of interpenetrating planes, matter condenses at the center of the canvas in golden-brown hues, intimating flesh without citing its exact color and in striking contrast to the cold blue, dissolved periphery. Volume, modeling, and spatial recession are suggested, as is the portrait likeness, in a drastically systematized and implicitly ironic application of Cubo-Futurist vocabularies.

Felixmüller's interpretation uses Futurist means to Expressionist ends. The premise of the portrait is subjective since it interprets the presence of a close friend; the means, however, depend on a determined, logically extreme visual linguistics. By transforming the face from a balanced, organic structure into an irregular, faceted network, Felixmüller presents a charged physical presence rather than an accurate record of appearance. He referred to the last years of World War I as his "Storm and Stress" phase, and sought what he called "absolute form" by fragmenting his subjects in an analytic mode. His 1919 manifesto, "Artistic Creation," passionately and vehemently sums up his intentions:

> We are not one-sided: not only because we are Cubist painters—but because we are Cubists of life as well —saturated by postures of form and tossed about in life, struggling in the stream of the age! Therein lies the foundation of our truth of the representation of life and our concepts. Pondering, soul and body saturated —dynamism everywhere. Explosive power sensed in its finest nuance and incomprehensible. Therefore, definition of space and form, not as illusion, not as impression, "appearance," but truthful expression from within, "vision." From within as well: movement, dynamism like the earth: streams of the power of nature shove earthquakes into man; not in the individual ego, but in all creatures and things.
> *The style* is determined by the spirit-era of our time: its character "is our style": speed, mechanics, politics, religiosity, luxury, war, our war, our express trains, aeroplanes, autos, hospitals, street fights—the revolution of humanity, its public and its ego.[1]

C. D. G.

1. "Wir sind nicht einseitig: nicht nur weil wir kubistische Künstler sind—sondern weil wir auch Kubisten des Lebens sind —durchdrungen von Formstellungen und auseinandergeworfen im Leben, strudelnd im Strom der Zeit! Da ist der Grund unserer Wahrheit der Wiedergabe des Lebens und unserer Vorstellungen. Vertieft, durchdrungen die Seele und Körper—Dynamismus allseitig. Explosive Kraft fühlbar bis in feinste Differenz und unfassbar. Daher Bestimmung des Raumes und der Körper, nicht als Illusion, nicht als Eindruck 'Anschauung,' sondern wahrhaft Ausdruck von innen her 'Vision.' Von innen her auch die Bewegung, Dynamismus gleich der Erde: Ströme der Kraft der Natur stösst Erdbeben im Mensch; nicht im einzelnen Ich, sondern aller Kreatur und allen Dingen.
"*Der Stil* bestimmt von der Geist-Ära unserer Zeit; ihres Charakters 'ist unser Stil': Schnelligkeit, Mechanik; Politik, Religiösität; Luxus, Krieg; unser Krieg, unsere Schnellbahnen, Äroplans, Autos, Lazarette, Strassenkämpfe—die Revolution des Menschen, seine Öffentlichkeit und er selbst." Conrad Felixmüller, "Künstlerische Gestaltung: Manifest," *Das Kestnerbuch*, ed. Erich Küppers (Hanover: Kestner-Gesellschaft, 1919), 142.

38 Conrad Felixmüller
*Portrait of Otto Ritschl (Painter
from Wiesbaden) (Bildnis Otto
Ritschl [Maler aus Wiesbaden]),
1920*

Oil on canvas
85 x 75 cm (33¹/₂ x 29⁹/₁₆ in.)
Signed u. l. "Felixmüller"; monogrammed and dated verso
"FM20"; inscribed verso
"No. 197"

Provenance: Heinrich Kirchhoff, Wiesbaden; Frankfurter Kunstkabinett Hanna Becker vom Rath; Galerie Michael Hasenclever, Munich.

Exhibitions: Milwaukee, Patrick and Beatrice Haggerty Museum of Art, Marquette University, *A Focus on Images: Sense and Form*, 9 November 1984–1 June 1985; Milkwaukee Art Museum, *Hidden Treasures: Wisconsin Collects Paintings and Sculpture*, 11 September–1 November 1987; Los Angeles County Museum of Art, *German Expressionism 1915–1925: The Second Generation*, 9 October–31 December 1988 (traveled to Fort Worth Museum, 2 February–9 April 1989; Kunstmuseum Düsseldorf, 18 May–9 July 1989; Halle, East Germany, Staatliche Galerie Moritzburg, 9 August–30 September 1989), cat. no. 49 (as *Portrait of Otto Ritsdil*).

This portrait of the artist and critic Otto Ritschl marks a transition from Conrad Felixmüller's self-consciously "modern" late Expressionism to a style marked by simplification and condensation of forms. The painting's obvious debt to Expressionism, however, remains evident in the flattened volumes, strident brushwork, and, except for the dark suit jacket, flamboyant color scheme. Compared with the manner of the earlier *Portrait of Elfriede Hausmann* (cat. no. 37), Felixmüller's formal vocabulary here is solid and sober: the former Cubo-Futurist splintering and spatial complexity have been modified so that only Ritschl's facial features are askew, while the remainder of the image takes on an almost immobile solidity.

In a certain sense, Felixmüller's focus on an immediate environment in tangible, recognizable form, represents a reaction against the more self-referential goals of Expressionism. That reaction manifests itself visually in solidly rendered objects or portraits. Portraiture was a major part of Felixmüller's oeuvre, evidence of his conviction that the human being is art's primary concern, as he stated in his 1925 manifesto, "Concerning Art":

> Art is an historical matter, because it is the expression of human society. The aesthetic impulse is therefore of subordinate importance. Even more so in these days of economic upheaval and spiritual collapse. Deprivation and misery concentrate thoughts and feelings in reality, and their interpretation is precise, brief and pointed. Economic, political, religious, and technical-scientific ideas constantly influence the character of our art, grant it the seal of disintegration or renewal, of revolution or romantic rapture. Its attitude towards life and humanity is critical, analytical, and rational. Art's content is created from the thoughts and

events of the day, and in every crucial case, it is partisan participation. The *human being* is consciously placed at the center of art; but he is no longer an unaccountable and unrestrained presence in it, but one full of social responsibility. In this sense, art becomes significant action. And the more it becomes so, the more it will lose the esoteric element of styles alienated from the world and the times, and of subjective world views —in order simultaneously to take hold of, to comprehend, and to adopt our daily life with greater intensity.[1]

Felixmüller preferred to represent the people of his society, typically those whose political sympathies closely matched his own. In this sense, portraiture is representative of the social obligation he thought to be a prerequisite of art. Ritschl, identified as an intellectual by his pince-nez and nervous demeanor, by the awkwardness of his clasped hands, shared Felixmüller's radical artistic and political convictions. Here, Felixmüller presents a type that is recognizable as a product of a specific era, and also fulfills his stipulations for responsible art.   C. D. G.

1. "Kunst ist eine historische Angelegenheit, da sie der Ausdruck menschlicher Gesellschaft ist, das ästhetische Moment ist dabei von untergeordneter Bedeutung. Noch mehr im heutigen Augenblick wirtschaftlicher Zerrüttung, geistiger Zusammenbrüche. Not und Elend konzentrieren Gedanken und Gefühle real, und ihre Interpretation ist sachlich, kurz und betont. Wirtschaftliche, politische, religiöse und technisch-wissenschaftliche Ideen beeinflussen ständig den Charakter unserer Kunst, geben ihr den Stempel der Auflösung oder des Neuwerdens, der Revolution oder der romantischen Schwärmerei. Ihre Einstellung zum Leben und zum Menschen ist kritisch, analytisch und rationell. Ihr Inhalt ist aus den Gedanken und Ereignissen des Tages geschöpft, und in jedem entscheidenden Falle ist sie Parteinahme. Der *Mensch* ist bewusst in den Mittelpunkt der Kunst gestellt; er ist in ihr keine rechenschaftsfreie und schrankenlose Erscheinung mehr, sondern voller gesellschaftlicher Verantwortung.

"In diesem Sinne wird Kunst zur zielvollen Handlung. Und je mehr sie es wird, desto mehr verliert sie das esoterische Element zeit- und weltfremder Stile und subjektiver Weltanschauung—um gleichzeitig mit grösserer Intensität unser tägliches Leben zu erfassen, zu begreifen und aufzunehmen." Conrad Felixmüller, "Über Kunst," in *Künstlerbekenntnisse*, ed. Paul Westheim (Berlin: Propyläen Verlag, 1925), 313.

39   Ernst Fritsch
Woman with Babushka (Frau mit Kopftuch), 1927

Oil on canvas
84 x 63.5 cm (33^{1}/$_{8}$ x 25 in.)
Signed and dated l. l. "E. Fritsch 1927"; inscribed and signed verso "Frau mit Kopftuch. E. Fritsch/ Wilmersdorf, Homburgerstr. 2"

Provenance: Kunsthaus Lempertz, Cologne.

In 1927, when he painted *Woman with Babushka*, Ernst Fritsch received the Great State Prize for study at the Villa Massimo in Rome. The first such prize granted by the Prussian Academy since World War I, the remarkable award may have provided the impetus for Fritsch's self-portrait of that year:[1] the painting is testimony to his person, but also to a degree of success revealed by such signs of respectability as the coat with kerchief peeking nattily from the breast pocket, checked tie, and bowler hat. Standing stiffly in a park setting, his large hands folded self-consciously in front of him, the artist displays an uneasy pride in his prosperity, as if the bourgeois clothes, obviously new, were more emblematic of his newfound status than a customary part of his attire. The self-portrait functions less as a study of personal psychology, character, or even physiognomy than as an investigation of a type, a recent arrival in the ranks of the middle class.

Woman with Babushka echoes the composition and presentation of the 1927 self-portrait. In a landscape with brick buildings—factories or tenements, most likely—and groups of trees, a young woman poses in a dark, mended cloth coat with a pink scarf covering her hair, cropped short as was popular at the time. Like Fritsch in his self-portrait, she clasps her large, unmanicured hands prominently in front of her. Setting, clothing, and mien indicate that the sitter is a working woman, not identified by name and thus an anonymous representative of her class. The painting subverts the traditional portrait's accentuation of individual difference and idiosyncrasy. In this sense, *Woman with Babushka* forms a conceptual complement to the self-portrait, with particular features signaling the subject's social and occupational situation. Both works reveal a kinship with August Sander's book of photographs *Antlitz der Zeit* (1929), in which individual appearances are similarly adapted to images of social classes and professions to present the "face of the times."

Fritsch employs the rationalism of *Neue Sachlichkeit*, its cold empiricism and denial of personal contact, in an effort to lend portraiture the apparent objectivity of scientific observation. Stylistically and ideologically, however, he does not approach the harsh verism of such painters as Otto Dix or Christian Schad. Eschewing their detailed precision and their emphasis on the accidentals of surroundings, Fritsch betrays, instead, his own prior attachment to naïve art in the simplified, airless setting with its isolated structures. His exact positioning of the figure before the landscape screen reflects a traditional portrait format that had also been adopted by photographers. Color, with the shock of pink babushka serving as focal point, recalls the subjective palette, borrowed from Robert Delaunay and Marc Chagall, that had characterized Fritsch's paintings earlier in the 1920s.

Framed by the pink babushka, the woman's face shifts out of its organic axis just sufficiently to imbue the image with a playful breath of unreality. The softened verism of Fritsch's approach is also seen in his retention of modeling brushstrokes and in the volumetric presence of the figure. She possesses the same three-dimensionality and weight found in Fritsch's *Bathers* (1927), an eclectic fusion of 1920s Neoclassicism and naïve painting recalling works by Karl Hofer and the romantic *Sachlichkeit* of Georg Schrimpf. Fritsch's female worker is monumentalized in her isolation within this syncretic process, but also made presentable in the context of the Academy, Berlin's large annual art exhibitions, and other institutions supported by the state and by middle- and upper-class audiences. The portrait is an art about the proletariat, not of or by the proletariat. Politically, therefore, its subject matter is neutralized while remaining attached to the formulations of more radical *Neue Sachlichkeit* imagery.
                    A. I. S.

1. *Self-Portrait (Selbstbildnis)*, 1927, Malte Fritsch Collection, Hedemünden, illus. in Wieland Schmied, *Neue Sachlichkeit und Magischer Realismus in Deutschland 1918–1933* (Hanover: Fackelträger-Verlag Schmidt-Küster GmbH, 1969), 27, no. 184.

40   "Fuhrmann"
Mardi Gras (Fasching), 1936

Charcoal, pen and ink on paper
50 x 31.8 cm (19^{11}/$_{16}$ x 12^{1}/$_{2}$ in.)
Signed and dated l. l. "Fuhrmann/ 36"

Provenance: Galerie 1900–2000, Paris.

In 1936, apparently in Paris, the artist who signed his work "Fuhrmann" rendered a recollection of German life prior to Adolf Hitler's rise to power three years earlier. This café scene of a Fasching, or Mardi Gras, masquerade is populated by a cast of characters representing the Weimar bourgeoisie as viewed by its artist critics: over-indulgent men, fat and bald, carouse with flagrantly exhibitionist women, clearly past the prime of youth. Sensuality without warmth or emotion informs relationships in which Fuhrmann's women offer themselves to the possessive grasping and groping of salacious men. Using shifting points of view in a tilted perspective, with figures jammed together and overlapping, the artist depicts an unstable, crowded space whose inhabitants assiduously seek to gratify their instincts for pleasure. The external world is excluded and a substitute artificiality has been imposed. A false crown sits on the head of a woman who leans back to display bared breasts to her corpulent drinking companion. Behind her, another customer dressed as a cowboy from a Karl May novel—a double fiction—emits a cloud of foul smoke into the face of an attending waiter.

Nicotine, alcohol, and jazz music from a three-man combo in the background heighten the prurient behavior of the partygoers in their ambience of falsehood. The small figures of a piano player, saxophonist, and an additional musician, rendered in childlike linearity, lack both the corpulence and size of the café's patrons. Along with the wait-er, who looks on impassively, the hired band is contrasted to the raucous revelers. Not part of the artist's indictment of this bourgeois hedonism, the servers and musicians are nevertheless forced to contribute to it. The drawing condemns a society whose depravity, if we can judge from this scene, advanced its own downfall. Implicitly, the degeneracy exhibited here prepares the way for the society's collapse and its transformation into a Fascist state, a manifestation of late capitalism. Sober, the Fasching celebrants would be contributors to the coffers of the Nazi party.   B. T. Y.

41   "Fuhrmann"
Lovers Dressing (Sich kleidendes Liebespaar), 1936

Charcoal, pen and ink on paper
50 x 33.5 cm (19^{11}/$_{16}$ x 13^{3}/$_{16}$ in.)
Signed and dated l. l. "Fuhrmann/ 36"

Provenance: Galerie 1900–2000, Paris.

A notice tacked onto the door in this interior identifies the setting as a hotel room; the "lovers" dressing are an unattractive prostitute and her cigar-puffing customer, who briefly rented room, bed, and woman. The style and content of the drawing, in a manner common in the 1930s, form a variation on works of the early and mid-1920s, echoing the voice of postwar social criticism but applying it to the context of Nazi confrontations and triumphs. Such appropriations testify to an overwhelming despair in which independent inventiveness is rejected as an artistic goal and emulation of earlier work antagonistic to the Fascist, capitalist, and bourgeois foe remains the sole viable alternative to submission.[1]

The artist who signed his work "Fuhrmann" worked in a manner closely related to that of Karl Arnold, Otto Dix, and George Grosz, whose drawings and cartoons mocking Weimar society appeared in moderate socialist as well as radical Communist publications. In the early thirties, these three became models for younger artists seeking to express political commitment in their work. Here, Fuhrmann skillfully emulates Arnold's flowing line, like a late remnant of *Jugendstil* elegance fallen on hard times, and fuses it with renditions of the physical types witnessed more acidly by Grosz and Dix. An image results whose synthesized components coexist uneasily, but whose critique gains impetus through its revivification of once familiar scenes of condemnation, like old political slogans applied in a more desperate historical conjunction once reason ceases to operate.   B. T. Y.

1. Also see, in this collection, the works by Bruno Voigt, cat. nos. 157–170.

42 "Fuhrmann"
In the Brothel (Im Bordell), 1936

Charcoal, pen and ink on paper
50 x 33.7 cm (19¹¹/₁₆ x 13¹/₄ in.)
Signed and dated l. l. "Fuhrmann/
36"

Provenance: Galerie 1900–2000, Paris.

The presentation of a young prostitute to a potential customer by a procuress has been a stock motif in erotic imagery at least since Félicien Rops's 1870s etching *Ma Fille, M. Cabanel*.[1] Frequently, the scene includes a clothed man watching a woman disrobe, as in this drawing by "Fuhrmann." Setting and props follow standard brothel iconography, with an overstuffed armchair, a plant stand with a small palm, a side table on which a drink, ashtray, and several books are displayed, and a heavy curtain behind which purchased sex is performed. Also consistently present in these scenes is a repulsive middle-aged customer who wears a business suit, smokes a cigar, and sports a cane to indicate his success in the exploitative capitalist economy. Acting as intermediary in the transaction at hand is a madam whose heavy makeup fails to hide her aging, degenerate features (the effects of syphilis are implied) and whose elaborate clothing fails to improve her vulgar appearance.

As she stands for the man's inspection, the prostitute also poses for the viewer, who judges not her physical allure but the morality of the scene taking place. Signs of ennui, exhaustion, and resignation can be read in her face, inviting pity or compassion, while the skull-like head of the madam and the coarse, quasi-mechanical features of the client inspire only loathing. With the man's class identity established, the purchase of the prostitute implicates capitalism's commodification of all labor and laborers. In this, Fuhrmann maintains an attachment to the practices of preceding German artists who visualized Karl Marx's comments on prostitution and capitalism in a similar fashion.

The premises of the drawing, both stylistic and ideological, are thus those of Weimar Germany's political left, retained without variation in the altered context of 1936, after the Republic had ceased to be. It is a perception of a past Germany seen by someone no longer capable of judging the Germany then present. Ironically, Fuhrmann imbues his scene of prostitution with the nostalgia of the expatriate and exile for whom contemporary conditions in the country that was fled cease to be reality. The frozen recollections of a world lost overpower observation and clothe even condemned vice in the aura of distance and memory.   B. T. Y.

1. Illus. in Victor Arwas, *Félicien Rops* (London: Academy Editions, 1972), pl. 5.

43 "Fuhrmann"
The Church Controls (Unter der Macht der Kirche), 1936

Charcoal, pen and ink on paper
49.6 x 32.7 cm (19¹/₂ x 12⁷/₈ in.)
Signed and dated l. l. "Fuhrmann/
36"

Provenance: Galerie 1900–2000, Paris.

In this caricature of a religious procession passing through a city street, a fat bishop scowls as he marches with folded hands under a canopy carried by a group of priests. Two attending clerics with incense and a candle prepare the procession's way. At the edge of the street, worshipers kneel and bow their heads, each transformed into a docile donkey: in this drawing by "Fuhrmann" religion, the "opiate of the people" according to Karl Marx, induces stupidity and submissiveness.

The overt antipathy towards religion, and particularly towards Roman Catholicism, displayed in Fuhrmann's drawing is not frequent in the imagery of the Weimar Republic. Although George Grosz, for example, often castigates clergymen who serve the state and bourgeois capitalist interests more than their purported Christian ideals, or who spout meaningless religious platitudes to people starving or condemned to death, his critique is of an institution and its representatives, not of the common believer or the faith itself. Fuhrmann's vitriolic image may have personal sources—the drawing is incorrect in details of the vestments and aspects of liturgical practice, and thus indicates little direct knowledge of Catholicism—but it certainly also is a response to the Church's readiness to sign a concordat with Adolf Hitler's regime and its apparently quiescent acceptance of Fascism and Nazism.

The drawing, however, does not address the specific historical situation, but attempts a universal indictment. The physiognomies of bishop and priests repeat those features Fuhrmann and his precursors reserved for German capitalists and other representatives of the bourgeoisie, but in no other respect does the drawing indicate a German setting. Fuhrmann's concern is not limited to Catholicism in Nazi Germany, but opposes the effect of Catholic discipline and teachings on humanity, in the recalled vocabulary and imagery of artists from Weimar's political left.
                B. T. Y.

44 "Fuhrmann"
The Rulers (Die Herrscher), 1936

Charcoal, pen and ink on paper
49.7 x 33.7 cm (19¹/₂ x 13¹/₄ in.)
Signed and dated l. l. "Fuhrmann/
36"

Provenance: Galerie 1900–2000, Paris.

Caricaturists during the French Revolution first identified the parasites of society as the aristocracy, clergy, and military. The stock types of decadent nobleman, fat bishop, and fancy-uniformed general were often depicted borne on the back of a personified common people, who are thus painfully maintained in a position of subservience while their strength is expended in supporting the very institutions that suppress them. In the imagery of the Weimar Republic, as in George Grosz's 1926 painting *The Pillars of Society (Stützen der Gesellschaft)* (Staatliche Museen Preussischer Kulturbesitz, West Berlin), social leeches also include the judiciary, newspaper editors, capitalists and bankers, petty bourgeoisie, and proto-Fascist hurrah patriots, in accordance with the altered conditions of postwar, postrevolutionary Germany. Represented in newspapers, popular magazines, and political tracts, the hooknosed capitalist smoking a cigar, paunchy clergyman with stubble on his cheeks, monocled aristocratic diplomat in formal attire, and square-jawed military officer with bristling Kaiser Wilhelm moustache were ubiquitous in Weimar's political iconography.[1]

Historically removed from such imagery, "Fuhrmann," with a sure and practiced hand, adopts and emulates it in this drawing of 1936. Capitalist and diplomat could be—and, in the political imagery of the 1930s, were—associated with any Western industrialized nation, and the cleric's robes and low-crowned hat appear as a pastiche of passé Lutheran and Roman Catholic dress. The military figure who dominates the foreground, supporting and supported by the trio behind him but also their overbearing despot, wears a uniform with German military emblems—oak leaves, an eagle on the cap, and medals in the shape of a cross formé—but is otherwise as generic as his companions. Using the established types of 1920s Germany, Fuhrmann delivers a general indictment of capitalist society following models in cartoons in the international Communist press. If the few indications we have of this artist's identity have been read correctly, his politically volatile drawing is that of a German exile in France, conflating and confusing democratic and capitalist institutions with those of Weimar Germany in accordance with a Stalinist ideology that failed to distinguish between Fascism, Nazism, and other forms of political conviction in capitalist democracies.   B. T. Y.

1. The types of the capitalist (with features such as the hooked nose identifying him as Jewish), diplomat, and clergyman—but significantly not the military officer —were also appropriated by Nazi and other right-wing cartoonists in their propagandistic efforts, thereby disseminating these caricatures even further in Weimar society.

45 "Fuhrmann"
The Suicide (Selbstmord), c. 1936

Charcoal, pen and ink on paper
50.5 x 32.5 cm (19⁷/₈ x 12¹³/₁₆ in.)
Signed l. l. "Fuhrmann"

Provenance: Galerie 1900–2000, Paris.

A suicide in a barren, crumbling tenement interior was a common icon in imagery of Weimar Germany's political left, particularly during the period of economic turmoil that followed World War I and continued until the "normalization" of the mid-twenties. The hopeless worker, unemployed and starving, who finds in death the sole solution to his desperate condition represented the extreme result of capitalist exploitation; his tragedy provided an unequaled source of pathos and rage for audiences sharing the artists' political convictions and moral indignation.

As in the other drawings bearing this signature, "Fuhrmann" retrieves the iconography of Weimar's radical art in *The Suicide*. A gaunt, impoverished man is shown dangling by a hastily made noose from a large nail, the only "decoration," except for a calendar page, on the walls of his otherwise bare room. The chair he kicked out from under him lies under a wooden table along with an empty wine bottle. On the table, an empty cooking pot, a single photograph, some letters, and a pencil accompany a scribbled suicide note. Focusing on the squalor of the man's room, the bare essentials of his former precarious existence, and the melodramatic instruments and sentimental embellishments of his final act, the artist narrates a tale of lonely surrender to hopelessness.

Fuhrmann effectively employs the devices of Otto Dix, George Grosz, and Rudolf Schlichter, but within a totally transformed context. By 1936, the date of this drawing, Adolf Hitler had been in power for three years and imposed his regime with ruthless determination. Earlier beliefs that his term of office would be brief, and that with its demise the capitalist system would also collapse under a proletarian revolution, had proven to be ideological illusions. Cells of resistance within Germany were few and ineffective; exile was the only alternative to repression and probable imprisonment. However, many German exiles found life in their host countries bleak. Having traded political persecution for impoverishment and isolation, they were unable to adapt to the alien society. It is this reality that Fuhrmann appears to render, more than that of ten years earlier. The emphasis on letters and photographs on the table suggests separation from beloved persons and a homeland which had become inhospitable but for which there was, psychologically and professionally, no substitute. For the destitute exile spit out from his home, as for the proletarian laborer in the images of the 1920s, death offered a way out of despair and starvation.   B. T. Y./R. H.

46 Otto Gleichmann
Street Scene (Strassenszene), 1921

Gouache, tusche, brush and ink on paper
23 x 31.3 cm (9¹/₁₆ x 12⁵/₁₆ in.)
Signed and dated l. l.
"O. Gleichmann. 1921"

Provenance: Galerie Michael Hasenclever, Munich.

In Otto Gleichmann's amusing but somehow ominous *Street Scene*, a boy restrains his barking dog, pulling tightly at its leash as they encounter a pack of strays while out on an evening walk. Encircling the youth and his pet, four dogs sniff and prowl, causing a commotion that draws the attention of several passersby. This common moment of modern urban life—dogs rushing together to play or fight, and their owners attempting to keep them apart—becomes a genre scene, rendered as if by a child for whom pets and their masters constitute an excitingly charged, visionary reality.

Like Paul Klee, Gleichmann devised a sophisticated style derived from children's and amateurs' art, manipulated according to Cubist and Futurist stylistic principles. Line is executed in a playful, scratchy manner, as if by a still unpracticed hand. Consistency of size is replaced by emphasis on the central figures of the boy and his dog, who appear out of scale with their surroundings. Buildings are outlined façades with irregular windows and doors; perspective is fragmented or ignored. In contrast to these naïve mannerisms is Gleichmann's use of color to emulate atmosphere and light. Textured paper shimmers through silvery gray wash to suggest light reflecting from cement surfaces in the dusk of early evening. *Street Scene* is a nocturne, but Whistlerian melancholy is here supplanted by noisy confrontation and apprehension mixed with amusement.

Although Gleichmann is relatively little known today, he was widely recognized during the late teens and the twenties. Alfred Flechtheim and Paul Cassirer, established dealers of modern art, published portfolios of his prints and sponsored exhibitions of his paintings. He was generously praised and supported by such critics as Theodor Däubler and Paul Westheim, whose aesthetic ideology—like that of Flechtheim and Cassirer—took shape in the international modern movement that preceded World War I. They were advocates of an established "avantgarde," liberal in their inclinations but cool to extreme artistic experimentation and political engagement, concerned with applying traditional concepts of quality to modernist convictions. With his willed individual style, subjective fantasy, and masterly manipulation of materials, Gleichmann ably met their demands for an art that transcended or transformed mundane reality.

Däubler first summed up these critical assessments and celebrations of Gleichmann's work in 1918 and repeated them yearly until 1922, thereby also bracketing the years of the artist's greatest reputation:

The creatures he presents are often plantlike, somewhat light-deprived, but perhaps also at the point of finally seeing the light after all. But no decisions lead them to ... They even grow like vines back into their own souls. Their roots are grounded in the ego. They sprout from no ego in the great world-forest. They derive from a tiny egolet, as if from a flower pot. In very little sun. But things are okay.[1]

B. T. Y.

1. "Die Wesen, die er bringt, sind oft pflanzenhaft, etwas lichtarm, jedoch vielleicht schon dabei, endlich doch das Licht zu sehen. Aber keine Entschlüsse führen sie dazu. Sie wachsen sogar wie Geränke zurück in ihre Seele. Ihr Wurzeln ist im Ich begründet. Sie keimen aus keinem Ich im grossen Weltwalde. Sie kommen aus einem winzigen Ichlein, wie aus einem Blumentopf, hervor. Bei sehr wenig Sonne. Doch es geht." Theodor Däubler, "Otto Gleichmann," *Feuer,* 1919/20: 522, as reprinted in *Im Kampf um die moderne Kunst und andere Schriften,* ed. F. Kemp and F. Pfäfflin (Darmstadt: Luchterhand, 1988), 186.

47 Otto Griebel
The Naked Whore (Die nackte Nutte), 1923

Watercolor over pencil on paper
40.6 x 29.1 cm (16 x 11½ in.)
Signed, dated, and inscribed l. r.
"Otto Griebel/23/Die nackte Nutte"

Provenance: Collection Martha Dix; Otto Dix Stiftung, Hemmenhofen; Galerie Remmert and Barth, Düsseldorf; Galerie Michael Hasenclever, Munich.

Exhibition: Düsseldorf, Galerie Remmert und Barth, *Die Dresdener Künstlerszene 1913–1933,* 1987, cat. no. 51.

In depicting this prostitute, a common motif of the 1920s, Otto Griebel has eliminated any stylistic artifice. Paring down his technique, eschewing caricature and formal experimentation, Griebel creates a haunting and commanding vision of a member of the exploited underclass. Watercolor, applied sparingly and very thinly, is used here to create a spartan surface, with sharp pencil lines visible through the transparent color. The woman is set against an aqua blue background, which has a clinical coldness to it, and which accentuates the gray pallor of her skin. Overtly frontal, she is brought up close to the picture plane, her legs cropped by the bottom edge of the canvas. Her torso is afforded the central part of the composition, and, although she is almost completely undressed, her body is displayed so frankly that the image's titillating, sensual impact is minimized. Only the red hat, vaguely reminiscent of female genitalia, has a direct sensual allusion in its shape and color, as heavily made-up and shadowed eyes emerge in riveting confrontation beneath it, and red lips echo its form.

Wearing stockings, garters, and black bloomers pulled down to reveal pubic hair, the prostitute functions as a matter-of-fact advertisement for the service she offers, callously and unemotionally. Her intense eyes, perhaps, recall the iconography of the *femme fatale,* but otherwise she appears as document of the profession she embodies and its efficient practice: since her earnings depend on the number of customers she can accommodate, sentimentality and feeling are luxuries she cannot afford.

In the process of portraying her, Griebel all but dehumanizes the woman. His inscription identifies her generically, using the vulgar term "whore." Unlike Otto Dix or Rudolf Schlichter, Griebel does not accent her sexuality by means of graphic representations of exposed genitals, but presents her in a dispassionate act of visual reporting that echoes her own dispassionate approach to sex. Hovering somewhere between the ridiculous and the pathetic, his is a cold and grotesque portrayal of a woman reduced to her physical body, to the commodity she so unabashedly displays.

C. D. G.

48 Rudolf Grossmann
Portrait of Wolfgang Gurlitt and Frau Tilly Christensen-Agoston (Porträt Wolfgang Gurlitt und Frau Lily Christensen-Agoston), c. 1930?

Pencil on paper
34.3 x 47.5 cm (13½ x 18¹¹/₁₆ in.)
Inscribed l. r. "Gurlitt"

Provenance: Wolfgang Gurlitt Estate, Munich; D. Thomas Bergen Collection, New York and London.

Rudolf Grossmann, like John Hoexter (see cat. no. 64) a frequent patron of Berlin's bohemian Romanisches Café and Café des Westens on Kurfürstendamm, is best known for his informal drawings and hand-colored engravings depicting Germany's personalities and night life during the teens and twenties. Well-connected in artistic and social and circles, and an unrepentant dandy, he often sketched artists, dealers, and critics as they sat together and conversed in the cafés; his innumerable portraits reproduced in fashionable intellectual periodicals, such as *Kunst und Künstler (Art and Artists)* and *Die Weltbühne (The World Stage),* provide a virtual inventory of Weimar society. Here, he portrays the prominent art dealer Wolfgang Gurlitt, who published many of Grossmann's graphics, along with his secretary, Tilly Christensen-Agoston. In fluid contours, Grossmann has captured their salient features, using a swift and malleable line to achieve the spontaneous and uncomposed look that is typical of his style. The portrait conveys the impression of having been drawn rapidly, with little thought, as if it were a compulsive act of reportage, unplanned and unposed, vibrant and vital in its effect.

Grossmann took neither himself nor his subjects too seriously, maintaining an attitude of knowing skepticism, insistent informality, and gently mocking humor. In a self-characterization written shortly after World War I, Grossmann, who was descended from a family of Baden artists, identified himself as someone born with six toes and then contrasted his own training and concerns with those of his ancestors:

My grandfather painted images of saints in church cupolas. His grandson started out in the whores' quarters of Paris. Never exercised in the Cubist gymnasium, never learned the Expressionist balance-beam movements. Nonetheless, people of

more than bourgeois significance maintained that even then, as I made the journey through France's brothels with [Jules] Pascin, I had Futurist and Expressionist elements in my art sooner than many a dodo who today programmatically whores for immortality with them. I don't worry about it. The great gesture of reaching for immortality leaves me cold and I am not in the habit of taking things like art so seriously that I forget life because of them. I do not draw for the sake of fame, but because my whims compel me to do it. And, I hope at least—if nothing else—to have given the Germans the spectacle of how to make the essence and the goals of human behavior apparent in playful fashion and with an elegance that takes nothing seriously, but nevertheless is penetrating.[1]

The portrait of Gurlitt and Christensen-Agoston is demonstrative of this attitude of mixed fascination and amused skepticism. All pretense of formal portraiture is gone, replaced by Grossmann's lightly stylizing naturalistic rendering of the reclining gallery publisher staring intently in the direction of his secretary. Wearing a fashionable hat whose brim nearly covers her eyes, Christensen-Agoston gestures in conversation while slouching in a chair. She wears the modified suit with slacks, shirt, and tie that were the uniform of Weimar's liberated "New Woman" during the late 1920s and early 1930s, the target of reactionaries who decried the appearance of women in men's clothing as a visible sign of a supposed decline in morality that accompanied woman's new public presence and political role. Absolute nonchalance characterizes employer and employee, and only the bulk of Gurlitt's form provides an indication of his determining role in this relationship of apparently easy equality. Traditional hierarchies are broken down in Grossmann's double portrait, and supplanted by the representation of a reformed society soon to be suppressed.

C. D. G.

1. "Mein Grossvater malte Heiligenbilder auf Kirchenkuppeln. Der Enkel begann in Paris im Hurenviertel. Turnte nie im kubistischen Turnsaal, erlernte nicht die expressionistische Bauchwelle. Gleichwohl behaupteten Menschen von überbürgerlicher Bedeutung, dass schon damals, als ich mit Pascin die Reise durch die Bordelle Frankreichs machte, ich futuristische und expressionistische Elemente in meiner Kunst mehr und eher gehabt, als mancher Nebbish, der programmatelnd heute damit Unsterblichkeit erbuhlt. Ich kümmere mich nicht darum. Die grosse Geste nach Ewigkeit liegt mir nicht und ich vermag nicht, Dinge wie Kunst so wichtig zu nehmen, dass ich das Leben darüber vergässe. Ich zeichne nicht aus Ruhm, sondern weil meine Launen mich dazu zwingen und ich hoffe, wenn auch nicht mehr, so doch immerhin den Deutschen das Schauspiel gegeben zu haben, wie menschliche Gebaren auf spielerische Weise und mit der Eleganz, die nichts wichtig nimmt, aber dennoch ergründet, Letztes und Wesentliches offenbart wird." Rudolf Grossmann, "Selbstcharakteristik," *Das Kunstblatt* 5 (1921): 143–144.

49 George Grosz
The Family (Die Familie),
c. 1916

Reed pen, brush and ink on paper
28.4 x 22 cm (11³/₁₆ x 8¹¹/₁₆ in.)
Signed l. r. "Grosz"

Provenance: Ernest Rathenau, Berlin,
Hamburg, and New York.

In his critical campaign against German society and its institutions, George Grosz sought to reveal by means of ridicule the often repulsive traits of the dominant classes, their decadence, perverse values, and hypocrisies. His drawings and paintings were weapons in this self-declared battle, presented in the German Communist Party's political periodicals, but even more frequently in art magazines, galleries, exhibitions, and investment-worthy lithographic portfolios. He followed in this the statutes of the Union of Communist Artists, or "Red Group," whose presiding officer he was in 1924 and which called for "exploitation of bourgeois art exhibitions for propaganda purposes."[1] His relationship to the art market affirmed his own observations on the situation of the artist in late capitalist societies:

> Today's art is dependent on the bourgeois class and shall die with it; the artist, possibly without wishing to be so, is a banknote factory and an investment machine of which the rich exploiter and the aesthetic fop makes use in order to invest his money more or less advantageously, in order to appear both to himself and to society as a patron of culture, which also seeks him out.[2]

Exploiting the institutions and desires of his proclaimed enemy, Grosz prevented use of his art as "a type of flight from this 'uncouth' world to a better star, into the lunatic world of their fantasy, into a purer paradise bereft of political parties and civil wars," by focusing his imagery precisely on those factors his patrons wished to deny to their consciousness.[3] He created variations on his drawings, permitting their message to be duplicated repeatedly, finally to be reproduced as photolithographs in limited-edition portfolios. Elements of *The Family* are thus reiterated in at least three different drawings, one of which appeared in the Berlin Dada journal *Die Pleite (Bankruptcy)*, and then in 1923 as the second plate in his vituperative pictorial attack on German middle-class values and politics, *Ecce Homo*.

Through a distillation and exaggeration of physical and attitudinal aspects of German social groups, Grosz produced easily recognizable types to act out the foibles of their class. In *The Family*, a bourgeois couple enjoys a leisurely walk in a mountainous landscape which, in *Ecce Homo*'s sequence of drawings, contrasts to the turmoil and indiscriminate crowding of Berlin streets.[4] The man's middle-class identity is established by his hat, fitted walking coat and trousers, celluloid collar and tie, glasses, and cane—all indicative of old-fashioned values and economic well-being. At his side, his wife wears an aproned dirndl and a hat, simplified, modish adaptations of

South German folk costume. As in many of Grosz's depictions of women, her clothing is transparent to reveal her naked body, and also the child she carries in her womb. The flowers blossoming nearby, including the bleeding heart emblematic of sentimental attitudes towards love, link Grosz's image to countless saccharine prints, magazine covers, illustrations, and photographs drawing conceptual equations between young women, springtime, and budding blossoms. Grosz, however, presents a mature woman, no longer sexually attractive but obviously sexually active as she fulfills her role of propagating her race and class.

The mountain setting, with its ornate sanatorium in the background at the right, is unusual in Grosz's typically urban imagery.[5] Indeed, the husband's severe attire and the wife's consciously countrified costume indicate that these two urbanites are out of their normal habitat: he on a brief visit, she for *Erholung*, or rest, as she awaits the birth of the child. Their dress, either out of place or mimicking local costume, suggests an inappropriate sense of propriety and middle-class conformity. Grosz's couple exists in a world of uniforms selected according to social status, profession, or temporary location without sincerity or conviction.

Grosz also mocks the relationship of husband and wife. As she walks next to him, her arm passively entwined in his, she becomes an extension of his presence, servilely allowing herself to be led. Like his walking stick and cigar, she gives testimony in her ample figure to his prosperity and his pride in his possessions. Her accented sexuality and pregnancy identify her *raison d'être* as a biological guarantee of heirs through which property is maintained in the family and comes to dominate the human lives with which it is associated. The two dogs provide a footnote commentary, echoing the biological relationship of man and woman. What the dogs in their instincts lack, however, is the sense of ownership that submits all relationships to those of property, domination, and subordination.

If the woman in *The Family* is reduced to sexual functions and a possessed object, this is not so far removed from what Grosz himself announced as a woman's role. In a letter to his friend Otto Schmalhausen, he wrote in 1918:

> Just between us, I can't stand "depth" in women; generally it is combined with an ugly predominance of masculine qualities, angularity, and poor thighs. I subscribe to the same view as [Alfred] Kerr (the critic): "Intellect is my prerogative and no one else's."[6]

Grosz views women solely in sexual terms, either as empty-headed, "feminine," and thus desirable, or as intelligent, "masculine," and ugly. On the subject of women, the very possessive and dominating attitudes he criticized in the German bourgeoisie, he shared with them.   S. L. D.

1. "Ausnützung bürgerlicher Kunstausstellungen für Propagandazwecke." "Manifest der Vereinigung kommunistischer Künstler 'Rote Gruppe,'" *Die Rote Fahne* 57 (1924), as reprinted in *Manifeste Manifeste 1905–1933*, vol. 1 of *Schriften*

deutscher Künstler des zwanzigsten Jahrhunderts, ed. Diether Schmidt (Dresden: VEB Verlag der Kunst, n. d.), 319.
2. "Die heutige Kunst ist abhängig von der bürgerlichen Klasse und wird mit ihr sterben; der Maler, vielleicht ohne dass er will, ist eine Banknotenfabrik und Aktienmaschine, deren sich der reiche Ausbeuter und ästhetische Fatzke bedient, um sein Geld mehr oder weniger lukrativ anzulegen, um vor sich und der Gesellschaft als Förderer der Kultur, die auch danach ist, dazustehen." George Grosz, "Statt einer Biographie," in Grosz and Wieland Herzfelde, *Die Kunst ist in Gefahr* (Berlin: Malik Verlag, 1925), as reprinted in *Manifeste Manifeste*, 257.
3. "... eine Art Flucht aus dieser 'pöbelhaften' Welt auf einen besseren Stern, in das Mondland ihrer Phantasie, in ein reineres, partei- und bürgerkriegsloses Paradies." Ibid.
4. Plate 1 of *Ecce Homo* depicts Berlin's Friedrichstrasse; plate 2 is the variant of *The Family*.
5. For the identity of the building as sanatorium, compare the drawing titled *Sanatorium*, with its similar structure, in *Neue Jugend* 11/12 (1917), reprinted in *Pass Auf! Hier Kommt Grosz: Bilder, Rhythmen und Gesänge 1915–1918*, ed. Wieland Herzfelde and Hans Marquardt (Leipzig: Philipp Reclam, 1981), 27.
6. "Unter uns: ich scheisse auf die Tiefe bei Frauen, meistens verbinden sie damit ein hässliches Überwiegen männlicher Eigenarten, Eckigkeit und Schenkellosigkeit; ich denke wie Kerr (der Kritiker): 'Jeist hab ick alleene.'" George Grosz, *Briefe 1913–1959*, ed. H. Knust (Reinbeck: Rowohlt, 1979), 58. This letter of 3 March 1918 is cited and translated by M. Kay Flavel, "Über alles die Liebe: Food, Sex, and Money in the Work of George Grosz," *Journal of European Studies* 13 (1983): 279, and idem, *George Grosz: A Biography* (New Haven and London: Yale University Press, 1988), 43.

50 George Grosz
Dive (Kaschemme), c. 1917

Brush and ink on paper
37.5 x 32 cm (14³/₄ x 12⁹/₁₆ in.)
Signed l. r. "Grosz"

Provenance: Galerie Franke, Munich; Galerie Wolfgang Ketterer, Munich.

Exhibition: University Art Museum, University of Minnesota, Minneapolis, *Berlin: Art and Metropolis—Works on Paper 1912–1932*, 8 September–11 October 1987.

In this drawing, George Grosz depicts a tavern where three men sit together at a table to smoke, drink, and talk. Derived from villainous stereotypes in popular illustration and film, Grosz's low-life types suggest the criminal element of the Berlin underworld: one figure wears a long, curling moustache, another bites a cigarette holder in his mouth with an evil sneer; dark shadows surround his eyes. In the upper right corner of the drawing, another figure with furrowed brow hunches over a table on which an old oil lamp is perched. Without electricity, this disorganized cellar café boasts only bare tabletops, bare floors and walls, and, at the upper right, an overturned chair.

Grosz's style in this work simultaneously recalls bathroom graffiti and chil-

dren's drawings. In his autobiographic reminiscences, published with Wieland Herzfelde in the pamphlet *Art Is in Danger* in 1925, Grosz remembered consulting these primitive graphic sources:

> I drew, for example, a table around which the regular patrons of the beer hall *Siechen* were seated like fat red globs of meat compressed into ugly gray sacks. In order to arrive at an appropriately drastic and crudely blunt style which could do justice to the coarseness and repulsiveness of my subjects, I studied the most unspoilt manifestations of artistic instincts: in pissoirs I copied folkloristic drawings, to me the expression and most immediate translation of strong feelings. Children's drawings, too, inspired me, because of their unambiguous immediacy. Thus, gradually I arrived at a razor-sharp style which I applied to recordings of my observations, dictated at the time by my absolute rejection of humanity.[1]

Grosz speaks here from the viewpoint of his radical convictions of the 1920s, when he rejected the superiority of an ego over the anonymity of the mob, and valued instead humanity's collective identity, notably the identifying consciousness of the proletariat. His attitudes towards art then caricatured perceived bourgeois aesthetic values, especially the extreme subjective individualism of Expressionism, much as his drawings caricatured the appearance of social types. Grosz subverts Expressionism's adulation of the capacity for unspoiled self-expression apparent in the work of children and folk artists, in which, Vassily Kandinsky argued, "the inner sound of the subject is revealed automatically." According to Kandinsky, these untrained artists are able "to ignore the external ... [and] ... to express the abiding internal in such a form that it emerges and affects very forcefully."[2]

Grosz identifies not naïve votive paintings but crude toilet-stall graffiti as folk art, and praises children's drawings not for their "inner sound" but for their external veracity, thus reversing or debasing Kandinsky's Expressionist search for archetypal spirituality while simultaneously appropriating it in a transformed, materialist aesthetic. The coarse, sketchy quality of line in *Dive* identifies and reveals the harsh atmosphere of the bar. By depicting it in a graffiti-derived style, Grosz likened the late-night café to a place where graffiti might appear, as a social analogue to the pissoirs in which he found the paradigms of his style.   S. L. D.

1. "Ich zeichnete z. B. einen Stammtisch im Bierhaus Siechen, wo die Menschen wie dicke rote Fleischmassen in graue hässliche Säcke gepresst sassen. Um zu einem Stil zu gelangen, der drastisch und verblümt die Härte und Lieblosigkeit meiner Objekte wiedergab, studierte ich die unmittelbarsten Manifestationen des Kunsttriebes: Ich kopierte in Pissoirs die folkloristischen Zeichnungen, sie erschienen mir als der Ausdruck und die kürzeste Übersetzung starker Gefühle. Auch Kinderzeichnungen regten mich ihrer Eindeutigkeit wegen an. So kam ich allmählich zu einem messerharten Stile, dessen ich zur Aufzeichnung meiner da-

mals von absoluter Menschenverneinung diktierten Beobachtungen bedurfte." George Grosz, in Grosz und Wieland Herzfelde, *Die Kunst ist in Gefahr* (Berlin: Malik Verlag, 1925), as reprinted in *Manifeste Manifeste 1905–1933*, vol. 1 of *Schriften deutscher Künstler des zwanzigsten Jahrhunderts*, ed. Diether Schmidt (Dresden: VEB Verlag der Kunst, n. d.), 348.

2. Vassily Kandinsky, "Über die Formfrage," in *Der Blaue Reiter*, ed. Kandinsky and Franz Marc (Munich: Piper Verlag, 1912), 92, as translated in Klaus Lankheit, ed., *The "Blaue Reiter" Almanac* (New York: The Viking Press, 1974), 174, 175.

---

51 George Grosz
To Them Peace Is Assured (Ihnen ist der Friede gesichert), 1919

Pen, brush and ink on paper
47 x 36 cm (18¹/₂ x 14³/₁₆ in.)
Inscribed l. l. "Johannis 19" ("[St.] John's [Day] 19"); inscribed l. c. "Ihnen ist der Friede gesichert"; estate stamp verso

Provenance: Estate of the artist; private collection, Germany; Christie's, London and Munich.

George Grosz's opposition to war and the military was already apparent during the initial days of World War I. Although he volunteered—as did most of his contemporaries for reasons ranging from ardent nationalism to the privileges volunteers enjoyed over draftees—he was able to obtain a medical discharge within a few months. After returning to Berlin, he joined the pacifist artistic and literary circle associated with Franz Pfemfert's periodical *Die Aktion* (*Action*). By 1916, he was working with Wieland Herzfelde and John Heartfield on the activist journal *Neue Jugend* (*New Youth*) and on establishing the radical-left publishing house, Malik Verlag. The prints he produced at this time for his *Little Grosz Portfolio* (*Kleine Grosz Mappe*) were critical of imperial German society, but it was only with the end of the war and the relaxation of military censorship that he was able to publish his most overt anti-military drawings, such as this one. Included in *The Face of the Ruling Class* (1921), the fourth volume of Malik Verlag's "Little Revolutionary Library,"[1] the drawing is among Grosz's most pessimistic indictments of German militarism and its consequences.

Using his title ironically to identify a view of war graves, Grosz depicts a vast expanse of land pockmarked by bomb and artillery craters. Save for a few weeds and scraggly flowers growing from the dried, cracked, violated earth, there are no signs of life. Instead, crosses stretch in uneven rows towards the horizon, marking countless makeshift graves. A single soldier's helmet, either English or American, hangs on one of the crosses, but no inscription identifies the "hero" honored with this decoration. It is a bleak vision of the results of World War I, in which over eight million soldiers died. Dated to the feast of St. John the Baptist, 24 June,

the drawing commemorates midsummer's day for 1919, the day that traditionally celebrates the beginning of summer and the planting of new crops. But according to Grosz's perception, death was the crop of 1919; peace was assured only to those who had already died; for the surviving it was far from certain.

On 16 June, the German delegation at Versailles had received the final peace conditions from the Allies; in response, the government of Philipp Scheidemann resigned rather than accept the "dictated peace." On 21 June, the German fleet held captive at Scapa Flow was scuttled by order of Admiral Ludwig von Reuter to avoid its confiscation in the peace process. Summer solstice was further marked by the burning of French flags by German soldiers and by Field Marshal von Hindenburg's public rejection of the peace treaty (while he secretly informed President Ebert that the military was incapable of resisting an Allied invasion). Despite these and other vocal protests, the treaty was reluctantly accepted under the new government of Gustav Bauer, although with objection to the clause naming Germany as the aggressor and instigator of the war. Peace now seemed "assured."

Grosz's drawing is a bitter commentary on these events and the revanchism, prevalent among Allies and Central Powers alike, which threatened the peace process. With the motif of the Tommy's helmet, however, rather than the steel helmet of the Kaiser's troops, Grosz seems to be directing his accusatory judgment more towards the situation in Germany than in England or France. The attitudes of the German military and opportunistic politicians towards peace seemed a greater danger than the reparations demands of the Allies, and by summer solstice in 1919 it had become clear that the military's power, prestige, and ambition remained as much a component of the fledgling republic's social order as had been the case in the German Empire.

Efforts by soldiers' councils to introduce military reform failed once the Ebert regime agreed to the Supreme Command's conditions for support. In the winter and spring of 1918 and 1919, military and allied units of Freikorps troops were used to suppress Spartacist and other left-wing revolts against the moderate republic. Attempting to quell revolutionary activity and establish law and order, the civilian government became dependent on the remnants of an imperial military over which it had no control. Simultaneously, leaders of the armed forces promulgated the myth of a civilian betrayal which absolved them of responsibility for Germany's defeat and fostered a revanchist chauvinism within their own ranks and among the German population. The deaths of two million German soldiers from 1914 to 1918 failed to affect the military's entrenched position.

Picturing fields of Allied dead, their anonymous graves monuments to German militarism, Grosz condemns his compatriots' continued refusal to recognize the role that glorification of the military had played in the Kaiser's provocative foreign policies. On summer solstice in 1919, the events surrounding

the Treaty of Versailles and the enduring power of an unreformed German military inspired Grosz to provide, with this grim drawing, a prophecy of future German military adventurism and additional countless deaths. The prophecy was fulfilled on 1 September 1939.

S. L. D.

1. George Grosz, *Das Gesicht der herrschenden Klasse: 55 politische Zeichnungen*, Kleine revolutionäre Bibliothek, vol. 4 (Berlin: Malik Verlag, 1921), 62.

---

52 George Grosz
Orgy (Orgie), c. 1922

Watercolor, pen and ink on paper
50.5 x 49.5 cm (19⁷/₈ x 19⁷/₁₆ in.)
Signed l. l. and l. r. "Grosz"; inscribed l. l. "N° 43"

Provenance: Galerie Thomas Borgmann, Cologne; Konrad Mönter, Düsseldorf; Fischer Fine Art, London.

Orgy relates to watercolor drawings published by Grosz in 1923 in his collection of sardonic imagery, *Ecce Homo*.[1] Under the motto "Behold the Man," whose Latin form echoes precedents ranging from depictions of the scourged Christ to Nietzsche's intellectual autobiography, Grosz combined eighty-four drawings and sixteen watercolors of 1915 to 1922 that presented his perceptions of human nature. Together, the drawings confirmed his cynical transformation of the messianic Expressionist slogan "Man is good" into "Man is not good—but a beast."[2] Perversity, overindulgence, cruelty, and persecution characterize the inventory of human behavior Grosz provides. Although not among *Ecce Homo*'s images, *Orgy* serves much like an index, a compendium or digest, of the book's pictorial conclusions. A woman, her bared breast emerging from her chemise, dispassionately kisses a more ardent, clothed, moustached middle-class man. A wealthy, bald burgher has fallen off his chair and slouches drunkenly at a table covered with the detritus of drink and food, a bottle held precariously in his hand and a cigar stuck in his mouth as he belches wine. In the background, a woman defecates into a chamber pot and the legs of a man are seen disappearing up steps to leave behind this subterranean, disjointed scene of human ruination. Excessive consumption, purchased satisfaction, base animal functions—these, and these alone, characterize both the humanity that inhabits Grosz's watercolor image and the society to which he bears witness.

Following publication of *Ecce Homo*, Grosz was charged with offending public morality. His defense was that he depicted life as he saw it; moreover, he argued, his work served educational and moral purposes as it exaggerated the antithesis existing between reality and the ideal. The court found him guilty of depicting "all the perversity into which a person could possibly fall" and fined him 6,000 Reichsmarks.[3]

R. H.

1. George Grosz, *Ecce Homo* (Berlin: Malik Verlag, 1923; facsimile eds. New York: Brussel & Brussel, Inc., 1956; New York: Grove Press, 1966; and Hamburg: Rowohlt Verlag, 1966).

2. "Der Mensch ist nicht gut—sondern ein Vieh." George Grosz, "Statt einer Biographie," in George Grosz and John Heartfield, *Die Kunst ist in Gefahr* (Berlin: Malik Verlag, 1925), as repr. in *Die Zwanziger Jahre: Manifeste und Dokumente deutscher Künstler*, ed. Uwe M. Schneede (Cologne: DuMont Buchverlag, 1979), 61. Grosz first published this text in *Der Gegner* 2, no. 3 (1920–21) and, as an autobiographical statement, in Willi Wolfradt, *George Grosz*, Junge Kunst, vol. 21 (Leipzig: Klinkhardt & Biermann, 1921).

3. ". . . die ganze Perversität, auf die irgendein Mensch verfallen kann." Because court records of Grosz's trial and fine cannot be located, this incident, repeatedly mentioned in the literature on Grosz, has been called into question by Ludwig Leiss, *Kunst im Konflikt: Kunst und Künstler im Widerstreit mit der "Obrigkeit"* (Berlin and New York: Walter De Gruyter, 1971), 330–331. Recently, however, Kay M. Flavel, "Über alles die Liebe: Food, Sex and Money in the Work of George Grosz," *Journal of European Studies* 13 (1983), 287, n. 40, has cited an account published in *Das Tagebuch*, 23 February 1924, 240–248; it has not been possible to corroborate this reference.

---

53 George Grosz
Street Scene, Berlin (Strassenszene, Berlin), c. 1924

Watercolor, pencil, pen, brush and ink on paper
58.4 x 46 cm (23 x 18¹/₈ in.)
Signed l. l. "Grosz"

Provenance: Mr. and Mrs. Joseph Randall Shapiro, Oak Park, Ill.; B. C. Holland, Chicago.

Exhibitions: Chicago, Museum of Contemporary Art, *Selections from the Joseph Randall Shapiro Collection*, 20 December 1969–1 February 1970, cat. no. 95 (as *Berlin Street*, 1917); Milwaukee, Patrick and Beatrice Haggerty Museum of Art, Marquette University, *A Focus on Images: Sense and Form*, 9 November 1984–1 June 1985; Milwaukee, UWM Art Museum, University of Wisconsin, *Reactions to the War: European Art, 1914–1925*, 2 November–14 December 1986, cat. no. 21 (as *Berlin Street*); West Berlin, Berlinische Galerie, Museum für Moderne Kunst, Photographie und Architektur im Martin-Gropius-Bau, *Ich und die Stadt: Mensch und Grosstadt in der deutschen Kunst des 20. Jahrhunderts*, 15 August–22 November 1987, cat. no. 62.

Street Scene, Berlin is one of numerous urban scenes that focus on class characterization and contrasts as George Grosz perceived them in Germany both during and after World War I.[1] In this instance, a bakery shopwindow richly adorned with bread and cake serves as backdrop before which, from foreground to background, three passersby are arranged: a chauffeur or deliveryman; a police official with cap, sword, and satchel indicating his rank and bureaucratic position; and a nanny who pushes a baby carriage. Sharing the illumination of street and shopwindow, the trio also share the employ of the city's dominant bourgeois class. Nurse, policeman, and male domestic wear the uniforms of their professions; they are functionaries of the middle class, dependent on its prosperity, submissive to its control, preserving order or engaged in the tasks that contribute to the material comfort of their employers.

Single-mindedly obedient to their assignments, they parade resolutely past the old blind man standing in the darkness of a recessed doorway. He wears the drab, worn, field-gray coat issued to him during the war in which—so Grosz stages the scene—he lost his eyesight and health. Now he appears stooped and shriveled, a castoff of society, ignored as he attempts to sell lottery tickets, and seems (literally, if the lines of Grosz's drawing are followed) to dissolve into the building against which he leans.

But the ironic antithesis of prosperity and deprivation that artists of the left used as a constant formulation of capitalist society here receives a more subtle analysis. Grosz does not represent the formulaic fat burgher gorging himself in a sidewalk café or embracing recently purchased luxuries, who in the process of his ostentatious consumption ignores or denigrates the unfortunate proletarian or veteran victimized by capitalist institutions. Instead, the servants of this prototypical bourgeois are shown sharing his callous attitudes. (Even the muzzled dachshund urinating near the doorway may be said to be in servitude.) The servants, too, now refuse to acknowledge the plight of members of the very class from which they derive. Betraying the proletarian class struggle, they form an alliance of submission with their bourgeois exploiters.

If the style of this watercolor is less harsh, more volumetric in its rendering than Grosz's previous works, *Street Scene, Berlin* is also less insistent on a dichotomy between capitalist and proletarian, between exploiter and exploited. In comparison with his Dada- and *Scuola metafisica*-inspired works, this drawing thus marks both a stylistic and an ideological transformation. The significantly simplified Communist vision of class struggle that Grosz presented in terms of pitiful or heroic workers and demonic burghers, soldiers, and capitalists here shifts to a critique of the institutions through which the social order is maintained and of a human psychology accepting of injustices and inequalities. Grosz recognizes an intermediate class, employed by such capitalist institutions as the police, the small firm, or family, who adopt the ideology of their employers. They insist on separating themselves from their origins and on distinguishing among themselves in accordance with supposed differences of rank and status, but are unable to lose their subordinate social position and socially or monetarily to enter the ranks of the class they emulate and envy.[2] It is, similarly, the institutions and their functionaries that Grosz attacks in his autobiographical essay "Summing Up":

Today I no longer hate people indiscriminately; today I hate their bad institutions and the people in power

who defend these institutions. And if I have any hope at all, it is this: that these institutions and that this class of people that protect them may disappear. It is to this hope that my work is dedicated. Millions of people share this hope with me, and they are not the art professors, not the art patrons, not the ones who buy art. Whether or not my work should therefore be called art is dependent on the question of whether or not one believes that the future belongs to the working class.[3]

S. L. D. / R. H.

1. The watercolor has previously been dated c. 1923, by Eberhard Roters, for instance, in Roters and Bernhard Schulz, eds., *Ich und die Stadt: Mensch und Grossstadt in der deutschen Kunst des 20. Jahrhunderts* (West Berlin: Nicolaische Verlagsbuchhandlung, 1987), 198. Careful comparison with other works by Grosz of the mid-1920s suggests, however, that *Street Scene, Berlin* is closer stylistically to works of 1924–25, prior to the artist's trip to Paris.
2. It is useful to recall here Siegfried Kracauer's observations, originally published in 1930, concerning Germany's white-collar workers: "The widespread addiction in bourgeois Germany to distinguishing oneself from the masses through some sort of ranking or status, even if it is only imagined, makes a collective identity difficult even among the employed themselves" ("Die im bürgerlichen Deutschland ausgeprägte Sucht, sich durch irgendeinen Rang von der Menge abzuheben, auch wenn er nur eingebildet ist, erschwert den Zusammenhalt unter den Angestellten selber"). Kracauer, "Die Angestellten: Aus dem neuesten Deutschland," in *Schriften*, vol. 1 (Frankfurt a. M.: Suhrkamp, 1971), 275.
3. "Heute hasse ich die Menschen nicht mehr wahllos, heute hasse ich ihre schlechten Institutionen und die Machthaber, die diese Institutionen verteidigen. Und wenn ich eine Hoffnung habe, so ist es die, dass diese Institutionen und dass die Menschenklasse, die sie schützt, verschwinden. Dieser Hoffnung dient meine Arbeit. Mit mir teilen Millionen Menschen diese Hoffnung, es sind dies nicht Kunstsachverständige, nicht Mäcene, nicht Kaufkräftige. Ob man daher meine Arbeit Kunst nennt, ist abhängig von der Frage, ob man glaubt, dass die Zukunft der arbeitenden Klasse gehört." George Grosz, "Abwicklung," *Das Kunstblatt* 8, no. 2 (February 1924): 38. This statement was previously associated with the watercolor under discussion by Eberhard Roters, in Roters and Schulz, *Ich und die Stadt*, 198. Roters's conclusion, however —that Grosz shows understanding and compassion for the ordinary person here and recognizes that he is one of them himself—diverges from our interpretation of the work.

54 George Grosz
Sidewalk Café (Strassencafé), c. 1923–24

Brush and ink on paper
50 x 39.2 cm (19¹¹/₁₆ x 15⁷/₁₆ in.)
Stamped l. l. "Grosz"; estate stamp verso

Provenance: Estate of the artist, Princeton, N. J.; Aaron Berman Gallery, New York.

George Grosz divides this scene diagonally into two parts by means of the low wall separating a sidewalk from an outdoor café. On the upper side of the diagonal, a man in a smoking jacket sits at a cloth-covered table, smokes a cigarette, and drunkenly grasps a champagne glass and bottle in his hands. This image of decadent indulgence is contrasted to what appears on the other side of the wall: the supine form of a barefoot man, his face skull-like and his body cramped from spasms of hunger, either dying of starvation or already dead. Another gaunt figure turns to confront the viewer at the bottom of the scene; only his head is visible, with a face drawn and thin, and eyes that gaze accusingly but without focus.

Separated by the diagonal are two antagonistic worlds, one of ostentatious consumption, the other of public deprivation. Grosz accents this confrontation stylistically as well as iconographically, representing the realm of the drinker with firm, consistent, precise lines, and the other with jagged, irregular, brushed forms. Elegance and squalor are thus echoed and reasserted in the means of their rendition as disjunctive, discordant realities incapable of merging, one set off against the other.

Such juxtapositions of plenty and drastic deprivation are a standard *topos* in Grosz's work, with a particular concentration from 1923 to 1925 in his published collections of drawings *The Day of Reckoning Will Come!* and *The Mirror of the Bourgeoisie*.[1] The intrusion of poverty into the context of abundance, of the starving poor into the feasts of the rich, is a persistent motif among artists of the 1920s, a contemporary reconfiguration of the biblical parable of the rich man who lives in splendor while the beggar Lazarus lies dying at the manor gates, yearning for scraps from the rich man's table.[2] Lazarus is rewarded for his misery by the joys of heaven after death, while the rich man suffers in eternal fire and receives no compassion, just as he gave none in life.

Lazarus's counterparts in the 1920s receive no such compensation, however; their deaths only constitute one aspect of their suffering. "It's true," Grosz wrote in his introduction to *The Mirror of the Bourgeoisie*, "life would be without meaning and purpose were it not for this one goal: the struggle against the stupidity and arbitrary brutality of today's possessors of power."[3] The class struggle alone would bring salvation in dialectical opposition to the existing capitalist order. The insider/outsider juxtaposition of Grosz's drawing would find no resolution, only a violent overthrow and reversal of its order.

S. L. D. / R. H.

1. *Abrechnung folgt! 57 politische Zeichnungen*, Kleine revolutionäre Bibliothek (Berlin: Malik Verlag, 1923; reprint, Frankfurt a. M.: Makol Verlag, 1972); *Der Spiesser-Spiegel: 60 Berliner Bilder nach Zeichnungen mit einer Selbstdarstellung des Künstlers* (Dresden: Carl Reissner Verlag, 1925; reprint, New York: Arno Press, 1966). Also compare the watercolor *Insider and Outsider* (1925), collection Carlo Ponti, Rome, illus. in Hans Hess, *George Grosz* (London and New Haven: Yale University Press, 1984), 142, where, however, it is incorrectly dated to 1926.

2. Luke 16: 19–21.
3. ". . . das Leben wäre sinnlos und zwecklos, wenn es nicht den einen Sinn hätte, den Kampf gegen die Dummheit und willkürliche Brutalität der heutigen Machthaber." Grosz, *Spiesser-Spiegel*, 12.

55 George Grosz
Seated Woman (Sitzende), 1923

Brush and ink on paper
63 x 46 cm (24³/₄ x 18¹/₈ in.)
Stamped l. l. "21 Feb 23"; verso: *Pensioners (Pensionäre)*, c. 1923, brush and ink

Provenance: Marlborough Fine Arts Ltd., London.

During 1923 and 1924, George Grosz produced numerous studies after the woman depicted in this drawing. With her broad features, stocky body, plain clothing, and characteristic hat, she became for him a surprisingly sympathetic image of the German middle-class woman. Seated as in this drawing, she served as prototype for an untitled illustration accompanying an article on the Wertheim Department Store in the January 1928 issue of *Der Querschnitt* (*The Cross Section*), the periodical whose liberal political and aesthetic policies represented the attitudes of the enlightened middle-class intelligentsia.[1] The image later became known as *In the Waiting Room*, but this title apparently did not originate with the artist.[2]

The drawing of the monumental seated bourgeoise captures an idea and pose which Grosz could manipulate and apply in further works based on this study of a model. A similar process is revealed by the drawing on the verso of this image, which represents two aged pensioners. Wearing a military coat with epaulets and sporting a moustache much like that of Field Marshal von Hindenburg, the standing man clearly is a retired army officer. The other man, his coat, tie, and pince-nez functioning like the uniform of a successful businessman, relaxes while he smokes a cigar. Grosz injected the two figures, separate or together, into other compositions. The retired officer, for example, stands little altered with his haughty hands-in-pockets pose on the steps of a grandiose manor house, presumably spoils of his service to the fatherland, in *The Mirror of the Bourgeoisie*.[3]

The drawings on either side of this sheet thus provide a remarkable insight into Grosz's working habits. Such figure studies comprised a vast dictionary of images which the artist consulted as he worked out his compositions. Self-quotation permitted or confirmed Grosz's reduction of the complexities of human society and physiognomy to a system of limited types. The drawings serve as individual specimens for a systematic visual analysis and categorization of the Weimar populace. Meanings and contexts are altered and shifted to apply to the social commentary Grosz intended according to predetermined conclusions.

S. L. D.

1. Frank Gettings, *George Grosz* (Washington, D. C.: Smithsonian Institution Press, 1978), 24, cat. no. 15.
2. *Im Wartezimmer*, illus. in Galerie Meta Nierendorf, *Ohne Hemmung* (West Berlin: Galerie Meta Nierendorf, 1963), fig. 105.
3. George Grosz, *Der Spiesser-Spiegel: 60 Berliner Bilder nach Zeichnungen mit einer Selbstdarstellung des Künstlers* (Dresden: Carl Reissner, Verlag, 1925; reprint, New York: Arno Press, 1966), pl. 21.

---

56 George Grosz
Street Scene (Strassenszene),
c. 1923

Pen and ink on paper
22.1 x 17.2 cm (8¹¹/₁₆ x 6¾ in.)
Signed l. r. "Grosz"

Provenance: Galerie Wending, Amsterdam.

In accordance with George Grosz's conviction that art should become a weapon in the class struggle, *Street Scene* represents an effort once again to critique the establishments of society. The well-dressed man who saunters down a city street in this drawing is identified as middle-class by specific attributes: the handkerchief in his suit pocket, celluloid collar, walking cane, monocle, and feathered hat. Grosz frequently reused figures from his drawings, injecting them into varied contexts as required, and this man appears also in the collected drawings of *The Mirror of the Bourgeoisie*, published in 1925.[1] His appearance there is slightly modified; walking with obvious self-satisfaction next to a chubby woman, presumably his wife, he sports an Iron Cross on his coat, a swastika on his lapel, and a Hitler-like moustache—indications of his former military service as well as his present reactionary political attitudes.

The woman in *Street Scene* is not identical with the one in the published drawing, nor is her connection to the man as straightforward. Here, she stands at the edge of the sidewalk and looks towards the passing fop with a wide grin and a broad wink. Well-fed and fashionably dressed, she appears also to be the model in a large drawing of 1923 (cat. no. 55) and a central figure in another drawing, published in the collection *Love above All* in 1930, where she wears a cloche hat and the identical fur-trimmed coat.[2] *Street Scene* lacks the narrative clarity of Grosz's published drawings and paintings of the time, which suggests it might be considered a study. In it, Grosz experiments with the components of a situation, using middle-class figure types according to the categories of his illustrations, but the result is more one of ambiguity than trenchant critique. The woman's wink might be a mocking response to the aged dandy as he walks past, an obvious parody of the amorous attention he seems to wish to attract. Her aggressiveness, on the other hand, in conjunction with the man's more passive role, is characteristic of encounters between prostitutes and potential customers in other Grosz drawings. By her expansive figure and middle-class clothing, however, she might be recognized as a less-than-respectful *Hausfrau* or office worker, perhaps also less than respectable and in futile search of supplemental income in Grosz's misanthropic world. A clear reading of her relationship to the monocled ex-military man cannot be attained. The drawing defies resolution, projecting contradictory significations, and is thus unusable in the context of visual weaponry in the class struggle, although its components could be, and indeed were, recycled in other images as appropriate ammunition against "the compact majority—brutal mass stupidity."[3]   S. L. D./R. H.

1. George Grosz, *Der Spiesser-Spiegel: 60 Berliner Bilder nach Zeichnungen mit einer Selbstdarstellung des Künstlers*, (Dresden: Carl Reissner Verlag, 1925; reprint, New York: Arno Press, 1966), pl. 11.
2. *Nach Geschäftsschluss (At the End of the Business Day)*, in George Grosz, *Über alles die Liebe: 60 neue Zeichnungen* (Berlin: Bruno Cassirer Verlag, 1930; reprint, New York: Dover Publications, 1971), pl. 105. The moustached, monocled man of the Fishman Collection drawing becomes a haughty military officer arriving at a reception or party in *Es ist erreicht (Goal Attained)*, pl. 75.
3. "Die kompakte Majorität—brutale Massendummheit." Ibid., 11.

---

57 George Grosz
Funeral (Begräbnis), c. 1927

Pen, brush and ink on paper
48.3 x 63.3 cm (19 x 24⅞ in.),
sight
Not signed; verso: unfinished ink drawing of two figures

Provenance: Galerie Paul Cassirer, Berlin; private collection; Galerie Meta Nierendorf, Berlin; Galerie Wolfgang Ketterer, Munich.

Exhibitions: West Berlin, Galerie Meta Nierendorf, 1962–63; University Art Museum, University of Minnesota, Minneapolis, *Berlin: Art and Metropolis*, September–October 1987.

With an eye for anecdote, George Grosz renders a funeral cortege with mourners following beneath black umbrellas, a pedestrian doffing his hat in respect, and a young woman, taking no notice, protecting her fashionable clothing under a dainty umbrella. With minimal means, leaving most of the paper blank, Grosz displays his mastery of ink drawing. Black ink applied heavily in broad areas lends an almost coloristic quality to the image, a sense of texture and volume, notably in the funeral procession; this effect is countered by the thin lines that describe the passersby and urban surroundings, with a few, slightly curved accents sufficing to indicate three-dimensional presence. The cortege spreads frieze-like across the paper, providing focus for a scene that exists in quietly balanced equilibrium.

Funeral contrasts significantly to Grosz's earlier city scenes, with their heightened agitation and figures overlapping and cutting into one another like two-dimensional graffiti. Absent, too, is the sharp cynicism of works such as the 1915 funeral scene, *Grin and Bear It! (Aushalten!)*, published in the proto-Dada, pacifist periodical *Neue Jugend (New Youth)* in 1916.[1] In that image, a sharp critique of German wartime society, Grosz depicted a funeral carriage followed by goose-stepping mourners in the background. The foreground is dominated by a prostitute, a man in a top hat with a child's coffin under his arm, and several other passersby, none of them paying the least attention to the cortege. A product of Grosz's hatred of World War I, *Grin and Bear It!* bitterly parodies one of imperial Germany's best-known slogans exhorting citizens to suffer the deprivations of war for the sake of the fatherland, promising the spoils of victory in recompense. Grosz's drawing shows none of this patriotic selflessness, however, and, instead, presents a society in which isolated individuals, suspicious of one another, are hardened against death, ignoring its presence as they proceed with their mundane, increasingly impoverished lives.

Funeral demonstrates a different style and tone. The vulgar, angular, gesticulating figures in Grosz's works of the teens and early twenties have been supplanted by precise, if simplified, representations of contemporary fashion—the slender, "athletic" female figure, and the man in suit and hat, both comfortably tailored. The drawing is more a descriptive record than a political critique. No longer do disconnected ink scratches caricature figures and forms representative of social classes; instead, gently drawn lines curve into fundamentally naturalistic renditions of frequently encountered types of individuals.

Grosz's tone became less vitriolic for several reasons after 1925. A trip to the Soviet Union during the summer of 1922 left him disillusioned with the Marxist system—or so he recalled after World War II, attempting to counter accusations that he was a Communist sympathizer. His continuing contributions, even after 1922, to KPD-sponsored publications, such as the satirical *Der Knüppel (The Cudgel)*, clearly put in question the extent of his purported disillusionment, or perhaps indicate that he still embraced the principles of Marxism while rejecting their Russian application. It is possible that, when Grosz expanded his gallery contracts to include the venerable dealer Alfred Flechtheim, he acted in response to a KPD-initiated tactic of infiltration, bringing his critical work into one of the very galleries that dealt with the most investment-worthy contemporary art.[2] Through Flechtheim, Grosz also began to provide drawings for the liberal periodical *Der Querschnitt (The Cross Section)*, which, unlike the contemporaneous *Der Knüppel*, did not tolerate an uninterrupted series of socially critical images.

Whether shifts in Grosz's political convictions or the demands of his increasingly appreciative audience, or both, were responsible for his altered style and content, he first applied them consistently in drawings he created during a stay in France in the winter of 1924/25.[3] His caustic vision was made yet more benign by a second French trip in 1927, to Provence. It is likely that *Funeral*, in which the open-style hearse is a French rather than German type, resulted from this second trip and that it was then included in 1929 in Grosz's first exhibition of drawings at the renowned Galerie Bruno Cassirer in Berlin.[4] Ironically, just a few years previously, in the pamphlet *Art Is in Danger*, Grosz had singled out the Galerie Cassirer to demonstrate the plight of modern artists:

> Should the purpose of our striving be to be admired in galleries? To imagine that Grünewald would have exhibited his Isenheim Altarpiece at Cassirer's throws a harsh spotlight on the problematic position of the artist in today's society. He's caught in a dead end: deprived materially, he is usually possessed by an idealism, a unique fascination with the future, with eternity.[5]

It is possible, however, to reconcile the apparent contradiction between Grosz's pronounced antagonism to the bourgeois art world and his ostensibly enthusiastic embracing of its venues. In light of the 1924 founding manifesto of the Communist artists' Red Group, the presence of Grosz's art in the luxuriously appointed gallery could serve as a kind of camouflage through which politically and socially engaged drawings could deliver their messages with less resistance. The politeness of *Funeral* in 1927 was a strategic pose.   S. L. D.

1. Illus. in Hans Hess, *George Grosz* (New Haven and London: Yale University Press, 1985), 51, no. 37.
2. See n. 1, cat. no. 49.
3. In accounting for this shift in Grosz's work, the example of a more gentle but nonetheless critical socialist art produced by Frans Masereel, with whom Grosz spent much time while in Paris, should not be ignored.
4. It appears probable that the inscription at the lower left of the drawing, "No. 132 Cassirer," relates to this exhibition.
5. "Sollte dies der Zweck unseres Strebens sein, in Galerien bewundert zu werden? Die Vorstellung, Grünewald hätte seinen Isenheimer Altar bei Cassirer ausgestellt, beleuchtet krass die problematische Stellung des Künstlers in der heutigen Gesellschaft. Eine Sackgasse: Materiell gequält, ist er meist von einem Idealismus, einer eigenartigen Begeisterung besessen für die Zukunft, für die Ewigkeit." George Grosz, in Grosz and Wieland Herzfelde, *Die Kunst ist in Gefahr* (Berlin: Malik Verlag, 1925), as reprinted in *Manifeste Manifeste 1905–1933*, vol. 1 of *Schriften deutscher Künstler des zwanzigsten Jahrhunderts*, ed. Diether Schmidt (Dresden: VEB Verlag der Kunst, n. d.), 346.

---

58 John Heartfield (?)
Family (Sunday Walk) (Familie [Sonntags-Spaziergang]),
c. 1919–21

Watercolor, collage, pen and ink over pencil on paper
28 x 21.3 cm (11 x 8⅜ in.)
Not signed

Provenance: Andrew Sinclair Collection, London; Piccadilly Gallery, London; private collection, Palm Beach, Fla.

Exhibitions: Milwaukee, UWM Art Museum, University of Wisconsin, *Reactions to the War: European Art, 1914–1925*, 2 November–14 December 1986, cat. no. 22; Atlanta, High Museum of Art, *Art in Berlin 1815–1989*, 14 November 1989–14 January 1990, cat. no. 49 (as George Grosz, *Sunday Family Walk*, c. 1923).

Previously attributed to George Grosz, this unsigned watercolor derives from the time of Grosz's collaboration with John Heartfield while both participated in Berlin's Dada activities. Working together as the collective Dada-monteur Grosz-Heartfield, they produced "meta-mechanical constructions" that fused elements of drawing, watercolor, and collaged newspaper photographs into didactic or tendentious compositions proclaiming Dada's rejection of Expressionist individualism in favor of a radical, world revolutionary, collective humanity. Rather than maintain the glorification of a single artist and artist's hand, they formed their depersonalized Dada entity, an extraordinarily inventive partnership of cynical humor, anti-bourgeois criticism, and material experimentation.

The process of pictorial manufacture in these meta-mechanical constructions, first exhibited during the summer of 1920 at Berlin's *International Dada Fair* in the Kunsthandlung Dr. Otto Burchard, was twofold and demanded interaction. Either Heartfield or Grosz would seek out photographs or postcards that could serve as initiating components of the image; the other was then entrusted with augmenting these found elements with drawing and color. Most surviving works have been attributed predominantly to Grosz; even when Heartfield is known to have participated in their production, he has been accorded the lesser role except in studies devoted to his work.[1] The attribution of the current work to Grosz alone therefore is not surprising, but it collapses under careful analysis.

Comparison of the figures and their drawing style to documented works by Grosz from 1919 to 1925 demonstrates significant divergence from his habits of drawing. Although related to Grosz's bourgeois types, the figures do not correspond precisely to any others in his work, a fact in itself remarkable given his practice of reusing established figures repeatedly in various drawings (see, for example, cat. nos. 48, 54, and 55). There is a concern with details—dramatically hooked noses, folds and wrinkles in the face, the individualized eyebrows—that is uncharacteristic of Grosz. The lines themselves are more carefully, uniformly, even fussily drawn than in Grosz's works, where lines are typically broken, interrupted, varied, and jagged. Similarly, the plotting out of the drawing with penciled indications, over which ink and watercolor are applied, is virtually unknown in Grosz's mature work, and implies a mentality such as Heartfield's—more accustomed by this time to creating page layouts than to rapid, frequent, and persistent sketching of innumerable scenes, rendered directly with ink on paper, without the mediation of preliminary pencil drawings.[2]

If Grosz is not responsible for the drawing in *Family (Sunday Walk)*, he may, however, have selected the collage elements. He employed similar perspectival scenes in meta-mechanical constructions, such as *"Daum" Marries Her Pedantic Automaton "George"*....[3] Heartfield's collages around 1920, on the other hand, focus on lettering and pictures of such objects as signage, telephone horns, automobile wheels, ball bearings, or watches, all motifs lacking from this image.[4] When it is noted that the watercolor technique with its spotty modulations is also unlike that of Grosz, the conclusion that this construction is largely by Heartfield becomes yet more inescapable.

The family on a Sunday outing, walking together through the countryside and enjoying nature, was a subject repeatedly considered by German Dada and *Neue Sachlichkeit* artists such as Dix or Grosz (see cat. nos. 28 and 48). Heartfield's family, however, walks a city street beneath a threatening sky, past freight trains, high-rise apartment blocks, and a public urinal plastered with overlapping posters. The signs of natural growth that do appear—three scrawny trees—are stunted, bereft of life, and alien to their surroundings. Walking wet pavements, watched by idle workers from a nearby sidewalk, this urban family inhabits a deprived environment. Their class identity, however, is difficult to determine, as is the purpose of this walk, which is surely not the Sunday stroll as which it has been customarily identified.

The parents with their gaunt, drawn faces and rumpled clothing are accompanied by their daughter, who wears a fur-collared coat, beribboned hat, and high button shoes, and carries a book under her right arm. With open mouth and closed eyes, she may be crying, and the pale, resigned look of her mother represents a significantly different response from the ruddy, grimacing grin of the father. Given their clothing, the family may be middle-class, while the run-down industrial neighborhood in which they find themselves may refine this identification to petty bourgeois or to a family proletarianized in the economic turmoil of the postwar years. But where this family is going and to what end is not clear. The girl's book or notebook would appear to be an iconographic clue whose precise meaning remains unknown, leaving this family walk among the depressing environment of the city a mysterious affair.[5]

R. H.

1. See, for example, attributions of the cover design for the program for Walter Mehring's puppet play, *Einfach Klassisch*, performed at the Berlin cabaret *Schall und Rauch*: the artist is identified as Heartfield/Grosz by Roland März in *John Heartfield: Der Schnitt entlang der Zeit—Selbstzeugnisse, Erinnerungen, Interpretationen* (Dresden: VEB Verlag der Kunst, 1981), 56, and as Grosz-Heartfield by Hans Hess in *George Grosz* (New Haven and London: Yale University Press, 1985), 106, pl. 92. In this work, where previously existing watercolor-and-ink renderings were cut out and recombined in a new format for the cover design, there is a noticeable inconsistency of drawing style that suggests both artists made roughly equal contributions.
2. Because Heartfield's drawings are little known, these conclusions must remain somewhat tentative. Virtually ignored due to the impact of his photomontages, few of the drawings have been published, but see the examples reproduced by März, *John Heartfield*, 153 and 249.
3. Galerie Nierendorf, West Berlin. Illus. in Hess, *George Grosz*, 103.
4. Heartfield's inventory of collage elements approximates Raoul Hausmann's more than Grosz's and in attitude forms a prelude to his later photomontages with their revised images of photographed reality. See the collage elements in *Leben und Treiben in Universal City 12 Uhr 5 Mittags (Life and Livelihood in Universal City at 12:05 in the Afternoon)* of 1919, illus. in März, *John Heartfield*, 52.
5. In a letter to me, dated 6 June 1990, George Grosz's son, Peter M. Grosz, gives as his opinion that neither Grosz nor Heartfield was involved in any way in the creation of *Family (Sunday Walk)*. While I agree that the drawing is clearly not by Grosz, for reasons outlined in this entry and after re-examining Heartfield drawings of 1919–20, I continue to consider as correct the attribution to Heartfield and to regard as feasible the conjecture that Grosz may have been responsible for aspects of the collage, given the two artists' working habits at the time.

59 Erich Heckel

Dangast Village Landscape with Canal (Dangaster Dorflandschaft mit Kanal), 1909

Oil on canvas
69.7 x 80 cm (27 7/16 x 31 1/2 in.)
Monogramed and dated l. l. "EH 09"
Vogt 1909–9 (as *Dorfstrasse [Village Street]*)

Provenance: Private collection, U.S.A.

Exhibition: Milwaukee Art Museum, *Hidden Treasures: Wisconsin Collects Paintings and Sculptures*, 11 September–1 November 1987.

Following the example of Max Pechstein, Erich Heckel spent the spring of 1909 in Italy, visiting Rome, Florence, Ravenna, and Fiesole. He returned to Dresden in time to help hang the exhibition, at the Galerie Emil Richter in June, of the artists' group *Brücke* (Bridge), among whose founding members he had been in 1905. That summer, he joined Ernst Ludwig Kirchner and Doris "Dodo" Grosse at the Moritzburg Lakes, then, in September, met Karl Schmidt-Rottluff and Rosa Schapire at Dangast, a small fishing village on the marshy lands of the Jadebusen inlet of the North Sea. Heckel spent several summers with Schmidt-Rottluff in Dangast; according to Gustav Schiefler, the Hamburg jurist who was among *Brücke*'s early and most supportive patrons, "there [Heckel] discovered a feeling for the expansiveness of space and the corporeality of the sky; the sea and its atmosphere communicated both these to him.... Objects submitted to the totality of the surroundings to such a degree that space, air, and light appear as the actual carriers of the sensation."[1]

Painted on coarse canvas covered by a white slip, parts of whose surface are left bare amid the actively brushed oil paint, this fall landscape derives from Heckel's time of interaction with Schmidt-Rottluff. With its dramatically rich and immediate contrasts of blue, red, yellow, and green, the painting depicts one of the innumerable drainage canals that cut through the meadows and moors of the Oldenburg area.[2] The golden-walled houses of Dangast block the horizon of the flat North Sea landscape.[3] Produced during the most intense and inventive period of the *Brücke* artists' cooperative approach to their work, Heckel's painting shares its vocabulary with contemporary works by the other members of the group while simultaneously pronouncing individual variations upon it that prefigure what Kirchner and Schmidt-Rottluff would adopt a few months later in 1910.

After viewing Etruscan tomb paintings and other Etruscan works at the Villa Giulia in Rome, Heckel opted for an increasing simplification of his imagery and compositional order. Vincent van Gogh's Auvers landscapes remain apparent as prototypes, as do the Divisionist brushstrokes of modified Neo-Impressionism and the color orchestrations of Fauvism, but the rhythm of actively applied marks and of vitalized subdivisions are less significant in this work than in the paintings of 1907 and 1908. Here, Heckel treats color in terms of large, interlocking planes that intersect with the flamboyant linear webs of black outlines and dark, silhouetted tree branches.

Spatial drama is introduced by means of a compositional formula he frequently employed, a central, cutting diagonal which here, in the shape of the deep blue canal, provides a dominating sense of perspectival depth in the midst of the network of other landscape components. With its directionally oriented brushstrokes, and with its paler blues interspersed with patches of white priming and threatened by streaks of darkness, the sky further enlivens the painting's spatial reading: it counters the canal's striving for distance with a determined dislocation forward, an expansiveness that appears to surround houses and trees and evolve generously towards the imagined picture plane, or even to spill into the space beyond the limits of the image.

With its broad, intensely colored planes fused with a vocabulary of active brushstrokes that suggest subjective immediacy, Heckel's *Dangast Village Landscape with Canal* contains the components of *Brücke's* mature style, lacking only the sharp angularity of forms that would be adopted by the group in 1910. Within an illusion of generative spontaneity and unreserved impulsiveness, the image is precisely constructed and controlled in its effect. Ludwig Justi, then Director of the Berlin National Gallery, where he built up the finest German museum collection of Expressionist art, recognized this dialectic of spontaneity and construction in 1921 when he replied to accusations that Heckel's works involved the "annihilation of form":

...for the truly artistic masters among our youth—and only they are of account—the opposite is the case: in their works, pictorial form is more powerful and firmer than it was for decades before them. As in older art, it is once again the essential goal of their work. A piece of reality is not arbitrarily excised and transferred onto the canvas, but rather form is constructed from an inner process of observation....

Nature is not viewed soberly and objectively as a model for masterly brushwork; it is not studied carefully in its color and light values in order to be directly rendered, but rather the artist... senses the life of nature behind external appearance—just as a hundred years earlier Caspar [David] Friedrich did—and he recognizes the mysterious being behind the external appearance of things which alone makes them truly valuable to him.... The pictorial form and structure of which we spoke, the scaffolding of planes and lines, of colors and light values: these are the external manifestations of inner vitality.[4]

Justi posits the artist as visionary perceiver of nature's inner essences, its realm of abstract ordering principles, and recognizes in the cohesive structure of the painting a pictorial equivalent to nature's hidden order. Rather than emulating the external surface of landscape, however, Heckel constructs, according to Justi, an intuited surrogate or structural scaffolding and a means of measure within the painted image. Following this argument, the simultaneity or dialectical cohesion of stabilizing construction and subjective empathy then constitute the vitality of Heckel's landscapes.

Shortly before Justi, in another testimony deriving from the circle of patrons closely identified with Heckel, Schiefler summarized the effect by means of a musical analogy that juxtaposed passages of minor and major keys: "...the power of these contrasts is tamed by means of his feeling for measure—here his sense of spatial organization. The antagonisms are neutralized and sound forth together in sustained, great and gentle chords."[5] *Dangast Landscape with Canal* provides one of the first truly major manifestations of this dialectical construct in Heckel's mature work. Of the landscapes painted in the company of Schmidt-Rottluff in 1909, it is among the most exemplary, guiding Schmidt-Rottluff and Kirchner towards their own more structurally revealing landscapes of 1910.[6]   R. H.

1. "Dort fand er das Gefühl für die Weite des Raumes und die Körperlichkeit der Luft; das Meer und seine Atmosphäre haben ihm beides vermittelt.... Gegenstände ordnen sich dem Ganzen der Umgebung so ein, dass Raum, Luft und Licht als die eigentlichen Träger des Eindrucks erscheinen." Gustav Schiefler, "Erich Heckels graphisches Werk," *Das Kunstblatt* 2, no. 9 (1918): 286.
2. Paul Vogt, *Erich Heckel: Monographie mit Werkverzeichnis* (Recklinghausen: Verlag Aurel Bongers, 1965), no. 1909-9, identifies the painting as *Dorfstrasse* (*Village Street*), not as a canal scene. Since Vogt knew the work solely from black-

and-white photographs, he must have read the variegated deep blue of the canal waters as representing a path. The identity of this diagonal area as a canal is certain, however. In Heckel's works, there are no examples of dirt roads appearing deep blue as in this painting; consistently, they are rendered instead in browns (tending towards burnt umber), oranges, or reds as expressive intensifications of local color. Nor would a North German road have the wide berm with bushes such as line the embankments of the canal in this painting. The title in Vogt's catalogue is therefore incorrect; a title inventorying the painting's contents more appropriately has been substituted here.
3. Compare the identical color scheme in *Windmill Near Dangast* (*Windmühle bei Dangast*) (Vogt 1909-29), Wilhelm Lehmbruck Museum, Duisburg, which also appears to make use of the same type of canvas.
4. "...Zertrümmerung der Form.... bei den wahrhaft künstlerischen Meistern unserer Jugend—und auf sie allein kommt es an—ist das Gegenteil der Fall: bei ihnen ist die Bildform kräftiger und fester, als wie es in Jahrzehnten vorher gewesen war, ist wieder, wie in alter Kunst, das eine wesentliche Ziel des Schaffens: es wird nicht ein Stück Wirklichkeit ausgeschnitten und auf die Leinwand übertragen, sondern es wird aus innerer Anschauung eine Form gebaut....
"Die Natur ist nicht sachlich-nüchtern betrachtet, als Vorbild für ein meisterliches Pinselgewirk, genau in Farbwert und Lichtwert gesehen und übertragen, sondern der Künstler, stark und zugleich zartempfindend, fühlt das Leben in der Natur—wie hundert Jahre früher Caspar Friedrich, ahnt ein geheimnisvolles Sein hinter der äusseren Erscheinung der Dinge, das sie ihm erst wahrhaft wertvoll macht.... Die Bildform, von der wir sprachen, das Gefüge von Flächen und Linien, Farben und Helligkeit, ist die Aussenseite der inneren Lebendigkeit." Ludwig Justi, "Naturwiedergabe und eigenes Bildgesetz," *Deutsche Allgemeine Zeitung*, 7 August 1921, reprinted in Zdenek Felix, ed., *Erich Heckel 1883–1970: Gemälde, Aquarelle, Zeichnungen und Graphik* (Munich: Prestel Verlag, 1983), 223–224.
5. "...die Macht der Gegensätze wird durch das Gefühl für das Mass—hier das Raumgefühl—gebändigt; die Widersprüche gleichen sich aus und klingen in gehaltenen, grossen und weichen Akkorden zusammen." Schiefler, "Erich Heckels graphisches Werk," 292.
6. Compare, for example, this work with Schmidt-Rottluff's *Village Path in Dangast* (*Dorfstrasse in Dangast*), c. 1910, Lothar-Günter Buchheim Collection, illus. in Elvehjem Museum of Art, *Expressionism: The Buchheim Collection* (Feldafing: Buchheim Verlag, 1983), cat. no. 248, where a similar combination of radical perspective effects and interlocking planes with active brushwork is employed.

60   Erich Heckel
Men at a Table (Männer an einem Tisch), 1913

Watercolor, gouache, brush and ink on paper
20.7 x 39.3 cm (8 1/8 x 15 1/2 in.)
Signed and dated l. r. "E. Heckel/ 13"

Provenance: Henry Schlesinger Estate, Berkeley, Calif.; Sotheby-Parke Bernet, Los Angeles.

Exhibitions: University Art Museum, University of Minnesota, Minneapolis, *Berlin: Art and Metropolis—Works on Paper 1912–1932*, 8 September–11 October 1987.

In 1912, Erich Heckel painted *Two Men at a Table*, a work Gustav Schiefler identified as "following Dostoevsky-like thought patterns."[1] During the next year, the artist returned several times in drawings and woodcuts to this motif of the table, the interior, and two antagonistic men confronting each other beneath a variant of Hans Holbein the Younger's *Dead Christ*.[2] Judging from the persistent repetition and variation, Heckel must have placed particular value on the image, or, as Schiefler indicates, perhaps was dissatisfied with the solutions he found in his effort "...to grant visible form to a psychological content."[3]
The series of variations is continued in this representation of three men drinking and conversing at a round table. With their blue clothing and visored caps, they appear to be workers or fishermen, either in Hamburg or the Baltic Sea village of Osterholz, which Heckel visited for the first time during the summer of 1913. From the left, another man holds a glass as he walks to join them, and a fifth man is seated at a table in the background, drinking alone, his head propped in one hand as he holds a pipe with the other. The gray-green atmosphere of the interior and the heavy, dark scaffolding of black outlines and interlocking pieces of furniture overpower the content of the scene, and, in combination with the extended horizontal format, lend it a melancholic or depressive mood as the individuals at the round table are placed in confrontation with each other.
It is difficult to discern why Heckel appeared so obsessed with this motif in 1912 and 1913, but its consistency in his imagery implies remarkable personal commitment. Schiefler's reference to Dostoevsky's *The Idiot* implies a psychological state of contemplation and despondency, and is worded to suggest that the mood was Heckel's rather than that of his images. If this is so, it must have been associated with the event of the time that had the greatest emotional as well as professional impact on Heckel, the dissolution of the artists' group *Brücke*, to whose collectivist principles he had been the most committed. The scene of the three silently conversing men, with another coming to join them and the remaining one isolated in the background, may be a direct reference to *Brücke*'s fate at this time, as Max Pechstein was expelled from the quartet of artists and Otto Mueller briefly joined before they decided to dissolve their union altogether. This biographical reading, however, while attractive, remains conjectural. The precise meaning of Heckel's "Dostoevskian" compositions—of which this is among the most complex and, in its careful working and reworking in different media, suggestive of a project for a painting never carried out—remains elusive.   R. H.

1. "Dostojewskischen Ideengängen folgend...." Gustav Schiefler, "Erich Heckels graphisches Werk," *Das Kunstblatt* (September 1918): 286.
2. For a consideration of the woodcut version of the image, see Reinhold Heller, *Brücke: German Expressionist Prints from the Granvil and Marcia Specks Collection* (Evanston, Ill.: Northwestern University, Mary and Leigh Block Gallery, 1988), 72–73.
3. "...einem seelischen Inhalt sichtbare Gestalt geben...." Schiefler, "Erich Heckels graphisches Werk," 287.

61   Hein Heckroth
Ada, c. 1924?

Watercolor on paper
39.7 x 32.2 cm (15 5/8 x 12 5/8 in.)
Signed u. c. "Heckroth"

Provenance: Collection Ada Heckroth, Frankfurt a. M.; Galerie Lempertz, Cologne.

Although the Hessian artist Hein Heckroth is best known for his stage and film-set designs, especially his drawings for the film *The Red Shoes* which won him an Oscar Award in 1949, he practiced painting throughout his career and exhibited regularly during the 1920s as well as after World War II. Works of the early twenties, such as this depiction of the artist Ada Meier, whom Heckroth married in 1924, reflect the Constructivist aspects of *Neue Sachlichkeit*. Not striving for a visual likeness, Heckroth here draws on the examples of George Grosz's automaton pictures and Carlo Carrà's Metaphysical Painting to create a surreal homage.[1] Realized in sharply defined forms which evoke a metallic patina, his yellow and red female mannequin has a pristine, mechanistic quality reinforced by the perfectly hemispherical breasts, cylindrical neck, and ovoid head. Without face or hands, and with only the essential and stereotypical aspects of the female form, Heckroth's image becomes the schema of a woman.
In contrast, the classicizing profile in the lower right corner is more lifelike and human. Although abstracted, facial features and wavy hair are clearly delineated. The two images offer views of a woman idealized, and neither can be taken as a verifiable likeness of Ada. In this strange, airless environment, Ada becomes an elusive symbol, impossible to decipher. Similarly, the space itself is illogical, deliberately disorienting. The big blue door in the background, for example, is too large for its frame. The bare interior suggests an attic, but curtains and an isolated wall element or screen on the left may indicate a stage set or the backstage area of a theater. With its exaggerated perspective and fragmented flooring, Heckroth's spatial organization is ambiguous; the mannequin inhabits the extreme foreground, on a plane with the profile face, but can also be read further back, in a vaguely defined middle ground. With its articulated shadows and static appearance, its lack of atmosphere or coherent spatial order, the scene achieves an unnatural effect, a disquieting mystery as its vari-

ous components confront each other directly but without explicable relationship.

These aspects, which treat the metaphysical and highlight the irrational elements of existence, appealed to German artists in the immediate aftermath of World War I. Offering an escape that is not idyllic, such a constructed and insistently unaccountable reality became a way of questioning the underlying assumptions of the order of a world which had been torn asunder by war and revolution. Using this common vocabulary, Heckroth's concept of Ada is simultaneously calm and tense in its composition as it suggests a disturbing new mechanized, overly mathematical order that defies rational comprehension.   C. D. G.

1. For examples of Grosz's automaton pictures of the early 1920s, see Hans Hess, *George Grosz* (New Haven and London: Yale University Press, 1985), 102–105.

62 Otto Herbig
The Tower (Der Turm), 1923

Oil on canvas
74.5 x 56 cm (29³/₈ x 22¹/₁₆ in.)
Signed and dated l. r. "Herbig 23"; signed and dated verso on original frame "Otto Herbig 1923"

Provenance: Galerie Ferdinand Möller, Berlin; Wilhelm Valentiner, Berlin and Detroit; Brigid Valentiner-Bertoia, Barto, Pa.; Olympia Gallery, Philadelphia.

Exhibition: Berlin, *Juriefreie Kunstschau*, 1924, cat. no. 513.

Otto Herbig is among the artists recently identified, with justification but questionable usefulness, as part of a group of "Expressive Realists" active in Germany between the wars but also continuing to work in the post-1945 era.[1] The attempt to associate Herbig with such a school indicates a desire for a more inclusive art history than that which is commonly practiced, and also demonstrates the resistance of Herbig's work to accepted stylistic categories or art movements. His training and formative artistic contacts account to some extent for this resistance. The late Impressionism of Lovis Corinth and the modified *Jugendstil* of Hans Olde and Albin Egger-Lienz contributed to his initial education, and laid the foundations for stylistic moderation, consciously modern but not innovative or radical.

More significant, however, was Herbig's proximity to Erich Heckel during their service in the German medical units stationed in Ostende during World War I. Heckel himself had undergone a dramatic stylistic shift, from the vibrant Expressionist colorism of his *Brücke* years to a more subdued palette and a more gently stylized, at times almost classicizing, form. Herbig adopted Heckel's altered Expressionist vocabulary, substituting, while still at Ostende, a more viscous paint application for Heckel's thinned pigments in scenes of sailors' bars and

military mental wards as well as landscapes. After the war, such works by Herbig and others who focused on their military experiences attracted immediate critical notice. Herbig's presence in the group of artists associated with Heckel gained him attention beyond the merits of his tentative efforts; his paintings were constantly compared with Heckel's, resulting in critical reservations to the effect that individuality remained elusive, "but a serious working process is constantly visible."[2]

Paul Westheim in 1923 was the first critic to announce the end of Herbig's apprenticeship to Heckel:

I have followed Herbig's development for the last four or five years. He presented the products of his beginnings with such stuttering uncertainty, as an admitted not-yet-being-able, that a large portion of goodwill was necessary just to concern oneself with such laborious efforts.... But now it seems to me that he has progressed far enough to warrant speaking of him. Recent exhibitions showed one or another painting by him that deserved our interest .... An intimate sense of compassion streams into his creation, granting it qualities of experience and vitality. Rigor and significance emerge from his humane compassion, which perhaps does not bring greatness but is necessarily sincere and true. Possibly, in order to do such expressions justice, we have to recognize that the human has its existential rights in art as much as does the super-human.[3]

There was consistent agreement among critics that what enabled Herbig to arrive at a point of independence was his altered subject matter, which established a position distinct from that of other artists of the time. The new paintings constituted a personal statement informed by compassion and tender intimacy in motifs of motherhood and of children; he began to focus on such themes in 1921, with images of his pregnant wife and, subsequently, of his son, Tyl.

The subject matter induced an altered formal vocabulary, as Herbig noted in a series of aphoristic observations on his work in 1934:

Characteristic of my work is its intense accentuation of content...the image is inspired by that which gives to my own human life a sense of significance and form.... It is wonderful to have a child around me in the studio. The continuous possibility of seeing and drawing is very important. In this persistent togetherness discoveries are made. But it is also true that only someone created to find is going to be able to do so.... The painter holds a child on his arms and sees the tender, white little head against the blue-silver of the spring sky; little hands reach out for the sickle of the moon. The sum of this expression, this color and form, must result in a tone in which we should be able to hear God.[4]

Herbig's ambition is to concentrate pictorially the emotive aura he assigns to his own responses to a child's presence and perception of the world. The attitudes of Expressionism, which tended

to present the child as the potential adult and particularly stressed a child's promise of sexual maturation, are rejected for one in which Herbig becomes a sympathetic but unintrusive observer who records affectionately the child's own world and its inherent reality.

In *The Tower*, Herbig's son, little more than two years old, is shown playing in his father's studio. The tonality of the painting is dark; dominant browns create a Rembrandt-like ambience within which the silver-gray building blocks and a diaphanous curtain shimmer subtly. A rug on the floor, a dark window, and a small painting propped against the wall complete the evening setting that father and son share. From the envelope of brown-black, the blond pale head of Tyl glows ethereally, attracting all attention to itself and to the task on which he focuses, the careful placement of a final cylindrical block onto his precariously balanced tower. Concentration, eye, hand, and tower alone constitute the reality of which the child is aware as all else dissolves into a realm of nearly indistinguishable shadows and undefined forms.

The seriousness of the child's world is presented, but from the fond and perhaps nostalgic view of the proud parent, who is uniquely capable of sharing Tyl's sense of accomplishment, his tense and joyous discovery of another skill mastered while the blocks sit shakily one on top of the other. What others judge ordinary and inconsequential, the child defines as magical and wondrous in Herbig's painting, at significant remove from the problems of proletarian deprivation and from the maudlin cuteness that dominates images of children by other artists of the 1920s. Produced within the enclosed, protected realm of the artist's own family and domestic life, *The Tower* is "...almost still life, half-dreamed," according to Paul Fechter, "from the surrounding and inner world of children, which remains accessible to [Herbig], and to which he grants a tender, lingering expression that never encroaches upon the child's realm with sentimentality."[5]   R. H.

1. In an effort to identify systematically artists who adopt neither the total subjectivity of Expressionism nor the pristine verism of *Neue Sachlichkeit*, Rainer Zimmermann coined the term "expressive realism" in *Die Kunst der verschollenen Generation: Deutsche Malerei des expressiven Realismus von 1925–1975* (Düsseldorf and Vienna: Econ Verlag, 1980). Like most attempts to distinguish stylistic groupings, Zimmerman's definition rests on subjective perceptions, especially as the spectrum between expressive and realist is a broad one, with criteria indicating at what point one becomes the other not identifiable beyond an "I-know-it-when-I-see-it" assertion. Because both book and concept spotlight a number of artists (many of whom are represented in the Fishman Collection) otherwise neglected in histories of German art, however, Zimmermann's study deserves special commendation.
2. "Doch ist ernstes Schaffen stets sichtbar." Willi Wolfradt, "Ausstellungen," *Das Kunstblatt* 6 (1922): 89.
3. "Seit vier oder fünf Jahren verfolge ich die Entwicklung von Herbig. Seine Anfängerschaft gab er so ganz als stammelnde Unsicherheit, als eingestandenes

Nochnichtvermögen, dass schon eine ganze Portion guter Wille dazu gehörte, überhaupt auf derlei Mühungen einzugehen.... Wenn man auf ihn einging, dann konnte es immer nur mit Vorbehalten geschehen. Auf den letzten Ausstellungen gab es das eine oder andere Bild von ihm, dass Interesse abnötigte.... Eine Innigkeit des Empfindens strömt in die Gestaltung ein, macht sie erlebt und durchblutet. Straffung und Bedeutung ergeben sich aus einer menschlichen Ergriffenheit heraus, die nicht unbedingt gross, aber unbedingt echt sein muss. Vielleicht müssen wir, um solchen Äusserungen gerecht werden zu können, zu der Erkenntnis gelangen, dass neben dem Übermenschlichen auch das Menschliche sein Daseinsrecht in der Kunst hat." Paul Westheim, "Atelierstreife II," *Das Kunstblatt* 7 (1923): 202–205.
4. "Charakteristisch für meine Arbeit ist die starke Betonung des Inhalts...[dass] die Gestaltung sich fast ausschliesslich entzündet an dem, was meinem menschlichen Leben Inhalt und Gestalt gibt.... Es ist schön das Kind im Atelier um sich zu haben. Die ständige Möglichkeit, zu sehen und zu zeichnen, ist sehr wichtig. In diesem dauernden Zusammensein werden die Funde gemacht. Freilich findet nur derjenige, der zum finden geschaffen ist.... [D]er Maler hält das Kind auf dem Arm, er sieht das zarte, weisse Köpfchen vor dem blausilbernen Frühlingshimmel; die Händchen greifen zur Sichel des Mondes. Die Summe dieses Ausdruckes, dieser Farbe und Form ergäbe einen Klang, durch den wir Gott hören müssten." Otto Herbig, "Aufzeichnungen aus dem Jahre 1934," in Galerie Döbele, *Otto Herbig 1889–1971* (Ravensburg: Galerie Döbele, 1980), 10.
5. "...halb geträumt[es] Stilleben aus der ihm immer noch zugänglichen Um- und Innenwelt der Kinder..., [mit einem] zärtlich schwebenden, aber niemals die Grenzen des kindlichen Kreises mit Sentimentalität verletzenden Ausdruck." Paul Fechter, in *Deutsche Allgemeine Zeitung*, 1941, cited ibid., 13.

63 Karl Jakob Hirsch
Martin Buber Mourning in a Jewish Cemetery (Der trauernde Martin Buber in einem jüdischen Friedhof), c. 1920

Watercolor over pencil on paper
35.5 x 28.5 cm (14 x 11¹/₄ in.)
Not signed

Provenance: Galerie Arno Winterberg, Heidelberg.

Descended from a noted Orthodox Jewish family, Karl Jakob Hirsch repeatedly addressed Jewish themes in his art, and was especially drawn to the teachings of Martin Buber (1878–1965). Buber's fusion of Jewish mysticism and utopian convictions, injected into the context of the German Revolution in 1919, resulted in Hirsch's collection of fervently Expressionist, messianic verse, prose poems, and drawings titled *Revolutionary Art (Revolutionäre Kunst)*. This watercolor shares with those drawings the late Expressionist vocabulary but, unlike them, does not celebrate the dead heroes—Karl Liebknecht, Rosa

Luxemburg, and Eugen Leviné—of the failed Revolution; it represents an alternative prophet, theological rather than political, whose philosophy of I and Thou foresaw a reformed humanity without violence or class conflict.

The theologian is depicted weeping beneath a tree in a Jewish cemetery. On one side of the tree is propped an open casket displaying the pale, amorphous shape of a corpse. Buber's figure is bent in grief, his body almost shriveled in contrast to the large head—a common iconography of the supremacy of spirit over flesh. His sorrowful posture is echoed in the tree and its branches, so that nature mystically empathizes with human emotion, echoing and augmenting it. Hirsch's use of intensely somber colors imbues the scene with a mood of solemnity. A similar "spiritual" emphasis is suggested by his broad application of color and the heavy black outlines that recall stained-glass windows and may point to Hirsch's study in Paris with Maurice Denis, to his adaptation of Synthetism in an effort to create a modern religious art.

It is likely that some specific incident or text inspired this strange image, but its particular source remains unknown. Is the corpse an identifiable individual and, if so, who is depicted? Or does the corpse in combination with the several tombstones represent death more generally? Is this a commentary, around 1920, on Jews who died fighting in the German army or who were among the martyrs of the Revolution and the suppressed uprisings of 1918 and 1919? Does Buber mourn the futility of these deaths? Is this corpse, as the size may indicate, perhaps a child who died during the disastrous epidemic of Spanish flu at the end of World War I? Or did Hirsch intend the watercolor to illustrate some of Buber's writings or to serve as frontispiece to a book? To these questions, answers are lacking; the image functions as a component in a pervasive sense of despondency and grief among the German political left as the Republic repressed hopes of significant reform and the deaths of war and revolution lost salvific significance.

B. T. Y.

64 John Hoexter
Clown in Profile (Ein Clown im Profil), c. 1920 (c. 1929?)

Gouache on toned paper
28.1 x 19 cm (11¹/₁₆ x 7¹/₂ in.)
Signed u. r. "JHOEXTER"

Provenance: Galerie Bassenge, West Berlin.

In accounts of Berlin's artistic haunts —the Café des Westens, also known as Café Grössenwahn (Megalomania), and the Romanisches Café—John Hoexter is a constant presence.[1] Infrequently active as an illustrator, essayist, and poet, he was a virtual personification of bohemia, ostentatiously rejecting bourgeois normalcy, mocking established values, making the café his home. Sarcastic in his art, the Dante and Ahasver of Berlin's bohème, he was recorded by Leo von König, his

teacher at the school of the Berlin Museum of Applied Arts, in a painting titled *Bohème-Café* (1909):[2] depicted in the company of the actress Spela Albrecht, Hoexter slouches at the edge of a table, head propped in his hand, eyes drooping, collar undone, behind a collection of partially emptied glasses. Sylvia von Harden, poet and essayist, recalled him as "a man with long black hair, glittering mouselike eyes, waxen complexion, with those trembling hands, and that nervous voice—painter, morphine addict…."[3] Similarly, Kurt Hiller, leader of the poets and artists of the New Club and the Neo-Pathetic Cabaret, in which Hoexter participated from 1909 to 1911, remembered him as the embodiment of decadence:

He was undernourished and stoop-shouldered, had a pale face with warts; mocking words were constantly on his lips, and his eyes beamed with gentleness. He was everything but a "megalomaniac," but of course he was very well read and judgmental especially outside his own "field." Not infrequently I heard from his mouth sparkling aperçus with philosophical significance. In addition, it was generally known that he was a drug addict…. How this…artist, so very unpopular because of his refined air of detachment, supported himself, none of us knew. His (discreet) begging campaigns in the Café were accepted as the most natural thing imaginable, and we assumed, too, that some rich patrons helped keep his head above water.[4]

Before World War I, Hoexter contributed satirical drawings, poems, and polemical essays (on Russian anti-semitism and on the cruelty of hunting) to Franz Pfemfert's *Die Aktion* (*Action*). In 1919, he served as first editor-illustrator for the Dada journal *Der Blutige Ernst* (*In Bloody Earnest*), for which he invented the title. Dadaist Walter Mehring later recalled that Hoexter was "…not a Dadaist, but a vagabond dadaizing independently."[5] Mehring remarked that little was known about Hoexter's paintings and that the authenticity of one canvas, belonging to a Berlin lawyer, was questioned by "experts."[6] His ironic comments about Hoexter's oeuvre may be exaggerated; nonetheless, Hoexter published no drawings at all between 1920 and 1928.

A date of 1920 for this gouache is thus highly approximate. Stylistically, *Clown in Profile* follows the general characteristics of fashionable, stylizing illustrations found in periodicals and books from Art Nouveau in the 1890s to Art Deco in the 1920s: flat forms, intense color contrasts with little modulation, idiosyncratic linear patterns, pronounced brushwork. There is little to identify a personal vocabulary. But the motif of the clown—the vaudeville or circus entertainer, an outsider existing at the edges of society and condoned by it—is a common symbol for the artist and an apt analogue for Hoexter's bohemian, drug-dependent persona. As a disguised self-portrait, *Clown in Profile* appears to be a kind of *Gelegenheitsarbeit*, an incidental work not commissioned. The emphatic sig-

nature consisting only of the name Hoexter, as if it alone represented all that need be known, as if it identified a notorious personality or a memorable relic of a past age, reinforces this notion.

When the Café des Westens closed in 1929, Hoexter illustrated his own recollections in book form, *This Was Our Life: 25 Years Berlin-Bohème*.[7] Because *Clown in Profile* trades on his notoriety as a bohemian archetype, it may date to the period of publication of these anecdotes. By the time Hoexter had collected his impressions, the bohemian quarter had been transformed, frequented now by tourists and by various artists and writers of the left. When the Nazis came to power in 1933, these remnants of Berlin's bohemia, too, were quickly destroyed. The conservative critic Friedrich Hussong, of Alfred Hugenberg's newspaper *Berliner Lokal Anzeiger* (*Berlin Local Gazette*), then rejoiced over the end of the "shameless dictatorship" of the "democratic intelligentsia" and its "perversities." "They are gone," he reported, "All those people who alone could be heard—they have been silenced. The ones who were everywhere, who alone seemed to be anywhere—now they are no longer visible."[8]

Hoexter, too, became "invisible," a non-person as both Jew and bohemian. A few days after the Kristallnacht in 1938, he sent a last letter to von König, to thank him for his support and bid a final farewell: "The works one should have been able to expect from me never matured," he wrote, "but nonetheless, especially in recent years, the voices have increased who see my entire existence as exemplary in and of itself and artistically-philosophically as an influential legend." He intended to follow the example set under the reigns of preceding "insane tyrants" and, like Seneca and Cato, to take his own life as release from "constantly increasing degradation," but confessed that he was still "an unpracticed suicide."[9] On 16 November 1938, his unpracticed intention became reality; he took poison and then hanged himself from one of the trees of the Grünewald.

R. H.

1. Both cafés were located near the Kaiser Wilhelm Memorial Church.
2. Private collection, Hamburg. Illus. in Martin Gropius Bau, *Berlin, Berlin: Die Ausstellung zur Geschichte der Stadt* (West Berlin: Nikolai, 1987), 435.
3. "ein Mann mit langen, schwarzen Haaren, glitzernden Mäuseaugen, gelber Gesichtsfarbe, mit zitternden Händen und nervöser Stimme—Maler, Morphinist…." Sylvia von Harden, "Erinnerungen an einst…," *Imprimatur* 6 (1969): 188, reprinted in *Expressionismus: Aufzeichnungen und Erinnerungen von Zeitgenossen*, ed. Paul Raabe (Olten and Freiburg i. B.: Walter-Verlag, 1965). For an English translation, see Sylvia von Harden, "Memories of Days Gone By," in *The Era of Expressionism* (Dallas: River Run Press, 1965), 189.
4. "Er war hagerkrumm, weissgesichtig mit Warzen, ständigem Spottwort und (fast messianischen) Güteaugen. Er war alles andre als 'grössenwahnsinnig', aber freilich sehr bewandert und urteilstüchtig gerade auch jenseits seines 'Faches'. Ich hörte nicht selten aus seinem Munde glänzende Aperçus philosophischen Inhalts. Daneben galt er allgemein als rauschgift-

süchtig…. Wovon dieser wegen seiner aparten Feinheit ganz unpopuläre… Künstler eigentlich lebte, wussten wir alle nicht. Seine (diskreten) Pumpzüge im Café wurden als das Selbstverständlichste vom Selbstverständlichen aufgenommen; auch vermutete man, dass irgendwelche reichen Gönner ihn über Wasser hielten." Kurt Hiller, undated letter to Alfred Bergmann in Bergmann, *John Hoexter: Ein Denkstein*, 19. Jahresgabe der Grabbe-Gesellschaft (Detmold: Grabbe-Gesellschaft, 1971), 15–16.
5. "…nicht Dadaist, sondern ein auf eigene Faust dadaisierender Vagant." Walter Mehring, *Berlin Dada: Eine Chronik mit Photos und Dokumenten* (Zurich: Arche, 1959), 63–64.
6. "In contrast," Mehring continued, "no matter how it might be tapped, Hoexter's phenomenal encyclopedic knowledge was never questioned by the 'Café Grössenwahn' artistic bohemia. A liver disease turned him into a morphine addict, and necessity into a genius at borrowing. But his appearance—his gaunt, almost oxidized figure—only raised his credibility as a moribundus who had less than two days to live, which is why every sympathizer—whether colleague or patron —donated just enough for basic essentials —money for two more days of morphine!" ("…doch niemals [wurde] in der 'Café Grössenwahn'-Kunstbohème Hoexters phänomenales Gesamtwissen – man konnte es aufschlagen, wo man wollte [angezweifelt]. Ein Leberleiden hatte ihn zum Morphinisten gemacht, und die Not ihn zum Pumpgenie. Doch sein Aussehen, seine ausgemergelte, gleichsam oxydierte Gestalt erhöhte nur noch seine Kredite eines Moribundus; dem man höchstens noch zwei Tage zu leben gab, weswegen ihm jeder Mitfühlende, ob Kollege, ob Gönner das allernotwendigste spendierte: das Geld für noch zwei Tage Morphium!"). Ibid.
7. John Hoexter, *So lebten wir: 25 Jahre Berliner Bohème* (Berlin: Biko Druckerei, 1928).
8. "Sie sind nicht mehr da. Die Leute, die allein zu hören waren—sie sind unhörbar geworden. Die Allgegenwärtigen, die allein vorhanden schienen—sie sind nicht mehr da." Friedrich Hussong, *Kurfürstendamm: Zur Kulturgeschichte des Zwischenreichs* (Berlin, 1934), 7, as cited by Hermann Kähler, *Berlin: Asphalt und Licht —Die grosse Stadt in der Literatur der Weimarer Republik* (East Berlin: Das Europäische Buch, 1986), 55.
9. "Die Werke, die man von mir hätte erwarten dürfen, sind nie gereift—wohl aber mehrten sich gerade in den letzten Jahren die Stimmen, die mein ganzes Dasein als solches beispielhaft und künstlerisch-philosophisch als eine fortwirkende Legende empfinden…. wahnsinniger Tyrannen…. dauernd wachsenden Entwürdigung…. Ich bin noch ein ungeübter Selbstmörder." John Hoexter, letter to Leo von König cited in Bergmann, *John Hoexter*, 43.

65 Richard Hohly
Two Unemployed Men (Zwei Arbeitslose), 1929

Charcoal, pen and ink on heavy paper
42.5 x 53 cm (16³/₄ x 20⁷/₈ in.)
Monogrammed and dated verso "RH 1929"

Provenance: The artist; Galerie Schlichtenmeier, Grafenau.

Exhibitions: Grafenau, Galerie Schlichtenmeier, *Welt der Figur*, 1 July–29 August
1989, cat. no. 135.

Like Bruno Voigt (see cat. nos.
157–170), Richard Hohly was among
the artists who emerged around 1930,
resurrecting styles, themes, and motifs
that had been prevalent earlier in the
twenties but that had lost their currency
during the economic prosperity after
1925. With the onset of the Great Depression in 1929, however, poverty and
unemployment regained their relevance
as subjects, and artists revived a
monumentalizing, stylized realism to
document proletarian misery as well as
resilience.

Paralleling a general downswing in
the world economy, German unemployment began to rise during the
winter of 1928 and 1929, reaching over
two million at the end of January for
the first time since the inauguration of
the unemployment insurance system,
and escalating by another million before the end of February. When unions
in the metals industry went on strike to
protest planned wage cutbacks, seeking, instead, better wages and a forty-
eight-hour work week, industry-wide
lockouts followed, with over 213,000
union and non-union workers affected.
By the time of the New York stock
market crash on Black Friday, 15 October 1929, with agricultural failures
and increasing bankruptcies among
small businesses, Germany's economy
had already reached a point of serious
crisis.

Hohly's image captures the defeated
mood of two anonymous unemployed
laborers in 1929. In broadly stroked
dark masses, with finely brushed lines
defining the contours of the despondent
men, Hohly recalls Karl Arnold's
technique, but with an overlay of Käthe
Kollwitz's figural proportions and her
empathetic use of dramatic gesture.
The workers are seated on a bench,
their despair evoked by slumped postures: the man on the left slouches forward with head in hand; his companion
leans back, hands folded in inactivity,
head lowered in resignation. Although
there is an overt concern with the emotional state of these figures, Hohly does
not investigate individual idiosyncracies, psyches, or even physiognomies. Instead, with their generalized,
monumental qualities and listless attitudes, his workers are symbols of a
widespread social malady and share a
common fate. Formerly the very
foundation of industrial might, lending
their bodies and skills to the production
of wares and profits, they have become
the rejects of the economic system in
which they labored. Superfluous, self-
absorbed, they sit isolated, deprived of
the activity that once shaped their lives.

C. D. G.

66   Karl Holtz
Farmer's Child (Bauernjunge),
c. 1921

Pencil on paper
28.5 x 19.8 cm (11 1/4 x 7 13/16 in.)
Not signed; Holtz estate stamp
verso

Provenance: Estate of the artist; Galerie
Bodo Niemann, Berlin; Galerie Michael
Hasenclever, Munich.

Karl Holtz delivered his first caricature
to *Die Rote Fahne (The Red Flag)*, the
newspaper of the newly formed Communist Party of Germany, in 1918.
During the following years, however,
he worked mostly for Franz Pfemfert's
Die Aktion (Action) and the less radical
satirical periodicals of the Free Social
Democratic Party. Holtz participated
throughout the 1920s in exhibitions
fostering the left's causes, such as Otto
Nagel's 1926 workers' exhibitions at
Berlin department stores:

The department store is the appropriate place. We showed only works
that could be readily understood by
the masses and also had direct relevance to them in terms of subject
matter. The number of visitors was
large. Some 160,000 people, mostly
laborers and clerical workers, went
through the four public exhibitions
. . . . This was not a selected public,
but the usual shoppers of the store.[1]

Despite his interest in producing art for
the lower classes and in activating these
classes for art, Holtz did not join any of
the radical artists' groups of the twenties, such as the Grosz-Heartfield Red
Group of 1924, nor did he become a
member of the Communist Party. Like
other artists, such as Magnus Zeller (see
cat. nos. 182–185), who sympathized
with the Weimar Republic's political
left, Holtz dedicated aspects of his work
to the political effort but otherwise remained separated from it, attempting to
cordon off his personal life from the
public proclamations of his drawings
and cartoons.

Holtz's pencil drawing of a boy in a
rumpled sailor suit derives from his
travels in 1920 and 1921 in rural areas of
northern and southern Germany. German farmers at the time were criticized
for excessive profits and for refusing to
sell their wares to needy city
populations—which may be among the
reasons for Holtz's interest in depicting
this boy, who stands before a porch and
passageway joining a farmhouse and
barn.[2] Unlike proletarian children in
contemporaneous drawings by, for example, Otto Dix (see cat. no. 26) and
Bernhard Kretzschmar (see cat. no. 83),
this child with close-cropped hair is
well nourished. As he poses for the
artist, stiffly and self-consciously, his
gaze turns downward, avoiding eye
contact, but Holtz's precise modeling
of the head grants a solidity which
transforms the boy's mood into one of
stubborn stability. The youth's striped
sailor suit with short pants represents
middle- and upper-class children's fashions of the prewar years, which continued into the twenties, signaling
simultaneously childhood and Imperial
German naval ambitions.[3]

Holtz contrasts this young boy with
his generational counterparts in the city
in multiple ways. His sturdy pose and
clear complexion differ from the haggard appearance and sallow, sore-
scarred skin of children of the urban
working class. The conservative clothing bespeaks his parents' conservative
politics, while more makeshift dress
finds links to proletarian political iden-

tity. The airy, open farmyard—the
bare white paper functions to represent
sunlight—acts as the antithesis of gray
cement courtyards closed in by high-
rise walls. Set in a discourse with depictions of the proletarian child, Holtz's
farm boy embodies the environmental,
economic, and class distinctions of
Weimar Germany.   R. H.

1. "Das Warenhaus ist der geeignete Ort.
Man zeigte ausschliesslich Werke, die von
der Masse ohne weiteres verstanden werden konnten und dazu ihr auch inhaltlich
Beziehung hatten. Der Besuch war sehr
stark. Rund 160000 Menschen, meist Arbeiter und Angestellte, gingen durch die 4
gezeigten Ausstellungen. . . . Es handelte
sich um keine gesiebten Besucher, sondern um das übliche Warenhauspubli-
kum." Otto Nagel, "Die Krisis der bildenden Kunst und das Volk," *Sozialistische Monatshefte* 33, no. 10 (1927), as
cited in *Otto Nagel: Leben und Werk
1894–1967* (Oberhausen: Städtische
Galerie Schloss Oberhausen, Ludwig-
Institut für Kunst der DDR, 1987), 47.
2. Previous identification of this drawing
as *Worker's Child (Arbeiterjunge)* is clearly
incorrect, in view of the background
buildings with a chicken nearby.
3. See Ingeborg Weber-Kellermann,
"Kindheit im Matrosenanzug," in *Fin de
siècle: 100 Jahre Jahrhundertwende* (West
Berlin: Elefanten Press, 1988), 6ff.

67   Karl Hubbuch
Self-Portrait (Selbstbildnis), 1924

Lithographic crayon on heavy
paper
52 x 36.4 cm (20 7/16 x 14 5/16 in.)
Inscribed and signed at bottom
"Zeichnungen u. Lithos/von/
Karl Hubbuch" (Drawings a[nd]
Litho[graph]s by Karl Hubbuch)

Provenance: Estate of the artist; Galerie
Michael Hasenclever, Munich.

Exhibitions: Frankfurt, Galerie Tittler,
Zeichnungen und Lithos von Karl Hubbuch,
October 1924; Munich, Galerie Michael
Hasenclever, *Karl Hubbuch*, 1981,
cat. no. 28; New York, Solomon R. Guggenheim Museum, *German Realist Drawings of the 1920's*, 15 May–6 July 1986
(traveled to Cambridge, Mass., Busch-
Reisinger Museum, Harvard University,
26 July–28 September 1986; Graphische
Sammlung, Staatsgalerie Stuttgart, 25 October–28 December 1986), cat. no. 66; Atlanta, High Museum of Art, *Art in Berlin
1815–1989*, 14 November 1989–14 January 1990, cat. no. 152.

This large drawing served as an in-
house poster for Karl Hubbuch's exhibition at the Galerie Tittler in Frankfurt
in 1924, an unusual function for a
unique drawing, especially since the exhibition also included lithographs, the
medium of choice since the nineteenth
century for exhibition posters.[1] The
irony is heightened by the fact that
Hubbuch had just accepted a position to
teach lithography at the Karlsruhe
Academy. Incorporating this irony
within the commentary of his technique, Hubbuch summarizes his artistic
concerns in the style and iconography
of this programmatic self-portrait.

The artist presents himself striding
down a street, before a massive neo-

Baroque façade, perhaps of a train station. Typically, he combines attention
to details—buttons and seams on his
jacket, capitals and stringcourses on the
structure behind him—with broad
areas of blank surface. Deep shadows
appear, only to dissolve precipitously
into light; soft shading gives way to
hatching. A nervous vision is implied,
one that focuses intensely on an object,
then shifts rapidly to another element,
gliding over intervening passages. The
resultant image, in which highlights al-
ternate dramatically with dark areas,
suggests nocturnal illumination despite
the brightness, and motion—the jerky
movement of figures in early black-
and-white films—despite the apparent
stasis of the scene.

Within the realistic proportions of
this self-portrait, Hubbuch has emphasized the eyes, enlarging them unnaturally beneath furrowed brows. The
device is one regularly used by German
draftsmen, the most notable prototype
being Caspar David Friedrich's *Self-
Portrait* of 1810.[2] Accentuated eyes are a
by-product of the intense stare into a
mirror that accompanies self-portraiture, but both Friedrich and Hubbuch
exaggerate the effect, drawing attention
to the eyes as the essential focus of their
images. Within the aesthetics of
Romanticism, Friedrich's gaze serves as
reference to his soul, as "expression of
an effort-filled exploration of his own
ego."[3] Hubbuch's stare is more confrontational; within the smoothly rendered volume of his face, the eyes are
like shields that project outward, not
inward. He probes not his own psyche
but the environment that contains him.
In the re-imagined mirror into which
he stares as he renders his portrait,
Hubbuch sees reflected the street with
its automobiles, Wilhelmine buildings,
and grinning passersby.[4]

The ostensible realism of Hubbuch's
image provides the means for his judgmental perception and presentation. Although objectivity is implied in the fas-
tidious rendering of detail and the
naturalistic depiction of figures and
buildings, the sharp division between
background and foreground, and the
collapse of space separating the two
while distinctions of scale are maintained, reveal a highly subjective, individual point of view. The size of the
artist in relation to his surroundings is
amplified; with his head cropped at the
top of the composition, he seems over-
sized, too large for the confines of the
image. He is dislocated, moreover,
from the other figures by a blatant variation in demeanor. While those behind
him are smiling or quizzical, Hubbuch
seems angry and disgruntled. He glares
out of the picture to confront the viewer
with a penetrating gaze, the enlarged
eyes his most prominent feature. Hubbuch's emphasis on the faculty of sight,
as well as his exaggerated physical
proportions, endow him with prophetic importance. The placard advertising
his work, and his placement among
people representing the social mainstream indicate the centrality of his role
as an artist to his function in society.
But, as an artist Hubbuch also envisioned himself as separate, an outsider
who observes rather than participates,
from the vantage of his professional
exile.   C. D. G.

1. Hubbuch produced several hand-drawn images, each similar to the other, to serve as posters for his exhibition of lithographs. See the related drawing, for instance, in a Karlsruhe private collection, illus. in Marlene Angermeyer-Deubner, *Neue Sachlichkeit und Verismus in Karlsruhe* (Karlsruhe: Verlag C. F. Müller, 1988), no. 5.
2. East Berlin, Staatliche Museen, Nationalgalerie, illus. in Helmut Börsch-Supan, *Caspar David Friedrich* (Munich: Prestel Verlag, 1990), 34.
3. "Der Ausdruck einer angestrengten Erforschung des eigenen Ich...." Helmut Börsch-Supan and Karl Wilhelm Jähnig, *Caspar David Friedrich: Gemälde, Druckgraphik und bildmässige Zeichnungen*, Studien zu Kunst des 19. Jahrhunderts, Sonderband (Munich: Prestel Verlag, 1973), 305.
4. The individual characterization of the three figures suggests they may be portraits, but their identity is unknown.

68 Karl Hubbuch
The Waitress (Die Saaltochter), c. 1926

Watercolor, tusche, pencil on paper
99.5 x 50 cm (39³/₁₆ x 19¹¹/₁₆ in.)
Signed l. r. "Hubbuch"

Provenance: Galleria del Levante, Munich; Fischer Fine Arts, London; Galerie Michael Hasenclever, Munich.

Exhibitions: London, Hayward Gallery, Arts Council, *Neue Sachlichkeit and German Realism of the Twenties*, 1978–79, cat. no. 166; Munich, Galerie Michael Hasenclever, *Karl Hubbuch: Werke der zwanziger Jahre*, 1979, cat. no. 5; Karlsruhe, Badischer Kunstverein, *Karl Hubbuch 1891–1979* (traveled to West Berlin, Neue Gesellschaft für Bildende Kunst; Hamburg, Kunstverein), 1981–82; Munich, Galerie Michael Hasenclever, *Überblick 10 Jahre Galerie Michael Hasenclever*, October–November 1982, cat. no. 85; Milwaukee, UWM Art Museum, University of Wisconsin, *Reactions to the War: European Art, 1914–1925*, 2 November–14 December 1986, cat. no. 23; West Berlin, Berlinische Galerie, Museum für Moderne Kunst, Photographie und Architektur im Martin-Gropius-Bau, *Ich und die Stadt: Mensch und Grossstadt in der deutschen Kunst des 20. Jahrhunderts*, 15 August–22 November 1987, cat. no. 95.

Karl Hubbuch here isolates the hardships of a single individual in specific terms of her economic class. His subject, by the very nature of her profession, is perpetually relegated to a subservient position. The toll taken by her labor is abundantly evident: although we see only the woman, in profile, and her milieu is not rendered, her thin form, dark sunken eyes, and slumped posture are clear indications of excessive work and fatigue. Hubbuch is not interested in her personality; despite the clarity of her features, she remains a type, as any suggestion of individual will, desire, or demeanor is largely suppressed. Wearing the uniform apron and black dress, she becomes wholly identified with her profession, which, in turn, is determined by her low economic and social status. Because she

works for those who can afford her services, she is to be presumed exploited by the privileged classes, a fact made poignant by her generally haggard appearance.

In this image and others, Hubbuch avoids conventional anecdote and sentimental formulas calculated to evoke sympathy. Like many artists of his generation, he opted for emotional detachment to portray a tangible, physical kind of oppression, rather than the vague psychological torment that had been associated with Expressionism. By the time Hubbuch depicted this exhausted proletarian, *Neue Sachlichkeit* was certainly well-established; with minimal means, he conveyed in this drawing the primary goals of the movement. Whereas Expressionists rendered their perception of alienation in the fervent pitch of a romanticized angst, their artistic successors, such as Hubbuch, reacted against this approach by delineating, deliberately without emotion, the palpable realities of class struggle.   C. D. G.

69 Karl Hubbuch
Detective Story (Leichter Krimi), 1924

Watercolor, pencil, colored pencil, ink on paper
54.1 x 41.9 cm (21¹/₄ x 16¹/₂ in.)
Signed l. l. "Hubbuch"

Provenance: Galleria del Levante, Munich; Galerie Michael Hasenclever, Munich.

Exhibitions: Munich, Galleria del Levante, *Karl Hubbuch*, 1971; Stuttgart, Württembergischer Kunstverein, *Realismus zwischen Revolution und Machtergreifung 1919–1933*, 1971; Innsbruck, Galerie im Taxis-Palais, *Aspekte der Neuen Sachlichkeit*, 1972; Bremen, Kunsthalle, *Karl Hubbuch*, 1974; Bergen, Bergens Kunstforening, *Kunst, Kamp, Kritikk: Tyveårenes sosialkritiske tyske kunst* (traveled to Oslo, Henie-Onstad-Kunstsenter; Stavanger, Kunstforening), 1976–77; Paris, Centre Georges Pompidou, *Paris-Berlin 1900–1933*, 12 June–6 November 1978; London, Hayward Gallery, Arts Council, *Neue Sachlichkeit and German Realism of the Twenties*, 1978–79; Karlsruhe, Kunstverein, *Karl Hubbuch 1891–1979* (traveled to West Berlin, Neue Gesellschaft für Bildende Kunst; Hamburg, Kunstverein), 1981–82; New York, Solomon R. Guggenheim Museum, *German Realist Drawings of the 1920's*, 15 May–6 July 1986 (traveled to Cambridge, Mass., Busch-Reisinger Museum, Harvard University, 26 July–28 September 1986; Graphische Sammlung, Staatsgalerie Stuttgart, 25 October–28 December 1986), cat. no. 65.

Using his typically precise but understated technique, Karl Hubbuch has created a puzzling image unquestionably disturbing in its narrative. A man and woman are the protagonists in *Detective Story*, but their relationship and activities are far from coherent. The man is seated precariously on the arm of a park bench, which juts forth suggestively between his legs and beneath the partially unbuttoned fly of his

trousers; the phallic reference is augmented by the cane that rests between his legs, hooked over his left thigh. He reads a novel, but inexplicably his head is shrouded by a hood from whose slit one blue eye peers at the tiny book. As he reads, he appears to beat his head with his right fist. His clothing is an improbable combination of pressed shirt and vest with a workman's loose blue trousers, which have slipped to the hips. One sleeve and a pant leg are rolled up; the pants' pocket bulges with unknown contents. His vest is partially undone, a watch fob dangles from the pocket, which contains a note of inflation currency. A slipper dangles from the man's left foot.

Seated on the bench proper is a red-haired woman, who wears a light coat or smock, unbuttoned but pulled together, falling loosely to reveal her right shoulder as well as a pink slip and a matching garter above her right knee. She leans forward intently, a look of concentrated dismay or perhaps terror on her face, her hands clutching claw-like at the bench. She presses her legs together but her feet are planted apart, as if she were prepared to get up quickly. Near her left foot, a woman's hat—presumably her own, since its color matches her shoes—is suspended, or has fallen to the ground.

Behind the two figures is a lake from which rise a medieval fortress and a contemporary highrise. On the shore, other buildings are clustered, crowds of people stroll along the beach, and a pier on which a single man walks extends out over the water. On the lake itself, various boats are docked, a sailboat passes, with a figure in a rowboat nearby, and a small steamer appears on the other side of the pier. Finally, a rose emerges near the arm of the man reading, apparently part of a bush behind him, accompanied by the frond of another plant.

Despite its great detail, the image remains cryptic. The little book is identified only by the word *Roman* (novel) and a picture, perhaps of the author. Since what is seen, however, is the book's back cover, even this may refer, not to the book itself, but to another being advertised there. The book, the very center of the drawing, can thus be distinguished only by its small size as belonging to the class of cheap thrillers and other pulp literature. For the francophile Hubbuch, the association of novel and rose may have suggested the *Roman de la Rose*, but it is unlikely that the individual depicted would be reading a medieval French poem and the association is therefore misleading.

The ambiguity of the little novel also permeates virtually every other aspect of the image. In the very public setting of a bench on a populous lakeshore, the couple's disheveled clothing is totally out of place. Moreover, the woman's head casts a pale shadow onto the background, which may thus not be an actual lakeshore but the image of one, a photographer's backdrop possibly. Is the setting then a photographer's studio, and the black cloth over the man's head a photographer's hood? If so, what is being photographed, or in what activity are the man and woman brought together? The proximity of the two as they are joined in the incon-

gruous world of Hubbuch's drawing suggests interaction, but their postures deny it. The man is absorbed in his mysterious novelette and is apparently unaware of the woman's presence. She, in turn, stares straight ahead, not at him, and responds to what she sees with tense apprehension.

While Hubbuch obscures the logic of the work, he also supplies indications of violence and perversity. The composition and structure of the drawing, with the man seen at the left foreground while reading, follows a tradition of dream and thought depictions, where the figures surrounding the thinker/dreamer are fantasies or dreams made visible. If this option is accepted, then the woman and the lake would both be projections of the pulp novel the man is reading in the privacy of an unseen setting. In the manner of such literature, she may well be a victim or intended victim, probably of sexual violence. The reader's raised, clenched fist could then be a partial acting out of the novel's events, while the metaphorical arm of the bench reveals an additional response to the activities in which he now participates through his imagination.

The apparent coarseness of his clothing and the greater fineness of hers, as well as her stylish coiffure, could then be reconciled, since the two exist in different realities. But why would the reader hide his head beneath the hood with its triangular eyehole? Even if ashamed of the literature he is reading, if alone, he hardly need bury his head beneath a black cowl. And what causes the shadow that falls sharply across his raised arm? If the woman's unbuttoned clothing and hiked slip suggest sexual activity, and her distressed appearance indicates the possibility of rape, there are no other indicators of either imminent or recent attack. Her hat, moreover, remains unexplained, both in terms of its position and its lack of relationship to her otherwise informal outfit.

Hubbuch's scene is constructed so as to suggest various possible readings, but the collage of its components fails to come together in a single narrative. The woman's pose and expression, the sinister hood, and the man's clenched fist all lend the work an overpowering sense of violence, actual or pending. The horror, however, is in the viewer's imagination and can find no resolution. It is the drawing itself, in its individual elements and their bizarre conjunction, that is the detective story of the title. The little book is a foil distracting from the actual mystery. Hubbuch's drawing is a series of visual clues with no solution except the recognition that it is its own detective story.   R. H.

70 Karl Hubbuch
Martha with Raincoat (Martha im Regenmantel), c. 1926–27

Pencil with watercolor on heavy paper
71.2 x 55.2 cm (28 x 21¹¹/₁₆ in.)
Signed l. r. "Hubbuch"

Provenance: Galleria del Levante, Munich; Galerie Michael Hasenclever, Munich.

Exhibitions: Bergen, Bergens Kunstforening, *Kunst, Kamp, Kritikk: Tyveårenes sosialkritiske tyske kunst* (traveled to Oslo, Henie-Onstad-Kunstsenter; Stavanger, Kunstforening), 1976–77; London, Hayward Gallery, Arts Council, *Neue Sachlichkeit and German Realism of the Twenties*, 1979; Milwaukee, Patrick and Beatrice Haggerty Museum of Art, Marquette University, *A Focus on Images: Sense and Form*, 9 November 1984–1 June 1985; New York, Solomon R. Guggenheim Museum, *German Realist Drawings of the 1920's*, 15 May–6 July 1986 (traveled to Cambridge, Mass., Busch-Reisinger Museum, Harvard University, 26 July–28 September 1986; Graphische Sammlung, Staatsgalerie Stuttgart, 25 October–28 December 1986), cat. no. 68; University Art Museum, University of Minnesota, Minneapolis, *Berlin: Art and Metropolis—Works on Paper 1912–1932*, 8 September–11 October 1987.

Karl Hubbuch met the model Martha in 1926; she posed for him for the next year, until his marriage to Hilde Issai. Martha appears here standing near a lightly rendered column and a doorway. Her figure dominates the image, in size and placement as well as in degree of detail. With his meticulous drawing technique, largely derived from drawings by Albrecht Dürer and other sixteenth-century German draftsmen, Hubbuch sharply delineates figure and clothing. Fine outlines, varying in thickness, identify Martha's features and the simple raincoat she wears, its belt, pockets, and cuffs. Precise pencil strokes represent individual strands of hair, or define the wide eyes, full lips, nose, and ears (including the tiny hole in the lobe for an earring).

The drawing's surface, however, is quantitatively devoted much less to such description than to large expanses of unmarked paper, which appear as background atmosphere as well as highlighted, rounded forms and folds. The sense of remarkable detail that emanates from Hubbuch's drawings collapses in such an analysis. The drawings gain their interest and unique drama precisely from this conjunction of blankness and seemingly unlimited detail. Dialectically, one modifies the other as the two components—emptiness and precision—synthetically form the illusion of the drawing.

Hubbuch combines thin gray washes with penciled scumbling to produce an effect of sharp light on the front of Martha's coat, generating volume and undulating folds, transforming the raincoat into a kind of still-life element in this portrait. Facial planes, in contrast, lack almost all detail and modeling. The neck in shadow and the dark surrounding mass of hair cause the face to emerge three-dimensionally, with the faintest shading of the right half of the face adding to this sense of volume. Martha's sensuously broad lips and large eyes, almost independent in the composition, cast shadows, attracting all focus to them. Hubbuch's remarkable use of color also contributes to this privileging of eyes and mouth. The most intense color is reserved for the lips, rendered, ironically, in a highly muted red of thin watercolor. The soft coloration of eyes and hair diffuse some of this single accent of gray-red.

Hubbuch's approach is one of understatement and subtlety. The frontal image is gently shifted: Martha turns slightly leftward, but she looks to her right, as if pausing somewhere to listen, facing in the direction of the sound. Her serious expression shows concern, melancholy, attention, a tender concentration oblivious to artist and viewer. She watches, but is herself necessarily watched as Hubbuch intensely but sympathetically duplicates her image in a classically reserved rendering.

C. D. G.

71 Karl Hubbuch
In the Theater Loge (In der Theaterloge), c. 1928–29

Watercolor over pencil on paper
80 x 43 cm (31^1/$_2$ x 16^7/$_8$ in.), sight
Signed l. r. "Hubbuch"; inscribed verso "In der Theaterloge"
Verso: *Head of a Woman (Mädchenkopf)*, watercolor

Provenance: Galerie Michael Hasenclever, Munich.

Exhibition: Karlsruhe, Badischer Kunstverein, *Karl Hubbuch 1891–1979* (traveled to West Berlin, Neue Gesellschaft für Bildende Kunst; Hamburg, Kunstverein), 1981–82.

A young woman in the audience of a theater turns away from the stage: it is a motif such as Edgar Degas would have selected, an unguarded moment revealing the ordinary to be extraordinary. In his scenes of everyday activity, it is to Degas that Karl Hubbuch, the perennial observer of modern German life during the 1920s, is most readily comparable. Both artists feign a detachment that lends their images a particular poignancy but, ironically, also a willed artificiality, as if the (unaware) observed is posing for the observer. Here, Hubbuch documents a momentary distraction, a sudden turn of the head to satisfy curiosity as wide eyes search the dim ambience of the theater.

The dark hues of this watercolor recreate the experience of a darkened theater, where one is typically part of a crowd, although in this case a sense of isolation prevails. Hubbuch's work is complex in its treatment of space, reality, and perception. Although the woman is shown from behind, and the action of the stage is presumably below and in front of her, her attention is focused upwards and to the left. The cropping of forms within the image extends this disjunctive aspect: the woman's head is intersected by the picture's edge, her torso by the seat back, and the seats again by the picture edge. Fragmentation, diverging directional orientation, and spotlight illumination combine to grant the image an unresolved tension, the appearance of movement unnaturally stopped, like a single frame within a film waiting to continue.

C. D. G.

72 Willy Jaeckel
Barges on the Spree (Frachtkähne auf der Spree), 1913

Oil on artist's board
51 x 71 cm (20^1/$_{16}$ x 28 in.)
Signed and dated l. r. "Jäckel 13"

Provenance: Karl und Faber, Munich.

Exhibition: West Berlin, Berlin Museum, *Stadtbilder: Berlin in der Malerei vom 17. Jahrhundert bis zur Gegenwart*, 19 September–1 November 1987, cat. no. 132.

In 1913, Willy Jaeckel lived on Cuxhavener Strasse in Berlin-Moabit. *Barges on the Spree* depicts a neighborhood near his studio, where the river bows at the Hansabrücke and the dome of St. John's Church is visible in the background.[1] The scene is presented as if from a window of a building bordering the river, the viewpoint slightly higher than the backs of the longshoremen at the river's edge, and all axes open to travel the distance of the water towards the horizon. The naturalistic colors —grays, rusts, browns, and greens —suggest the dull physicality of the working-class neighborhood in terms of its dominant tones, although the bright reflections on the water also appear as a celebration of light along the riverfront. The overall impression is less one of specific locale, however, than of rigorous formal relationships.

Jaeckel's composition is anchored by the bridge in the center of the image, which stabilizes the dynamic diagonals of barges, houses, and river's edge. The loose brushwork and angular oppositions create a sense of the river's current on what appears to be a rainy day. The barge on the right sways away from its moorings; the second barge around the river's bend drifts from the opposite direction. The warm rust accents of men, barges, and houses establish a rhythmic flow down the river and into the distance, countered by the horizontal bridge and the verticals of the buildings on each side of the river. This movement downriver, moreover, is contrived against the actual current indicated by the lift of the barges. Jaeckel's painting is thus informed by a subtle dynamism, a series of points and counterpoints like those employed by Expressionist painters, but rejecting their strident coloration in favor of a more cohesive Impressionist palette.

A composition similar to *Barges on the Spree*, the lithograph *Canal in Berlin*, appeared in 1916 in the first issue of *Der Bildermann (The Picture-Board Man)*, published by Paul Cassirer to replace his jingoistic *Die Kriegszeit (Wartime)*. In the new periodical, *Kriegszeit*'s battlefield images were replaced by more neutral scenes of civilian life, landscapes, and allegories generally antagonistic to war, if not to the specific conflict then in progress. Moderately left-wing and humanitarian, *Der Bildermann* embodied Germany's increasing war weariness, envisioning a world of art from which the realities of violence and deprivation had been filtered. In this context, Jaeckel's image is not simply a genre-type cityscape or formal study; associated with *Der Bildermann*'s mild opposition to war, it also conjures up a return to normalcy, a retrieval of prewar life unaltered, especially as juxtaposed to the poem printed below it, "Flowers of the Poor" by Walter Heymann, who had been killed in action:

> I love the flowers that in poor peoples' tiny gardens can be seen:
> Pansies and daisies,
> Dark blue, pink, yellow, brown, and green
> In amongst each other preen,
> Richer hued than a meadow's broad bouquet,
> Of joy and yearning they have much to say.
> Wildly they push beyond the bed; each wants to get out.
> No spot of earth from which they do not shout.
> Proud as Sunday and bereft of shame,
> They display themselves like garish goods behind a shopwindow's pane.
>
> And in the summer boasts that stranger, oleander,
> While singing in the door:
> From Italy I came so far.
> When through darkened window-eyes dusk shyly enters,
> Those whom life indoors makes tame,
> Push against their window pane;
> For in the green outdoors there burns in incendiary red:
> Fuchsia (just like a radish head),
> Flax and red, red poppy
> Throng together and make so happy
> Those who suffer in abject poverty.
> But those who fertilize with poorness
> Laugh and flourish with the best.
> And at night carnations have such wonderful scents.
>
> Poor people's love of colorful garish flowers is intense.[2]

With its sentimental concern for a profusion of flowers as relief from the dreariness of poverty, Heymann's poem may seem the antithesis of Jaeckel's image of cement and stone, of docks and anonymous longshoremen along the River Spree. Both poet and painter, however, highlight a sense of the picturesque and artistic order. They transform reality willfully into an admirable aesthetic experience designed to transcend the limitations of life's uncontrollable forces, disruptions, and disorder. From imperfection and incompleteness they construct an ideal memory of peacetime urban existence waiting to be retrieved.　B. T. Y.

1. The location was identified by Rolf Bothe, in *Stadtbilder: Berlin in der Malerei vom 17. Jahrhundert bis zur Gegenwart* (West Berlin: Berlin Museum, 1987), 238–239.
2. "Armer Leute Kleingarten-Blumen lieb ich sehr:/Stiefmutter und Tausendschön,/schwarzblau, rosig, gelb, braun, grün/mittendurcheinander blühn/bunter als ein Wiesenstrauss,/plaudern Lust und Sehnsucht aus./Drängen wild vom Beet; jedes will herfür./Lassen auch kein Fleckchen Boden leer./Sonntag-eitel ohne Scham/rufen sie wie Krämers Schaufensterkram./Und sommers rühmt sich vor der Tür/der fremde Oleander:/weit vom Land Italien kam ich her./Wenn aus finstern Fenster-Augen Dämmer ängstlich droht,/Schmiegen sich die drinnen bleiben/zimmerzahm dicht an die Scheiben;/brennt es doch im Grün entzündlich rot:/Fuchsien (wie Radieschen)/Flax und rotes Lieschen/mittendurcheinander zwängen/sich die vor

die Armut drängen./Die sich von der Armut mästen,/lachen und gedeihn am besten./Und des Nachts die Nelken duften schwer./Arme Leute lieben bunte grelle Blumen sehr." Walter Heymann, "Die Armeleute-Blumen," *Der Bildermann* 1, no. 2 (1916): n. p.

73 Willy Jaeckel
Hand-to-Hand Combat in a Trench (Kampf im Schützengraben), 1914

Pen, ink, ink wash on engraving paper
43.2 x 41 cm (17 x 16 1/8 in.)
Signed l. r. "W. Jäckel"; inscribed l. l. "Kampf im Schützengraben"

Provenance: Private collection, Germany; Galerie Wolfgang Ketterer, Munich.

In this brutal drawing, Willy Jaeckel depicts a German charge into a Russian defensive trench in 1914. Using a quasi-Baroque style which accents the light and shadow of heavy uniforms while suggesting the movement of muscular bodies beneath them, Jaeckel presents a cropped, crowded view of the conflict that permits no visual escape. His triangular composition peaks in the figure of a German soldier thrusting a bayonet into the throat of a falling Russian. The victim grasps at the blade entering his neck, his features distorted in a scream, his eyes already blank as they stare towards the sky. Behind him, another Russian soldier tears at his chest and falls against the wall of the trench; at his feet, a third Russian already lies dead. In the background, others surrender or attempt to flee.

Although Jaeckel gives indications that the scene is part of a larger military action, the three gruesome deaths are his focus. The Germans drop into the trench, massive, powerful figures, but there is no heroism here, only men killing one another mercilessly, even when resistance has ended. The dying soldiers, moreover, are individuals, helpless—not the anonymous, ruthless enemy depicted in German propaganda. For Jaeckel, death in battle is human, harsh, and violent. In this respect, the drawing relates to the artist's series of ten lithographs, *Memento Mori*, published by I. B. Neumann in 1915. Ernst Cohn-Wiener, Jaeckel's first biographer, described the prints as "visions of war filled with wretched dying, murder, rape, fantasized horror," and proclaimed them "the modern version of [Goya's] 'Disasters of War,' the first declaration of war against the war of 1914."[1]

The motif of a bayonet charge figures in the first of these lithographs, and also in the related painting of 1915, alternatively titled *Assault (Sturmangriff)* or *Bloodbath (Gemetzel)*.[2] The drawing *Hand-to-Hand Combat in a Trench* appears to be a preliminary study for either the lithograph or for the central portion of the painting, where a German infantryman—his face distorted in a grimace or shout—begins forcefully to jab a bayonet into the throat of an unarmed Russian, who grabs the blade with both hands as he collapses backwards from the impact, screaming in pain.

Jaeckel produced painting, prints, and drawing after the Battle of Tannenberg of 25 to 30 August 1914, in which the Russian advance into East Prussia was halted. It was the first major German victory on the Eastern Front. The battle resulted in the Eighth Army Commander, General Field Marshal Paul von Beneckendorff und Hindenburg, being hailed as the savior of East Prussia; he was an effective symbol of German military might for the remainder of the war, as well as during the years of the Weimar Republic, whose hesitant president he became in 1925. In his honor, a gargantuan wooden statue was erected in Berlin's Königsplatz, in front of the Victory Column which commemorated the Franco-Prussian War of 1870–71. In innumerable popular images, Hindenburg was then depicted as a colossus whose military greatcoat, like the mantle of a medieval Madonna, protected the German people, or cast a shadow eastward across a map of the Balkans while minuscule Russian soldiers shrank back in terror.

In the context of such nationalist posturing and mythologizing, Jaeckel's image is one of stark inhumanity. To Cohn-Wiener, who felt that viewers "must be so overcome by the mercilessness of this brutal annihilation that no uplifting thoughts of heroism are possible," Jaeckel's conceptions seemed "remarkably courageous in the midst of the 'state-sponsored' cheers of others."[3] The drawing presents men joined against men, not myths and idealized champions prevailing over personifications of subhuman evil. Indeed, humanity and nobility characterize none of the protagonists of Jaeckel's imagined scene. If *Hand-to-Hand Combat in a Trench* celebrates German military triumph after the Battle of Tannenberg, its celebration is severely tempered by the realization that human degradation was an even greater victor.

B. T. Y. / R. H.

1. "... Kriegsvisionen voll Verrecken, Mord, Notzüchtigung, phantastischem Grauen. Eigentlich die modernen 'Desastres,' die erste Kriegserklärung gegen den Krieg von 1914." Ernst Cohn-Wiener, *Willy Jaeckel*, Junge Kunst, vol. 9 (Leipzig: Klinkhardt & Biermann, 1920), 8.
   Several sources indicate that the portfolio was banned by German authorities (see, for example, the exhibition catalogue *Willy Jaeckel 1888–1944: Gemälde, Pastelle, Graphik* [Regensburg: Museum Ostdeutsche Galerie, 1975]); it has not, however, been possible to confirm this.
2. The painting, since destroyed, is illustrated in Cohn-Wiener, *Willy Jaeckel*, pl. 3. For a discussion of the lithograph and its relationship to the painting, see Ingrid Stilijanov-Nedo, *Willy Jaeckel 1888–1944: Das druckgraphische Werk* (Regensburg: Museum Ostdeutsche Galerie, 1987), 14–15.
3. "Unerhört mutvoll zwischen den 'staatlicherseits gebilligten' Hurrahgeschrei der Anderen.... müssen von der Erbarmungslosigkeit dieser brutalen Vernichtung so überwältigt werden, dass kein Gedanke an den Heroismus sie erheben kann...." Cohn-Wiener, *Willy Jaeckel*, 8.

74 Willy Jaeckel
Thinker (Denker), c. 1916

Gouache on vellum
33 x 30.1 cm (13 x 10 3/4 in.)
Signed l. l. "W. Jaeckel"

Provenance: Private collection, England; Christie's, London.

The title of Willy Jaeckel's *Thinker* is not the artist's, but rather descriptive of the unknown man depicted in a traditional contemplative pose with head propped in his hand. The image is clearly a portrait, however, in which the sitter gazes steadfastly at the viewer, his features individualized and fully revealed—the broad forehead, dark brown eyes, bushy moustache, and cleft chin. His conjunction with a landscape dominated by factory buildings and a dam suggests, moreover, that he is an industrialist, possibly the owner or a major administrative official in the company to which this factory complex belongs.

After serving briefly as a cartographer in the army during 1915, Jaeckel received special leave to paint four frescoes for the employees' dining room of the Bahlsen Cookie Factory in Hanover, a major supplier of the German military's biscuit rations. It is likely that the business contacts provided by the Bahlsen assignment established the occasion for this portrait, although Jaeckel had already begun to gain recognition as a portraitist before the war. In style and imagery, the gouache appears to date from the transitional years around 1916, as Jaeckel moved away from the monumental mannered compositions of 1914 and 1915, in which figures dominated or blocked out the landscape (see cat. no. 73).

Ludwig Meidner's apocalyptic images ironically seem to be the antecedents for the background Jaeckel selected for his industrial portrait. The dark, foreboding sky, explosive flash of sunlight, and undulating landscape forms seem almost copied from Meidner's projections of urban doom. But if Meidner's intent is to render the collapse of a world, Jaeckel's active factory buildings and bright sunburst over churning waters traversed by barges and bordered by heavy cranes point more towards human domination of the land with salvific light breaking through storm clouds. As an attribute of the meditative industrialist in the foreground, the panorama functions as his creation, the product of his pensive concern and logical, successful planning. His mind, not his hands, constructed the complex over which he presides and on which, as in a Baroque apotheosis, divinely guided sunlight casts its benign illumination. Monumental in effect despite its small size, the portrait celebrates industrial might, accomplishment, and prosperity brought on by the demands of war and the insatiable appetite of Germany's military machine during 1916 and 1917.

B. T. Y.

75 Richard Janthur
Illustration for Rudyard Kipling's "Jungle Book" (Illustration zu Rudyard Kiplings "Dschungelbuch"), c. 1920

Watercolor, brush and ink on paper
42.7 x 33.8 cm (16 13/16 x 13 5/16 in.)
Monogrammed l. c. "RJ"

Provenance: Wilhelm Valentiner, Berlin and Detroit; Brigid Valentiner-Bertoia, Barto, Pa.; Olympia Gallery, Philadelphia.

Exhibition: University Art Museum, University of Minnesota, Minneapolis, *Berlin: Art and Metropolis—Works on Paper 1912–1932*, 8 September–11 October 1987.

Artist-designed and illustrated books experienced a resurgence in Germany immediately after World War I. In part this appears to have resulted from an effort to produce objects whose value could survive the postwar economic turmoil. Much as gold and jewelry traditionally provided stability and assurance during times of war and its aftermath, art was discovered as an investment commodity during World War I by a relatively large portion of the upper bourgeoisie.[1] Prints and books extended this opportunity to a broader public, and art galleries and publishers generated a remarkably extensive output of fine-art books, well designed and representative of new as well as more accepted stylistic tendencies.[2]

In 1919, Richard Janthur began illustrations for the first of eight books for Wolfgang Gurlitt, whose Berlin gallery published graphics and several series of books, most notably *Die neuen Bilderbücher (The New Illustrated Books)*, by many recognized modern German artists, from Max Klinger and Lovis Corinth to Max Pechstein and Heinrich Zille. Issued in editions of one hundred to 250, Janthur's volumes contained original lithographs, frontispieces, and chapter headings with initials designed by the artist; the books were devoted to Asian and Near Eastern myths and fairy tales, as well as occidental literature, such as Jonathan Swift's *Gulliver's Travels* and Rudyard Kipling's *Jungle Book*, celebrating "the mysterious East." It is to Kipling's story of Mowgli, the human tiger cub, that this watercolor relates, although it does not appear in the published book of 1921. Most likely, it represents a rejected frontispiece.

From the published illustrations we can identify the characters depicted on this sheet. The moment is Mowgli's first encounter with human beings after he had been stolen from his tribe and raised in the jungle by a tiger, here transformed into a leopard. Mowgli is allied compositionally with the leopard in the background, as they confront a tribesman whose stark visage looms large in contrast to the boy's familiar jungle world. Janthur uses ambiguous symbols to represent the natural landscape—a plain on the edge of the jungle, where a small village of tribespeople lived—as well as its inhabitants. An arc spanning the center of the image is reminiscent of a bow; arrows with which the tribespeople hunted appear to the right of the leopard. These shapes also symbolize the trees and undergrowth of the thick jungle. An abstracted symbol of the sun emits colorful rays that penetrate the dark vegetation.

Janthur uses a thick calligraphic line to accentuate the figures; hatched lines on the boy's body represent teeth marks where Mowgli's wolf brothers had playfully nipped him as a child. These marks horrified the tribespeople who saw them as indications that Mowgli was not entirely human. Mowgli was thus forced to prove his exceptional manhood by killing the tiger that had originally kidnapped him. He did this with the help of his jungle family and wolf brothers, and was vindicated in the eyes of the tribe, but ultimately chose to return to the jungle. Janthur's image hints at the confrontations that take place in the story "Tiger-Tiger," presenting the tribesman with painted face and the leopard looming over his meeting with Mowgli. With its primitivizing, stylized elements, its conjuring of an Asian with the imagined features of a Native American, Janthur's drawing ably represents Expressionism's—and Germany's—fascination with fictionalized adventures of exotic lands and peoples, a substitute reality of seemingly limitless permutations.   B. T. Y.

1. For a discussion of the German art market during and immediately after World War I, see Otto Karl Werckmeister, *The Making of Paul Klee's Career, 1914–1920* (Chicago: University of Chicago Press, 1989), passim.
2. According to the incomplete catalogue in Lothar Lang, *Expressionist Book Illustration in Germany, 1907–1927* (Boston: New York Graphic Society, 1976), well over half the 380 works listed were published from 1918 through 1921. It should be noted that the concern with well-designed books extended not only to limited editions but also to inexpensive editions available to the general public.

76 Grethe Jürgens
Orange Cart (Apfelsinenkarren), 1923

Watercolor, pencil on paper
26.8 x 23.9 cm (10^1/$_2$ x 9^7/$_{16}$ in.)
Signed and dated l. r. "G. Jürgens 23"; signed and inscribed on removed matting "Grethe Jürgens/Apfelsinenkarren"

Provenance: Kunstsammlung Pelikan, Hannover; Galerie Krokodil, Hamburg; Galerie Michael Hasenclever, Munich.

Art of the 1920s from Hanover often conveys a predilection for simplicity and naïveté. Typically, Grethe Jürgens's *Orange Cart*, focusing on an ordinary object in a familiar environment, presents an unassuming, prosaic element of modern life. The vending cart, with its mound of orange fruit and repetitive rounded forms, is afforded such singular attention as the subject of this picture that it acquires a freshness and an exaggerated significance bordering on the surreal. All other elements

are secondary, fragmentary, like the word *Friseur* (barber) on the shop behind the cart, only partly visible. Even the human presence is relegated to the background, where, with a handkerchief poised near her face, the vendor is seen blowing her nose. The white shock of handkerchief calls attention to the figure, but also makes the work more emphatically mundane both in content and action. Jürgens perceives the city in all its informality, fragmentation, and intimacy.

The bright hues of the fruit and the jaunty, striped awning contrast with the brownish tones of the street. With her background in illustration, Jürgens was attracted to the bold colors that were becoming typical of advertising techniques. Yet she avoids antinaturalistic intensification and, instead, merely allows the colorful effects she observed in fruit and cart to emerge from their environment, all the more decorative for their repetitive patterning. Her approach compares with that of Erich Wegner (see cat. nos. 175–179), another Hanover artist, whom Jürgens knew, in that forms in his work are usually reduced to geometric shapes, deliberately crude in their simplification. Similarly, Jürgens emphasizes pattern, contour, and rough outlines, and often derives her unpretentious subjects from the street or other everyday milieus.

While Jürgens shares subject matter with a number of Weimar Germany's artists, she differs from many in that she does not treat the themes of violence and exploitation common to much *Neue Sachlichkeit* imagery. Although certain of her works feature the unemployed and destitute, her pictures do not have the acrid castigation of works by Otto Dix, George Grosz, or Rudolf Schlichter. Jürgens is more merciful and optimistic in her treatment of modern life. While her works are often documentary and reflective of the contemporary, her social criticism is generally more subdued.   C. D. G.

77 Grethe Jürgens
Factory Entrance (Fabrik Eingang), 1923

Watercolor, gouache, colored pencil on paper
20.6 x 17.5–17.9 cm (8^1/$_8$ x 6^7/$_8$–7^1/$_{16}$ in.)
Signed and dated l. r. "Jürgens '23"

Provenance: Kunstsammlung Pelikan, Hannover; Galerie Krokodil, Hamburg; Galerie Michael Hasenclever, Munich.

A single figure stands next to a factory entrance in Grethe Jürgens's intimate watercolor drawing. Flat, matte, complementary colors form geometric patterns set off against one another to render a street curving past a single arched lamppost, alongside a small train loaded with coal, towards the masses of towers and sheds in the background. The bright sunlight of midmorning—a clock indicates the time as 10:35—illuminates walls and road and defines wires and scaffolding against the sky.

An early work by Jürgens, one of the representatives of *Neue Sachlichkeit* in Hanover, *Factory Entrance* derives from her everyday environment; she worked for the Hackethal Wire and Cable Factory and produced illustrations for industrial trade periodicals. In its geometry of forms, this watercolor retains qualities of mechanical and blueprint drafting, but the severity of these is countered by Jürgens's accentuation of freehand drawing—dark, assertive, broad lines of black pencil. The lines wriggle over smooth paper, alter their values, refuse to adhere to color contours, and generate interlocked webs that cut softly across defined surfaces. *Factory Entrance* is a reality transformed in the process of vision, something subjectively known and encompassed within the personal world of the artist.

In her 1932 essay, "Recipes for a Beneficial Visit to an Art Exhibition," Jürgens commented that artists should concern themselves with the actuality of everyday encounter and achieve images marked by the lessons of geometric abstraction, without submitting to its fantasies.

[This leads to] the discovery of an entirely new world. We paint pots, garbage heaps, and suddenly see things in a totally new way, as if we had never seen a pot before. We paint a landscape, trees, houses, cars, and we see the world anew. Like a child, we discover a world of adventure. We see the structures of technology with totally different eyes when we paint them or see them in new paintings. The unemployed, homeless, and beggars are depicted, but not because they are "interesting types," and also not because we want to appeal to the social conscience and compassion of society, as Käthe Kollwitz, for example, does, but rather because suddenly we see that in these figures is the strongest expression of our era.[1]

Factory Entrance thus functions without overt sententiousness. Its colors, forms, and rendition attain intrinsic values as they sympathetically render the concrete structures and setting of industry. Gone is Expressionism's passionate transformation of visual experience into an analogue of intense emotion; substituted is calm contemplation guided by affectionate perception.

In 1923, however, as Germany's economy foundered and inflation was joined by increasing unemployment, the silence and inactivity at midmorning in this factory yard lend the watercolor its particular aesthetic of calm. The lone figure gazes without anticipation, opposite a sign that warns of automobile traffic—significantly missing from this image—Jürgens chose the scene for its gentle geometry and discovered in it a quiet sense of order that also bespoke the absence of prosperity.   C. D. G./R. H.

1. "... die Entdeckung einer ganz neuen Welt. Man malt Töpfe, Schutthaufen und sieht mit einemmal diese Dinge ganz anders, so, als hätte man nie vorher einen Topf gesehen. Man malt eine Landschaft, Bäume, Häuser, Fahrzeuge, und man sieht die Welt neu. Man entdeckt wie ein Kind ein abenteuerliches Land. Man sieht die technischen Gebilde mit ganz anderen Au-

gen, wenn man sie malte oder auf neuen Bildern sah. Es werden Arbeitslose, Landstreicher oder Bettler gemalt, aber nicht, weil sie 'interessante Typen' sind, und auch nicht weil man, wie Käthe Kollwitz zum Beispiel, an das soziale Gewissen und an das Mitleid der Gesellschaft appellieren will, sondern weil man plötzlich sieht, dass in diesen Gestalten der stärkste Ausdruck unsrer Tage liegt." Grethe Jürgens, "Rezepte zum erspriesslichen Besuch einer Kunstausstellung," *Der Wachsbogen* 5, no. 6 (1932), as reprinted in *Die zwanziger Jahre: Manifeste und Dokumente deutscher Künstler*, ed. Uwe M. Schneede (Cologne: DuMont Buchverlag, 1979), 145.

78 Grethe Jürgens
Spectators at a Traveling Circus (Zuschauer im Vorstadtzirkus), 1931

Watercolor on paper
68.6 x 49 cm (26^{15}/$_{16}$ x 19^1/$_4$ in.), sight
Signed and dated l. l. "Jürgens/1931"; inscribed verso "Zuschauer im Vorstadtzirkus"

Provenance: Galerie H. Remmele, Giessen; Galerie Michael Hasenclever, Munich; Barry Friedman, Ltd., New York.

Exhibitions: Hanover, Kunstverein, *Neue Sachlichkeit in Hannover*, 1974, cat. no. 36; London, Piccadilly Gallery, *German Realists 1918–1933*, 15 March–16 April 1977; Munich, Galerie Michael Hasenclever, *Realismus der Zwanziger Jahre: Bilder, Zeichnungen, Druckgraphik*, 14 October–15 November 1980, cat. no. 60.

A frequent motif since at least the eighteenth century, the circus gained increasing popularity in art from the 1880s onwards. Paintings and posters focused on entertainers, especially clowns and acrobats, who had symbolic value beyond their actual role as performers. Grethe Jürgens's *Spectators at a Traveling Circus* departs from this model: depicting neither the spectacle itself nor the glitz or tragedy of individual performers, she represents, instead, three spellbound members of the audience. A proletarian family, inhabitants of an industrial suburb, gaze upwards at an aerial act not seen by us, but whose high wire and other supports are clearly present. A tightrope and trapeze, and a wagon wheel at the lower left establish the circus environment; a drab tarpaulin gracing the image center separates the world of entertainment from the world of multi-family dwellings, with their black and red rooftops and smoking chimneys in the background.

It is a makeshift reality the spectators have entered, and in it their consciousness is lifted to the extraordinary, as if they were witnesses to a supernatural vision in the heavens above. We experience this transformation in the intensity of their gazes, especially the open-mouthed awe of the child. Despite their temporary transport into a realm of wonder, however, they remain inhabitants of a gray reality whose skies fill with smoke and whose trees struggle to survive. For us, spectators of these spectators, Jürgens distills the scene, extracting glamor, leaving the dregs of workaday qualities. These she renders with remarkable care, finely indicating forms with a subtle play of lines, soft volumes, and tender shadows.

In her advice to viewers in 1932, Jürgens warned that contemporary art should not be judged according to the "masterpieces of a happier time." The unheroic verity of the present, not dreams of past artistic or patriotic glory, should be sought in modern art; viewers should relinquish their demands for elevation into an aesthetic realm of eternal values:

I consider it a barbaric concept of culture to recognize in it, not obligations, but rather means to greater comfort and greater enjoyment. Art gets plopped as spiritual whipped cream onto the culture pudding. Art is the cloak with which people adorn and warm themselves, or it is just a decorative splotch of color on the wall. In reality, viewers would be enriched much more if they could resolve to view art in a totally different manner; that is, to contribute something instead of enjoying passively.

People with a feeling for art need no encouragement to go along this path. For the others, their interest is insufficient and they need to develop understanding first. For this, it seems to me that it is important that they first stop thinking so much about "eternal values" and think more about the relationship of our time to its art. Our times are rich in significant events. They are a devouring chaos only to someone who closes himself off from them and flees from raw reality to an idyllic isle of the dead.[1]

Jürgens accepts the circus and its world of fantasy in her drawing as an invitation to recognize the mundane reality from which it emerges. The spectators absorbed in a high-wire act participate in a drama of psychological conversion and translation whose significance resides in its testimony to the here and now.   C. D. G.

1. "...Meisterwerken einer glücklicheren Zeit.... Es scheint mir eine barbarische Auffassung von Kultur zu sein, in ihr keine Verpflichtung, sondern nur ein Mittel zu grösserer Bequemlichkeit und grösserem Genuss zu sehen. Als geistige Schlagsahne wird die Kunst auf den Kulturpudding getan. Die Kunst ist der Mantel, mit dem man sich schmückt und wärmt, oder sie ist nur ein dekorativer Farbfleck an der Wand. In Wirklichkeit würde man ja viel mehr bereichert, wenn man sich zu einer ganz anderen Kunstbetrachtung entschliessen könnte; nämlich mitzuarbeiten, statt zu geniessen.
"Menschen mit künstlerischem Gefühl gehen von selbst diesen Weg. Für die anderen genügt das Interesse nicht, sie müssen das erst erwerben. Dafür scheint es mir wichtig, dass sie zunächst etwas weniger an die 'Ewigkeitswerte' denken und mehr an die Beziehungen der Zeit zur Kunst. Unsere Tage sind reich an Ereignissen. Für den, der sich vor ihnen verschliesst und von der rauhen Wirklichkeit auf die idyllische Toteninsel flüchtet, werden sie ein Chaos, das ihn verschlingt." Grethe Jürgens. "Rezepte zum erspriesslichen Besuch einer Kunstausstellung,"

Der Wachsbogen 5, no. 6 (1932), as reprinted in *Die zwanziger Jahre: Manifeste und Dokumente deutscher Künstler*, ed. Uwe M. Schneede (Cologne: DuMont Buchverlag, 1979), 144.

79   Georg Kinzer
Woman at a Mirror (Frau vor dem Spiegel), 1932

Oil, tempera on canvas
73.5 x 64.5 cm (28^{15}/₁₆ x 25^{7}/₁₆ in.)
Monogrammed and dated l. r.
"GK 32"

Provenance: Juro Kubicek, Berlin; Galerie Nierendorf, West Berlin; Galerie Brockstedt, Hamburg.

Exhibitions: West Berlin, Haus am Waldsee, *Neue Sachlichkeit*, 26 September–29 October 1961; West Berlin, Galerie Nierendorf, *Die 2oer Jahre*, 1971; Stuttgart, Württembergischer Kunstverein, *Realismus zwischen Revolution und Machtergreifung 1919–1933*, 1971, cat. no. 90.

An old table and a wooden shipping crate support the mirror into which Georg Kinzer shows a woman gazing as she combs her greasy hair. The label on the crate ends with the syllable "stolz" (pride), implying a variation on the theme of vanity. However, unlike traditional *vanitas* imagery, with its attendant wealth and luxury, Kinzer's picture is a display of poverty: the woman's comb is missing teeth, paper peels from the back of her mirror, and her dressing table is bare except for a red garment and scant signs of femininity—five hairpins and a floral barrette. The fifty-pfennig price on the crate further indicates a cheapness incompatible with more typical *vanitas* emblems.

Kinzer uses a sharp-focused realism to examine the physiognomy of the woman primping. Her beauty is subverted by vaccination scars on her arm, wrinkles on her face, and bumps on her nose. Heavy and strong, with ponderous breasts and flabby arms, she is much older than her youthful lingerie would suggest. Her exaggerated features show the signs of a difficult life, yet she retains a sense of pride in her attempt to dress up.

In a style shared by many *Neue Sachlichkeit* painters, Kinzer presents a caricatured contrast to images of fashion-conscious women of the period. He captures the details of the woman's toilette with precision and clarity, but in a detached manner that leaves the viewer with an ambiguous message: Kinzer neither condemns nor exalts the situation he depicts, but exploits it for its pathetic-humorous potential. The old-master technique of mixed oil and tempera with fine glazes diminishes any sense of subjectivity, any trace of the artist's hand and brush. Kinzer's *Neue Sachlichkeit* thus represents a revival of the themes and manner of the mid-1920s. Supplanted by less strident, more romantic forms of realism, the earlier, engaged realism that had emerged during the years of inflation was perceived as "academic" once prosperity returned.[1] That prosperity was short-lived, however, and the very critics who had rejected *Neue Sachlichkeit*'s

political wing saw new relevance in it. Paul Westheim, for instance, reviewing an exhibition in 1931, described the new work as a "protestation against a world order which is, after all, the antithesis of order," and continued:

Most of these works were created as much as ten or more years ago. It is remarkable that so much that seemed like crassest exaggeration then, fits the current situation extremely well. It almost appears as if the unsuspecting artists, who looked at the world from its nether side, had greater perception than those who stood so tall in their superiority that they had to fall out of the clouds first.[2]

Sachlichkeit, Westheim concluded about Kinzer's art, represented "not a tendency, but a very German tradition" whose perceptions of a world no longer prosperous or just, of a society no longer democratic or orderly, took on a peculiar new urgency during the early 1930s.   B. T. Y.

1. Paul Westheim, "Die Ausstellung der jungen Maler und Bildhauer in der Deutschen Kunstgemeinschaft, Berlin," *Das Kunstblatt* 12 (1928): 8.
2. "...Protestation gegen eine Weltordnung, die ja das Gegenteil von Ordnung ist. Die meisten dieser Blätter sind vor zehn und mehr Jahren schon entstanden. Das Merkwürdige ist, dass so vieles, was damals wie krasse Übertreibung erschien, bestürzend auf die heutige Situation zu passen scheint. Fast will es erscheinen, als ob die ahnungslosen Künstler, die die Welt bloss von unten gesehen haben, mehr Ahnung gehabt hatten als diejenigen, die in ihrer Überlegenheit so hoch droben standen, dass sie erst mal aus den Wolken fallen mussten." Westheim, "Ausstellungen," *Das Kunstblatt* 15 (1931): 300.

80   Ernst Ludwig Kirchner
Small Café Society (Kleine Café Gesellschaft), c. 1910

Pen, ink, ink wash on yellow paper
16.8 x 22.8 cm (6^{5}/₈ x 9 in.)
Not signed.

Provenance: Stuttgarter Kunstkabinett; Dr. Isermeyer, Hamburg; Galerie Wolfgang Ketterer, Munich.

Exhibition: University Art Museum, University of Minnesota, Minneapolis, *Berlin: Art and Metropolis—Works on Paper 1912–1932*, 8 September–11 October 1987.

In this image of a group at a café table, Ernst Ludwig Kirchner uses a motif common to Impressionist, *Jugendstil*, and Expressionist artists, and represents a scene typical of Germany's café culture early in this century. The "snapshot" composition suggests immediacy and a candid, frozen moment: it is as if the artist, seated at an adjacent table, had turned suddenly and glimpsed the group of three, registered their presence without concern for details or refinements, and swiftly recorded what he saw. Kirchner's deft drawing implies his habit of sketching from life, making studies and drypoint renderings while

sitting in cafés or music halls, and later using these studies in paintings and other prints. However, the careful positioning of the figures in their "random" poses and the addition of ink wash counter this conclusion and indicate, instead, a precisely orchestrated, finished drawing in which the air of informality is consciously preserved.

Kirchner privileges process in this drawing, in accordance with his and other *Brücke* artists' principles during their early years in Dresden. Lines and forms seem quickly rendered and figures are juxtaposed in a montage-like manner, without spatial transitions or atmospheric harmony, to serve as signs of the artist's interaction with his materials. The two women in stylish feathered hats appear in another drawing, *People in a Public House (Menschen im Lokal)*, dated to 1910.[1] Comparison of *Small Café Society* with other Kirchner drawings and photographs allows identification of the woman on the left as Doris "Dodo" Grosse, the artist's companion in Dresden from 1906 until 1911. A date of late 1910 would thus seem reasonable for this drawing, prior to Kirchner's extended absence from Dresden in early 1911 and his decision later that year to move to Berlin.[2]

Small Café Society presents an image of modernity that contrasts sharply with Kirchner's primitivism and *Brücke*'s return to nature in a search for liberation from an oppressive bourgeois society. His simultaneous celebration of nudity as freedom and of artificiality and urbanity in fashionable cafés represents the contradictions inherent in the attitudes of many German artists and writers towards modern life. The range of cafés, however, offered identity with a class and a milieu; the German bohème in various cities of the Empire identified itself and its radical allegiances in part through the cafés its members frequented, as Helmut Kreuzer summarized in his insightful study of the bohemian phenomenon: it was in the café that the bohemian found his public and fulfilled his needs for provocation and for self-presentation.[3]

The café became "a stage," Kreuzer notes, "for roles played partially for one's comrades, partially for the 'burghers'"; and it yielded possibilities for observation of individuals sitting "motionless behind coffee glasses already emptied in the morning."[4] For artists such as Kirchner, the café fulfilled a variety of practical purposes, providing contacts with friends and patrons, ideas about current artistic directions both in conversations and in a rich selection of periodicals, attachment to social reality beyond the segregated milieu of the studio, and a source of imagery and impressions. "In this sense," Kreuzer concludes, "the café is the culmination of the real, *the* scene of life liberated and concentrated."[5]   B. T. Y.

1. Illus. in *Ernst Ludwig Kirchner: Zeichnungen und Pastelle*, ed. Roman Norbert Ketterer with W. Henze (Stuttgart and Zurich: Belser, 1979), 28.
2. Previously, the date of 1911 was assigned to the drawing, on the assumption that it depicted a Berlin café.
3. Helmut Kreuzer, *Die Bohème: Beiträge zu ihrer Beschreibung* (Stuttgart: J. B. Metzler, 1968), 202.

4. "...eine Bühne... für Rollen, die man teils vor seinesgleichen spielt, teils vor 'Bürgern'.... [die Möglichkeit] reglos hinter den schon am Vormittag geleerten Kaffeegläsern [zu sitzen]." Ibid.

5. "In diesem Sinne ist das Café die Kulmination des Wirklichen, *der Schauplatz* des entfesselten und gesteigerten Lebens." Ibid.

81 Immanuel Knayer

Locomotive (Lokomotive), c. 1927

Watercolor, brush and ink on paper
13.6 x 19.5 cm (5³/₈ x 7¹¹/₁₆ in.)
Signed l. r. "Knayer"

Provenance: Galerie Schlichtenmaier, Grafenau; Galerie Michael Hasenclever, Munich.

Exhibition: Böblingen, Städtische "galerie contact," *Immanuel Knayer 1896–1962: Gemälde, Aquarelle, Zeichnungen, Druckgraphik*, 25 March–2 May 1987, cat. no. 28.

The industrial landscape, its inhabitants and machines were constant subjects in Immanuel Knayer's work when he moved to Düsseldorf in 1921 to escape the authority of his parents, who opposed his career as an artist.[1] After his initial stay in the Rhineland, Knayer resumed studies at the Stuttgart Academy of Fine Arts, but returned repeatedly to the Ruhr area, which remained the preponderant source of his imagery. Railroads, train yards, and workers' dwellings particularly attracted his attention in small drawings and watercolors, such as this one, whose color scheme and especially dramatic use of rust red are shared with works reliably dated to 1927.[2]

Despite the artists' common training at the Stuttgart Academy, Knayer's industrial landscapes exhibit none of the precisionist verism of Volker Böhringer's views of Stuttgart's industrial suburbs (see cat. nos. 9, 10). After experimenting with hard-edged images overlayed with geometric faceting, Knayer turned to forms with softer contours in shallow space, with intersecting rectangular planes and linear webs. The locomotive of this watercolor is seen against a network of posts, wires, and tracks. Knayer's palette of gray and red echoes the very stuff of industry; the textures of iron and rust and the puffs of smoke emitted from the train are almost more palpable than the tenement houses behind them. The buildings are bathed in a trembling wash of color, a rust-red reflection of the signal lights that dissolves the walls into amorphous clouds contained by dark outlines and fixed by the regular rhythm of their windows and the linear tangle of electric and telegraph wires. The colors of the signaling mechanism and its latticed support, just to the left of composition center, influence the entire image, as they flash and regulate the traffic on the tracks below.

The steam locomotive, celebrated for its power during the 1920s and 1930s by artists and writers (and musicians, as in Arthur Honegger's *Pacific 231*), here takes on a gentler presence. A miniature model rather than an overpowering dy-

namo of glistening steel, the engine trails a billow of white smoke through the dark urban surroundings, from which only a rough wall separates it imperfectly. Rendering this gray environment, Knayer imbues his watercolor with a softened objectivity: a touch of poetry enters the work, subverting both the exaggerated pathos of Expressionism and the puritanical sobriety of *Neue Sachlichkeit*. The artist shared this aim with others at the Stuttgart Academy, students of Christian Landenberger and Robert Breyer who rejected the dominant teachings of Adolf Hölzel, with their abstract tendencies, affirming instead the contemporary world and a quality of personal involvement. Founders of Stuttgart's New Secession in 1929, these artists embraced the prototype of a valued Impressionism, frequently with socially critical attitudes, injected with Expressionism's empathetic concerns and abstraction's constructed geometries. Representative of this school of painting, Knayer's small watercolor, by its very size, proclaims a personal element and intimacy foreign to most *Neue Sachlichkeit* work. Documenting industrial reality, Knayer does not render this reality neutrally but translates it into a private realm, reconstructing the world in nuanced miniature.   C. D. G.

1. Harry Schlichtenmaier, "Zum Leben und Werk Immanuel Knayers," in Böblingen, Städtische "galerie contact," *Immanuel Knayer 1896–1962: Gemälde, Aquarelle, Zeichnungen, Druckgraphik* (Grafenau: Galerie Schlichtenmaier, 1987), 7.

2. See, for example, the signed and dated watercolor *Landscape in the Rhineland (Landschaft im Rheinland)*, illus. ibid., 34, no. 27.

82 D. W. Koeppen (?)

A Woman of 1934 (Eine Frau von 1934), 1934

Watercolor over pencil, pen and ink on paper
25.3 x 29.7 cm (10 x 11³/₄ in.)
Monogrammed and dated l. r. "K 34"

Provenance: Galerie Michael Hasenclever, Munich.

Exhibition: Munich, Galerie Michael Hasenclever, *Aquarelle und Zeichnungen der Zwanziger Jahre*, 1 March–4 April 1987, cat. no. 52.

The identity of D. W. Koeppen is unknown, and no further works by this artist have been discovered. Since the full name existed only on matting lost prior to 1987, it is possible that a misreading of the signature is involved. In 1938, at the exhibition *Art allemande libre (Free German Art)* in the Maison de la Culture, Paris, watercolors were exhibited by Margarete Koeppen, who may be identical with, or related to, the present artist; firm evidence, however, is currently lacking. In a review of the exhibition for the Parisian émigré newspaper, *Pariser Tageszeitung*, Paul Westheim described her works as "disciplined in *Neue Sachlichkeit*, but nonetheless saturated with a certain undertone of humanity."[1] This charac-

terization, in conjunction with the watercolor medium and the anti-Nazi ideology, could apply to *A Woman of 1934* as well, but is too general to allow any conclusive judgment to be made.

With spotlight clarity and focus on a narrow sidewalk stage, a bakery window and a park serving as backdrop, Koeppen presents an ironic scene of domestic virtue. A monumental, buxom blond woman, accompanied by her little girl, pushes a baby carriage along one of the innumerable streets named for World War I field marshal Hindenburg—later president of the Weimar Republic who appointed Hitler chancellor. The unseen tiny inhabitant of the pram waves a miniature swastika flag, announcing an early and precocious attachment to the victorious "German ideology." In the park, other women, too, push carriages filled with newborn citizens for the year-old Thousand Year Reich.

The face of Koeppen's woman expresses the delight and self-satisfaction to be found in Nazi propaganda images, posters calling for blond "Healthy Mothers" or "Happy Mothers" who produce similarly blond, healthy, happy children. "The mission of woman is to be beautiful and to bring children into the world," Joseph Goebbels pronounced in his novel *Michael: A German Fate in Diary Form* in 1924.[2] Hitler, too, repeatedly expounded his conviction that women's rights were most appropriately protected by providing them with the possibility of being mothers:

> An unlimited range of work opportunities exists for women. For us the woman has always been man's most loyal comrade in work and in life. I am often told: You want to drive women out of the professions. Not at all. I wish only to create the broadest measure of possibility for her to cofound her own family and to be able to have children, because by so doing she most benefits our *Volk!*[3]

During the summer of 1933, the German state inaugurated legislation to encourage women to fulfill these visions of regenerated maternal femininity by means of marriage incentives. Up to one thousand Reichsmarks, one-fifth of an average worker's annual wage, were to be paid to couples who married, provided the wife ceased working outside the home and both partners were certifiably "Aryan"; a "bachelor tax" imposed a surtax on the earnings of unmarried Germans; birth control and abortions were outlawed or strictly limited; marriage loans were introduced whose principal would be reduced with the birth of each child; income tax deductions for children were increased so that families with six or more children paid no tax at all; and the fifth child in a family could have such prominent national leaders as Hindenburg or Hitler himself as godfather.[4]

Statistics collected in 1934 indicate the apparent success of these pronatal policies. Marriages that year increased by almost 2 percent over those of 1933 and 4 percent over those of 1932, while births came to 18 per thousand Germans, compared with 14.7 in 1933. These rates did not match those of the early 1920s, but Nazi officialdom and

eugenics professors could nonetheless conclude that German women were indeed enthusiastically giving babies to the Führer, fulfilling their role in the National Socialist program, in which "soil provides the food, woman supplies the population, and man performs the deeds."[5]

Wheeling her flag-waving gift to the German *Volk* towards the nearby landscaped square—it would surely soon become Adolf-Hitler-Platz—the woman in Koeppen's image falls into the mold established by the newfound champions of German motherhood. Abundantly healthy, she is the mother of genetically approved children. Koeppen succeeds in transforming the maudlin grins of Nazi propaganda into a double-chinned smile of self-satisfaction in this well-fed German mother, whose pale blue eyes show little sign of thought or intelligence. In its satiric commentary, *A Woman of 1934* presents a variation of *Neue Sachlichkeit*'s numerous street scenes. The basic components of George Grosz's *Street Scene, Berlin* (cat. no. 53) are present: sidewalk, street, house façades, shopwindow, and passersby; Grosz's bitter commentary on Weimar social realities, however, is transformed, ominously so, despite the overlay of sugary charm. The bakery shop's display is bounteous still and, unlike Grosz's beggars, the woman is surely able to afford its wares. But this prosperity is obtained at a significant price: the bustle and traffic and diversity of Grosz's Berlin is gone. There are no men in this picture as the *Hausfrau* walks her children; she performs the duties of her sole appropriate profession while the men exist in their world of labor and regimented politics. Emptied of life, Hindenburg Strasse is the setting for mindless political submission and indoctrination as the baby-sized flag flutters over the carriage to signal acceptance of the Führer's will.

B. T. Y. / R. H.

1. "Die... in Neuer Sachlichkeit gestrafften und dabei doch von einem gewissen Unterton von Menschlichkeit durchbluteten Aquarelle der Marg. Koeppen." Paul Westheim, "Rundgang durch die Deutsche Kunstausstellung in der Maison de la Culture," *Pariser Tageszeitung* 837, 9 November 1938, reprinted in Badischer Kunstverein, *Widerstand statt Anpassung: Deutsche Kunst im Widerstand gegen den Faschismus 1933–1945* (West Berlin: Elefanten Press, 1980), 140.

2. Joseph Goebbels, *Michael: Ein deutsches Schicksal in Tagebuchblättern* (Munich: Zentralverlag der NSDAP, Frz. Eher Nachf., 1929), 41, cited and trans. by George L. Mosse, *Nazi Culture: Intellectual, Cultural and Social Life in the Third Reich* (New York: Grosset & Dunlap, 1966), 41.

3. Adolf Hitler, Speech to the National Socialist *Frauenschaft*, reported in *Der Völkische Beobachter*, 13 September 1936, as cited and trans. ibid., 39.

4. Claudia Koonz, *Mothers in the Fatherland: Women, the Family and Nazi Politics* (New York: Saint Martin's Press, 1986), 149–150, 185–186.

5. Unidentified Nazi source, cited ibid., 178. The present translation differs somewhat from that provided by Koonz.

83 Bernhard Kretzschmar

Standing Boy (Stehender Knabe), 1921

Pencil on paper
37 x 30.7 cm (14¹/₂ x 12¹/₈ in.)
Signed and dated l. r.
"B. Kretzschmar. 21"

Provenance: Galerie Michael Hasenclever, Munich.

Exhibition: Munich, Galerie Michael Hasenclever, *Überblick: Zehn Jahre Galerie Michael Hasenclever*, 1982.

The twentieth century, Ellen Key announced in 1900 in the title of her popular and influential book, would be "The Century of the Child."[1] The imperialist ambitions of Europe's nations prevented the Swedish feminist's prediction from coming true in the manner she foresaw. Despite this, her calls for pedagogical reform, for protecting children against the ills of industrial society, fostering their mental health, and recognizing their unique needs formed the basis of innumerable political, cultural, and religious tracts issued by advocates of reactionary, conservative, liberal, and radical ideologies alike. Artists, too, shared in the exploration of the modern child's identity: they emulated children's art, recorded and interpreted children's physiological and psychological transformations, and depicted children's environments—the bright bourgeois playroom as well as the dark, cement-covered tenement courtyard.

During the 1920s, as political parties and religious sects formed youth organizations to shape this newly recognized social segment into adjuncts to their ideological struggles, the child continued to be a frequent subject of artists' attention.[2] In scenes of the petty bourgeois, proletarian, and small farmer's milieu of Friebelstrasse in Gostritz, at the southern edge of Dresden, Bernhard Kretzschmar brought to depictions of children the same concentration on detail and search for significance with which he approached the world of workers, handymen, and office employees. Perhaps intended as a component in a painting, this drawing of a boy is without reference to surroundings, but the single figure suffices to suggest an entire environment. The boy, presented in a casual pose, drawn from life, was probably someone Kretzschmar repeatedly observed; despite the self-conscious and tentative gesture, the child seems unaware of the artist's gaze, as if accustomed to it.

The boy wears no shoes, and only a simple smock over his shirt with its rolled-up sleeves. Kretzschmar renders head and face with more detail and volume than the rest of the figure, drawing particular attention to them and to the excessively large, staring eyes with their deeply shaded sockets. With his spindly legs and scrawny arms, and a head too large for this weak body, the boy seems a victim of malnutrition, one of the acute problems of the late- and post-war years, especially among Germany's poorer classes. Kretzschmar quietly addresses this issue in *Standing Boy*, but is also concerned with the boy's psychological state. The facial expression and guarded clasping of the hands convey a boyish bashfulness, reinforced by the figure's slightly off-center placement and his protective sideways stance.

Except for the child's abnormal physical development and modest clothing, Kretzschmar offers no clues as to the boy's circumstances. Conspicuously lacking playfulness or youthful energy, the boy has a pensive look; while sadness is not overtly expressed, his spirit seems to have been dampened by his state of need. The drawing is a reminder that children were the hardest-hit victims of capitalist exploitation and of war. "The proletarian child is the most forsaken creature under the sun," wrote Otto Rühle, the radical founder of the independent German Communist Workers' Party (KAPD).[3] In two separate books, *Das proletarische Kind* (*The Proletarian Child*) (1922) and *Die Seele des proletarischen Kindes* (*The Soul of the Proletarian Child*) (1925), Rühle suggested that the Weimar government was remiss in the degree of its provision for the needs of workers' children. Such a critique also underlies Kretzschmar's refined drawing, whose precision and delicacy of rendering augment the poignancy of the subject.

C. D. G.

1. Ellen Key, *The Century of the Child* (New York and London: G. P. Putman's Sons, 1909), translated from the German, *Das Jahrhundert des Kindes* (Berlin: S. Fischer, 1903), translated from the Swedish, *Barnets Århundrade* (Stockholm: Bonnier, 1900).
2. In addition to this drawing by Kretzschmar, see representations of children by Fritz Burmann, Otto Dix, Otto Herbig, Karl Holtz, Wilhelm Lachnit, and Martel Schwichtenberg (cat. nos. 22, 26, 62, 66, 84, and 142 respectively).
3. "Das proletarische Kind ist das verlassenste Geschöpf, das es unter der Sonne gibt." Otto Rühle, *Die Seele des proletarischen Kindes* (Dresden: Verlag Am Anderen Ufer, 1925), 22.

84 Wilhelm Lachnit

Boy in Sailor Suit (Knabe in Matrosenjacke), 1923

Carpenter's pencil on paper
46–45.7 x 33.4 cm
(18¹/₈–18 x 13¹/₈ in.)
Signed and dated l. r. "Lachnit 23"; inscribed and dated verso "Knabe in Matrosenjacke 1923/Z."

Provenance: Collection Peter Hielscher, Dresden; private collection, Germany; Galerie Bodo Niemann, Berlin; Galerie Michael Hasenclever, Munich.

Exhibitions: West Berlin, Neue Gesellschaft für Bildende Kunst, *Wem gehört die Welt: Kunst und Gesellschaft in der Weimarer Republik*, 1977 (traveled to Stockholm, Moderna Museet, 1978), cat. no. 345; Munich, Galerie Michael Hasenclever, *Aquarelle und Zeichnungen der Zwanziger Jahre*, 1 March–4 April 1987, cat. no. 55 (as *Arbeiterjunge*).

One of a group of young Dresden artists around Otto Griebel and Bernhard Kretzschmar who exhibited in the studios of the portrait photographer Hugo Erfurth, Wilhelm Lachnit shared their radical political convictions, dedicating his work to the cause of the working class as represented by the German Communist Party. Like Otto Dix (see cat. no. 26), Griebel, and Kretzschmar (see cat. no. 83), Lachnit portrayed proletarian children regularly, depicting signs of poverty and disease while simultaneously celebrating survival. For Lachnit, and for other socially critical artists, the child became an icon of pathos and deprivation, among the most effective emblems of capitalism's victims.

In *Boy in Sailor Suit*, Lachnit's focus on the boy's head and torso, his emphasis on the face, with its pronounced jaw and sunken cheeks, provides a clear indication of malnutrition. The boy's hair, moreover, is thin and falling out; shadows around his mouth suggest raw skin. His sailor blouse does not hide the fragile condition of his little body: distended joints, fleshless arms, sunken chest. Gazing without focus through large eyes and lifting his head slightly, the child displays the symptoms of tuberculosis. Lachnit relies for this effect on concrete forms rather than expressive distortions, and the very palpability of the image yields a pathetic representation. Rendered in sharp, delicate contours, the boy's head looms large, overpowering with its visual weight the scrawny body supporting it. Situating the boy in an empty, windowless corner of a room, the artist creates a visual vortex; the space becomes not only bare, but also constricting, a poignant visual metaphor for the child's state of existence.

"Wilhelm Lachnit," a critic for *Das Kunstblatt* observed in 1926, "is a gentle and quiet artist who imparts a gentle delicacy even to the most desolate of worlds. That is in general the remarkable aspect of this younger generation . . . that it refuses to be intimidated, that with strong feelings it says yes to life 'despite everything'."[1] Drawn during Lachnit's last year as a student of the Dresden Academy, *Boy in Sailor Suit* counters the pathos of the depiction with its monumental presence. The boy's figure fills virtually the entire drawing and dominates the spare space within which he appears, an articulated identity amidst anonymity, a determined manifestation of life in an environment of stark emptiness. Shortly before his death in 1962, Lachnit summarized the aspirations he had long held for his work, declaring, "I want to produce something absolutely gigantic, absolutely severe, absolutely classic and yet filled with the perfume of life. It should show people living on in hope and, at the same time, all the horror that is destroying them."[2]

C. D. G./R. H.

1. "[Lachnit] ist ein weicher und stiller Künstler, der seine sanfte Zärtlichkeit auch über die ödeste Welt legt. Das ist ja überhaupt das Wunderbare dieser jungen Generation . . . dass sie sich nicht unterkriegen lassen, dass sie mit starkem Gefühl 'trotzdem' zu diesem Leben sagen." Hildebrand Gurlitt, "Von jungen Dresdner Künstlern," *Das Kunstblatt* 10 (1926): 260.
2. "Ich möchte etwas schaffen, ganz gigantisch, ganz streng, ganz klassisch und doch voller Duft. Es soll die Menschen zeigen, wie sie hoffend leben und das ganze Schreckliche zugleich, das sie zerstört." Wilhelm Lachnit, cited in East Berlin, Staatliche Museen, Nationalgalerie, *Schönheit und Bedeutung im Werk Wilhelm Lachnits* (East Berlin: Staatliche Museen, Nationalgalerie, 1980), n. p.

85 Franz Lenk

Blooming Cactus (Blühender Kaktus), 1931

Watercolor on paper
40.8 x 29.2 cm (16 x 11¹/₂ in.)
Signed and dated l. c. "1931 F. Lenk"

Provenance: Galleria del Levante, Munich; Galerie Michael Hasenclever, Munich.

Exhibitions: Innsbruck, Galerie im Taxis-Palais, *Aspekte der Neuen Sachlichkeit*, 1972; Milan, Rotanda Basana, *Il Realismo in Germania*, 1971–72; Vienna, Museum des 20. Jahrhunderts, *Neue Sachlichkeit und Realismus: Kunst zwischen den Kriegen*, 1977.

In 1927, Emil Utitz, a former advocate of Expressionism, celebrated the new objectivity in the work of Franz Lenk and others, with its emphasis on "the order, clarity, and severity of things" and its preference for "the most common objects: dishes and bottles, prickly cacti, and cheeses with holes. Their being," Utitz continued, "appears almost painfully before us, naked, unadorned. Yet mystery surrounds the objects, not applied to them but residing within them as something indescribable."[1] Like artists of the Italian *Scuola metafisica* or the verist school of Surrealism, *Neue Sachlichkeit* painters utilized a cold, sharp focus on still-life objects precisely silhouetted in an airless and static atmosphere. Their vision was hyper-detailed, their surfaces smooth and polished, without a sense of the artist's brush. Apparent objectivity was proclaimed in their precise "scientific" or mechanical examination of facts, but this approach also imbued objects with an alienating distance and deprived them of organic life, the potential of movement or change. Reified in this fashion, the subjects of *Neue Sachlichkeit* gained the mysterious quality Utitz discerned. Common objects in common contexts lost their commonality.

Utitz's inventory of *Neue Sachlichkeit* still-life motifs includes everyday household objects; prickly cacti would seem out of place on his list were it not for their frequent portrayal by Franz Lenk, Alexander Kanoldt, Georg Scholz, and Georg Schrimpf. "Especially favored," Utitz observed, "are prickly cacti, possibly because a breath of the exotic surrounds them, but also because of their clear, austere bodily structure, so strangely enigmatic."[2] Lenk's single flowering cactus, its every detail itemized in an extraordinarily dry watercolor technique, is isolated in a shadowy ambience vaguely suggesting a window. In its iconic seclusion and glowing emergence from darkness, the plant achieves Utitz's mystery, and is incapable of being subsumed into any genus because of its extreme individuality. It seems an organic embodiment of radical structural principles as its marvelous, luminous blossom extends precariously from a long, slender stem arising from the squat, serrated cactus itself as if in defiance of logic.

Favored in International Style interiors, the cactus was also a preferred plant of the arrived middle class. Dramatic and exotic but requiring little care, it was representative of a well-to-do household in which social and professional demands prevented extensive gardening or other customary signs of prosperity and taste. The Bavarian chronicler Oskar Maria Graf recalled in *Das Leben meiner Mutter* (*The Life of My Mother*) how his brother, newly prosperous with a coffeehouse in the small town of Berg on Lake Starnberg, boasted of his cacti, seeing himself attached through them to a system of bourgeois values which superseded his peasant origins:

> I took walks with Annemarie, and we tore down the [Nazi's anti-Semitic] posters. After coming home, I showed them to Maurus and wanted to discuss them. But he hated politicizing and showed me his newest cacti, which he had recently come to love passionately.
>
> "Here, you've just got to look at this," he called out, "isn't this much more interesting than all that political palaver? Look at how a plant like this slowly, bit by bit takes on a truly remarkable plastic shape!...Just the other day, somebody told me that old Goethe raised cacti! I can't understand why they don't interest you!... Instead, you always come with your politics! As if they don't *always* do their politics without us." Carefully, he rubbed the flat of his hand over the prickly-fine needles and his face took on an almost tender expression.[3]

Maurus's cacti acted as a distraction from the day's realities; they were an aesthetic presence more intriguing, more vital than life itself. Appreciation of them marked the attainment of a certain social status, and the link to Goethe demonstrated both the cactus owner's good taste as well as his respect for the past. The cactus, gingerly embraced and fondled, affirmed and justified middle-class complacency; its cultivation could be substituted for political awareness and replace social sensitivity.

Lenk's watercolor was a prelude to on oil and tempera painting, *Blooming Cactus* of 1933 (estate of the artist, Schwäbisch-Hall). With the cactus clearly set on a window ledge next to an additional plant, in front of a sober, airless landscape, the painting follows a *Neue Sachlichkeit* cactus "portrait" formula that contrasts the potted plant in an interior to an open, extensive landscape. The cactus is thus seen much as in German Romanticism single individuals were depicted gazing through open windows, yearning for release into infinite nature. The cactus again is a substitute, an update of the Romantic compositional formula, but with a different signification. Rather than yearning for release in a panentheistic universe, the cactus blooms behind the protection of a glass window. Its very existence depends on this divorce from the alien Northern environment. An artificial life removed from nature itself, the plant lives not in its own soil but deliberately isolated from it. The cactus then is a metaphor, perhaps for the modernist art Lenk decried, perhaps for the condition of urban humanity.

Lenk's own art in the late 1920s and early 1930s represented a romanticized *Neue Sachlichkeit*, focused on aesthetic and sentimental values while seeking contacts with an audience that had been alienated by "... the convoluted and complex paths of art problems that the past decades brought."[4] Lenk called for art to return to spiritual content, to a realm of secularized religious salvation found in careful contemplation. He insisted, in addition, on an art free of foreign influences, dependent instead on German tradition: "Despite all sensuality of appearance," he wrote in 1931, "art should lead us back to the realm of faith.... There is no theory that leads there, but perhaps quiet, calm, and strength rooted in the soil.... Art demands quiet and its own native soil in order to grow. No plant thrives if it is persistently pulled out of its soil."[5] S. L. D. / R. H.

1. "Ordnung, Klarheit, Strenge erscheinen... die schlichtesten Gegenstände: Teller und Flaschen, stachelige Kakteen und löcherige Käse. Ihr Sein steht fast stechend vor uns, nackt, ungeschminkt. Doch umwittert Geheimnisvolles die Dinge, das aber nicht an sie herangetragen wird, sondern das in ihnen als etwas Unaussprechbares liegt." Emil Utitz, *Die Überwindung des Expressionismus* (Stuttgart: Fenk Verlag, 1927), 140.
2. "Besonders beliebt sind stachelige Kakteen, mag sein, weil der Hauch des Exotischen sie umspinnt, aber auch wegen ihrer klaren, herben, körperlichen Struktur." Ibid., 141.
3. "Ich machte Spaziergänge mit der Annemarie, und wir rissen die [antisemitischen] Zettel ab. Heimkommend, zeigte ich sie Maurus und wollte diskutieren. Der aber hasste das Politisieren und zeigte mir seine neuesten Kakteen, die er in der letzten Zeit leidenschaftlich liebte.
"'Da, das musst du dir einmal genauer anschauen,' rief er, 'ist das nicht weit interessanter als der ganze politische Schmarren, wie so eine Pflanze nach und nach eine ganz sonderbare plastische Form kriegt?... Neulich hat mir einer erzählt, dass auch der alte Goethe ein Kakteenzüchter war! Ich versteh' nicht, dass dich das nicht interessiert!... Immer kommst du mit deiner Politik! *Die* wird doch immer ohne uns gemacht.' Er fuhr behutsam mit der Innenfläche seiner Hand über die stachlig-feinen Borsten und bekam dabei ein fast zärtliches Gesicht." Oskar Maria Graf, *Das Leben meiner Mutter* (New York, 1940; reprint, Munich: Deutscher Taschenbuch Verlag, 1982), 534.
4. "... die verzwickten und verzweigten Wege der Kunstprobleme, die die letzten Jahrzehnte gebracht haben...." Franz Lenk, "Was ich will," *Die Kunst* 32 (1931), reprinted in Uwe M. Schneede, ed., *Die zwanziger Jahre: Manifeste und Dokumente deutscher Künstler* (Cologne: DuMont Buchverlag, 1979), 288.
5. "Ein Bild sollte bei aller Sinnlichkeit der Erscheinung in das Gebiet des Glaubens führen. Dafür gibt es für den Gestalter keine Regel noch ein Rezept. Keine Theorie führt dahin, vielleicht aber ruhige, gleichmässige und bodenständige Kraft.... Die Kunst will Ruhe und eigenen Boden haben zum Wachsen. Keine Pflanze kommt zum Blühen, wenn man sie immer wieder aus der Erde reisst." Ibid.

86 Käthe Loewenthal
Black Ducks (*Schwarze Enten*), c. 1924

Pastel on paper
29.4 x 38.4 cm ($11^1/_2$ x $15^1/_8$ in.), sight
Monogrammed l. l. "KL"

Provenance: Estate of the artist; Neue Münchner Galerie, Munich.

Scenes of barnyard fowl were a popular genre in German art, beginning with nineteenth-century naturalists, who emulated Dutch Baroque precursors. With the introduction of the illustrated press, such images were in constant demand as magazine covers, illustrations, and vignettes, sentimental or entertaining representations of country fauna for a primarily urban readership. The scenes suggested an unfettered, unspoiled life in close contact with nature as an idyllic alternative to city experience, or provided animals with quasi-human characteristics in amusingly narrative genre pictures. By the latter part of the century, animal paintings had developed such a large market that specialized training in animal portrayal was introduced into the curriculum of German academies.

Despite this history in academic art, mass market illustrations, and kitsch, images of domestic fowl continued in the "high art" of Expressionists and progressive painters, such as Edvard Munch and Emil Nolde. Although Käthe Loewenthal studied animal painting at the Berlin Academy under the Impressionist Leo von König, her pastels are closer to these non-academic precedents, which departed from illusionistic anecdote and idyll in favor of more consequential presentations. Her work is difficult to characterize according to standard art-historical perceptions of the 1920s. Surviving works suggest that Loewenthal projected into the decade an earlier Synthetist vocabulary, retaining an attachment to Expressionism and to the example of Ferdinand Hodler, her first teacher. Perceiving in nature analogues to human existence, she infused it with the devotional attitudes of her adopted Christian panentheistic empathy. There are parallels to her approach in neo-Romantic landscapes by Franz Lenk and even Otto Dix early in the 1930s, but Loewenthal did not share their *sachlich* stylistic conviction.

In *Black Ducks*, she depicts five large fowl against a blue-green ground. Wooden duck boxes jut sharply into the background of the composition to form two sides of an irregular triangle that contains and frames the horizontal pattern of ducks in the foreground. Loewenthal repeats the wedge shape beneath the ducks in an amorphous echo of melding pastel colors, implying puddles and grassy mounds. Subtle tonal gradations, surface sheen, and shades of light and dark render the ducks' space ambiguous, counteracting the aggressive perspectival recession of the nest boxes. The dark silhouettes of the ducks emerge within this coloristic and spatial play of nuance as precise, characteristic shapes, solid and individualized in contrast to the ambiguity and repetitive geometry that surrounds them. Isolated within the composition, the ducks are enveloped by pale auras as if further to distinguish their animal life from their environment, and their current freedom from the confinement of the nesting cages above them.

It is difficult, moreover, to view Loewenthal's work without recalling her fate as a born Jew in Adolf Hitler's Germany and her death in a concentration camp. Even the apparently ingenuous motif of black ducks becomes retrospectively transformed into a subjectively perceived analogue to threatened confinement and possible butchery. The inhuman sentence imposed on Loewenthal in 1942 overshadows the intended concerns of the image that confronts us, and deprives it of independence. For us it is impossible to retrieve its innocence. B. T. Y. / R. H.

87 Käthe Loewenthal
Children at the Edge of a Village (*Kinder am Dorfrand*), c. 1924

Pastel on paper
29.8 x 39.5 cm ($11^3/_4$ x $15^1/_2$ in.)
Monogrammed l. l. "KL"

Provenance: Estate of the artist; Neue Münchner Galerie, Munich.

Exhibition: Munich, Neue Münchner Galerie, *Käthe Loewenthal*, 1985.

Käthe Loewenthal transforms a naturalistic vision of a village landscape into an image of foreboding by mixing black into all the colors along the horizon line. Blue sky melts into dark storm clouds and a bright path diminishes on a sweeping curve into shadowed meadow. Two children walk alone along the road, their forms and surroundings slowly engulfed by darkness. The formulation of mood-filled landscape with dramatic perspective and flattened forms Loewenthal has retained from her training with Ferdinand Hodler, as well as from the examples of Vincent van Gogh and Edvard Munch. Through them, in turn, she maintains the aesthetic ideals of Romanticism, focusing on a rural setting and experience, removed from the governance of industry and metropolis in a timeless environment where nature prevails. Human existence is subordinated to nature's overpowering force, whose eternity embodies the qualities of the divine.

Loewenthal spent most summers after 1912 in the town of Vitte on the island of Hiddensee in the Baltic Sea—that year, her sister had purchased an old fisherman's hut there—and it is likely that this pastel derives from one of these stays.[1] Joining the two sisters on the North German island were their mother and another sister, accompanied by her children, so that the months spent in Vitte became times of renewed family identity and linkages. The pastel, in this context, gains the potential of subjective witness as well as bearing testimony to Loewenthal's adherence to Expressionist and Romantic landscape standards, with the town pehaps symbolic of a refuge found, an area of protection from an encroaching and threatening environment. Much of

Loewenthal's surviving imagery contains similar indications of storms, but also of isolated trees or other surrogates of human presence that stand alone, vulnerable and battered, in antagonistic surroundings, much as the two children do here. A Jewish convert to Christianity, a Jew in a society increasingly hostile to Jews, a woman living in close companionship with another woman, working in a profession dominated by men, Loewenthal lived in psychological isolation, longing for integration but not achieving it. In 1909, she had noted with bitterness and hope:

If only I were a man and could speak as my heart speaks—to speak it out loud, talk with human beings: in a small circle at a round table as well as to the entire people from a lofty standpoint without a woman's imposed limitations.... [I believe a time will come] when woman's apparent limitations can be resolved in a natural state of being human ... when a woman will be able to speak openly and publicly about everything and to everyone... and still... be seen and respected as a woman, and her speech as that of a human being.[2]

B. T. Y. / R. H.

1. Erich Heckel, too, spent part of the summer of 1912 on Hiddensee, but no contacts between the two artists are known. Loewenthal's closeness in much of her work to aspects of *Brücke* art, however, make the possibility of such a meeting an intriguing art-historical prospect.
2. "Wär ich ein Mann und könnte da reden, wie mir es im Herzen redet—nach aussen hin, Reden zu den Menschen: im kleinen Kreise, am runden Tisch wie zu allem Volk von hoher Warte aus, ohne weibliche Gebundenheit.... [Ich glaube, die Zeit wird kommen, in der das] äusserliche Gebundensein des Weibes aufgehen kann in ein natürliches Mensch-sein .... wo ein Weib öffentlich und nach aussen hin reden kann, von allem zu allen... und sie doch als Weib angesehen und respektiert wird und ihr Reden als das eines Menschen." Cited by Ingeborg Leuchs, "Einleitung," *Käthe Loewenthal: Ein Erinnerungsbuch* (Munich: Neue Münchner Galerie, 1985), n. p.

88 Elfriede Lohse-Wächtler
Nightclub Balcony (Ausblick im Nachtlokal), 1930

Pastel on paper
72.5 x 55 cm (28 1/2 x 21 5/8 in.)
Monogrammed and dated l. r.
"ELW / 30"

Provenance: Schacht and Westrich, Hamburg; Galerie Brockstedt, Hamburg; Galerie Michael Hasenclever, Munich.

Like other women artists of the 1920s in Germany, such as Else Meidner and Martel Schwichtenberg, Elfriede Wächtler found marriage a problematic experience. Her dedication to her talent prevented her from subordinating herself and her work to the socially prescribed domination of a husband. Political convictions, rooted in the programs of the German Communist Party, as well as an ostentatious bohemianism,

included the equality of women and men but failed to provide the personal and psychological means whereby two careers could unfold simultaneously and without conflict. Extreme financial distress and bankruptcy proceedings contributed to the failure of the artist's marriage to Kurt Lohse, which ended in divorce in 1931. For Lohse-Wächtler, this process and its poisonous antagonisms brought a nervous breakdown early in 1929, and an eight-week treatment at the psychiatric clinic in Friedrichsberg. The experience of her own and other women's mental and physical sufferings in the sanatorium provided her with the means to the personal, mature vocabulary that had eluded her previously, as the Hamburg critic Anna Banaschewski summarized when the pastel *Portraits from Friedrichsberg* (*Köpfe von Friedrichsberg*) were exhibited:

What happened? A young woman artist, early revealed to possess a multifaceted talent, who with severe self-criticism engaged in the search for her own identity and failed to find it, burdened by numerous artistic and just as many personal problems, likable in her honesty as draftsman and painter and in her searching gaze, remarkably cultivated in her sense of color, remarkably ambitious and seldom banal, who nonetheless failed to attract attention to herself, this woman artist undergoes an unexpected development during eight weeks whose results are nothing short of exciting. A creative flood breaks loose—but—and this is absolutely fundamental—she is not the blind tool of some power raging through her; she is in control of countless technical possibilities; she is the wise observer, the viewer with deep psychological intuition. What initially appeared as the burial, the closing off of human-artistic potential, reveals itself now as one of those great crises in the life of a creative individual from which a rich stream bursts forth in powerful eruption, the illumination that follows temporary darkness.[1]

Banaschewski's observations depend on popular beliefs in the kinship and fragile separation of creative genius and madness, and testify to heightened contemporary interest in the art of schizophrenics and others affected by forms of apparent mental illness. Vincent van Gogh, committed to the asylum at Saint-Rémy, is the unacknowledged prototype of this interpretation of Lohse-Wächtler. The pastels demonstrated her newly achieved artistic maturity as well as her compassionate insight into the physical-psychological sufferings of her fellow patients, with no hope of cure, isolated in the realities of their fantasy or silently awaiting the terminal effects of cancerous tumors or sclerosis. "She has captured the essence of their being," the critic claimed, "and psychiatrists even consider the specifics of [the patients'] psychological illness to be recognizable in her images."[2] With a gift of "psychological intuition," she is capable of revealing through her imagery the hidden contortions of the other inmates' disturbed souls, competing in the subjectivity of her art with the scientific objectivity of medical diagnosis and, implicitly, surpassing it.

This celebration of Lohse-Wächtler's artistic genius also coincides with the discovery of the art of mental patients by an increasingly larger audience. Since the publication of Hans Prinzhorn's *Artistry of the Mentally Ill* in 1922,[3] his international collection of some six thousand works by patients in mental institutions was the material of popular as well as art-historical and psychiatric admiration, curiosity, and study. After seeing drawings, paintings, and sculptures from the collection, Alfred Kubin, for example, identified them as "miracles of the spirit of art" which had "dawned forth from the depths, distant from anything thoughtful-rational, and needs must enrich both creativity and enjoyment. Herein resides their value, that they are indicative of the universal; and that, too, is why it was with a feeling of sublime joy that I responded to them."[4] Positive links between the perceived archetypal art of the mentally ill and modern art were also discovered, so that Prinzhorn concluded in 1929, "if the art of these alienated individuals so closely approximates contemporary art, it is because it corresponds to the most hidden aspirations of our era."[5]

Banaschewski's insistence that Lohse-Wächtler's drawings were not the result of a "blind force raging through her" distinguishes the trained artist's work from that of the other clinic inmates, while also positing a quality of immediacy common to both. Like the drawings of Prinzhorn's patients, Lohse-Wächtler's pastels are presented as products of an indefinable subconscious drive which permits her to empathize with the sufferings of those around her and to render their subjective reality as a shared reality of the times. A similar perception of an objectified subjectivity is likewise to be read in Lohse-Wächtler's more characteristic imagery, which she derived, like numerous other artists of the decade, from Hamburg's bars, nightclubs, and brothels; she devoted much of her work to these themes after her release from Friedrichsberg.

The denizens of this demimonde of entertainment and commercial sex, like the clinic's patients, were of a reality distinguished from that of rational normalcy. Rendered in garish colors, in alternating flashes of light and dark, with a linear ductus that resists stasis and with juttingly irregular strokes of pastel, the audience in *Nightclub Balcony* gazes down at a dance floor or stage beyond the limits of the drawing. The diagonal orientation and sharp spatial jumps from foreground to background and down into the central nightclub arena lend a dislocating sense of instability to the scene. Dominant in the image is the bright red back of a woman, her sinewy arms bare, her blond hair cropped short, turned sharply to the right to show a profile with a large red-tinted eye, heavy lips, and bared teeth. Separated from her by a tabletop and glass, leaning or disintegrating against the picture edge, is a dark-clothed man, his face and body virtually dissolved as a distorted, drunken vision in scumbled black-blue pastel shading with smears of red. Grimacing faces and swipes of color likewise characterize the other customers arranged behind him along

the balcony edge, beneath a flutter of striped banners.

In a revived Expressionist manner, Lohse-Wächtler duplicates the electrified, agitated vision of the nightclub patron. If her portraits from the clinic were efforts in revealing her fellow patients' psychological states, not her own, the nightclub scene likewise interprets the responses of its participants. Unlike Expressionism's aesthetic of personal revelation, in which the image was deemed to pictorialize the artist's psychological dynamic, Lohse-Wächtler's concern is less with her own psyche than with that of the world she witnessed. The object, not the subject, is primary, although in a self-determining subjective treatment of the object. Her ever-varying linear rhythms characterize, codify, and contain her figures, but precariously, tentatively. Despite the power of her colors and their bold application, Lohse-Wächtler's images betray an underlying frailty in which they question the power of their own existence. "Perpetual dissatisfaction with what she created drives her restlessly towards new works," Banaschewski commented, maintaining a fundamental identity between the reality Lohse-Wächtler chose to depict and her own subjective being.[6] Distinctions disappear, and Lohse-Wächtler's scenes of Hamburg nightlife, because of her participation in it, become as much scenes of her own life as of an empathetically rendered external other. R. H.

1. "Was ist geschehen? Eine junge Malerin, deren vielfältiges Talent sich früh zeigte, die in strenger Selbstkritik einen Weg suchte und ihn noch nicht fand, beschwert von viel künstlerischer und ebenso viel menschlicher Problematik, sympathisch durch ihre zeichnerisch-malerische Ehrlichkeit, den suchenden Blick, beachtenswert kultiviert in ihrem Farbempfinden, beachtenswert fleissig, selten banal, aber keineswegs auffallend, macht innerhalb acht Wochen eine Entwicklung durch, die aufregende Perspektiven hat. Ein Schaffensstrom bricht hervor—aber—und das ist sehr wesentlich—sie ist nicht blindes Werkzeug einer durch sie jagenden Kraft, sie ist die Beherrscherin zahlloser technischer Möglichkeiten, die kluge Beobachterin, die mit tiefer psychologischer Intuition Schauende. Was anfangs als Zudeckung, Abschnürung menschlich-künstlerischer Potenz erschien, zeigt sich als eine jener grossen Krisen im Leben eines Schaffenden, aus der in heftiger Eruption ein reicher Strom bricht, Aufhellung nach flüchtiger Verdunkelung." Anna Banaschewski, "Friedrichsberger Köpfe: Zeichnungen von Elfriede Lohse-Wächtler," *Der Kreis* 6 (1929): 307.
2. "Sie hat die Essenz ihres Wesens festgehalten, und sogar die Eigenart ihrer psychischen Erkrankung ist für den Psychiater meist aus den Bildern ablesbar." Ibid., 308.
3. Hans Prinzhorn, *Die Bildnerei der Geisteskranken* (Berlin: Springer Verlag, 1922); trans. Eric von Brockdorff as *Artistry of the Mentally Ill: A Contribution to the Psychology and Psychopathology of Configuration* (New York: Springer Verlag, 1972).
4. "... Wundern des Künstlergeistes, die aus Tiefen jenseits alles Gedanklich-überlegten heraufdämmern und Schaffen und Anschauen beglücken müssen. Hierin liegt der Wert, der ins Allgemeine weist;

darum war es auch ein Gefühl erhebendster Freude, mit dem ich diese Eindrücke aufnahm." Alfred Kubin, notations of 1922 cited by Stefanie Poley, "'...und nicht mehr lassen mich diese Dinge los': Prinzhorns Buch 'Die Bildnerei der Geisteskranken' und seine Wirkung in der modernen Kunst," in Heidelberger Kunstverein e. V., *Die Prinzhorn-Sammlung: Bilder, Skulpturen, Texte aus Psychiatrischen Anstalten (ca. 1890–1920)* (Königstein/Taunus: Athenäum Verlag, 1980), 58.

5. "...si l'art des aliénés touche de si près à l'art contemporain, c'est qu'il correspond aux aspirations les plus secrètes de notre époque." Hans Prinzhorn, "Apropos de l'art des aliénés," *Variétés* 1 (1929): 577–581, as cited by Werner Janzarik, "Der bildnerische Ausdruck seelischen Krankseins als projektiver Stimulus," in Heidelberger Kunstverein, *Die Prinzhorn-Sammlung*, 6.

6. "...die ewige Unzufriedenheit mit dem Geschaffenen treibt sie rastlos zu neuem Schaffen." Banaschewski, 310.

---

89 Elfriede Lohse-Wächtler
Lissy, 1931

Watercolor over pencil on paper
68 x 49 cm (19^1/$_4$ x 26^{13}/$_{16}$ in.)
Monogrammed and dated l. r.
"ELW/31"

Provenance: Galerie Krokodil, Hamburg; Galerie Brockstedt, Hamburg; Galerie Michael Hasenclever, Munich.

Lissy, the subject of this watercolor, stands provocatively in a brilliant red, formfitting dress, her left hand on her hip, her right hand ostentatiously displaying a cigarette holder. Seen in three-quarter view, she turns her blond head towards the viewer and gazes over her bare shoulder from deeply shadowed eyes, a questioning smile or perhaps inquisitive sneer on her heavy lips. A cocktail glass, testimony to the fashion in Germany for American-style mixed drinks, appears on a marble-topped table as another of Lissy's attributes as she presides over a bar or café such as Elfriede Lohse-Wächtler regularly depicted in the early 1930s. A couple sits at another table in the background, the grotesquely caricatured faces and bodies functioning as shadowed blues within which shine the red, pink, and white of lips, skin, and teeth. With its directly juxtaposed reds —spilling from one area into another, providing a continual skipping accent —and blues, its pinks, greens, and yellows, the watercolor is executed in the effulgent color scheme Lohse-Wächtler favored at this time as an analogue of psychologically tense excitation and sensual confrontation.

Her presence in a bar alone, as well as her provocative clothing and flirtatious deportment, identify Lissy as a prostitute, or at least as a woman whose physical appeal constitutes part of her public, professional identity—if not a prostitute then perhaps the owner of the bar. The ambivalence projected here contrasts significantly to more common representations of prostitutes by Weimar Germany's male artists. In those images, prostitutes function as ciphers of commercial availability,

posed in windows, displaying themselves, or otherwise arousing the approval of potential male (usually bourgeois) customers. The impersonal nature of the commercial transaction and the reduction of women to commodity are emphasized. Women's subjugation is acknowledged in such instances, but as the prostitutes' sexual appeal, their unveiled sexual organs, and the process of their negotiations are foregrounded, the images also emerge as voyeuristic projections in which the male artist participates in the very practices presented for condemnation. Given a determining male gaze in combination with the character of the scenes depicted, in which women overtly play roles of commercial self-presentation and sexual objectification, such ambivalence may be inevitable, although the personal attitudes of Otto Dix, George Grosz, or Rudolf Schlichter towards women often would seem to be more condoning than condemning of the practices they portray.

Lohse-Wächtler's *Lissy* is a relatively rare example of a woman treating female sexuality in a commercial context, one where both observer and observed are women, but the code of vision remains male-determined.[1] Provocatively eccentric in her own life and appearance, Lohse-Wächtler frequented Hamburg's demimonde and such socially ostracized institutions as gypsy camps after her release from the Friedrichsberg clinic; the milieu and inhabitants of these became the major focus of her art. In her study of Lissy, the frequently elevated or inferior position for the imagined viewer that characterizes Dix's or Schlichter's images of women, implying either domination or subordination, is supplanted by direct confrontation. Viewer and subject are on the same level, equal, with neither in a position of power in relation to the other. Lissy, however, with her red dress and her imposing figure extending from upper to lower edge of the drawing, dominates the scene in which she appears and demands that she be the focus as she gazes attentively out at the beholder. While Weimar Germany's male artists usually fetishize the sexual aspects of a model's body—whether nude or clothed—such as breasts, buttocks, or genitals, Lohse-Wächtler explores the totality of the figure, rendering its general form beneath the tight dress but not valuing any particular area more than another. Instead, the aging flesh of the hands and arms becomes a major factor, testimony to fading youth, while Lissy's heavy makeup similarly signals a struggle against the loss of those qualities deemed attractive to her male customers.

The practiced turn of her body loses something of its provocativeness in conjunction with these testimonials to age, denoting habitual action, not impetuous response or flirtatious action. Like the red dress, cigarette holder, and makeup, posture and gesture are part of a professional vocabulary which is beginning to lose its effectiveness. Lissy, in Lohse-Wächtler's presentation, is a woman poised at the edge of the loss of livelihood. Her ability to attract men according to the established norms of the institutions of commodified sexuality is threatened by the unavoidable

processes of time, whose symptoms Lohse-Wächtler presents with precision, without commentary except for what is implied in an empathetic confrontation in equality.   R. H.

1. Also see the works by Jeanne Mammen, cat. nos. 90–92.

---

90 Jeanne Mammen
The Journey Home (Heimfahrt), 1920s

Black chalk on paper
38.5 x 31.25 cm (15^1/$_8$ x 12^1/$_4$ in.)
Signed l. r. "J. Mammen"

Provenance: Fischer Fine Art, London; Piccadilly Gallery, London.

A little-explored aspect of Weimar Germany's artistic production are the drawings, watercolors, and pastels that appeared weekly as covers, illustrations, or reproductions in numerous popular periodicals. These journals ranged from general interest and humor magazines, such as *Simplicissimus* and *Uhu (Owl)*, via liberal intellectual reviews like *Die Weltbühne (The World Stage)*, to those aimed at special audiences, including *Der Junggeselle* for bachelors, the fashion magazine *Die Dame (The Lady)*, and the nudist movement's *Die Schönheit (Beauty)*. Max Beckmann and Karl Hofer were among the major artists who contributed to these efforts; others, such as Rudolf Grossmann (see cat. no. 48), were artists who focused on drawings and prints or who were professional illustrators. At the end of the 1920s, Jeanne Mammen was one of the most prolific and admired of the artist-illustrators, as is apparent from the critic Kurt Tucholsky's open letter to her:

The tender, aroma-filled watercolors you publish in various periodicals and satirical journals so far surpass the undisciplined scribblings of most of your professional colleagues that we owe you a small declaration of love. Your figures are clearly presented; they are both charming and severe; and they leap forth from the paper as if they were of flesh and blood. In the delicatessen shop which your employers open up for us weekly or monthly, you are virtually the sole delicacy available.[1]

Mammen depicts the world of women among themselves and in society with men. Her motifs of lovers in restaurants and bars, on park benches, or at dances, her scenes of flirtation and prostitution, of show girls and lesbians, are common to the work of many male artists of the time, but, like Elfriede Lohse-Wächtler (see cat. nos. 88–89), Mammen often reveals an otherwise rare sensitivity and empathy towards her female characters, even if they are presented judgmentally. In *The Journey Home*, the foreground focus is on a young woman, fashionably clothed in a fur-trimmed coat, with a chic coiffure of short-cut hair, who shares a nocturnal cab ride with her male companion, similarly at-

tired in formal evening wear. As she gazes out of the cab at the passing street life and lights, he is unceremoniously slumped over, oblivious to her and soundly asleep.

Mammen orchestrates the lights and shadows of her image, registering the three-dimensional fading into two in order to grant the woman a presence and corporeal reality which the man lacks. His dark form melts into the shadows of the cab's interior, so that he appears as a collection of disjointed, powerless body parts and clothing fragments, nothing more than gloved hands, white scarf, top hat, and an undifferentiated face deprived of individuality. She, however, is alert and erect, her entire form in light, and her head turns to face a world beyond both the taxi and the drawing. Feline-like, with heavily made-up eyes transformed into sharply attentive slits, her face emerges from the enveloping softness of her luxurious fur collar to register both boredom and disdain.

Among Mammen's frequent themes is that of the unequal pair, the young woman who is an older man's object of desire. Age distinctions in these images signal overt psychological distance. *The Journey Home* is a variation on the theme, as the separation and alienation between the self-assured woman and the unconscious man sharing the taxi is palpable. The façade of elegance and glamor is pierced, and the couple's intimacy is characterized as one of proximity alone.   R. H.

1. "Die zarten, duftigen Aquarelle, die Sie in Magazinen und Witzblättern veröffentlichen, überragen das undisziplinierte Geschmier der meisten Ihrer Zunftkollegen derart, dass man Ihnen eine kleine Liebeserklärung schuldig ist. Ihre Figuren fassen sich sauber an, sie sind anmutig und herb dabei, und sie springen mit Haut und Haaren aus dem Papier. In dem Delikatessenladen, den uns Ihre Brotherren wöchentlich oder monatlich aufsperren, sind Sie so ziemlich die einzige Delikatesse." Kurt Tucholsky, "Antwort an Jeanne Mammen," *Die Weltbühne* 25, no. 32 (6 August 1929): 225.

---

91 Jeanne Mammen
Berlin Street Scene (Berliner Strassenszene), c. 1927–29

Watercolor over pencil on vellum
33.8 x 48.4 cm (13^1/$_3$ x 19 in.)
Signed u. l. "J. Mammen"

Provenance: Private collection, Germany; Hauswedell and Nolte, Hamburg.

In his lengthy study on morality in the post-World War I era, Magnus Hirschfeld, founder of the Institute for Sexual Research in Berlin, published this watercolor under the title "The Street Is There for the Traffic."[1] It is not known whether this *double-entendre* reflects Jeanne Mammen's own title, since Hirschfeld frequently adapted titles to suit his text. In periodicals of the 1920s, however, Mammen's works often bore similar humorous explanatory quotations and titles, supplied by the artist or at times by her editors. The scenes are thus designed to receive supplementary verbal accompaniment, to be suggestive of a narrative potential in terms of brief aperçus, often with comic overtones as befitted the satirical journals for which Mammen worked. It is in the image's capacity to do this, not in the accuracy or authorship of titles and commentaries, that *Berlin Street Scene* finds its identity.

Mammen's setting is a sidewalk café on the fashionable thoroughfare of Kurfürstendamm, where, on the far less fashionable level of an attic, she had her studio. Hirschfeld's title refers to the throng of pedestrians on the sidewalk and to the street traffic indicated by a passing double-decker bus rising above them. "Traffic," however, also alludes to the women offering themselves in the traffic of prostitution, most notably the one wearing a fox stole at the far right who turns to look seductively over her shoulder, and possibly to several other single or paired women in the scene. Their stylish clothing and setting may identify them, moreover, as middle-class women who, so Hirschfeld's study reported, turned in apparently large numbers to part-time prostitution as a means of improving their financial situation during the 1920s:

Appalling is the growth of prostitution in all countries in the decade from 1919 to 1929. It consisted not only of the women registered and hygienically supervised by the police, but also of all those girls and women who escaped police supervision and followed the "horizontal profession" under various more or less successful disguises. . . . Not a few housewives sold their bodies in order to improve their economic situation. . . . The number of "the secret" stood in glaring disproportion to the "official ones." Numbers are usually boring, but, nonetheless, it should be mentioned here that, besides the 6,000 registered prostitutes in Berlin, an army of 60,000 of "the secret" . . . were on the street.[2]

Whether or not Hirschfeld's statistics are accurate, they point to a perception, exploited by the watercolor's attributed title, of the prevalence of prostitution in Berlin.

While Mammen's display of women on Kurfürstendamm can serve such a perception of "hidden" prostitution, as the watercolor focuses on the life of Berlin's street at night it also celebrates the city's prosperity during the few years before the onset of the Great Depression in 1929. The café is crowded with well-dressed patrons taking pleasure in drinks and conversation as a waitress rushes among them and the sidewalk swarms with prosperous Berliners. Where artists such as George Grosz had earlier depicted sidewalk cafés (see cat. 54) as callous oases of plenty in a city populated by war cripples and starving children, Mammen's Berlin, rendered in elegant muted tones of violet, brown, gray, and red, is a city in which misery and deprivation no longer have a place—or are kept at a distance from this scene of seeing and being seen, of consumers and the pleasures awaiting them.

Mammen distributes vignettes of physiognomic characterization and

psychological expression throughout the image, such as the man walking on the sidewalk at right, his head proudly held high above the crowd, while the young woman on his arm slouches, bored or even depressed, at his side. In the café, in the foreground, a teenaged girl—not yet graduated to stockings, she wears knee-socks with her short skirt—sips a drink through a straw. She, too, slouches forward and appears submissive next to her large, erect, domineering mother seated at the same table, observing the street traffic coldly as her daughter obediently slurps the drink from her glass. Fat, moustached men in the café behind her similarly speak of a society in which personal bullying and domination are accepted norms of behavior, belying the gentility and subtlety of Mammen's colors.

R. H.

1. "Die Strasse dient dem Verkehr," in Magnus Hirschfeld, *Zwischen Zwei Katastrophen*, rev. ed. of *Sittengeschichte der Nachkriegszeit*, vol. 2 of *Sittengeschichte des 20. Jahrhunderts* (Hanau a. M.: Verlag Karl Schustek, 1966 [orig. ed., 1930], 379.
2. "Ungeheuer ist die Prostitution in allen Staaten innerhalb der zehn Jahre von 1919–1929 angewachsen. Sie setzten sich nicht nur aus den bei der Polizei Registrierten und gesundheitlich Kontrollierten zusammen, sondern auch aus all den Mädchen und Frauen, die sich der Aufsicht der Polizei entzogen und unter mehr oder weniger geschicktem Deckmantel dem 'horizontalen Gewerbe' nachgingen . . . . So manche Ehefrau verkaufte zur Verbesserung ihrer wirtschaftlichen Lage ihren Körper . . . . Die Zahl dieser 'Heimlichen' stand in einem schreienden Missverhältnis zu der der 'Öffentlichen.' Zahlen sind meist langweilig; dennoch sei hier erwähnt, dass neben 6000 eingeschriebenen Prostituierten in Berlin ein Heer von mindestens 60 000 'Heimlichen' . . . auf den Strich ging." Ibid., 377.

92 Jeanne Mammen
Boring Dollies (Langweilige Puppen), c. 1927–30

Watercolor over pencil on paper
38.7 x 28.5 cm (15¹/₄ x 11¹/₄ in.)
Signed u. l. "J. Mammen";
inscribed on matting l. l.
"Langweilige Puppen"

Provenance: Gallery La Boetie, New York; Hauswedell and Nolte, Hamburg.

Ennui is a subject Jeanne Mammen addressed repeatedly in her work of the late 1920s. Typically, the scenes involve prosperous members of Weimar society, often stylishly dressed and coiffured younger women in the company of older men. The implications of degeneracy, of women bought and kept, are unmistakable and persistent components of these scenes, which update the traditional motif of the unequal pair. Conventional imagery, however, or that of Otto Dix and George Grosz during the 1920s, accents the obvious disparity between the wrinkled, wizened, shriveled men in these relationships and their voluptuous, robust companions, frequently to the point of caricature as the men's salacious appetites are accentuated. Mammen's

focus is on the women and on the physical and psychological effects of the barter in which they exchange their freedom for a life of idleness and material luxury.

A variation on this theme, *Boring Dollies* depicts two young women in the company of a female clown doll. As the red-headed woman stares upwards into space and the other smokes a cigarette in mannered fashion, neither communicates with the other. Elegant pearl and ivory necklaces subtly highlight their refined but understated wardrobe to bespeak a sense of casually accepted prosperity. The silence and inactivity, the postures and facial expressions of these women, their withdrawal into a cool somnolent self-contemplation, identify this self-indulgent affluence with tedium. The clown doll serves as an attribute of entertainment, of repeated and routine performance which disguises the person of the performer beneath an alternative reality of masks and makeup. Mammen's title, meantime, describes the "dollies" of her watercolor not in terms of the women's own ennui, but as being as boring as they are bored, as failing to arouse any action or interest.

The writer Erich Kästner portrayed similar women in his ironic popular poems characterizing and satirizing Weimar society, as in "Refined Daughters in Conversation":

The one sits. The other reclines.
They talk a lot. The time goes by.
They don't let it bother them.
The one reclines. The other sits.
They talk a lot. The sofa sweats
As it listens to their stupidity.

They are built so effectively
and have such very refined skin.
What might it cost per yard?
Their corners they have rounded off.
And they wear makeup so that their mouths
and bodies will not suffer rust. . . .

Their head is pretty and pretty empty.
But they still feel quite satisfied.[1]

Like their silent counterparts in Mammen's watercolor, Kästner's prattling women pass their time and wait mindlessly, bored.

Boredom and melancholy, however, could take on additional meaning in Weimar Germany. Significantly, Kästner himself was criticized as dissatisfied and melancholic by his fellow writer Walter Benjamin. But Kästner's melancholy, Benjamin concluded, "is due to routine. For to be submissive to routine means to have sacrificed one's idiosyncracies, to have betrayed the gift of being horrified."[2] Benjamin, moreover, attributed this melancholic state, which results in inactivity, to Germany's left-wing intellectuals and publicists in general, accusing them of having transformed revolutionary reflex and social concern into objects of amusement, empty shells of comfort incapable of political action. For Benjamin, melancholy was a symptom of a society no longer capable of combatting its own ills and evils, a society increasingly inured to its own insensitivity.

R. H.

1. "Die Eine sitzt. Die Andre liegt./Sie reden viel. Die Zeit verfliegt./Das scheint

sie nicht zu stören./Die Eine liegt. Die Andre sitzt./Sie reden viel. Das Sofa schwitzt/und muss viel Dummes hören./ Sie sind sehr wirkungsvoll gebaut/und haben ausgesuchte Haut./Was mag der Meter kosten?/Sie sind an allen Ecken rund./Sie sind bemalt, damit der Mund/ und die Figur nicht rosten. . . ./Ihr Kopf ist hübsch und ziemlich hohl./Sie fühlen sich trotzdem sehr wohl." Erich Kästner, "Höhere Töchter im Gespräch,", in *Gesammelte Schriften*, vol. 1, *Gedichte* (Zurich: Atrium Verlag, 1959), 208–209.
2. " . . . kommt . . . aus Routine. Denn Routiniertsein heisst, seine Idiosynkrasien geopfert, die Gabe, sich zu ekeln, preisgegeben haben." Walter Benjamin, "Linke Melancholie," in *Ausgewählte Schriften*, vol. 2, *Angelus Novus* (Frankfurt a. M.: Suhrkamp Verlag, 1966), 458; trans. Ben Brewster as "Left-Wing Melancholy. (On Erich Kästner's New Book of Poems)," *Screen* 15, no. 2 (Summer 1974): 30.

93 Herbert Marxen
The Seamstress (Die Schneiderin), 1927

Oil on canvas
51.5 x 47.5 cm (20¹/₄ x 18³/₄ in.)
Monogrammed and dated u. l.
"HM/27"; monogrammed and inscribed on stretcher "HM/Die Schneiderin/"

Provenance: Galerie Brockstedt, Hamburg

A dressmaker's form, one of the ubiquitous emblematic presences in 1920s painting, dominates Herbert Marxen's composite image portraying, according to its title, a seamstress. Framing this semi-abstract black form that dominates the foreground are a nude woman and a white shift on a hanger suspended from a nail. Otherwise the gray interior is empty, save for a pin cushion, tape measure, pins and needle, and an iron displayed on a table as further signs of the seamstress's trade.

Marxen was active primarily as a commercial artist, cartoonist, and illustrator in Flensburg, a city in Schleswig-Holstein in the far north of Germany. Through his academy studies and contributions to the satirical journals *Jugend* and *Simplicissimus*, he was also associated with Munich's artistic milieu. His major aesthetic concern was a moderately stylized imagery that would find widespread comprehension among the German public. His painting, however, belongs to a more private world where ambiguity is generated through montage-like juxtapositions of disparate but related elements. Stylistically, in its muted and limited color scale, in the simplicity of the composition with a few accented and focused elements, and in the classicizing proportions of the female nude, *The Seamstress* is related to the work of such Munich artists as Georg Schrimpf or Max Radler (see cat. nos. 127–129). Its imagery, however, departs significantly from Munich practices, with their clearly defined, Biedermeier interiors and landscapes. Here, the dressmaker's form overpowers the entire image as a dark, multivalent presence shifting from human anatomical reference to bell, bulb, or cloche hat and to virtual abstraction.

The primary motif of the painting, it is ironically the least precisely delineated, a black shape that reads as a void, the most hermeneutically malleable of the objects represented.

The constructed, adjustable tailor's dummy, denying or anticipating color, waits to shape and carry a woman's dress. The white shift nearby similarly signals a woman's body as an absence through which the plain, unadorned garment gains its physical and functional rationale. Both shift and tailor's dummy are thus determined in their appearance by an external model; totally dependent, they lack a self-generated identity. The naked woman at the left, her arms raised in a beauty pose that reveals the totality of her body as she gazes to the side, perhaps into a mirror beyond the picture frame, becomes the measure for the forms that share her pictorial world.

Her nakedness prevents a reading of the image as a slightly stylized rendering of a fitting at a seamstress's shop; the woman would certainly wear undergarments while trying on the clothing made to her measure. Marxen's title, moreover, suggests that the painting is less a recorded scene than the evocation of a portrait, although not a physiological likeness, in a manner similar to Hein Heckroth's *Ada* (cat. no. 61). If the painting is such a multiple representation of a person, the multiplicity is reduced to more specific terms by means of the seamstress's bodily presence and—because of her otherwise superfluous nakedness—sexual identity, in conjunction with the hallmarks of her profession.

The accentuation of the seamstress as woman suggests a further refinement of this decoding. The depicted elements of her trade are passive ones, awaiting some action upon them or shaped according to functional demands. Such active tools of the seamstress's trade as her scissors or sewing machine, or indications of the actual, completed products of her art, are significantly missing from the scene, as are her customers. Accompanied by attributes whose essential meaning lies in their pliancy and receptivity, the naked woman, too, partakes of these qualities. Like the dressmaker's form, she demands to be shaped and provided with an identity, or perhaps literally to carry an identity other than her own, if the vaguely womb-like shape of the dressmaker's dummy is taken into account. *The Seamstress* then appears as Marxen's imaging of female receptivity, a woman's lack of independent identity, and her need for the external determination of clothing measured and provided, presumably, by a man.   R. H.

94   Frans Masereel
Accordionist in a Tavern (L'Accordéoniste au cabaret), 1927

Oil on canvas
49.8 x 64.9 cm (19⁹/₁₆ x 25⁹/₁₆ in.)
Monogrammed and dated l. r.
"FM/1927"
Vorms 108

Provenance: Jan Tyssen, Brussels; Kunsthaus Lempertz, Cologne.

Best known for his acerbic and poignant socio-political woodcuts, which served as book illustrations or independent "novels in pictures," the self-taught Flemish artist Frans Masereel was a major influence in the Germany of the 1920s. Part of the small group of European refugees that gathered in Geneva during World War I, Masereel produced woodcut illustrations for the pacifist newspapers *Demain (Tomorrow)* and *La Feuille (The Newspaper)* which attracted the attention of Germany's political left. An appreciative critic noted in 1930 that "during a time when nearly all intellectuals failed to support their convictions and hardly a single one remained true to the principles of socialism, he remained steadfast and did not participate in the 'betrayal by the intellectuals.'"[1] Book illustrations for works by Romain Rolland, Emile Verhaeren, and Walt Whitman, and several series of anti-war woodcuts corresponded to both the aesthetic of Expressionism and the ideology of the moderate as well as radical left, who praised Masereel for having "extended the folklike and social character of woodcut art....In his hands it became dynamic as never before."[2] With his revolutionary idealism and extraordinary inventiveness of image and form, Masereel gained the favor of such otherwise antagonistic authors as Bertolt Brecht, Rainer Maria Rilke, Thomas and Heinrich Mann, Hermann Hesse, and Kurt Tucholsky. Masereel's literary supporters represented a remarkably broad spectrum of political affiliation, from center to extreme left, such as virtually no other artist enjoyed at the time.

After purchasing a fisherman's hut in Equihen, near Boulogne-sur-Mer, in 1924, Masereel turned increasingly to oil paint as his preferred medium, and developed a personal style of massive figures and muted colors, frequently with gray-green and brown-gold dominant, that served as an extension of the social realism developed in Belgium at the end of the nineteenth century by Constantin Meunier. Political commitment remained a major component in these harbor scenes, but not in overt images of urban rebellion or the drudgery of proletarian existence. Instead, Masereel's fishermen are silent monuments to a life unchanged and unchanging in its struggle with the sea and in the comforting communal protection offered in small taverns glowing with a golden light. The degree to which such perceptions corresponded to France's largest fishing port, a center of both the fishing and canning industries, and also a significant naval site, is at best dubious, and they should be recognized as idyllic projections by both Masereel and the audiences he was addressing.

In *Accordionist in a Tavern*, Masereel structures his figures in a light that alternately shades and sharply illuminates as it gently breaks through the dark ambience of the painting. Seated on a wine-red bench between two tables, the accordionist is only partially highlighted, a dark figure against a wall of yellow ocher. Emerging ponderous and gray from the shadows, he dominates the scene with the fused mass of his body and his accordion, and is situated as if he and it were the source of the light surrounding them. This light becomes a metaphor for his music as it transforms the somber atmosphere of the tavern and plays off the bodies of two women seated nearby. The light links them to the musician despite their spatial and existential separation, while the ship above them—not a modern steamer but a nineteenth-century sailing vessel that completes the painting's nostalgic mood—indicates the life of the men absent from the painting.

Alone, the women are joined in the music and the imagined presence of the sea with its full-rigged ship. Their pensive waiting is pulled from its melancholy ambience by the accordionist's melodies. Like the music, moreover, the bodies of these women, whose revealing clothing suggests they may be harbor prostitutes, wait to offer their comfort to the toiling men of the sea once they enter the tavern's dim shelter. The scene as Masereel painted it appears atemporal, removed from present and past and transformed into an eternal present, calm and unalterable, as if to state majestically but despondently that such a life has always been, and always shall be, the perpetual contrast to the "electric vitality of the metropolis, the life of automobiles and subway stations, of ghostly all-night bars and overfilled trains."[3]   C. D. G.

1. "In einer Zeit, in der beinahe alle Intellektuelle versagten und kaum einer den Idealen des Sozialismus treu blieb, hat er standgehalten und 'Den Verrat der Geistigen' nicht mitgemacht." Nico Roost, "Frans Masereel," *Kunst der Zeit* 1, no. 12 (September 1930): 267.
2. "...Masereel hat...die Volkstümlichkeit und den sozialen Charakter der Holzschnittkunst erweitert....Unter seinen Händen ist sie dynamisch geworden wie nie vorher." Ibid., 265.
3. "...die elektrische Vitalität der Grossstadt, das Leben der Autos und unterirdischen Bahnhöfe, der gespensterischen Nachtlokale und der überfüllten Züge." Ibid., 269.

95   Frans Masereel
Seaman with a Woman (Marin et femme), 1928

Oil on canvas
72.5 x 60.1 cm (28⁹/₁₆ x 23⁵/₈ in.)
Monogrammed and dated l. l.
"FM/1928"

Provenance: Frank Crowninshield, New York; Walter O. Schneider, Beverly Hills.

Exhibition: Windsor, Ontario, Art Gallery of Windsor, *A Tribute to Frans Masereel*, 1981.

In 1930, Georg F. Hartlaub, who organized Frans Masereel's first major German retrospective at Mannheim that year, contrasted the artist's paintings to his woodcuts and compared them to an orchestra's rich sonority, as opposed to "more pointed, rhythmical chamber music." Has the artist changed totally since he began every summer in Boulogne-sur-Mer to conquer anew the atmosphere and scent of the sea, the tangle of ships' masts a[nd] smoke stacks, the warm darkness of seamen's taverns, the broad gait of the fishermen and seafarers? Certainly, war and inflation, the cripplingly present, terrible actuality, are over. Many another artist has heard the message of increased calmness. But Frans Masereel['s]...apparent transformation is only self-development, a clear willingness to reveal the central kernel of his being....Essentially, Masereel has always remained a lyricist, a pantheist, an enthused believer attentive to "the music of the world." ...Life's figures gain through him a mysterious sense of distance, and sometimes it seems to us as if this artist does not present the conditions and actions of our time except in the way a ballad or a melancholic-harsh street song might report on forgotten events.[1]

Hartlaub discovers in the paintings "the Flemish, original Netherlandish face of the modern metropolitan Masereel," the stable foundation in the quiet and patient characteristics of his ancestry that supported his existence in the "most convulsion-filled concentrations of the whirlpool of life on our planet."[2] Perpetual values are perceived in the paintings that provide the counterpoint to the political, moral, and psychological indictments of Masereel's narrative woodcuts.

The figures in this painting are visionary formulations, emerging light from enveloping darkness. Using broad spatula strokes to compose brick-shaped areas of color which shape light, dark, and image, Masereel generates an interior, a single wall with a bench and table before it. Seated on the bench, his arms heavy on the table, gazing directly out of the painting: a man in seaman's cap, jacket, and sweater. Sitting opposite him, seen in profile, her eyes downcast and head bent forward: a woman in a low-cut dress who may be a prostitute, waitress, or tavern entertainer. The two do not speak to one another, nor communicate; silence is their bond. A triangular composition joins their quasi-geometric forms, producing an effect of firm stability. Masereel avoids individualizing features in favor of a physiognomic type common to the Franco-Flemish fishermen and seafarers among whom he spent his summers, away from the constant motion and transformation of the cities he otherwise inhabited. The submissive position of the woman within the supportive triangular configuration generated by the seaman, her contemplative turn inward contrasted to his determined stare forward and outward, their existence side by side as coloristic as well as psychological foils, the irreducible simplicity of clothing and surroundings—these form the unalterable world of the archetypal humanity Masereel proposes.

The history of the painting provides a further augmenting commentary. Like Jean-François Millet's peasants a century earlier, Masereel's nobly proportioned, silent, and monumental fishermen appealed strongly to upper-class collectors—industrialists, financiers, and entrepreneurs—both in Europe and North America. Soon after it was painted, *Seaman with a Woman* entered the collection of Frank Crowninshield, publisher of the New York woman's magazine *Vanity Fair*. Identified incorrectly but appropriately for the context in the February 1933 issue as *Sailors' Café, Marseilles*, the painting accompanied Paul Morand's article "Marseilles: Chicago of the Latin World." It served as a visible complement to Morand's inventory of "the blue café where the sailors are signed on . . . false identification papers are sold . . . [and] Marseilles gangsters get their death sentences reprieved, as one might elsewhere have a fine for speeding remitted."[3] Marseilles, with its popular "picturesque" reputation for adventure, romance, and intrigue, "where the most astonishing human flotsam and jetsam in the world is encountered," better suited the demands of *Vanity Fair*'s editors than the far less recognizable Boulogne-sur-Mer; it was not specificity of site but its ability to conjure forth "aromas—popular, gustatory, nocturnal" that recommended Masereel's painting.

Displayed in *Vanity Fair*'s Manhattan offices and featured in the magazine's pages along with advertisements informing readers that "society women know the right way to reduce fat" or celebrating "what Packard has done for the fine car buyer of 1933," the painting provided an aestheticized rusticity, a view of a life simpler and less complex than that of the New York society and changing fashions presented in the magazine. It was the world of European "natives" sought out by American tourists, to be gaped at and adulated, visited briefly as a refreshing contrast to a modern urban reality, and far removed from the radical socialism Masereel advocated.   R. H.

1. ". . . eckigere, rhythmischere Kammermusik. . . . Hat der Künstler sich ganz verwandelt, seit er allsommerlich in Boulogne-sur-mer den Dunst und Geruch des Meeres, das Gewirr der Schiffsmasten u. Schornsteine, das warme Dunkel der Schifferkneipen, den breiten Gang der Fischer und Seefahrer für sich wieder neu erobert? Gewiss, Krieg und Inflation, das lähmend Gegenwärtige, furchtbar Aktuelle sind vorüber. Beruhigung hat sich auch andern Künstlern mitgeteilt. Aber Frans Masereel hat sich nicht 'umgestellt,' . . . seine scheinbare Wandlung ist nur Selbstentfaltung, deutlicheres Erkennenlassen des eigentlichen Wesenskerns . . . . Im Grunde ist der Künstler Masereel immer Lyriker geblieben, Pantheist, berauschter Gläubiger, hinhorchend auf die 'Musik der Welt'. . . . Die Figuren des Lebens erhalten bei ihm eine geheimnisvolle Distanz, und bisweilen ist uns, als lebe dieser Künstler die Zustände und das Getriebe unserer Tage nicht anders nach, als wie eine Ballade oder ein melancholischschriller Bänkelsang, verschollene Ereignisse meldend." Georg F. Hartlaub, "Frans Masereel," *Deutsche Kunst und Dekoration* 33 (February 1930): 304.
2. ". . . das vlämische, altniederländische Gesicht des modernen Grossstädters Masereel . . . . krampfigste Ballungen des Lebenswirbels auf unserem Planeten." Ibid.

3. Paul Morand, "Marseilles: Chicago of the Latin World," *Vanity Fair* 39, no. 6 (February 1933): 32.

96   Frans Masereel
The Green Smokestack
(*La Cheminée verte*), 1929

Oil on canvas
71.5 x 90.5 cm (28^1/$_8$ x 35^5/$_8$ in.)
Monogrammed and dated l. r.
"F. M. 1929"; signed and dated verso center "Frans Masereel/ 1929"
Vorms 164

Provenance: Galerie Joseph Billiet, Paris; Lucien Lefevre-Foinet, Paris; F. Ehrmann, Prague and Australia; Sotheby Parke-Bernet, New York; Feigl Gallery, New York.

Exhibitions: Mannheim, Kunsthalle, *Franz Masereel: Das gesammelte Werk*, November 1929, cat. no. 47; Amsterdam, Stedelijk Museum, *Frans Masereel*, February 1930, cat. no. 29; Munich, Städtische Galerie, *Frans Masereel*, March–April 1930, cat. no. 44; Windsor, Ontario, Art Gallery of Windsor, *A Tribute to Frans Masereel*, 1981; Milwaukee, Patrick and Beatrice Haggerty Museum of Art, Marquette University, *Modern Masters*, 9 July–7 November 1990.

"I was always of the opinion," Frans Masereel commented in 1939, "that the fact of the artist handling pencil and brush does not necessarily distance him from the community or make him blind to human and social events. He can also be a witness to the times in which he lives. . . . For me, nothing else would be conceivable."[1] *The Green Smokestack*, a view of a harbor city from the deck of a freighter, accentuates contemporaneity, the machinery of seafaring, and the pragmatic structures of warehouses and tenements that line the harbor shores. The artist depicts a social milieu. Instead of offering an allegedly objective and concrete depiction, he evokes an ambience: heavily applied paint renders the substance of smoke, soot, and rain-filled clouds from whose darkness the city materializes, its wet pavements shimmering gold and silver. But it is the green-blue chimney of the foreground, along with the lifeboat, boom, and air intakes, that lend personality to the scene. Their warm colors enfold protectively the small figure of a seaman who appears among them, as if to draw him out of the city's bleak impersonality into the world of ships and the sea.

That world was an object of particular fascination to Masereel, even before he began to spend his summers in Norman fishing villages. Recalling his acquaintance with George Grosz, for example, he attributed their friendship in part to their mutual attraction, during Grosz's visits to Paris, to "harbors, accordion players, and sailors."[2] This surely overdetermines and simultaneously reduces in significance the friendship of the two artists, but does provide an indication of the degree to which Masereel saw these motifs as composing a world and a world view. His sailors, however, do not take on the sinister quality of Grosz's nor the sexual obsession of Otto Dix's; they approach

in spirit the many sailor and port scenes of Erich Wegner (see cat. nos. 175, 177), who similarly recognized in the seafarer an archetype in which emotions and life situations are distilled, to be presented in elemental simplicity and clarity.   C. D. G.

1. "Ich war immer der Auffassung, dass die Tatsache, dass der Künstler Pinsel und Stift führt, ihn nicht unbedingt von der Gemeinschaft entfernen, ihn für das menschliche und soziale Geschehen nicht blind machen müsse. Auch er kann ein Zeuge der Zeit, in der er lebt, sein. . . . Für mich wäre es nicht anders denkbar." Frans Masereel in the preface to the woodcut album *Du Noire au blanc—Von Schwarz zu Weiss* (Zurich: Precht Verlag, 1939), cited by Peter Riede, *Frans Masereel* (Wiesbaden: Altstadtgalerie in der Wegemannstrasse, 1986), n. p.
2. ". . . Häfen, Akkordeonspieler und Matrosen . . . ." Frans Masereel, "Besuche in Berlin," in *Berliner Begegnungen: Ausländische Künstler in Berlin 1918 bis 1933—Aufsätze, Bilder, Dokumente,* ed. Klaus Kändler, Helga Karolewski, and Ilse Siebert (East Berlin: Dietz Verlag, 1987), 196.

97   Frans Masereel
Inner Harbor (Bassin de port),
1932

Oil on canvas
73 x 60 cm (28^3/$_4$ x 23^5/$_8$ in.)
Monogrammed and dated l. r.
"F. M. / 1932"
Vorms 323

Provenance: Galerie Joseph Billiet, Paris; Walter O. Schneider, Beverly Hills.

Exhibitions: Kunstverein Winterthur, *Frans Masereel*, March–April 1933; Paris, Galerie Joseph Billiet, *Frans Masereel*, 1933, cat. no. 18.

An American critic in 1939 wrote about Frans Masereel as a prototypical Flemish artist, the embodiment of a national character:

A brooder like his countrymen . . . Masereel dwells often upon the overcast northern skies, the moist countryside and threatening storm . . . . Masereel broods, too, about the toilers of sea and soil, and he envelops his passion sometimes in salty clarity, other times in rising fumes of color . . . .[1]

The description is less of Masereel than of the world of his paintings, inhabited by fishermen and their women of the harbor towns in northern France, not Belgium, as the critic assumed. What is more significant for Masereel than their exact nationality, however, is the capacity of his silent fishermen to represent a nobler, more essential and existential humanity beyond the limitations of national or ethnic difference. That the result is ambiguous in terms of its connotations or applications is indicated by the history of *Seaman with a Woman* (cat. no. 95), especially when viewed in conjunction with Masereel's invitation to visit the Soviet Union in 1935 and his continuing support of the radical left's causes. His images, which could be appreciated in the society homes and offices of capitalism's sky-

scraper cathedrals in Manhattan, found equal admiration according to the norms of Stalinist Socialist Realism. Not unjustifiably, the German novelist and critic Stefan Zweig recognized in the uncommon diversity and contradiction of Masereel's audiences an "imaginary democracy," and concluded that, "because he can experience the entirety of the world, his effect is also on the totality; because spiritually he belongs to no single class, he is capable of moving the common people and the diverse peoples."[2]

Masereel's paintings in 1928, *Das Kunstblatt* was surprised to report, "demonstrate a remarkable development. Development into the painterly. The surface is conceived as coloristic unity; the color harmony is—remarkably tastefully—nuanced. What once was manifesto now is painting."[3] *Inner Harbor* matches these characterizations of a "new" Masereel, apparently supplanting the old Masereel of pictorial novels and social commitment with refined variations in light, shade, and subtle accents of color. As in many of his paintings, a central light source, the unseen moon still close to the horizon and blocked from view by the towering mass of a freighter's hull, illuminates unevenly all objects in this nocturnal scene. The silver-white moonlight and its shimmering reflections on the water cast a diffused light on the darkly silhouetted vessels, pier, and on the longshoreman who walks in the foreground, his hands shoved into his pockets and his shoulders hunched against the chill of the night. Depicting the fishing port of Boulogne-sur-Mer, Masereel emphasizes the transformative functions of melodramatic lighting—as well as the overwhelming impact of marine technology and its machinery on the harbor. The dark waters, crowded with ships, tugs, and barges, and the moonlit sky, filled with discharged smoke and soot, are the sole remnants of the industrially churning seashore. Isolated, the man is the single cipher of life.

Masereel accents the monumental strength of ships and harbor installations, the submission of nature to industrial power, but also implies the indestructible resistance of humanity. Close to the center of the painting, his hunched back seeming to support the ship's prow looming behind him, the man is the final focus of the inner harbor in the Belgian artist's vision. "For me that is the incomparable power that emanates from Masereel," Stefan Zweig wrote, "a sense of the world's own energy, fullness and unending life supported by a pure and strong manliness."[4] A naïve idealism and fundamental optimism informs Masereel's images: muscular and invincible, his fishermen and workers dominate the world around them as men (to whom women, too, are necessarily subordinate) aware of their strength, in control of their destiny, resilient, and resisting the powers that seek to suppress them.
                R. H.

1. Anonymous, "Masereel: Brooding Fleming," *Art Digest* 14 (15 October 1939): 6.
2. ". . . einer imaginären Demokratie . . . . Weil er die ganze Welt fühlt, wirkt er eben wieder auf die Gesamtheit, weil er

keiner Klasse geistig angehört, ist er fähig, auf das Volk und die Völker zu wirken." Stefan Zweig, "Frans Masereel, der Mann und Bildner," in Wolfgang Tenzler, ed., *Über die Schönheit hässlicher Bilder: Dichter und Schriftsteller über Maler und Malerei (1880–1933)* (East Berlin: Buchverlag Der Morgen, 1984), 423.

3. "...zeigen eine bemerkenswerte Entwicklung. Entwicklung ins rein Malerische. Die Fläche wird als koloristische Einheit begriffen; die Farbgebung ist—erstaunlich geschmackvoll—nuanciert. Was Manifest war, wird nun zum Bild." Anonymous, "Neue Bilder von Masereel," *Das Kunstblatt* 12 (1928): 200.

4. "Das ist für mich die unvergleichliche Gewalt, die von Masereel ausgeht: Weltkraft, Fülle und unendliches Leben, von einer reinen und starken Männlichkeit getragen." Zweig, "Frans Masereel," 423.

---

98 Else Meidner
Double Portrait: Else and Ludwig Meidner (Doppelbildnis Else und Ludwig Meidner), 1933

Black chalk on paper
29 x 21.7 cm (11⁷/₁₆ x 8¹/₂ in.)
Inscribed and dated l. r. "Herrn Dr. Gollop und Frau Gollop am 17.VII.33 von Else Meidner" (To Dr. and Mrs. Gollop from Else Meidner on 17 July 1933)

Provenance: Dr. Max Gollop, Berlin; Galerie Arno Winterberg, Heidelberg.

Else Meyer married Ludwig Meidner in 1927, and struggled consistently thereafter to maintain her independence as an artist while also working jointly with her husband. The two maintained separate studio spaces and schedules, but Ludwig Meidner nonetheless frequently sought to adjust her images according to his own perceptions. She, in turn, habitually portrayed him, caricatured him, and thus submitted him to her perceptual control during his painting campaigns as he struggled with his own canvases. Late in the 1920s, Else Meidner began to develop a reputation for her portraits and received several awards; her work was included in *Das Kunstblatt*'s 1929 review of contemporary German portraiture.

Else Meidner's aesthetic approach is gentler than her husband's: a palpable atmosphere and Impressionist softening hovers around the contours in her drawings. Here, her self-portrait emerges from a massing of values; she avoids precise lines in favor of light and dark tones to define a sharply illuminated face gazing steadfastly out at the viewer. At her side, Ludwig Meidner appears to inhabit a different world. Lines, not volumes, generate his likeness, which is simplified into its salient characteristics subjectively accentuated. He faces no viewer; instead, his attention is drawn totally by his wife, as if she were the agent through whom reality was filtered for him. Separation and confrontation, a tense existence in independent but interrelated worlds are implied both in the image and in its stylistic disjunctions.

Else Meidner's career, so promising during the early 1930s, was quickly interrupted, however. The turmoil and persecution of the Nazi era, exile in wartime London, and repeated conflicts with Ludwig Meidner drastically reduced her artistic production until the early 1950s. Only after separation from her husband did her work resume more consistently, but focused now increasingly on the extraordinary religious visions she experienced. These slowly but inexorably supplanted the actuality of everyday life for her. Alone, she formulated her own reality.   R. H.

---

99 Ludwig Meidner
Self-Portrait (Selbstporträt), 1912

Oil on canvas
74.9 x 58.3 cm (29¹/₂ x 23 in.)
Monogrammed and dated l. r. "LM/1912"

Provenance: Ernest Rathenau, Berlin, Hamburg, and New York.

After a sojourn in Paris financed by one of his aunts during 1906 and 1907, Ludwig Meidner returned to Germany to do his obligatory year of military service. When he failed to fulfill the physical requirements of the peace-time army, however, he resumed his work as artist in Berlin. Impoverished, and for three years finding little money for painting supplies, he spent most of his days in public reading rooms, hungry. His mind absorbed by Charles Baudelaire, Friedrich Hölderlin, Friedrich Nietzsche, and Walt Whitman, he also wandered the edges of the city, where new industrial construction brutalized and scarred the retreating landscape. Impressionism, Fauvism, and Vincent van Gogh in eclectic fusion leave their traces in the paintings he completed but could not exhibit.

In 1911, by chance, Meidner received support in the amount of 100 marks per month, obtained with the aid of Max Beckmann, and was finally able to paint regularly. He concentrated on scenes of the industrializing city and, more incidentally, on aspects of his studio. Depictions of his living space, bed, and domestic furnishings contrast with the denatured anonymity of the suburban cityscape, and are initial indications of a fascination with his own conscious and unconscious life. Over the next year, more than ten painted or drawn self-portraits marked the beginning of Meidner's persistent self-representation, in an unequalled explosion of self-investigations that study his features under varied conditions, from innumerable vantage points, at different times of day, that focused on his head or on the artist at his easel painting or, pencil in hand, drawing.

Produced during the summer of 1912, with thinned pigments and a palette limited to greens and red, this self-portrait celebrates Meidner's newly discovered satisfaction in being able to practice his profession. His gaunt face, his head with hair almost all fallen out, his bright sunken eyes, testify to the strain of his years of near starvation. But light, the greenish blue light of a gaslamp, bathes his arms and shoulders to lend strength to the jagged excitation and jumble of dark green that otherwise defines body and limbs. At the level of his eyes, his raised brush points to the canvas on which the portrait is taking shape as an agitated recollection of Van Gogh and as testimony to Meidner's own anguished self-perception:

...one summer, I was dirtied from head to foot with mites, deprivation, and insanity. I shall never forget it, because it made me old, and the plans of my youth were scattered to the winds and my determination was tested.

Stuck into a painter's smock so covered with paint stains as to be stiff as armor, armed with an insatiable palette and snarling brushes, I stood there during the entire night, never vacillating, and painted myself before the grimacing mirror. No one disturbed. Gas stove, teapot, and tobacco pipe were my murmuring companions. Heat puffed at me like a fire storm. Painting stretchers creaked. The window was wide open and the stars rained like rockets down around my glacier-bare baldness. How the prison green of my studio burned my skin. Sun never stabbed its bloody knives in here. But I became as tan as if it were August. Within me, the desert's summer boiled with its vultures, skeletons, and barking thirst. Within me were cries for crackling far-off lands and the trumpet calls of future catastrophes. Did I not always have to include traces of blood and raw wounds?! Did I not prefer for backgrounds comets' tails and bursting volcanoes?! I scratched, rubbed, and honed my colors. But I scratched miserably at my body, hung with its armor of paint, that burned as the mites crawled all over it.

...Oh but then came happy moments. I shoved the painting as far as possible away from me and saw a trembling brow, a moon-like body stretching. Always in my pictures my crippled hand grasped the palette like a shield, prepared to ward off attack. You, my sole shield, weeping with color, in the pain of eternally gray days of work.[1]

Suffering from rashes, uncomfortable in the unusual summer heat, alone, Meidner generated his own companions in the populations of his self-portraits. Grinning, grimacing, searching, they surrounded him while he brushed and molded yielding oil pigments into the configuration of yet another *Doppelgänger*, a ghostly duplicate of himself.   R. H.

1. "...einen Sommer besudelt über und über mit Krätze, Not und Verrücktheit werde ich nicht vergessen können, denn er hat mich alt gemacht, und meine Jugendpläne sind zerweht und mein Mut ist brüchig geworden.

"In einem Malkittel steckend, der, mit geronnener Farbe bedreckt, wie ein Panzer steif war, mit nimmersatter Palette gegürtet und fletschenden Pinseln, so stand ich, nicht wankend, die ganze Nacht und malte mich selbst vor dem grimassierenden Spiegel. Ich blieb ungestört und nur Gaskocher, Teekops, und Tabakpfeife waren meine murmelnden Gefährten. Hitze keuchte wie bei einer Feuerbrunst. Die Keilrahmen knackten. Weit offen stand das Fenster, und die Sterne regneten wie Raketen um meine gletscherblanke Glatze. Wie mich die Kerkerfarbe des Ateliers verbrannte. Sonne stach nie ihre blutigen Messer hinein. Aber ich wurde braun wie der August. In mir kochte der Wüstensommer mit Geiern, Skeletten, und gellendem Durst. In mir schrie es nach knatternden Fernen und den Posaunenstössen künftiger Katastrophen. Musste ich nicht auf meine Selbstporträts immer Blutrinnsale hineinmalen und zerfressene Wunden?! Liebte ich nicht auf allen Hintergründen den Kometenschweif und brandende Vulkane! Ich kratzte, rieb, und wetzte meine Farben. Aber elend zerrte ich dabei am Leibe, der, verhängt vom Farbenpanzer, glühte in der Krätze grässlichem Gewimmer.

"...O, dann kamen selige Minuten. Ich rückte das Bild weit weg von mir und sah eine zuckende Stirne, einen mondhaften Leib sich recken. Immer hielt auf meinen Bildern die zerkrümelte Hand die Palette wie einen Schild zur Abwehr bereit. Du mein einziger Schild, farbentränender, in der Pein des ewigen Werktags." Ludwig Meidner, *Septemberschrei: Hymnen/Gebete/Lästerungen* (Berlin: Paul Cassirer, 1920), 6–7.

---

100 Ludwig Meidner
My Nocturnal Visage (Mein Nachtgesicht), 1913

Oil on canvas
66.7 x 48.9 cm (26¹/₄ x 19¹/₄ in.)
Monogrammed and dated c. r. "LM 1913"

Provenance: Gertrud von Lutzau, Berlin and Rodenkirchen am Rhein; Richard Feigen Gallery, New York; Dr. and Mrs. Gerhard Strauss, Milwaukee.

Exhibitions: Berlin, Paul Cassirer, *Ludwig Meidner*, January 1918; Milwaukee Art Center, *Ludwig Meidner: Apocalyptic German Expressionist (From the Collection of Marvin and Janet Fishman)*, 4 June–18 July 1976 (as *Night Visage*); Chicago, Museum of Contemporary Art, *Art in a Turbulent Era: German and Austrian Expressionism*, 10 March–30 April 1978 (as *Self-Portrait [My Night Vision]*); Ann Arbor, University of Michigan Museum of Art, *Ludwig Meidner: An Expressionist Master*, 20 October–20 November 1978, cat. no. 2 (as *Night Visage*); Fine Arts Galleries, University of Wisconsin-Milwaukee, *German Expressionism from Milwaukee Collections*, 22 January–11 March 1979, cat. no. 90 (as *Night Visage [Self-Portrait]*); New York, Solomon R. Guggenheim Museum, *Expressionism: A German Intuition 1905–1920*, 14 November 1980–18 January 1981 (traveled to San Francisco Museum of Modern Art, 19 February–26 April 1981), cat. no. 301a (as *My Night Visage [Self-Portrait]*); London, Royal Academy of Arts, *German Art in the 20th Century: Painting and Sculpture 1905–1985*, 11 October–22 December 1985 (traveled to Staatsgalerie Stuttgart, 8 February–27 April 1986), cat. no. 74 (as *My Night Visage*); West Berlin, Berlinische Galerie, Museum für Moderne Kunst, Photographie und Architektur im Martin-Gropius-Bau, *Ich und die Stadt: Mensch und Grossstadt in der deutschen Kunst des 20. Jahrhunderts*, 15 August–22 November 1987, cat. no. 135; Atlanta, High Museum of Art, *Art in Berlin 1815–1989*, 14 November 1989–14 January 1990, cat. no. 35.

Indicative of the significance of the subjective ego as the source of their art, self-portraiture was a favorite genre among Expressionist artist. Their numerous self-portraits also point to the value they attached to the figure of the artist as alienated and prophetic visionary to profane bourgeois society. Among Expressionists, Meidner painted or drew his own mirrored image even more frequently than the others, as his self-portraits testified to his energetic interaction with paint and vision in the construction of an alternative world of invented imagery, the product of his fevered imagination.

He painted at night, his dark studio illuminated by glimmers of flame from a stove or by the glare of a light bulb overhead. Surrounding him was nocturnal blackness, while from his mirror his own face—eyes large and intensely observant—shone yellow and red, deeply shadowed, as if providing its own illumination. Paint, canvas, and brush were the sole external presences he recognized:

A swarm of Paris blue on bare chalk ground; cynical, bleating zinc yellow; white with ivory black: the tints of aged, bedridden invalids; static green next to cinnabar screams; umber, bright cadmium, and fiery ultramarine—in general, existence has to be contained by fat, bursting tubes of oil paint. You've got to lock yourself within four ash-gray studio walls, romp before big canvases, cuss to yourself, get mad, scratch your crotch, and hold one hell of a palette in your fist.

To myself, I conjure up the most grandiose things: apocalyptic turmoil, Hebrew prophets, and hallucinations of mass graves—because imagination is all that matters, and nature be hanged. But it's not enough: tubes splitting from oil matter more, almost, because paints help paint, help invent, help celebrate. Sometimes I stand dumb and empty before my easel and grin stupidly to myself with unshaven, freckled cheeks; then an outline suddenly leaps from those viscous chrome-colored dung patties, the vermilion starts to scream and beneath my bristled brush the marvelous hubbub of an entire world constructs itself....

You have to be able to drink. Always have a rum bottle on your night table. A painter has to gorge himself. Then ideas will come like Brueghel's. Fantasy rises up from a full belly. You have to have a screaming laugh, like a prole, and blow snot from your nose, and shout curses with the best of them. Then, too, it's good to lean far out a window, make faces at the stars and amuse the moon with dirty jokes. And then, artist, you've got to work like a dog. Push up to the easel with a mighty shove. Don't worry about styles and such notions, or about what they say in cafés. Paint your own stuff, all your loathsomeness and sanctity, out of yourself....

My easel groans and presses against my beer belly. I rage with varnish. Sticky brushes recall the poverty of existence. Chrome-green leaves me cold. And cobalt blue reminds me of my little-boy days when I bit the tails off salamanders. I'm a brush fanatic, actively, slyly, shamelessly, and incorrigibly. I think evil thoughts and my painting enthusiasm drools and shouts hurrah. Sometimes I grin happily. I marvel at my canvases. From now on, I'll paint nothing but ecstatic scenes. I'm not afraid. But sometimes the grave's darkness opens wide before me.

It's night, half-past one.

In my breast, the unpainted plague victims, necrophiliacs, and starving wet-nurses cry out. Cramped fists and grimacing faces threaten me on walls. I walk surrounded by violent dreams. I'm so afraid. The night is silent and throbbing.

What a true artist desires: umber with zinc yellow and Paris blue! A bottle of rum! One hell of a palette! An insatiable lover and a hand stretched out towards the stars![1]

Meidner's ecstatic prose poem celebrating the act of painting, written about 1916 and published two years later, isolates his image within the engulfing darkness of night, his studio, his psyche. The apparent disorder of brushstrokes in *My Nocturnal Visage*, the juxtaposition of colors and disregard for stylistic fixity are seen in Meidner's paean to his artistic process as laws of his inner life, lived in isolation, deliberately crude in defiance of social conventions. The text parallels his self-portrait, which thus presents a visionary and self-indulgent ascetic who endures the sufferings of a deprived, deranged, victimized humanity, and who sees the omnipresence of death's darkness. Portrait and poem portray a "true artist," an Expressionist archetype, the artist not only as he saw himself but as he wished to be seen: vital and active in an imperialist society collapsing in entropy.   R. H.

1. "Gewimmel von Pariserblau auf blanken Kreidegründen; zynisches, meckerndes Zinkgelb; Weiss mit Elfenbeinschwarz: das Kolorit der alten Bettlägerigen, Permanentgrün neben Zinnobergeschrei; Umbra, helles Kadmium und feurig Ultramarin—überhaupt muss das Dasein von fetten, strotzenden Ölfarbentuben eingeengt sein. Man muss sich fest einschliessen in vier aschengraue Atelierwände, vor grossen Leinwänden herumturnen, einsam schimpfen, wütend sein, sich kratzen und eine Donnerwetter-Palette in der Faust haben.

"Ich denke mir die grossartigsten Dinge aus, apokalyptische Gewimmel, hebräische Propheten und Massengrab-Halluzinationen—denn der Geist ist alles, die Natur kann mir gestohlen bleiben. Aber das genügt nicht: die ölstrotzenden Tuben sind noch wichtiger, weil die Farben mitmalen, miterfinden, mitfeiern.

"Ich stelle mir manchmal blöde und ausgeleert vor die Staffelei und grinse in meine unrasierten, sommersprossigen Backen hinein; da hüpft aus den zähen Chrom-Fladen auf einmal ein Umriss heraus, das Zinober fängt zu schreien an und eine wunderbare Wirrwarr-Welt baut sich allmählich unter meinen Borstpinseln auf....

"Man muss saufen können. Immer eine Rumflasche auf dem Nachttisch. Ein Maler muss viel fressen. Dabei hat er breughelische Einfälle. Tollheiten steigen aus dem prallen Bauch. Man muss Gelächter brüllen wie ein Prolet, dröhnend sich schneuzen, gemeine Flüche zum besten geben. Dann auch ist es gut, sich weit aus dem Fenster zu beugen, die Sterne anzuulken und den Mond mit Zoten zu beglücken. Nachher sollst du feste schuften, Maler. Schiebe dich mit gewaltigem Ruck vor die Staffelei. Kümmere dich nicht um Schulen und vorgefasste Meinungen, noch um das Gerede der Caféhäuser. Mal' deinen eigenen Gram, deine ganze Verruchtheit und Heiligkeit dir vor dem Leibe....

"Meine Staffelei knurrt und bäumt sich gegen meinen Bierbauch. Ich wüte mit dem Krapplack. Klebrige Pinsel mahnen mich an die Erbärmlichkeit des Daseins. Chromgrün lässt mich kalt. Und Kobalt erinnert mich an meine Kleine-Jungen-Tage, wenn ich Molchen die Schwänze abbiss. Ich bin ein Pinselfex, rührig, schlau, schamlos und unverbesserlich. Ich hege böse Gedanken und mein Malfanatismus geifert und hurra't. Manchmal lächle ich vor Glück. Ich bestaune meine Leinwände. In Zukunft werde ich nur noch extatische Szenen malen. Ich fürchte mich nicht. Nur manchmal klastert jäh Grabes-Finsternis vor mir auf.

"Es ist nachts halb zwei.

"In meiner Brust schreien die noch ungemalten Pestkranken, Leichenschänder und hungernden Ammen. Mich bedrohen verkrampfte Fäuste und wiehernde Grimassen an den Wänden. Ich schreite wie in gewalttätigen Träumen umfangen. Ich habe schreckliche Angst. Die Nacht ist schweigend und dröhnt.

"Dies ist die Sehnsucht des wahren Malers: Umbra mit Zinkgelb und Pariserblau! Eine Rumflasche! Die Donnerwetter-Palette! Die zügellose Geliebte und die Hand ausgestreckt nach den Sternen!" Ludwig Meidner, *Im Nacken das Sternemeer* (Leipzig: Kurt Wolff Verlag, n. d. [1918]), 17–18, 23–25.

101 Ludwig Meidner
Street Scene (Strassenszene),
1913

Ink, tusche over pencil, with white highlighting, on paper 39.8 x 50 cm (15^5/$_8$ x 19^5/$_8$ in.) Signed and dated l. c. "L Meidner 1913"

Provenance: Galerie Michael Pabst, Munich; D. Thomas Bergen Collection, London and New York.

Exhibitions: South Bend, Ind., Snite Museum of Art, University of Notre Dame, *The Graphic Work of Ludwig Meidner: Drawings and Prints from the D. Thomas Bergen Collection,* 1972; Ann Arbor, University of Michigan Museum of Art, *Ludwig Meidner: An Expressionist Master,* 20 October–19 November 1978, cat. no. 14; West Berlin, Berlinische Galerie, Museum für Moderne Kunst, Photographie und Architektur im Martin-Gropius-Bau, *Ich und die Stadt: Mensch und Grossstadt in der deutschen Kunst des 20. Jahrhunderts,* 15 August–22 November 1987, cat. no. 138.

The nocturnal street where disruptive shafts of light intersect with sheets of darkness became one of Ludwig Meidner's favored motifs during 1913. The views of gasometers and construction sites dominant in his previous cityscapes gave way to avenues, canyons of façades, sidewalks, and pedestrians caught up in the pictorial excitement of Meidner's deconstructive style. In 1914, when the city had been a major and persistent theme in painting for over half a century, in his most famous essay, "Instructions for the Painting of Pictures of the Metropolis," he admonished his fellow artists:

We must at last begin to paint our real homeland, the metropolis which we love endlessly.... First thing is: to learn to see, to learn to see more intensively and correctly than our predecessors. Impressionist vagueness and lack of precision are of no use to us. Superceded perspective no longer means anything to us and cramps our creativity.... Second concern—and no less significant—is that we begin to work. We can't carry our easels into the hustle and bustle of the streets to read (while squinting) "tonal values." A street does not consist of tonal values, but is a bombardment of hissing window rows, cones of light racing among every kind of vehicle and a thousand hopping balls, bits of people, billboards, and roaring, formless masses of color.[1]

Meidner's manifesto-like text, lashing out against Impressionism on the pages of *Kunst und Künstler,* the periodical that most avidly supported German Impressionist art, betrays a knowledge of F. T. Marinetti's "Futurist Manifesto," published in translation by Herwarth Walden in *Der Sturm* in 1913. But Meidner's essay also reveals an artist of immense ambition, willing to match his art against that of contemporaries and the past, defining his work as visionary rather than imitative, and proclaiming its superior ability to render the essential character of modern urban life. His *Street Scene* participates in this confrontational dialogue with past and present, much like an effort to demonstrate the basic principles of his "instructions."

Berlin, Meidner asserted, should be depicted only in black and white. His paintings clearly break with this dictum, which his ink drawings more readily fulfill. Similarly, the paintings most often present Meidner's visionary projections, and less frequently the experience of contemporary urban life in streets and cafés. Produced in the artificial light of his studio, the drawings function as diary entries after the passing of a day, recording the immediate encounters and characteristics of the city whose streets Meidner roamed, preferring night to day, the artificial illumination of streetlamps to the glow of sunlight.

Street Scene, in the manner of James Ensor and Edvard Munch, concentrates on the milling crowds that jostle through the city's asphalt canyons, between banks of darkness rhythmically disrupted by streams of lighted windows. Like a sharp triangular wedge, the sky pierces the closed ranks of façades, cutting down to the cramped flow of pedestrians below, pointing into the head of the central passerby. Seen only in disjointed fragments, this figure is disrupted and confused, as hands, arms, and shoulders slice into his profile and his face is obliterated by the juggernaut nose and cap brim of a military officer in the foreground. The cap, directly under a cone of light emanating from a streetlamp, dominates the entire scene, drawing all movement toward it. Its wearer, in turn, stands gesturing in conversation with a second officer as the two, in mirrored confrontation, visually overpower by their size and placement all other occupants of the street. Behind them, a crowd of men—the absence of women in almost all of Meidner's street scenes is notable—rush past; some glance at the officers; all avoid them.

Because of the forceful presence of these officers, the drawing, from 1913, has been associated with premonitions of World War I.[2] The contention can be neither proven nor disproven. Far from being an admirer of military personnel or prowess, Meidner seldom included soldiers in his drawings or paintings before the war, preferring instead to accentuate the city's civilian appearance and its democratic process of destroying social rank and inequality among the inhabitants of its streets. The soldiers here thus do take on a unique significance, breaking with Meidner's more typical imagery. Around their self-oriented gesticulating and central position, the encircling mass of men must move and adjust.

In 1911 and 1912, a series of international crises centered around military activity, notably the second Morocco Crisis in which French and German interests conflicted, and the ongoing Balkan Wars which threatened to involve Austria-Hungary (with whom Germany was allied) and Russia. Forebodings of war might well have haunted Germans less sensitive than Meidner. But Street Scene, unlike the artist's contemporary paintings of city bombardments, does not depict war, but rather relatively standard street activity. The military emphasis demands a different explanation.

If not war itself, then the ability to wage war may be the content of the two officers'—for us, silent—conversation. The Reichstag elections of 1912 for the first time brought majority control of the imperial parliament to the Socialist Party of Germany and their allied Progressive People's Party. An internal political crisis, exacerbated by an outbreak of large-scale strikes, rather than a foreign military crisis, threatened German society that year, and in it the armed forces, too, had a major role. Among the Socialists' policies was the rejection of imperialist military expansion and a demand for reduced military spending. With proof of nothing more than premonitions of war, it is possible that Meidner's two officers are discussing the potential loss of their dominant position in the society that surrounds them.   R. H.

1. "Wir müssen endlich anfangen, unsere Heimat zu malen, die Grossstadt, die wir unendlich lieben.... Das erste ist: dass wir sehen lernen, dass wir intensiver und richtiger sehen als unsere Vorgänger. Die impressionistische Verschwommenheit und Verundeutlichung nützt uns nichts. Die überkommene Perspektive hat keinen Sinn mehr für uns und hemmt unsre Impulsivität.... Zu zweit—und das ist nicht minder wichtig—müssen wir anfangen zu schaffen. Wir können unsre Staffelei nicht ins Gewühl der Strasse tragen, um dort (blinzelnd) 'Tonwerte' abzulesen. Eine Strasse besteht nicht aus Tonwerten, sondern ist ein Bombardement von zischenden Fensterreihen, sausenden Lichtkegeln

zwischen Fuhrwerken aller Art und tausend hüpfenden Kugeln, Menschenfetzen, Reklameschildern und dröhnenden, gestaltlosen Farbmassen." Ludwig Meidner, "Anleitung zum Malen von Grosstadtbildern," Kunst und Künstler 12 (1914): 312. For a translation by Victor Miesel of the full text as "Introduction to the Painting of Big Cities," see Ludwig Meidner: An Expressionist Painter (Ann Arbor: University of Michigan Museum of Art, 1978), 30–31, reprinted in Miesel, ed., Voices of German Expressionism (Englewood Cliffs, N. J.: Prentice-Hall, Inc., 1970), 111–115.
2. Miesel, in Ludwig Meidner, 63.

102   Ludwig Meidner
Grand Café Schöneberg, 1913

Pen, brush and ink over pencil
40.6 x 47 cm (15^{15}/$_{16}$ x 18^1/$_2$ in.)
Signed and dated u. r.
"L. Meidner 1913"; inscribed l. l.
"Grand Café Schöneberg"

Provenance: E. and T. Grochowiak, Recklinghausen; Hauswedell and Nolte, Hamburg; D. Thomas Bergen Collection, London and New York.

Exhibitions: Recklinghausen, Kunsthalle, Ludwig Meidner, 1963 (traveled to West Berlin, Haus am Waldsee, 1964; Darmstadt, Kunstverein, 1964); South Bend, Ind., Snite Museum of Art, University of Notre Dame, The Graphic Work of Ludwig Meidner: Drawings and Prints from the D. Thomas Bergen Collection, 1972; Ann Arbor, University of Michigan Museum of Art, Ludwig Meidner: An Expressionist Master, 20 October–19 November 1978, cat. no. 15; West Berlin, Berlinische Galerie, Museum für Moderne Kunst, Photographie und Architektur im Martin-Gropius-Bau, Ich und die Stadt: Mensch und Grossstadt in der deutschen Kunst des 20. Jahrhunderts, 15 August–22 November 1987, cat. no. 130.

In his recollections of prewar Berlin, Ludwig Meidner describes dividing his time among the studio where he worked and slept, the street, and the café. For him the café was a place of transformation, a place of fantasy in which the amusement was atmosphere, music, and a parade of people, eccentric, broken off from the society outside. The café in Meidner's extended Expressionist prose poem becomes a place of recuperation:

> You café full of pleasure—oh magical hall—you paradise of the living. You soul of the times. You swinging bell of the present. You school of higher spirits. You rendezvous of speeding strugglers. You tumultuous arch of the poets. You hall, cathedral, airship, volcano, cage, grotto and ditch, dung hole and hour of worshipers.... In your tumultuous glowing brightness I flare up. I dance over to your marble basins. Is life not lived without purpose, all the difficult hours of the day....?! Am I not always envious, venomous, lustful, and totally cried out?! But you—living being, coffeehouse, trembling, itching, and stuffed full with unusual pleasures—ban from my earthly shell—from this clashing, gaudy skull, this oceanic, moonlit breast—chase from my copper-red

existence the gesticulations of spleen, the winds of world pain, the catafalques of longing, sending them out into the shattering air. With your armchairs, woven chairs, and grinding mirrors, you are the stage of boastful evening dress, of traitors, cheaters, amusers; you are the valley of artist adventurers; you are the audience and the hall for imposing rhetoricians.... Now I sit in the midst of it all, the pasha of eternity.... The mirrors grimace. Lamps illuminate faces creased with anger. The ceiling mirrors my disgruntled disposition. My fingers move like dancing mice on the trembling marble tabletop, the circus ring. I am in the café and drink the tea.[1]

Meidner's preferred café was the Café des Westens, popularly known as Café Grössenwahn (Megalomania), which other artists, poets, and various members of Berlin's bohemia regularly frequented. The Grand Café Schöneberg, however, lacked such literary and artistic associations; its clientele was more bourgeois. In Meidner's drawing, the café's orchestra performs, and its violin soloists serenade with calming salon music. In the foreground, a couple sits at a round table, the man in dark suit with folds of fat supporting his bald head, the woman a secondary presence, her face a caricatured frown.

Perspectival exaggerations and inconsistencies disrupt and enliven the café interior. The vaulting arches fan out into intersecting lines from which chandeliers sway. These arches and undulating chandeliers form the ultimate key elements in the visual connotation of the drawing: as line meets line in depth and moving forward, leaning right and tending left, the drawing participates in the swaying rhythms of waltzes, polkas, and marches. It renders visible the serenade of the orchestra, but disturbed by the vertigo of Meidner's choppy counterpoint, the intruding rhythms formulated by his pen strokes, and an overlay of bohemian rejection.   R. H.

1. "Du Café voll Wonne—o zaubrische Halle—du Paradies der Lebendigen. Du Seele der Zeit. Du schwingende Glocke des Diesseits. Du Schule hoher Geister. Du beschwingter Kämpfer Rendezvous. Du tumultuöse Arche der Dichter. Du Halle, Dom, Luftschiff, Vulkan, Käfig, Gruft und Kluft, Dungloch und Stunde der Beter.... Ich flamme auf in deiner tosenden Gluthelle. Ich tanze zu deinen marmornen Bassins hin. Ist das Leben nicht umsonst gelebt, alle die schwierigen Stunden des Tags....?! Bin ich nicht immerfort gierig, geifernd, feil, und ganz verheult?! Doch du Lebendiges, du Caféhaus, zuckend, juckend und seltener Freuden gerammelt voll, jagst aus meinem irdischen Gehäus—diesem grellen kunterbunten Schädel, dieser ozeanischen, mondhellen Brust—treibst aus meinem kupferroten Dasein die Gebärden des Spleens, Winde der Weltlust, Katafalke der Sehnsucht heraus zu schmetternder Luft. Du bist mit deinen Sesseln, Korbstühlen und fletschenden Spiegeln, Tribüne der flunkernden Fräcke, der Traiteure, Chikaneue, Amüseure, Tal der artistischen Abenteurer, der imposanten Herren Rhetoriker Parkett und Spielsaal .... Nun sitz ich mitten drin, Pascha der Ewigkeit.... Die Spiegel grimassieren.

Lampen glühen in Zornesfalten. Die Decke spiegelt meine mürrische Frisur. Meine Finger zucken wie Tanzmäuse auf bebender Marmorplatte Zirkus Rund. Ich bin im Café und trinke den Tee." Ludwig Meidner, Im Nacken das Sternemeer (Leipzig: Kurt Wolff Verlag, n. d. [1918]), 29–31.

103   Ludwig Meidner
Apocalyptic Landscape
(Apokalyptische Landschaft)
1913

Oil on canvas
67.3 x 80 cm (26^1/$_2$ x 31^1/$_2$ in.)
Monogrammed and dated l. r.
"LM/1913"
Verso: *Landscape (Landschaft)*,
c. 1913, oil.

Provenance: Galerie I. B. Neumann, Berlin and New York; Addison Gallery, Phillips Academy, Andover, Mass.; Paul Cantor Gallery, Beverly Hills and New York; Clifford Odets, New York and Los Angeles.

Exhibitions: Pasadena Art Museum, German Expressionism, 23 April–4 June 1961, cat. no. 170; Milwaukee Art Center, Ludwig Meidner: Apocalyptic German Expressionist (From the Collection of Marvin and Janet Fishman), 4 June–30 July 1976, cat. no. [1]; Bloomington, Indiana University Art Museum, German and Austrian Expressionism 1900 to 1920, 23 October–3 December 1977, cat. no. 68; Chicago, Museum of Contemporary Art, Art in a Turbulent Era: German and Austrian Expressionism, 10 March–30 April 1978, cat. no. 22; Ann Arbor, University of Michigan Museum of Art, Ludwig Meidner: An Expressionist Master, 20 October–19 November 1978, cat. no. 1; London, Royal Academy of Arts, German Art in the 20th Century: Painting and Sculpture 1905–1985, 11 October–22 December 1985, cat. no. 76 (traveled to Stuttgart, Staatsgalerie, 8 February–27 April 1986); West Berlin, Berlinische Galerie, Museum für Moderne Kunst, Photographie und Architektur im Martin-Gropius-Bau, Ich und die Stadt: Mensch und Grossstadt in der deutschen Kunst des 20. Jahrhunderts, 15 August–22 November 1987, cat. no. 127; Los Angeles County Museum of Art, The Apocalyptic Landscapes of Ludwig Meidner, 12 October–17 December 1989 (traveled to West Berlin, Berlinische Galerie, Museum für Moderne Kunst, Photographie und Architektur im Martin-Gropius-Bau, 1 February–8 April 1990), cat. no. 5.

In 1916, inducted into the German imperial army, Ludwig Meidner was stationed near Kottbus as a translator and guard at a camp for prisoners of war. He began to compose ecstatic prose poems which fuse confessional autobiography, visionary ruminations, and pathos-laden diary entries. In these, Meidner recounts how the nearby city attracted him, promising relief from the drudgery and discipline of the barracks, allowing immersion in the excitement of a supra-personal existence in the desperate community of cafés, bars, and erotic frustration. Turning to writing as an expressive substitute for painting and as a means of psychological relief from his despondency, Meidner conjured visions of urban color that contrasted with field-gray uniformity, in language reminiscent of the apocalyptic fantasies of his prewar paintings:

Sometimes, when at night I feel driven towards the city, my insolent brow dipped low, behind me the sea of stars, when I race undeterred through the distance... then I am surrounded by cloud-screams, a far-off beating of wings, and by creatures, human and dark and panting. The moon burns down on my hot forehead. We sail through the distance, I and my shadow, that stretched-out cur. Just now I had a wild quarrel with myself, punished my groin with accusations, scratched at myself with mocking sophistry —and now through the plains, cavalcades of pain, I crush my heated breast.
... The city approaches. Already it crackles against my body. On my skin, its cackling burns. I hear its eruptions echo in the back of my head.
Houses approach. Catastrophes explode from out their windows. Stairwells silently collapse. People laugh beneath the ruins. Walls are thin and transparent. Masks are nailed too hard to skulls. In beds, unspeakable things happen. Children piddle. Female clerks await their lovers. Already they are masturbating from boredom.... The streets slowly become smoother. Street lamps carelessly throw away their beams and everybody gets hit.... After a while, the streets fill up. The asphalt shouts out. Horrible turmoil. Machine noise.... Neighing of derailed streetcars, sneezing of older ladies, and philosophical discussions among shoemakers occupy the area. Shop-windows fire brand-new dummies out into the world. In the shopwindows the new great era gasps limpingly. Wives and women shove their big stomachs through the cold weather. And newspaper hawkers, satiated with beets, trundle twittering behind.
Tumult arises. The department store's walls bulge with heat. In cataracts of electric light their sweat hurtles down on us. The floors bark. Thousands press their exhausted bodies. A world of boxes hails down from ceilings. Clouds of vice hover above it, woven into thundering petticoats.[1]

Meidner's violent vision of a vitalized urban environment consists of fragmented scenes and sensuous perceptions as he rushes panting towards the city and then runs through its streets. Nothing is seen clearly, nothing is stable; everything is volatile, stabbing at him. He pushes his oversensitized, short and enfeebled body through air, light, smell, and sound; each element physically protests his progress.

Human masses bubble past, creatures from distant stars, cascades in purple.... crash into walls, sink down droning into asphalt.
The city screams out, towered steep and to the sky. It stretches to its full length like a crocodile into the distance, expands like fireworks into

the winds. It pours balconies down on me. It gnaws at my guts.... It coagulates into an avalanche and hurls itself, with thunder, into the moon.[2]

The city is for Meidner an experience of disruptions, an alluring reality that defies consumption. In his febrile state, it becomes an anxious image of impending doom, thrilling in the specter of its own explosive end.
Words and images in 1916 echo those of earlier years, of 1912 and 1913 when Meidner painted his first apocalyptic urban views.[3] He perceived the city in both instances during states of extreme agitation, with a mixture of despair and exhilaration. During the war, Meidner's depression, resulting from repressive military life and duties, found rebellious release in the agitation of the city. In 1912 and 1913, poverty and a deficient diet, extraordinarily hot summers, and festering skin rashes joined with nights of unprecedented productivity, his first exhibitions, and initial critical success. In 1916, with the same vocabulary he employed to describe nights in Kottbus, he called forth memories of the paintings, their production, and their conflicting destructive-creative content:

I build up towers of houses in dancing landscapes, moon sickles above them. Six hours long I gasp for air before the easel. Cloud-clenched day arrives before I throw myself into bed.... And again night sees me within its walls. With broad bristled brush I row around hills and jagged boulders, with my forefinger and the ball of my hand I squish the heavenly goo. Suppressed cries in my heart, I navigate the high trail the moon leaves in the sky. I remain unbroken and wonderfully cleft in brow. Call Bosch and Brueghel my favorite brothers. Tubes of umber are emptied in a flash. Vermilion rattles around the shaking heads of refugees diagonally across the picture and zinc-yellow lightning flashes crack the ribs of barren plains.
A steamer sails along a river. Thinly a silvery footpath dangles over the waves. A man, the pig, trips lightly along it.... then: crack, it breaks. Splash, screams! Pleading calls to God.
House-monsters bend and shake off many a suicide. Cathedral tumbles leftward into the landscape. Not a single whimper! Only the stench that streams forth from the bedrooms of innumerable lust-filled people. Why do so many zeppelins darken the moon?!! There, one smacks down onto the roofs. Human paste drips down onto my hat.
These are the nights through which I am dragged! My soul flutters around my paints. On my brush's point my soul smiles and sings with the chorale of my viscous forests. Heat burns all around me; passionate songs seek to burst out of me; a terrible power rumbles through my chest.[4]

In thickly applied paint, dominated by a Prussian-blue sky and a burnt-umber earth streaked with black, *Apocalyptic Landscape* conforms almost exactly to

this description, presenting a city within boulder-filled landscape cut by a river and bordered by mountains. A broken tree branch, eerily leglike in tone and configuration, appears in a foreground crevice, accompanied by Meidner's caricatured self-portrait, hand raised to his head in a gesture of fear or bewilderment. Within the landscape, planes shift in raw explosions of white light, a shadowed figure is collapsed in the center, and buildings writhe as steamboats ply the foaming river that curves through the city. From the darkness of the mountain range in whose valley the city nestles, a burst of white and clouds of black erupt into the star-filled night sky. A fiery orange sun, encircled by a corona of red, hangs isolated in the poisonous green of the horizon.
From this itemization of the picture's components, it is not truly apparent that an apocalyptic scene, as in biblical narratives of the end of the world, is what Meidner depicted. Indeed, while the rocky brown landscape is certainly desolate as its sole growth consists of twisting highrises, only the disturbing brilliance of white highlights indicates anything abnormal in a mildly Cubist nocturnal scene, where factories continue to pour smoke through their chimneys and ships churn up the river. It is in response to the imposed whiteness, however, that the houses warp and bend, as if seeking to escape its impact. The effulgent zinc white emerges in rays and streams from behind the mountains, not the red flow of lava but an unnatural eruption of light that deprives even the sun of radiance and reappears in heavy steam-like clouds behind Meidner's alarmed self-projection in the foreground. Its source hidden, the light remains mysterious; its failure to match the expressive gold and red volcanic bursts and meteor trails in Meidner's other apocalyptic landscapes suggests its source is different from these natural cataclysmic events. The eerie white eruption requires another explanation, a man-made source in a burst of intense artificial light, the nocturnal glow of a nearby city perhaps, or the powerful blast from a bomb.
The incomprehensibility of the intruding force in the landscape grants it apocalyptic connotations, as the grisly light transforms night into shadowed day. The central silhouette of a figure reclining or fallen, arm raised before its face in a protective movement, and Meidner himself in the foreground seeming to run in panic from the scene provide the sole human response.[5] They suffice, however, in conjunction with the disjointed transitions from extreme light to dark, to communicate a sense of terror—although the artist, judging from the self-portrait caricature, maintains a certain ironic distance even while immersed in the catastrophic event. It is less the actuality of destruction or pain that reveals the scene's significance than the multiplication of connotative details: the barren landscape painted as if covered by mud-stained snow, the twisted houses, broken tree branches, nocturnal sky, burning sun, and the blinding whiteness that encroaches everywhere. In these details and in the artist's disjunctive technique, the image approximates the prewar Ex-

pressionist poetry of Jakob van Hoddis and Georg Heym, members of the literary-artistic Neo-Pathetic group of which Meidner was a cofounder in 1912. Even specific motifs in *Apocalyptic Landscape* find echoes in Heym's "But All at Once a Great Dying Occurs":

The forests rustle in an ocean of flame....

But boatmen ply their ships uncertainly.
On gray streams the great barges roam

In sheets of rain and darkness.
Through empty bridges' empty cries, and cities
That collapse like empty graves,
And the emptiness of wintry, spreading plains.

Short is the light that storms now cover...

But beggars sit about and sing their songs
Their hands outstretched throughout the land,
And eyes look up through blood-soaked sockets.

Distance is sought by the last flock of birds,
And along the way the tiny votive pictures
Are isolated in the wintry earth.[6]

In 1919, with the benefit of hindsight informed by World War I, Meidner wrote that in 1912 he had painted his anxieties out of himself in "Last Judgments, worlds' ends, and morbid songs, because in those days the great world-engulfing storm already cast an acid-yellow shadow onto my hand that groveled with my brush."[7] Like most other postwar recognitions of prewar prophecies of the international conflagration of 1914 to 1918, Meidner's foreknowledge of World War I is at least open to question. While precise motivations for his scenes of cataclysm and apocalypse cannot be determined, his fascination with scenes of universal destruction was clearly common before 1914 among a multitude of German artists and writers.[8] Similarity of concept points not to influence but to the contemporaneity of the concerns of Meidner and the Expressionist poets in the years immediately preceding World War I. Their wintry visions of catastrophic destruction posit an extreme cultural pessimism and nihilism as they regarded uneasily and with distaste the society and time in which they lived, their bohemian rejection driven into the ecstatic terror of annihilation.   R. H.

1. "Zuweilen, wenn es mich nachts zur Stadt hintriebt, verwegene Stirne tief getunkt, im Nacken das Sternemeer, wenn ich längshin die Fläche sause... sind Wolkengeschreie um mich her, flackernde Gebüsche, ein fernes Flügelschlagen und Menschenkerle, dunkel und fauchend. Der Mond brennt an meinen heiseren Schläfen. Wir durchsegeln den Raum, ich und mein Schatten, der lange Hund. Eben hatte ich noch ein wildes Gezänk mit mir selbst, peinigte meinen Unterleib mit Vorwürfen, zerkratzte mich mit höhnischem Gewitzel—und jetzt durch die Ebene hin, Kavalkade des Schmerzes, zertrümmert die heisse Brust.

"... Es naht die Stadt. Sie knistert schon an meinem Leibe. Auf meiner Haut brennt ihr Gekicher. Ich höre ihre Eruptionen in meinem Hinterkopf echoen.

"Die Häuser nahen. Ihre Katastrophen explodieren aus den Fenstern heraus. Treppenhäuser krachen lautlos zusammen. Menschen lachen unter den Trümmern. Wände sind dünn und durchsichtig. Schädel haben zernagelte Fratzen. In Betten geschehen unerhörte Dinge. Kinder pullen sich ein. Kontoristinnen warten auf ihren Beischläfer. Sie masturbieren schon aus Langeweile.... Die Strassen werden allmählich glatter. Laternen schmeissen ihre Lichtstrahlen einfach weg und jeder kriegt was ab.... Allmählich werden die Strassen voll. Der Asphalt brüllt auf. Furchtbares Getümmel. Maschinenlärm .... Gewieher entgleister Strassenbahnen, Niesen älterer Damen und philosophische Gespräche der Schuhmacher beschäftigen den Raum. Schaufenster feuern funkelnagelneue Attrappen in die Welt hinaus. In Schaufenstern keucht hinkend die grosse Zeit. Damen und Weiber schieben ihre Dickbäuche durch das kalte Wetter. Und Kolporteurskinder, von Kohlrüben gesättigt, trudeln zwitschernd hinterdrein.

"Tumult steht auf. Warenhauses Wände bauchen aus vor Hitze. In Glühlichtkatarakten stürzt ihr Schweiss auf uns herab. Die Etagen bellen. Tausende pressen sich die matten Leiber. Eine Welt der Schachteln prasselt von den Decken. Der Unzucht Wolken schweben darüber hin, verweben sich den donnernden Unterröcken." Ludwig Meidner, *Im Nacken das Sternemeer* (Leipzig: Kurt Wolff Verlag, n. d. [1918]), 26–28.

2. "Menschenscharen brodeln vorbei, Kreaturen ferner Gestirne, Kaskaden in Lila.... stürzen in die Wände, versinken dröhnend im Asphalt.

"Die Stadt kreischt auf, steilgetürmt und weltenhoch. Sie dehnt sich krokodilisch lang, schnellt wie ein Feuerwerk in alle vier Winde. Sie bestürzt mich mit ihren Balkonen. Sie knattert in meinen Eingeweiden.... ballt sich dick wie eine Lawine und stürzt donnernd in den Mond hinein." Ibid., 29.

3. For discussion and illustrations of Meidner's apocalyptic landscapes, see Carol S. Eliel, *The Apocalyptic Landscapes of Ludwig Meidner* (Los Angeles: Los Angeles County Museum of Art, and Munich: Prestel Verlag, 1989).

4. "Ich mauere Häusertürme in tänzelnde Mondsichellandschaften. Sechs Stunden keuche ich vor Staffeleien. Es wird wolkengeballter Tag, ehe ich ins Bett stürze.... Und die Nacht sieht mich wieder in ihren Mauern. Ich rudere mit breiten Borstpinseln um Hügel und Felszacken herum, quetsche mit Zeigefinger und Ballen den Himmelbrei. Erdrückte Schreie im Herzen, so geht es mit der hohen Bahn, die der Mond am Himmel macht. Ich bin ungebrochen und herrlich stirnzerklüftet. Nenne Bosch und Breugel meine besten Brüder. Die Umbratuben sind im Nu geleert. Zinnober raschelt um die Wackelköpfe der Fliehenden diagonal über das Bild und die Zinkgelbblitze schlagen kahlen Flächen die Rippen ein.

"Ein Steamer treibt den Strom entlang. Dünn hängt der silberne Steg über dem Gewoge. Das Menschenschwein trabt drüber her.... da: rux, es kracht. Gischt, Geheul! Rufe zu Gott.

"Häuserungetümer biegen sich und schütteln manchen Selbstmörder ab. Kathedrale purzelt nach links in die Landschaft hinein. Kein Gewimmer! Nur Gestank strömt aus den Nachtlagern zahlloser Lüsterner. Warum verdunkeln so viele Zeppeline den Mond?!! Da klatscht einer auf die Dächer hinab. Menschenbrei rinnt auf meinen Hut.

"Durch solche Nächte werde ich geschleift! Meine Seele umflattert meine Farben. Auf der Spitze des Pinsels lächelt die Seele und singt mit dem Choral meiner pastosen Wälder. Hitze umbrandet mich; heisse Gesänge wollen aus mir heraus; eine furchtbare Gewalt rumort in meiner Brust." Meidner, *Im Nacken das Sternemeer*, 18–19.

5. The isolated figures on the road in the central background might be considered to be running in flight, but their size is such that a specific visual reading of their postures is not possible.

6. "Die Wälder rauschen wie ein Feuermeer.... / Die Schiffer aber fahren trüb im Ungewissen / Auf grauem Strom die grossen Kähne treibend / In schiefen Regens matten Finsternissen. / Durch leerer Brücken trüben Schall, und Städte / Die hohl wie Gräber auseinanderfallen, / Und weite Öden, winterlich verwehte.... / Die Bettler aber, die die Lieder grölen, / Sitzen im Land herum, mit langen Händen, / Und weisen ihre roten Augenhöhlen. / Die Weite sucht die letzte Vögel-Herde, / Und an dem Weg die kleinen Gottesbilder / Sind einsam in der winterlichen Erde." Georg Heym, "Auf einmal aber kommt ein grosses Sterben...," in *Georg Heym*, ed. Karl Ludwig Schneider and Gunter Martens, "sammlung dialog 46, texte" (Munich: Nymphenburger Verlagshandlung, 1971), 68. The poem was originally published in a posthumous collection edited by Kurt Pinthus and Erwin Loewenson (Georg Heym, *Dichtungen* [Berlin: Kurt-Wolff-Verlag, 1922]).

7. "... Jüngste Gerichte, Weltuntergänge und Totenschädelgesänge, denn in jenen Tagen warf zähnefletschend das grosse Weltengewitter schon einen grellgelben Schatten auf meine winselnde Pinselhand." Ludwig Meidner, "Mein Leben," in Lothar Brieger, *Ludwig Meidner*, Junge Kunst, vol. 4 (Leipzig: Klinkhardt & Biermann, 1919), 12. For citations of additional texts in which Meidner presents his paintings as premonitions of war, see Eberhard Roters, "The Painter's Nights," in Eliel, *Apocalyptic Landscapes*, 63 ff.

8. For considerations of Vassily Kandinsky's and Franz Marc's similar premonitions of World War I in apocalyptic guise, see Reinhold Heller, "Kandinsky and Traditions Apocalyptic," *Art Journal* 43, no. 1 (Spring 1983): 19–26, and my review of books on Kandinsky and Marc, *Art Journal* 39, no. 4 (Summer 1980): 313–325. Similarly, Donald Gordon, *Expressionism: Art and Idea* (New Haven and London: Yale University Press, 1987), 15–18 and 41–47, no longer follows traditional views of these apocalyptic paintings as premonitions of war, but posits a relationship among the apocalyptic, Nietzsche, and belief in "creation through destruction." This model is followed by Eliel, *Apocalyptic Landscapes*, 17–19. Roters, "The Painter's Nights," ibid., 65–68, reasserts the sense of impending doom present in society during the years before 1914, with emphasis on the sinking of the Titanic as "an omen of retribution for society's overweening pride." For an overview of apocalyptic motifs in art, see Richard W. Gassen and Bernhard Holecek, eds., *Apokalypse: Ein Prinzip Hoffnung? Ernst Bloch zum 100. Geburtstag* (Ludwigshafen: Wilhelm-Hack-Museum; Heidelberg: Edition Braus, 1985). An extensive but nonetheless very partial discussion of escatological motifs in German Expressionist literature is provided by Christoph Eykman, *Denk- und Stilformen des Expressionismus* (Munich: Francke Verlag, 1974), 44–62.

104 Ludwig Meidner

Südwestkorso, Berlin, Five O'Clock in the Morning (Südwestkorso, 5 Uhr früh), 1913

Carpenter's pencil, pencil on paper
42.1 x 56.6 cm (16½ x 22¼ in.)
Signed and dated r. l. r.
"L Meidner/1913"; inscribed l. r. "Südwestkorso. 5 Uhr früh"
Verso: *Portrait of a Boy in Sailor Suit (Porträt eines Knaben in Matrosenanzug)*, c. 1913, pencil.
Collector's seal u. l., flower with monogram "H. H."

Provenance: Hannah Höch, Berlin; Galerie Pels-Leusden, Berlin; Frankfurter Kunstkabinett Hanna Becker vom Rath; Bert Van Bork, Evanston, Ill.

In 1913, Ludwig Meidner lived in impoverished circumstances in a studio at Wilhelmshöher Strasse 21, adjacent to the major thoroughfare of Südwestkorso, in the Friedenau district of southwest Berlin. With its streetcar tracks and overhead wires, rows of multistory houses bordering broad sidewalks, and clumps of recently planted trees, Südwestkorso was for Meidner virtually an archetype of the modern city street. The wide avenue, its direction accented in this drawing by the parallel metal furrows of its tracks, provides a broad view into the distance, an allusion of endless extension with the continuing rhythmic sameness of its bordering buildings. The apartments with deep shadows cast by their protruding balconies form a fragmented pattern of faceted surfaces shifting from highlighted white to penumbral darkness. Vast emptiness looms in the central expanse of the drawing, the street deserted in the sharp, distorting illumination of an early summer morning. The vibrancy of Meidner's pencil strokes that appear as repeated parallel patterns, the deep black of the thick and soft lead of a carpenter's pencil, and the rubbing of the surface transform the image from a naturalistic perception to an existentially interpretive one, but one rooted in careful observation of visual phenomena, not in abstracting formal vocabularies.[1]

In his 1913 essay "Instructions for the Painting of Pictures of the Metropolis," Meidner vividly and accurately described the compositional principles applied in *Südwestkorso*:

> Important for the compositional aspects [of an image] is the area of focus. It is the most intensive part of an image and the focal point of the composition. It can be placed anywhere, in the middle, right or left of the center, but for principles of composition one should select a position somewhat below the center of the image. One should also be careful that all objects in the focal area be clear, sharply and unmystically presented. Within the focal area we see upright lines as strictly perpendicular. The further they move away from the focal area, the more the lines will incline. If we stand, for example, in the middle of a street, then the houses before us, far away, will be seen as vertical and their window rows seem to correspond to popular ideas about perspective, because they converge towards the horizon. But the houses near us to the side—we only half see them—seem to totter and fall apart. Here lines that in reality run parallel to one another shoot up steeply and intersect. Gables, chimneys, windows are dark, chaotic masses, fantastically foreshortened, multivalent.[2]

The artist's own experience of a scene is primary, and the image is asked to conform to the peculiarities of that artist's vision in its accidental deformations of the known visual world.

Meidner's introduction of distortion and his selection of the site and time of the drawing, however, also function to impart a more psychologically subjective content to the drawing. The emptiness of the center is all-determining. Drawn early in the morning, after Meidner had painted through the night as was his practice, the broad avenue of Südwestkorso, otherwise filled with pedestrians and traffic, is deserted and without movement, a void whose exaggerated perspective draws the lines of the bordering houses into itself vertiginously. R. H.

1. Meidner's dependence on visually present distortions of surfaces, primarily through intense light and light reflections, rather than on Futurist or Cubist principles of faceting in the creation of his "apocalyptic" effects is noted by Charles W. Haxthausen, "Images of Berlin in the Art of the Secession and Expressionism," in *Art in Berlin 1815–1989* (Atlanta: High Museum of Art, 1989), 68. Also see Reinhold Heller, "'The City Is Dark': Conceptions of Urban Landscape and Life in Expressionist Painting and Architecture," in *Expressionism Reconsidered*, Houston German Studies I, ed. Gertrud Bauer Pickar and Karl Eugene Webb (Munich: Wilhelm Fink Verlag, 1979), 46–48.

2. "Wichtig für das Kompositorische ist der Blickpunkt. Er ist der intensivste Teil des Bildes und Blickpunkt der Komposition. Er kann überall liegen, in der Mitte, rechts oder links von der Mitte, aber aus Kompositionsgründen wähle man ihn etwas unter der Mitte des Bildes. Es ist auch zu beachten, dass alle Dinge im Blickpunkt deutlich seien, scharf und unmystisch. Im Blickpunkt sehen wir aufrechtstehende Linien senkrecht. Je weiter vom Blickpunkt entfernt, desto mehr neigen sich die Linien. Stehen wir zum Beispiel geradeausblickend mitten auf der Strasse, so sind vor uns, weit unten, alle Häuser senkrecht zu sehen und ihre Fensterreihen scheinen der landläufigen Perspektive Recht zu geben, denn sie laufen dem Horizont zu. Doch die Häuser neben uns—wir fühlen sie nur mit halben Augen—scheinen zu wanken und zusammenzubrechen. Hier schiessen Linien, die in Wirklichkeit parallel laufen, steil empor und schneiden sich. Giebel, Schornsteine, Fenster sind dunkle, chaotische Massen, fanatisch verkürzt, vieldeutig." Ludwig Meidner, "Anleitung zum Malen von Grossstadtbildern," *Kunst und Künstler* 12 (1914): 314.

105 Ludwig Meidner
Street (Strasse), 1913

Brush, pen and Chinese ink with
white highlighting on paper
54.6 x 45.1 cm (21¹/₂ x 17³/₄ in.)
Monogrammed and dated l. r.
"LM/1913"

Provenance: Frankfurter Kunstkabinett
Hanna Becker vom Rath, Frankfurt a. M.;
D. Thomas Bergen Collection, London
and New York.

Exhibitions: Frankfurter Kunstkabinett
Hanna Becker vom Rath, *Ludwig Meidner:
Zeichnungen 1902–1927*, 5 March–25 April
1970, cat. p. 9; South Bend, Ind., Snite
Museum of Art, University of Notre
Dame, *The Graphic Work of Ludwig
Meidner: Drawings and Prints from the
D. Thomas Bergen Collection*, 1972; Ann
Arbor, University of Michigan Museum
of Art, *Ludwig Meidner: An Expressionist
Master*, 20 October–19 November 1978,
cat. no. 12 (as *Street in Berlin at Night*);
Milwaukee Art Center, *Ludwig Meidner:
Apocalyptic Expressionist (From the Collec-
tion of Marvin and Janet Fishman)*, 4
June–18 July 1976, cat. no. [8]; Milwaukee
Art Museum, *German Expressionism from
Milwaukee Collections*, 21 June–11 March
1979, cat. no. 91; West Berlin, Berlinische
Galerie, Museum für Moderne Kunst,
Photographie und Architektur im Martin-
Gropius-Bau, *Ich und die Stadt: Mensch und
Grosstadt in der deutschen Kunst des 20. Jahr-
hunderts*, 15 August–22 November 1987,
cat. no. 136; Los Angeles County
Museum of Art, *The Apocalyptic Land-
scapes of Ludwig Meidner*, 12 October–17
December 1989 (traveled to West Berlin,
Berlinische Galerie, Museum für Moderne
Kunst, Photographie und Architektur im
Martin-Gropius-Bau, 1 February–8 April
1990), cat. no. 16.

In this view from his studio window,[1]
Ludwig Meidner vitalizes the nocturnal
Berlin street within an agitated web of
crisscrossing lines and angles, sharp illumination, and undifferentiated black
silhouettes. From the artist's elevated
viewpoint, the house façades extend
down and backwards, behind a net of
bare tree branches in the foreground, as
if the mathematical laws of perspective
had been reversed. The result, as in
many of Meidner's images from 1912
through 1914, gives the appearance of
walls about to collapse. The effect is
furthered by the explosive disruption of
the sky through starlight and the glow
of the city below, and by the ominous
undiluted darkness of broad shadows
spreading over walls and pavements.

As in other works of 1913, the drawing of a Berlin street corner obeys the
pragmatic principles Meidner expounded in his "Instructions on the
Painting of Pictures of the Metropolis":

In nature we do not recognize light
everywhere; often we see nearest to
us very large of surfaces that appear
to be almost solid and seem to be
without light, while here and there
we feel heaviness, darknesses, un-
vitalized matter. The light appears to
flow. It shreds things. We very
clearly feel light in tatters, in stripes,
in bundles. Entire complexes weave
in the light and appear to be transparent—but then again between
them solidity, opacity in broad
masses. Between tall rows of houses
we are blinded by a tumultuous interplay of light and dark. Planes of

light rest broadly on walls. In the
middle of a throng of heads, a rocket
of light bursts. Between vehicles in
traffic, suddenly light flashes forth
brightly. The sky pushes towards us
like a waterfall. Sharp contours stag-
ger in the blinding light. Flocks of
right angles flee in whirling rhythms.
Light causes all things to move in
space. Towers, houses, lanterns seem
to be suspended or to swim.[2]

R. H.

1. The corner house of the drawing is in-
correctly identified as the Villa Kochmann
in Dresden by Carol S. Eliel, "The
Apocalyptic Landscapes of Ludwig
Meidner," in *The Apocalyptic Landscapes of
Ludwig Meidner* (Los Angeles: Los Angeles
County Museum of Art, and Munich:
Prestel Verlag, 1989), 19, n. 14. This type
of spired corner house, however, appears
frequently in Meidner's images of Berlin-
Friedenau (see cat. no. 104) and is a characteristic of that city neighborhood.
2. "Wir nehmen in der Natur nicht überall
Licht wahr; wir sehen häufig ganz vorn
grosse Flächen, die wie erstarrt sind und
unbelichtet scheinen, wir fühlen da und
dort Schwere, Dunkelheiten, unbewegte
Materie. Das Licht scheint zu fliessen. Es
zerfetzt die Dinge. Wir fühlen deutlich
Lichtfetzen, Lichtstreifen, Lichtbündel.
Ganze Komplexe wogen in Licht und
scheinen durchsichtig zu sein—doch da-
zwischen wieder Starrheit, Undurchsich-
tigkeit in breiten Massen. Zwischen hohen
Häuserreihen blendet uns ein Tumult von
Hell und Dunkel. Lichtflächen liegen breit
auf Wänden. Mitten im Gewühl von Köpfen zerplatzt eine Lichtrakete. Zwischen
Fahrzeugen zuckt es hell auf. Der Himmel
dringt wie ein Wasserfall auf und ein.
Seine Lichtfülle sprengt das Unten.
Scharfe Konturen wanken in der Grelle.
Die Scharen der Rechtecke fliehen in wir-
belnden Rhythmen.
"Das Licht bringt alle Dinge im Raume
in Bewegung. Die Türme, Häuser, Later-
nen scheinen zu hängen oder zu schwim-
men." Ludwig Meidner, "Anleitung zum
Malen von Grossstadtbildern," *Kunst und
Künstler* 12 (1914): 300.

106 Ludwig Meidner
*Street with Passersby (Strasse mit
Passanten)*, 1913

Pen, brush and Chinese ink over
pencil on paper
53.8 x 46 cm (21³/₁₆ x 18¹/₈ in.)
Signed and dated l. r.
"L Meidner 1913"

Provenance: Kunsthaus Lempertz, Cologne; D. Thomas Bergen Collection,
London and New York.

Exhibitions: Recklinghausen, Kunsthalle,
Ludwig Meidner, 1963 (traveled to West
Berlin, Haus am Waldsee, 1963; Darm-
stadt, Kunstverein, 1964); South Bend,
Ind., Snite Museum of Art, University of
Notre Dame, *The Graphic Work of Ludwig
Meidner: Drawings and Prints from the
D. Thomas Bergen Collection*, 1972; Ann
Arbor, University of Michigan Museum of
Art, *Ludwig Meidner: An Expressionist
Master*, 20 October–19 November 1978,
cat. no. 11; West Berlin, Berlinische
Galerie, Museum für Moderne Kunst,
Photographie und Architektur im Martin-
Gropius-Bau, *Ich und die Stadt: Mensch und

Grosstadt in der deutschen Kunst des 20. Jahrhunderts*, 15 August–22 November 1987,
cat. no. 137.

In this nocturnal street scene, set in Berlin, Ludwig Meidner breaks up planes
and surfaces, disembodies figures, and
duplicates rhythms with a formal consistency unusual in his work. The
streetlamps at the center of the image
cast their intense light onto houses, destroying their solidity, causing them to
break from their vertical axes. The
street and sidewalk appear to heave as
irregularly shaped light and dark planes
intersect sharply and without shaded
transitions. Figures move as dark
shadows through this visual turmoil, a
disjointed multitude of legs and torsos
in parallel echoing rhythms.

In its regular faceting and geometric
disruptions, the drawing approximates
more closely than most of Meidner's
works effects found in paintings by
Robert Delaunay and the Italian Futurists exhibited in 1912 and 1913 at Herwarth Walden's *Der Sturm* gallery. To
these paintings Meidner turned as examples adaptable to the task of providing an accurate image of the modern
metropolis and its life:

. . . the metropolis must be depicted.
What the problems are has already
been said in the manifestos of the
Futurists—not in their clumsy paintings, however—and Robert Delaunay three years ago inaugurated
our movement with his grand conception of the "Tour Eiffel." This
year, in a few painted efforts and in
more successful drawings, I too have
put into practice what I call for here
in theory. And all younger talents
should immediately begin working
and flood all our exhibitions with
representations of the metropolis.[1]

Meidner's urban scenes, so often identified solely as harbingers of apocalyptic
doom, are radical celebrations of the
modern city's inner vitality. The fragmented forms in *Street with Passersby*
testify to a reality that shifts and
changes persistently as it is observed
and experienced. Bursts of light provide the excitement of fireworks, not
the shattering explosions of bombs. A
vision of lights orchestrates urban appearance, granting mystery to the mundane and exhilaration to the common-
place.

R. H.

1. ". . . die Grossstadt muss gemalt werden.
"Es ist schon in Manifesten der Futuri-
sten—nicht etwa in ihren Machwer-
ken—gesagt worden, wo die Probleme
liegen und Robert Delaunay hat vor drei
Jahren mit seiner grossartigen Konzeption
des 'Tour Eiffel' unsere Bewegung inau-
guriert. Auch ich habe in diesem Jahre in
einigen malerischen Versuchen und
gelungeneren Zeichnungen praktisch das
getan, wofür ich hier theoretisch eintrete.
Und alle jüngeren Talente sollten sogleich
an die Arbeit gehen und alle unsere Ausstellungen mit Grossstadtschilderungen
überschwemmen." Ludwig Meidner,
"Anleitung zum Malen von Grossstadtbildern," *Kunst und Künstler* 12 (1914): 304.

107 Ludwig Meidner
*Coffeehouse Scene (Stammtisch-
szene)*, 1913

Pen and ink with white highlighting over pencil on paper
60 x 40 cm (23⁵/₈ x 15³/₄ in.)
Signed and dated u. c.
"L. Meidner/1913"

Provenance: Collection Kirste, Recklinghausen; Collection Dr. Scheele, Recklinghausen; Frankfurter Kunstkabinett Hanna
Becker vom Rath, Frankfurt a. M.

Exhibitions: Recklinghausen, Kunsthalle,
Ludwig Meidner, 1963 (traveled to West
Berlin, Haus am Waldsee, 1964; Darmstadt, Kunstverein, 1964); Milwaukee Art
Center, *Ludwig Meidner: Apocalyptic German Expressionist (From the Collection of
Marvin and Janet Fishman)*, 4 June–18 July
1976; University of Wisconsin-Milwaukee, Fine Arts Galleries, *German Expressionism from Milwaukee Collections*, 22
January–11 March 1979, cat. no. 92; West
Berlin, Martin-Gropius-Bau, *Berlin, Berlin: Die Ausstellung zur Geschichte der Stadt*,
1987, cat. no. 27/36 (as *Berliner Caféhaus*).

Around their reserved table in *Coffeehouse Scene*, four café habitués sit listening intently to the declamations of a
younger fifth, whose features recall
those of the pioneering Expressionist
poet Jakob van Hoddis as depicted by
Meidner in 1913.[1] Nocturnal darkness
is broken by the large intruding electric
light bulbs, mercilessly shooting artificial light down onto bald crowns, a
shiny marble tabletop, and emptied
glasses. Sharing this circle of light, reflections bouncing off their heads like
halos of modern secular enlightenment,
the quintet forms a cenacle of verbal intensity and concentration, partaking of
the prophecies of their own words. The
age difference between listeners and
speaker suggests a state of transition, as
youth passionately proclaims its new
doctrines and discoveries, insisting on
supplanting precursors who have become comfortable in the bohemian im-
perative they once constructed.

Unmistakable sarcasm suffuses
Meidner's drawing in the caricatured
physiognomies, stretched bodies, and
agitated atmosphere of darting white
and broken black. The café, which
Meidner praised for its ability to attract
the intellectual and artistic life of Berlin,
to transport its customers into a transformed reality (see cat. no. 102), here
receives a more judgmental portrayal.
A pathos of recognition mirrors the en-
closing wall of adjoining heads that
separates the table's discussion and
proclamation from external intrusion.
The group's fervor fails to transcend
the limits its round table has defined.
Self-generated and self-contained, the
energy of this bohemian encounter remains, according to Meidner's presentation, ineffective in breaking through
the darkness that surrounds them.

It is likely that the setting of Meidner's scene is Berlin's major bohemian
café, the Café des Westens, or one of its
imitations. A less impassioned but
similarly ironic representation of this
"Café Megalomania" and its clientele
was recorded in the booklet celebrating
the café's twentieth anniversary just before World War I, unwittingly marking
the end of an era of Berlin's bohemian
life:

> Everybody in Berlin, even in its furthest suburbs, who poeticizes, daubs in paints, stages acts and in recent times, in these glorious times of the cinotype, makes films, comes to the Café des Westens. They consider as lost any day they fail to breathe this unique atmosphere resting heavily on the heads of visitors, impregnated by spiritual paroxysms, filled with the smoky fog of cigarettes and cigars. Here in the Café the grand exchange of ideas takes place, here the battles of the cliques are fought. Here each day someone formulates a new philosophy as an aside, existences are annihilated, new heroes enthroned, everything criticized that one did not create oneself. Here the great mocking laughter of a superior humanity sounds. Here everyone waits for his moment of power, for that great moment when he will have something of significance to say. In the one corner *Der Sturm* blows supreme, in the other tender Neo-Pathetic winds stir, but all are served with the same loving care, and the Pilsner and goulash taste good to all alike.[2]

It was in the corner of "Neo-Pathetic winds" that Meidner himself belonged. His first major exhibition, shared with Jakob Steinhardt and Richard Janthur, was with the *Pathetiker* group at Herwarth Walden's *Der Sturm* gallery during November 1912. The exhibition traveled from Berlin to three further cities, with fifteen paintings and additional drawings. Together with other Expressionist artists, including Erich Heckel, and poets such as van Hoddis, Rudolf Leonhardt, Paul Boldt, Theodor Däubler, and Gottfried Benn, the exhibiting group issued a small-circulation periodical, *Das Neue Pathos* (*The New Pathos*). As a program they adopted an attitude formulated by the German Idealist philosopher Friedrich Schelling. They believed, as had Schelling before them, that art should further Enlightenment ideals of human freedom and knowledge, with the final goal of revealing the Idealist essence of existence and the transcendental order of reality, but that art should also seek its sources in the events and existential problems of contemporary life.[3]

To increase awareness of philosophical ties to the late eighteenth and early nineteenth century and to revitalize them were the declared goals of the loosely-knit group of artists and intellectuals known as *Die Pathetiker* (The Ones Filled with Pathos). They addressed the present in terms of critiques that had been devised as the industrial revolution was making its first forays in Germany, critiques which after a hundred years had still failed to be acted upon. Their resurrecting of an impassioned plea from German Romanticism proclaimed their desire to maintain links with the past, to seek an essential identity in tradition while simultaneously invoking innovation. That they saw their poetry and images as capable of transforming society is testimony to their optimism and idealism, but also to their naïveté in the face of unprecedented economic, social, and political forces unleashed in the years prior to World War I. Although Meidner's drawing is ironically critical and perhaps even cynical as it foregrounds the self-containment of Expressionism's bohemian café society, its fervent style shows it to be caught up in the very same attitudes. R. H.

1. Meidner's portrait drawing was published in *Die Aktion* 5, nos. 7/8 (13 February 1915): 90, and included as an illustration in Kurt Pinthus's fundamental anthology of Expressionist poetry, *Menschheitsdämmerung: Symphonie jüngster Dichtung* (Berlin: Ernst Rowohlt Verlag, 1920; reprint, Hamburg: Rowohlt Taschenbuchverlag, 1959), 105.
2. "Alles, was in Berlin bis in die weitesten Vororte dichtet, malt, bildhauert, schauspielert und in letzter Zeit, in der glorreichen Zeit des Kientopps, filmt, kommt in das Café des Westens. Man empfindet jeden Tag als einen verlorenen, wo man nicht diese eigentümliche Luft geatmet hat, die geschwängert von geistigen Paroxysmen, durchweht von Zigaretten- und Zigarrenqualm auf den Köpfen der Besucher lagert. Hier im Café ist der grosse Gedankenaustausch, hier werden die Schlachten der Cliquen geschlagen. Hier werden Weltanschauungen täglich aus dem Ärmel geschüttelt, Existenzen vernichtet, neue Helden auf den Thron gehoben, Kritik geübt an allem, was man nicht selbst geschaffen hat. Hier wird das grosse Hohngelächter des Übermenschen angeschlagen. Hier wartet jeder auf den Augenblick der Macht, auf diesen grossen Augenblick, wo auch er einmal wirklich etwas zu sagen haben wird. In der einen Ecke rast der Sturm, in der anderen säuseln zarte neopathetische Winde, aber allen wird mit gleicher Liebe die Schale Haut serviert, und allen schmeckt gleichzeitig gut das Pilsener und das Gulasch." *Café des Westens: Erinnerungen vom Kurfürstendamm*, 2d ed., "Randfiguren der Moderne" (Hanover: Postscriptum, 1988), 26–27.
3. Friedrich Wilhelm von Schelling, in *Das Neue Pathos* 1, no. 1 (1913), as cited in Kunstamt Wedding, *Jakob Steinhardt: Das graphische Werk*, ed. Stefan Behrens (West Berlin: Kunstamt Wedding, 1987), 29.

108 Ludwig Meidner

Apocalyptic Vision (Apokalyptische Vision), 1913

Ink over pencil on paper
54.9 x 43.6 cm (21⁵/₈ x 17³/₁₆ in.)
Signed and dated l. u. l.
"L. Meidner/Dezember/1913"

Provenance: Hauswedell and Nolte, Hamburg.

Exhibitions: University Art Museum, University of Minnesota, Minneapolis, *Berlin: Art and Metropolis—Works on Paper 1912–1932*, 8 September–11 October 1987; Los Angeles County Museum of Art, *The Apocalyptic Landscapes of Ludwig Meidner*, 12 October–17 December 1989 (traveled to West Berlin, Berlinische Galerie, Museum für Moderne Kunst, Photographie und Architektur im Martin-Gropius-Bau, 1 February–8 April 1990), cat. no. 18.

After World War I, Ludwig Meidner titled many of his earlier works, from 1912 through 1914, in apocalyptic terms so that they might acquire an aura of prophecy. Meidner's own profligacy with the word "apocalyptic" has in turn encouraged its application, in art-historical studies, to his prewar city scenes, landscapes, and various figurative compositions, frequently without proper justification.[1] The present "apocalyptic vision" has been viewed in these terms, resulting in a notable misidentification of Meidner's content.

Depictions of catastrophes ranging from the sinking of the Titanic to visions of world destruction were frequent during the crisis-ridden time preceding World War I.[2] Meidner's scenes clearly partook of this vocabulary as he portrayed comets and meteors crashing to earth, rivers flooding their banks, cities burning and exploding, revolutions erupting, and people fleeing in terror or already dead in streets and landscapes. The chiliastic disasters thus presented seek out neither guilty nor innocent, male nor female; they find their victims without prejudice or bias. Meidner, however, habitually represented his image of humanity through figures of men alone, as if women did not share the earth or experience its catastrophic end.[3] Exceptions to this tendency therefore demand particular notice and explication beyond that of universal disasters or visions of apocalypse.

Apocalyptic Vision, recently recognized as conveying a "sense of threat of modern urban life" as "a demonic male figure, spotlighted from above, [who] victimizes a group of women,"[4] is an urban nocturnal scene set in a street in which, in terms of Meidner's characteristic stylistic vocabulary, streetlamps cut façades and surfaces into faceted planes, agitating the entire composition in sharp, shifting disjunctions of black and white. A pyramidal arrangement of figures occupies the center of the scene, with a man at the apex of the triangle whose base and sides are formed by gesticulating women. The man, however, does not menace the women; indeed, they run at him from the nearby houses and surround him. Neither apocalyptic nor threatening towards these women, the scene needs closer reading to be deciphered.

At the lower left of the drawing, a female figure lies on the pavement, one hand clawing the air, the other grasping a bunch of hair. Her dress is pulled open to expose breasts, pubic hair, and vulva. One woman in the central group looks towards her; the others focus on the man above them, reaching up towards him, grabbing at his legs. They represent the active violence of the scene in their vehement gestures, the Baroque contortions of their bodies, and their screams and shouts. The man climbs a lamppost to escape them, a desperate and futile action in response to the women's pursuit. His mouth, too, is open in a shout while his body, a disjointed jumble of angular intersections, seems to disintegrate beneath the sharp illumination of the large streetlamp. Surrounded by the flapping remnants of his jacket, his penis is exposed beneath a fringe of pubic hair.

Deciphered in this fashion, the scene is more appropriately titled "Woman's Revenge" or "Avenging Women" as it represents women who attack the rapist they have trapped at the top of the lamppost. Having violated the woman lying in the street, he is caught up in the alarm that, presumably, arose as she screamed and struggled to resist. The terror of her response remains apparent even now in her desperate gestures. Meidner renders her figure with broad, heavy strokes of brush and ink that contrast the shorter, brittle pen strokes used to represent her exposed, vulnerable sexuality. Curving, agitated, massed black brushstrokes also characterize the active company of women, suggesting the energy of their anger and their determination to take revenge. One, at the left, aims a pistol at the rapist who clings to the ineffective refuge of the lamppost.

Scenes of rape and sexual violence towards women are not infrequent in German art prior to World War I, and proliferate after it. Usually, the artist either emphasizes the horror of the violation, or assumes an essentially bemused voyeuristic attitude. Meidner's scene is unique in its accentuation of women's defensive solidarity and in the representation of their fears and wrath in response to the terror of rape. He succeeds in presenting the pain of the victim as well as the rage of women in the face of rape; and he neither mythologizes the rapist nor debases him into a caricature of a criminal type, a member of an antisocial underclass whose socio-psychological profile and otherness acquits "ordinary" men of guilt in the patterns of sexual violence. Meidner's rapist is characterized, if at all, by his ordinariness, his lack of distinction other than in his aggressively—now vulnerably—exposed genitals. The rapist, desperate and powerless as he climbs up his lamppost while the mob of irate women tears at his legs and trousers, is everyman.

Misidentified—significantly, one cannot but conclude, by a male-dominated world of art galleries, museums, and collectors—as an "apocalyptic vision," Meidner's scene of rape, of its horror, and of women's outrage is deprived of its significance. Properly identified, it is an extraordinary statement, perhaps unique in its time, whose sources demand clarification within the complex and conflicting attitudes Meidner displays towards women in his work. Within the repertoire of Expressionism's celebrations of female sexuality and availability, of women's universal, passive receptivity to male sexual desire, Meidner's image forms a remarkable commentary, the necessary corrective which its misidentification has denied. R. H.

1. For discussion of the term "apocalyptic" and its application, see Reinhold Heller, "Kandinsky and Traditions Apocalyptic," *Art Journal* 43, no. 1 (Spring 1983): 19–26, and Richard W. Gassen and Bernhard Holeczek, eds., *Apokalypse: Ein Prinzip Hoffnung? Ernst Bloch zum 100. Geburtstag* (Heidelberg: Edition Braus, and Ludwigshafen: Wilhelm-Hack-Museum, 1985).
2. For a fragmentary overview, see *Apokalypse: Ein Prinzip Hoffnung?*, 197ff.
3. Among Meidner's "disaster" depictions (the term is more suitable than "apocalyptic" for much of this imagery), female figures appear as major actors only in the lost paintings *Cholera* and *Lamenting Women* (*Klagende Frauen*), both of 1912, illus. in Carol S. Eliel, *The Apocalyptic Landscapes*

of *Ludwig Meidner* (Los Angeles: Los Angeles County Museum of Art, and Munich: Prestel Verlag, 1989), 16, and in *Judgment Day* (*Der Jüngste Tag*) of 1916 (West Berlin, Berlinische Galerie), illus. ibid., 58.
4. Eliel, "The Apocalyptic Landscapes of Ludwig Meidner," in *Apocalyptic Landscapes*, 45.

109 Ludwig Meidner
Of the Terrible Doubt of Appearances (Die Ungewissheit der Erscheinungen), 1914

Ink over pencil on paper
47 x 42.5 cm (18^1/$_2$ x 16^3/$_4$ in.)
Signed and dated l. r.
"L. Meidner 1914"; inscribed
u. r. "Die Ungewissheit der Erscheinungen"

Provenance: Galleria del Levante, Munich.

Exhibitions: Milan and Rome, Galleria del Levante, *Disegni di Ludwig Meidner*, 1965; Washington, D. C., Hirshhorn Museum and Sculpture Garden, *Utopian Visions*, 1983; West Berlin, Berlinische Galerie, Museum für Moderne Kunst, Photographie und Architektur im Martin-Gropius-Bau, *Ich und die Stadt: Mensch und Grossstadt in der deutschen Kunst des 20. Jahrhunderts*, 15 August–22 November 1987, cat. no. 142.

At his inaugural exhibition as member of the *Pathetiker* group in 1912, Ludwig Meidner included a now lost painting titled *Soul of Walt Whitman* (*Die Seele Walt Whitmans*). The homage to the American poet functioned as a coded reference to Meidner's own urban images, the vitalized metropolitan streets and avenues that seem to make visible Whitman's enthused inventories of city sights:

> What hurrying human tides, or day or night! . . .
> Thou portal—thou arena—thou myriad of the long-drawn lines and groups!
> (Could but thy flagstones, curbs, façades, tell their inimitable tales;
> Thy windows rich, and huge hotels —thy side-walks wide;) . . .
> Thou visor'd, vast, unspeakable show and lesson!^{1}

More than such an indication of a general kinship of attitudes, this drawing demonstrates Meidner's direct dependence on Whitman: its title echoes that of Whitman's poem "Of the Terrible Doubt of Appearances":

> Of the terrible doubt of appearances,
> Of the uncertainty after all, that we may be deluded,
> That may-be reliance and hope are but speculations after all,
> That may-be identity beyond the grave is a beautiful fable only,
> May-be the things I perceive, the animals, plants, men, hills, shining and flowing waters,
> The skies of day and night, colors, densities, forms, may-be these are (as doubtless they are) only apparitions, and the real something has yet to be known. . . .^{2}

Meidner's drawing, highly composed and artificial in comparison with his other works, is cryptic. Like Whitman's poem, it questions the reality of appearances as its imagery shifts in and out of readability and generates a world of doubt and elusive visions.

Meidner's setting is urban, but not the canyons of streets with linked house façades of his other cityscapes; here, rows of independent houses or villas are set on a hill, beneath a stylized tree which spreads heavy branches and shading leaves. Banks of clouds fill the sky, releasing streams of rain. A road or walkway traverses the foreground, with a single male figure striding across it. He raises one arm and turns his head to look towards the viewer; his shadow echoes and repeats his form, extending it to engender a ghostly second configuration.

The rationality of the scene collapses in its center, where a bizarre apparition emerges. It may represent the face of a woman, the features not confined by outlines, the hair in frizzy curls.^{3} The composition of this face, however, splits into two unlike halves, to transform it into a pair of disembodied heads joined in a kiss. The fantastic scene, an Expressionist ghost story, is further deprived of logic by a gaunt hand which reaches up towards the kissing profiles, its bony fingers picking at a configuration not unlike a perspectival rendering of a piano's ebony and ivory keys. Another claw-like hand reaches into the drawing from the lower left and a monstrous face (in the company, perhaps, of others) resides in the corner at the lower right.

As its Whitmanesque title suggests, Meidner's drawing indeed places appearances in doubt. The initial recognition of a cityscape is denied without being rejected as the overlay of a world of ghoulish fantasy is applied. The title fails, however, to clarify the drawing's meaning, and only a biographical incident may provide some further context for the image. In 1914, Meidner, highly self-conscious about his appearance, persistently rejected by women,^{4} and at least uncertain about his own sexual orientation, fell in love:

> . . . a star [rises] in your heart and you skip around like a young boy, for God's face has revealed itself to you in unbelievable love. God's fullness has dulled you as if with scented rainfall. . . .
> To have a woman to love. Race around for weeks on end, be confused, sleep with her and kiss her. Ignore your work and forget God . . . then, as if by chance, to watch an aged woman die outside the night refuge beneath a shower of stars, and then to creep away totally overcome by remorse, deeming kisses, lovemaking, and beloved worthless.^{5}

The conflation of death and love, the remorse for sexual activity are familiar syndromes, but usually among adolescents, not thirty-year-old men. Meidner's ambivalence towards his relationship is apparent within this poeticized confession, and is repeated in somewhat different form as a renunciation of woman later in his autobiographical prose poem:

> I had lost the woman I loved. She was never true to me, but I loved her like someone allowed to love only this one single time. For several months, I ignored work, calling, and God, and sat down for innumerable, begging, and pleading love letters. She, the little actress in Munich, from time to time tossed a scrap of paper my way too, and I grasped it hungrily and nibbled away at it happily. And after each one of these contentless bits of paper, I sent ten-page-long oaths of fealty to Munich. Then she borrowed fifty marks from me and left me. That was enough. Never will I beg and plead again.^{6}

Meidner's drawing of the unreliability of appearances, viewed in this context, may be a commentary on the falseness of either this woman or women in general. The kiss, superimposed onto a woman's head, lacks fixity and fades in and out of other forms in the drawing, as does the music that accompanies it. The man, his shadow intact signifying his preserved reality, turns his back on this bodiless specter.

But such a biographical reading, even if tantalizing, fails to take into account the remaining aspects of the drawing: the setting unusual for Meidner, the grasping hands, gargoylesque faces, and shifting shadows that take on shape only to cast doubt on their own appearance. If the drawing is indeed Meidner's effort to visualize love as illusion, he has inserted it into a vision that continually defies both consistent reading and recognition of its content in a world of personal apparitions while "the real something has yet to be known. . . ." R. H.

1. Walt Whitman, "Broadway," *Leaves of Grass*, in *Complete Poetry and Collected Prose* (New York: The Library of America, 1982), 624.
2. Walt Whitman, "Of the Terrible Doubt of Appearances," ibid., 274. The reference to Whitman in Meidner's title is noted by Victor Miesel, *Ludwig Meidner: An Expressionist Master* (Ann Arbor: University of Michigan Museum of Art, 1978), 20, n. 23.
3. In its components, ranging from curlicued hair to amorphous facial shape, the face compares with others of women in Meidner's urban scenes, such as *Grand Café Schöneberg* (cat. no. 102).
4. "I am always by myself. No girl loves me. No woman will sleep with me" ("Ich bin immer für mich allein. Kein Mädchen liebt mich. Keine Frau will bei mir schlafen"). Ludwig Meidner, *Im Nacken das Sternemeer* (Leipzig: Kurt Wolff Verlag, n. d. [1918]), 35.
5. ". . . ein Stern [geht] in deinem einfachen Herzen auf und du hüpfest wie ein Junge, denn Gottes Angesicht hat sich in ungeheurer Liebe in dir aufgetan. Gottes Fülle hat dich wie duftender Regenfall betäubt. . . .
"Eine Geliebte haben. Wochenlang rasen, verwirrt sein, beischlafen und küssen. Arbeit liegen lassen und Gott vergessen . . . dann wie zufällig, in leisem Sternenfall eine Greisin sterben sehen vor nächtlichem Spital und sich wegstehlen, sehr zerknirscht und Küsse und Beischlaf und Geliebte gering halten." Ibid., 40.
6. "Ich hatte eine Geliebte verloren. Sie war mir niemals treu gewesen, aber ich liebte sie wie einer, der nur dieses eine Mal lieben darf. Ich liess ein paar Monate Arbeit, Berufung und Gott im Stich und

setzte mich hin zu unzähligen, bettelnden Liebesbriefen. Sie, die kleine Schauspielerin in München, warf mir gelegentlich auch einen Wisch auf den Tisch, den ich gierig aufgriff und ganz zerknabberte vor Seligkeit. Und ich sandte nach jedem dieser inhaltslosen Scheine zehn seitenlange Schwüre nach München. Dann lieh sie sich fünfzig Mark und liess mich im Stich. Das genügte. Ich werde nie mehr betteln gehn." Ibid., 62.

110 Ludwig Meidner
Battle (Schlacht), 1914

Pen, brush and ink on paper
64.9 x 50.6 cm (25^9/$_{16}$ x 19^{13}/$_{16}$ in.)
Signed and dated l. c.
"L Meidner 1914"

Provenance: Collection Kirste, Recklinghausen; Kunsthaus Lempertz, Cologne; Kunstkabinett Helmut Tenner, Heidelberg; Frankfurter Kunstkabinett Hanna Becker vom Rath, Frankfurt a. M.; Kornfeld & Klipstein, Munich; D. Thomas Bergen Collection, London and New York.

Exhibitions: Heidelberg, Kunstkabinett Helmut Tenner, *Ludwig Meidner*, 1968; Frankfurter Kunstkabinett Hanna Becker vom Rath, *Ludwig Meidner*, 20 November–24 December 1969; Frankfurter Kunstkabinett Hanna Becker vom Rath, *Ludwig Meidner*, 5 March–25 April, 1970; South Bend, Ind., Snite Museum of Art, University of Notre Dame, *The Graphic Work of Ludwig Meidner: Drawings and Prints from the D. Thomas Bergen Collection*, 1972; Ann Arbor, University of Michigan Museum of Art, *Ludwig Meidner: An Expressionist Master*, 20 October–19 November 1978, cat. no. 20; Milwaukee, UWM Art Museum, University of Wisconsin, *Reactions to the War: European Art, 1914–1925*, 2 November–14 December 1986, cat. no. 31 (as *Schlact* [sic]).

A version of the drawing published as number 7 in Ludwig Meidner's 1915 portfolio *War* (*Krieg*),^{1} *Battle* depicts a French artillery unit in whose midst an exploding grenade or shell brings violent death. In the manner of Alfred Rethel's woodcut series devoted to the Revolution of 1848, *This, Too, Is a Dance of Death* (*Auch ein Totentanz*),^{2} Meidner melds this scene of contemporary reality with the traditional skeletal emblems of Death, guiding actors in the carnage who perch on or peer around the cannon and wave a grimacing banner, a rallying standard that calls for additional human sacrifice. Continuing aspects of his apocalyptic scenes during the first months of World War I, Meidner's *Battle* grounds their chiliastic visions in current events as cities are bombarded by cannons, bombs, and grenades, whose smoke here darkens the sun as if to inaugurate the eternal night of the end of time.

Meidner was immediately affected by the war. Although initially he failed to pass the military physical because of his substandard size and various ailments, he was placed in reserve with the possibility—a reality after 1916—of being called to active service. Returned from Dresden to Berlin, he allied himself with the left-wing, pacifist periodical *Die Aktion*, where he published drawings of corpse-strewn battlefields and crowded military hospitals.[3] The death in battle of Ernst Wilhelm Lotz, the poet with whom Meidner had worked in Dresden in 1914, also may have served as motivation for these scenes of death and destruction meted out now by men rather than by uncontrollable cosmic forces.

In *Battle*, a Baroque whirl of lines characterizes war's savage devastation—imagined by Meidner from photographs and written accounts—in a graphic analogue. The diagonal division of the drawing into compartments of black and white further adds to its disruptive quality as it represents the central grenade explosion whose force tosses bodies outward towards the drawing's edge. The terror and force of the explosion are condensed in the soldier at the lower right. Rendered in faceted surfaces and swirling lines, he screams out as his hands and feet are torn from his body and fly off into the surrounding conflagration. The quasi-Cubist vocabulary of disjuncture Meidner employs is linked to an actual dismemberment of the *poilu*'s body, and the Futurist dynamism of the composition is the result of the grenade's explosive force. Stylistic devices are deprived in this image of their abstraction, are transformed into similes of violence and destruction.

The composition, with a shouting figure in the foreground backed by a scene of conflagration and battle, echoes Meidner's earlier updating of Eugène Delacroix's *Liberty on the Barricades* (1830) in a 1913 painting titled *Revolution* or *Battle on the Barricades*.[4] In that painting, however, it was the personification of triumphing revolution who waved the banner to rally the struggling masses; now it is Death who beckons others to follow in his suicidal entourage. The shouting figure, moreover, is divested of any heroic dimension, no longer calling to revolt but screaming in pain as his body is ripped to pieces. The earlier allegorical summons to revolution and heroic conflict has been subverted and rendered into its antithesis, a grim scene of death and destruction with reference to nothing but more death and destruction.

Meidner's pessimistic conclusion about the futile devastation of the World War is akin to Rethel's earlier response to the failed Revolution of 1848. In the autumn of 1914, such perceptions countered the popular euphoria and official optimism that shaped German reactions to the outbreak of war. Indeed, German troops had triumphed in August 1914 at the Battle of Tannenberg in the east and, in the west, quickly marched through Belgium, appearing to head for Paris. In September, however, with the losses of the Battle of the Marne, the German advance halted, and the relative stagnation, deadly in its effect, of four years of trench warfare set in. German propaganda images, focusing on Tannenberg and on the heroes of the Marne, presented scenes of victory, of German "warriors" overcoming the French, in a concerted media effort to maintain German civilian belief in German invincibility.

Like Willy Jaeckel's contemporary *Hand-to-Hand Combat in a Trench* (cat. no. 73), Meidner's *Battle* in part uses the vocabulary of state-sponsored propaganda art as it depicts enemy soldiers being overpowered, defeated and dying. The victims of war are French, as their uniform caps make clear, much as Jaeckel's were clearly Russian, and in this identification links to German propaganda efforts necessarily exist. A similar focus on recognizably French *poilus* characterizes most other images in Meidner's portfolio *War*, moreover, as it does his other drawings of wartime violence in 1914 and 1915, but significantly not those published by Franz Pfemfert in *Die Aktion*. Indeed, Meidner's persistent depictions of dying French soldiers may have contributed to the break between him and Pfemfert after 1916. The ambivalence that characterizes Meidner's scenes of apocalyptic destruction, in which the celebration of destruction coexists with terror, extends into *Battle* and the other plates of *War*.

However, in the portfolio the accentuation of French victims may also be a device to circumvent German censorship. While sharing its vocabulary, Meidner simultaneously subverts the content of official imagery that celebrates war and demands that Germans be seen victorious over their enemies in combat. In Meidner's drawing, no human combatant prevails. The grenade is not hurled by muscular German infantrymen; it has no visible source. If the dismemberment of French soldiers in *Battle* is to be considered worthy of applause by the German public, the public is also denied its accustomed ability to recognize German power and nobility as the cause of enemy deaths. Death in Meidner's drawing is, instead, an anonymous force, a grenade or bomb that lacks identity other than as a modern instrument of mass death. Without aim or apparent origin, the projectile brings death to those who chance to be near. Riding the cannon in Meidner's drawing, Death alone is the victor.   R. H.

1. For a second version of the drawing, titled *The Cannon (Die Kanone)*, formerly in the collection of Wolf Schön, Cologne, see Thomas Grochowiak, *Ludwig Meidner* (Recklinghausen: Verlag Aurel Bongers, 1966), 100, pl. 48.
2. For illustrations and extensive discussion of Rethel's woodcuts, see Peter Paret, *Art as History: Episodes in the Culture and Politics of Nineteenth-Century Germany* (Princeton: Princeton University Press, 1988), 104–130.
3. Meidner's war-oriented drawings published in *Die Aktion* are: *Battlefield (Schlachtfeld)*, 4, nos. 48/49 (5 December 1914), title page, the first work depicting a wartime motif published by *Die Aktion*; *Dedication Page for Die Aktion (Widmungsblatt für Die Aktion)*, 5, nos. 1/2 (2 January 1915), title page, whose original drawing, not included in this exhibition, is also in the Marvin and Janet Fishman Collection; *Battlefield (Schlachtfeld)*, 5, nos. 5/6 (30 January 1915), 58, in an issue illustrated throughout by Meidner; and *Military Hospital (Lazarett)*, 5, nos. 20/21 (15 May 1915), title page.
4. *Revolution (Auf den Barrikaden)*. Grochowiak, *Ludwig Meidner*, 95, pl. XIII.

111 Ludwig Meidner
Self-Portrait (Selbstporträt), 1915

Carpenter's pencil on paper
49.5 x 36.5 cm (19$\frac{1}{2}$ x 14$\frac{3}{8}$ in.)
Signed and dated l. r. "Ludwig Meidner/1915"

Provenance: Ernest Rathenau, Berlin, Hamburg, and New York.

As Germany's armies demanded more and more recruits following the initial enthusiastic enlistments of August 1914, Ludwig Meidner, too, was placed in reserve training, although his short stature and physical ailments prevented him from being called into active service for over a year. Living and working in Berlin, associating with the pacifists and war resisters around Franz Pfemfert, Meidner contributed drawings to Pfemfert's periodical, *Die Aktion*. The present self-portrait derives from this period of anxiety and uncertainty as Meidner, like others previously rejected for military service, awaited the inevitable call.

The gaunt, wide-eyed, and moustached face with its minimal fringe of hair remains much as in the artist's previous self-portraits, but the raised hand is an unusual addition to Meidner's typically exclusive focus on the head. His gesture is unclear, except that it shows his fingers, stiff from arthritis, as testimony to his lack of fitness for military duty. There may be accusatory overtones to Meidner's display of his partially crippled hand: like a paralytic exhibiting his suffering to God, he waits for the miracle of a cure.

Despite his physical handicaps, Meidner guided pencil and pen with remarkable assurance. Short, jabbing lines, trembling and shifting in value but heavy with the soft lead of a carpenter's pencil, make up this self-portrait, providing a likeness with economy of detail and in an agitated style. The harsh impress of pencil into paper, almost pushing through the surface, suggests an intensity, almost violence, in Meidner's drawing process that recalls his own poetic description:

Fear not the empty whiteness of the paper. Do not lose heart! There the wild world, horrible uncertainty are to be found—and here is your spirit and your heated will to produce a new world, a purer, more subdued world closer to God than the chaotic, confused one all around us. . . .
Fear not the visage of man, which is a reflection of divine glory, but more often is a feast of slaughter with bloody scraps of flesh. Bring the forehead's frown, root of the nose and eyes close together. Like a burrowing animal, bore down into the inexplicable ground of the pupils and the whites of your sitter's eyes and do not let your pen rest until you have tied your sitter's soul to your own in a pathetic bond. Sink down into the intimacy, into the moist and fearful intimacy of a pair of lips. Observe the point or the scarred softness of the chin. The ornament of the ear should charm you again and again, as should the flaming hair, the waves of hair, the ashes of hair around gaunt cheeks; the prickly bristles, the little

hairs at the mouth should be a pleasant taste for your flitting pen.[1]

R. H.

1. "Fürchte dich nicht vor der leeren Weisse des Papiers. Sei unverzagt! Dort ist die wilde Welt, die schreckliche Ungewissheit—und hier ist dein Geist und dein heisser Wille eine neue Welt zu schaffen, eine reinere, gebändigtere, Gott nähere Welt als die chaotische, wirre, da ringsherum. . . .
"Fürchte dich nicht vor dem Antlitz des Menschen, das ein Abglanz himmlischer Herrlichkeit ist, aber noch häufiger ein Schlachtfest mit blutigen Fetzen. Nimm Runzelstirne, Nasenwurzel und Augen eng zusammen. Bohr dich wie ein Wühltier in den unerklärlichen Pupillengrund und das Augenweiss deines Gegenübers und lass' deine Feder nicht rasten, bis du deines Gegenübers Seele mit der deinen zu einem pathetischen Bunde vermählt hast. Versenke dich in die Innigkeit, in die feuchte und schreckliche Innigkeit eines Lippenpaares. Beachte die Spitze oder zernarbte Weichheit des Kinns. Das Ornament des Ohres soll dich immer wieder entzücken und die lodernden Haare, die Haarwellen, die Haar-Asche um dürre Wangen, die stechenden Borsten, die Härlein um den Mund seien ein Wohlgeschmack für deine flitzende Feder." Ludwig Meidner, *Im Nacken das Sternemeer* (Leipzig: Kurt Wolff Verlag, n. d. [1918]), 32–33.

112 Ludwig Meidner
Self-Portrait (Selbstporträt), 1916

Ink over pencil on paper
43.5 x 34.9 cm (17$\frac{1}{8}$ x 13$\frac{11}{16}$ in.)
Monogrammed and dated l. r. "L. M./1916"

Provenance: Private collection; Kornfeld und Klipstein, Berne; Galleria del Levante, Munich; D. Thomas Bergen Collection, London and New York.

Exhibitions: South Bend, Ind., Snite Museum of Art, University of Notre Dame, *The Graphic Work of Ludwig Meidner: Drawings and Prints from the D. Thomas Bergen Collection*, 1972; Ann Arbor, University of Michigan Museum of Art, *Ludwig Meidner: An Expressionist Master*, 20 October–19 November 1978, cat. no. 29.

Despite constraints imposed on his artistic activity by military duty at a prisoner-of-war camp, Ludwig Meidner drew numerous portraits and self-portraits during 1916. The process of sketching, of intimate contact through pencil and pen with the physiognomies of soldiers and prisoners, brought relief from the sufferings of inadequate clothing and shelter. "Ah, to draw in the midst of war's miseries," he wrote later. "To bury oneself in the pockmarked lunar landscape of a man's physiognomy. Soon one reaches the ground of his soul. . . ."

This self-portrait drawing presents Meidner in a consciously held pose. Fingers touch his raised chin and eyes gaze up towards heaven in an expectant ecstasy:

It's necessary to use a sharply pointed instrument; a nib pen, sharp needle, or hard chalk. You, graphic artist, must not fuss around in "painterly" fashion and bluff your way through.

Your line has to break forth from inner life. You must have a diabolical wind in your nerves. You are moon-mad. Your blood must be a boiling ocean.

Poetry deep within, and a sharpened, expansive, glowing line; a line that sits prophetically just right, that expresses everything, that can be made only one time. The music of your expansive breast and your fire-swinging hand which an angel guides for you. That is more important than anything else. That leads to the great work.

Draftsman of these days, you ecstasy-filled male person! You know your tools. You know how much depends on every single stroke, every dot over every "i." You possess an immense sense of responsibility because from your soul no unfinished, ugly and impure images may come forth. . . .

Drawing brings good health, happiness, and faith in God.[2]

The rhapsodic pose and paean to drawing suit the hymnic exultation of Meidner's book of Expressionist prose poems, *Im Nacken das Sternemeer* (*At My Back, a Sea of Stars*), which he wrote during his years of military service. Confessional ruminations, pronouncements on artistic practice, hymns to a newly recovered God fill the book, and drawings of prophets, beggars, and saints interact with its texts. The self-portrait in which Meidner raises hand to chin and eyes to the heavens above him, seeking answers to his doubts, is the book's second frontispiece, immediately before an unbounded litany: "What beats in my brain, what drips in my breast? All is so strange to me."[3]

R. H.

1. "Ah, zeichnen im Elend des Krieges. Sich eingraben in die zerlöcherte Mondlandschaft einer männlichen Physiognomie. Man gewahrt bald den Grund seiner Seele. . . ." Ludwig Meidner, *Septemberschrei: Hymne/Gebete/Lästerungen* (Berlin: Paul Cassirer, 1920), 4.
2. "Man muss mit spitzem Instrument ans Werk gehen; Kugelspitzfeder mit Stau, scharfer Nadel, oder harter Kreide. Du Graphiker darfst nicht 'malerisch' wursteln und bluffen. Dein Strich muss aus innerem Leben hervorbrechen. Du musst einen höllischen Wind in deinen Nerven haben. Du Mond-Toller, dein Blut soll ein kochendes Meer sein.
"Die Poesie tief drinnen und der geschärfte, expansive, glühende Strich; der Strich, der hellseherisch richtig sitzt, der alles ausdrückt, der nur einmal gemacht werden kann. Die Musik deiner weitatmenden Brust und die feuerbeschwingte Hand, die ein Engel führt. Darauf kommt es an. Das ist wichtiger als alles andre. Das führt zum grossen Werk.
"Zeichner dieser Tage, du ekstasenreicher männlicher Mensch! Du kennst deine Mittel. Du weisst, wie sehr es auf jeden Strich, auf den I-Punkt ankommt. Du hast ein ungeheueres Verantwortlichungsgefühl, denn deiner Seele dürfen nicht hässliche, unfertige und unlautere Gebilde entspriessen. . . .
"Zeichnen macht gesund, heiter, und gottgläubig." Ibid., 32–33.
3. "Was schlägt in meinem Hirn, was tropft in meiner Brust? Es ist mir alles unbekannt." Ibid., 9.

113 Ludwig Meidner
Beggar (Bettler), 1916

Pen, brush and ink over pencil on paper
58.5 x 45.7 cm (23 x 18 in.)
Monogrammed and dated l. l.
"LM/1916"

Provenance: Kunsthaus Lempertz, Cologne; Frankfurter Kunstkabinett Hanna Becker vom Rath, Frankfurt a. M.; D. Thomas Bergen Collection, London and New York.

Exhibition: South Bend, Ind., Snite Museum of Art, University of Notre Dame, *The Graphic Work of Ludwig Meidner: Drawings and Prints from the D. Thomas Bergen Collection*, 1972.

Late in 1915 and in 1916, Ludwig Meidner produced a series of ink drawings of isolated figures that act out states of extreme existential excitation. Eleven of these, in addition to his self-portrait (cat. no. 112), he collected as plates for his book *Im Nacken das Sternemeer* (*At My Back, a Sea of Stars*). *Beggar* is the fourth of these, appearing in association with a text that characterized his early Berlin existence:

Often I sat on a bench, totally incapacitated by pain, and over and over again I counted my years wasted and continuing to be lost in poverty and hunger. I fed anger within me and anarchism. I had my eyes out for others like me.

I recognized you right away, my brothers in fate! Homeless, abandoned old women, men without work or a home, of uncertain step, unseeing eyes, trudging alone so pleadingly. Did I not sometimes walk behind you for hours on end and did not my own misery seem less as a result?![1]

Beggar is a self-portrait raised to the level of universality. Barefoot, one hand raised imploringly, the other cupped in hope of alms, a bowl with a few coins at his side, the mendicant with Meidner's features sits on the ground. A bedroll or rock is depicted behind him, but otherwise no indication of place or time distracts from the anguished figure rendered monumentally so as to fill the space of the paper, pushing towards its edges. The beggar is Meidner; the beggar is Lazarus, seated at the gates of the rich man's estate and pleading for crumbs.

R. H.

1. "Oft sass ich auf einer Bank, ganz erstarrt vor Schmerz und zählte mir immer wieder meine verlorenen Jahre, die in Armut und Hunger hinsiechenden Jahre auf. Ich nährte Wut in mir und Anarchismus. Ich hatte den Blick für meinesgleichen.
"Ich erkannte euch gleich, Schicksalsbrüder! Obdachlose, verlassene alte Frauen, Männer ohne Arbeit und Heim, unsichern Schritts, blicklosen Auges, so flehentlich dahinwankend. Ging ich nicht manchmal stundenlang hinter euch her und wurde nicht mein Unglück geringer dabei?!" Ludwig Meidner, *Im Nacken das Sternemeer* (Leipzig: Kurt Wolff Verlag, n. d. [1918]), 20–21.

114 Ludwig Meidner
Prophet (Prophet), 1916

Brush, pen and ink over pencil on paper
57.7 x 45 cm (22³/₈ x 17¹¹/₁₆ in.)
Signed and dated r. c. r
"L Meidner/1916"

Provenance: Kunsthaus Lempertz, Cologne; D. Thomas Bergen Collection, London and New York.

Exhibitions: Recklinghausen, Kunsthalle, *Ludwig Meidner*, 1963 (traveled to West Berlin, Haus am Waldsee, 1963; Darmstadt, Kunstverein, 1964); South Bend, Ind., Snite Museum of Art, University of Notre Dame, *The Graphic Work of Ludwig Meidner: Drawings and Prints from the D. Thomas Bergen Collection*, 1972; Ann Arbor, University of Michigan Museum of Art, *Ludwig Meidner: An Expressionist Master*, 20 October–19 November 1978, cat. no. 27.

Bald and bearded, pointing ecstatically towards the heavens, Ludwig Meidner's *Prophet* appears among the confessional, anguished prose poems in *Im Nacken das Sternemeer* (*At My Back, a Sea of Stars*). A translation into modern Europe of Old Testament figures previously rendered by Christian Baroque painters, the drawing is a synthesizing testimony to Meidner's Jewish ancestry and religion, now reaffirmed after years of denial, and to his personal and artistic formation within the culture of contemporary Germany. For him, these aspects of his life were fused inextricably, incapable of separation, but threatened in the military morass of the winter months of 1916. As the war stretched further into its second year of brutality, deprivation, and death, he was called up to serve as a guard at prisoner-of-war camps:

Is it the end-of-March snow that hurts me so?!!

On this cold earth, oh how long already, the winter firmament hammers onto my poor exhausted brain. The earth's pores will not open. The trees will not leap, clouds not thaw, houses not green, and my hands not smile in the stream of a new, thirsting day.

I am an artist, something of a poet as well; but now, a slave of the times, appearing like a robber with revolver and butcher's knife dangling at my side—but too cowardly, oh woe, too lacking in courage, and too much in despair to grant an ear to God's voice. . . .

Is this earth not as alien to me and as horrifying as the entrails of a trampled corpse?! This sky as noisy as pits of mad dogs?!! And the firmament at night is ice cold. The stars are drunk and not as gentle as those of my spiritual, my true, inner home. Here there are no flowers. Never, never shall I forget that such a hard, grass-less earth exists, that there is such moldy sand bereft of warmth. Ugh! and these fulminating pines, of which my torturers are so proud, are they, too, God's trees, cool, speckled parasols?!

Oh these torturers! Oh this humanity sunk down to the level of beasts! It's better not to speak of them! How the fate of our poor continent tears at my breast every day!

Old, proud Europe!. . . I do not know what will come of it. God is slandered. Law disappears. Poets, visionaries, prophets of goodness and all righteous people, all lovers of a greater humanity that our earth once generated are now swept away. The flood leaves behind a miserable mercantile generation and our Christians' sun chokes to death behind violent horizons. I cannot understand the men of these tortured days. Never, never will I comprehend what compels them. I can only give myself up, with passionately folded hands, to my devotions, to my yearning for God, to my spiritual visions. . . . But then when I think of my brothers in the large courtyard over there, of the Frenchmen, Russians, Romanians . . . whenever I march past the penal company, this screaming line of murderers, Apaches, and ruthless criminals. . . . Oh, this weeping wound that runs with the excretion of revulsion, bloodthirstiness, and anger . . . then I choke down into myself silently and duck down on my side, deep into the March snow. . . .[1]

R. H.

1. "Ists der Ende-März-Schnee, der mir so weh tut?!!
"Auf dieser kalten Erde, ach wie lange schon! hämmert das Wintergestirn auf mein erbärmlich mattes Hirn. Der Erde Poren wollen nicht aufbrechen. Die Bäume wollen nicht hüpfen, Wolken nicht tauen, Häuser nicht grünen, und meine Hände nicht lächeln im Strom eines neuen, lechzenden Tags.
"Ich bin ein Maler, ein wenig Dichter auch; aber jetzt ein Knecht der Zeit, anzusehen wie ein Räuber, mit Revolver und Schlachtmesser an der Seite—aber zu feig, ach! zu mutlos und verzweifelt, um der Stimme Gottes Gehör zu geben. . . .
"Ist mir diese Erde nicht so fremd und grässlich wie zertretener Leiche Gedärm?! Dieser Himmel lärmend wie die Zwinger toller Hunde?!! Und das Nacht-Firmament ist eisern. Die Sterne sind betrunken und nicht lind wie die meiner geistlichen, meiner wahren, inneren Heimat. Hier sind keine Blumen. Nie, nie werde ich vergessen, dass es auch so harten gräserlosen Erdboden, so schimmeligen, wärmelosen Sand gibt. Huh! und diese fulminanten Föhren, auf die meine Peiniger so stolz sind, sind das auch Bäume Gottes, kühle, gesprenkelte Sonnenschirme?!
"O diese Peiniger! O diese in die Tierheit herabgesunkenen Menschen! Rede lieber nicht von ihnen! Wie mir unsres armen Kontinents Geschick jeden Tag die Brust aufreisst! Altes, stolzes Europa!. . . Ich weiss nicht was noch wird. Gott wird geschmäht. Das Recht verschwindet. Dichter, Seher, Künder der Güte und alle Gerechten, alle hohen Menschheitslieber, die nur unsre Erde zeugte, werden weggeschwemmt. Die Sintflut lässt ein elend merkantilisches Geschlecht am Leben und unsre Christen-Sonne verröchelt hinter gewalttätigen Horizonten. Ich verstehe die Männer dieser verzerrten Tage nicht. Nie, nie werde ich ihr Treiben fassen. Ich gebe mich nur mit inbrünstig gefalteten Händen meiner Andacht, meiner Gottes-Sehnsucht, meinen geistlichen Gesichten hin. . . . Aber wenn ich dann an meine Brüder denke, im grossen Hofe drüben, die gefangenen Franzosen, Russen, Rumänen . . . wenn ich jedesmal an der Straf-Kompanie vorbeischreite, dieser kreischenden Linie von Mördern,

Apachen, und Wüterischen. . . . O, dieser heulenden Wunde, die von Ekel, Blutgier und Wut aufspringt . . . dann würge ich stumm in mich hinein und duck' mich tief zur Seite in den März-Schnee. . . ." Ludwig Meidner, *Im Nacken das Sternemeer* (Leipzig: Kurt Wolff Verlag, n. d. [1918]), 69–71.

115 Ludwig Meidner
Self-Portrait (Selbstporträt), 1916

Brush, pen and ink on paper
47 x 39 cm (18¹/₂ x 15⁵/₁₆ in.)
Monogrammed and dated l. c.
"LM/1916"

Provenance: Private collection; Sotheby, London.

As World War I continued into its second and third year, German manpower needs escalated while the number of men available decreased. In 1916, Ludwig Meidner was pressed into military service along with others previously considered unfit. "When we all stood there together," Meidner wrote, "sickly boys next to clubfooted men and shaky old beards, then it looked as if a cheeky band of robbers had lost its courage and now came crawling back to the cross."[1]

The self-portrait drawing shows Meidner even more gaunt than in previous years. Posed at an angle, he seems precariously balanced, as if listening for suspicious noises or intrusions on his clandestine drawing efforts. More than earlier pen drawings, this one appears rushed. The ink splatters as the saturated pen is scratched over the paper surface, or fades as ink supply in the nib dwindles.   R. H.

1. "Wenn wir alle so dastanden, schwächliche Knaben neben Hinkfüssen und wakkeligen Runzelbärten, dann war es anzusehen, als ob verwegne Räuberbande den Mut verloren hätten und nun zerknirscht zu Kreuze kroch." Ludwig Meidner, *Septemberschrei: Hymnen/Gebete/Lästerungen* (Berlin: Paul Cassirer, 1920), 3.

116 Ludwig Meidner
Landscape with Birch Tree (Landschaft mit Birke), 1919

Oil on canvas
30 x 34.5 cm (11³/₄ x 13¹/₂ in.)
Signed and dated l. l.
"L. Meidner 1919"

Provenance: Dr. Wilhelm R. Valentiner, Berlin and New York; Villa Grisebach, West Berlin.

The work in oils produced by Ludwig Meidner immediately after World War I remains little known, and appears to have been limited in amount. Much of Meidner's energy was absorbed by the publication of his writings, by the various exhibitions of his work at Paul Cassirer's noted Berlin gallery, at the Kestner Gesellschaft in Hanover, and at I. B. Neumann's gallery in Berlin, and by preparation of Lothar Brieger's monograph in the series *Junge Kunst*

212   Catalogue

(Young Art), which included new works in ink, watercolor, gouache, and tempera (see cat. no. 117). Indeed, as Meidner presented himself in the revised version of the *Junge Kunst* volume in 1923 works of 1918–19 do not exist, aside from watercolor visions of prophets, a drawn self-portrait, and a portrait engraving.[1] Since this self-representation by Meidner still shapes our perception of the artist, recent publications and exhibitions devoted to his work have continued to ignore the oils of the immediate postwar period. *Landscape with Birch Tree* thus provides a remarkable opportunity to fill this gap in our knowledge of Meidner's career, but the lack of contemporary oils by him makes it difficult to place the work in a meaningful context.

Considering Meidner's urban orientation and his prewar challenge to artists to paint the modern city, this landscape with its view of the battered remnants of a birch tree beneath a darkly threatening sky is surprising. Indeed, such a pure landscape, unpopulated and without buildings or other signs of civilization, would seem to be without parallel among his mature works. The notably careful writing of his signature in brilliant red, contrasting to the dark and muted colors of the landscape itself, and using Gothic lettering rather than his usual *Süterlinschrift*, may indicate that Meidner wished to underline the work's uniqueness by accenting the name of the artist as unavoidable complement of the image. Perhaps the landscape derives from the region around Bernstadt in Silesia, where Meidner lived briefly with his mother following his release from the army, but in its generalized, tortuously rolling hills that lack individualizing features the scene is more easily read as an imagined one, a subjective projection rather than the rendering of an actual encounter with nature. With its virulently active brushwork, the landscape then appears rather like an extended signature, a seismograph of personal involvement that resembles a transfigured self-portrait.

Isolated trees such as Meidner's birch have been surrogates for, or extensions of, a human presence in landscape depictions at least since Caspar David Friedrich and Johan Christian Clausen Dahl included them in their Romantic iconography of loneliness and embattled endurance. Meidner borrows this device and adapts it to a vocabulary of composition, color, and activated brushwork that overtly emulates Vincent van Gogh. These eclectic components of the painting indicate a kind of retrospective recognition, a harkening back to earlier prototypes and models which Meidner had sought out from 1909 to 1911 as he strove to shape the individual vocabulary of his art. It is as if Meidner, a decade later, were announcing a renewed period of transition, a deliberate effort to shift his previous identity towards a revised vision of art and reality that would serve the altered reality emerging after war and revolution.

As a member of the Work Council for Art, formed by German artists late in 1918 in order to place their collective efforts at the service of constructing a socialist revolution from the Empire's

defeat, Meidner wrote in his manifesto "To All Artists, Poets, and Musicians" that the "bloodstained" wages of the bourgeoisie—"that ugly beast of prey lusting for victims, the thousand-headed emperor of tomorrow, the atheist and Anti-Christ"[2]—must be rejected by artists and a new identification sought with the working class:

Oh, during this dark day may we be guided by the divine voice: Justice and Love! With body and soul, with our hands we must join in.

For socialism is at stake—that is, Justice, Freedom, and Love of Humanity—*God's order in the world![3]*

Meidner's purposeful but desperate optimism did not survive the violence of 1919, however, and for his adherence to communal activity and socialism he substituted an increasingly withdrawn introspection and religiosity. If a direct parallel can be drawn between *Landscape with Birch Tree* and Meidner's intellectual and ideological retreat into social pessimism—and such correlations are always restricted in their value—then the painting's battered tree and dark sky, its rejection of the contemporary, its implication of a turn towards a highly individualist, mystical aesthetic, all make visible the resisted alienation and renewed isolation that Meidner experienced in 1919.   R. H.

1. Ludwig Meidner, *Eine autobiographische Plauderei,* Junge Kunst, vol. 4, rev. ed. (Leipzig: Klinkhardt & Biermann, 1923), pl. 8–9, 11–12.
2. " . . . das hässliche Raubtier, den beutelüsternen, tausendköpfigen Kaiser von Morgen, den Gottesleugner und Anti-Christ!" Ludwig Meidner, "An Alle Künstler, Dichter und Musiker," *Das Kunstblatt* 3 (1919), as repr. in *Die Zwanziger Jahre: Manifeste und Dokumente deutscher Künstler,* ed. Uwe M. Schneede (Cologne: DuMont Buchverlag, 1979), 43.
3. "O, leite uns an diesem dunklen Tag die göttliche Stimme: Gerechtigkeit und Liebe! Mit Leib und Seele, mit unseren Händen müssen wir mittun.
"Denn es geht um den Sozialismus —das heisst: um Gerechtigkeit, Freiheit und Menschenliebe—*um Gottes Ordnung in der Welt!"* Ibid.

117 Ludwig Meidner
The Call at Daybreak (Der Schrei vor Tagesanbruch), 1920

Watercolor, gouache over pencil on light cardboard
67.4 x 50.5 cm (26¹/₂ x 19⁷/₈ in.)
Monogrammed and dated l. r.
"L. M. 1920"

Provenance: Collection Kirste, Recklinghausen.

Exhibitions: Recklinghausen, Städtische Kunsthalle, *Ludwig Meidner,* 1963 (traveled to West Berlin, Haus am Waldsee, 1963; Darmstadt, Kunstverein, 1964); Ann Arbor, University of Michigan Museum of Art, *Ludwig Meidner: An Expressionist Master,* 20 October–19 November 1978, cat. no. 3 (as *Shriek Before Daybreak*); Milwaukee, Fine Arts Galleries, University of Wisconsin, *German Expressionism from Milwaukee Collections,* 22 Janu-

ary–11 March 1979, cat. no. 96 (as *Cry of the Day*); Milwaukee, UWM Art Museum, University of Wisconsin, *Reactions to the War: European Art, 1914–1925,* 2 November–14 December 1986, cat. no. 32 (as *Cry at Daybreak*).

In 1919, in response to a perceived need of Germany's post-revolutionary socialist society, the Leipzig publishing house of Klinkhardt & Biermann began issuing a series of brief artists' monographs, *Junge Kunst (Young Art)*, designed to make studies of contemporary art available at low cost to a wide public. The first three volumes, devoted to Max Pechstein, Paula Modersohn-Becker, and the sculptor-architect Bernhard Hoetger, considered early practitioners or precursors of German Expressionism. The fourth volume, by Lothar Brieger, presented Ludwig Meidner as representative of the generation following them, the prototype of "the primitives of a new artistic era" who explode the conventions of the past and announce the precepts of renewal, unable, however, to realize fully the principles they espouse:

Someone of such brilliant potential as Meidner cannot bring perfection, cannot bring order, and indeed cannot do so simply by virtue of his time and of his position in that time. Innovators stand not only at the heights but also at the entrance of a new era. . . .

It is extraordinarily difficult to demand acknowledgment of the primitive from a time that believes itself to be washed by the waters of culture's greatest achievements and that has just behind it a war which, with immeasurably more accomplished means, recalls the most gruesome battles of primeval man. In our time this has been precisely the martyr-like and embattled position of young artists of Meidner's type, has been the posture of martyr and struggler adopted by all primitives: that they have always had to introduce a new culture after an overly refined one has choked to death on its own excesses, that in them over and over again the self-awareness of the soul revolted against overly luxurious materiality.[1]

Brieger's "primitives" are the progenitors and innovators. As a corrupted age approaches its end, they announce the vocabulary of the coming era, which others are to take up, develop, and refine. But they themselves are doomed never to achieve the greatness their own vocabulary makes possible. "It cannot, and may not, be denied," Brieger contended, "that the new language still stutters."[2]

To accompany Brieger's text as first published, numerous drawings from Meidner's prewar period were selected: scenes of cafés and city streets; prophet figures from his book *Septemberschrei (September Outcry)*; portraits of "prophets" of the new age, Expressionist poets such as Johannes Becher and Alfred Mombert; and Meidner's own self-portrait, *My Nocturnal Visage* (cat. no. 100). Text and images thus combined to proclaim a rejuvenated, reformed humanity and the new era of art that would accompany it. The past was marked by destruction and the violence of national conflicts; the future promised a new, spiritualized humanity. Meidner introduced his autobiographical summary in the book with a similarly naïve optimism, the short-lived euphoria of postwar months:

At first you chase around blind and confused on numerous side roads on the way towards the blinding goal. But nonetheless one day the great, safe main avenue opens up and confusion disappears like fog and everything becomes simple and marvelous.[3]

Four years later, in 1923, Klinkhardt & Biermann issued a second, expanded edition of the book, with more and different illustrations and a new text, now written by Meidner himself. Instead of proposing a process of discovery which, despite halting starts, leads to a definable goal and positions the artist in the role of society's prophet, Meidner now proposes a withdrawal inward, a dialogue between artist and art in which the studio is the realm of greatest extension:

It is a wonderful hour, in the afternoon at five, when a broad sky appears over Berlin after dark winter months; when the cool light of spring falls through the large window onto the many pencils and the empty bottles and boxes, and I can draw bent over my drawing board. The books, the old rusted canvases, alarm clock, teapot, and herring bowl—everything is in its place. Turpentine and acid lightly scent the room, smells so sweet for an aritst.

How marvelous is such a studio, no matter how small! Nowhere would I rather be than in my studio . . . . Here is isolation, essentiality and introspection; here, the place of observation and prayer—and here I am my own guest and engage in conversation with myself, and I work and eat and drink and sleep, and will die one day in the studio, or so I hope. . . . Because the world, that is insanity, error, and temporality—but the true world, that is the inner world when you enter the silence and listen and there hear the true word speak within you.[4]

Dedicated to his sister Helene, a female extension of himself, the book indicates a transformation in Meidner's art. A few portraits, introspective rather than ecstatically expansive as earlier, and ink drawings of interiors remain, but the frontispiece declares a new theme, the artist's vision of supernatural destruction, his *Apocalyptic Landscape* (cat. no. 102). Childhood drawings of flagellants and the Jews in exile introduce the selection of images that follows the text. Meidner confesses repentance and a return to the faith of his Jewish ancestors:

. . . If you [are] . . . filled with longing for the eternal, then do not go to false prophets, occultists, and theosophists, nor to the teachings of Buddha and Laotse, which today are on everyone's lips, but unlock your heart to old verses and psalms that you learned in your childhood. Perhaps in them, who today have to stand ignored like pitiable beggars and are no longer noticed by anyone,

you will discover unanticipated and beneficent treasures.

Yes, that is where salvation, peace, happiness, and permanence exist beyond the days of this earth![5]

Saul of Tarsus is depicted preaching and in ecstacy; Jews carry Torah scrolls, Bible readers enter states of ecstasy, psalmists sing their verses towards heaven in Meidner's reformed imagery. Central within the selection of reproductions is a self-portrait drawing of 1919, Meidner in the act of drawing; juxtaposed is the watercolor-gouache *The Call at Daybreak*.

A barefoot man, dressed in red and blue, sits in a large shell and appears to hover slightly above the landscape, where a single dark house stands. Massive and contorted, the volumes of legs and arms supplant all else in his twisted posture; his art-historical ancestors are in Michelangelo's Sistine Chapel ceiling and in the prophets and saints of Baroque church frescoes. "They are manly, unyielding and yet gentle people, these greatest witnesses to our Creator and Lord."[6]

Meidner's prophet reaches out with a burning torch which touches the sky and ignites flame-like clouds of white in its blue darkness. An allegory of dawn, he gesticulates zealously with the clenched fist of his left hand held up to his head. His mouth is open to call out the daybreak introduced by his torch. "Oh and I,"—Meidner, who spent his nights painting and saw daybreak come with fear and relief—"filled with gentle visions and never escaped from the night, now carry night into day. Earth trembles beneath me, wind calls out and the demons of houses take away my breath, my hearing, the light of my eyes. I am day-blind and stumble through its blinding glory."[7]   R. H.

1. ". . . die Primitiven der neuen künstlerischen Zeit. . . . Eine geniale Potenz wie Meidner ist kein Vollender, kein Ordner und kann es seiner Zeit und seiner Stellung in dieser Zeit nach auch garnicht sein. Die Schöpfer stehen nicht nur auf der Höhe, sie stehen vielmehr auch am Eingang eines jeden Stils. . . .

"Es ist ungeheuer schwer, das Bekenntnis zur Primitivität von einer Zeit zu verlangen, die glaubt mit allen Wassern der reifsten Kultur gewaschen zu sein und die eben erst einen Krieg hinter sich hat, der mit ungleich grösseren Mitteln an die grausamsten Kämpfe der Naturvölker erinnert. Das eben ist die Märtyrer- und Kämpferstellung dieser jungen Künstler vom Schlage Meidners in unserer Zeit, ist die Märtyrer- und Kämpferstellung aller Primitiven gewesen: Dass sie immer am Ende einer an sich selbst erstickten Überkultur gegen sie ein Neues heranführen mussten, dass in ihnen immer wieder das Selbstbewusstsein der Seele gegen die zu üppig gewordene Materie revoltierte." Lothar Brieger, *Ludwig Meidner*, Junge Kunst, vol. 4 (Leipzig: Klinkhardt & Biermann, 1919), 14. Like many of the other texts in the series, Brieger's was previously published in Klinkhardt & Biermann's periodical, advertised as "tribune of the new time and the conscience of the new art," *Der Cicerone* 11, no. 4 (27 February 1919): 69–75.
2. "Es kann und darf nicht bestritten werden, dass die neue Sprache noch stammelt." Ibid., 13.
3. "Zuerst rennt man blindlings und bestürzt auf unzähligen Nebenwegen dem

blendenden Ziele zu. Eines Tages tut sich aber dennoch die grosse sichere Hauptstrasse auf und die Verwirrungen zergehen wie Nebel und alles wird einfach und wunderbar." Ludwig Meidner, "Mein Leben," ibid., p. 15.
4. "Das ist eine schöne Stunde, nachmittags um fünf, wenn ein heiterer Himmel über Berlin steht, nach schweren Wintermonaten; wenn das kühle Frühjahrslicht durchs grosse Fenster auf die vielen Bleistifte und die leeren Flaschen und Kisten fällt und überm Brett gebückt ich zeichne. Die Bücher, die alten verrosteten Leinwände, Weckeruhr, Teetopf, und Rollmopswanne—alles ist an seinem Platz. Nach Terpentin und Säure duftet es leis im Raum, Gerüche, die ein Maler so gern hat.

"Wie fein ist so ein Atelier und wär' es noch so klein! Nirgendwo bin ich lieber als in meinem Atelier. . . . Hier ist Abgeschiedenheit, Wesenheit, und Einkehr; hier der Ort der Betrachtung und der Gebete—und hier bin ich bei mir selber zu Gast und halte Zwiesprache mit mir selber und ich arbeite und esse und trinke und schlafe, und werde auch einmal sterben im Atelier, so hoffe ich wohl. . . . Denn die Welt, das ist das Närrische, Verkehrte, und Vergängliche—aber die wahre Welt, das ist die inwendige Welt, wenn du in die Stille gehst und lauschest und dort das wahre Wort im Innern reden hörst." Meidner, *Eine autobiographische Plauderei*, Junge Kunst, vol. 4, rev. ed. (Leipzig: Klinkhardt & Biermann, 1923), 5–6.
5. "Wenn Du . . . voller Sehnsucht [bist] nach dem Überzeitlichen, so gehe nicht zu den falschen Propheten, Okkultisten und Theosophen, noch zu den Lehren des Buddha und Laotse, die heute in aller Munde sind, sondern schliesse Dein Herz den alten Sprüchen und Psalmenversen auf, die Du in Deiner Kindheit gelernt hast, vielleicht wirst Du in ihnen, die heute wie armselige Bettler abseits stehen müssen und von Niemand mehr beachtet werden, ungeahnte und beglückende Schätze finden.

"Ja, dort ist das Heil, Frieden, Seligkeit und Dauer über den Erdentag hinaus!" Ibid., 13–14.
6. "Es sind männliche, unbeugsame und dennoch milde Menschen, diese grössten Zeugen des Schöpfers und Herrn." Ibid., 8.
7. "O und ich, zarter Gesichte voll und nie entglitten der Nacht, trag nun die Nacht in den Tag hinein. Boden wanket unter mir, Wind schreiet und die Dämonen der Häuser nehmen mir Atem, Ohr und Augenlicht. Ich bin tagblind und taumle in der blendenden Herrlichkeit." Meidner, *Im Nacken das Sternemeer* (Leipzig: Kurt Wolff Verlag, n. d. [1918]), 55.

118   Ludwig Meidner
Self-Portrait (Selbstporträt),
1923

Oil on artist's board
59.1 x 47 cm (23¼ x 18½ in.)
Monogrammed and dated u. l.
"LM 1923"

Provenance: Karl und Faber, Munich.

Exhibitions: Milwaukee Art Center, *Ludwig Meidner: Apocalyptic German Expressionist (From the Collection of Marvin and Janet Fishman)*, 4 June–18 July 1976,

cat. no. [4]; Los Angeles County Museum of Art, *German Expressionism 1915–1925: The Second Generation*, 9 October–31 December 1988 (traveled to Fort Worth Art Museum, 2 February–9 April 1989; Düsseldorf, Kunstmuseum, 18 May–9 July 1989; Halle, Staatliche Galerie Moritzburg, 9 August–30 September 1989), cat. no. 142.

The colors Ludwig Meidner employs in this self-portrait are essentially the same greens, reds, blues, and browns as in *My Nocturnal Vision* (cat. no. 100), painted ten years earlier, but this similarity only accentuates the distance separating the two images. The 1913 painting existed in a dialectical relationship with Vincent van Gogh's *Self-Portrait with Easel* (1889), accepting and adapting its vibrant color, physiognomic interpretation, and schema of the subject as suffering, isolated seer, the prototypical characterization of the Expressionist artist.[1] Meidner emerges defiant, glowing with the heat of his colors, from the surrounding darkness in the 1913 self-portrait; in 1923, the contrast is less pronounced and the artist's posture more passive.

Wearing a dark coat over a blue smock, Meidner in this later self-portrait acknowledges the muted interior in which he poses. A painting rests, face to the wall, behind him as does a vase filled with brushes instead of flowers, but dark, clean, and unused. Light strikes his head, forming shapes evenly from brightness to shadow; the softly molded brushstrokes are not the agitated, snaking, wriggling paths of color of 1913, but curving, contouring touches which blend areas of the face gently together.

Meidner's oeuvre emerged in disruptions, in a series of disjunctive leaps interspersed with periods of relative inactivity as artist. The first of these fractures occurred on his return to Germany from Paris in 1907; for over three years, Meidner then produced little, to emerge in his Neo-Pathetic Expressionism in 1912. This new phase lasted, marked by consistency of quality and style, until World War I; for two years after 1916, Meidner's primary concern was his writing, and he considered abandoning painting altogether. A religious conversion, his return to the Judaism of his ancestors, accompanied Meidner's adoption of the neo-Baroque manner of his prophet images, a revised celebration of his prewar ecstasies and apocalypses, but affirming the integrity of figures and objects as the earlier works had not. In 1923, however, in response to *Das Kunstblatt*'s survey of artists and critics concerning a "new Naturalism" in art, Meidner described a calmer manner in his work, firmly rejecting his rapturous postwar imagery:

For my part, I cannot do without direct contacts with nature, and believe that all romantic exaltation will increasingly give way to a more contemplative concept of nature. Greater respect for the object—that is what I now tell myself every day![2]

Meidner's "greater respect for the object" was linked to his newfound faith, which demanded reverence for God's creation, the living beings and nature that surrounded him. The act of painting became one of re-creating God's beneficent donation of the world:

I am totally concerned with the object in a painting. What could possibly be more important than the objects of this world? They are a thousand times closer to us than all the world's ideas. And the great truths of faith, too, are not ideas, but objects which are comprehensible through the senses. A painting without objects from the real world is a great foolishness and of use only to fools and snobs. . . .

"Truly wise, and one who has learned more from God than from man, is he for whom all objects are significant for what they are, not for what they are called or for why they are valued by man"—thus in a beautiful book from the Middle Ages. Even if all worldly people and all artists overflow with praise for the purely artistic, I myself will always celebrate more and more those masters who enrich my heart and who turn my innermost being in love towards Him who is the greatest of all Masters and who endows the greatest of talents.[3]

Meidner privileges the visual over the verbal as providing a more essential communication, but the visual in terms of a search for underlying realities that reveal a divine purpose. He praises the Nazarene artist Peter von Cornelius and such German late Gothic painters as Hans Multscher, who opted for a limited palette, unlike their contemporaries. Their works, like those he himself now produced, Meidner considered as contemplatively involved with a tactile reality, in contrast to the false sensuousness of coloristically rich works, including his own youthful paintings, which he now thought removed from the divine and as leading to ultimate darkness.

The self-portrait is conceived according to these principles. Its muted color harmonies with their earthen presence accent the figure within a continuous construct, a human countenance emerging from the primordial clay from which God formed it. Abandoning the anger and confrontation of the 1913 self-portrait, in this self-image Meidner proclaims softly but fervently: "Yesterday I was another. Today I am renewed. It is your love which has achieved this, oh Thou God of essential kindness."[4]   R. H.

1. Formerly New York, Collection John Hay Whitney; illus. in J.-B. de la Faille, *The Works of Vincent van Gogh* (New York: Reynal & Co., 1970), no. 626.
2. "Ich für meinen Teil komme ohne unmittelbare Naturberührung nicht aus und glaube, dass mehr und mehr alle romantischen Exaltationen besonneneren Naturauffassung Platz machen werden. Grössere Ehrfurcht vor dem Objekt—rufe ich mir jetzt jeden Tag zu!" Ludwig Meidner, in response to "Ein neuer Naturalismus?? Eine Rundfrage des Kunstblatts," *Das Kunstblatt* 6 (1922): 382.
3. "Mich fesselt so sehr der Gegenstand eines Bildes. Was ist auch wichtiger als die Gegenstände der Welt? Sie sind uns tausendmal näher als alle Ideen der Welt. Und die grossen Wahrheiten des Glaubens sind auch keine Ideen, sondern Dinge, die sinnlich wahrnehmbar sind. Ein Gemälde

ohne Gegenstände der realen Welt ist eine grosse Torheit und nur dem Narren und Snob ein Gewinn. . . .

"'Der ist wahrlich weise und mehr von Gott denn von Menschen gelehrt, dem alle Dinge das gelten, was sie sind und nicht das, was sie vom Menschen geschätzt werden'—so heisst es in einem schönen Buche des Mittelalters. Mögen auch alle Leute von Welt und alle Künstler überströmen im Lobe der rein künstlerischen Kunst, so will ich selber für mich immer mehr jene Meister feiern, die mein Herz reicher machen und die mein inwendiges Zuwenden in Liebe dem grössten aller Meister und Geber aller guten Gaben." Ludwig Meidner, *Eine autobiographische Plauderei*, Junge Kunst, vol. 4, rev. ed. (Leipzig: Klinkhardt & Biermann, 1923), 8–10.
4. "Ein Anderer war ich gestern. Ein Neugeworener bin ich heute. Das hat deine Liebe getan, du grundgütiger Gott!" Ludwig Meidner, "Von der Liebe Gottes," *Das Kunstblatt* 6 (1922): 206.

---

119   Ludwig Meidner
Portrait of a Young Woman from Poland (Portrait of a Polish Jewish Woman—Domestic Servant) (*Porträt eines jungen Mädchens aus Polen [Porträt einer polnischen Jüdin—Dienstmädchen]*), 1929

Oil on artist's board
70 x 50 cm (27³/₈ x 19⁵/₈ in.)
Monogrammed and dated u. r. "LM/29"; inscribed on stretcher verso "Porträt eines jungen Mädchens aus Polen" and "Porträt einer polnischen Jüdin—Dienstmädchen"

Provenance: Collection Kirste, Recklinghausen; Kunsthaus Lempertz, Cologne.

Exhibitions: Recklinghausen, Kunsthalle, *Ludwig Meidner*, 1963 (traveled to West Berlin, Haus am Waldsee, 1963; Darmstadt, Kunstverein, 1964); Milwaukee Art Center, *Ludwig Meidner: Apocalyptic German Expressionist (From the Collection of Marvin and Janet Fishman)*, 4 June–18 July 1976, cat. no. 5.

Around 1923, Ludwig Meidner adopted a naturalism of muted tones with variations on browns and grays; he maintained this manner of painting until 1936 when he fled Germany to avoid further Nazi persecution. *Portrait of a Young Woman from Poland* represents the accomplishments, but also the problems, of Meidner's style of the 1920s. The scheme of the image is a standard one of portrait painters and photographers, showing the Polish servant posed at a slight angle away from the artist, while turning her head in his direction to lend movement to the image. Like many of his female subjects, the Jewess is presented from a slightly elevated position, so that she looks up to him both physically and metaphorically. The viewpoint signals Meidner's ambivalence towards women, notable in 1929 several years after his unexpected marriage to the young artist Else Meyer. Their relationship was marked by career conflicts and her efforts to preserve her independence

and identity despite his desire to dominate, their respective positions paralleled in her adherence to liberal Jewish views while he became increasingly orthodox and dogmatic.

Meidner complained in 1929, tongue in cheek but nonetheless with a tone of serious accusation, that throughout his twenty-five-year career he had received only three portrait commissions: "one was paid for, the other was not completed, and the third was rejected."[1] In addition to painting self-portraits, he portrayed models, artist and poet friends he knew in Berlin, or, as in the case of the Polish servant, members of his or acquaintances' households. Meidner's choice of sitters is predicated either on personal closeness or his socially superior position: not permitted to exist outside their relationship to him, his subjects are extensions of his own ego. *Portrait of a Young Woman from Poland* accordingly reads more as a projection of Meidner's personality than as an interpretation of his sitter's, a series of negations rather than affirmations.

Painted in uniform thickness, wet-in-wet on a colored ground, the image is composed of controlled, almost hesitant strokes of the brush, limited in their visibility, denying the virulent gestures of his earlier, Expressionist works. "I have to consider myself one of that mass [of Expressionist artists] for whom not even a cock crows anymore, and that in their own lifetime," Meidner complained sarcastically, "and this totally without foundation, because I am after all a significant person, at least within my own family, a correct husband and a busy painter, likewise within my family, since my wife, too, impetuously flirts with the artist's trade."[2] Else Meidner's work caused him further to question his own abilities and value as artist. Her work, he felt, surpassed his own and rendered it superfluous. He looked back to his most celebrated works of the 1910s and wished he could resume the impetuous relationship with painting they represented. Unable to do so, however, he rejected them in order to justify the timid accuracy of his subsequent style: "We painted like oxen then, who stuffed colors down and went on binges with them and never looked very closely as to whether somebody's schnoz sat correctly in the middle of the face or was sliding more towards the right ear—it was miserable draftsmanship, and we called it 'ecstasy.'"[3]

Meidner's son, David, was born in 1929; the artist's role within his own family was altered as a result, and the marriage given new configuration as Else Meidner was now not only a mother but received significant publicity and awards through *Das Kunstblatt* for her portraiture. Self-doubt and an all-too-understandable pessimism in the face of contemporary political events marked Meidner's attitudes, and he yearned to withdraw into himself, freed of the necessity to produce art:

No longer do I expect great things [of myself]: because now for me greatness consists of yearning and losing oneself; and that I quietly contemplate is wiser than all heartfelt effusions. . . . Now I have time to stride calmly. May frenzy and ardour and

fury remain distant to me. Peace, peace—a voice now says deep within me.[4]

The portrait of the Polish servant embodies just such calm, a denial of concious excitement; however, for Meidner, the Jewish painter in Germany, the peace and tranquility for which he yearned eluded him. Frenzy, ardour, and fury combined with persecution in 1933.   R. H.

1. ". . . wurde mir nur einer bezahlt, der andere wurde nicht beendet und der Dritte nicht angenommen. . . ." Ludwig Meidner, "Eigenlob stinkt nicht oder Lustiger Traktat über Porträtmalerei," *Das Kunstblatt* 13 (1929): 68.
2. ". . . ich [muss] mich selber . . . zur Masse derer rechnen, nach welchen kein Hahn mehr kräht, schon zu ihren Lebzeiten, und dies ganz zu unrecht, denn ich bin immerhin ein bedeutender Mensch innerhalb meiner Familie, ein korrekter Ehemann und ein tüchtiger Maler, ebenfalls innerhalb meiner Familie, da auch meine Ehefrau ungestüm dem Malerhandwerk frönt." Ibid., 65.
3. "Wie die Heuochsen malten wir dazumal, welche die Farben frassen und soffen und nicht genau hinschauten, ob die Gusche richtig mitten ins Gesicht gepflanzt ward oder mehr ans rechte Ohr rutschte—ein miserabeliges Gezeichne war das; das Resultat nannte man dann 'Ekstase.'" Ibid., 68.
4. "Keine grossen Dinge erwarte ich mehr: denn das ist mir gross, das Sichsehnen und Sichverlieren; und dass ich ruhig mich besinne, ist weiser als alle Herzenstaumelei. . . . Nun habe ich Genüge an stillem Schreiten. Fern sei mir Krampf und Brunst und Raserei. Friede, Friede—sagt tief eine Stimme in mir." Meidner, *Gang in die Stille: Erbauungsbuch* (Berlin: Euphorion Verlag, 1929), 11.

---

120   Walter Meyer-Vax
The Editor (Der Redakteur), 1929

Oil and pencil on canvas
140 x 76 cm (55³/₁₆ x 29¹⁵/₁₆ in.)
Signed l. c. r. "Meyer-Vax"; dated l. r. "V.29"

Provenance: Neue Münchner Galerie, Munich.

Exhibition: Berlin, Prussian Academy of Fine Arts, *Einsendungen für den Grossen Staatspreis*, 1930.

Against the background of a yellow-beige screen and red rug, Walter Meyer-Vax presents a newspaper editor holding the product of his labor. The editor stares alertly and directly out of the canvas, standing confidently, one hand on his belt; wearing a dark suit and tie, spats and a homburg hat, he occupies a position of power and pride. Meyer-Vax constructs this figure with heavy, planar strokes, and scratches isolated details on spats and suit. His broad orchestration of volume and planes, as well as the stark posture and composition, indicate his indebtedness to his teacher, Karl Hofer. The simple design with its flat forms is reminiscent of *le Douanier* Rousseau's full-length portraits, but also of Edvard Munch's extended series of full-length portraits of men.[1] This stylistic amalgam of naïveté and sophistication results in an imposing image, in which the figure becomes representative, not of an individual, but of a class and profession. Self-conscious and self-assured, the editor observes society observing him, determined in his cool reserve.

The extreme partisanship and ideological determinism of the German press might be read into this image, but its confident tone had already become illusory by 1929. At that time, 147 daily papers reported the news in Berlin and proclaimed political and cultural convictions that ranged across the full multi-party spectrum of Weimar ideologies.[2] However, three major publishing houses—Mosse, Scherl, and Ullstein—dominated Berlin's newspaper scene, each printing a multiplicity of papers and maintaining a certain uniformity in the daily press despite the apparent kaleidoscopic diversity. The dominance of capitalist publishing houses devoted to classical humanistic standards had effectively collapsed after Alfred Hugenberg, standard-bearer of extreme right causes and monopoly capitalism, surreptitiously gained control of the Scherl Verlag, adding its list to the more than five hundred newspapers he owned in other German cities.

Hugenberg's purchase in 1921 of the Wolff Telegraph Bureau, providing a subscription service to news stories, secured his reactionary influence over the German press even beyond the particular newspapers he owned and controlled directly. By the mid-1920s, he had concluded his reorganization of the Scherl Verlag and added a cheap daily tabloid to the firm's already numerous publications. In 1926, Scherl's employees numbered over six thousand, including 130 editors; it had become the cornerstone of Hugenberg's press syndicate.[3] As his entrepreneurial success and consolidation of a huge propaganda network demonstrates, command of the publishing industry and subordination of editorial staff was paramount to gaining political power in the Weimar Republic. Conflicts between editorial and publishing responsibilities thus became explosive as the publishing business grew in economic power. The rights and roles of editors and publishers in determining the form, content, and policies of newspapers were highly disputed, as the fight for the Journalists' Law in the mid-twenties reveals.

This law proposed that the editor's responsibility would be situated "within the limits of the agreement specifying the general political, economic, and cultural orientation of the publication," and was defined as "the shaping and representation of the intellectual content."[4] This legal definition of the editor-publisher relationship and the state support of editorial prerogatives it implied, however, was ultimately denied. By the end of the twenties, the press had become big business, and emphasis shifted from responsibility to profit and then to controlled political propaganda and, with it, to the final subordination of editor to publisher. By the time Meyer-Vax painted *The Editor*, newspapers had ceased to be perceived as a major source

of income and became, instead, primarily transmitters of ideology. Traditional canons of quality were dismissed; mass marketing supplanted journalistic worth. The virtual monopoly on information addressed to middle- and lower-class audiences was further aided by increasingly frequent governmental restrictions on press freedom. In 1933, the Nazi government encountered little resistance in transforming the bourgeois press, by means of emergency decrees, into an instrument of totalitarian propaganda and social control. Meyer-Vax's independent editor was supplanted by the Party functionary.   B. T. Y.

1. Meyer-Vax's appreciation of Munch's work is also indicated by his traveling to Norway after being awarded the Great State Prize of the Prussian Academy of Fine Arts in 1930.
2. In total, 2,633 newspapers and periodicals were then headquartered in Berlin, more than half the roughly five thousand dailies and weeklies published throughout Germany; as the American scholar Oron J. Hale has observed, the German press surpassed that of all other countries as educational and cultural medium. Hale, *The Captive Press in the Third Reich* (Princeton, N. J.: Princeton University Press, 1964), 2.
3. John A. Leopold, *Alfred Hugenberg: The Radical Nationalist Campaign Against the Weimar Republic* (New Haven and London: Yale University Press, 1977), 15. Leopold analyzes the clandestine approaches that characterized Hugenberg's entrepreneurial successes as well as his involvement in the campaign against democracy in Germany as chairman of the board of directors at Krupp's, as director of a propaganda syndicate, and as chairman of the German National People's Party.
4. Hale, *The Captive Press*, 10.

121   Ernest Neuschul
Nude Girl (Jung-Mädchen Akt), 1930

Oil on canvas
99.8 x 65.2 cm (29¹/₄ x 25¹¹/₁₆ in.)
Signed l. l. "Ernest Neuschul"
Inscribed and dated on stretcher verso "Jung-Mädchen Akt, 1930"; artist's stamp

Provenance: Galerie Nierendorf, West Berlin.

Exhibition: West Berlin, Galerie Nierendorf, *Herbst '84*, 1984.

Reminiscent of Edvard Munch's *Puberty* (1893) in composition and motif, Ernest Neuschul's depiction of a naked girl sitting on the edge of a bed is strikingly different in mood and effect. In Neuschul's painting, poverty is an underlying theme: only a few rumpled sheets cover the child's mattress; no rugs warm the earthen floor under her feet. It is a room of simple necessities the girl occupies, harshly illuminated by a sharp glare which highlights her knees, chest, and forehead. Her hair is roughly cut, short, and black, her skin dark in tone. Her head, bent forward, almost touches the upper edge of the painting, so that she seems constrained, trapped and pinned like a specimen in

an immovable display. The girl's resigned pose and the spare compositional format, in which she forms a vertical crosspiece, together with her silent expression and the dingy tonality of the painting, induce a mood of melancholy or deprivation.

Neuschul emphasizes the austerity of lower-class setting and life. In this he echoes documentary photographs that similarly attempted to expose the unhealthful conditions suffered by urban inhabitants, especially by the proletariat. If Neuschul avoids the extremes of both physical deformity and squalor that photographic reportage foregrounded in its effort to generate shock and sympathy among middle-class viewers, it is at least partly because of the altered ideological and political context since the publication of most of those socially critical photographs in the teens and twenties.

With her black hair and tallowish skin, Neuschul's child in 1930 appeared an antithesis to persistent popular and Nazi propaganda images fostering ideals of Nordic beauty, blond and fair, cultivated in sunlight and nature. Such healthful, outdoor advantages are denied to the young girl in Neuschul's image, but rather than transforming her into a caricature of "degenerate" physiognomy—as in Nazi representations of "lesser" racial types—Neuschul imparts to her an implicit nobility of resistance, of determined existence. She becomes not only a representative of her class and social milieu, but a plea for reform, for recognition of her humanity and the need to change the conditions of her life.   B. T. Y.

122   Hermann Niehaus
Prole (Prolet), 1924

Watercolor, gouache, pen and ink on paper
50.8 x 40.4 cm (20 x 15⁷/₈ in.)
Signed and dated l. l. "Niehaus/ 24"; signed and dated on mat l. r. "Hermann Niehaus/1924"; inscribed on mat l. l. "Prolet"

Provenance: Christie's, London.

In this strange and disturbing image, the North German artist Hermann Niehaus has depicted a member of Hamburg's working class in the aftermath of the uprising of October 1923 led by the German Communist Party (KPD). The year was among the most crisis-filled periods of the Weimar Republic's crisis-filled history. Inflation raged unabated, the mark dropping from a value of 18,000 to the dollar in January to 40 billion to the dollar by late October. France sent troops to occupy the entire Ruhr area after the Allied Reparations Commission declared Germany in arrears in the reparatory delivery of coal. Efforts at passive resistance in the Ruhr were countered by force of arms while France also supported efforts to establish separatist states in the Rhineland. In August, the cabinet of Wilhelm Cuno resigned after losing the support of the Socialist Party of Germany (SPD), and Gustav Stresemann formed the first of the

Great Coalition governments that delegated cabinet positions to representatives from the moderate right to the moderate left. Strikes broke out in the major industrial centers. In Bavaria, the Nazi party's increasing belligerence under Adolf Hitler culminated in the failed putsch of 8 and 9 November, while other right-wing forces continued to seek autonomy from the central government in Berlin. The constitutionally formed coalition governments in Thuringia and Saxony, consisting of members of the SPD and KPD, were removed from power by a decree from the central government and with the aid of national troops. A state of military emergency was imposed on the entire German nation. Worsening economic conditions were aggravated further by food scarcities and widespread hunger.

In Hamburg, the city senate, dominated by moderate SPD policies, failed to meet the needs of the city's extensive working-class population, and imposed a local state of military emergency to counter general unrest. Despite this, strikes and demonstrations remained almost daily occurrences, in part guided by a militant and growing KPD in which Ernst Thälmann was gaining a leading position. During October, plans were made for a revolutionary uprising to begin in Hamburg with a general strike, a signal to workers throughout Germany to topple the bourgeois democracy and inaugurate a workers' and peasants' regime. During the morning hours of 23 October, police precinct stations were attacked in Hamburg-Barmbeck, the police disarmed, and their weapons requisitioned by workers. Initial successes, however, could not be sustained. Over six thousand police reinforcements were dispatched with armored cars and artillery to put down the revolt. Workers cut down trees and tore up paving stones to construct defensive barricades, directed sniper fire at attacking government forces from the rooftops of tenements, and for two days prevented wholesale occupation of the city's proletarian quarters. But disunity within their leadership, inability to rally the population as a whole, and recognition of the superior equipment and numbers of the police caused the workers to break off their revolt on the evening of 24 October. The next day, they dispersed and resumed their restive existence within the gray environment of their tenement homes.

It is this army of discontent and deprivation that Niehaus's *Prole* exemplifies, a concretization of his class identity. With muted blues and grays, touched by somber reds and incisive yellows like the ashes and embers of past conflagrations, the image presents a bleak environment dominated by the spattered, shadowed façade of a high-rise tenement, its windows barred, and by smoking factory chimneys. Wearing a blue worker's blouse, the proletarian looms in the foreground. His large head is not so much situated in, as mapped onto, the two components of his world, the factory and the tenement. A gray-blue pallor tints his gaunt face, which is marked and chiseled by Niehaus's late Expressionist faceting. The wrinkles and scars of age, weather, and worry augment his expression of insurmountable sadness, concern, and despair. Entrapped in his environment, he has no means of escape; the failure of the previous year's uprising leaves imprinted only a message of hopelessness.

C. D. G. / R. H.

123 Felix Nussbaum
Park of Antiquities (Antiken-park), 1931

Oil on canvas
60 x 72 cm (23⁵/₈ x 28⁵/₁₆ in.)
Signed and dated l. r. "Felix Nussbaum 1931"; signed and inscribed verso "Felix Nussbaum 'Antikenpark'"

Provenance: Dr. Hans Cürlis, Berlin; estate of Dr. Hans Cürlis; Villa Grisebach, West Berlin.

Exhibition: Osnabrück, Kulturgeschichtliches Museum, *Felix Nussbaum*, 6 May–18 August 1990.

Felix Nussbaum's fate as a Jew in Nazi Germany and his murder at Auschwitz necessarily separates him in our perception from the other artists that practiced a modified realism in Weimar Germany, accepting neither the radical solutions of abstraction or of engaged social criticism, nor submitting to the demands for a saccharine, academic naturalism that dominated conservative traditionalist approaches. The spirit of *le Douanier* Rousseau imparts to these works "a childlike, unaffected grace of vision, for which the world transforms itself into a complex of toys and amusing innocence," as a sympathetic critic stated in *Kunst unserer Zeit* (*Art of Our Time*), the modest periodical published by the organization *Künstler-Selbsthilfe* (Artists' Self-Help) to explain contemporary art to German workers.[1] In Nussbaum's case, as in that of Käthe Loewenthal (see cat. nos. 86, 87), we tend to overlay this "amusing innocence" retrospectively with an aura of threat and terror shaped by the Holocaust.

Nussbaum began producing images of sport and gymnastics, an established genre in the art of Weimar Germany, in 1929. However, his work is without the celebration of muscular skill and coordination, of machine-like strength and precision, that characterizes the sport imagery of such artists as George Grosz, Ernesto de Fiori, or Karl Hubbuch. *Park of Antiquities* depicts a wrestling match sponsored by the German Gymnastics Society (as the banner indicates), but the intense training and accented proto-professionalism of the society are seen only in the masterful, textbook-like wrestling holds of the two protagonists. The wrestlers themselves appear more like dolls or transformations of Philipp Otto Runge's nineteenth-century portraits of children than as celebrants in the ceremony of a sport of strength, muscular control, skill, and intense competition. By virtue of their size and placement in the painting, the two wrestlers dominate the composition, but nonetheless appear strangely entrapped within the walled courtyard, its neoclassical building, and the anonymous black mass of onlookers. Muted colors add to this de-

nial of sport's excitement and excitation, and increase the strangely melancholic tone of the painting.

The conclusion reached in 1930 by the moderate critic Willi Wolfradt, one of Nussbaum's early champions, that "Nussbaum paints a nightmare consisting of sugared icing and marzipan" appears appropriate.[2] After Auschwitz, however, the sugar and marzipan have lost their sweetness, leaving for us only the bitter, acid recognition of the nightmare.

R. H.

1. ". . . eine kindlich unbefangene Grazie der Anschauung, der sich die Welt in lauter Spielzeug und drollige Unschuld verwandelt." Willy Wolfradt, "Zu den Bildern von Felix Nussbaum," *Kunst der Zeit* 1, nos. 10/11 (July–August 1930): 248.
2. "Nussbaum malt . . . ein[en] Albtraum aus Zuckerguss und Marzipan." Ibid., 249.

124 Felix Nussbaum
Train Station at Alassio (Bahnstation in Alassio), 1933

Gouache on paper
49.5 x 65.5 cm (19⁷/₁₆ x 25³/₄ in.)
Signed and dated l. r. "Felix Nussbaum 1933"
Junk/Zimmer 109

Provenance: Willy Billestraet, Brussels; Roger Katz, Brussels; Burgman Family Collection, Brussels; Tzwern-Aisinber Fine Arts, Brussels; Galerie Michael Hasenclever, Munich.

Exhibition: Osnabrück, Kulturgeschichtliches Museum, *Felix Nussbaum*, 6 May–18 August 1990.

On 8 August 1932, Felix Nussbaum received notice from the Prussian Ministry of Science, Art, and Education that he had been awarded a six-month stay at the Villa Massimo in Rome in the competition for the Academy's coveted Rome Prize.[1] Although it provided no stipend, the award brought the thirty-one-year-old master student enviable official recognition. From the sale of several drawings as covers to the liberal periodical *Der Querschnitt* (*The Cross Section*), Nussbaum was able to support himself while in Rome. The loss of some 150 paintings during a fire in his Berlin studio late in 1932 was a major setback for him, both financially and psychologically, but he continued to work assiduously, so that a six-month extension of his stay at the Villa Massimo was granted in March 1933.

"Nussbaum presented a sensible, narrow-chested appearance, shy by nature, but totally devoted to his art. He was seldom seen. [He] had no discussions [with me] concerning his work."[2] In this rather curt characterization, Nussbaum was recalled in 1978 by Arno Breker, a fellow student at the Villa Massimo in 1933 and soon to become one of Adolf Hitler's most favored sculptors. Hitler was appointed Chancellor of the German Reich on 30 January while Nussbaum was in Rome, and the impact of his repressive regime was almost immediately felt at the Prussian Academy's Roman extension. Students began spying on each other;

suspicion supplanted the previous atmosphere of cooperation and trust; Nussbaum, the only Jewish student that year, was slapped by another Rome Prize recipient, the painter Hubertus Count von Merveldt. In April, Joseph Goebbels visited Mussolini in Rome and also met with the Villa Massimo artists; a month later, Nussbaum's grant for study there was withdrawn. Leaving his work behind to be sent after him, Nussbaum departed abruptly for the Italian seaside resort town of Alassio.

In Rome, Nussbaum had depicted city streets and the nearby campagna; antiquities were absent from his images, except as ruins in several works apparently responding to the sudden collapse of his career at the Villa Massimo. In Alassio, similarly, he avoided noted landmarks as motifs, and selected, instead, fishing boats, houses with balconies, or narrow passageways, with only fragmentary views of the Mediterranean or the seashore. Perhaps for reasons of economy, he continued as he had in Rome to work primarily in gouache, not oils. His imagery is one of calm and silence. Despite the turmoil and discrimination he had experienced, when writing to the Villa Massimo's director to obtain his abandoned possessions, he reported, "My painting is coming remarkably easily to me now. I am full of good cheer!"[3]

This gouache focuses on the modest train station at Alassio and on the single set of tracks that pass before it, almost parallel to the picture plane. At the center of the image, posts and a heavy wire block access to a track crossing, but ineffectively as the black cable has been stretched and bent by those who had circumvented its obstruction. On the road to the right, a prominent sign identifies the town; a single automobile and a pedestrian pass by, while another, larger figure of a man stands to the left, on the opposite side of the crossing. Two telegraph poles, slender echoes of the squat foreground crossing markers, serve as vertical accents, framing the station with its roof tower and a limited view of the bay. An irregular rhythm of verticals thus generates a zigzag movement between foreground and middleground, and across the picture's matte surface. Nussbaum's palette is limited to warm browns, light ocher, dark green, blue, and stark white, all mixed with, or surrounded by, black. Broad, planar strokes of varied texture, juxtaposed in constructive units of contrast and complement, compose the forms. Relaxed order dominates. While symbols of modernity are included, they are submitted to the same naïve rendering as landscape, building, and figures.

As news reached him of the dismissal of Jewish academy professors in Germany and of the first concerted Nazi actions against Jews in business, and with his own departure from the Villa Massimo still fresh in his mind, Nussbaum welcomed Alassio, with its quiet beaches and fishermen, as a refuge from which to await the collapse of Hitler's government. As his parents prepared to leave Germany for sanctuary in Switzerland or Italy, Nussbaum's imagery gained a degree of tranquility rare in his

previous work. His artistic efforts at this moment presented a cerebral exile and an emotional refuge, perhaps not without resignation, with subject matter that exults in simplicity.

C. D. G. / R. H.

1. For the text of Nussbaum's notification, see Peter Junk and Wendelin Zimmer, with Manfred Mainz, *Felix Nussbaum: Leben und Werk* (Cologne: DuMont Buchverlag, and Bramsche: Rasch Verlag, 1982), 87–89.
2. "Nussbaum war eine sensible, schmalbrüstige Erscheinung von scheuer Natur, aber der Arbeit ganz ergeben. Man sah ihn selten. Eine Diskussion über seine Arbeit war nicht gegeben." Arno Breker, letter dated Düsseldorf 27 April 1978, cited ibid., 92.
3. "Das Malen geht mir leicht von der Hand. Ich bin vollen Mutes!" Felix Nussbaum, letter to Herbert Gericke dated 11 June 1933, cited ibid., 96.

125 Felix Nussbaum
Self-Portrait (Selbstbildnis), 1935

Gouache on paper
64.4 x 50.2 cm (25³/₈ x 19³/₄ in.)
Signed and dated u. c. "Felix Nussbaum 1935"

Provenance: Willy Billestraet, Brussels; Roger Katz, Brussels; Burgman Family Collection, Brussels; Tzwern-Aisinber Fine Arts, Brussels; Galerie Michael Hasenclever, Munich.

Exhibition: Osnabrück, Kulturgeschichtliches Museum, *Felix Nussbaum*, 6 May–18 August 1990 (as *Selbstbildnis mit Malertuch*).

After the months spent in Alassio and other towns of the Italian Riviera, Felix Nussbaum went to Rapallo to join his parents, who had fled Germany in 1934 and come to Italy by way of Switzerland. Homesick for Germany, feeling guilty at having left, the parents returned to Cologne early in 1935; Nussbaum went with Felka Platek, whom he would later marry, to Paris, then to the Belgian seaside resort of Ostende, where the Nussbaum family had vacationed frequently and had several acquaintances, and where they arrived on 2 February. In a remarkable interview with the Belgian art critic Emile Langui published in the Flemish newspaper of the Belgian Workers' Party, *Vooruit* (*Forward*), Nussbaum recalled, just months before the outbreak of World War II:

Afraid and aimless, I wandered along the Italian Riviera for some time, even wrote a novel there, but painted little. All my time was occupied by my constant search for rest and a new fatherland. Living nowhere, I roamed around with hastily sketched watercolors rolled up as my baggage. . . . Switzerland, France, Paris, until finally the Belgian border opened up to offer salvation. In Ostende I began to work again, drew and painted valiantly. I resist and do not grow tired. I'm all right.[1]

Living in an attic apartment, Nussbaum earned money, according to Langui, by decorating plates with pictures of elephants, giraffes, and palm trees, but remained determined to continue his art: "Between having to earn money and other daily worries and disruptions that we uprooted ones have to bear, I do not lose my will for good work."[2] Langui saw in Nussbaum's paintings a "tender sense of joy, an unartificial naïveté that does not exclude humor" and believed that the "gentle, shy figure" of the artist could be discerned in his work, a fundamentally idealistic project "in which his entire personality has been fixed."[3]

After Nussbaum's emigration to Belgium, he painted self-portraits with increasing frequency, both as records of his appearance and survival and as symbolic or metaphorical statements of the plight of the Jewish German exile and refugee. A vast emptiness surrounds Nussbaum in this self-portrait. Doubly identified by a beret to signal pride in his profession and by a prayer shawl-like drapery over one shoulder to indicate his Jewishness, he is alone. Tall green walls, rendered in fine tones applied thickly in irregular brick-like formations, cut together in a corner behind him; the dark form of a door leads nowhere, acting as a barrier more than an exit. Nussbaum's head, relegated to the lower half of the picture, is in three-quarter profile, his mouth slightly twisted as if suppressing a smile or a comment. Although his gaze is directed out of the painting, he avoids direct visual contact with the viewer; his oblique glance suggests a furtive, cautious circumspection.

There is an art [Langui wrote of Nussbaum's work] which remains unknown. It works without capital, without public, without press. It is not sold, is pushed from the streets, and lives in attics, where it shivers in the cold and hungers, hungers.

It is the art of the banished, of the countryless, of the German and Austrian refugees who earn their bread God-knows-where and God-knows-how, and who, despite their rumbling stomachs and their worn-out shoes, continue to pursue the eternal dream of beauty and truth.[4]

Nussbaum continued his pursuit in refugee camps, hidden away in attics, and in Nazi internment camps for five and a half years after Langui's interview. At the end of July 1944, on the last train to transport deportees from Belgium, he was shipped to Auschwitz. On 9 August, according to the research of Belgian authorities, Nussbaum's efforts to capture an ideal of art, which saw its own existence as a last fragile emblem of hope and humanity, were terminated in the Nazi gas chambers.

C. D. G. / R. H.

1. "Ängstlich und ziellos schweifte ich längere Zeit an der italienischen Riviera entlang, schrieb dort sogar einen Roman, malte aber wenig. Die fortwährende Suche nach Ruhe und einem neuen Vaterland nahm meine Zeit ganz in Anspruch. Nirgends wohnhaft zog ich umher mit hastig notierten Aquarellen zusammengerollt als Gepäck.... Schweiz, Frankreich, Paris ... bis sich endlich die Grenze von Belgien erlösend öffnete. In Ostende begann ich wieder zu arbeiten, zeichnete und malte fleissig. Ich wehre mich und werde nicht müde. Es geht." Felix Nussbaum, quoted in Emile Langui, "Inter-

views op mansarden: Felix Nussbaum —de zachte humor in ballingschap," Vooruit: Orgaan der belgische werkliedenpartij, 5 February 1939. German translation from an exhibition brochure, Kulturgeschichtliches Museum Osnabrück, "Dauerausstellung Felix Nussbaum" (Osnabrück: Stadt Osnabrück, n. d.), 3. We are grateful to the staff of the David and Alfred Smart Museum of Art, University of Chicago, for making a copy of this article available.
2. "Zwischen Geldverdienenmüssen und sonstigen alltäglichen Sorgen und Ruhestörungen, die wir Entwurzelten zu tragen haben, verliere ich nicht den Willen zu guter Arbeit." Nussbaum, cited in German by Langui, "Interviews op mansarden," n. p.
3. "... von einer zärtlichen Glückseligkeit durchdrungen, einer unschuldigen Grazie und einer ungekünstelten Naivität, die Humor nicht ausschliesst ... zarte, schüchterne Erscheinung ... in dem die ganze Persönlichkeit festgelegt ist." Langui, ibid., translated into German in Kulturgeschichtliches Museum Osnabrück, "Dauerausstellung Felix Nussbaum."
4. "Es besteht eine Kunst, die unbekannt bleibt. Sie arbeitet ohne Kapital, ohne Publikum, ohne Presse. Sie verkauft sich nicht, sie wird von der Strasse gestossen, und lebt in Bodenkammern, wo sie vor Kälte zittert und hungert, hungert.

"Sie ist die Kunst der Verbannten, der Heimatlosen, der deutschen und österreichischen Flüchtlinge, die Gott weiss wo und Gott weiss wie an ihr Brot kommen, und die trotz ihres knurrenden Magens und ihrer durchgelaufenen Schuhe weiter dem ewigen Traum von Schönheit und Wahrheit nachjagen." Langui, ibid., translated into German in Kulturgeschichtliches Museum Osnabrück, "Dauerausstellung Felix Nussbaum," 2.

126 Hermann Max Pechstein
Tempest (Sturmlandschaft), 1911

Oil on canvas
65.4 x 65.4 cm (25³/₄ x 25³/₄ in.)
Signed and dated l. r.
"Pechstein/1911"

Provenance: Private collection, U. S. A.

Max Pechstein was the only member of the artists' group *Brücke* with extensive academic training as a painter; he was also recipient of a coveted fellowship for study in Rome, and enjoyed contacts among artists and art markets in Paris and Berlin. Pechstein thus played a major part in enabling the Dresden Expressionists to participate in German and international efforts to establish a viable modern art movement around 1910. He was the first of the Dresden group to move to Berlin, obtained recognition for *Brücke* within the New Secession, and joined Ernst Ludwig Kirchner in founding MUIM, the Institute for Modern Instruction in Painting (Moderner Unterricht in Malerei), in 1911. Although the artists frequently worked apart, during their times together and in their communal exhibitions they shared their painting experiences, each supporting the other in exploring a common stylistic vocabulary within which individual variation was fostered.

Pechstein spent the summer of 1911 with his young bride, Lotte Kaprolat, at the Baltic fishing village of Nidden (then in East Prussia, today in Lithuania). He had first visited it in 1909 but, he later wrote, "this summer ... enchanted me from beginning to end." He recalled in his memoirs the excitement of many hours of profitable work as well as the exhilaration of experiencing nature: "[We] walked barefoot over the sand of the dunes, through the cool grass of the forests. ... From sun-up to sundown, we roamed out of doors and only returned home after dark."[1] The motif of the low, wind-battered pines in *Tempest*, which cling precariously to the sandy soil and whose branches twist dramatically up to their thick crowns of densely thatched needles, derives from these daylong excursions through the wooded East Prussian dunes. Significantly, Erich Heckel was simultaneously depicting, at Prerow on the Baltic Sea, similar seashore settings, as was Kirchner during his summer stay on the island of Fehmarn.[2]

With the pines' rust-red trunks generating a sinuous pattern throughout the composition and lending it cohesion, the image vibrates with intense color juxtapositions of red and blue, green and golden orange, interspersed with heavy applications of spiky black outlines and shadows. All sense of stasis is removed in the view over the top of a dune, through the intertwined tree trunks, out onto the blue waters of the bay, which subdivides the composition into alternating horizontal bands of light and dark. Repeatedly, color relationships, insistent outlines, and areas of blank white canvas confuse the illusion of depth and space without totally destroying it. The view onto the Baltic is one of inherent contradictions and antitheses in which the components are arranged in an additive, montage-like fashion, persistently unstable in their relationship to each other as well as to the totality of the composition.[3]

Pechstein's coloristic intensity can be found in paintings of 1911 by Heckel and Kirchner with similar motifs; in other ways, however, his work departs from theirs. During their summer stays in northern Germany, both the other artists increased the flatness of their forms, emphasizing broad planes rather than the play of discrete brushstrokes. Pechstein retains the separate strokes with their reference to the activity of creation, using Vincent van Gogh as a prototype. The *Brücke* painters had worked through Van Gogh's impact four or five years previously; Pechstein's revival of an earlier model at this time was possibly in response to the phenomenal popularity and success Van Gogh was enjoying in Germany in 1911, as several museums purchased major works by him. The flickering brushstrokes and dependence on black outline, in conjunction with the tendency towards angular form, also represent the importation of effects derived from the Expressionist woodcut into Pechstein's paintings, much as Heckel and Kirchner were doing to grant a unified appearance to their work, both paintings and prints.

Pechstein's reluctance to follow the more drastic solutions of the other

Brücke painters points to a lingering resistance to change, a demand to retain values—even controversial ones, such as those embodied in the work of Van Gogh—discovered in past art and continued in the present. Pechstein's academic past, so significant for the group's initial development, was by 1911 inserting a greater distance between his work and that of his compatriots. In 1912, when the Berlin Secession invited him to exhibit apart from *Brücke*'s communal identity, Pechstein accepted.

R. H.

1. "Dieser Sommer ... berauschte mich von Anfang bis Ende. Ich hatte viele beglückende Stunden der Arbeit, die mir einen Schauer über den Rücken herabrieseln liessen. Nach wie vor ... ging es auf blossen Füssen über den Sand der Dünen durch das kühle Gras des Waldes .... Von Sonnenaufgang bis zum Untergang weilten wir draussen und kehrten erst in der Dunkelheit zurück." Max Pechstein, *Erinnerungen*, ed. Leopold Reidemeister (Wiesbaden: Limes Verlag, 1960), 50–51.
2. See Heckel's watercolor *Path through Dunes* (*Weg durch Dünen*), Brücke Museum, West Berlin, illus. in Leopold Reidemeister, *Das Brücke-Museum* (West Berlin: Brücke Museum, 1984), 99.
3. The sensation of instability and movement, which can be viewed as analogous to that of wind blowing through the scene, surely accounts for the painting's current title, *Tempest*. There is no documentation to indicate whether Pechstein used this title, but it is unlikely. Failing other evidence, the painting should more correctly bear a simple descriptive title such as *Dune with Scrub Pines*.

127 Max Radler
Woman in a Doorway (Ausblickende), 1930

Watercolor on heavy paper
30.7 x 22.6 cm (12¹/₁₆ x 8⁷/₈ in.)
Signed and dated l. r. "Max Radler. 1930"; inscribed and dated r. "Meiner Schwester/ Margarete/zum 17. Geburtstag/ 29. 5. 1930" (To my sister Margarete on her 17th birthday 5/29/1930)

Provenance: Margarete Radler, Munich; Galerie Michael Hasenclever, Munich.

Max Radler's picture, presented to his sister on her seventeenth birthday, is representative of the Munich school of *Neue Sachlichkeit*. The work displays none of the timely verist brutality so common in the Berlin, Dresden, or Karlsruhe schools. Instead, aspiring towards a universal statement, the image is generalized, the mood contemplative, reflecting the influence of Georg Schrimpf in its calm atmosphere and heavy, statuesque figure. The simple composition consists of a female figure seen from the back, gazing onto a landscape of gently rolling hills. At the center of the image, an expanse of blank tan-toned paper represents a small body of water. The young woman's features remain hidden from view as she looks out over the lake; the three-quarter rear profile Radler has provided is bereft of detail, and the woman's bare feet and generic clothing further minimize personal and cultural specificity. The elementary forms and the broad volumes of the body lend the work visual and emotional steadiness.

Although the pensive woman remains anonymous, her spatial proximity to the viewer and her relation to nature are central to the work's meaning. Withholding particulars of who, what, and where, Radler invites the viewer to partake in the contemplation of nature along with the figure seen from behind, much in the manner of Caspar David Friedrich's paintings a century previously. In the typical scheme of Romantic works by Friedrich and Moritz von Schwind, a tradition very much recalled in compositions by Schrimpf as well, a figure indoors is seen from the back, gazing through an open window. The juxtaposition of interior and exterior suggests the dichotomy between domesticity and nature, closed spaces and open ones, confinement and unbridled freedom. The open window in Romanticism became a metaphor for spiritual longing that simultaneously presented and prevented a journey to the unknown realms of nature.[1]

The allusion to meditation and longing is appropriate to the transitional state of a birthday, and particularly the seventeenth, a pivotal but elusive moment in the transformation from youth to maturity. In her classical contrapposto pose, the young woman leans against the wall, which becomes a mechanism of solidity, safety, and restraint. Although she does not look through a window, she is still sheltered by an interior space. Before her is a railing, and below, near the water, a stairway is visible. Radler has thus metaphorically presented his sister on the threshold of adulthood, which she thoughtfully considers. Yet, with her left arm held behind her back, she still leans against the symbolically protective wall of her childhood. Radler indicates the trepidation and uncertainty that confronts her in the transition, and treats it as a universal rite of passage.

C. D. G.

1. See Lorenz Eitner, "The Open Window and the Storm-Tossed Boat: An Essay in the Iconography of Romanticism," *Art Bulletin* 37 (December 1955): 281–290.

128 Max Radler
Urban Scene with Train (Stadt-landschaft mit Eisenbahn),
c. 1930

Oil on canvas
55.2 x 80.2 cm (21³/₄ x 31⁹/₁₆ in.)
Signed l. r. "Max Radler"

Provenance: Estate of the artist; Galerie Michael Hasenclever, Munich.

Around 1930, Max Radler completed several industrial landscapes which testify to his continued interest in the urban environment and the milieu of the worker, the major motif of his work other than that of the female figure. *Urban Scene with Train* consists of only a minimum of greenery, while the concrete of the roadway and overpass pro-

vides the pervasive, dominant texture of the image. Radler has used the basic construction of a landscape, which relies on a broad field of vision and a clearly delineated skyline or horizon. He has, however, transposed the formula often reserved for nature to the industrial world.

Radler's image is nearly unpopulated, so that the mechanical means of production and especially their context become the primary focus. The triangular concrete slab that connects the hill and the train track occupies the center of the canvas. Carrying freight instead of passengers, the locomotive looms over the upper left half of the canvas, while the factory governs the right. The bottom third of the painting is consumed by the road, presumably built recently to access the industrial areas on the city's outskirts. A single figure appears, awaiting a streetcar and dwarfed by the tall signpost. The painting documents industrialization and, more importantly, an awareness of it that was common among *Neue Sachlichkeit* artists. Other painters, including Franz Radziwill, Erich Borchert, and Gustav Wunderwald, were intent on rendering this aspect of modernity. *Urban Scene with Train*, like certain works by these artists, is unsettling in its spirit of depersonalization. The essential absence of humanity is made even more palpable by the lone figure who stands near the road. Existence appears largely mechanized as the human is made insignificantly small and the train, road, and bridge become dominant.

Radler's statement about industry is deliberately ambiguous, with distinctly positive and negative qualities. The structure of industry, depicted in the precise language of *Neue Sachlichkeit*, becomes infused and synonymous with energy and efficiency. Yet simultaneously, the environment appears dehumanized and artificial. Thus the notion of an "urban landscape," in light of the German landscape tradition in which nature became a receptacle and paradigm of spiritual expression, is ironically transferred to the mechanized world bereft of spirit, a constructed world of containing measure rather than the infinity of divine creation.

C. D. G.

129 Max Radler
Woman at Her Toilet (Mädchen bei der Toilette), 1931

Pencil on paper
48.1 x 22.5 cm (18⁷/₈ x 9¹³/₁₆ in.)
Signed and dated l. r. "M. Radler 1931"

Provenance: Galerie Michael Hasenclever, Munich.

Around 1928, Max Radler became increasingly interested in the cause of labor and produced images of workers and proletarian demonstrations. While *Woman at Her Toilet* does not present an overt political message, it is replete with the artist's sympathies towards the working-class woman depicted, the modesty of her demands, and the purity of her rudimentary surroundings. Seated on a wooden chair, her feet

soaking in a tin washtub, she is central and dominant in the composition. Avoiding anatomical particulars, Radler renders her figure in broad, volumetric masses, with subtle gradations of light and dark eliciting a sense of roundness more geometric than fleshy.

While the simple activity of the young woman is the focus of Radler's image, the interior provides a crucial context, a complex construction of rectangular spatial articulations, the edges of which are hard and bare. Vertical elements, evenly dispersed throughout, lend the drawing visual stability; the edge of the cabinet door, the vertical edge of the window, the chair's legs and back frame, the stove pipe, and the corner where the walls meet are axes which unify and anchor the image. Radler achieved balance by counteracting straight edges with curved ones and complementing and opposing visual elements to create a continuity of actions and reactions. For example, the open cabinet door to the left discloses a black void, but is offset by the window above, opened in the opposite direction to reveal a great expanse of space and light.

By means of these careful balances, Radler establishes a classical order, immobility, and stillness. It is thus easy to overlook the humble conditions that distinguish the image as a subtle statement about class. The room lacks any adornment. The cabinet seems bare and the basin is basic and functional; even the chair, not soft and upholstered, is of the simplest wood construction. The slippers to the right indicate that this is the woman's home, with the stove heater in the background and a clothesline strung above it, an article of clothing hung out to dry. The nook suggests an attic room, cheaper, that is, than one on a lower level.

Radler has revived a traditional formula, the toilet of Venus, in a modern idiom, and used a working-class type in his reinterpretation. This is no conventional commentary on feminine vanity: everything about the drawing projects a spartan existence. The woman's slightly bent posture and soaking feet suggest a respite after a hard day's work. Frugality is implied in the conspicuous absence of material possessions. And the freshly washed item hanging behind the woman indicates an honest virtue that derives from dignity and self-respect, which transcend social class. The modesty of this woman's life is further reflected in Radler's own style, which relies on solid, basic volumes rather than technical flourish. Spare and unspectacular like its subject, understated in its politics, the drawing represents a remarkably rigorous agreement of form and content.

C. D. G.

130 Hans Rilke
Mother and Son (Mutter und Sohn), 1924

Watercolor, pen and ink, pencil on paper
46.5 x 30.5 cm (18¹/₄ x 12 in.)
Signed and dated u. r. "Hans Rilke 1924"

Provenance: Dr. Wietz, Düsseldorf; Joern Wietz, Düsseldorf; Galerie Wolfgang Ketterer, Munich.

Associated with the Düsseldorf gallery of Mother Ey during the 1920s, as well as with the artists' organization *Das Junge Rheinland (The Young Rhineland)*, Hans Rilke shared that group's fascination with amateur painting and naïve art. Contacts with the retired industrial manager Adalbert Trillhaase, who began drawing and painting at the urging of the artist Otto Pankok, particularly fostered this interest. After Trillhaase's work was included in the 1922 *Das Junge Rheinland* exhibition, the Sunday painter's stylistic vocabulary began to be emulated by Otto Dix, Rilke, and Gert Wollheim, in part as a means of effecting a shift from Expressionist- and Futurist-inspired imagery to a more object-oriented one.[1]

Apparently presented to Rilke's dentist in exchange for treatment,[2] the portrait of a mother and son is based on a pre–World War I photograph, judging from the pose of the two figures and their clothing. The sharply delineated heads, partially distorted in their proportions, are made to appear as if they had been inaccurately cut from an existing image and pasted into the new composition, where their scale does not coincide with that of the bodies. Adding to this montage effect are the irregularly cut edges of the cheap drawing paper; the entire drawing is made to emulate an old photograph, colored and crudely cut from its album. Large eyes, simply rendered noses and lips, itemized indication of hair, and flattening of body forms, moreover, are common features in work by amateur painters or teenaged children.

Rilke thus applies a variety of strategies in *Mother and Son* to generate an impression of an aging photograph with a rubbed and flaking surface which has been transformed, colored, and cut out by a child or artistically unschooled individual. The charm and innocence traditionally attributed to these now become associated with Rilke's refined emulation of naïveté. In an overlay of connotations, while admiration of untutored artists' works is clearly present, an attitude of irony and amusement likewise is injected in the degree of sophisticated technique and understanding required to render this neo-naïve effect. Remnants of a Dada desire to confuse apparent meaning and expression remain in this effort skillfully to betray appearance, confounding the image's reading and reception.   R. H.

1. For discussion of this aspect of Dix's work, see cat. no. 28, *Sunday Outing.*
2. Information conveyed by Joern Wietz to Marvin Fishman.

131 Marcel Ronay
Sailor and Girl (Matrose und Mädchen), 1929

Oil on panel
54.1 x 42.8 cm (21¹/₄ x 16¹³/₁₆ in.)
Monogrammed and dated l. l. "M. Ron/29/[?]"

Provenance: John Denham Gallery, London; Galerie Michael Hasenclever, Munich.

Born in Hungary of Jewish parents and trained in Vienna, Marcel Ronay was one of many Central and Eastern European artists who participated in Germany's artistic life during the first three decades of this century. But unlike Vassily Kandinsky or Lázló Moholy-Nagy, for example, Ronay did not introduce innovations on which German artists would build. Instead, like Hugo Scheiber (see cat. no. 136), he presented a vocabulary already tried and explored, flavored with his personal idiom but also relatively divorced from the concern with content that marks the work of his German contemporaries. The result accentuates style rather than meaning, and anecdote rather than significant narrative.

The motif of sailor and prostitute in the entertainment district of a seaport forms part of the stock repertoire of German artists, from Otto Dix's recollections of sailors on leave in Belgium during World War I to Erich Wegner's fonder visualizations of shore leave encounters (see cat. nos. 177, 179), akin perhaps to Hans Albers's numerous films set on Hamburg's waterfront, the *Waterkant*. Indeed, the sailor in bars, cafés, and brothels, or in a street with a prostitute linked in his arm, became an international artistic icon during the 1920s, appearing in works by artists as diverse as Belgium's Frans Masereel (see cat. no. 95) and the American Stuart Davis. Ronay thus partakes of a recognizably marketable image, and applies to it an idiosyncratically personal and belated variation on Synthetic Cubism to achieve in 1929 a tone of fashionable modernity.

With the brothel *Zum Seemann* (*At the Sign of the Sailor*) ostentatiously exhibiting a trademark red lantern in its doorway, and a dock crane and warehouses in the background, Ronay's sailor and his companion have just entered into their encounter. She grabs his arm and he turns in response towards her, lips pushing forward, as if in anticipation of meeting hers, offered in close proximity. The scene may, however, not be what it at first glance seems to be. Ronay, in land-locked Austria, certainly had no regular contact with harbors and sailors, so it is likely that the scene is an imaginatively constructed one, or represents a brief visit to a North German seaport. The sailor, moreover, with his repeated flaunting on clothing and in tatoos of an anchor motif that emulates the stylized letter "M" in Ronay's monogram, is less a seaman than someone dressed to play the role.

The prostitute likewise bears none of the hallmarks of sexual display found in other representations of practitioners of her trade, and, instead, is dressed demurely as she awkwardly ensnares her prospective customer beneath the prototypical street lantern. With its faceting recalling the sets of Expressionist films such as *The Cabinet of Dr. Caligari*, its strong spotlight effects, its trite setting, and its role-playing actors, Ronay's painting appears as a willed fiction, a theater production on a fashionable Viennese stage, the latest melo-

drama recounting the fall of a young woman from virtuous respectability to the infamy of prostitution, a *Dirnentragödie* in which she of course retains the purity of heart that is her fundamental character trait.   R. H.

---

152 Christian Schad
Narcissus (Narziss), 1927

Pencil, pen and ink, watercolor and tusche with splatter technique on paper
18.3 x 12.9 cm ($7^3/_{16}$ x $5^1/_{16}$ in.)
Signed and dated l. l.
"Schad/27"

Provenance: Estate of the artist, Stuttgart; Kunstkabinett G. A. Richter, Rottach-Egern; Villa Grisebach, West Berlin.

Exhibitions: West Berlin, Staatliche Kunsthalle, *Christian Schad*, 1980; New York, Solomon R. Guggenheim Museum, *German Realist Drawings of the 1920's*, 15 May–6 July 1986 (traveled to Cambridge, Mass., Busch-Reisinger Museum, Harvard University, 26 July–28 September 1986; Graphische Sammlung, Staatsgalerie Stuttgart, 25 October–28 December 1986), cat. no. 91.

Celebrated for his pristine, coldly detailed portrait paintings, Christian Schad devoted his drawings to scenes from café life, homosexuals' clubs, and sexual narratives. For the exquisite recording of minutiae that characterizes his paintings, he substituted in drawing a linear style that concentrated on nuanced movements of continuous outlines, attenuated and constantly on the verge of breaking. Splattered ink provides shading and creates a dialectic of depth and flatness against which the outlined, reserved figures become ironically volumetric.

Narcissus is one of several drawings intended as illustrations for short stories by Walter Serner, with whom Schad had collaborated on issues of the Zurich Dada journal *Sirius* in 1916. Here, Schad's typically attenuated figures are rendered with watercolor and ink washes, while preciously applied touches of color lend accent to the narrative. In a snow-covered park with weather-worn, leafless trees, a well-dressed young woman stops suddenly in horror and stares at the exposed genitalia—strategically hidden from the viewer by her outstretched arm—of an exhibitionist. With pants lowered to his knees and coat thrown wide open, he stands with his back arched to reveal himself to her, an unavoidable barrier in her path. Schad further accentuates the object of the woman's horrified gaze by dangling a bright red scarf —whether hers or his is unclear—from the man's groin to his knees. The red coloration is picked up at intervals throughout the watercolor—at the base of the background bushes, on the woman's cheeks, and on the man's nipples. The center of his sexual arousal thus echoes throughout the image, like the woman's gasp, a visual analogue to her soundless response also present in her embarrassed blush.

The man's face and identity are cut by the picture edge, but nonetheless are sufficiently seen to reveal a smile of pleasure and amusement. The woman expresses her response with arms spread in surprise, her mouth open, and her cheeks flushed pink. If exhibitionists can clearly be threatening to women at least psychologically, in Schad's scene such connotations are absent and, instead, comical bemusement marks his rendering of the occurrence. With reference to the Greek mythological youth whose major enjoyment was his own reflection in a pool, Narcissus here is a well-to-do young man—witness his fur coat—whose pleasure is in self-display to the astonished gaze of a demure, unsuspecting *Hausfrau*. As Narcissus ultimately collapsed and died in his inability to embrace the watery object of his desire, so here the exhibitionist may well be in the process of losing his tumescence without the benefit of an embrace, with only the "reflection" of the woman's shocked response before him, having arrived at the climax of his effect. Schad's comedy is heavy-handed and insensitive, while certainly implicitly gynephobic. The humor intended in the drawing, however, is unmistakable.   S. L. D.

---

153 Josef Scharl
Portrait of a Worker (Arbeiterbildnis), 1925

Oil on canvas
105 x 78.6 cm ($41^3/_8$ x $30^7/_8$ in.)
Signed and dated l. l.
"Jos. Scharl/1925"

Provenance: Galerie Lempertz, Cologne; Barry Friedman Ltd., New York.

Exhibition: Cologne, Galerie Lempertz, *Die Kunst der verschollenen Generation*, 1980.

Seated informally in an old wooden armchair, Josef Scharl's monumental worker fills almost the entire canvas. Hands folded between spread legs, his powerful, frontal figure projects a sense of dignity and innate worth. The collarless blouse, jacket, and heavy pants function as a uniform of his profession. Scharl's characteristic painting technique involves a heavy surface, rhythmically swirled into regular peaks and valleys of pigment that sculpt the worker's face and hands into a rough, wrinkled skin that seems marked by years of experience and hard labor.

The placement and pose of the figure, the artificial, tilted space with its exaggerated perspective, as well as the thick, agitated paint surface, all testify to the significance of Vincent van Gogh for Scharl. *Portrait of a Worker* is much like a pendant to *La Berceuse* (1888), a male proletarian parallel to the female peasant archetype Van Gogh painted in Arles rocking the cradle of the world. The dark, glowing palette, however, seems more akin to Van Gogh's earlier portraits of Dutch peasants at Nuenen, whose brownish colors recall the very earth in which the farmers and miners labor. In both Van Gogh's and Scharl's

works, concern is with the individual, his spiritual nobility and fate; there is a Romantic sensibility to suffering and a Romantic faith in divinely determined human worth, applied to the struggles of the working class. Seen as a representative less of his class, however, than of existential endurance, the image of Scharl's worker emerges much as Scharl himself did in Albert Einstein's eulogy to him in 1955:

Everything about Scharl was true, genuine, and unspoiled. He had gazed into the tragedy and abyss of human existence and had a deeper capacity for suffering than most men, but he could not be permanently depressed by anything. His radiant sense of humor and the strong interest he took in his fellow men always triumphed over discouragement and paralyzing resignation. Though fate had not dealt kindly with him, he remained so rich in inner strength that he could always give encouragement and support to weaker natures.[1]

      B. T. Y

1. Albert Einstein, "Josef Scharl," *Print* 9, no. 4 (March–April 1955): 20.

---

154 Josef Scharl
Battered Prostitute (Misshandelte Dirne), 1931

Oil on canvas
87.4 x 56.3 cm ($34^7/_{16}$ x $22^3/_{16}$ in.)
Signed and dated l. l.
"Jos. Scharl/1931"

Provenance: Prof. Dr. Aloys Greither, Munich; Prof. Dr. Helma Greither, Munich.

With its straightforward documentary manner, full frontality, and intense lighting, Josef Scharl's *Battered Prostitute* recalls a police photograph, an image used as evidence. Against a dark background, we see the three-quarter figure of a woman, her hands behind her back, naked except for earrings, necklace, and a yellow garment draped over her arms and shoulders, in effect accentuating rather than covering her nakedness. Her head and body are shaved, her face is barren of expression. Gaps appear among her teeth, and her bruised body, especially her neck, testifies to beatings and attempts at strangulation. The source of her mistreatment is not clear in the midst of her unabashed display; but the title of the painting, announcing her profession, leads us to suspect the potential perpetrators of this violence against her: a sadistic customer, her pimp, or the police.

In the late 1920s, prostitution was a volatile issue. The "Bremen Morality Scandal" erupted from the 1926 publication of the story of a young woman in Bremen, *Killed by Life*.[1] The book described how any young woman even suspected by the police to be a prostitute could, by means of surveillance and compulsory hospital treatment, be made into a social pariah, and thereby into a prostitute.[2] By 1927, police brutality had become a strong political issue among feminists opposing state regulation of prostitutes. Nineteen thirty-one, the year Scharl painted *Battered Prostitute*, saw demonstrations by women demanding the right to abortion and birth control; it was also the year of Berlin's great exhibition *Frauen in Not (Women in Need)*, devoted to the plight of women in contemporary German society. Although Scharl's image was not in that exhibition, it is an example of aesthetic social consciousness that comments on women "killed by life," on women in need.

Women were also victims in 1931 of roving bands of SA men who, when not assaulting Communist or Socialist party members or Jews, frequently sought out lower-class prostitutes, shaved their heads, and marched them through the streets with placards around their necks declaring their "crimes"—especially sexual contact with Jews. It is this abuse of the prostitute and what she symbolized that Scharl's image implies. Where Expressionist poets and painters had heralded the prostitute as a symbol of liberation from Wilhelmine society, many of the socially engaged artists of the 1920s and 1930s saw prostitution as an effect of capitalist economic conditions.

The extreme aestheticization, the deliberate "art" of *Battered Prostitute*, contrasts dramatically—even melodramatically—to the harshness of the subject matter of the naked woman, battered and exposed. Compositionally, the image is firmly anchored, simple, and iconically monumental. With its unctuous surface of thickly applied pigment, aesthetic interplay of color and forms, and striking contrast of light and dark, it offers itself as an object of delectation. Blues and pinks, greens, yellows, and black—the colors of bruises and flesh—melt into one another with a subtle delicacy which counteracts the linear forcefulness of the figure's silhouette against the background.

Conceptually, beauty and ugliness constitute the painting, to serve montage-like as disjointed, jarring modifiers of one another. With the injection of paint's visual sensuality, Scharl displaces and subverts the apparent neutrality of the documentary photograph that serves as antecedent and model for the image. If Fascism involved not only the aestheticization of politics, but also the aestheticization of violence and terror, then Scharl's painting is a horrifying premonition in the factuality of its witness.   B. T. Y.

1. M. I. Breme, ed., *Vom Leben getötet* (Freiburg: Herder Verlag, 1926).
2. Elisabeth Meyer-Renschhausen, "The Bremen Morality Scandal," in *When Biology Became Destiny: Women in Weimar and Nazi Germany*, ed. Renate Bridenthal, Atina Grossmann, and Marion Kaplan (New York: Monthly Review Press, 1984), 90.

135   Josef Scharl
Soup Eater (Suppenesser), 1932

Oil on canvas
115 x 92.5 cm (45⁷/₈ x 36¹/₄ in.)
Signed and dated l. l.
"Jos. Scharl/1932"

Provenance: Private collection, Germany; private collection, New York.

Exhibition: Nuremberg, *Nürnberger Kunstausstellung*, 1932.

Beggars have long been a persistent motif in European painting, their depiction emphasizing either picturesque poverty or impoverished misery. During the nineteenth century, this dual approach continued, although realist artists tended to accent deprivation and social isolation. During the years of Weimar Germany, beggars again became a staple concern of artists, notably in the immediate postwar era as revolution, repression, and economic disruption resulted in a significant increase in beggars' visibility in German cities. The crippled war veteran sitting on the bare sidewalk, selling matches or simply slumped against a wall, his hand held out in a desperate effort to gain compassion from indifferent bourgeois passersby, was thus represented in numerous variations by Otto Dix, George Grosz (see cat. nos. 32 and 53 respectively), and other artists of the political left. After the return of economic prosperity in 1925, this theme declined as a focus of artistic attention, as beggars presumably also became rarer sights in German cities. With the onset of depression in 1929, however, as unemployment in Germany reached a higher rate than in any other industrial country, beggars once more gained the attention of artists and writers, achieving something of an apotheosis in G. W. Pabst's filming of *The Threepenny Opera* by Bertolt Brecht and Kurt Weill in 1931.

Beggars, workers, and the unemployed figure in the imagery of Josef Scharl as well. In his dramatic *Soup Eater*, Scharl depicts a gaunt and disheveled man, wearing a rumpled dark suit and loose tie, seated awkwardly on a doorstep. His gnarled hands and haggard face are highlighted as focal points of the scene. Hunched protectively over a small bowl of soup, the apparent reward for pleas at a kitchen door, he eagerly ladles the liquid into his mouth, opened wide in avid anticipation, while the concavity of his hollowed eye sockets and cheeks echoes that of the soup bowl. Anxiously feeding himself, the soup eater moves with an urgency that suggests an animal-like instinct, totally subordinating his personality to this one absolute action. Soup eating has become his identity.

Scharl employs exaggerated gesture to signal the beggar's manic state, starvation warded off briefly by the charity of unseen benefactors with this humble meal. The suit and tie speak of a more respectable past and identify the beggar as one of the victims of economic disaster, deprived of job and livelihood, expelled from the material comforts of the class of employees. The heavy, built up, tracked surface of the painting, its insistently dark bituminous physical presence, extends the sense of dirt and

soiled existence and provides a constructed analogy to the existential distress of the starving beggar. Scharl's image is contemporaneous with John Heartfield's poster *Capitalism Robs Them of Their Last Piece of Bread (Das letzte Stück Brot raubt ihnen der Kapitalismus)*, produced for the German presidential elections of March 1932, which depicts a starving child clinging desperately to a slice of bread. Painted the year Adolf Hitler received 11.3 million votes, *Soup Eater* confirms the intensity of the hunger issue as a forceful political concern at the time.   B. T. Y.

136   Hugo Scheiber
Anxiety (Self-Portrait) (Angst [Selbstporträt]), c. 1920–22

Oil on cardboard mounted on board
48 x 48 cm (18⁷/₈ x 18⁷/₈ in.), sight
Signed l. r. "Scheiber"

Provenance: Estate of the artist; Christie's, New York, sale of 19 May 1981, no. 283 (as *Angst*).

Born and trained in Hungary, Hugo Scheiber was a figure in Budapest's bohemian artistic circles much like John Hoexter in Berlin. After the revolutionary soviet republic collapsed in 1919, Scheiber left Hungary for Vienna and there had his first successful exhibition—of Futurist-Expressionist street and café scenes and portrait heads—at the gallery of Max Hevesi. Scheiber would spend most of the following decade in Germany, among a large group of Hungarian émigré artists associated with Herwarth Walden, his gallery and periodical, *Der Sturm*. Walden began in 1920 to champion Hungarian Constructivist artists associated with the periodical *MA*, especially László Péri and László Moholy-Nagy, but did not become significantly interested in Scheiber until three years later. When a Hungarian translation of Walden's manifesto-like book *Einblick in Kunst: Expressionismus, Kubismus, Futurismus (Insight into Art: Expressionism, Cubism, Futurism)*, first published in 1917, was being prepared, Walden augmented the original illustrations with works by Scheiber and Béla Kádár.[1]

Scheiber was then featured in an exhibition at Walden's Berlin gallery in January 1924, and again the next month, in conjunction with Moholy-Nagy and a collection of Peruvian tapestries. Constructivist art gained Walden's vocal support from 1920 to 1923, supplanting the Expressionism he had advocated earlier. Shortly after the exhibition of predominantly Constructivist Soviet Russian art at the Galerie van Diemen in Berlin, Walden's exhibition policy began to demonstrate a greater inclusiveness and a renewed endorsement of expressive figuration in painting. He displayed Scheiber's self-portraits and café scenes, created during the artist's years in Vienna from 1920 through 1922, next to Moholy-Nagy's Constructivist paintings and photographs, interspersed with tapestries by

Peruvian Indians, and granted all three equal status.

In his *Anxiety (Self-Portrait)*, Scheiber breaks with the Futurist-inspired works he had produced in Hungary during the late teens, and reintroduces a more directly referential portrait likeness, only slightly stylized. Expressiveness is achieved largely through the indication of an extreme psychological state: his mouth is depicted wide open in a scream, or perhaps a yawn. The Viennese Expressionist painters Richard Gerstl, Egon Schiele, and Max Oppenheimer had portrayed themselves with similar physiognomic emphasis and exaggeration, in emulation of the series of sixty-nine idiosyncratic self-portrait "character heads" by the eighteenth-century Viennese sculptor Franz Xaver Messerschmidt.[2] In each of the portrait busts, Messerschmidt represented himself with features frozen in exaggerated grins, frowns, yawns, and other expressions. Scheiber's *Anxiety (Self-Portrait)* indeed approximates Messerschmidt's *The Yawner*, of which a cast was displayed at the Zichy Museum in Budapest,[3] and should be recognized as a conscious homage. Where Messerschmidt presses his eyes tightly closed, however, Scheiber's eyelids are shown half-lowered, as if he were gazing at himself while fighting to ward off sleep, possibly the result of overindulgence in drink, as the red nose and cheeks suggest. The anxiety reference of the title, apparently supplied by Scheiber's estate to correspond to the art market's demand for angst in Central European art, misrepresents the content of the image.[4]

Scheiber's self-portrait, with its muted and limited color range, marked contrasts of light and shade, and pronounced linear patterning, represents a transition from his works of the teens to the numerous Art Deco-related self-portraits he painted later in the 1920s. The humor and self-irony present in them are less evident in *Anxiety (Self-Portrait)*, but the eccentric yawning motif, distorted proportions of the head, and clown-like red nose introduce an unmistakable sense of the comic here as well. Eberhard Roters's characterization applies most aptly: he discovers in Scheiber's style "a uniquely unproblematic synthesis of Expressionist and Cubist formal elements that unites effortlessly with constructive, decorative, fashionably chic, comical, and travestying qualities."[5] The dark, muddy color and the Messerschmidt allusion, however, also add a somber note to the work. In the aftermath of war, in the midst of deprivation and defeat, after revolution and the violent imposition of a Fascist dictatorship in Budapest, the painting's humor functions like a mask, adopted from Messerschmidt, to hide and deny a mundane, overpowering misery and despair. "I had only my strong constitution to thank for my survival," Scheiber wrote in 1923, "because last year I often had nothing to eat."[6]   R. H.

1. Julia Szabó, "Der Expressionismus und die ungarische Kunst von 1915–1927: Anfänge des Expressionismus in Ungarn," in Neue Galerie und Museum Bochum, *Wechselwirkungen: Ungarische Avantgarde in der Weimarer Republik* (Marburg: Jonas

Verlag für Kunst und Literatur, 1986), 94.

2. Maria Pötzl-Malikovna, *Franz Xaver Messerschmidt* (Vienna and Munich: Jugend und Volk, 1982), 243–266, nos. 67–123.

3. Ibid., *Der Gähner*, 245, no. 71.

4. The title *Angst* was associated with the painting at the time of its auction at the sale *German Expressionist Paintings, Drawings and Sculpture*, Christie's, New York, 19 May 1981 (lot 283). There is no other documentation for the title, nor any exhibition history of the painting to indicate what title, if any, Scheiber applied to the work. It should be noted that the common representation of anxiety or fear includes staring, wide-open eyes in conjunction with a gaping mouth, not the half-closed eyes of this depiction.

5. "...eine eigenartig unbekümmerte Synthese aus expressionistischen und kubistischen Formelementen, die konstruktive, dekorative, modisch-mondäne, komische und travestierende Züge mühelos in sich vereint." E[berhard] R[oters], "Hugo Scheiber: *Mädchen*," in Roters and Bernhard Schulz, eds., *Ich und die Stadt: Mensch und Grossstadt in der deutschen Kunst des 20. Jahrhunderts* (West Berlin: Nicolaische Verlagsbuchhandlung Beuermann, 1987), 218.

6. "Nur einer glücklichen Konstruktion hatte ich es zu verdanken, dass ich noch aushielt, denn voriges Jahr hatte ich oft nichts zu essen." Hugo Scheiber, "Autobiographische Notizen (1923)," in *Wechselwirkungen*, 127.

157 Rudolf Schlichter

Circus Children (Zirkuskinder), c. 1924–25?

Pencil on paper
49.8 x 41.6 cm (19⁹/₁₆ x 16³/₈ in.)
Signed l. l. "Rudolf Schlichter";
inscribed l. r. "Zirkuskinder"

Provenance: Hauswedell and Nolte, Hamburg.

In 1919, Rudolf Schlichter moved from the south of Germany to Berlin. Joining the Communist Party, he also participated in the *International Dada Fair* and, in effect, renounced his prior academic training in Stuttgart and Karlsruhe. Following the example of George Grosz, he adapted the hard-edged, quasi-mechanical figure style and spatial paradoxes of the Italian *Scuola metafisica* in socially critical but often hermeneutically ambiguous images. By 1923, his style had shifted towards a delicate naturalism characterized by sensitively drawn contours and finely modeled surfaces, with manipulated spatial relationships still testifying to his earlier Dada convictions. Stylistically consistent thereafter, Schlichter's work is difficult to date precisely; he often practiced different modes of drawing simultaneously, letting either subject matter or function determine his formal vocabulary.

Circus Children has previously been dated to 1919 and considered to display Dada influence, apparently because of the caricature-like rendering of the horse and rider in the left background. What seems Dadaesque initially, however, can be identified in this circus setting as a clown wearing a large mask and "riding" a cloth-and-wood horse that fits around his waist. Rather than a comic distortion, the clown is a veristic if schematic figure, consistent with Schlichter's style of the mid-twenties. A common feature of his compositions at this time is the concentration, usually towards the center, on an area of highly detailed, carefully modeled figures or figure fragments; emanating from this area, the drawing becomes increasingly less detailed, more schematic and tending towards outline. In *Circus Children*, a triangular grouping of a clown and two girls occupies the center, one girl seated while the other walks past. An erotic tension links the three, focused in the dark-haired girl with large eyes and accented lips such as Schlichter favored in his female models. She sits in an open, relaxed pose and wears a form-fitting tricot, short bloomers, and laced boots; the clown stares down at her and she in turn gazes towards the passing blond girl. To this scene of implied sexual potential, the background clown and two circus workers serve as contextualizing attributes.

Although Schlichter included all the components of a circus environment, the joyful ambience typically associated with the circus is replaced by a sinister and haunting quality. A popular motif in German art of the 1920s, the circus or sideshow frequently functioned as an extended metaphor for contemporary life and politics. Here, however, Schlichter seems interested in the circus more as a world outside conventional social and moral prescriptions. Circus performers, generally separate from mainstream society because of their nomadic life, were considered exempt from the strictures by which others were bound. The sense of abandon, absence of bourgeois morality, and touch of perversity appealed as well on a personal level to Schlichter, who was repeatedly depicted by fellow artists as an obsessive boot fetishist and masochist.

In his preferred motifs during the 1920s of violent Wild West scenes and sadistic and voyeuristic sexuality, Schlichter manifests interests shared by virtually all the male artists of the Berlin Dada group, who saw themselves participating in the class struggle on the side of the proletariat. The relationship between the German Communist Party's view of women workers as equal to men and these artists' gynephobic sexual fantasies is problematic. Because they desired an activist art, they may have intended their sexually exploitive scenes as a means of consciousness-raising for an otherwise insensitive audience, but such work also fed the search for vicarious sensationalism among that same audience and contributed to the very attitudes the artists sought to resist. Similarly, sexually aberrant practices could be attributed to the decadent bourgeois or to social outsiders like circus performers and bohemians, while the sexual life of the productive worker is either not depicted—other than in the children that are its product—or is deemed more wholesome and natural. Sexual exploitation, including child abuse and sadism, then characterizes the capitalist society that the artists, in league with workers, are combatting.

But such pictorial indictments by means of graphic depiction necessarily participate in the mores they condemn, and the border between condemnation and celebration is a fluid one, difficult to identify. The appeal of these images to artists sensitive to human dignity and to their audiences is an historically determined problem whose configuration continues to be elusive. Schlichter's ambiguously defined *Circus Children* is but one component of the larger dilemma, its significatory possibilites and intentions as conflicting as those of the more explicit scenes Schlichter produced.

C. D. G.

158 Georg Scholz

Nightly Noise (Nächtlicher Lärm), 1919

Oil on canvas
56.8 x 50.9 cm (22³/₈ x 20 in.)
Signed and dated l. r. "Scholz 1919"; inscribed, signed, and dated on stretcher "Nächtlicher Lärm Georg Scholz 1919"

Provenance: Private collection, Germany; Galerie Michael Hasenclever, Munich.

Exhibition: Berlin, November Group, *Grosse Berliner Kunstausstellung*, 1919.

Wounded in service during the final months of World War I, Georg Scholz was hospitalized and then joined his family in the small town of Grötzingen, near Karlsruhe, to continue his recuperation. With a wife and child to support, he eked out an existence by means of commercial design and book illustration, but Scholz was also active in the volatile political and artistic life of revolutionary Germany. He joined the Communist Party in 1919, and was one of the seven founding members of Group Rih, Karlsruhe's short-lived, eclectically anti-academic branch of the November Group. Named for the Arabian stallion in a novel by Karl May, Group Rih in 1919 published a list of guiding principles for a proposed art periodical:

> Freedom of subject as corrective against a society art pushing its wares with the permissive ethics of commercial interests. Freedom and independence for the individual. Rejection of those forms of fantasy that permit a continuation of philistine pleasure and enjoyment. Freedom of means to achieve these goals . . . . [R]ecognition to the forms of expression belonging to the anti-social art of so-called children and madmen . . . not as rational achievements of consciousness, but rather as a form of expression subordinate to its own laws and to whose recognition and estimation this publication shall be open.[1]

Although the periodical envisioned by Group Rih never materialized, these principles, based in the radicalized humanistic aims of late Expressionism, informed Scholz's style at the time the list was compiled. In *Nightly Noise*,[2] for example, whose compositional logic is indebted to Edvard Munch's *Scream* (1893), Scholz employs the Futurist-inspired faceting, geometric abstraction, and heightened color contrasts characteristic of postwar Expressionism. Bright reds and yellows are juxtaposed with dark greens, while touches of blue appear as accentuated intrusions. In the immediate foreground, a large red bearded man runs towards the viewer, thin legs raised in an energetic gallop, arms flailing, his hat fallen behind him as he calls out, shouts, or screams. Near him, jagged, yellow-red starlike forms signal explosive impact, while a second, caftan-clothed figure runs drunkenly in the middle distance, balancing unsteadily on one foot, arms and bottle and head fragmented and multiplied in alcoholic vision.

The cause of this panic appears in a wedge-shaped green form whose tip pushes into the painting to be defined by the beard and open mouth of the foreground figure. Isolated, in color and shape echoing one eye of the red alarmed man as if to indicate the sight that caused his distress, a blue-gray triangular shape marches on shiny points into the scene. A highly stylized emblem of a police or military uniform, its apex is shaped by a red collar and the unmistakable black leather *Pickelhaube* helmet, a hallmark of reactionary German armed authority.

With its riotous explosions and hysterically shrieking figures, the painting depicts a disruption of nocturnal revelry. The turmoil is in response to the entrance into a city neighborhood of troops, their appearance reduced to the triangular helmeted emblem. Two readings of the image are suggested. The first is of a simple genre scene in which carousers are dispersed by an admonishing policeman; running from this preserver of order, they are even noisier than they were before his arrival. Such lightly sarcastic commentary appears in other contemporaneous works by Scholz, but in *Nightly Noise* coloristic and compositional intensity exceed the requirements of a genre motif. Notably, the agitation of the foreground figure certainly surpasses that of tipsy fright. His wild gestures, scream, and the harsh dissonance of red and yellow marking his head indicate greater danger, as does the sharp impact of the wedge shape extending from the military-police configuration into his head. The yellow-red explosive stars around him are marks of violence, not of a harmless confrontation between overly rambunctious revelers and a cautioning policeman. The chaos of the scene is more extreme than humorous, and the invasion of the depersonalized military figure is more powerful in its panic-inducing results than the routine round of a policeman on the beat.

The painting's temporal coincidence with events in Germany and Eastern Europe, together with Scholz's socialist convictions and the political commitment of his work, suggest that the image is more drastic in intent. By 1919, the artist had had persistent experience of the military terror and destruction of civilian life that *Nightly Noise*, in a final reading, appears to represent: Scholz had witnessed both war and numerous suppressions of radical left-wing uprisings throughout Germany—and the red of the foreground figure, while certainly part of an iconography of excitement, may also be politically significant in this context. Caftans, beards, and the fallen high-crowned, round black hat may indicate a setting, moreover, in a ghetto of Orthodox Eastern European Jews during the war or the ensuing revolutions, although the marked stylization of all figures and forms makes certain identification difficult. Whether or not such an interpretation is justified, the meaning of Scholz's painting is more sinister than comic in a year when Karl Liebknecht, Alfred Rosenberg, Kurt Eisner, and Eugen Leviné were among the victims of military and paramilitary terror activities.

The artist's radical Expressionism in this image was intended to facilitate instinctive communication with a broad-based, popular audience in the collective effort to destroy the possibility of "philistine pleasure and enjoyment." The excited dissonance of his colors and geometrically transmuted forms suggest a psychic state rather than the narration of a particular event. But for Scholz, as for Rudolf Schlichter, through whom he established contacts with Berlin artists, the shift from this expressive mode to the more iconoclastic opposition of Dada was easily achieved. Within a year, Scholz had rejected the manner of *Nightly Noise* and turned to structured, more illusionistic imagery, still politically committed, using elements of simulated photomontage. He showed these new works at the *First International Dada Fair* in Berlin in 1920.

Noting this development in Scholz's style, a critic described his work in the early twenties: "Polemical elements dominate; merciless struggle is proclaimed and carried out with brutal candor against all smugness, all inflexibility, all hearty philistine sentimentality, all constipated sexuality, all capitalist crudeness, all fatherlandish stupidity."[3] Scholz retained the coloristic sensitivity and expressiveness of such previous works as *Nightly Noise*, as well as his political motivation, but "the desire for universal understanding led to objectivity, to a clear comprehension of his figures, to heightened representation of material texture."[4] For him, as for others, Expressionism had provided invaluable lessons in communicative intensity, but the lure of the objective and material linked to his political convictions demanded that he reject Expressionism's speculative, individualistic, and therefore bourgeois, capitalist "vivisection of the psychic."[5]   R. H.

1. "Freiheit des Subjekts als Korrektiv gegenüber der mit labiler Ethik Geschäftsinteressen wahrenden Gesellschaftskunst. Freiheit und Selbstleben des einzelnen. Aberkennung der Phantasieformen, die dem Philister das Geniessen gewähren. Freiheit der Mitteln, diese Ziele zu erreichen.... Sie ist bestrebt, die Ausdrucksformen der gesellschaftsfeindlichen, der vermeintlichen Kinder- und Krankenkunst ... nicht als rationale Bewusstseinsleistung, sondern als eigenem Gesetz unterworfener Ausdruck, zu dessen Erkennung und Wertschätzung das Organ freigelegt werden soll." Catalogue insert reprinted in *Zehn Jahre Novembergruppe*, special issue of *Kunst der Zeit* 3, nos. 1–3 (1928): 24.
2. The ambivalent meaning in Scholz's title should be noted: *Nächtlicher Lärm*, here

translated as "Nightly Noise," might also mean "Alarm at Night." Inscribed on the stretcher along with the artist's signature and the date of 1919, *Nächtlicher Lärm* is Scholz's original title, as is also confirmed by the title on a preparatory sketch for the painting in the Scholz estate (see *Georg Scholz: Ein Beitrag zur Diskussion realistischer Kunst* [Karlsruhe: Staatliche Kunsthalle, 1975], 194, no. 25). An old label on the stretcher, however, bears the alternative title *Nächtlicher Schrei* (*Nightly Scream*), apparently used in an exhibition after 1919.
3. "Die polemischen Elemente herrschen vor; aller Sattheit, aller Verbortheit, aller herzigen Banausen-Sentimentalität, aller gepfropften Sexualität, aller kapitalistischen Roheit, aller vaterländischen Dummheit wird unerbittlicher Kampf angesagt, der mit brutaler Offenheit geführt wird." Hans Curjel, "Zur Entwicklung des Malers Georg Scholz," *Das Kunstblatt* 7 (1923): 260.
4. "...das Bemühen nach allgemeiner Verständlichkeit führte zur Gegenständlichkeit, zu klarer Fassbarkeit der Figuren, zu zugespitzter Stoffmalerei...." Ibid., 261.
5. "Vivisektion des Psychischen..." Ibid., 257.

139 Franz Theodor Schütt
Young Woman before a Window (*Junge Frau vor dem Fenster*), 1929

Gouache, pencil on paper
47 x 27.3–32 cm
(18 1/2 x 10 3/4–12 5/8 in.), sight
Signed, inscribed, and dated l. l.
"Schütt / Stettin 29"

Provenance: Galerie Brockstedt, Hamburg.

In this image by Franz Schütt, a young woman, her blond hair cut into the modified page boy fashionable during the late 1920s, stands before a window buttoning her lacy white camisole-bloomers. Her expensive undergarments and shiny silk stockings contrast distinctly with the deteriorating, gray stucco façades seen through the window, which signal a lower middle- or working-class neighborhood. The city setting, stylish lingerie, and position at an open window suggest that this woman is someone accustomed to being observed, even half-clothed. She is observed this time as well, implicitly by Schütt and the viewer who takes his place, but also by a seated woman, her skirt informally raised above her knees, whose reflection appears in a mirror at the upper right of the picture. It is likely, too, that Schütt's model, standing and turning, her brows knit in concentration, is looking into another mirror beyond the picture's field.

Schütt has staged a triple interplay of observation and reflection. Artist and viewer observe a woman gazing at herself in an unseen mirror and watched by someone not depicted but reflected in another mirror. The ricochet of watching and watched, reality and reflection, is carried further if the windows across the street are recognized as both reflecting and seeing presences focused on the person posing before her open window. The woman, therefore, in heavy

eye shadow and lipstick, is not only adjusting her clothing but also her representation for the outside world. Schütt's depiction investigates a complex dynamic of actuality and representation, illusion and consumption.

His gouache technique is matte and dry, permitting the sharp juxtaposition of precisely delineated forms. Details are further accented in pencil; the lace border on the lingerie, for example, with its pattern of holes, is rendered by indenting the wet paper with a pencil point. Light entering through the window highlights the tensely drawn fabric of the white underclothes, which focus attention on breasts, hips, and buttocks, and aid in transforming the model into a sexual fetish. As she has been seduced by the fashionable undergarment, a revealing uniform in which her sexual existence is packaged as if in wrapping paper, she, too, functions as a seductive commodity being observed and tested by her seated companion, by the staring windows of the somber façades, and finally by artist and viewer, presumed to be male. Representation and reflection, along with self-alienation and otherness, construct a complex dynamic of fetishization and consumption in which the artwork itself, as object, false reality, and commodity, forms the final component.

B. T. Y.

140 Karl Schwesig
Out to the Demonstration (*Heraus zur Demonstration*), 1931

Watercolor, ink and tusche on paper
23.9 x 29.8 cm (9 7/16 x 11 13/16 in.)
Signed and dated l. l.
"K. Schwesig 1931"

Provenance: Galerie Remmert und Barth, Düsseldorf; Galerie Michael Hasenclever, Munich.

Exhibitions: Brussels, Goethe-Institut, *Karl Schwesig 1895–1955: Gemälde—Graphik—Dokumente*, 2 February–15 March 1986, cat. no. 26; Düsseldorf, Galerie Remmert und Barth, *Karl Schwesig: Ausgewählte Werke 1920–1955*, 17 September–19 November 1988, cat. no. 65.

On 15 March 1931, the number of unemployed in Germany was officially announced to be 4,980,000; by the end of the year, the number had risen, even according to the government's underreporting, to a record 5,666,000. Almost every second German worker was unemployed. Private industry and the national government, by means of a series of emergency decrees, systematically lowered wages while also reducing working hours, a measure that affected some three million employed. On 25 February, the Communist Party of Germany (KPD) organized an International Day of the Unemployed in the major cities to protest government policies and the drastically worsening condition of the workers. A predictably regular aspect of these demonstrations and strikes were the violent clashes between KPD members and Nazi counter-demonstrators; typically as

well, the police responded primarily by arresting a number of the KPD demonstrators.

A KPD member in Düsseldorf, Karl Schwesig repeatedly recorded assemblies of unemployed workers, demonstrations, and the groups of blue-uniformed policemen that political and economic developments called out onto the city's streets in 1931.[1] *Out to the Demonstration*, set among the tenement row houses of one of Düsseldorf's workers' districts, identifies the slogan of its title as that of the KPD, and links it to another painted exhortation, posted on a wall near the center of the picture, "Workers Come Out." Schwesig devotes the central foreground to a quartet of jack-booted policemen, who dominate the street or square in which they stand. Although outnumbering the police, the workers are dispersed as smaller, less densely formed figures throughout the remainder of the watercolor's space, visually inferior and narratively threatened by the four domineering dark blue presences, pistols at their sides. As workers turn their backs to the police and stand gazing beyond the edges of the image, the scene is one of expectation. The two signs announce a demonstration, and workers assemble loosely beneath and near them, mindful perhaps that during the Ruhr miners' strikes in January three workers had been killed in encounters with the police. With the psychological tension of the event generated through the spacing of his figures, Schwesig's workers and police wait in silence.

There is, however, no indication of an organized demonstration, no marchers rallying together in columns, no banners announcing the slogans and goals of a mass protest. Instead, in this section of the workers' quarters men stand idly or walk without purpose and in isolation. There are no conversations, no consultations, no signs of communication. These workers depicted by Schwesig in 1931 are idle, without jobs, without apparent hope, and even the scrawled signs admonishing them to political action are without effect. There is no demonstration, only the debilitating despair and general misery of unemployment and the brutal threat provided by the squared-off group of intimidating policemen.

R. H.

1. A selection of these drawings is illustrated in Galerie Remmert und Barth, *Karl Schwesig: Ausgewählte Werke 1920–1955* (Düsseldorf: Galerie Remmert und Barth, 1988), 41.

141 Martel Schwichtenberg
Portrait of a Woman (Seated Woman with Flowers) (*Mädchenbildnis [Sitzende mit Blumen]*), c. 1920–21

Oil on canvas
94.5 x 78 cm (37 1/4 x 30 3/4 in.)
Signed l. r. "Schwichtenberg"

Provenance: Galerie Ferdinand Möller, Berlin; private collection, New York; Galerie Brockstedt, Hamburg.

In 1920 and 1921, Martel Schwichten-berg and Robert W. Huth, recently married, summered in the Pomeranian fishing village of Jershöft to paint with Karl Schmidt-Rottluff. Of the two young artists, Huth more closely emu-lated the former *Brücke* painter, so much so that the critic Paul Westheim accused him of "being knee-deep in Schmidt-Rottluff." Schwichtenberg, on the other hand, was "more feminine, more talented," according to Westheim, who likened her tasteful paintings to Gobelin tapestries.[1] Such comparisons of the couple continued throughout the 1920s and surely con-tributed to the problems that beset the marriage, causing Schwichtenberg fre-quently to escape from Berlin and her husband, whose response to the critical denigration of his art in favor of his wife's, although not known, is unlikely to have been entirely acquiescent.

Portrait of a Woman serves to test as-pects of the critic's appraisal. In this garden scene, Schwichtenberg presents a woman seated on a bench as a mass of variegated dark blues and flesh tones surrounded by green, red, and white shapes infused with light. These lighter colors push the figure forward, giving her a sense of volume and presence. Contrasts of light and dark, and jux-tapositions of different values of the same color, produce an effect seen in works by Paula Modersohn-Becker. The contemplative calm of the sitter, her proportions, self-assured gaze, and relaxed relationship to her surround-ings, as well as the informal emblematic use of flowers, recall Modersohn-Becker's images of Worpswede women painted fifteen years earlier.

This reliance on Modersohn-Becker, however, is only part of Schwichten-berg's consciously synthetic style. Schmidt-Rottluff's precedent emerges in the color values and spatial concep-tion of the painting, both of which de-pend on his postwar art, adapted now to the compositional prototype of Modersohn-Becker. Schwichtenberg's portrait achieves a unique dynamism while accenting, as neither of her mod-els did, the painting's planar organiza-tion, its tapestry-like surface cohesion. The result is an appearance of subjectiv-ity composed of determined, objective, synthesizing efforts. One critic associ-ated with Schwichtenberg thus wrote in 1930 that "it would be quite amiss to look for psychological interpretation in these works. Their greatest merit lies in the aggressive, unsentimental simplic-ity with which the forms are consis-tently rendered."[2] Schwichtenberg's aesthetic is not the microscopic obser-vation of external nature that charac-terizes much *Neue Sachlichkeit* painting, but depends instead on a careful proces-sing of pre-existing styles. Sidestepping modernism's demand for individualis-tic invention, she adopts a posture of eclecticism that constitutes a hitherto unrecognized link to postmodern Ger-man painting of the 1970s and 1980s.

B. T. Y.

1. ". . . über die Kniee in Schmidt-Rott-luff . . . fraulicher, geschickter. . . ." Paul Westheim, "Atelierstreife II," *Das Kunst-blatt* 7 (1923): 209.
2. Flora Turkel-Deri, "Berlin Letter: Ex-hibition Flechtheim Gallery," *Art News* 29 (27 December 1930): 6.

142 Martel Schwichtenberg
Girl in Red Striped Skirt (*Mäd-chen in rotgestreiftem Kleid*),
c. 1920?

Oil on cardboard
70.8 x 49.8 cm (27⁷/₈ x 19⁵/₈ in.),
sight
Signed l. r.
"M. Schwichtenberg"

Provenance: Galerie Ferdinand Möller, Berlin; Dr. Wilhelm R. Valentiner, Berlin and Detroit; Brigid Valentiner Bertoia, Barto, Pa.; Olympia Gallery, Philadel-phia.

As a young woman, Martel Schwich-tenberg was employed as a designer at the Bahlsen Cookie Factory in Hanover. Bahlsen was applying war-time profits towards innovative pack-aging design and an extensive new building campaign, including a factory and a workers' colony (never com-pleted), which called for fresco cycles, stained-glass windows, and other appli-cations of the "art in the workplace" philosophy. For Schwichtenberg, just twenty years old and with minimal for-mal training in art, painting and design at Bahlsen provided a significant affir-mation of her talent and value as an art-ist. It meant, too, that her decision not to study mathematics in preparation for a job as a grade school teacher—the type of modest ambition considered ap-propriate for the daughter of a govern-ment clerk—was viable and respect-able, and not a prelude to a life of lazi-ness or bohemian excess.

Schwichtenberg sought models for her synthetic style primarily among early German Expressionists. Con-sciously eclectic and thus bereft of Ex-pressionism's emotive subjectivity, her work might be classified as a restate-ment of her artistic ancestry, but melded into a searching, never fixed de-mand for a personal vocabulary. *Girl in Red Striped Skirt* serves as an overt homage to Paula Modersohn-Becker and her portraits of the blond, blue-eyed peasant children of Worpswede, and in the act of homage elucidates Schwichtenberg's own position as a woman artist during the years follow-ing the German November Revolution.

Schwichtenberg first viewed a major collection of Modersohn-Becker's work in 1917 at the Kestner-Gesellschaft in Hanover. The exhibi-tion of 119 paintings was arranged with the aid of Bernhard Hoetger, the ar-chitect-sculptor under whose direction Schwichtenberg worked at Bahlsen. Modersohn-Becker had become both an ideal and a model for young women artists by 1920. She was acclaimed as an innovator of Expressionism along with the artists of *Brücke* and *Der Blaue Rei-ter*. Repeated exhibitions in German museums were devoted to her work, as was the second volume of *Junge Kunst* (*Young Art*), a series that sought to propagate modern German art in brief but extensively illustrated mono-graphs.[1]

Hoetger reminisced in the book about his friendship with Modersohn-Becker, and characterized her as ". . . someone who loved life and culti-vated it, took personal responsibility for it, never took advantage of a situa-tion for her own profit."[2] She was pre-sented as the prototype of the modern woman painter, absolutely dedicated to her art but also appropriately feminine: "Paula Modersohn did not lose her womanhood as woman artist, and to be a woman means to be forever and al-ways an unprogramatic person," the book proclaimed with uneasy ambi-valence.[3] Accordingly, her image re-mained that of a naïve and humble woman, recognizing her call to motherhood (and dying for it), and working for the joy of her art, an art of "chaste sensuality" whose great genius posterity recognized.

The ideal of Modersohn-Becker was joined to the romantic socialism of the Worpswede artists' colony, which Schwichtenberg visited during the summers of 1918 and 1919 along with Hoetger, Heinrich Vogeler, Karl Jakob Hirsch, and the art publisher Georg Biermann. After moving to Berlin and establishing her independent studio in Sybelstrasse, Schwichtenberg joined the November Group, with its radical but idealistic program of applying art to the struggle for a vaguely imagined socialist future of worldwide fraternity. The poets Johannes R. Becher and Theodor Däubler, as well as the museum director Wilhelm R. Valen-tiner, further encouraged art-oriented social activism, a concern for humanity and for a society which art would con-struct free of capitalist exploitation and militarist adventurism.

Girl in Red Striped Skirt may well rep-resent a peasant child of Worpswede, a descendant of the models for Moder-sohn-Becker's portraits. Using thinned oil paints, however, Schwichtenberg replaces her prototype's heavy model-ing, technical experimentation, and muted palette with flat forms and bright, complementary colors. Her sketch-like rendering transforms cloth-ing, arms, facial features, hair, and doorway into a pattern of intercon-nected, simplified shapes. Schwichten-berg emphasizes the painting as both synthetic planar construct and hand-crafted object. The painting's function in a larger decorative context that ex-ploits the "chaste sensuality" of natural materials is likewise echoed in the sim-ple, gold-tinted, rough wooden frame, in accordance with the Expressionists' adaptation of the arts-and-crafts ideals practiced at Worpswede.[4]

In portraying children, Modersohn-Becker had been seen—especially by her male advocates—as expressing her own desire for children, and this was sentimentally celebrated as an affirma-tion of her womanhood. Schwichten-berg's painted homage similarly turns to a child, possibly in recognition of the motif as one already expected of her, since she had recently married and was persistently associated in art criticism as one half of the "Schwichtenberg-Huth artist couple." The plain background of *Girl in Red Striped Skirt*, the child's un-sophisticated posture, large bright blue eyes, and the melancholy tilt of her head give the young farm girl a wistful quality, a shy reticence combined with a seriousness seemingly beyond her age. In all this Modersohn-Becker con-tinues to be the prototype, but the sen-sitivity with which Schwichtenberg renders the contemplative mood of the girl also becomes a significant hallmark

of other artists' renderings of children in the Weimar Republic. A pathos, not infrequently associated with signs of malnutrition or tuberculosis, from which gentle sentimentality cannot be removed despite all efforts at objective observation, separates *Neue Sachlichkeit* conceptions by Otto Dix, Otto Herbig, or Bernhard Kretzschmar from Moder-sohn-Becker's earlier images of chil-dren. Schwichtenberg's painting forms a transition linked to the earlier ideals of Hoetger and Worpswede but existing in the radicalized political and economic environment of Germany after the col-lapse of the Empire in 1918.

B. T. Y. / R. H.

1. The first volume of *Junge Kunst* pre-sented Max Pechstein as the premier Ex-pressionist; the third was dedicated to Bernhard Hoetger. This trio of artists —Pechstein, Modersohn-Becker, Hoet-ger—functions as a conceptual prelude to contemporary German art and its pos-sibilities as seen in the work of "first-gen-eration" Expressionists. Schwichtenberg's contacts with the *Junge Kunst* circle in-cluded not only Hoetger but also the pub-lisher Georg Biermann.
2. ". . . ein Mensch, der in eigener Verant-wortung das Leben liebte und ausbaute, keine Situationen benutzte, um Vorteile zu erreichen." Bernhard Hoetger, "Erin-nerungen an Paula Modersohn," in C. E. Uphoff, *Paula Modersohn*, Junge Kunst, vol. 2 (Leipzig: Klinkhardt & Bier-mann, 1920), 12.
3. "Paula Modersohn verlor als Künstlerin nicht ihr Frauentum, und Frau sein, das heisst immer und ewig ein unprogram-matischer Mensch sein." Uphoff, *Paula Modersohn*, 6.
4. Paint traces, corresponding to the pig-ment of the painting, on the inner edge of the frame suggest it was applied by the artist herself.

143 Martel Schwichtenberg
Snowy Landscape II
(*Schneelandschaft II*), c. 1922

Oil on canvas
67 x 82.2 cm (26³/₈ x 32³/₈ in.)
Not signed

Provenance: Galerie Ferdinand Möller, Berlin; Wilhelm R. Valentiner, Berlin and Detroit; Brigid Valentiner Bertoia, Barto, Pa.; Olympia Gallery, Philadel-phia.

Exhibition: Berlin, Galerie Ferdinand Möller, 1922.

In her rapid exploration of styles during the early 1920s, Martel Schwichtenberg remained preoccupied with painting's function in an architectural setting. A concern with the flat surface and its re-lationship to the wall, whether in mu-rals or in plainly framed oil paintings, informs her work, which often ap-proaches a tapestry-like effect.[1] *Snowy Landscape II* is a study of white to-nalities and muted blues interspersed with black and brown in the soft un-dulating forms of a mountain land-scape. The abstract, stylized forms and broad planes of color outlined with black follow French Synthetist practices established during the 1880s. By the time Schwichtenberg applied this Gauguin-inspired technique, it had been filtered through the works of Edvard Munch, *Brücke*, and *Der Blaue Reiter*, with Gabriele Münter's views of Murnau's Alpine surroundings most closely approximating this painting.

The monochromatic emphasis of *Snowy Landscape II* functions as an antidote to the intense colorism Schwichtenberg derived from Karl Schmidt-Rottluff's work during 1920 and 1921, and for which several critics repeatedly faulted her. Echoing the subtler palette of Münter, she also adopts a more insistently neo-naïve manner of rendering her scene. Simple, flat shapes of remembered reality generate a childlike, charmed world of stability, order, and harmony which serves as foil to the turmoil of German life during the 1920s. It is also a scene of a world outside Berlin, viewed during one of her frequent efforts to escape the conflicts of an unstable marriage. Unpopulated, the mountain landscape offers an isolated bucolic refuge, a protected tranquility fantasized by Schwichtenberg on the controlled reality of her canvas surface.

B. T. Y.

1. Compare Paul Westheim's negative judgment in 1927, that in a painting by Schwichtenberg, "the concept of 'surface' is understood too much in the sense of flat" (". . . der Begriff 'Fläche' [ist] zu sehr im Sinne von flach genommen"). Westheim, "Die Ausstellung der jungen Maler in der Deutschen Kunstgemeinschaft, Berlin," *Das Kunstblatt* 11 (1927): 143. Also compare Schwichtenberg's relief sculpture, whose shallow carved surfaces approach woodcut blocks in appearance, as noted by Gerhard Wietek in Los Angeles County Museum of Art, *German Expressionist Sculpture*, ed. Stephanie Barron (Los Angeles: Los Angeles County Museum of Art in association with the University of Chicago Press, 1984), 189.

144   **Richard Seewald**
Landscape with Rocky Cliffs and Goats Overlooking the Sea Near Positano (Felsenlandschaft mit Ziegen und Blick auf das Meer bei Positano), 1924

Watercolor over pencil on paper
35 x 28.5 cm (13³⁄₄ x 11³⁄₁₆ in.)
Signed and dated l. l. "Seewald 1924"

Provenance: Estate of the artist; Karl und Faber, Munich.

The small southern Italian town of Positano, romantically dotted with antique and medieval ruins, became a fashionable vacation resort during the 1920s. Richard Seewald preceded the German tourists there in 1923, when he left Munich at the invitation of his friend the Italian Prince Leone Massimo, who arranged the trip and an exhibition. Seewald found the landscape monumental and alluring, and decided to remain near Positano, where he discovered a unique interaction of traditional folk customs and remnants of medieval life and classical antiquity.

These multiple components form the basis for this watercolor. The deep blue waters of the Tyrrhenian Sea stretch westward from a steep, rocky promontory. Gnarled trees stand isolated as dark, intricate linear patterns among grass-covered projections of land and boulders. A herdsman and his goats climb the steep, irregularly twisting system of steps that surmount arched remnants of medieval fortification and lead to a precariously perched, characteristically cubic house. Nearby, silhouetted against the sky, a woman carries a water jug; her form, deep blue, bright white, and terra-cotta, summarizes the tones of the watercolor in an intensity not matched elsewhere; she becomes the focus and goal of the image. A solemn, idyllic mood is generated, a persistent reality, unchanging through time, linked to nature, silent in perpetual sunlight.

Seewald's imagery and style recall the simplified, classicizing naturalism of nineteenth-century Biedermeier painters. He developed this mode in Munich in conjunction with artists such as Georg Schrimpf and Max Radler (see cat. no. 127), although he does not share their concern with the monumental human figure. After the turmoil of war and revolution, in which Munich's artists played a prominent role, Seewald escaped to a quiet realm, removed from contemporary German life, projecting a melancholically recalled, vaguely defined past. His solution to the inflationary reality of the Weimar Republic is an attachment to an artistic style that mediates the present as it postulates a personal, social, and environmental harmony in a clearly structured, unproblematic world.

The Cologne critic Luise Straus-Ernst, usually a relatively neutral recorder of modern art in the 1920s, recognized the simplicity of Seewald's work as an indication of his conscious commitment to an innocence of conception and a concern with essentials alien to other figurative painters of the time:

During his entire development . . . Seewald has always kept himself removed from the broad mainstream. Neither consciously nor unconsciously has he belonged to any of the great artistic movements of recent times. The unrestrained emphasis on one's own personality, which manifested itself in Expressionism, never was comfortable for him. His reverence for the form and essence of all creatures and things was too great for that. And it is precisely this love of everything growing and becoming that prevents him today from following "Neue Sachlichkeit." Faced with the experience of nature, which is the alpha and omega of his work, he is unable to muster the cool objectivity that is the defining characteristic of this movement. Despite Seewald's artistic sophistication, he approaches every new experience without preconceptions and with a joy such as only children are capable of otherwise. And that explains why Seewald is to be counted among the very few artists of our time whose paintings and drawings can speak directly and with

understanding to children and be comprehended by them immediately. And that, perhaps, is the best that could ever be said about any artist.[1]

Seewald invited the harrowed citizens of Weimar Germany to forget the political and economic, the moral and social transformation of their milieu and to imagine a simpler, surer, calmer existence. To him, Positano represented eternity.

B. T. Y.

1. "Seewald ist während seines ganzen Werdens . . . immer etwas abseits von der grossen Strasse gegangen. Er hat weder bewusst noch unbewusst irgend einer der grossen künstlerischen Bewegungen der letzten Zeit angehört. Das hemmungslose Betonen der eignen Persönlichkeit, das sich im Expressionismus manifestiert, war ihm niemals gemäss. Dazu war seine Ehrfurcht vor der Gestalt und dem Wesen aller Geschöpfe und Dinge zu gross. Und eben diese Liebe zu allem Gewachsenen und Gewordenen ist es auch, die ihn heute hindert, der 'neuen Sachlichkeit' zu folgen. Vor dem Erlebnis der Natur, das Anfang und Ende des Schaffens bedeutet, bringt er die kühle Objektivität nicht auf, die wesentliches Merkmal dieser Bewegung ist. Trotz aller künstlerischen Kultur tritt er jedem neuen Erleben voraussetzungslos und froh gegenüber, wie es eigentlich sonst nur Kinder vermögen. Darum gehört auch Seewald zu den ganz wenigen Künstlern unserer Zeit, die in ihren Bildern und Zeichnungen unmittelbar und verständlich zu Kindern sprechen können und ohne weiteres von ihnen verstanden werden. Und das ist vielleicht das Beste, was man überhaupt von einem Künstler sagen kann." Luise Straus-Ernst, "Neue Arbeiten von Richard Seewald," *Das Kunstblatt* 11 (1927): 355.

145   **Friedrich (Fritz) Skade**
Young Woman (Junge Frau), c. 1925?

Watercolor over pencil on paper
47.8 x 32 cm (18¹¹⁄₁₆ x 12⁹⁄₁₆ in.)
Signed l. r. "F. Skade"

Provenance: Hugo Erfurth, Dresden; Kunsthaus Lempertz, Cologne.

One of a group of artists, including Otto Griebel, Wilhelm Lachnit, and Hans Grundig, who exhibited at the Graphics Cabinet of Hugo Erfurth in Dresden, Fritz Skade shared their radical political convictions and the exact observation reflected in their images. As early as 1925, however, Will Grohmann, a young critic linked to the group, warned that the stylistic and other similarities and the apparent influence of Otto Dix did not suffice to define Skade's work:

Kindred origins and attitudes towards the human figure (landscape as yet plays no role at all) result at first sight in an external similarity, but Skade's vision and sensation are totally instinctive and independent, as his direct response to an object already indicates. The very wide range of his graphic modes of representation extends from the silverpoint-like outline of a woman's body to the

brutally true blunt-end drawings with charcoal and crayon that arouse one's sense of touch. Something proletarian, unspoiled resides in his greedy comprehension and representation of a human figure, in the sensuous moistness of a brushstroke as in his direct, almost agressively violent coarseness. He has drawn workers' children whose expression borders on social caricature, but these images also contain love, a feeling for the cohesion of the genus humanity.[1]

Comparing Skade's standing red-headed woman in underwear and stockings with Griebel's *The Naked Whore* (cat. no. 47) supports aspects of Grohman's appraisal. Griebel's aging prostitute, her red hat functioning both as incongruous emblem and caricaturing commentary, is viewed frontally, mercilessly in every detail, every crevice and wrinkle of her body and face. Her nakedness is examined and presented dispassionately, as if she were a specimen pinned for display against the aqua-colored background. Skade's image, too, presents a frontal view and an eschewal of surroundings that could relieve or distract from the figure. Unlike Griebel, however, Skade displaces his model from the geometric center of the composition, and permits some space between her and the top edge, while also depicting more of her legs. He thus avoids the unrelenting rigidity of Griebel's image. Instead of being trapped between top and bottom edge, Skade's woman shifts her posture in an almost classical contrapposto, which suggests both movement and awkwardness, an imbalance that echoes in its signification the uneven hems of her homely, practical cotton undergarments.

Rosy-cheeked, her red hair standing out in uneven spikes from her head, she gazes through clear blue eyes at her portrayer/viewer, with no hint of seductiveness and with no suggestion of the pernicious *femme fatale* that informs Griebel's *The Naked Whore*. The hesitancy of this proletarian model is also echoed in Skade's technique, in which the pencil drawing shifts and changes, avoiding the honed contours of Griebel's nude, as if the artist were as inexperienced in his craft as the novice model is in hers. Similarly, the artist's focus is never fixed, but allows gentle transitions across areas of color and body, virtually dissolving the woman's facial features to permit her eyes to shine forth in all their lucidity.

Unlike Dix, with his frequently mocking and violent attitudes towards women, or George Grosz, with his obsessive accentuation of simultaneously revulsive and provocative sexuality, Skade demonstrates a gentle empathy with his red-headed proletarian model. In her awkwardness and despite her partial undress, her lack of efforts at sexual display, the young woman assumes a recognizable personality independent of that male control which Skade's fellow artists refused to relinquish. Borne out by this sensitive watercolor is Grohmann's concluding point that Skade accents the unifying genus of humanity, not the distinctions of class, age, or sex.

R. H.

1. "Verwandte Herkunft und Einstellung zum Menschen (die Landschaft spielt noch gar keine Rolle) ergibt auf den ersten Blick eine äussere Ähnlichkeit, aber Skades Sehen und Empfinden sind ganz triebhaft und unabhängig, das beweist schon die umittelbare Reaktion auf das Objekt. Der Umkreis seiner zeichnerischen Vortragsmöglichkeiten ist sehr gross und geht von der silberstiftzarten Umrisslinie eines Mädchenkörpers bis zur brutal wahren, den Tastsinn reizenden Vollzeichnung mit Kohle und Fettkreide. Etwas Proletarisches, Unverbrauchtes steckt in seinem gierigen Erfassen und Wiedergeben eines Menschen, in der sinnlichen Feuchtigkeit des Strichs wie in seiner geraden, fast gewalttätigen Derbheit. Er hat Arbeiterkinder gezeichnet, deren Ausdruck die soziale Karikatur streift, aber es ist auch in diesen Blättern Liebe, Gefühl für die Zusammengehörigkeit der Gattung Mensch." W[ill] Grohmann, "Fritz Skade," *Der Cicerone* 27 (1925): 97.

146 Alice Sommer
Two Sisters (Zwei Schwestern), 1925

Pencil on toned paper
64 x 48.2 cm (25³/₁₆ x 19 in.)
Signed and dated l. r. "A. Sommer 25"; monogrammed and dated u. r. "9. Februar 1925/ A. S."

Provenance: Estate of the artist, Dresden; Galerie Saxonia, Munich; Galerie Brockstedt, Hamburg.

In her large drawing of two sisters, Alice Sommer uses concrete formal means to achieve a psychologically penetrating portrait. Adhering to the stylistic principles of *Neue Sachlichkeit* in her accentuation of volume, surface, and illusion, Sommer nonetheless retains the aura of Expressionism in her emphasis on subjective interpretation, hints of distortion, and use of space as psychological construct. In the corner of a barren interior, the sisters are seen from a high vantage point, as if by an adult who has entered the room and looks down on the girls. The viewer's superior position implies a power that contrasts with the children's huddled, diminished, and vulnerable presence before the towering walls, whose juncture the girls echo in their own juxtaposition. The sharp light, coming perhaps through a door suddenly opened, casts intense highlights and mysterious shadows as it intrudes into the comfortable ambience of a room which is no longer the girls' alone.

Rendered with a remarkably refined drawing technique, the girls sit idle on the floor, without toys, dolls, or games to define their childhood personalities. One dressed in a play smock, the other in a knit dress, they stare without focus in front of them, at the floor or into an unknown space. There is no communication, only a silence marking their immobility and their self-enshrouded existence, which even their physical closeness fails to surmount. Lacking the charming characteristics usually associated with a child's room, the sterile interior in which the girls pose is more

akin to a hospital or sanatorium ward than a playroom. Their own dejected demeanor and failure to take note of the viewer likewise suggest a realm foreign to the cheerful curiosity common to children. Protectively, fearfully avoiding an outside world, the girls seem alienated from what surrounds them, inhabiting psychological realities solely their own.   C. D. G.

147 Alice Sommer
Portrait: Head of a Woman (Porträt Mädchenkopf), 1925

Oil on board
48.5 x 23.9 cm (19¹/₁₆ x 9¹/₄ in.)
Signed, dated, and inscribed in pencil verso "Porträt Mädchenkopf/A. Sommer Dresden/24. Februar 25 [altered to read '22']"

Provenance: Estate of the artist, Dresden; Galerie Saxonia, Munich; Galerie Brockstedt, Hamburg.

Exhibition: Dresdner Kunstgenossenschaft, Annual Exhibition, 1925?

Alice Sommer received her artistic training in Dresden at the Painting School for Women and then, as one of the first women admitted, at the Dresden Academy. It was a time of radical activity by artists of the Dresden Secession Group 1919, but while Otto Dix, Conrad Felixmüller, and Otto Griebel pushed Expressionism in the directions of Dada and political activism, Sommer was practicing traditional lessons of draftsmanship. She apparently established no contact with these artists only a few years older than herself, some of them fellow academy students; nor does her surviving work indicate any interest in their art or ideological position. But by 1925, although exhibiting with the conventional Kunstgenossenschaft (Art League), Sommer was evincing a tendency towards the neo-objectivist verism shared by artists associated with the galleries of photographer Hugo Erfurth and of Mother Ey in Düsseldorf. Their incisive, socially critical imagery, however, does not emerge in her paintings, nor is overt sexuality or violence an aspect of her aesthetic. Instead, she presents a psychologically more introspective world, one less assertive, more questioning, more groping as she faces and mirrors the life that surrounds her.

Portrait: Head of a Woman is conceived in a somber tonality whose dominant blacks in costume and background lend the image a seriousness and solemnity augmented by the vertical format, with its traditional implication of the dominance of spirit over matter, mind over body. Rendered in glowing, golden earth tones and brown-reds, capped by roughly cut, short brown hair, the volumetric head of the unknown woman contrasts with and dominates the encompassing darkness. The head alone emerges as a tactile reality with carefully modeled features, which mold the direction and appearance of meticulously located brushstrokes, each distinguishing a plane or highlight in the

dramatic terrain of face and neck. Sommer's technique is dependent on nineteenth-century realist prototypes, and the more distant model of Rembrandt, but the unflinching observation of faults and flaws, and the transformation of volumes, surfaces, and planes into distinctly juxtaposed realms of shaping and defining color—these are the hallmarks of the realism of the 1920s, conscious of the practices of Expressionism and Cubism while applying them to images that deny their subjectivist and abstracting principles.

Sommer visualizes a woman whose deep-blue eyes, beneath the extended meander of joined eyebrows, are bifocal: one eye gazes ahead, slightly upward; the other turns definitively downward. An uneasy ambivalence results, demanding a perpetually shifting responding gaze from the viewer. The stillness and calm of the portrait are thereby destroyed, supplanted by an indeterminate motion of conflict akin to that established by the landscape of folds, sinews, and muscles, highlighted and deeply shadowed, of the woman's throat. Tense and unstable, the neck is still the insistent, distracting base for the topography of the head. The mouth, turned down and slightly open, seeming to shape a sound without uttering it, concentrates the note of contradiction and inactive ambivalence at the painting's center. While focused on the accidentals of external appearance, Sommer orchestrates the pictorial components to produce a suggestively psychological rendering of irresolution.

Without documentation, the inspiration for this portrait of a woman's disturbed state of indecision, with its contending centers of attention, cannot be identified. Although it is not a self-portrait in the sense of a physiognomic likeness,[1] one is tempted to view the painting as a concealed self-portrait, capturing a frame of mind. That during the 1920s in Germany a sensitive and ambitious woman—such as Sommer's artistic career with its repeated recognition of extraordinary achievement indicate her to have been—would suffer from conflicting aspirations is understandable. Less than two years after creating this portrait head, Sommer married, and stopped painting.[2]   R. H.

1. In 1925, Sommer was not yet thirty, and this image is of a woman significantly older, perhaps in her forties or fifties.
2. No biographical or professional data indicates why Sommer changed the date in the verso inscription from 1925 to 1922: her reason for doing so thus remains unclear.

148 Jakob Steinhardt
Self-Portrait (Drawing for an Exhibition Poster: Die Pathetiker) (Selbstporträt [Zeichnung für ein Ausstellungsplakat: Die Pathetiker]), 1912

Pen and ink over charcoal, pencil, with white highlighting, on paper
43 x 30 cm (16⁷/₈ x 11³/₄ in.)
Monogrammed and dated r. l. r. "J. St./1912"; inscribed l. r. "Pathetiker-Plakat"

Provenance: D. Thomas Bergen Collection, New York and London.

Exhibition: Jerusalem, Bezalel Museum, *Steinhardt*, February 1962, cat. no. 41.

In November 1912, the three Silesian artists Jakob Steinhardt, Ludwig Meidner, and Richard Janthur exhibited for the first time in Herwarth Walden's *Der Sturm* gallery as *Die Pathetiker* (The Ones Filled with Pathos). In styles indebted to French Cubism and Italian Futurism, examples of which Walden had exhibited earlier that year, the artists seemed to one critic to represent "an increase in the spiritual in the artwork," manifested through "often grotesque exaggeration."[1] Steinhardt later recalled:

> We wanted to give content to our images, great, arousing content. We wished to produce an art that would move people and humanity and not just satisfy the aesthetic cravings of a small clique among them. We were fascinated and excited by our painted and unpainted pictures and were convinced that with them we were introducing a new era in art.[2]

Announcing the exhibition, a programmatic visual statement of the artists' concerns, was the poster making use of Steinhardt's self-portrait focused on his head and a surrounding cityscape. The emotionalism of the artists and their identification with the dynamics of the metropolis is stylistically reflected in the poster's panoply of broken, jagged lines, rapidly executed in differing thicknesses. The city assumes an animistic quality in its implied upheaval, complemented by the angular, disfiguring outlines of the human form. The heavier lines delineating Steinhardt's facial features, and especially the pensive dark eyes, mannered neck, and ovoid head (reminiscent of El Greco), underscore the feeling and humanity of the figure rather than its volumetric form. This heightens the sense of the city as locus of powerful technological potential and of dehumanizing materialism. The implication of tumultuous motion and the fragmentation of the artist's stroke are Futurist techniques adapted by Steinhardt, as they were by Meidner, to the common theme of the metropolis, yet they symbolize the artist's pessimistic anxiety more than they manifest the sights, sounds, and smells of a "living" city.   A. I. S.

1. "Vertiefung des Geistigen im Kunstwerk ... das oft zu grotesken Übertreibungen führt." Walter Georgi, "Die Pathetiker," *Deutsche Kunst und Dekoration* 31 (1912–13): 438.
2. "Wir wollten den Bildern Inhalte geben, grosse erregende Inhalte. Wir wollten eine Kunst schaffen, die Volk und Menschheit packen und nicht nur den ästhetischen Bedürfnissen einer kleinen Schicht dienen sollte. Wir begeisterten und erregten uns an unseren gemalten und nicht gemalten Bildern und waren überzeugt, dass wir damit eine neue Ära in der Kunst herbeiführen würden." Undated statement, cited in *Jakob Steinhardt: Das graphische Werk*, ed. Stefan Behrens (West Berlin: Kunstamt Wedding, 1987), 9.

149 Jakob Steinhardt
Recollection of the War (Kriegserinnerung), c. 1919

Lithographic chalk on paper
43 x 40 cm (16^{15}/$_{16}$ x 15^3/$_4$ in.)
Stamped l. l. and l. r. "Jakob Steinhardt"

Provenance: Estate of the artist, Jerusalem; Gallery Ben Ami, Tel Aviv.

During World War I, Jakob Steinhardt served in the German army in Lithuania and Macedonia as an official photographer of war victims, graves, and memorials. As the end of the war appeared imminent during the fall of 1918, he deserted and joined other debilitated soldiers in a painful trek back to Germany, where he arrived in Nuremberg in a state of physical and psychological collapse. Finally returned to his parents' home in Zerkow, he suffered a nervous breakdown. Recollections of the horrors of war, especially as they affected the civilian population of conquered and embattled lands, and particularly in Eastern Europe's Jewish ghettoes, informed his work during the time of recovery, functioning as a means to purge himself of the terror the memories continued to hold for him. Viewing paintings Steinhardt exhibited in 1922, the critic Julius Elias wrote in *Der Tag (The Day):*

> Jakob Steinhardt, shaken and trembling with awareness of the fate of his people as he experienced it in the deepest distress of war, is as moving and opens our hearts just as much as a painter as he has as draftsman. He is possessed by passion, but it is under a shadow. When will this great talent no longer work under the torment of his visions, but in the light of their joy?[1]

This drawing of a wartime recollection represents German soldiers in the foreground, entering a burning city. Depicted in close file, their spiked helmets dominant, they appear as an anonymous force in the right foreground, pushing forward, only one breaking rank to gape moronically at the scene before them.[2] In the street, civilians run in terror, their faces transformed into skulls, chaos marking their movement. As they seek to escape the invading troops and the combat apparent in the background, one of them is shot and collapses, arms flailing. Sharp contrasts of light and dark, differences in drawing technique, inconsistencies of scale, and a persistent breaking up of forms contribute further to the agitation of the scene and its representation.

Images of German troops entering villages in strict order, in closed ranks amid the destruction their powerful armaments caused, were a stock feature of wartime propaganda. The monumental nobility of Germany's armed men was contrasted to the inferior humanity of enemy soldiers conquered in such scenes. Civilian suffering did not exist in the propagandistic repertoire of armies clashing with armies. Steinhardt's drawing undermines this official fiction with his own witness to wartime barbarity and the pain of civilians trapped in the advance and retreat of brutal combatants. It is a testimony

of sympathy rare even among vociferous opponents of the war, who rendered their own and their comrades' agony, or the depravity and callousness brought on by war's inhumanity, but not the fate of civilian populations. Steinhardt's visions of torment reveal, clearly, the barbarity of men in battle, but they reveal all the more his own gentle, tragically powerless compassion for the war's most helpless victims.

R. H.

1. "Jakob Steinhardt, nach wie vor fieberhaft gerüttelt und geschüttelt von der Tragödie seines Volkes, die er in tiefen Kriegsnöten erlebte, ergreift als Maler und öffnet unser Herz wie einst als· Zeichner. Er hat Leidenschaft, doch sie ist beschattet. Wann wird diese starke Begabung nicht mehr unter dem Zwang, sondern unter dem Glück der Gesichter arbeiten?" Julius Elias, review in *Der Tag*, 1922, as cited in *Jakob Steinhardt: Das graphische Werk*, ed. Stefan Behrens (West Berlin: Kunstamt Wedding, 1987), 12.
2. The isolated soldier is identical with one in Steinhardt's etching *Kriegserinnerung (Schnapsschenke)* (1920), ibid., no. 106, illus. p. 39. The two works are comparable stylistically as well, although in their motifs they share only this soldier in profile.

150 Jakob Steinhardt
Couple at a Table (Paar am Tisch), c. 1920?

Pencil, charcoal on toned paper
29 x 21.8 cm (11^7/$_{16}$ x 8^5/$_8$ in.)
Signed, dated, and inscribed l. l.
"Herrn Cohop/von Jakob Steinhardt/Mai 1920"

Provenance: Karl und Faber, Munich.

In an insightful and highly informative essay written in 1928 on Jews in art, the Jewish critic Karl Schwarz described the world of Jakob Steinhardt as one "saturated with a melancholy magic." In Steinhardt's images, Schwarz observed,

> [T]he Jew is represented in the insurmountable confines of his ghetto existence. His figures bear the marks of their fate. The artist depicts their silently plaintive complaint, their sorrow, their despair, and their religious ecstasy, and often he causes us to shudder before his visionary fantasies.[1]

In a similar manner, Steinhardt himself defined the world he represented in his work around 1920 as having its foundation in his wartime experience of Jewish ghettoes:

> In 1915, I was a soldier in Lithuania; there I came to know the Jewish people: their small towns, the grayness of their quotidian life, their sufferings, their fervent, impassioned prayers, their sacred sabbaths, their old men, mature men, and sons who, removed from the times and their events, investigate the word of God and patiently await their great mission. These people moved me as nothing previously had, to the very

depths of my being. All my works from that day to this have been produced under the impression of this experience.[2]

Thus, a melancholic deprivation characterizes Steinhardt's images of this time, reflecting the patient suffering of his people and his own testimony to their silent bravery.

Whether overtly Jewish or not, the couple in this drawing partakes of the overwhelming despondency dominant in Steinhardt's surviving scenes of Lithuanian Jewish life, most rendered during the time he spent in Zerkow recovering from a nervous breakdown. With their elongated forms defined in languid curves and suggesting the haggard appearance of hunger and starvation, the woman and elderly man sit at a table before a small bowl and a wine bottle. Deep shadows and remnants of Cubist faceting heighten the darkness of the emotive ambience.

But an unusual touch of the erotic, lacking in Steinhardt's work since the beginning of World War I, also emerges in this work. The woman is nude, her bare breasts accented in the center of the image as she bends towards the man, who appears, however, to be oblivious to her presence. Posed in an active diagonal, turning as she appears to enter the drawing from the left, she injects a sense of movement into the otherwise passive composition, and provides a contrast to the man's lethargic posture and demeanor.

The work may relate to changes in Steinhardt's life around 1920, after his recuperation in Zerkow. When he returned to Berlin, the artist received commissions for illustrations to several books by Jewish authors and for a Haggadah; Fritz Gurlitt also published Steinhardt's portfolios of woodcuts and lithographs devoted to aspects of Jewish life. Through Gurlitt, Steinhardt met Minni Gumpert, who introduced him to Berlin society, joined him in cafés, and otherwise significantly transformed his melancholic, vagabond life. Slowly he broke out of the dejection that had marked him since the war. Set at the small round table of a café, this scene may then be representative of Gumpert's entry into Steinhardt's life, to present her gently erotic vitality as counterforce to his pessimism and gloom.

R. H.

1. ". . . in schwermütige Magie getaucht, den Juden in unüberwindbaren Grenzen seines Galutdaseins erschaut. Seine Gestalten tragen ein Verhängnis. Der Künstler malt die stille Klage, die Trauer, die Verzweiflung und die religiöse Ekstase und lässt uns vor seinen visionären Gesichten oftmals erschauern." Karl Schwarz, *Die Juden in der Kunst* (Berlin: Fritz Gurlitt Verlag, 1928), 129.
2. "1915 war ich Soldat in Litauen; dort lernte ich das jüdische Volk kennen: Seine Städtchen, seinen grauen Alltag, seine Leiden, seine inbrünstigen, leidenschaftlichen Gebete, seine heiligen Sabbate, seine Greise, Männer und Söhne, die, weitab von Zeit und Geschehnissen, das Wort Gottes erforschen und geduldig ihrer grossen Mission harrten. Diese Menschen haben mich, wie nie etwas zuvor, bis ins Innerste ergriffen. Unter dem Eindruck dieses Erlebnisses sind alle meine Arbeiten von jener Zeit an bis auf

den heutigen Tag entstanden." Jakob Steinhardt, in *Das Graphische Jahr* (Berlin: Verlag Fritz Gurlitt, 1921), 53.

151 Jakob Steinhardt
Plague (Seuche), c. 1922-23?

Pen and ink, ink wash on paper
42 x 50 cm (16^1/$_2$ x 19^{11}/$_{16}$ in.)
Signed l. r. "J. Steinhardt"

Provenance: Gordon Gallery, Tel Aviv.

Among the major German artists of the prewar and Weimar years, Jakob Steinhardt, along with Ludwig Meidner and Jakob Hirsch, identified with, and celebrated, more than any others their Jewishness. Jewish motifs appear early in Steinhardt's work; at the 1912 premiere of *Die Pathetiker* at Herwarth Walden's *Der Sturm* gallery, his works concentrated on biblical scenes, such as The Dance around the Golden Calf, or depictions—in two paintings, an engraving, and a drawing—of the prophet Jeremiah. Similar subjects dominated Steinhardt's imagery until he entered the armed forces after the outbreak of war in 1914. It was the experience, in Eastern Europe during the war, of Jewish communities in small Lithuanian towns that brought full identification with his Jewish heritage, as he recorded in his diary:

> During cold dark days, our regiment marches into Lithuania. A long country road, filthy snow. Just before a small town, we came to a halt, exhausted and thirsty. Near the road, I see a small ramshackle wooden house, drag myself inside to let myself be given something to drink. A half-dark room. An old woman sits hiding in a corner and next to her a girl at a sewing machine. Where have I seen this old woman before? She wears a wig like the one my great-grandmother wears in a picture hanging in our home in Zerkow. I never saw this woman in my life—and yet I know her, this old Jewish mother, and she knows me and gives me tea and from a hiding place she gets some little cakes, and we speak like old, old acquaintances and in this poor small room I feel as if I were at home.
>
> Soon I was lying in the trenches of the Eastern front. There hunger and cold and death reigned.[1]

A member of the victorious German army, Steinhardt enters the unpromising home of an impoverished citizen in an occupied country, and there finds an identity that, contrary to all expectations, links directly with his own home and ancestry. The small household of an indigent Lithuanian Jew embraces him and brings the comfort of a known heritage, while the experience in his own nation's military among the comrades of his regiment is one of alienation and death. The hunger, cold, and death he encounters in the trenches are not only those of warfare, but more fundamentally existential. His primary identity, the contentment of belonging and sharing, is not with the field-gray uniforms of the Kaiser's army, but with the Jewish woman whose home he invaded, and where he was welcomed and food was shared with him as member of a family with a common heritage, religion, and values.

After recovering from the effects of war, and having become an advocate of Zionism, Steinhardt translated his witness to the lives, historical experience, and mores of Lithuania's unassimilated Jews into artistic imagery. In portfolios of etchings and woodcuts, he depicted motifs from Lithuanian Jewish life, both present and past. From this repertoire derives the bearded patriarch wearing timeless caftan-like clothing and highlighted amid the dark ambience of this drawing. Collapsed within a mass of other tortured figures, their mouths open in screams, their eyes and arms raised to implore heaven for deliverance, he embraces and shelters a small child who clings desperately to his body in a trusting, doomed search for protection. A Jewish community is here threatened with annihilation, as such communities had been throughout history in pogroms, wars, and plagues. The aged as well as the newborn are submitted to an unseen but overpowering threat hidden within the enveloping darkness to bring anxiety, despair, and death.

At the 1912 *Pathetiker* exhibition, Steinhardt displayed several images of apocalypse and universal destruction, thematically similar to Meidner's works in the same exhibition. During the next year, to these motifs of chiliastic disaster Steinhardt added Last Judgments and floods, but also pogroms in which Eastern European onion-domed buildings line streets where bearded, defenseless Jewish men are surprised, trapped, and beaten by shapeless mobs brandishing clubs and swords while swilling courage for their attack from raised bottles. The hundreds of Russian pogroms at the time of the 1905 revolution form the context of these images within Steinhardt's inventory of apocalyptic themes prior to World War I; after the war, as he concentrated more directly on representations of the Jewish experience, he surprisingly did not resume his depiction of pogroms, nor is violence against Jews an aspect of his rendered war memories.

After 1918, repression and subsistence-level existence shape Steinhardt's images of Jewish life, but mass death is brought by starvation and epidemics, not by pogroms. Perhaps—and ironically, in view of new guarantees of freedom in the Weimar constitution and the vocal rejection of anti-Semitism in Lenin's revolutionary Russia—Steinhardt considered pogroms a scourge of the past, not of the present or future; plagues and starvation, however, decimated vast portions of Eastern and Central Europe's population, both Jewish and gentile, after World War I, and were a significantly greater problem for the small Jewish communities there.

This drawing of Jewish death has previously been identified as a pogrom, but such a reading is indefensible in the context of Steinhardt's work of the early 1920s. Stylistically close to his graphics of Jewish life published in 1922, the drawing also relates thematically to their depictions of plagues. No attacking mobs are present, nor other signs of external violence. Instead, it is darkness that encompasses the mountain of humanity and destroys the fading light of life that plays around them. As they collapse in emaciated weakness and terror, their fleshless faces do not so much scream out as gasp desperately for breath, hands clutched to their throats. Viewed more than fifty years after its production, Steinhardt's *Plague* gains a new terror. Not an image provoking condemnation of past pogroms, its depersonalized mass of Jews gasping for breath today necessarily recalls Nazi gas chambers, so much more effective in the annihilation of Jewish life and culture in German-occupied Eastern Europe than pogroms had ever been.　　　　　　　　　　R. H.

1. "In kalten dunklen Tagen marschiert unser Regiment in Litauen ein. Eine lange Landstrasse, kotiger Schnee. Kurz vor einem Städtchen rasteten wir, ermüdet und verdurstet. Ich sehe am Wege ein armseliges Holzhäuschen, schleppe mich hinein, um mir ein Getränk geben zu lassen. Ein halbdunkler Raum. In einer Ecke versteckt sitzen eine alte Frau und daneben ein Mädchen an einer Nähmaschine. Woher kenne ich die alte Frau? Sie trägt eine Perücke, wie meine Urgrossmutter, deren Bild in Zerkow in unserer Wohnung hängt. Ich habe diese Frau nie in meinem Leben gesehen—und doch kenne ich sie, diese alte jüdische Mutter, und sie kennt mich und gibt mir Tee und holt aus einem Versteck ein paar kleine Küchelchen, und wir sprechen wie alte, uralte Bekannte, und ich fühle mich in diesem armen Stübchen wie zu Hause.

"Bald lag ich im Schützengraben an der Ostfront. Dort war Hunger und Kälte und Tod." Jacob Steinhardt, undated diary entry cited in *Jakob Steinhardt: Das graphische Werk*, ed. Stefan Behrens (West Berlin: Kunstamt Wedding, 1987), 10.

152　**Georg Tappert**
Woman with Monkey (Reclining Nude with Baboon) (Frau mit Affen [Liegender Akt mit Pavian]), c. 1913

Oil on canvas
60 x 67.5 cm (23⅝ x 26½ in.)
Signed u. r. "Tappert"; signed verso "Tappert" and "Tappert"; signed and inscribed on stretcher, "Tappert/Frau mit Affen"
Wietek 136

Provenance: Estate of the artist; Ernest Raboff Gallery, Los Angeles; Mr. and Mrs. Fred Bartman, Los Angeles; Sotheby Park-Bernet, New York.

Exhibitions: New York, Hutton Galleries, *German Expressionism,* 9–23 May 1964; West Berlin, Berlinische Galerie, *Georg Tappert: Ein Berliner Expressionist 1880 bis 1957,* 28 November 1980–25 January 1981, cat. no. 11 (dated 1911).

As if it were an Expressionist revision of Edouard Manet's *Olympia* (1863), Georg Tappert's *Woman with Monkey* presents a reclining nude in an interior in the company, not of a cat, but of a baboon. In its overt reference to modern art's ancestry, Tappert's painting indicates both his artistic ambitions and the attitudes towards women perpetuated in the odalisque. If Manet's *Olympia* displayed sexual aggression in somewhat comic form, as T. J. Clark has argued,[1] Tappert has done likewise, but with the empathic posture of Expressionism informed by contemporary German perceptions of female sexuality. In *Woman with Monkey,* Tappert replaces the Parisian boudoir with a generic "tropical" setting. His nude gazes at the viewer with dark eyes—her face is otherwise without detail except for the shadow of a nose and the red smear of a mouth—while she raises and crosses her legs to hide her sex but also to reveal her vulnerability. A descendant of Paul Gauguin's Tahitians, she is surrounded by motifs of verdant foliage and red flora, and shaded by a voluminous brown canopy which opens onto a brief expanse of blue suggesting water or sky.

Tappert constructs a vision of exotic feminine voluptuousness as brown skinned, red nippled, black haired, continuing in the nude's green-shadowed body the coloristic crescendo of her ambience. Browns, reds, blues, and greens visually generate the warmth of a tropical atmosphere and supplant the subtle white harmonies in which Manet indulged. The scene, however, is a studio conceit. The canopy and brightly patterned blanket emulate those set up by *Brücke* artists in their studios as a celebration and approximation of "primitive" life and of nature.[2] The baboon with his red, moon-shaped posterior functions as part of this pseudo-African world of Expressionist decor, but also as an attribute of his mistress. A commentary in the manner of late nineteenth- and early twentieth-century images that found humor or coyness in the suggestive juxtaposition of naked women and animals,[3] Tappert's baboon assigns to the nude, by implication, the sexual promiscuity traditionally associated with monkeys,[4]

Within this signifying setting, Tappert posed the model, today known only as "Betty," to whom he devoted a series of frankly sensual paintings, drawings, and prints during 1912 and 1913. In a 1913 lithograph, *Two Female Nudes (Zwei Frauenakte),*[5] Tappert rendered Betty twice, reclining in a corner of the studio; in one of her dual manifestations, she assumes a pose similar to—and most likely the source of—the pose of *Woman with Monkey,* propped against a cushion and lying on the patterned blanket or rug that also appears in the painting. The Oceanic queen who confronts us in *Woman with Monkey* has thus been conjured forth, not from ethnographic sources, but through filtered artistic interpretations of voyeuristic encounters—in Manet, Gauguin, *Brücke* artists, and Tappert's own depictions of Betty.

The exhibitionist and perpetually receptive nude Tappert and other Expressionists envisioned is one element in a primitivizing project. Rehearsing the arguments of Jean-Jacques Rousseau and the Romantics, Expressionists imagined a purer, more natural existence among the natives of Africa and the South Pacific, to which capitalist, industrialized Europe was perceived as the unhealthy antithesis. Max Pechstein, on his way to the German Pacific colony of Palau, promised a concerned colonial official "not to destroy [the natives'] habits derived from nature with the vacuity of Europe," and assured him that he "yearned for Palau with . . . feelings of respect for the anticipated, unsullied unity of nature and human beings."[6] Primitive existence in nature was to the civilized European an absolute Other, something to be yearned for and which could be restored, as Pechstein discovered in the South Seas:

Since I myself grew up among simple people and with nature, I have no difficulty in establishing a kinship with this abundance of new impressions. I need not adjust much. What I received in Dresden, Italy, France, and Berlin in terms of the experience of culture reveals itself as what it was in truth all the time: as superficial frill to be doffed effortlessly. From within myself leaps forth with uninhibited joy the boy of old, as whom I entered into friendship with animals and flowers, with fields and streams, and lived with no difficulty among fishermen, farmers, and workers. From a most profound feeling of human community, I could approach the South Sea islanders fraternally.[7]

Pechstein's recollections typify the conviction that, once returned to a more natural, more innocent life, humanity would be transformed, and a renewed sense of community would supplant existing animosities. Nature, like the primitive with which it was identified, was a value concept. Available to the Expressionists as a symbol of this Other was a reified notion of woman as allied to ". . . the world of nature and natural processes, particularly sexuality and reproduction."[8] In confronting the (male) viewer and celebrating her nakedness while the baboon proclaims her sexuality, Tappert's nude accents her otherness, her existence as antithesis to the superficial, cerebrally ordered world of men. She offers, instead, a return to nature, to an essential existence in which struggles of the ego dissolve in passionate community.　B. T. Y. / R. H.

1. Concerning *Olympia,* see T. J. Clark, *The Painting of Modern Life: Paris in the Art of Manet and his Followers* (New York: Alfred A. Knopf, 1985), and Werner Hofmann, *Nana,* 2d rev. ed. (Cologne: Du Mont Buchverlag, 1974).
2. The possibility that this may be one of the *Brücke* studios cannot be dismissed. Tappert's close association with *Brücke* is concentrated in the initial years of the New Secession and the Jury-Free Art Show, 1910–13.
3. Perhaps the best known of these are the prints of Edvard Munch's lithograph series *Alpha and Omega* (1908–09), which narrates Omega's infidelity to Alpha by means of a variety of animals ranging from stags and bears to snakes and pigs. For a very incomplete, obsessive, and sententious anthology of such woman-animal confrontations, see Bram Dijkstra, *Idols of Perversity: Fantasies of Feminine Evil in Fin-de-Siècle Culture* (New York and Oxford: Oxford University Press, 1986), 289ff.
4. The most extensive discussion of simian iconography, which does not extend into

the twentieth century, however, is Horst W. Janson, *Apes and Ape Lore in the Middle Ages and the Renaissance*, Studies of the Warburg Institute, vol. 20 (London: Warburg Institute, University of London, 1952).

5. A signed and dated impression of the lithograph was included in the retrospective exhibition *Georg Tappert 1880–1957* (West Berlin: Akademie der Künste, 1961), 20 (illus.), cat. no. 72. One of few works dated by Tappert, it provides a date by association for the painting, which displays similar stylistic characteristics. Tappert translated *Woman with Monkey* into a lithograph apparently printed in 1914 (although, failing concrete evidence, 1913 would also seem to be a possible date), which provides a *terminus ante quem*. Tappert habitually created graphic versions of his painted compositions at roughly the same time as the paintings, and there is no compelling reason to believe that in this case he translated a painting some three years old. Since in the lithograph the nude has also been identified as Betty, who posed for Tappert during 1912 and 1913 this, too, would indicate a date of c. 1913 for the painting. Gerhard Wietek, *Georg Tappert 1880–1957: Ein Wegbereiter der Deutschen Moderne* (Munich: Karl Thiemig, 1980), "Werkverzeichnis der Gemälde," cat. no. 136, notes incorrectly that the date "[19]11" follows Tappert's signature on the painting. In fact, the painting is not dated, and stylistically as well as thematically should be grouped with other works of 1913.

6. "…ihre naturgebundenen Gewohnheiten nicht durch europäische Nichtigkeiten zu zerstören … mit … Gefühlen der Achtung für die zu erwartende, unentweihte Einheit von Natur und Mensch nach Palau sehnte." Max Pechstein, *Erinnerungen*, ed. Leopold Reidemeister (Wiesbaden: Limes, 1960), 55.

7. "Selbst unter einfachen Menschen und mit der Natur aufgewachsen, finde ich unschwer ein Verhältnis zu dieser Fülle neuer Eindrücke. Ich muss mich nicht allzusehr umstellen. Was mir Dresden, Italien, Frankreich und Berlin an Kulturerfahrung gebracht haben, erweist sich als das, was es in Wahrheit gewesen ist: als äusserer Behang, der mühelos abgeschüttelt wird. Aus mir selbst springt mit froher Unbefangenheit der Junge heraus, als der ich mit Tieren und Blumen, mit Ackern und Wasserläufen Freundschaft geschlossen habe und ohne Mühe mit Fischern, Bauern und Arbeitern lebte. Aus tiefstem Gefühl der Menschengemeinschaft konnte ich mich den Südseeinsulanern brüderlich nähern." Ibid., 78.

8. Barbara D. Wright, "'New Man,' Eternal Woman: Expressionist Responses to German Feminism," *German Quarterly* (Fall 1987): 588.

---

153 Georg Tappert
Woman in a Café (A Cup of Hot Chocolate) (Dame im Café [Eine Tasse Schokolade]), c. 1917

Oil on canvas
82 x 76 cm (32¼ x 29¹⁵/₁₆ in.)
Signed u. l. "Tappert"
Wietek 174

Provenance: Estate of the artist; Galeria Conkright, Caracas; private collection.

Exhibitions: West Berlin, Grosse Berliner Kunstausstellung, *Georg Tappert: Gedächtnisschau*, 1958; Kassel, Kunstverein, *Georg Tappert: Gedächtnisausstellung*, 1959; Fulda, Stadtschule, *Berliner Künstler: Fritsch—Luckner—Tappert*, 1960; West Berlin, Akademie der Kunst, *Georg Tappert 1880–1957: Gedächtnis-Ausstellung*, 1961; New York, Leonard Hutton Galleries, *A Retrospective Exhibition of Paintings by Georg Tappert*, 22 April–16 May 1964, cat. no. 17 (as *At the Tea Room* and dated 1911); Los Angeles, Ernest Raboff Gallery, *Georg Tappert*, 1965; Caracas, Galeria Conkright, *German Expressionist Painting*, 1966; Rome, Villa Massimo, 1984; Milwaukee, Patrick and Beatrice Haggerty Museum of Art, Marquette University, *A Focus on Images: Sense and Form*, 9 November 1984–1 June 1985; West Berlin, Berlinische Galerie, Museum für Moderne Kunst, Photographie und Architektur im Martin-Gropius-Bau, *Ich und die Stadt: Mensch und Grossstadt in der deutschen Kunst des 20. Jahrhunderts*, 15 August–22 November 1987, cat. no. 197; Los Angeles County Museum of Art, *German Expressionism 1915–1925: The Second Generation*, 9 October–31 December 1988 (traveled to Fort Worth Art Museum, 2 February–9 April 1989; Kunstmuseum Düsseldorf, 18 May–9 July 1989; Halle, Staatliche Galerie Moritzburg, 9 August–30 September 1989), cat. no. 189.

For Expressionists as well as for their Impressionist, Naturalist, and *Jugendstil* predecessors, the café held connotations that ranged from bourgeois self-satisfaction and complacency to countercultural bohemian revolt.[1] Georg Tappert's *Woman in a Café*, arguably his most frequently reproduced and exhibited painting, is commonly cited as exemplary of Expressionist representations of Berlin's café society.[2] Although tantalizingly suited to such perceived historical patterns, this reading of Tappert's image of a fashionable blond seated at a table with a cup of hot chocolate before her is beset with problems that demand a reevaluation of the painting's dating and signification.

Despite the tendency to regard *Woman in a Café* as paradigmatic of Tappert's work, the painting in many ways is atypical of his art. The stylistic vocabulary in its totality appears in none of his other paintings, although components of it do. Most characteristic of *Woman in a Café* are the systematic, if modified, Cubo-Futurist faceting of the major forms, the single dominant color, precise contours, and rigidly symmetrical composition. A cluster of images from 1916 through 1919, displaying the mixed faceting technique, suggests that *Woman in a Café* derives from this time as well; but these paintings exhibit looser brushwork and more fluidly defined forms, less static and hierarchic compositions, and a varied palette. Without any stylistic parallel, comparative dating of *Woman in a Café* becomes almost arbitrary within this three-year period.[3] The painting is bracketed, on the one hand, by the beginnings in 1916 of the artist's use of Cubo-Futurist elements in compositions retaining a degree of illusionism and, on the other, by the point in 1919 when the faceting subsumes the image to a degree verging on abstraction.

The motif of a café interior is likewise unique among the paintings of these years, and, indeed, is relatively rare in Tappert's entire oeuvre. Compositionally and thematically closest to

Woman in a Café is *Maruschka* of 1910 (Wietek 126), which shows a woman in profile seated at a café table, but its quasi-Impressionist style otherwise fails to relate to the later painting at all.[4] External evidence as to the date of *Woman in a Café* is also lacking. The earliest record of its exhibition, according to Gerhard Wietek, principal cataloguer of Tappert's work, is the memorial exhibition in Berlin in 1958. Although Tappert made a linocut repeating the painting's composition in reverse, no dated impressions of the print are currently known; he did not publish it or its reproduction in the several periodicals to which he regularly contributed from 1916 to 1920. Neither exhibition history nor the linocut are of aid in providing an accurate *terminus ante quem* for the painting.

Woman in a Café is a product of the last years of World War I, this much alone is certain. This temporal framework significantly separates the painting from other Expressionist café scenes produced during the relative prosperity of peacetime existence before 1914. For Tappert's image of a woman seated with her cup of chocolate amid the café's vermilion ambience, which extends even to the large plants echoing one another on either side of her, the context of wartime Berlin is a determinant that must be considered in a reconstruction of its meaning.

Tappert spent the last years of World War I stationed in Berlin and was able to live in his own home. After a hiatus caused by his first year of military service, he resumed painting. In contrast to virtually every other German artist, he never introduced scenes of military life, warfare, or its effects into his imagery, except in a few portraits of friends in uniform. He depicted a world of civilian life, especially of variety singers and dancers, that proffers a false reality of escape. Although she is not part of the sphere of sideshows otherwise favored by Tappert, the elegant woman in a café is an extension of their world of make-believe. She, too, exists in a fantasy divorced from contemporary events, echoing and extending prewar habits and circumstances. The reality of muddy trenches, barbed wire, machine guns, grenades, and millions of deaths does not intrude into the vermilion warmth of her café, with its marble-topped tables, silver trays, and china.

The civilian world of late wartime Berlin is also denied, its unheated homes and worn-out clothing, rampant hunger, striking workers, and wounded soldiers. The German chronicler Oskar Maria Graf described the bleak aspects of those years, so removed from Tappert's sumptuous depiction:

Almost every woman worked in the war industry, the men were in the army, and the children were left to their own devices. Food was severely rationed. And for every piece of clothing, for shoes, wood, coal, oil, and cooking alcohol, rationing coupons were needed. A wild black market in all these things emerged. The rich, who could pay any price, did not suffer. The poor slowly wasted away.[5]

Such conditions are conspicuously absent from Tappert's painting. As *Woman in a Café* denies the very existence of war, moreover, it might likewise be seen to reject contemporary events in art. Genre paintings of this sort, especially of civilian life in an urban setting, were rare at the time; café scenes such as Impressionists and Expressionists favored before 1914 had disappeared almost entirely from the repertoire of German artists.

Although signature and degree of finish indicate that Tappert considered *Woman in a Café* a completed work, he did not, so far as we know, exhibit the painting during his lifetime, despite numerous opportunities to do so. Had it been included, at the time of its creation, in any of the various artist-organized or government-sponsored exhibitions, *Woman in a Café* would have been surrounded by works focusing on war and its effects, or by landscapes and portraits, many with patriotic connotations. With its mannered amalgamation of Cubist, Futurist, and Expressionist elements—a fusion of the most "avant-garde" styles of the time, two of them imported from countries then at war with the German Empire—and its strident red coloration, Tappert's painting would surely have appeared an anomaly or anachronism.

Once identified as an image that rejected Germany's dominant artistic concerns while emulating non-traditional styles, how is *Woman in a Café* to be read? In it, Tappert eschews both the idealized realism and patriotic content of officially sanctioned art as well as the overt anti-war posture assumed among many non-traditional artists. With his subjects almost totally limited, except for the portraits, to entertainers and nudes, he created an inventory of representations fundamentally timeless in nature and proven by the "masters" of past art, dedicated to the principle of art's existence for posterity, not as a mirror of temporality. Within the neutrality of a genre motif, it could be argued then, *Woman in a Café* defended art against efforts to enchain it in functional didacticism.

This conclusion, however, demands significant modification, if not absolute rejection. Although Franz Pfemfert, editor of *Die Aktion* (*Action*), dedicated a collection of Gottfried Benn's poems in 1917 with the words "To my unpolitical Georg Tappert,"[6] Tappert was far from politically neutral, nor did he reject the possibility of art serving political ends. In an impassioned letter to Pfemfert on 20 November 1918, Tappert argued that non-naturalistic art failed to find resonance among the Marxist proletariat and for that reason was inappropriate as a tool of mass political action. Instead, he favored support of "an already firmly definable circle of international intellectuals, organizing a human society built on socialist foundations."[7] The external control of artistic expression was what Tappert rejected, not the employment of art in the struggle to give form to a new society. "We want to impart to the future our form of expression," he wrote, "but must not let that form be imposed on us by some functionary in the party or by the masses."[8] During the war and the November Revolution, he consistently presented his work within such activist, politically radical forums as Pfemfert's *Die Aktion* and the Dresden Secession Group's *Menschen* (*People*).

In 1918, Tappert also participated in the Mannheim exhibition *Neue religiöse Kunst* (*New Religious Art*), which provided institutional recognition to late wartime religious images paralleling poets' prophecies of a New Age and a New Human Being, an era when human kinship would replace national and capitalist competitiveness and belligerence. Such spiritual aspirations were apparent in Tappert's art for Gerhard Ausleger, Tappert's fellow editor at *Die Schöne Rarität* (*Beautiful Rarity*), who proclaimed that his friend's work represented:

> Dissolution in heaven and pain of being bound to earth, dual fate of humanity, grasped in singular intensity by implacable line; using form, the remarkable activity of true artists, to indicate old snares and pronounce the new path to the community of love: therein lies the significance of Georg Tappert's graphic work.[9]

Woman in a Café does not function overtly in such pronouncements of a reformed humanity, but it is nonetheless a painting that resonates in the milieu of late wartime Germany's activist artists. What is missing from *Woman in a Café* needs to be remembered to reconstitute this resonance. The environment of wartime deprivation receives no recognition in Tappert's painting as its opposite is presented—leisure, luxurious surroundings, fashionable clothing, and imported chocolate. *Woman in a Café* might have recalled pre-1914 prosperity, but it served even more as a vociferous contrast to life as experienced then by the majority of the German population. It was an image of ostentatious material display and consumption in the midst of war's material need, of hot chocolate served on silver trays rather than of substitute coffee brewed from acorns.

Seated in an interior where plants and skin tones submit to the inexorable artifice and orchestration of vermilion surroundings, Tappert's woman proudly lifts her head, dramatically to display her profile. *Hauteur* motivates the pose, which also permits Tappert to exaggerate nose and chin, to move the image towards caricature and away from portraiture or genre. There is in Expressionism's emphasis on subjectivity and exaggeration a danger of transforming all likeness into caricature; however, in Tappert's carefully crafted image the distortions appear less subjective, more a conscious manipulation of features to permit ridicule to enter this spectacle of *haute couture*, jewelry, makeup, and a coiffure of tight ringlets.

Perhaps, too, the deliberate amalgam of contemporary art styles devised by Tappert is an extension of his play on gaudy fashion, now proffering commentary on aspects of late Expressionist painting as well as on the art consumers already precipitously driving up the prices of works from the estates of Franz Marc and August Macke. Ironically predicting the stylistic effects of Art Deco that would appear during the 1920s, Tappert's *Woman in a Café* could

be read during the war's last two years as a parody not only of conspicuous consumption of rare food and clothing, but also of the turbulent rush after stylistic novelty among German artists and their patrons.

The context that permits such an interpretation of Tappert's painting was short-lived. In 1918, the Russian capitulation and the Treaty of Brest-Litovsk, the German spring offensive and its failure, the November Revolution, and the cease-fire significantly undermined the capacity of *Woman in a Café* to function as a relevant commentary on contemporary mores. The transformation of the image into a representative of Expressionist café scenes, as it is (as is nostalgically) seen today, had begun. Tappert chose not to exhibit the painting. R. H.

1. See cat. nos. 64 and 80.
2. See, for example, Eberhard Roters's catalogue entry in Roters and Bernhard Schulz, eds., *Ich und die Stadt: Mensch und Grosstadt in der deutschen Kunst des 20. Jahrhunderts* (West Berlin: Nicolaische Verlagsbuchhandlung Beuermann, 1987), 114. Significantly, Roters groups the painting among Expressionist works of 1911–13, outside its proper chronological context.
3. The standard catalogue of Tappert's paintings, contained in Gerhard Wietek, *Georg Tappert 1880–1957: Ein Wegbereiter der Deutschen Moderne* (Munich: Karl Thiemig, 1980), indicates that the dating of most paintings created after 1914 lacks documentation from the artist and is therefore determined relatively according to constructed temporal groupings, although photographs of works with dating indicated on the photographs by Tappert were also used. None of the entries provides indication as to the source of the dates provided, whether it be subjective stylistic grouping or external documentation.
4. Also compare the two versions of *Die Loge*, in which a woman appears similarly in profile, with her features silhouetted against a large, dark round hat. Wietek's listing identifies the major concentration of café interiors in Tappert's work as c. 1928 (Wietek 286–289).
5. "Fast jede Frau arbeitete in einem Kriegsbetrieb, die Männer standen im Feld, und die Kinder blieben sich selbst überlassen. Die Lebensmittel waren streng rationiert. Auch für jedes Kleidungsstück, für Schuhe, Holz, Kohle, Petroleum, und Spiritus brauchte man Bezugsscheine. Ein wilder Schleichhandel mit alledem kam auf. Die Reichen, die jeden Preis bezahlen konnten, litten nicht. Die Armen siechten langsam dahin." Oskar Maria Graf, *Das Leben meiner Mutter* (New York, 1940; reprint, Munich: Süddeutscher Verlag, 1978), 435.
6. "Meinem unpolitischen Georg Tappert." Franz Pfemfert, as cited by Wietek, *Georg Tappert*, 46.
7. ". . . den schon heute fest zu umschreibenden Kreis der internationalen Intellektuellen, organisieren eine menschliche Gemeinschaft, die auf sozialistischem Boden stehend. . . ." Georg Tappert, as cited ibid., 50.
8. "Wir wollen dem, was werden soll, unsere Ausdrucksform aufprägen, uns diese aber nicht von irgend welchem Parteigewaltigen oder der Masse aufzwingen lassen." Ibid.
9. "Verschollenheit im Himmel und Leid des Erdverhafteten, Zwie-Geschick des Menschenseins, erfasst in einmaliger Dringlichkeit unverrückbarer Linie; aus

Form, ungeheuerlicher Aktivität der wahrhaften Künstler, alte Verklammerungen weisend und möglichen Weg sagend zur Gemeinschaft der Liebe: ist Bedeutung des graphischen Werkes Georg Tapperts." Gerhard Ausleger, "Der Graphiker Georg Tappert," *Die schöne Rarität* 2, no. 12 (1918/19), reprinted in *Schrei in die Welt: Expressionismus in Dresden*, ed. Peter Ludewig (East Berlin: Verlag Der Morgen, 1988), 65.

---

154 Georg Tappert
Waiting (Erwartung), c. 1927

Pen and ink on parchment
31 x 24 cm (12³/₁₆ x 9¹/₂ in.)
Signed l. l. "Tappert"; inscribed and signed on matting l. l. "Erwartung", l. r. "G. Tappert"

Provenance: Galerie Rolf Ohse, Bremen; Karl und Faber, Munich.

In 1916, Franz Pfemfert devoted an issue of *Die Aktion* to the Alsatian Expressionist writer Heinrich Schaefer and to drawings and woodcuts by Georg Tappert.[1] Two of the drawings, essentially small vignettes, inaugurated the series *Dunkel Winkel*, in which Tappert depicted various frequenters of Berlin's "dark corners"—hotel maids and waitresses, prostitutes and their pimps. *Waiting* continues the artist's treatment of these motifs some ten years later, but with greater attention to milieu and in a simplified linear style, which ironically places renewed emphasis on volume after Tappert's faceting, Cubo-Futurist experiments of the late teens.

The image is of three buxom women at the doorway to a restaurant. The two large women in the foreground, standing casually with their hands in their pockets or behind their backs, wear common clothes—smock, skirt, and short-sleeved sweater—and show heavy legs with feet stuffed uncomfortably into tight high-heeled shoes. They look out of the drawing as if anticipating someone's arrival, as the title also suggests. Framed by the doorway, the third woman wears a fashionably short, pleated skirt, hip-length jacket, and hat;[2] in her left hand, she flaunts a cigarette.

Tappert's title makes apparent that the women are prostitutes. Plays on the words "Erwartung" (anticipation, waiting) and "Bereitschaft" (preparedness, readiness, on call) abound in captions to popular semi-erotic illustrations of the 1920s representing aspects of prostitutes' lives, usually with a degree of heavy-handed but effective coyness and salacious humor similar to Tappert's exaggeration of breast size.[3] Age differences are often implied or explicit in such imagery, with older, misshapen prostitutes now retired from their trade (and at times accompanied by their children) overseeing thinner, more fashionable young women or seeking customers for them.

The scene of three women independently plying their erotic trade, linked neither to a brothel nor to a male pimp, demonstrates the altered situation of prostitutes in Germany towards the end

of the 1920s. Brothels were outlawed in 1927 (although technically they had been illegal in Prussia since 1871), but prostitution itself ceased to be considered officially illegal. Even before these developments, the number of brothels had declined in what several observers saw as an outcome of women's new social and legal status in the Weimar Republic:

> The dying out of brothels in Germany is not only a result of official measures, but also a consequence of attitudes among the prostitutes themselves in accordance with the developments of the time. The drive towards the independence of women, that emancipation that has also led to a reduction of true pimping, militates against the enslavement which necessarily follows upon entry into a brothel.[4]

Nevertheless, the Law to Combat Venereal Disease did little to counteract the effects of policed registration, through which prostitution received official consent and often forced continuation: removal of one's name from the police list of registered prostitutes (as potential carriers of disease) was virtually impossible.[5] There is no evidence that Tappert intended this drawing to comment on the victimization of women and their entrapment in this system of registration, but his image is indicative of the persistence of prostitution and the unlikelihood of women being able to withdraw from its practice, despite their "emancipation" under the law. B. T. Y.

1. *Die Aktion* 6, nos. 37/38 (16 September 1916).
2. The drawing previously has been dated to c. 1921. The short-skirted costume worn by this figure, however, suggests the fashions of 1926 to 1928.
3. An extensive anthology of such illustrations, international in character, is to be found in Magnus Hirschfeld, ed., *Zwischen zwei Katastrophen*, 2d rev. ed. of *Sittengeschichte der Nachkriegszeit 1918–1930* (Hanau: Verlag Karl Schustek, 1966).
4. "Das Aussterben der Bordelle in Deutschland ist nicht allein eine Auswirkung behördlicher Massnahmen, sondern auch eine Folge der innerlichen, mit der Zeitentwicklung schreitenden Einstellung der Dirnen selbst. Der Drang nach Selbständigkeit der Frau, jene Emanzipation, die auch zu einem Zurückgehen der echten Zuhälterei geführt hat, wehrt sich gegen die Sklaverei, die dem Eintritt in ein Bordell notwendigerweise folgt." G. Lehnert, as cited ibid., 398.
5. See ibid., 399–401, and Elisabeth Meyer-Renschhausen's insightful discussion of M. I. Breme's *Vom Leben getötet* (*Killed by Life*) and responses surrounding its publication in 1926, "The Bremen Morality Scandal," in *When Biology Became Destiny: Women in Weimar and Nazi Germany*, ed. Renate Bridenthal, Atina Grossmann, and Marion Kaplan (New York: Monthly Review Press, 1984), 87ff.

155 Georg Tappert
Woman's Head with a Red Cap
(Kopf mit roter Mütze), c. 1932

Oil on canvas
45 x 35.5 cm (17³/₄ x 14 in.)
Inscribed verso "Kopf mit roter
Mütze"

Provenance: Galerie Bassenge, Berlin.

Georg Tappert's painting presents a woman with short blond hair standing in front of a window or glass-paned door. Dressed in a brown jacket, blouse and tie, red beret and aqua earrings, she typifies the "unisex" look made popular by Marlene Dietrich, which drew the ire of conservatives decrying the emancipation of women, their increasing presence in public life, and their supposed neglect of the traditional responsibilities of "Kinder, Küche, Kirche" (children, kitchen, church). "The 'new woman,'" reports a recent sociological study of women in Weimar and Nazi Germany, "captured the imagination of progressives who celebrated her, even as they sought to discipline and regulate her, and of conservatives who blamed her for everything from the decline of the birth rate and the laxity of morals to the unemployment of male workers."[1]

Tappert's female figure here differs from those in most of his earlier imagery, who appeared primarily as nudes, entertainers, and prostitutes. Typologically, all these function in relationship to men, often impersonally; they are presented to arouse male pleasure. Such sexual reductivism is absent from this image, as is the overt subjectivity previously characteristic of Tappert. Here sexual role-playing and imagined exotic scenarios are replaced by a sense of reportage and observation. Even though he may have known this anonymous woman, the artist depicts her in a manner suggesting an impartial encounter, as if in a snapshot, capturing her in her own milieu as a self-determined person in an informal moment. The thinned oil paint, with its suggestions of fluidity and rapid execution, contributes to this effect, although the closure of the composition, lack of pentimenti, and juxtaposition of complementary colors (red cap against aqua windowpanes) indicate calculated manipulation by the artist. The abdication of subjectivity and the apparent dearth of commentary were certainly inspired by altered fashions in German art, but Tappert conjoins this approach with an alternative view of a woman, one that in its very neutrality implies an empathetic response not obvious in his earlier work.

By 1932, the extreme right's campaign against the Republic and modernity had become focused on three major figures of disdain and vilification: the Jew, the "new woman," and the modernist artist. All three represented degeneracy—racial, moral, and cultural—and were frequently conflated, each sharing the attributes and identity of the other. As Tappert neither glamorizes nor denigrates, but factually documents the mature woman's physiognomy, a testimony to life's experience, he also denies the charges of depravity and implicitly defends her values, those of the Republic, and the effort to shake off the shackles of Germany's authoritarian, Prussian past.

Contained within that is a defense of the artist as well, of his persistent advocacy of a contemporary style and content unimpeded by external control. Tappert's "new woman"—no longer new in the 1930s—is also a self-portrait in a society divided by class and ideology seeing its images in simplified slogans, in caricatures of reified equations.

B. T. Y.

1. "Introduction," *When Biology Became Destiny: Women in Weimar and Nazi Germany*, ed. Renate Bridenthal, Atina Grossmann, and Marion Kaplan (New York: Monthly Review Press, 1984), 13.

156 Georg Tappert
Country Street, Evening Mood
(Landstrasse, Abendstimmung),
1936

Watercolor over pencil on paper
24.8 x 33.5 cm (9³/₄ x 13³/₁₆ in.)
Signed and dated l. r. "Tappert
36"

Provenance: Galerie Wolfgang Ketterer, Munich.

Because of his earlier partisanship in Berlin's New Secession and the Arbeitsrat für Kunst (Work Council for Art), Georg Tappert was commonly associated with modern art during the 1920s. He was also seen as transmitting anti-traditional vocabularies to his students at the Berlin State School of Art. In 1933, as a result of this notoriety, he became one of the first victims of Nazism's antagonism to modern art. Early in February, his class was raided by uniformed Nazi troops and he was dismissed from his post. Alexander Kanoldt, newly appointed director of the School, was able to have Tappert reinstated, but four years later he was dismissed again and his art declared degenerate. During his four-year reprieve, Tappert shifted his focus from figural compositions to landscape, which had played a role in the early years of his career but had become incidental during the teens and twenties. A contemplative scene such as *Country Street, Evening Mood* thus represents a retreat, landscape serving as a politically neutral refuge from repression, although the very act of continuing to create art outside the dictates of the Nazi regime constituted a feeble act of resistance, as it did for other artists of the "Inner Migration."

The flat, simplified trees in *Country Street, Evening Mood* create a pattern of stylized verticals against a broad expanse of muted blues in the manner of mood, or "*Stimmung*," paintings. A single lamp glows yellow in contrast to the somber, dreamlike color scheme, but fails to illuminate the nocturnal landscape. The light that sheds no light, alone in the dusk, duplicates the formula of other mood paintings, but in 1936 also presents an ominous message of encroaching darkness, helpless isolation, and enforced silence. "Because it is silent," Walter Benjamin wrote, "nature grieves."[1] Tappert's scene similarly grieves in its absolute inability to speak. Lacking in precise statements, it represents an effort to avoid any overt mean-

ing other than that associated with contemplation and melancholy.

It is probable that this scene derives from Tappert's painting excursions with his classes to the western outskirts of Berlin. The small format makes the work portable and easily hidden, an image of resignation and despair. Here there is no statement of the heroic struggle, of German man conquering the land, that artists sympathetic to the regime projected in their landscapes. Instead, *Country Street, Evening Mood* echoes the silence of an artist passionate about the necessity and autonomy of art and the freedom to teach and produce art as a sign of the nobility of the human spirit. Adolf Hitler and World War II, however, destroyed this idealist motivation and faith in art for Tappert. Before the war's end, with his paintings declared degenerate and outlawed from public view, his studio in ruins, and no opportunity to teach, Tappert decided never to paint again.

B. T. Y.

1. "Weil sie stumm ist, trauert die Natur." Walter Benjamin, "Über Sprache überhaupt und über die Sprache des Menschens," in *Angelus Novus* (Frankfurt a. M.: Suhrkamp, 1988), 24; trans. Peter Demitz as "On Language as Such and on the Language of Man," in *Reflections: Essays, Aphorisms, Autobiographical Writings* (New York and London: Harcourt, Brace, Jovanovich, 1978), 317.

157 Bruno Voigt
The Boss: Thoughts of a Man Watching an Attractive Woman in a Café (Der Chef: Gedanken eines Mannes, der im Café eine attraktive Frau betrachtet), 1931

Pen, brush, ink over pencil on paper
34.6 x 40.1 cm (13⁵/₈ x 15³/₄ in.)
Monogrammed and dated l. r. "-V-/31"

Provenance: Staatlicher Kunsthandel der DDR, East Berlin.

Exhibitions: Leipzig, Galerie am Sachsenplatz, *Bruno Voigt: Aquarelle, Zeichnungen und Radierungen*, 31 August–28 September 1986, cat. no. 7; Milwaukee, Patrick and Beatrice Haggerty Museum of Art, Marquette University, *Berlin in the 1920s and 1930s: A City of Decadence, Revolt, and Chaos—Watercolors and Drawings of Bruno Voigt*, 11 June–2 August 1987, cat. no. 19.

In *The Boss*, Bruno Voigt presents the voyeuristic fantasies of a male capitalist. Using physiognomic exaggerations such as were commonly thought to signal stupidity, weakness, depravity, and self-indulgence, Voigt shows the Boss with porcine features: a low forehead, receding chin, large fleshy ears, furtively glancing eye, and a neck of layered fat. The jowl-faced Boss smokes a big cigar; his broken veins and bloodshot eyes testify to excessive drinking. Encompassed by projections of his pornographic thoughts, the Boss seems governed by his appetites, by degeneracy and dissipation. Outlining his form heavily so that it dominates the various surrounding sexual vignettes, Voigt at-

tempts to characterize the Boss as exploitive and misogynistic.

The nature of the vignettes indicates that the artist had a specific critique in mind. The sexual activity the Boss imagines as he regards an attractive woman, as the drawing's subtitle informs us, does not involve his own amorous encounter with her, nor does it concern any other active sexual event on his part. The scenes instead concentrate on sexual display, onanism, and implications of erotic interaction between women in the presence of a voyeur, presumably the Boss, since the scenes function within his imagination. In vulgar Marxist terms, it might be argued that, rather than participating in the "labor" of sex, he supervises it and gains satisfaction in the "labor" of others while not contributing to it himself. Voigt thus draws an analogy between the Boss's sexual role and his position in the economic life of society where, as boss, he controls and oversees the labor of others but is alienated from the actual process of production himself and is, in that sense, impotent.

As in his relationship to the workers subordinate to him, who are reified in terms of their labor, the Boss views women here solely as manifestations of their sexual function. Isolated emblems of aroused phalluses and testicles are interspersed among views of women —or, more correctly, fragments of women—dancing naked in chorus lines, displaying genitalia and breasts or buttocks, or engaged in masturbation. Mouths, eyes, legs, a whip, boots and shoes, a fetus proliferate as fetishistic objects. Bottles, glasses, bar and dance hall signage mix with the graffiti-like names of sexual organs. The orchestrated blatancy of women in poses of sexual display suggests the world of Weimar Germany's nude dance reviews, cabarets, and brothels—sexuality commodified and commercialized. Voigt's drawing might therefore be considered a critique of these capitalist establishments and their bourgeois clientele as personified in the Boss.

The number 175, repeated three times along the right side of the drawing, adds a particular focus to Voigt's commentary. Paragraph 175 of Weimar's Criminal Code, taken over from that of Imperial Germany without modification, outlawed homosexuality and bestiality, stating: "Unnatural carnal intercourse between males or between persons and animals is punishable with confinement." The reference to such proscriptions in the context of the Boss's erotic thoughts might imply his own homophobic anxieties. In its most emphatic presence in Voigt's drawing, however, 175 appears in conjunction with the lower torso and hand of a woman masturbating; the number 69, emblem of mutual oral sex, is inscribed like a tatoo on her thigh. The two numbers are associated elsewhere in the drawing as well, suggesting female homosexual relationships rather than the "unnatural carnal intercourse between males" specifically prohibited by paragraph 175.[1] The hieroglyph 69, as employed by Voigt in the Boss's thoughts upon seeing an attractive woman, indicates two women engaged in an act of mutual cunnilingus, with the Boss as implied fascinated witness.

Lesbian lovers caressing appear frequently in pornographic imagery, and male audiences have regularly been offered the spectacle of women engaged in sex in brothels and other locales of erotic entertainment. Voigt's Boss, the voyeuristic aficionado of women's erotic display, covertly resurrects such scenes by means of his conjoined numerical codes as a further item in an inventory of commodified sex available on male demand. Subjugation emerges finally as a hidden motif that links the various fragmented representations of women's sexual organs, limbs, lips, eyes, and disembodied heads. The drawing does figurative violence to women as it dissects and exhibits their isolated body parts; with the word *Mord* (murder) inscribed between the legs of the lower torso immediately beneath the Boss's hand and smoking cigar, the violence becomes a significant part of his sexual fantasies as well. His passive voyeurism only here becomes transformed into activity, in the violence and dismemberment of sex murder.   B. T. Y. / R. H.

1. Significantly, the Criminal Code did not proscribe "unnatural carnal intercourse between females," not because it condoned lesbian relationships, but because women legally lacked sexual identity except in the institutions of marriage (in terms of adultery) and prostitution.

158 Bruno Voigt
Capitalism Has Reached Its Apogee (Der Kapitalismus hat seinen Höhepunkt erreicht), 1932

Watercolor, pen and ink, splatter technique on paper
50 x 32.7 cm (19¹¹/₁₆ x 12⁷/₈ in.)
Monogrammed and dated l. l.
"-V-30.6.32"; inscribed, signed, and dated on matting "Der Kapitalismus hat seinen Höhepunkt erreicht/Bruno Voigt 1932"

Provenance: Staatlicher Kunsthandel der DDR, East Berlin; Neue Münchner Galerie, Munich.

Exhibitions: Munich, Neue Münchner Galerie, *Bruno Voigt: Gemälde, Zeichnungen, Graphik 1930–1948*, November 1983–February 1984; New York, Solomon R. Guggenheim Museum, *German Realist Drawings of the 1920's*, 15 May–6 July 1986 (traveled to Cambridge, Mass., Busch-Reisinger Museum, Harvard University, 26 July–28 September 1986; Graphische Sammlung, Staatsgalerie Stuttgart, 25 October–28 December 1986), cat. no. 120; Milwaukee, Patrick and Beatrice Haggerty Museum of Art, Marquette University, *Berlin in the 1920s and 1930s: A City of Decadence, Revolt, and Chaos—Watercolors and Drawings of Bruno Voigt*, 11 June–2 August 1987, cat. no. 21.

Bruno Voigt renders the subject of class conflict with a degree of specificity often missing in the works of his predecessors. Like many of Voigt's images, *Capitalism Has Reached Its Apogee* parallels a drawing by George Grosz, the January 1920 cover of the periodical *Die Pleite (Bankruptcy)*, also included in

the collected drawings of *The Face of the Ruling Class* (1921).[1] In both works, figures representing capitalism and the military are hanged as symbolic victims of the Communist revolution to which Grosz and Voigt dedicated their work. The differences between the two images correspond to the distinct approaches of their respective artists, both members of the Communist Party of Germany at the time they produced their drawings. By removing the two figures from any particular setting, Grosz abstracts the image so that it functions outside a temporal context. The two figures simply dangle from a wooden gallows, universal types testifying to the depravity of their class, without allusion to their executioners. The meaning of the drawing is completed by Grosz's ironic caption, "The capitalist and the military officer wish each other a blessed new year."

Voigt's image is ideologically more sophisticated. Using the arm of a tall crane as the gibbet on which his allegorical figures are hoisted, Voigt provides ready reference to a developed imperialist industrial society, "the apogee of capitalist evolution."[2] According to the 1928 Program of the Communist International, this evolutionary apex was the point at which capital and the military formed a noxious alliance, as most immediately seen in Weimar Germany. Voigt ironically identifies the crane, a triumph of modern industry, simultaneously as an apogee towards which capitalism strives and a gallows from which the corpses of capitalism and militarism dangle. He thus recalls Marx's comment that capitalism carries within itself the seeds of its own destruction, as echoed in the 1928 Program:

The epoch of imperialism which fulfills the process of producing the material conditions for socialism (concentration of the means of production, extensive nationalization of labor, strengthening of labor organizations) simultaneously intensifies the conflicts between the "great powers" and calls forth wars that lead to the collapse of unified world commerce. Imperialism therefore is decaying, dying capitalism. It is the final step in the development of capitalism in general. It is the initiation of the socialist world revolution.[3]

Thus, where Grosz was satisfied with an ironic condemnation of social ills and the prediction of revolution, Voigt injects a specific Marxist critique of a system that corrupts through its own progress. Voigt, moreover, situates his capitalist and military officer at the literal height of their careers in an industrial landscape. Marching down the road is a file of armed workers, carrying the red banners of the socialist revolution. The broken windows of the factory buildings testify to the violence of their struggle as it spreads triumphantly into the countryside while the emblems of capitalist domination hang above, strangled by instruments of their own making.   B. T. Y.

1. George Grosz, *Das Gesicht der herrschenden Klasse: 55 politische Zeichnungen*, Kleine revolutionäre Bibliothek, vol. 4 (Berlin: Malik Verlag, 1921), 66, published oppo-

site Grosz's *To Them Peace Is Assured* (cat. no. 51).
2. "... die höchste Phase der kapitalistischen Entwicklung." Programm der Kommunistischen Internationale, Sixth World Congress of the Communist International, Moscow, 1 September 1928, as reprinted in *Geschichte der deutschen Arbeiterbewegung*, vol. 4 (East Berlin: Dietz, 1966), 490.
3. "Die Epoche des Imperialismus, die den Prozess der Schaffung der materiellen Vorbedingungen des Sozialismus vollendet (Konzentration der Produktionsmittel, gigantische Vergesellschaftung der Arbeit, Erstarken der Arbeiterorganisationen), verschärft die Widersprüche zwischen den "Grossmächten" und ruft Kriege hervor, die den Zerfall der einheitlichen Weltwirtschaft herbeiführen. Der Imperialismus ist daher der verwesende, sterbende Kapitalismus. Er ist die letzte Etappe der Entwicklung des Kapitalismus überhaupt, er ist der Anbruch der sozialistischen Weltrevolution." Ibid., 491.

159 Bruno Voigt
Attack (Angriff), 1932

Watercolor, tusche on paper
50.8 x 35.9 cm (20 x 14¹/₈ in.)
Monogrammed and dated l. l.
"-V-/32"

Provenance: Staatlicher Kunsthandel der DDR, East Berlin.

Exhibitions: Leipzig, Galerie am Sachsenplatz, *Bruno Voigt: Aquarelle, Zeichnungen und Radierungen*, 31 August–28 September 1986, cat. no. 73; Milwaukee, Patrick and Beatrice Haggerty Museum of Art, Marquette University, *Berlin in the 1920s and 1930s: A City of Decadence, Revolt, and Chaos—Watercolors and Drawings of Bruno Voigt*, 11 June–2 August 1987, cat. no. 20.

The solidarity with which Bruno Voigt portrays the Communist resistance in *Attack* reasserts his belief in the efficacy of demonstrations opposing the industrial-military establishment. During the thirteen years of the Weimar Republic, labor/management antagonism and the concomitant division of classes were particularly acute. Depictions of conflict were thus a frequent concern of socially engaged artists such as Voigt. *Attack*, a scene based on numerous factory lockouts in the late 1920s and early 1930s, depicts a cigar-smoking industrialist in the foreground with his hands shoved in the pockets of his three-piece suit. He is placed in an urban setting of factory buildings and a church which no longer offers salvation or resolution to the grievances of the demonstrating workers.

Voigt depicted such workers in many of the etchings of unemployed he produced in 1931. In this image of labor on the march, there is a stylistic affinity to Rudolf Schlichter's pictures of the individual worker; Voigt, however, represents the workers as a solid mass, a unified class demonstrating for its class interests. The protesters are identified as Communists by the hammer and sickle on the banner they carry, as well as by the defiant salute of the clenched fist. Facing the workers and separating them from the industrialist, is a file of armed

soldiers with fixed bayonets, who prevent the marchers from entering the factory. It is a scene that took place frequently in 1932, depicted regularly in the *Arbeiter Illustrierte Zeitung (Workers' Illustrated Newspaper)* and other Socialist and Communist periodicals.

In 1932, the Anti-Fascist Action united Socialists, Communists, and Unionists in an effort to overcome the effects of monopoly capitalism. Demonstrations were organized to counter factory lockouts during which there were violent clashes between workers and the military and police units protecting industrial property. The situation had become especially critical after the Wall Street Crash of 1929 and the resultant depression. As the German economy collapsed and unemployment rose precipitously—in February 1932, 6.12 million were unemployed, including nearly half of the total trade union membership—demonstrations took on an undeniable urgency and provided opportunities for political organization, especially for the Communist Party of Germany (KPD).

Voigt's image presents the workers as a collective force combatting the advance of Fascism. The currency of the situation is captured by the words "work" and "bread" on the red banner, a common working-class slogan during the early and late years of the Weimar Republic. In 1932, a splinter political party even identified itself as "The Unemployed for Work and Bread" and was included on the ballot of 6 November. The wretchedness of the unemployed and the continued discontent of the working class fostered an upsurge of radicalism which enabled the KPD in the last phase of the Republic to overtake the Socialists in electoral districts of high industrial concentration: Berlin, Merseburg, Cologne, Aachen, East Düsseldorf, and West Düsseldorf. Voigt's image refers then to the tumultuous events of 1932, to the Communist political successes, and responds with the hoped-for organized front and ultimate victory over the encroaching Fascist regime.   B. T. Y.

160 Bruno Voigt
Potter's Lane, Weimar (Töpfergasse, Weimar), 1932

Pen and ink, splatter technique on blue-gray paper
46 x 46 cm (18¹/₄ x 18¹/₄ in.)
Signed, dated, and inscribed on matting l. l. "Bruno Voigt Töpfergasse Weimar, 1932"

Provenance: Staatlicher Kunsthandel der DDR, East Berlin; Neue Münchner Galerie, Munich.

Exhibitions: Munich, Neue Münchner Galerie, *Bruno Voigt: Gemälde, Zeichnungen, Graphik 1930–1948*, November 1983–February 1984; Milwaukee, Patrick and Beatrice Haggerty Museum of Art, Marquette University, *Berlin in the 1920s and 1930s: A City of Decadence, Revolt, and Chaos—Watercolors and Drawings of Bruno Voigt*, 11 June–2 August 1987, cat. no. 3.

In *Potter's Lane, Weimar* Bruno Voigt depends on the socially critical style of Karl Arnold, a noted contributor to the humor periodical *Simplicissimus*. The appropriation of a well-known artist's style was a conscious tactic on Voigt's part, designed to enhance the legibility of his narrative while avoiding the problem of stylistic innovation during a politically and economically volatile era. It was, in short, a deliberate rejection of artistic experimentation in favor of propagandistic effectiveness.[1] In this drawing, Voigt augmented Arnold's flowing linearity with a delicate splatter technique, using the blank areas of the pale blue-gray paper for contrast. Paper color immediately translates into a depiction of dusk; the splattering provides shading and smudging to suggest the run-down conditions of the neighborhood. The atmospheric effect of twilight, the temporal setting of sentimental mood paintings as well as Whistlerian nocturnes, associates the image with a maudlin romantic quality which is subverted by the subject matter of prostitution.

Like Arnold's illustrations, *Potter's Lane, Weimar* presents an anecdotal pictorial narrative. The setting, identified by the inscription, is the city of Weimar, significant politically as the site of the German Republic's constitutional assembly in 1919, but even more noted as the city of Goethe and Schiller, the font of classical German culture that served as the reified foundation of bourgeois education. Voigt presents none of this, however; instead, his evening nocturne depicts the prostitutes' quarter in Potter's Lane, the underside of the bourgeois system of values. With two naked prostitutes waiting at the window and a light beckoning over the door, a brothel occupies most of the right half of the drawing. Another woman, demurely dressed, approaches the doorway, presumably to begin her own shift in the labor of self-display and sale. Two men in the foreground slouch past the brothel, hands shoved into their pockets, while a third stares intently at a young woman in the left foreground. She is also the focus of the attention of one of the prostitutes and of a man with a bowler hat who stands in the background, half hidden behind the corner of a house.

The object of so many glances, including the viewer's, the young woman is the center of Voigt's narrative, which becomes a negative fairy tale, a sinister *Cinderella*. Wearing a plain jacket and skirt, she stands erect, her arms held tightly at her sides, hands slightly behind her hips, and shoulders back with her breasts lifted high. Despite her modest attire, her pose is a revealing one, which implicitly presents her body for examination. Yet her posture also betrays a sense of awkwardness, a degree of fear and naïveté, and her gaze seems wide-eyed with innocence. Her ambivalent deportment, her isolation from the other figures, and her youth render her vulnerable, the potential victim of those who scrutinize her.

At issue is a specific socio-economic situation in Weimar Germany, affecting the lives of many women in the late 1920s and early 1930s. The girl in Voigt's drawing is a newcomer to Potter's Lane, unable to find other means of support; not employed in the institutionalized house of prostitution, she competes unofficially and illegally for the same customers. Her bowler-hatted observer, attempting to keep out of sight, might be her pimp, or, more likely, a representative of the vice squad charged with controlling and patrolling the technically illegal trade in women's bodies and prepared to bring this novice prostitute into the state's surveillance system. The suspicious and quizzical gazes—whether the viewer's as her potential customer, the prostitute's as her antagonistic competition, or the policeman's as her cataloguer and registrar—all depersonalize her, deprive her of individuality, and render her a violable object. Unlike Cinderella, the young woman finds no princely salvation from her economic and personal degradation.

There is in Voigt's drawing an added subtext. With the prostitutes in the brothel idle and their young competitor still without a customer, even the business of sex during this economically depressed year of 1932 is suffering. The men who are the intended consumers of the sexual commerce walk past, slouching in postures of despondency, not availing themselves of their opportunities, apparently unable to afford this service in which their presence in Potter's Lane announces their interest. The scene, on the surface titillatingly anecdotal with its naked and available women associated with men, finally decodes as an indictment of Weimar's capitalist society, a representation of its deterioration, and a further prediction of its expected collapse. Karl Marx contended that "prostitution is only a *specific* expression of the *general* prostitution of the *laborer*...a relationship in which falls not the prostitute alone, but also the one who prostitutes."[2] For Voigt then, as for Marx, the failure of prostitution mirrors the general economic failure of Weimar's capitalist system.   B. T. Y./R. H.

1. For further observations concerning this aspect of Voigt's work, see cat. no. 161.

2. Karl Marx, *The Economic and Philosophic Manuscripts of 1844*, ed. Dirk, J. Struik, trans. Martin Milligan (New York: International Publishers, 1964), 133. Marx repeatedly uses prostitution as a simile for labor under capitalism in his writings, and although we make no claim for Voigt's knowledge of this particular text, the first publication of the *Manuscripts* in 1932 is a fortuitous circumstance worthy of note.

161 Bruno Voigt
Anti-War Demonstration (Antikriegsdemonstration), 1932

Watercolor, pen and ink, splatter technique, over pencil on paper
50.3 x 35.7 cm (20 x 14¼ in.)
Monogrammed and dated l. r. "-V- 13. 6. 32"; signed, dated, and inscribed on matting l. l. "Bruno Voigt Antikriegsdemonstration 1932"; inscribed on matting l. r. "In der Weimarer Republik"

Provenance: Staatlicher Kunsthandel der DDR, East Berlin; Neue Münchner Galerie, Munich.

Exhibitions: Munich, Neue Münchner Galerie, *Bruno Voigt: Gemälde, Zeichnungen, Graphik 1930–1948*, November 1983–February 1984; Milwaukee, Patrick and Beatrice Haggerty Museum of Art, Marquette University, *Berlin in the 1920s and 1930s: A City of Decadence, Revolt, and Chaos—Watercolors and Drawings of Bruno Voigt*, 11 June–2 August 1987, cat. no. 16.

Bruno Voigt's watercolor drawing of an anti-war demonstration divides into three sections that correspond to different social classes. In the foreground, fat-necked, bald, cigar-smoking industrial and financial leaders conspire with military officers as a nattily dressed war veteran—presumably a former officer, decorated with medals—nervously mops his brow. Drawn as a blue-uniformed file across the center of the image are four policemen who carry billy clubs, revolvers, and rifles with mounted bayonets. They separate, formally and physically, the foreground group from the train of countless marching workers and their banner proclaiming "Gegen den imperialistischen Krieg" (Against Imperialist War). The demonstrators mass back to the horizon line where Voigt has schematized a factory complex identified as a chemical concern of the conglomerate I. G. Farben.

The image of a peaceful protest, with marchers and capitalists segregated and protected by the police cordon, is reinforced by Voigt's balanced composition; but the sense of order is undermined by details that inject an uneasy anticipation into the demonstration. The tall, leather-helmeted police accompany the procession, but even more they contain it; any movement outside the pre-ordained line of march is met—as in the confrontation of a worker and a policeman beneath the arch of the banner—with firm resistance aided by a fixed bayonet and a (hidden) drawn revolver. With the proletarian group grimly marching in silence, the readiness of the police to do battle is indicative of the brutality and antagonism with which workers' demonstrations were met by Germany's "guardians of the peace." The political cabaret poet and essayist Kurt Tucholsky summarized the official attitude ironically in "Calm and Order":

When millions work, but cannot live,
When mothers to children watered milk do give—Then that's order.
When working people call out: "We want to be heard!
We should condemn whoever steals our work!"

Then that's disorder. . . .
The main thing is: Not to listen to the hungry.
The main thing is: No disruption in the country.
Just don't shout.
Give it time. Everything'll be fine.

Evolution will take care of everything.
That's what your representatives have discovered.

What if, by then, by six feet of earth you're covered?
Then on your graves they'll be able to read:
They were always quiet and orders did heed.[1]

During the last years of the Republic, peaceful demonstrations often became violent as police attacked almost at will. Demonstrating groups were confronted with specially drafted riot squads armed with billy-clubs, pistols, and rifles that were used at the least provocation. As the drawn revolver concealed behind the policeman's back in Voigt's image signals, the possibility of bloodshed was always imminent.

Demonstrations that exposed such brutality were also central to the tactics of the Communist Party and to popular politics at this time. By depicting the potential conflict between unarmed workers and armed police, Voigt refers to the concept that every protest march was a means of disclosing a civil war latent in the existing socio-political order. The Communist Party held that every war fought in an age of imperialism, regardless of the victor, is damaging to the proletariat: the anti-war slogan emblazoned on the protesters' banner had been a fundamental part of the Party's public position since the end of World War I. Significantly, Voigt's marchers file past the entrance to an I. G. Farben chemical plant such as produced weapons components. By placing his capitalist managers in the intimate company of military officers, Voigt also unmasks the alliance among capitalists, military, and monopolistic industries which prospered in Weimar Germany's waning years, as arms production and weapons development once again became major industrial and governmental concerns.   B. T. Y.

1. "Wenn Millionen arbeiten, ohne zu leben,/wenn Mütter den Kindern nur Milchwasser geben—Das ist Ordnung./ Wenn Werkleute rufen: "Lasst uns ans Licht!/Wer Arbeit stiehlt, der muss vors Gericht!"/Das ist Unordnung..../Die Hauptsache ist: Nicht auf Hungernde hören./Die Hauptsache ist: Nicht das Strassenbild stören./Nur nicht schreien./Mit der Zeit wird das schon./Alles bringt euch die Evolution./So hats euer Volksvertreter entdeckt./Seid ihr bis dahin alle verreckt?/So wird man auf euern Gräbern doch lesen;/Sie sind immer ruhig und ordentlich gewesen." Kurt Tucholsky, "Ruhe und Ordnung," in *Das Lächeln der Mona Lisa* (Hamburg: Rowohlt, n. d.), as reprinted in *Um uns die Stadt: Eine Anthologie neuer Grossstadtdichtung*, comp. Robert Seitz and Heinz Zucker (Berlin: Sieben-Stäbe, 1931), 70–71.

162 Bruno Voigt
Berlin Street Corner (Berliner Strassenecke), 1932

Black chalk, tusche, watercolor over carpenter's pencil on paper
57 x 44.9 cm (22⅜ x 17¾ in.)
Monogrammed and dated l. r. "-V-/13. 8. 32"

Provenance: Staatlicher Kunsthandel der DDR, East Berlin.

Exhibitions: Leipzig, Galerie am Sachsenplatz, *Bruno Voigt: Aquarelle, Zeichnungen und Radierungen*, 31 August–28 September 1986, cat. no. 44; Milwaukee, Patrick and Beatrice Haggerty Museum of Art, Marquette University, *Berlin in the 1920s and 1930s: A City of Decadence, Revolt, and Chaos—Watercolors and Drawings of Bruno Voigt*, 11 June–2 August 1987, cat. no. 4.

Berlin Street Corner resurrects a pictorial formula of postwar city scenes that had been employed by Otto Dix, George Grosz, and others in the early 1920s. In these images, war cripples, gaunt and haggard in tattered uniforms, usually seated on the sidewalk and propped against a wall, contrast with prosperous passersby. The *topos* of the ignored, begging war victim first became popular after the Napoleonic Wars, and was repeated with contemporizing variations after each of the numerous wars of the nineteenth century. In Germany after World War I, the major prototype was Ottomar Starke's lithograph of a one-legged beggar on crutches, apparently a war cripple although in civilian clothes, who watches a stylishly dressed, cigar-smoking young man walk pretentiously past, turning his head away from the embarrassing confrontation with the beggar's outstretched hat.[1]

The motif proliferated in paintings, drawings, prints, and photographs during the years after the War and Revolution while Germany's economy foundered, war pensions and compensations became increasingly inadequate, and programs for training maimed veterans proved ineffective. By the mid-1920s, however, Dix, Grosz, and other artists had ceased producing these images as prosperity and relative political stability returned: inflation was checked, the Dawes Plan revised Germany's reparation payments, and a new influx of foreign investment began. Voigt's image in 1932 therefore retrieves and revitalizes a theme that had lost its currency and popularity; this revival suggests an effort to draw a parallel between past and present. The familiar 1920s vocabulary makes Bruno Voigt's *Berlin Street Corner*—dated 13 August 1932—immediately legible.

Acknowledging the influence of Grosz, Rudolf Schlichter, and Karl Arnold on his early drawings and engravings, Voigt observed in 1986, "I do not consider that plagiarism, but rather a problem of the generation to which I belong."[2] For the twenty-year-old Voigt in 1932, the formulation of a personal and individual style—a hallmark of the modern artistic effort—was not a significant concern; his contribution to the struggle against Fascism, however, was. For artists in the late Weimar Republic and Third Reich, such as Voigt and the artist who signed his works "Fuhrmann" (see cat. nos. 40–45), styles previously developed in opposition to capitalism, militarism, and social exploitation provided an articulated anti-Fascist statement to be cited, adapted, and amplified.[3]

A closer reading of *Berlin Street Corner* reveals the political specificity of Voigt's critique. He depicts a legless war victim seated on the pavement, heavily shadowed by three distinct degrees of shading. This effect contributes

to the beggar's isolation and links him to the wall with its tattered posters. He has become part of the scenery, representing not an individual fate but a standard fixture of the class structure, the result of a decade of economic turmoil and disillusionment with the Republic. His plight makes overt the Republic's failure to solve the problem of the disabled. The middle-class consumers on their way to sales and cafés in the background hardly notice him, as he disintegrates slowly like the posters under which he begs. In all this, Voigt closely follows earlier prototypes.

It is with the inclusion of the posters that his political critique engages the present, the year 1932. On 20 July, a state of emergency had been declared in Prussia by the central government of Chancellor Franz von Papen, ostensibly to prevent a Communist putsch, for which there was no reliable evidence. It is to this event that one of the posters in Voigt's drawing refers, with the words "Standrecht" (Military Emergency), "Kommi," and "Putsch." The other poster encourages, with the charge "wähle" (vote), participation in the forthcoming general elections on 31 July. But the parliamentary processes of the Republic failed to address fundamental social problems and consistently supressed the left's political movements while condoning right-wing extremism. Voigt expresses his disenchantment with the Republic by juxtaposing the posters and the continuing problem of the unemployed and disabled in a callously unsympathetic bourgeois society. For Voigt as a member of the beleaguered Communist Party, such disappointment was particularly exacerbated after the July elections, in which the Nazis made unprecedented gains. Produced at a moment of historic crisis, the drawing is set up as a weapon against the danger of Fascism, a contribution to desperate tactics that weakly attempted to forestall a Nazi victory. B. T. Y.

1. Part of a series on war profiteering ironically entitled "The New Society" ("Die Neue Gesellschaft"), Starke's image appeared in *Der Bildermann*, 5 September 1916.
2. "... ich halte das nicht für ein Plagiat, sondern für eine Frage der Generation, der ich angehöre." Bruno Voigt, "Mein Lebenslauf," in *Bruno Voigt: Aquarelle, Zeichnungen und Radierungen* (Leipzig: Galerie am Sachsenplatz/Staatlicher Kunsthandel der DDR, 1986), 5.
3. A different point of view is presented by Wolfgang Thiede in *Bruno Voigt 1912–1988: Widerstandskunst 1933–1944* (West Berlin: AGO Galerie, 1988), 44, who understands a non-individualistic style as a search for anonymity to escape political persecution.

163   Bruno Voigt
Resignation (Resignation), 1932

Black chalk, brush, pen, ink, and watercolor on paper
40.4 x 36.2 cm (15¹⁵/₁₆ x 14¼ in.)
Monogrammed and dated l. r.
"-V-/20. 12. 32"

Provenance: Staatlicher Kunsthandel der DDR, East Berlin.

Exhibitions: Leipzig, Galerie am Sachsenplatz, *Bruno Voigt: Aquarelle, Zeichnungen und Radierungen*, 31 August–28 September 1986, cat. no. 49; Milwaukee, Patrick and Beatrice Haggerty Museum of Art, Marquette University, *Berlin in the 1920s and 1930s: A City of Decadence, Revolt, and Chaos—Watercolors and Drawings of Bruno Voigt*, 11 June–2 August 1987, cat. no. 13.

Bruno Voigt's *Resignation* is a study of poverty and psychological dejection, correlatives of the squalid living conditions to which the couple represented have resigned themselves. The walls of their tenement apartment are cracked and crumbling, an oil lamp indicates the lack of electricity, while a chamber pot, bowl, and pitcher show that running water and private toilet are also absent. An old coal stove with exposed pipe heats a coffeepot; there is no separate kitchen or cooking area. The single room, sparsely furnished with a table, chair, and bed, constitutes the couple's entire living space. The view through the window breaks the confinement of their surroundings but reaffirms the dreariness in which they live.

Voigt presents the couple in an intimate moment, as they prepare for bed some ten minutes after midnight. The man, weary and stoop-shouldered, wearing checked pajamas, sits on the edge of the bed with his eyes closed and jaw clenched; his heavy hairless head is bent forward despite his thick muscular neck. The focus of the image, however, is the seated woman, removing her stockings while holding a cigarette limply between the fingers of her right hand. A bottle and glass stand at her feet. Her pose is also one of despondency, without energy, submissive. Her slip is pulled up to reveal her genitals, increasing her vulnerability and defining the scene as a sexual one in which *Sachlichkeit* triumphs. With neither modesty nor flirtation, she prepares slowly to join the man waiting for her, both as resigned to their unemotional togetherness as to their poverty.

Artists of the 1920s resurrected in their ironic critiques of contemporary society the motif of the unequal pair, of the aged and ugly man accompanied by a beautiful young woman. George Grosz varied the theme in depictions of petty bourgeois couples, man and woman now equally repulsive as they undress, perform their personal toilet, and prepare matter-of-factly for the mating ritual. Voigt's drawing continues this treatment, but his actors appear to belong to the *Lumpenproletariat*. Unlike the determined proletarians he depicts in courageous moments of revolution and resistance, this couple embodies a heavy lethargy. Incapable or unwilling to seize control of their lives, they are stripped of optimism and affirmation.

Despair, Søren Kierkegaard stated with characteristic insight, is the sickness unto death, rendering action impossible, the sickness of self-rejection. Voigt's *Resignation* translates that existentialist adage into a Marxist observation of social conditions when, so the young Communist Party member believed, the proletarian revolution was imminent. B. T. Y.

164   Bruno Voigt
Attack (Angriff), 1932

Watercolor, ink on paper
45.7 x 29.2 cm (18 x 11½ in.)
Monogrammed and dated l. r.
"-V-/3. V. 32"

Provenance: Staatlicher Kunsthandel der DDR, East Berlin.

Exhibitions: Milwaukee, Patrick and Beatrice Haggerty Museum of Art, Marquette University, *Berlin in the 1920s and 1930s: A City of Decadence, Revolt, and Chaos—Watercolors and Drawings of Bruno Voigt*, 11 June–2 August 1987, cat. no. 18; West Berlin, Berlinische Galerie, Museum für Moderne Kunst, Photographie und Architektur im Martin-Gropius-Bau, *Ich und die Stadt: Mensch und Grossstadt in der deutschen Kunst des 20. Jahrhunderts*, 15 August–22 November 1987, cat. no. 201; Atlanta, High Museum of Art, *Art in Berlin 1815–1989*, 14 November 1989–14 January 1990, cat. no. 150.

Attack is one of several scenes of violent confrontations between workers and German government troops that Bruno Voigt produced in 1932 (see also cat. no. 159). In the foreground, behind a barricade, a wounded worker clutches his abdomen, blood streaming from his forehead and mouth as he looks back towards his comrades firing at approaching jack-booted, helmeted troops. Streetlamps and windows crash and barbed wire flies loose as gunfire explodes in defense of the neighborhood. Voigt's image, dated 3 May 1932, recalls events three years earlier, when police stormed Berlin working-class neighborhoods following illegal May Day demonstrations. Despite a ban issued by the Socialist Police Chief of Berlin, Karl Zörgiebel, the Communist Party of Germany (KPD) had called for street demonstrations to maintain the proletariat's right to march on its international holiday. An article in the Party organ, *Die Rote Fahne (The Red Flag)*, was addressed to the policemen of the city, assuring them that demonstrators would be unarmed.[1]

The KPD counted two hundred thousand workers who gathered for their traditional march through the streets of the city in defiance of the ban. Marching peacefully or returning from legal indoor rallies, they were brutally attacked by the police with billy clubs, rifles, and drawn pistols. Under the leadership of Red Front-Fighters' League members, the workers countered the attacks and attempted to fight their way into the city center. Workers, passersby, and onlookers were arrested and frequently beaten. The next day, the working-class districts of Berlin were sealed off and placed under virtual martial law. At Köslinger Strasse in Wedding and Hermannstrasse in Neukölln, barricades were set up spontaneously to deter the police troops' entry into the neighborhoods. Attacked by armored cars and personnel-carriers, the workers responded with rifle fire. By the evening of 3 May 1929, the bitter fighting had claimed thirty-one dead, none of them police officers. Two hundred people were wounded; twelve hundred arrests were made.[2]

An independent commission, composed of sympathetic writers, investigated the events and concluded that the KPD was not guilty of the deaths of early May; the commission instead placed "responsibility for these inhuman actions of the terrible Blood May of 1929 totally on the shoulders of Herr Zörgiebel."[3] While the national government was headed by the Socialist Hermann Müller, the actions of Blood May seemed to justify the Communists' refusals to cooperate with the Socialist Party. The Twelfth KPD Congress, meeting significantly in Berlin-Wedding in June 1929, accused the Socialists of being "Social-Fascists," "betraying and murdering workers."[4]

Voigt's image glorifies the May Day battles as it commemorates their anniversary and implicitly sustains the condemnation of the Socialist Party. But as much as *Attack* is an historical reflection, it also predicts a successful armed proletarian uprising such as the KPD advocated as the sole means of achieving the dictatorship of the proletariat. Despite the heroic proletarian casualty in the foreground and the damage to nearby buildings, it is the attacking police who throw up their arms as they encounter the workers' gunfire—in contrast to the outcome of Blood May. The scene of workers' resistance and triumph, moreover, is witnessed from their side of the barricade, situating both artist and viewer in their midst as comrades-in-arms in the final triumphant revolutionary struggle.

B. T. Y.

1. "We, the Communists, inform you, the police, that the class-conscious workers, who will march under the banners of the Communist Party in the streets tomorrow, have no desire for confrontation. They will therefore march unarmed. It is up to you to demonstrate that you are not totally submissive instruments of the officers" ("Wir, die Kommunisten, sagen euch, den Beamten, dass die klassenbewussten Arbeiter, die morgen unter den Fahnen der Kommunistischen Partei auf die Strasse gehen werden, kein Interesse an Zusammenstössen haben; darum werden sie unbewaffnet marschieren; an euch ist es, zu zeigen, dass auch ihr keine willenlosen Instrumente der Offiziere seid"). Cited by the Committee for the Investigation of the Berlin May Events, *Protokoll vom 1. Verhandlungstag nebst Anlagen*, ed. Rote Hilfe Deutschlands (Berlin, n. d. [1929]), 33, reprinted in Institut für Marxismus-Leninismus beim Zentralkomitee der SED [Sozialistische Einheitspartei Deutschlands], *Geschichte der deutschen Arbeiter Bewegung*, vol. 4, *Von 1924 bis Januar 1933* (East Berlin: Dietz, 1966), 514.
2. For a summary of the Blood May events, see Eve Rosenhaft, *Beating the Fascists? The German Communists and Political Violence 1929–1933* (Cambridge and New York: Cambridge University Press, 1983), 32–35.
3. "...die Schuld an diesen Unmenschlichkeiten des furchtbaren Blutmai 1929 Herrn Zörgiebel zuschieben!" *Protokoll*, 33, as cited in Institut für Marxismus, *Geschichte*, 514–515.
4. "Sozialfaschisten....Partei des Arbeiterverrats und des Arbeitermordes...." "Beschlüsse des XII. Parteitages der KPD," ibid., 519–522.

165 Bruno Voigt
In the Brothel (Im Bordell), 1932

Pen, brush, ink, watercolor on paper
46.6 x 42.2 cm (18¼ x 16½ in.)
Monogrammed and dated l. l.
"-V-/3. 8. 32"

Provenance: Staatlicher Kunsthandel der DDR, East Berlin; Neue Münchner Galerie, Munich; Galerie Michael Hasenclever, Munich.

Exhibitions: Munich, Neue Münchner Galerie, *Bruno Voigt: Gemälde, Zeichnungen, Graphik 1930–1948*, November 1983–February 1984; Milwaukee, Patrick and Beatrice Haggerty Museum of Art, Marquette University, *Berlin in the 1920s and 1930s: A City of Decadence, Revolt, and Chaos—Watercolors and Drawings of Bruno Voigt*, 11 June–2 August 1987, cat. no. 12.

In the foreground of Bruno Voigt's brothel scene, two customers sit at a table with a woman clothed in a red strapless dress, through which, impossibly, her pubic hair is visible. Behind them, one man leaves the room while a woman displays herself to two other clients. Such a scene could derive from numerous variations on Henri de Toulouse-Lautrec's images of Paris brothels in the 1890s, but Voigt characteristically subverts the situation by confronting the viewer with the disfigured face of one of the customers in the very center of the drawing. One of the man's eyes—or its empty socket—is covered with a cotton bandage and leather patch. His features are distorted and his malformed hand rests stiffly on the tabletop. Fourteen years after the end of World War I, he may still be one of its victims, forever maimed in the service of his country, or he may be the victim of other kinds of violence that permeated Weimar society during the Republic's closing years: crime, industrial accidents, police brutality, Nazi political strategies and Communist responses. Whatever the source of his wounds, he comes now well-dressed to this brothel, seeking to purchase the physical affection and comfort otherwise denied him.[1]

He is joined by another man, similarly wearing jacket and tie, his feet stretched rudely out to reveal spats covering his shoes, his fat neck spilling over his shirt collar, cigarette in hand, and stomach pushed forward in self-satisfaction. His display of prosperity mocks the misfortune of his companion, a victim of the bourgeois society he represents, and his callous demeanor contrasts to the look of horror that marks the face of the prostitute fated to sell the use of her body to one or both of these two repulsive customers. Voigt attempts to include a degree of humor in recording the prostitute's reaction, but in the process he succeeds only in accentuating the distasteful nature of the confrontation.[2]

Human relationships are here reduced to monetary exchange, and the woman as commodity is enslaved within a system that denies reality to her individuality, and recognizes only her body and its abuse while ignoring her existence as a person. Paragraph 180 of the Imperial German Criminal Code, which outlawed brothels in 1900, remained in effect during the years of the

Weimar Republic. As Voigt's image testifies, houses of prostitution nonetheless proliferated, justified through another paragraph (361/6) of the criminal code which permitted the police to subject prostitutes to medical examinations and registration. Brothels were then essentially formed under police protection with the fiction of safeguarding social health and morality; they were identified as "homes," their keepers as landlords. The officially sanctioned *Bordellierung* masked the hypocrisy of a state that punished women who did not comply with regulation and, even more obviously, failed to address the problem of the male customers who generated the demand for prostitution but were subjected neither to dehumanizing medical examinations nor to the ostracism associated with "houses of ill repute."

Indeed, brothels were sites where, like the two deformed—physically and/or morally—customers in Voigt's drawing, men otherwise incapable of intimacy or not offered it freely could demonstrate their manhood in easy, guaranteed sexual subjugation. During his commercial transaction with the prostitute, the deformed cripple could recall his destroyed wholeness and his bestial companion could confirm his strength. For the prostitute, however, there is no escape from the horror to which, as purchased goods, she must submit.

B. T. Y.

1. The inability of crippled war victims to obtain sexual satisfaction or compassion while nonetheless continuing to feel sexual desire is a theme that emerges very early in postwar art. For examples, see Magnus Hirschfeld, ed., *Sittengeschichte des Weltkrieges*, vol. 2 (Leipzig and Vienna: Verlag für Sexualwissenschaft Schneider & Co., 1930), 50, 54. Also compare George Grosz's frequent juxtaposition—especially in the drawing series *The Face of the Ruling Class*—of begging war veterans, many of them crippled, who are alone while caricatured capitalists and army officers enjoy the company of women. Grosz, *Das Gesicht der herrschenden Klasse: 55 politische Zeichnungen*, Kleine revolutionäre Bibliothek, vol. 4 (Berlin: Malik Verlag, 1921).
2. It is useful to compare the scene to Max Beckmann's lithograph *The Way Home (Der Nachhauseweg)* from the portfolio *Hell (Die Hölle)*, which in 1919 depicted the artist's encounter with a severely disfigured war victim, and in which a prostitute appears in the background. Voigt shifts the pathos of such a scene, focused on the horror of disfigurement, from the war victim (most probably based on previous artists' depictions rather than Voigt's actual experience) to the prostitute, and thus from a condemnation of war and its effects to a condemnation of Weimar social and economic forces and relationships.

166 Bruno Voigt
Street Fight (Strassenkampf), 1932

Watercolor and ink on paper
50.5 x 36 cm (19⅞ x 14¼ in.)
Monogrammed and dated l. r.
"-V-/32"

Provenance: Staatlicher Kunsthandel der DDR, East Berlin; Neue Münchner Galerie, Munich; Galerie Michael Hasenclever, Munich.

Exhibitions: West Berlin, Galerie Bodo Niemann, *Bruno Voigt*, 1986; Milwaukee, Patrick and Beatrice Haggerty Museum of Art, Marquette University, *Berlin in the 1920s and 1930s: A City of Decadence, Revolt, and Chaos—Watercolors and Drawings of Bruno Voigt*, 11 June–2 August 1987, cat. no. 17; West Berlin, Berlinische Galerie, Museum für Moderne Kunst, Photographie und Architektur im Martin-Gropius-Bau, *Ich und die Stadt: Mensch und Grossstadt in der deutschen Kunst des 20. Jahrhunderts*, 15 August–22 November 1987, cat. no. 202.

During 1930, the Communist Party organization Red Aid (*Rote Hilfe*) recorded the deaths of forty-four Party members at the hands of the Nazis' SA troops, fifty-two in 1931, and seventy-five during the first six months of 1932. The statistics testify to escalating violence during the last years of the Weimar Republic, as political parties propagated ideologies through paramilitary groups who engaged in street brawls and armed confrontations. The streets, Joseph Goebbels instructed his SA and SS troops in Berlin, must be conquered; his troops marched brazenly and with determined provocation into the workers' quarter of "Red Wedding," where loyalty to the Communist and Socialist parties dominated. "Wherever a Fascist dares to show his face in the quarters of the working class," responded the Communist Party newspaper *Die Rote Fahne (The Red Flag)*, "the workers' fists will light his way home. Berlin is red! Berlin will remain red!"[1] Local and national government action aggravated more than it countered the violence. Ideologically allied with the extreme right, the police often actively supported Nazi attacks on workers and others classified as socially "undesirable." On 10 June 1932, the Reichswehr was called upon to aid in suppressing political violence for the first time since the Spartacist uprisings and separatist movements of the early 1920s; the intervention of national troops resulted in fourteen deaths.

Bruno Voigt's *Street Fight* captures the bloodshed and horror of the street battles that had become a terrifying fact of German life, especially in the politically volatile urban centers. Rather than recording a particular scene or event of 1932, however, Voigt has resurrected the imagery of the early 1920s when Freikorps troops turned the arms and armor of World War I against the civilian population sympathetic to the Spartacist cause. In the drawing, helmeted and uniformed soldiers use tanks and cannons to attack the brick tenements and barbed wire barricades of a resisting proletariat armed with only knives, rifles, and fists. Bullets, gunsmoke, and broken bodies fill the sharply tilted space, but Voigt's focus is on individual heroic action. Two workers in the foreground violently counter the military's attack, one gouging out a soldier's eyes, his wounded companion stabbing another soldier in the head. From the broken window of a tenement, a worker's body dangles in futile martyrdom.

Possibly created for an aborted 1933 exhibition in Dresden by the Association of Revolutionary Artists of Germany, *Street Fight* presents contemporary events in the historical costume of 1918 to 1920. The street battles of Red Front and SA are transformed into valorous resistance against government-sponsored terror. Trapped in a situation of crisis, Voigt made no effort to continue the stylistic experimentation that marked the art of Weimar Germany, but rather exploited the vocabularies of progressive artists of the previous decade. Established style and iconography, readily recognized by viewers educated in artists' contributions to the political struggles of the Communist Party, legitimized the left's ongoing resistance by visually equating the brutal counterrevolutionary events of 1918 and 1919 with the Nazi's vicious street terror of the early 1930s.   B. T. Y.

1. *Die Rote Fahne*, 31 August 1929, as cited and translated by Eve Rosenhaft, *Beating the Fascists? German Communists and Political Violence 1929–1933* (Cambridge and New York: Cambridge University Press, 1983), 64.

167   Bruno Voigt
*The Revolution Will Triumph
(Die Revolution Siegt)*, 1933

Watercolor, ink, charcoal on paper
50.5 x 36 cm (19¹/₄ x 16 in.)
Monogrammed and dated l. l.
"-V-1933"

Provenance: Staatlicher Kunsthandel der DDR, East Berlin; Neue Münchner Galerie, Munich.

Exhibitions: Munich, Neue Münchner Galerie, *Bruno Voigt: Gemälde, Zeichnungen, Graphik 1930–1948*, November 1983–February 1984; New York, Solomon R. Guggenheim Museum, *German Realist Drawings of the 1920's*, 15 May–6 July 1986 (traveled to Cambridge, Mass., Busch-Reisinger Museum, Harvard University, 26 July–28 September 1986; Graphische Sammlung, Staatsgalerie Stuttgart, 25 October–28 December 1986), cat. no. 119; Milwaukee, Patrick and Beatrice Haggerty Museum of Art, Marquette University, *Berlin in the 1920s and 1930s: A City of Decadence, Revolt, and Chaos—Watercolors and Drawings of Bruno Voigt*, 11 June–2 August 1987, cat. no. 15.

The Revolution Will Triumph consists of two images, one overlapping the other. The dominant image, a transparent bust of a man with grotesque features, is a caricatured type used by German artists throughout the 1920s to represent capitalism and its bourgeois practitioners, the investors, bankers, and industrialists perceived as the primary profiteers of a corrupt social and economic system. Around his fat neck, cinched by a stiff white celluloid collar, the capitalist wears a tie inscribed with a swastika to indicate his political loyalties. His distorted face, with thick red lips, squinting eyes, and small forehead, suggests coarseness, stupidity, and decadence.

Through this overwhelming figure of capitalism, images of workers are visible, active as groups, struggling for

their cause, carrying red flags and wearing the hammer-and-sickle insignia of the Communist Party. Buildings crack, crumble, and fall as the proletarian revolution progresses against capitalist institutions evoked by the word "Shell" and the fragmentary "I. G. Farben" (Germany's major chemical firm, a monopolistic conglomerate) inscribed on factory walls. As if the system were turning in on itself, moreover, the smokestacks point like so many cannons at the capitalist's head. At the bottom right, a worker appears, wearing a cap and Communist emblem, and defiantly presents the closed-fist salute.

Bruno Voigt's drawing illustrates the revolution, with its forcible triumph over capitalist exploitation and repression, predicted by Karl Marx at the end of *The Communist Manifesto*: "Let the ruling classes tremble at a Communistic revolution. The proletarians have nothing to lose but their chains. They have a world to win."[1] Voigt, however, produced his image in 1933, either immediately before or even after Adolf Hitler was appointed Chancellor on 30 January. The triumph of Fascism, not Communism, set the context in which Voigt delivered his political message. It was a time of unprecedented defeat for the Communist movement in Germany: the Party was legally dissolved, its leaders arrested, and workers forced to join the Nazi pseudo trade union, the German Labor Front. As Hitler consolidated his power, organized labor resistance became virtually impossible, and a Communist revolution seemed an unrealizable utopian dream.

Despite all this, Voigt's *The Revolution Will Triumph* announces the artist's dogged conviction that workers will prevail. His optimism in the face of apparently unpromising political reality was anchored in Marxist-Leninist teachings on the nature of capitalism. It is significant that Voigt foregrounds his image with a personification of capitalism and that the red specter of revolution is directed against him. Where other artists of the late 1920s and early 1930s focused their visual attacks on the person of Hitler, identifying the political problem in terms of an individual, for Voigt the dictator was but the historical tool of larger economic forces. Hitler was a puppet supported and manipulated by moneyed interests, much as John Heartfield depicted him in the famous 1932 photomontage *Millions Stand Behind Me (Millionen stehen hinter mir)*, where Hitler's Nazi salute doubles as a hand receiving cash from a domineering figure of capitalism.[2] Voigt's capitalist displays allegiance to Fascism, but it is a temporary allegiance which—like the tie—could be changed according to the demands of the situation, to ensure continuing expansion and profit.

Voigt's depiction of the revolution's ultimate triumph therefore counters the ostensible victories of Nazism with the view shared by most Communist Party leaders at the time—that Hitler marked the final phase of capitalism and that his rule, necessarily short-lived, would soon generate the proletarian revolution. This belief proved to be tragically wrong, of course, but during the early months of 1933, despite increasing repression and governmental violence,

the Communist Party desperately adhered to the idea that Hitler's very success proved that capitalism was historically doomed. The workers' revolution could not be restrained, and in the final analysis, Voigt maintained, the proletariat's struggle to free itself would triumph.   B. T. Y.

1. Karl Marx, *The Communist Manifesto*, trans. Samuel Moore (Baltimore: Penguin Books, 1976), 120.
2. See Dawn Ades, *Photomontage*, rev. ed. (London and New York: Thames and Hudson, 1976), illus. 59.

168   Bruno Voigt
Cultivate the Music of the German Home (Pflegt deutsche Hausmusik), 1933

Pen and ink, watercolor over pencil on paper
48.7 x 40.7 cm (19³/₁₆ x 16 in.)
Monogrammed and dated l. r.
"-V-/18. 1. 1933"

Provenance: Staatlicher Kunsthandel der DDR, East Berlin.

Exhibitions: Leipzig, Galerie am Sachsenplatz, *Bruno Voigt: Aquarelle, Zeichnungen und Radierungen*, 31 August–28 September 1986, cat. no. 83; Milwaukee, Patrick and Beatrice Haggerty Museum of Art, Marquette University, *Berlin in the 1920s and 1930s: A City of Decadence, Revolt, and Chaos—Watercolors and Drawings of Bruno Voigt*, 11 June–2 August 1987, cat. no. 14 (as *Pfleger* [sic] *deutsche Hausmusik* [*Cultivator of German Chamber Music*]).

Bruno Voigt's use in this drawing of the oft-repeated slogan "Cultivate the Music of the German Home" is obviously ironic. Music is indeed being "cultivated," but the "home" is a brothel, and the family to whose high spiritual and cultural level this musical togetherness testifies consists of four prostitutes and their pimp. Germans, particularly conservative Germans, prided themselves on their appreciation of, and subjective identity with, music and the rich native tradition of folk song as well as of compositions by "German masters." Arthur Schopenhauer's philosophical conclusion in the nineteenth century that music represents a universal language superior to words and logic because it provides access to the essence of things (*das Ding an sich*) had long been transformed into a sentimental emoting deemed an appropriate response to the work of Ludwig van Beethoven, Franz Schubert, and Richard Wagner.

Music is the enemy of all artificial alienation and antagonism among people, Friedrich Nietzsche wrote; it is "the return to nature, and simultaneously the purification and transformation of nature . . . nature transformed into love."[1] In a fashion certainly abhorrent to the philosopher of the *Übermensch*, this concept found application in one of the most infamous nineteenth-century German academic paintings, *Temporary Quarters outside Paris (Im Etappenquartier vor Paris)*

(1894) by the long-time director of the Prussian Academy of Fine Arts, Anton von Werner.[2] The scene depicts German soldiers during the Franco-Prussian War of 1870–71, their boots muddied, in a French Rococo *palais*; they gather, gravely attentive, around a grand piano while two of their comrades perform a Schubert *Lied*. The soldiers, so recently recognized as enemies, are joined by the family of the concierge as music overcomes the enmity previously felt, and human heart speaks directly to human heart in a common language of unifying emotion and aesthetic appreciation.

Von Werner's unbelievable scene of musical harmony is echoed and undermined in George Grosz's *God's Visible Blessing Is with Me*, one of a series of drawings providing a contemporary interpretation of Friedrich Schiller's eighteenth-century play *Die Räuber (The Robbers)*.[3] Grosz depicts Christmas Eve in an interior crowded with a Christmas tree, fruits, toys, chairs, tables, and a piano. A fat, cigar-puffing father, his wife, daughter, and two young sons complete this image of ostentatious prosperity and insensitive self-satisfaction. What unites Grosz's unappealing upper middle-class family is, as in the case of Werner's Prussian infantrymen, music. Playing with a hobbyhorse, gazing at the candle-covered tree, or sitting back in full-bellied relaxation, the family members listen intently as the daughter, her eyes closed in overwhelming emotion, plays the piano and sings the familiar words "Silent night, holy night."

Grosz's bitter commentary on society's materialistic "robbers" sharing the spiritual experience of music is analogous to Voigt's depiction of the guardians of German music as prostitutes and pimps, likewise not representatives of a humanity that is spiritually and culturally uplifted or uplifting. The truisms about music's powers and what its appreciation represents in an individual or a people are crassly unmasked as fatuously false by both artists. But "Silent Night," it might be argued, does at least function as a visible-aural sign of the bourgeois family's formal or legal unity as the primary unit of society; in Voigt's image even this ameliorating aspect of music's role is denied, as the *Haus* of his *Musik* is clearly not a home.

The watercolor *Cultivate the Music of the German Home* was included in the first exhibition of Voigt's work in the United States, at the Haggerty Museum of Marquette University in 1987. In response to the exhibition, Voigt wrote in English to Marvin Fishman to express his gratitude for the collector's efforts on his behalf.[4] Accompanying the letter is a self-portrait caricature, the artist's head crowned with the laurel of victory, which Voigt signed "the former fairy-tale prince Bruno the Great." The humorous but apt commentary of the 1930s was not forgotten or lost even as illness brought the artist ever closer to the end of his career.   R. H.

1. ". . . Rückkehr zur Natur, während sie zugleich Reinigung und Umwandlung der Natur ist . . . die in Liebe verwandelte Natur." Friedrich Nietzsche, "Richard Wagner in Bayreuth," in *Werke in drei Bän-*

den, vol. 1, ed. Karl Schlechta (Darmstadt: Wissenschaftliche Buchgemeinschaft, 1966), 388.

2. Collection Staatliche Museen Preussischer Kulturbesitz, Nationalgalerie, West Berlin; illus. in Nicolaas Teeuwisse, *Vom Salon zur Secession: Berliner Kunstleben zwischen Tradition und Aufbruch zur Moderne* (West Berlin: Deutscher Verlag für Kunstwissenschaft, 1986), 52.

3. *Gottes sichtbarer Segen ist bei mir*, pl. 6, *Die Räuber: Neun Lithographien zu Sentenzen aus Schillers 'Die Räuber'* (Berlin: Malik Verlag, 1922); illus. in Hans Hess, *George Grosz* (New Haven and London: Yale University Press, 1985), 113.

4. "I have all the newspaper [articles] of my drawings of the exhibition in Milwaukee. The great exhibition of the Martin-Gropius-Bau in Western-Berlin: I have seen two drawings of my hand on loan by Mr. Fishman. I was very happy, it was a great honour for my work." Bruno Voigt, in an unpublished letter to Marvin Fishman, dated 1.6.88. The exhibition in West Berlin to which Voigt refers is *Ich und die Stadt* (15 August–22 November 1987), in which the present cat. nos. 164 and 166 by Voigt were included.

169 Bruno Voigt
Solicitation (Auf Animiertour), 1933

Pen and ink on paper
50.6 x 36.3 cm (19¹⁵/₁₆ x 14¼ in.)
Monogrammed and dated l. r.
"-V-/33"

Provenance: Staatlicher Kunsthandel der DDR, East Berlin.

Exhibitions: Leipzig, Galerie am Sachsenplatz, *Bruno Voigt: Aquarelle, Zeichnungen und Radierungen*, 31 August–28 September 1986, cat. no. 100; Milwaukee, Patrick and Beatrice Haggerty Museum of Art, Marquette University, *Berlin in the 1920s and 1930s: A City of Decadence, Revolt, and Chaos—Watercolors and Drawings of Bruno Voigt*, 11 June–2 August 1987, cat. no. 8.

With a manner of drawing reminiscent of Karl Arnold's and a subject more immediately associated with George Grosz, Bruno Voigt here depicts a prostitute soliciting in the streets of a German city. An atmosphere of twilight, created with an ink splatter technique such as Grosz, too, favored, permeates the scene, but the darkness is broken by intense streetlamps, automobile headlights, and illuminated signs advertising hotels and stores. Like the commercial messages and the other indications of the city's prosperity, the prostitute's figure breaks through the dusk, an advertisement of the commodity she offers.

The prostitute displays herself before a partially opened doorway, her arms akimbo, booted legs spread, and her coat open to reveal a transparent dress. Near her strolls a wealthy bourgeois in bowler hat, fur-collared coat, and tweed pants. The potential customer, however, has failed to stop and respond to her offers. Her pursed lips may signal a noisy and desperate effort to mock his rejection and regain his attention, but even her mockery accentuates her dependence and inability to control her own life or livelihood. Voigt's exagger-

ated and bemused depiction may be amusing; in its underlying content, however, it condemns precisely what it presents.

The scene unmasks the society fostering prostitution as one in which individual fates are ignored or subsumed to the prosperity of commerce and capital. Unable to earn a living in the modern city in any other fashion, the woman has transformed herself into a commodity. The debasing labor of her profession, its repeated failures and demands for yet further tiring self-presentation, is Voigt's actual subject matter. It is combined with the commentary of the run-down tenement before which she stands: even if successful, her efforts do not gain her access to the world of lights and material well-being that function as a backdrop to the scene.

B. T. Y.

170 Bruno Voigt
Self-Portrait (Selbstporträt), 1935

Oil, tempera on artist's board
59.5 x 39 cm (23⁷/₁₆ x 15³/₈ in.)
Monogrammed and dated l. r.
"-bV-[intertwined]/1935"

Provenance: Galerie Michael Hasenclever, Munich.

During the summer of 1933, Bruno Voigt's studio in Weimar, the studio of a young art student who had for several years participated in Communist Party-sponsored youth organizations, was raided by police and SA men in search of anti-Fascist images and other evidence of political activity branded illegal by the Third Reich. Nothing, apparently, was found—"I was still able to save my works, the day before police and SA came to my studio to clean up for me," the artist recalled a few months before his death in 1988[1]—but soon thereafter Voigt ended his studies at the local, now-Nazified art school, married, and moved back to his native city, Gotha. Secretly he continued to produce politically critical drawings and watercolors, private images that gave form to frustrated and necessarily repressed political convictions. To continue working publicly within the confines of the Third Reich, he copied German Renaissance paintings and learned their technique, mixing oil paint with tempera, layering glazes to obtain smooth surfaces, pristine and dry.[2]

In 1935, Voigt painted several portraits of friends and also this self-portrait, within the parameters of his life under Nazi rule. A market for these works did not exist, however. Voigt's self-portrait, like his political drawings and watercolors, found justification only in fulfilling his desire to provide visual formulation for his convictions, to engage in a private opposition which could not directly address his public target.

And one wanted to produce some sort of documentation, wanted to leave behind some kind of evidence, wanted to show it to acquaintances as well, so one wanted to be active

politically, or else said to oneself, when this time is past maybe then the possibility will exist to be effective politically. So it's totally wrong to claim we wanted to create artworks. At least I didn't want to create any.[3]

The result was political art incapable of being political. Frustrated resistance and enforced immobility are the necessary content of this self-portrait as Voigt struggles to define the reality within which he is prisoner and his identity is under attack.

He depicts himself in a fur-trimmed coat, white shirt, and dark tie; raising his right hand to his lapel, he gazes downward with a deep frown and firmly closed mouth. In the background, mammoth cement pillars create a barren and oppressive architectural setting reminiscent of Albert Speer's buildings. The image of Voigt demonstratively silent and contemplative contrasts with self-images preceding 1933 in which he appears as a raging figure violently kicking down symbols of capitalist society, routing bankers, police, soldiers, and Nazis. Those pictures represented youthful fury, Voigt explained in 1988: "You do not see here the party-line Communist but the shouting and screaming individual, the revolter who tramples everything that does not suit him."[4] A similar rage for destruction in the ferocious desire to prevent a Nazi victory and to supplant the ideology of capitalism characterizes his depictions of street and barricade battles during 1932 and 1933, as his opposition concentrated itself in scenes of anticipated confrontation, of a final mighty effort which would evict the Nazi and imperialist scourge from power and introduce a humane proletarian future. The hope expressed in this violence is extirpated in the self-portrait in 1935 and replaced by a quiet attempt to survive within the imprisoning architectural environment whose Fascist massiveness now substitutes for earlier city streets and proletarian housing.

Voigt's self-portrait, in its technique, theme, and composition, also serves as an homage to Albrecht Dürer. The fur-collared coat, muted colors, position of the hand, and nearly frontal portrait-bust format readily recall Dürer's famous self-portrait of 1500 (Alte Pinakothek, Munich). By associating his own image and art with the paradigmatic German artist of the past, Voigt affirms his claim to a national cultural heritage then being distorted and appropriated by the Nazi propaganda machine. He reveals himself as an alternative manifestation of German identity. The melancholic pessimism of his self-representation after two years of Nazi rule is, perhaps, countered by the determination communicated by knit brows, large gazing eyes, and the hand, grasping at the lapel, which begins to form a fist. These subjective indicators, like the very assertion of continuing presence that a self-portrait necessarily contains, signal resistance. The portrait of the artist is evidence left behind, a testimony to his refusal to submit, a rejection of Nazi dominance and oppression.

But if Voigt's self-portrait, created in the face of nationalistic extremism and

paranoia, confirmed the endurance of German traditions in 1935 despite their being commandeered by Hitler, the artist soon realized that his belief in those traditions and their ability to survive by power of will, unaltered and purified, was a mirage. Years later, he recalled a conversation with the painter Martin Pohle in the Kirchbach Valley, near Weimar, in the 1930s during a hay harvest:

We sat in a hay stack. Pohle had been released again a few days earlier from Buchenwald. They locked him up every so often, for no reason at all. He was an intellectual, was quite elegant, and that was enough. And I said to him: "Our country is so beautiful here. Isn't it truly beautiful here. The scent of hay—everything is so wonderful." And then he said to me: "We no longer have a homeland. We never will have one again." And the worst part is, it proved [to be true]—I never forgot that sentence —and I have to admit, he was right.... It grieves me, I was born here, speak the language, but I am not at home anymore.[5]

R. H.

1. "Meine Arbeiten hatte ich noch retten können, am nächsten Tag kamen Polizei und SA in mein Atelier, um bei mir aufzuräumen." Bruno Voigt, "Ein Stückchen Lebenslauf," in Wolfgang Thiele, *Bruno Voigt 1912–1988: Widerstandskunst 1933–1944*, (West Berlin: AGO Galerie, 1988), 199.

2. German Renaissance technique was emulated by other artists of the 1920s and 1930s, with Otto Dix perhaps the best known among them. Voigt's lifelong admiration for Dix, another native of Gotha, should be taken into account in any conjecture as to his motivation in adopting this traditional manner of painting.

3. "Und man hat da eine Dokumentation machen wollen, man wollte was hinterlassen, man wollte es auch Bekannten zeigen, also man wollte doch politisch wirken oder sagte sich, wenn die Zeit vorbei ist, ist vielleicht die Möglichkeit da, politisch zu wirken. Also, es wäre völlig verfehlt zu behaupten, dass wir Kunstwerke machen wollten. Ich habe jedenfalls keine machen wollen." Voigt, quoted in Thiele, *Widerstandskunst*, 77.

4. "Man sieht da nicht den linientreuen Kommunisten, sondern den rumtobenden Menschen, den Revoltierer, der alles zertrampelt, was ihm nicht passt." Ibid., 74.

5. "Wir sassen in einem Heuhaufen, der Pohle war zwei Tage aus dem Buchenwald wieder mal entlassen worden. Wurde immer mal eingesperrt, ohne Grund. Das war ein Intellektueller, war sehr elegant, und das genügte hier. Und ich sagte zu ihm: 'Unsere Heimat ist schön. Das ist doch sehr schön hier. Das Heu duftet—es ist alles schön.' Und da sagte er zu mir: 'Wir haben keine Heimat mehr. Wir werden nie wieder eine haben.' Und das schlimme ist, das hat sich [bestätigt]—ich habe den Satz nie vergessen—und ich muss ihm recht geben.... Das tut mir sehr leid, ich bin hier geboren, spreche die Sprache, aber ich bin nicht mehr zu Hause." Ibid., 104.

Christoph Voll
Nude near Stove (Akt am Ofen),
c. 1920

Watercolor, pen and ink on
paper
34.8 x 50 cm (13^{11}/₁₆ x 19^{11}/₁₆ in.)
Signed l. r. "C. Voll"; collection
stamp verso "Stadtmuseum
Dresden"; inventory no. K1921/
102

Provenance: Stadtmuseum, Dresden; Galleria del Levante, Munich; Galerie Michael Hasenclever, Munich.

Among the works confiscated from the Dresden City Museum in accordance with Nazi art policies, which identified modern art as degenerate, was this small, wistful watercolor by the Dresden sculptor Christoph Voll. During the 1920s, the City Museum had carefully and systematically acquired works by artists active in the Saxon city, from *Brücke*'s innovative Expressionism to the late Expressionism and emergent *Neue Sachlichkeit* of Otto Dix, Conrad Felixmüller, and other artists of the Dresden Secession Group 1919. The collection provided the basis for the most spectacular of the early Nazi exhibitions documenting the "cultural Bolshevism of 1918–1933," *Spiegelbilder des Verfalls in der Kunst (Reflections of Decay in Art)*, which opened on 23 September 1933 at the City Museum. The exhibition then traveled to other German cities, and in 1937 formed the conceptual core of the notorious exhibition *Entartete Kunst (Degenerate Art)* in Munich.

On the occasion of the Munich exhibition, at the opening of the counter-exhibition devoted to examples of Nazi-approved art at the newly completed House of German Art, Adolf Hitler formulated his most extensive condemnation of contemporary "art processors," to be countered in his Thousand Year Reich by a "truly German art":

Today's new era is at work on a new type of human being. . . . This type of human being, which we first saw step forth in its gleaming, proud, bodily strength and health before the entire world last year at the Olympic Games, this type of human being, my dear prehistoricizing art-stammerers, is the type of the new era; and you, what is it that you fabricate? Misshapen cripples and cretins, women who can only be viewed as repulsive, men who seem closer to animals than to humans, children who, if any alive were like that, would have to be considered a curse of God![1]

Hitler demanded an art that would be not time-bound, neither "modern" nor "not modern" but rather an "immortal revelation emanating from the deepest essence of a people."[2]

By his vehement actions and verbal perorations against the art of the Weimar years, Hitler deprived it of a primarily aesthetic existence and associated even its most harmless images with the values of a system antagonistic to his own. It is informative, therefore, to consider Voll's small *Nude near Stove*, one of the works that fell victim to the Nazi "cleansing of the German

temple of art," as a demonstration of a fundamental aesthetic ideology which after 1933 would not be countenanced. For with its orchestrated anaturalistic pastel coloration, its gentle stylizations of the female nude and her surroundings, its playful references to an antecedent non-Renaissance and non-Hellenic visual vocabulary, Voll's watercolor clearly meets the criteria of Hitler's vociferously impassioned condemnation of "unnatural smearings and blottings."[3]

In his speech, Hitler recalled the destruction by fire of Munich's Crystal Palace that had resulted in 1931 in the loss of numerous examples of German Romanticism. His House of German Art was intended to replace the former exhibition building, while the German Romantics, he opined, should serve as ". . . the most beautiful examples of [the] German search for the real and true nature of our people and for a sincere and decent expression of this internally sensed law of life."[4] To some extent, Hitler voiced standard philistine objections to the manifestations of art since Impressionism, but, in accenting the ideal of an inherently "German" art characterized by the values of the *Volk*, he added a further defining component. "We desire," he proclaimed, "an art which carries in it a recognition of [our] racial structure and therefore takes on an undivided unified appearance."[5] Undifferentiated unity would be the hallmark of his German art; individual characteristics would be increasingly denied, leaving regimentation and uniformity as the generally recognizable "eternal" manifestation of the *Volk*.

Voll's watercolor provides the antithesis of Hitler's demand for a German homogeneity. The subjectivity of his presentation is its most immediately apparent quality, pronounced in a style Voll affected around 1920. In woodcuts and drawings,[6] he favored rounded, varied strokes, formed into simplified contours of plump figures. The heads of these figures dominate, large ovals containing wide-open eyes (one usually larger than the other), linear nose, and button-like lips, with minimal indications of hair. African or Oceanic sculpture may be a vaguely recalled prototype, but significantly translated into a vocabulary Voll shared in Dresden with Lasar Segall, akin also to the drawings of Otto Gleichmann (see cat. no. 46). A personally shaped aesthetic is manifest, only in part due to conscious emulation, dependent on similar responses to the preceding stylistic explorations of Expressionism. The personal and temporal constitute the watercolor's fundamental connotation as it depicts nude and bath brush, stove and window in an interior warmly tinged with orange and pink. The image is person-, time-, and locality-bound while participating in a more extensive art project.

Hitler objected to precisely this "Jewish discovery of the time-bound nature of art," and in his speech demanded its replacement by "manifestations of eternity."[7] In its accentuation of variance and its implicit denial of an eternally determined racial expression, despite its lyrical tone and small size, Voll's demurely rendered nude was seen as a threat to Hitler's perception of his

future order. In the collection of the Nazified Dresden City Museum, it functioned subversively and was eliminated.

R. H.

1. ". . . Kunstproduzenten . . . wahrhaft deutsche Kunst. . . . Die heutige neue Zeit arbeitet an einem neuen Menschentyp . . . . Dieser Menschentyp, den wir erst im vergangenen Jahr in den Olympischen Spielen in seiner strahlenden, stolzen, körperlichen Kraft und Gesundheit vor der ganzen Welt in Erscheinung treten sahen, dieser Menschentyp, meine Herren prähistorisierenden Kunststotterer, ist der Typ der neuen Zeit, und was fabrizieren Sie? Missgestaltete Krüppel und Kretins, Frauen, die nur abscheuerregend wirken können, Männer, die Tiere näher sind als Menschen, Kinder, die, wenn sie so leben würden, geradezu als Fluch Gottes empfunden werden müssten!" [Adolf Hitler], "Hitlers Rede zur Eröffnung der 'Grossen Deutschen Kunstausstellung' 1937," in *Nationalsozialismus und "Entartete Kunst": Die "Kunststadt" München 1937*, ed. Peter-Klaus Schuster (Munich: Prestel Verlag, 1987), 247, 246, 250.
2. ". . . eine aus dem tiefsten Wesen eines Volkes entstammende Offenbarung." Ibid., 244.
3. ". . . unnatürlichen Schmierereien und Klecksereien." Ibid., 247.
4. ". . . die schönsten Vertreter [des] deutschen Suchens nach der wirklichen und wahrhaften Natur unseres Volkes und nach einem aufrichtigen und anständigen Ausdruck dieses innerlich geahnten Lebensgesetzes." Ibid., 246.
5. "[Wir wollen] uns eine Kunst wünschen, die . . . in ihr immer mehr der Vereinheitlichung [unseres] Rassengefüges Rechnung trägt und damit einen einheitlichen geschlossenen Zug annimmt." Ibid.
6. The most extensive collection of Voll's prints is documented in Eberhard Frommhold's exhibition catalogue, *Christoph Voll: Radierungen und Holzschnitte* (Munich: Galleria del Levante, 1981). No comprehensive presentation of his drawings and other two-dimensional works currently exists.
7. ". . . der jüdischen Entdeckung der Zeitgebundenheit der Kunst . . ." in contrast to "Ewigkeitserscheinungen." *Nationalsozialismus und "Entartete Kunst,"* 244.

---

172 **Aloys Wach**
Street Scene (Strassenszene),
c. 1914

Brown chalk on brown paper
43.4 x 31.5 cm (17^{1}/₈ x 12^{7}/₁₆)
Signed l. c. "Wach"

Provenance: Christie's, New York.

Using dense hatching and elongated forms in this drawing, Aloys Wach combines fragments from different scenes at varying perspectives to produce a subtle collage effect. Centered in the image is a man with hands awkwardly held together; behind him are two mysterious figures in conversation. At the lower left, a woman in three-quarter view extends her right arm in an enigmatic gesture, while in the background, buildings list and lean around a large streetlamp. Light falls sharply on the figures, producing harsh tonal contrasts, which Wach manipulates in quasi-Cubist faceting, lending the scene

a dematerialized, kaleidoscopic effect of unstable surfaces.

The style of Wach's image corresponds to that of other works dating from late in his Paris stay of 1913 and 1914, such as the linocut *Nocturnal Scene (Nächtliche Szene)*.[1] His mannered, attenuated figures with their expressive hands suggest the influence of Amedeo Modigliani, whom Wach met in Paris and whose work he studied, but the dissolving Cubo-Futurist facture and obscure narrative are uniquely Wach's own. In both linocut and chalk drawing, the light-streaked, shadowy street with its prominent lamp serves as setting for some kind of encounter. The actors are variations of a single pair, a man and a woman viewed in successive scenes. Both works translate as scenes of solicitation, using a medieval device of sequential images to render the passage of time and continuing action.

In Paris, Wach adopted a repertoire of motifs that encompassed "the poor, the fallen, the homeless, cafés with nightlife,"[2] which he imbued with a mystical appearance. Often suffering from lack of money and shelter himself, he recognized his community with these unfortunates and in his work offered compassion founded in a vague religiosity. Shifted into the realm of political activism, in Munich after the November Revolution of 1918, Wach transferred these same mystic perceptions to his celebrations of socialism, clothed in a more radical style. He remained, however, unorthodox both politically and religiously. His attachment to the cause of revolution gave way, after 1920, to service in the Catholic Church, which he later rejected following a bishop's criticism of his work. He subordinated all loyalties to the demands of his art as he perceived them, and—as he wrote of his teacher—to his own personal "religiosity, rising above every religion: the reverence and belief for and in humanity."[3]

B. T. Y.

1. Illus. in Neue Galerie der Stadt Linz, *Klemens Brosch, Carl Anton Reichel, Aloys Wach* (Linz: Neue Galerie der Stadt Linz, 1982), 85. Wach did not sign his works with this name until after World War I. In the present drawing, the signature is clearly an addition from this later time, rather than contemporary with the creation of the image.
2. "Arme, Gefallene, Obdachlose, Cafés mit Nachtleben. . . ." Aloys Wach, quoted by Carl Hans Watzinger, "Aloys Wach und seine Bilder vom obderennsischen Bauernaufstand 1626," in Ausstellungsgruppe Firesü, *Aloys Wach 1892–1940: Gedächtnisausstellung* (Braunau am Inn: Firesü, 1979), 32.
3. "Seine über jede Religion hinwegsteigende Religiösität: die Ehrfurcht und der Glaube vor und an die Menschheit." Aloys Wach, "Aloys Wach in einer Selbstdarstellung (1925)," ibid., 16. Wach's description was of Albin Egger-Lienz, but applies even more to himself.

173 Aloys Wach
Dedicated to Kapp (Kapp gewidmet), c. 1920

Pen, violet ink, watercolor on toned paper
30.6 x 23.4 cm (12^1/$_{16}$ x 9^1/$_4$ in.)
Signed l. r. "Wach"; inscribed l. r. "Kapp gewidmet" (dedicated to Kapp)

Provenance: Galerie Wolfgang Ketterer, Munich.

The inscribed title largely determines the reading of this watercolor-and-ink drawing of a man passing with raised hands through a mountainous landscape. "Dedicated to Kapp"[1] refers to Wolfgang Kapp, a minor government official from East Prussia, one of the founders of the ultra-conservative *Vaterlandspartei* (Patriotic Party) and member of the National Association formed in October 1919 to overthrow the newly constituted German Republic. In March 1920, Kapp was briefly proclaimed head of the government during the abortive Kapp-Lüttwitz putsch.

The immediate cause of this attempted coup was an order to reduce Germany's military by three-quarters and to disband major units of the Freikorps in accordance with the Treaty of Versailles. General Walther von Lüttwitz, commander of troops in central and eastern Germany, refused to obey, and instead ordered the elite Naval Free Corps Brigade Erhardt, previously used to suppress the Spartacist revolt in Brunswick and active in the violent campaign against the Bavarian Soviet Republic, to occupy Berlin. Friedrich Ebert's government fled the capital city. No directions were left for the remaining government workers by the fleeing ministers, but Ebert's press secretary did issue a call for a general strike. When Kapp attempted to take up the abandoned reins of government as chancellor, therefore, the city came to a standstill. As such members of the government bureaucracy who attempted to work also refused to carry out Kapp's orders, the putsch collapsed in disarray within five days. Kapp and Lüttwitz fled to Sweden; Ebert returned with the constitutional government to Berlin.

Aloys Wach's dedication to the leader of the failed putsch is ironic in its intention. The artist was closely identified with the Bavarian Soviet Republic; he had contributed title-page woodcuts in April 1919 to the *Münchner Neueste Nachrichten* (*Latest Munich News*) and *Bayerischer Kurier* (*Bavarian Courier*) while these two newspapers were controlled by the Action Committee of Revolutionary Artists. When the Erhardt Brigade and other Freikorps and national troops brutally suppressed the council government, Wach fled Munich.[2] Detained in Simbach for several days because of passport irregularities, he finally succeeded in escaping through the Alps to an isolated farm near Braunau-am-Inn in Austria. Induced by the anti-revolutionary activities of the Erhardt Brigade, Wach's flight could be connected to Kapp indirectly through the Brigade's support of the Kapp-Lüttwitz putsch a year later;

hence the motivation for the watercolor's sardonic dedication.[3]

The motif of the fleeing figure might be applicable to either Wach or Kapp, although the mountainous setting corresponds more to the artist's route of escape, and recognition of the work as a stylized self-portrait further fixes the drawing's reference to Wach's own successful but harrowing efforts to elude Erhardt's marauding troops.[4] With its adaptation of Cubist faceting and Expressionism's mannered gesture, *Dedicated to Kapp* maintains a stylistic vocabulary shared by other young Expressionists who lent their art to the short-lived Munich Soviet Republic. A naturalistic coloration and quasi-Gothic elongation of forms further testify to efforts to produce a communal, "elemental," revolutionary art. According to this program, "landscapes are no longer this or that spot on earth, but . . . cosmic experiences that find their formulation in spatial-rhythmic subdivisions of the surface, through which the universal vitality of events differentiates itself. . . ."[5]

Melding religious, mystical, and political action and experience, *Dedicated to Kapp* presents Wach's elusion of capture in a manner recalling religious iconography. Wach himself appears with arms raised in a variation of an orante pose, with his knees bent as if beginning to genuflect. He is barefoot as he nears bushes and trees, like Moses approaching the burning bush. Wach's escape is transfigured into an allegory of the experience of the divine as golden light reflects off mountaintops and illuminates his figure while he flees from houses in the valley into the uninhabited heights of the Alps. Dedicated to Kapp, the drawing almost maliciously contrasts Wach's salvation through escape to Kapp's flight in failure.

B. T. Y.

1. Gallery and collection records indicate a previous misreading of the inscription as "Rapp [sic] gewidmet." The drawing was identified by means of the descriptive title *Man with Uplifted Arms in a Mountain Landscape*.
2. For details of Wach's and other artists' involvement with the radical Munich regime in March through May 1919, see Joan Weinstein, "Art and the November Revolution in Germany, 1918–1919" (Ph. D. diss., University of California, Los Angeles, 1986), 205ff. Her account of Wach's work during this period and of his escape to Austria is the most complete one to date.
3. Written with pencil which is not used elsewhere in the drawing, it is likely that the dedicatory inscription was added to the completed drawing. Despite the link to Kapp, the drawing therefore cannot be dated to 1920 with certainty, although its Cubo-Expressionist vocabulary is representative of Wach's work during 1919 and 1920.
4. Compare the features of the running figure to those of Wach's woodcut portrait by Fritz Schaefler, *Der Weg* 1 (January 1919): 3, as well as to Wach's allegorical self-portrait in the etching *In Praise of Mathematics* (*Lob der Mathematik*), 1920, illus. in Ausstellungsgruppe Firesü, *Aloys Wach 1892–1940: Gedächtnisausstellung* (Braunau-am-Inn: Firesü, 1979), 11. The trees in full leaf would also seem to be more appropriate to Wach's late springtime escape than Kapp's late winter one.

5. "Landschaften sind nicht immer dieser oder jener Erdenfleck, sondern es sind kosmische Erlebnisse, die ihren Niederschlag finden in räumlich-rhythmischer Aufteilung der Fläche, wobei die allgemeine Bewegtheit des Geschehens sich zu konkreter Raumerfüllung differenziert. . . ." Kurt Gerstenberg, "Abstraktionismus," *Der Weg* 1 (January 1919): 6.

174 William Wauer
Portrait of Albert Bassermann (Porträt Albert Bassermann), 1918

Bronze, ed. 6/7 (cast 1945)
51 x 20 x 20 cm (20^1/$_{16}$ x 7^7/$_8$ x 7^7/$_8$ in.)
Inscribed on front of base "Albert Bassermann"; signed and numbered, r. "W. Wauer 6–7"

Provenance: Estate of the artist; Galerie Brockstedt, Hamburg.

Herwarth Walden remarked in 1918 that William Wauer had "created absolute sculpture," having "resolved the problem of forming reality in an immediately plastic fashion, that is, without imitating nature."[1] Wauer augmented this characterization of his sculpture in a letter to Ludwig Justi, Director of Berlin's National Gallery, in 1928:

Like all artists, I naturally give form to my "ideal man." I wish him to be true to his essence through his physiological substance. I want him, freed of everything human-all-too-human, to be totally charged with the rhythms of the task assigned to his being.

The artistic means I employ are the most primitive, most spare, and most direct ones I consider necessary. That is how my form came to be; it concerns itself more with the inner than the exterior person.[2]

A fundamental dualism that divides reality into a spiritual essence and a visible, material appearance underlies both statements, but there is also the conviction that the sensuous is capable of expressing, of literally giving body to, the spiritual. This theory forms the basis of Wauer's Expressionist aesthetic and approach to his sculpture.

In this bust of the actor Albert Bassermann (1867–1952), one of a series of monumental portraits of friends and colleagues Wauer produced in 1918 and 1919, the angular forms of Expressionism, dissected planes of Cubism, and swinging, energetic lines of Futurism are fused in a synthesis of artistic trends dominant in Germany and propagated by Walden's *Der Sturm* gallery at the end of World War I. Rising from a roughly square socle, with an arched, elongated neck, the bust exhibits the taut energy of a drawn bow. Mouth open and eyes wide, their forms echoed by the sharp-edged subdivisions of surrounding facial planes, Bassermann is portrayed forcefully declaiming a role on stage. The features combine to create an emotionally charged, empathetic

representation of an actor and his metier. A physical likeness is retained, surprisingly, in this process of pressing the sculpture into an analogue of the actor's defining function, the "task assigned to his being."

Bassermann appeared in the German premier of the Austrian playwright Hans Müller's *Der Schöpfer* (*The Creator*) in Berlin in November 1918, and this is most likely the date of Wauer's portrait bust. One of the major actors of German Naturalism, Bassermann also appeared in silent films produced by Wauer prior to World War I. He was celebrated for his capacity to use his body as well as his voice to project a heightened reality of both the person and the milieu of the roles he played:

Albert Bassermann was born with his entire physical being into Naturalism. He experienced it corporeally. . . . That Bassermann's tall, slender, harmonic, elastic figure became the support for a realism of detail . . . is the most undeniable sign of the necessity of his art. And a proof that . . . not external measure, but inner rhythm determines his bodily manner of portrayal, the rhythm of his body's movements which are obeyed by voice and limbs alike. . . . Every minute movement of his dramatic figure trembles in echo through the movements of his unprecedentedly empathetic, schooled, disciplined limbs, and continues in the modulations of his sharp, all-encompassing voice that contains every possible contrast within it. . . . It always emerges in the tones of conversation, the accents of daily life, and yet these are raised to a level of insight that is already an analysis, a translation.[3]

Wauer condenses this characterization of the actor into the tense rhythms of his sculpture, in which a spiritual, dramatic force seems to emerge from the concentration of forms representing eyes, nose, and mouth. He constructed a physical likeness of Bassermann, infused with passion.

S. L. D.

1. "Die absolute Plastik schuf [William Wauer]. . . . das Problem gelöst, das Gegenständliche unmittelbar plastisch, also ohne Nachahmung der Natur zu gestalten." Herwarth Walden, "Zur Formulierung der neuen Kunst," *Expressionismus: Die Kunstwende* (Berlin: Verlag Der Sturm, 1918), 104.
2. "Ich gestalte natürlich, wie alle Künstler, meinen 'Idealmenschen.' Ich wünsche ihn wesensecht aus seiner pysiologischen Substanz. Ich wünsche ihn befreit von allem Menschlich-Allzumenschlichen ganz eingespannt in den Rhythmus seiner Daseinsaufgabe.
"Die künstlerischen Mittel, die ich aufwende, sind die primitivsten, knappsten, und direktesten, was ich für notwendig halte. So ist meine Form entstanden, die sich mehr auf den inneren, als den äusseren Menschen bezieht." William Wauer, letter to Ludwig Justi, 5 June 1928, Archives of the National Gallery, East Berlin, as cited in Staatliche Museen zu Berlin, *Expressionisten: Die Avantgarde in Deutschland 1905–1920* (East Berlin: Staatliche Museen zu Berlin, Nationalgalerie and Kupferstichkabinett, 1986), 382.
3. "Albert Bassermann wurde in den Naturalismus mit seiner ganzen Physis

hineingeboren. Er empfand ihn körperlich. . . . Dass Bassermanns hohe, schlanke, harmonische, elastische Figur der Stützpunkt für einen detaillierenden Realismus wurde . . . ist das unwiderlegbare Zeichen für die Notwendigkeit seiner Kunst. Und ein Beweis, dass . . . nicht das äussere Mass, sondern der innere Rhythmus auch die körperliche Darstellungsform bestimmt: der Bewegungstakt des Leibes, dem die Stimme wie die Glieder gehorchen. . . . Jede Schwingung der dramatischen Gestalt zittert in den Schwingungen der beispiellos empfindlichen, geschulten, beherrschten Glieder nach und setzt sich fort in den Schwingungen der jähen, umspringenden, alle Gegensätze umfassenden Stimme. . . . Sie hat immer den Tonfall des Gesprächs, die Akzente des alltäglichen Lebens und diese doch zu einer Eindringlichkeit gesteigert, die schon Gliederung, die schon Übersetzung ist." Herbert Ihering, *Albert Bassermann,* vol. 3 of *Der Schauspieler: Eine Monographiensammlung,* ed. Otto Zoff (Berlin: Erich Reiss Verlag, n. d.), 12–13.

175 Erich Wegner
Little Mary (Die kleine Mary),
c. 1920

Oil on canvas
35.2 x 33.3 cm (13⅞ x 13⅛ in.)
Signed l. r. "Wegner"; inscribed
on stretcher verso "Die kleine
Mary"

Provenance: Estate of the artist; Galerie
Michael Hasenclever, Munich.

In *Little Mary,* Erich Wegner couples the subject of a lower-class prostitute with an incommensurately innocent style, so that acerbic content is tempered by his neo-naïve technique and an air of whimsy. Although Wegner takes up a theme many of his contemporaries used as a means of social criticism, the initial effect of the image is comparatively benign, even affectionate. The social facts that are the drawing's referent are thus transformed, but in this very transformation reality becomes perceived in antagonistic contrast to the playful humor of *Little Mary.*

The rough contours of the image, its simplified forms and inconsistent perspective, are typical features of paintings by untrained artists. Compositionally, the scene is reduced to its fundamental elements: a cot, a curtained window, a table with clothes tossed upon it, and a single bowl in the foreground. On the bed, with garishly made-up face, wearing only stockings, "Little Mary" reclines with legs carelessly spread, smoking a cigarette and gazing at the viewer—her customer. Despite the frank pose, lack of modesty, as well as self-conscious display, there is surprisingly little erotic allure. The sensuousness of the image, ironically, is in its color orchestration rather than in the nude depicted.

The theme of prostitution is emblematic of twenties iconography. As artists became increasingly committed to social issues in the postwar era, all aspects of city life, especially social ills, perversions, or exploitation of one class by another, came to be used as visual ammunition against explicit or covert

social policy. The Weimar government was regarded as ineffectual by most of the political left, and, by engaging provocative and often grotesque imagery, artists launched an attack on the new, reluctantly democratic regime. Wegner's depiction of "Little Mary" is therefore conspicuous in its apparent lack of social or moral condemnation. But a certain rebelliousness can be recognized in Wegner's disengagement. His combination of a style signifying innocence and a vulgar subject reflects a rejection of mainstream values.

Although her submissive pose is reminiscent of conventional formulas, "Little Mary" undermines the notion of the human body as ideal form as well as the demure posturing and false coyness of the conventional female nude. Her casual, receptive attitude, as well as the absorbent mat beneath her hips, are references to the business of sex, and augment the notion of sex without intimacy. Wegner stripped the painting of romantic overtones, but neither condemned nor glorified his subject. His unexpected combination of a deliberate artlessness and an image of what is often taken as a moral statement, together with his avoidance of the sensuousness normally associated with the subject and with the medium itself, undercut mainstream moral constraints and the hallowed trappings of art itself.

C. D. G.

176 Erich Wegner
*Mangling Done Here (Hier kann
gerollt werden),* c. 1923

Watercolor with gouache, brush
and ink over pencil on paper
30.3 x 26.6–27.1 cm
(11¹⁵⁄₁₆ x 10½–10⅞ in.)
Signed l. r. "Wegner"; estate
stamp verso

Provenance: Estate of the artist; Galerie
Kühl, Hanover.

Erich Wegner's predilection for the neo-naïve is given full expression in this unusual watercolor merging aspects of graffiti, children's drawings, and amateur art. Although comprehensible in its individual components, the image becomes tantalizingly cryptic in the sum of its parts, a playful anagram that eludes definitive interpretation as it represents a city street in juxtaposition with an idyllic, gold-tinged landscape. The center of the drawing is dominated by a window-like rectangle within which a large, naked woman appears, resting her arms on a red rug draped across the window ledge. Her outsize proportions break with the scale of the other figures, and her relationship to the remainder of the scene is further put into doubt as the "window" that frames her seems to balance on a short pole, like a sign or billboard. She is a prostitute displaying herself in the vitrine of a brothel, an advertisement to potential customers passing by, but whether she is physically present or merely a picture within a picture is an open question.

The prostitute is central to Wegner's image and world, both in placement and signification. In the foreground,

behind the corrugated wall of a public urinal, stands a man whose unseen action is repeated by the diminutive dog with lifted leg at the base of the prostitute's pole. The man, with short-cropped hair, a dark suit, collarless shirt, and bowler hat—the caricatured uniform of the underclass—may be a petty criminal or pimp; he glances over his shoulder at the approaching figure of a grinning policeman. In conjunction with the framed nude, they comprise a compositional triangle at whose apex she appears, their dominating sign, but the relationship among the three is not clear. In the background, another woman stands before a door whose heart-shaped sign announces a "house of love." On the foreground wall, a schematized mangle accompanies a notice announcing that pressing is done here, a play on the German "rollen"—to press or mangle, but also to roll around—as a not so coy reference to sex play.

The graffitied mangle and the sign accompanying it are covert advertisements for a house of prostitution and thus announce the overall theme of the drawing—or rather, they relate clearly to half the drawing, for a distinctly separate world in color, style, and setting takes up the section to the left and behind the prostitute. Here, a bright, hilly landscape appears with setting sun and a pair of lovers who stroll arm in arm past a dark pool towards a park bench and a copse of pines. Is this to be understood as the arcadian obverse of the commercialized love that is dispersed like the disjointed frames of a silent film throughout the remainder of Wegner's fantasy? Or is this park but another setting for the "rolling" advertised on the foreground sign, part of a bifocal allegory of sexual interplay?

More mundane is the recognition of the sunset scene as a splotched, cracked, and peeling wall. It, too, serves as advertisement, then, of the business in which the central prostitute is engaged. The sentimental heart on the brothel's door is echoed by the scene of romance on its façade. But the buxom figure at the drawing's center undermines all efforts at a narrative or illusionistic reading of the image. Her valanced window breaks into both the yellow idyll with its red sun and the urban red-light district with its whores, pimps, and policemen. She overpowers all that surrounds her. Or perhaps she is, after all, only a placard within Wegner's flatly rendered scene, the reproduction of herself on permanent display in a world where fantasy is the sole remaining reality.

C. D. G.

177 Erich Wegner
Sailor in Port (Hafenkneipe),
1923

Gouache, brush and ink on
heavy brown paper
32.8 x 24.7 cm (12¹⁵⁄₁₆ x 9¾ in.)
Signed and dated l. c.
"Wegner 23"

Provenance: Galerie Schoenbrunn, Frankfurt a. M.

During the 1920s, sailors as subjects attracted the attention of several German artists, and Erich Wegner, who had grown up in the port city of Rostock, was among those who celebrated the adventuresome but often prosaic existence of seafaring men. Generally, however, his sailors are seen, not at sea or even aboard ship, but on land, where they attend to basic needs and desires, ranging from food and drink to women. In this drawing, Wegner depicts a sailor on shore leave, but refers to life at sea by placing a picture of a ship prominently above the sailor's head. Crudely schematized like a primitive mask, the man's tanned face dominates the composition. The intense contrast between his ruddy complexion and the white pallor of his companion underscores their gender difference. While her proximity to the sailor suggests a sexual relationship, there is no sign of affection between them. Like the plates of food and bottles of liquor, the woman can be seen as another object of the mariner's corporeal appetites.

In this work and others, Wegner consciously sought the look of an amateur painter. The clashing color fields of *Sailor in Port,* contained by heavy contour lines, read as distinctly flat planes; awkward outlines become willfully childlike in their rough simplification. Wegner achieves a disjointed effect by registering each element separately, as if according to its own individual law of perspective: the sailor's face in rigid profile, the service counter receding towards the right, the plates tilting upward to display their contents. Deliberately manipulating the vocabulary of naïve painting, Wegner creates a visual analogue to the artless, sailor's world he depicts.

Sailors appeared in art at this time as foils to conventional and complacent segments of society. Frequently presented as outsiders, not bound by constraints of domesticity, they renounced the comfort and security of bourgeois life. Wegner articulated this very basic means of living by engaging a deliberately crude style that reflects the rough and rustic life of the sailor. These types of themes were also popularized in the written works of Joachim Ringelnatz (pseudonym for Hans Bötticher, 1883–1934), a poet and painter who performed and wrote satirical sailor pieces, unabashedly raw and earthy. Ringelnatz, who was of the same generation as many of the *Neue Sachlichkeit* artists, was friendly with members of the Dresden Secession, and his writings parallel some of the themes taken up by Wegner. *Kuttel Daddeldu,* his series of poems published in the early twenties, is also the title of a 1930 watercolor by Wegner. The poems concern a sailor's adventures, incorporating parody, trivial sentimentality, and montage techniques. Wegner, too, emphasized the crude and ordinary aspects of a sailor's existence. Works like *Sailor in Port* provide a visual corollary to the renunciation of bourgeois culture implicit in Ringelnatz's writings and, in their consciously neo-naïve style, reject conventional artistic standards as well.

C. D. G.

178 Erich Wegner
Woman at a Gate (Frau am Zaun), 1923

Gouache on heavy paper
37.3 x 25.3 cm (14³/₄ x 10 in.)
Signed and dated l. r.
"Wegner/23"

Provenance: Galerie Schoenbrunn, Frankfurt a. M.

As iconography and narrative are minimized, Erich Wegner's attempt to achieve the look of a Sunday painter becomes pronounced in *Woman at a Gate*. The setting is an industrial landscape, with factories visible in the distance on the left. Close to the picture plane and just behind the *repoussoir* fence, framed by gate, wall, and trees, Wegner's woman in Sunday best dominates this simple composition. Her large head appears to be mismatched with a narrow body; her torso, intersected by the gatepost, is awkwardly rendered with impossible proportions. Such inconsistencies reveal Wegner's calculated emulation of the naïve; however, while his prototypes generally tend towards fantastic or dreamlike subjects, and focus on a remembered past, he sought an innocent vision in realizing contemporary themes.

Flatness governs the work: although some objects—wall and sidewalk, for instance—do seem to recede into space, other forms, such as the woman's arm, are emphatically two-dimensional. There is an intentional visual incongruity among the various elements, a play between flat pattern and illusionistic devices, that reveals an academic foundation in conjunction with an assumed ingenuousness. The artist seems intent on describing minutiae, such as the lace on the collar and the leaves on the trees, while sacrificing illusionistically convincing formal and spatial relations. His attempt to record details, his predilection for firm outlines, and inconsistent treatment of space are all reminiscent of naïve art. In this respect, Wegner's approach also serves as a renunciation of the vehement emotionalism of Expressionism. In contrast to what were considered contrived Expressionist ploys, which emphasized interior life and valorized feeling, Wegner captured the guilelessness and naïveté of amateur painters, which came to be seen as fresh, unspoiled, and genuine. He attempted to record the visual facts of a scene piece by piece, much as a child would construct an image; while he renounced the cohesion of the composition, he attained a childlike simplicity and solidity in his forms.　C. D. G.

179 Erich Wegner
Couple with a Sailboat (Paar mit Segelschiff), 1925

Watercolor over pencil on paper
35 x 26 cm (13¹³/₁₆ x 10¹/₄ in.)
Signed l. l. "Wegner"; signed, inscribed, and dated verso "Erich Wegner/Paar mit Segelschiff 1925"

Provenance: Hauswedell and Nolte, Hamburg.

This watercolor is more restrained in subject matter and style than Erich Wegner's many earlier sailor scenes. The use of black contour line and simple geometric form, as well as the airless quality of space and general neonaïve style, relate Wegner's work to other Hanover artists of the twenties, such as Grethe Jürgens (see cat. nos. 76–78). Centered around a couple in a harbor tavern, the composition is pared down to just a few elements: pictures of ships adorn the walls; the rectangular table is carefully drawn in accurate if obvious linear perspective. It is primarily through line rather than modeling that Wegner conveys spatial depth. The beer glasses on the table, for example, are given three-dimensional form by clear contours, while the contents of the glasses appear as flat color. The room itself is a simple space, with the junction of floor and wall indicated only by two different shades of brown.

Pensive and still, the woman wears a blue, short-sleeved dress; the man, in uniform, sits at right angles to her. The mood is partially determined by the gesture of the woman, who tenderly places her arm around the sailor's shoulder. Their eyes are cast down, and the scene has a tangible melancholy and gentleness that is conspicuously absent in Wegner's earlier sailor scenes. The pictures in the background, typical of harbor tavern decor, also suggest the sailor's imminent departure, and set the context for the couple's sad resignation to another period of separation. The tenderness apparent in this work may have been a result of a new attitude towards relationships affected by Wegner's recent marriage. Through a simple, direct style, he created the wistful mood of lovers, of a lower social class, parting.　C. D. G.

180 Kurt Weinhold
The New Window Display (Die neue Auslage), c. 1929–30

Pen and ink on paper
46 x 59.2 cm (18¹/₈ x 23¹/₄ in.), sight
Signed l. r. "Kurt Weinhold"; inscribed l. r. "Die neue Auslage"

Provenance: Galerie Schlichtenmaier, Grafenau.

Kurt Weinhold's drawing of a lingerie shop window was aptly employed to illustrate the article on lingerie fetishism in the *Illustrated Lexicon of Sexology* of 1930.[1] The pen drawing generates an ambiguous reality in which the two sides of the shopwindow, inside and outside, intermingle. A similar confusion emerges within the window display as human figures, mannequins, and mannequin fragments are juxtaposed in such a way as to render the constructed figures more animate and sensuous than their living prototypes.

A fashionably clothed woman, seen from the back at the left, stands before the window applying lipstick. Like an incongruous mirror reflection, a man, apparently oblivious to her presence, confronts her from behind the glass; his actual position, however, is beyond the vitrine, within the access door leading from the store into the window display. As he supervises the activity and the array of lingerie around him, the accented configuration of the crotch and fly of his trousers, concluding in his right hand grasping a smoking cigarette, suggests that the pleasure he derives from the view of numerous female undergarments is not professional alone but part of a voyeuristic, masturbatory fantasy.

Near him kneels a woman, her posture submissive while, as a window decorator, she adjusts a pair of beribboned pantaloons on the base supporting a camisole-clothed dummy. Arms outstretched and head thrown back, this construction of feminine appeal is one of a trio of similar three-dimensional advertisements for silk undergarments and hosiery, their dance-like postures in strong contrast to the static bearing of the three accompanying people. The sense of erotic abandon among these life-sized dolls is countered, however, by the central mannequin's pose, which recalls a twirling dance but also, incongruously and disturbingly, a crucifixion.

This signal of suffering and pain is echoed in the display that proudly identifies Hautana brassieres as the best available. What appears initially as the image of a woman kicking her legs emerges as a composite of representation and disjointed body parts suggesting dismemberment, as does the isolated, disconnected leg resting between the passerby and the store manager. In Weinhold's drawing, the world of consumer goods merges with the reality surrounding it. The various levels of looking and desiring likewise become indistinguishable, so that voyeurism extends beyond consumerism in the image, indicting the world of the spectator. An undertone of violence disrupts the cohesion of these realms of fantasy and fantasy-emulation, as women are addressed as consumers in order themselves to become products, willing or unwilling, of male consumption and potential victims of violence.　B. T. Y.

1. *Bilder-Lexicon der Sexualwissenschaft* (Vienna: Verlag für Kulturforschung, 1930; reprint, Hamburg, 1961).

181 Gustav Wunderwald
Underpass (Spandau) (Unterführung [Spandau]), c. 1927

Oil on canvas
66.3 x 83.7 cm (26¹/₈ x 33 in.)
Signed l. r. "Gustav Wunderwald"; inscribed on stretcher "Wunderwald"

Provenance: Galerie Neumann-Nierendorf, Berlin; Fritz Martin, Hamburg; Galerie Brockstedt, Hamburg; Galerie Michael Hasenclever, Munich.

Exhibitions: Essen, Folkwang Museum, *Kunst und Technik*, 8 June–22 July 1928, cat. no. 777; West Berlin, Rathaus Tiergarten, *Gustav Wunderwald: Berlin im Bild*, 7–22 October 1950 (traveled to Heimat-museum Spandau, 5–19 November 1950), cat. no. 13; West Berlin, Haus am Lützowplatz, *Gustav Wunderwald*, 13 January–11 February 1962, cat. no. 35; West Berlin, Centre Française de Wedding, *Grosstadt Berlin: Horst Stempel, Gustav Wunderwald*, 30 May–22 June 1962, cat. no. 11; Hamburg, Galerie Brockstedt, 20 January–20 April 1965, *Malerei der 20er Jahre: August Dressler, Karl Hubbuch, Gustav Wunderwald*; Wuppertal, Kunst- und Museumsverein, Von-der-Heydt Museum, *Magischer Realismus in Deutschland 1920–1933*, 10 September–29 October 1967, cat. no. 115; Hamburg, Kunstverein, *Realismus in der Malerei der zwanziger Jahre*, 19 October–1 December 1968 (traveled to Frankfurt a. M., Kunstverein, 14 December 1968–2 February 1969), cat. no. 150; Duisburg, Wilhelm-Lehmbruck-Museum, *Industrie und Technik in der deutschen Malerei*, 7 May–7 July 1969, cat. no. 227; Stuttgart, Württembergischer Kunstverein, *Realismus zwischen Revolution und Machtergreifung 1919–1933*, 25 September–28 November 1971, cat. no. 170; West Berlin, Berlinische Galerie, *Gustav Wunderwald: Gemälde, Handzeichnungen, Bühnenbilder—Eine Ausstellung zum 100. Geburtstag des Künstlers*, 20 August–10 October 1982 (traveled to Albstadt, Städtische Galerie, 21 November 1982–2 January 1983), cat. no. 57.

Paul Westheim, the influential editor of *Das Kunstblatt*, is credited with having discovered the painter Gustav Wunderwald. With the lead article of the January 1927 issue, Westheim identified him as Berlin's Maurice Utrillo, painting without academic training, portraying the city naïvely as if from a childhood memory:

The homeland of this person, the milieu in which he grew up, consists of factory chimneys and tenement houses. If now in Berlin and Spandau he depicts metropolitan streets with their apartment houses, false gables, billboards, courtyards, factories, etc., then it may be a recollection and reinvolvement with youthful impressions. At least that is how he sees it. The melancholic charm of this world otherwise perceived as so lacking in charm has never left him. In the process, of course, he also avoided what other artists are accustomed to bringing to this world: social pathos and social romanticism....He saw it without pathos, soberly characteristic, saw it—if one can still say this here—with the intimacy of someone who belongs there....[1]

Westheim introduces Wunderwald to the German public as an autodidactic painter, awed by the majesty of art and its proprieties ("...for a long, long time, [he lacked] the courage to give form to this personal experience in a painting")[2] but encouraged by the neo-objective ethos. Innocence and cultivated contact with the contemporary are posited, in a manner similar not only to Utrillo but also to *le Douanier* Rousseau, so that Wunderwald appears within an established modern tradition that guarantees genuineness and sincerity. Like Adalbert Trilhaase among the artist-circle of Mother Ey in Düsseldorf, Wunderwald is presented as a German parallel to the French "peintres du sacre-cœur" then being exhibited at the Paris gallery of Wilhelm Uhde and praised as rejuvenators of modern art.

In 1920, Wunderwald's Berlin incorporated surrounding communities into Greater Berlin to become the third-largest city in the world, ranking behind only New York and London. Among the towns annexed was Spandau, the industrial suburb where the railroad underpass in this painting, featuring streetcar line 54, was located.[3] The composition is a variation on one that Wunderwald frequently employed, with a street cutting diagonally into depth in the center, but here provides a sharp break which extends the foreground horizontally. The train tracks and road pass in heightened perspective under the bridge, but the sidewalk, embankment, and pier at the left set forth a broad area from which the flow backwards is launched. This area also establishes the painting's horizontal format and the arrangement of bridge and wires that cross the street, so that two major receding diagonals intersect in a neutralizing "X." The potential for a single dominant direction and sense of accelerated movement is thus canceled. Despite the advancing vehicles, the scene is one of frozen motion and implicit quiet, denying the roar of the motorcycle and the rattle of the streetcar.

Colors, including the yellow of the trolley which seems enveloped by its surroundings, are muted beneath the gray sky in an atmosphere of dusk. Composition and color harmony combine in a dreamlike scene, the present transformed into recollection. Wunderwald invents a personal reality founded in his observations of the Berlin whose streets he wandered. "You know," the artist wrote to his friend Wilhelm Schmidtborn in 1926, "I really am a regular street urchin, I only come to life once I am in the street—but only when alone—then everything in me gets going."[4] The street with its persistent transformations and movement acts as an inspiring muse, but Wunderwald grants his city scenes of the most changeable sections of Berlin the naïve artist's permanence of memory.[5] Even the bird perched in isolation above the streetcar and smokestacks of Spandau seems forever immutable, the fixed image of a dream by the painter Westheim identified as the portraitist of Berlin.

R. H. / C. D. G.

1. "Die Heimat dieses Menschen, das Milieu, in dem er aufgewachsen ist, sind die Fabrikschlote und Mietskasernen. Wenn er jetzt in Berlin und Spandau Grossstadtstrassen mit ihren Mietshäusern, Brandgiebeln, Reklameschildern, Hinterhöfen, Fabriken usw. malt, so mag das ein Rückerinnern und Wiederaufgreifen von Jugendeindrücken sein. Wenigstens empfindet er das so. Ihn hat der melancholische Reiz dieser sonst als reizlos empfundenen Welt nie losgelassen. Wobei ihm freilich das abging, was andere Maler in diese Welt hineinzutragen pflegten: Sozialpathos und Sozialromantik.... Er sah sie unpathetisch, sachlich charakteristisch, sah sie, wenn man das hier noch sagen darf, mit der Intimität des Zugehörigen...." Paul Westheim, "Gustav Wunderwald," Das Kunstblatt 11, no. 1 (January 1927): 3–4.
2. "...lange, sehr lange [hatte er] nicht den Mut, dieses persönliche Erlebnis als Bild zu gestalten." Ibid., 4.
3. The underpass appears to be one at the juncture of Grenadier- and Stresowstrasse.

See Hildegard Reinhardt, "Gustav Wunderwald: Leben und Werk," in Berlinische Galerie, Gustav Wunderwald: Gemälde, Handzeichnungen, Bühnenbilder—Eine Ausstellung zum 100. Geburtstag des Künstlers (West Berlin: Nicolaische Verlagsbuchhandlung, 1982), 65.
4. "Weisst Du, ich bin der richtige Strassenjunge, ich krieg erst Leben sobald ich auf der Strasse—aber nur allein—bin, dann gehts los." Gustav Wunderwald, in a letter of 7 December 1926, cited by Eberhard Roters, "Wunderwald und Berlin," in Berlinische Galerie, Gustav Wunderwald, 9.
5. In his emphasis on stasis, deep perspective, and long cast shadows, Wunderwald is comparable with Giorgio de Chirico and the Scuola metafisica, as are other artists of German Neue Sachlichkeit in the 1920s. Major distinctions should be recognized, however, and temptations to collapse the two schools into a single stylistic attitude should be resisted. Among other distinguishing elements, the surfaces of Wunderwald's paintings should be taken into account, so sharply antithetical to the smooth, trackless surfaces of de Chirico.

---

182   Magnus Zeller
In the Insane Asylum (*In der Irrenanstalt*), c. 1919–20

Pencil on heavy gray paper
21 x 20.5 cm (8¼ x 8¹/₁₆ in.)
Signed and dated l. r. "Zeller"
Verso: Pencil drawing of a cat,
c. 1919–20

Provenance: Villa Grisebach, West Berlin.

In his lithographic portfolio *The Time of the Revolution* (*Revolutionszeit*) and related paintings, Zeller recorded both the overt and the covert face of the November Revolution and its effects on German life and society. His witness to war and revolution was not restricted to these seven scenes, however, and extended into numerous additional drawings, many having allegorical significance and commentary hidden beneath the apparent reportage of their imagery. In its depiction of a group of mental patients in the walled courtyard of their hospital, each isolated from the other, each enacting with exaggerated gestures a role that defies rational explanation, *In the Insane Asylum* employs an iconography of the insane that extends back to the nineteenth century and forward into the 1920s (see cat. no. 34).

Unlike the war-derived imagery of madness in works by Erich Heckel, Otto Dix, or Conrad Felixmüller, Zeller's scene does not focus on the derangement and tragedy of a single person resulting from the terrors of war and the military. Instead, madness is here a shared characteristic and situation, even if communication is necessarily lacking between the affected individuals. Two of the men are seated, one examining an absent object "held" between his hands, the other, with clasped hands, gazing intently into nothingness. More significant is the trio of standing men, accompanied by a shadowy fourth. One of them, his left foot raised onto a platform-like box, gestures emphatically, his speech addressed to no one. Behind him, a com-

panion stands in a pose of extreme pensiveness, while the third man presses his ear against a wall as if to listen intently to whatever is occurring on the other side. Agitated speech, melancholic thought, and furtive eavesdropping are depicted in a manner which suggests that, together, the individuals represent three aspects of a shared concern. Their clothing, moreover, is not the simple uniform of an asylum, but clearly the formal jacket with tails that constantly served to characterize diplomats and government officials in caricatures and other political imagery of the time.

If Zeller intended the three standing inhabitants of this asylum to be thus identified they may represent postwar national leaders. Their audience splits between enraptured, uncomprehending attention and self-absorbed disregard, but their own espionage, thought, and oratory is similarly lacking in significance. The babbling, cogitation, and activity of madmen, Zeller concludes pessimistically in this drawing, characterizes the times in which he lives and to which his art bears witness. The post-revolutionary world appears to him as an insane aylum, having lost all reason.

R. H.

---

183   Magnus Zeller
Thieves (*Diebe*), 1919

Watercolor on paper
29.8 x 36.2 cm (11¾ x 14¼ in.)
Signed and dated l. r. "Magnus Zeller / 1919"

Provenance: Private collection, Germany; Leo Spik Kunsthaus, West Berlin.

After returning to Berlin from the war in 1919, Magnus Zeller created a series of paintings and lithographs devoted to aspects of the November Revolution and its aftermath. One of these images, an oil painting titled *Thieves*, depicts a man and woman looting a village, fleeing from storage sheds with stolen sacks of grain. Zeller's lithograph of the motif, included in his portfolio *The Time of the Revolution* (*Revolutionszeit*) published in 1920, reverses the composition and alters several details. This watercolor represents an early crystallization of the image Zeller further worked out in the oil painting and print. While most of the modifications Zeller makes as he shifts from one medium to another are minor, an obvious change from watercolor to oil painting occurs in the artist's suppression of the motif of the dead dog in the foreground. A wish to simplify the composition may have motivated this change, but it is probable also that Zeller considered the pathos-laden canine corpse a distraction from the general commentary of the image on looting.

In the repeated images of *Thieves*, as in the lithograph series in total, Zeller presents the underside of the Revolution, not its glory or heroism. This is particularly apparent in the lithographs, which contain none of the scenes of struggle common to revolutionary imagery. Instead, Zeller contrasts a ball game in the street with a funeral procession for the Revolution's victims, public fairs with furtive looting. The activity of revolution is not represented at all, but serves as the implied background to the ordinary citizen's experience, to threats of theft and death, to public celebrations intended to mask the realities of violence, inflation, and deprivation. Chronicling his era through images of such diverse occurrences and emotions, Zeller alludes to fading hopes for a new socialist society after the failed Spartacist revolts of 1919. *Thieves* documents the emergence of depravity, and the horror and helplessness many people felt.

Zeller achieves this duality of objective and subjective worlds not only in his subject matter, but also through a congruence of naturalistic and Expressionist styles. In the watercolor, blue-gray tonal gradations grant a coloristic harmony to the naturalistic scene, yet the stylized, elongated figures and the distorted spatial effects lend the image a feeling of unreality. No horizontals or verticals anchor the picture, and the exaggerated perspective, causing the corners of the buildings to rush together, heightens the sense of agitation. The confused pictorial diminution and the rush of the fence on the left produce a disjunctive mood of frenetic instability. Finally, the Cubist faceting of light on the figures and foreground contrasts to the naturalistic light of the moon as it rises over the house gable.

This infusion of the naturalistic scene with a consciously subjective style effects a perpetual shifting between experienced reality and subjective response, much as the critic Paul Fechter observed in Zeller's work in 1921:

> The strange unreality of Zeller's world, which is simultaneously somehow horribly real, derives from the fact that this painter works solely from his own vision. He develops his image of the world quite simply without using any models, quite simply from this inner talent, from this purely receptive relationship to the external world. Magnus Zeller is one of those people who are separated only by a thin, fragile wall from the essence of the world, from the metaphysical.[1]

B. T. Y.

1. "...die seltsame Unwirklichkeit der Zellerschen Welt, die doch zugleich etwas erschreckend Wirkliches hat, wächst eben daraus, dass dieser Maler rein aus seiner Vision heraus schafft, dass er eben diese, über das nur rezeptive Verhältnis zur Welt hinausgehende Produktivität besitzt, und aus diesem inneren Besitz, ohne Modell, lediglich seine Vorstellung von der Welt entwickelt. Magnus Zeller gehört zu den Menschen, die nur eine dünne, zerbrechliche Wand vom Wesen der Welt, von der Berührung mit dem Metaphysischen trennt." Paul Fechter, "Magnus Zeller," Der Cicerone 13 (1921): 343.

184 Magnus Zeller
In Flight (Auf der Flucht), 1920

Watercolor over pencil on paper
30.4–31.3 x 22.6–23 cm
(12–12⁵/₁₆ x 8⁷/₈–9¹/₁₆ in.)
Signed and dated l. r. "Magnus
Zeller/1920"

Provenance: Galerie Bodo Niemann, Berlin; Galerie Michael Hasenclever, Munich.

The size, technique, nocturnal setting, and concern with non-heroic aspects of postwar Germany place this watercolor in the series of paintings and prints Magnus Zeller produced from 1919 to 1920 on the November Revolution and its aftermath. Like his earlier images, *In Flight* draws its subject matter from the contradictions of everyday life during the frightful times following the failed Revolution. The stylistic and compositional devices of *Thieves* (cat. no. 183) are here maintained to render a scene of pursuit in which demonic forces shape action and events. The simply historical and incidental thus become universal, providing a commentary on human nature and existential experience rather than a record of a specific event.

In Flight depicts a person, apparently a woman although this is not clear, who has donned a dark blue cloak to meld into the night. Discovered, the fugitive is now pursued by a man in brown uniform, presumably Russian. The artist produces a rush of energy through the diagonal lines and sweeping forms of the fleeing foreground figure, who engages the viewer with red-rimmed, staring, terrified eyes. Zeller juxtaposes the village houses to their surrounding fences in such a way that there is little room for spatial transitions; details such as the downspout and overhanging roofs emphasize the center of the image, where the hands of the uniformed man reach violently towards the fleeing victim.

Zeller arouses a sense of the unknown and makes it central to the scene. The transforming effect of blue, traditional color of night and mystery, pervades all objects and atmospheres in the image; it pushes the drama of pursuit away from illusion and narrative, and silences the panting, running noises, and screams of hunter and hunted. Soundless where sound is expected, the image exists in a refined realm between the visionary and the seen world, as Max Osborn also noted:

> We see scenes before us that are derived from an impression of reality and which openly acknowledge this to us. But we also feel: this report, this representation does not exhaust what was important for the artist. The reality of the presentation is simultaneously illuminated by a strange shimmer that derives from the world of dreams and visions in which the hidden core of the material, tangible world first begins to reveal itself precisely through the magic of its fantastic veiling.[1]

Osborn's recourse to a quasi-mystical language of imagined veils and hidden nuclei, despite its imprecision, aptly characterizes Zeller's work. He was an artist who shared the concerns and motifs of more radical artists, both politically and artistically, but refused to subscribe to their collective principles and aesthetic. His works retain an attachment to a world of nuance and melancholic contemplation that seems alien to the violence of revolution, inflation, and political assassinations, even as such contexts formed their imagery. He chronicles a time of transition, freezing its momentary events and thereby granting their very transience the effect of permanence. B. T. Y.

1. "Wir sehen Szenen vor uns, die einem Eindruck der Wirklichkeit entnommen sind und ohne Scheu davon erzählen. Aber wir fühlen: nicht diese Mitteilung, dies Abbild erschöpft das, worauf es dem Künstler ankam; die Realität der Schilderung ist gleichsam durchleuchtet von einem Schimmer, der aus der Sphäre des Traumhaften, Visionären stammt, in der sich der versteckte Kern der materiell greifbaren Welt gerade durch die Zauberei phantastischer Verschleierung erst enthüllt." Max Osborn, "Magnus Zeller," *Velhagen & Klasings Monatshefte* 43, no. 3 (November 1932): 217.

185 Magnus Zeller
Macabre Business (Makabre Sache), c. 1921–22?

Pencil on heavy Bütten
18 x 23 cm (7¹/₁₆ x 9¹/₁₆ in.)
Signed l. r. "Magnus Zeller"; inscribed verso "Makabre Sache"

Provenance: Villa Grisebach, West Berlin.

After World War I, Magnus Zeller became one of the leading artists of the Berlin Secession, recognized for his variations on a mannered, "Gothic" expressive style that avoided the radical stylizations and distortions of Expressionism while retaining its subjective accent. In paintings, drawings, prints, and book illustrations of 1919–20, his slender, elongated figures acted out scenes of revolution, counterrevolution, and exploitation. Thereafter, however, they tended to appear as despondent individuals escaping the burdens of everyday existence in bars and cafés, brothels and circuses, cocaine parties and spiritualist seances, but they also inhabited idyllic pastoral settings with lovers or shepherd families, enacted urban experiences of misery and deprivation, embodied religious visions, or participated in eerily mysterious responses to nature. Whatever the motif or subject, Zeller injected into the scenes a quality of the uncanny, the inexplicable, and the grotesque as his figures existed in a murky, shadowed darkness from which silence emanated amid flashes of sharply revelatory light.

Macabre Business, possibly a project for a book illustration similar to those that Zeller provided for Leonid Andreyev's *Red Laughter*, published in 1922,[1] exploits a Poe-like morbidity in a nocturnal setting as two men rush furtively past walls and fences while half-carrying, half-dragging a limp third figure between them. Are they carousers bringing an unconscious drinking companion home? Is a crime, a murder, being hidden as the body is lugged away to be discarded in a dark, remote corner of a city's uninhabited outskirts? The title of the drawing suggests the latter, but Zeller offers no further clues to the narrative underlying his visual equivalent of an E. T. A. Hoffmann tale of gory fantasy. R. H.

1. For two of the six engravings that Zeller contributed to Leonid Andreyev, *Das Rote Lachen: Bruchstücke aus einer aufgefundenen Handschrift*, trans. Arthur Luther (Berlin: Euphorion Verlag, 1922), see Lothar Lang, *Expressionist Book Illustration in Germany 1907–1927* (Boston: New York Graphic Society, 1976), 209–210.

186 Richard Ziegler
*Young Widow (The New Me)
(Junge Witwe [Das zweite Ich])*, 1922

Oil on canvas
102 x 61 cm (39¹/₂ x 24 in.)
Monogrammed l. l. "RZ"

Provenance: Neue Münchner Galerie, Munich.

Exhibitions: West Berlin, Berlinische Galerie, Museum für Moderne Kunst, Photographie und Architektur im Martin-Gropius-Bau, *Ich und die Stadt: Mensch und Grosstadt in der deutschen Kunst des 20. Jahrhunderts*, 15 August–22 November 1987, cat. no. 208; Atlanta, High Museum of Art, *Art in Berlin 1815–1989*, 14 November 1989–14 January 1990, cat. no. 52.

Germany suffered 2,700,000 deaths as a result of World War I, some four percent of the country's prewar population. An obvious consequence was a noticeable increase in the number of widows, a significant proportion of them young widows. The art of Weimar Germany presents two major responses to this phenomenon. Images like Otto Dix's *Beggar Woman* (cat. no. 32) demonstrate compassion for women's grief and personal loss, often with a recognition of the plight of many whose widows' pensions failed to provide sufficient means during a period of severe inflation. In other cases, the war widow is reduced to an object of male fantasy in which a woman, deprived of her sexual partner, satisfies erotic needs either in masturbatory dreams of her dead husband or in a life of sensual celebration and profligacy. The paradigmatic male vision of women as perpetually aroused and available sexual creatures is linked here with the theme of death, so that widowhood becomes a virtual substitute marriage joining eros and thanatos, sensuality and the black garb of mourning.

Richard Ziegler envisions a young widow in a fashionable interior, a variation of reds and blacks, the corner of a room outfitted with a full-length mirror and a slender chair on which are draped several items of women's underwear. On the wall hangs a small oval portrait, probably of the late husband, in a gold frame. The woman, tall and slender, is naked except for a black veil, transparent black shawl, and black stockings with green garters. Standing in a gentle contrapposto pose, with her pale back and buttocks turned towards the viewer, she contemplates her reflection in the mirror. A cross on a rosary-like necklace hangs between her breasts, which she cradles voluptuously in the drapery of her black shawl. With her face hidden beneath the widow's veil, she observes the transformation of her marble-like, classically posed body into the warm apparition in the mirror, slightly crouching in a posture of anticipated movement, her legs spreading beneath the dark triangle of her pubic hair as if she were preparing to leap.

Ziegler thus symbolizes, with perhaps misplaced humor, the transformation or "liberation" of an attractive woman from repressed, religious wife and mourning widow into someone newly aware of her body and her sexual desirability. Through the device of the mirror, she appears as two women: one, pale-skinned, composed of light colors, stands within a room whose space and time the viewer shares; the other, in contrast to this *hic et nunc*, is a fantasized figure in warm, vital reds and oranges, the "new me" of the painting's subtitle. The scene corresponds to Hanns Heinz Ewers's representation of a woman in his novel *Alraune*:

> She tore off her blouse, lowered her skirts, undid her corset and threw it crashing against the mirror. "I need a man." . . . Her shift slid to the floor. She stood naked before the mirror, pressed her breasts up with both her hands. "Who wants me?" she called out loud. "Come on in—all of you together! It's free today—because we're celebrating—half price for children and soldiers."[1]

Ewers's intermittently pornographic novel, a semi-Expressionist and quasi-mystical updating of medieval legends, was written before the War but not published until 1919. It immediately gained wide popularity and was staged during the early 1920s, by then conservatively hinting at artistic contemporaneity, facility, and relaxed morality. Ziegler's voyeuristic painting shares much of this characterization as it continues in the established, self-consciously witty pattern of depicting erotically aroused, promiscuous, recently widowed young women.

The painting gains a more menacing subtext, however, as Ziegler presents his widow without personal identity, her face darkly concealed behind her black veil. The viewer perceives her totally in terms of the sexual unreality of her mirrored proffered body, unaware of her personal self and unable or unwilling to discover it. This objectification, moreover, is complicated by the image of death. The cross between her breasts signals religious conviction, but also death lurking in red-nippled carnality. The veil falling over her face is like the sinister hood of an executioner, permitting her to become the anonymous instrument of death itself; the gold-framed portrait of her deceased husband doubles as a trophy of one of her victims. In league with death, the irresistible glow of the widow's mirrored reflection in Ziegler's painting offers a false reality to disguise the actuality of her cold body, offering for the (male) viewer the frisson of death and danger accompanied by sex. The young widow's "new me" is commodified and reified, a *femme fatale* adjusted to the anxieties of the postwar years.

A. I. S. / R. H.

1. "Sie riss ihre Bluse herunter, streifte die Röcke ab, löste das Mieder, warf es krachend gegen den Spiegel. 'Einen Mann will ich!'...Das Hemd glitt herab, nackt stand sie vor dem Spiegel, presste mit beiden Händen ihre Brüste hoch. 'Wer will mich?' rief sie laut. 'Hereinspaziert —alle zusammen! Kost' keinen Pfennig heut—weil Festtag ist—für Kinder und Soldaten die Hälfte'." Hanns Heinz Ewers, *Alraune: Die Geschichte eines lebenden Wesens* (Munich: Georg Müller Verlag, 1919), 129.

187 Richard Ziegler
Couple at Table (Paar am Tisch), 1927

Oil on canvas
100 x 75 cm (39³/₈ x 29⁹/₁₆ in.)
Monogrammed and dated l. r.
"RZ 1927"

Provenance: Neue Münchner Galerie, Munich.

Exhibitions: West Berlin, Berlinische Galerie, Museum für Moderne Kunst, Photographie und Architektur im Martin-Gropius-Bau, *Ich und die Stadt: Mensch und Grossstadt in der deutschen Kunst des 20. Jahrhunderts*, 15 August–22 November 1987, cat. no. 210; Atlanta, High Museum of Art, *Art in Berlin 1815–1989*, 14 November 1989–14 January 1990, cat. no. 51 (as *Couple in Café [Paar am (sic) Café]*).

In couple seated at a café table, whether romantically involved or not, has been represented innumerable times by painters of every nationality since the mid-nineteenth century. The motif also attracted German artists of the 1920s, who used it as a means of social commentary on leisure-time habits of the bourgeoisie, or as an occasion for exploring encounters between prostitutes and their potential clients, frequently sailors (see cat. 177). Seldom, however, is the eroticism of the scene as drastic as in Richard Ziegler's *Couple at Table* with its poisonously fluorescent coloration.

The marble-topped table ubiquitous in German cafés here has been moved into the related interior of a brothel's reception room, where customers are met, teamed up, and provided with entertainment and drinks prior to fulfilling their primary wishes behind a strategically placed curtain. It is such a curtain, brilliant red-violet and partially transparent, that borders the right edge of Ziegler's painting and through which the body of a young woman shimmers. Waiting with apparent patience for the activity behind the curtain to end in order that they might take their turn there, the couple at the table drinks (although with only one glass, reserved for the customer) and plays cards (with a deck consisting only of

hearts). Her body provocatively revealed in a slipping camisole, black silk stockings, and green garters, the blond prostitute presses herself against her customer and caresses his hand in a practiced effort to initiate or maintain his sexual arousal. While she glows with the impassioned red of the curtain behind her, he appears pale, the tones of violet in his face cool within an ambience of blue-greens. His head propped on his hand, a smoking cigarette in the corner of his mouth, a bemused smile on his face, he gazes down at her through veiled eyes, and only the play of his eyebrows indicates a response to her heated female flesh.

Ziegler's colors suggest the contrast between the client's relaxed reserve, appropriate perhaps to a frequent and nonchalant customer of such commercial sexual favor, and the vitality of the young harlot; in their unnatural tonality, they also imply a decadent artificiality such as characterizes much of Ziegler's work. Moreover, the caricature-like depiction of the figures conjoined with the vibrantly decorative color scheme lends the scene a dominant tone of voyeuristic amusement, an invitation to empathetic participation in what is presented as an airy sexual fantasy.

The prostitute in the brothel fulfills the male sexual fantasy of women's perpetual availability, while the man maintains a reserve that connotes control and superiority not without the implication of subjugation and possible violence. In the context of 1927, Ziegler's scene takes on additional significance. On 25 January of that year, the Reichstag promulgated the law against regimentation, through which houses of prostitution would be prohibited, to become effective in October. The law, intended in part to end the virtual enslavement that characterized life in police-supervised brothels, threatened the abolition of an institution, although the fact that brothels were already nominally illegal under the imperial and Weimar constitutions had previously proven such hopes or fears illusory, and would do so this time as well. Even before the law was passed, the number of brothels in Berlin had begun to decline, to be replaced by other establishments ranging from private lodges to massage parlors.[1] Ziegler's image of sexual barter represents a ritual deemed endangered, a nostalgic record of a passing institution as October 1927 neared.

R. H.

1. Magnus Hirschfeld, ed., *Sittengeschichte des 20. Jahrhunderts*, vol. 2, *Zwischen zwei Katastrophen*, rev. ed. (Hanau a. M.: Verlag Karl Schustek, 1966), 411–413.

188 Richard Ziegler
Springtime on Tauentzien Street (Frühling auf der Tauentzien), 1927
From the series *Springtime in Berlin (Frühling in Berlin)*

Oil pastel, brush and ink on paper
38 x 28 cm (15 x 11 in.)
Signed and dated l. l. "R. Ziegler 27"; monogrammed, on sidewalk, "RZ"; inscribed c. r. "Frühling auf der/Tauentzien"

Provenance: Neue Münchner Galerie, Munich.

Complemented by doggerel verse in Berlin dialect, Richard Ziegler's series of oil pastels *Springtime in Berlin* provides an anecdotal, witty survey of the German capital's informal public milieu, the quotidian life in streets and cafés during the prosperous years before the Great Depression. The object of Ziegler's observation is less an overview of the social fabric, however, than the display of women and their public presence as objects of male scrutiny within a spectacle of erotic projection.

The setting of *Springtime on Tauentzien Street* is one of the streets off Kurfürstendamm, with its fashionable cafés and representative buildings, that served as a major collection point for Berlin's numerous prostitutes. The scene was such that, forty years later, aged men continued to recall the place with erotically nostalgic amusement as a type of sexual cafeteria: "That whole street was filled with little girls. And older ones, who made themselves up to look like little girls. They all wore special clothes—mini-mini dresses—and they would swing their handbags ....There were cheap hotels all around, and dance halls...."[1] Ziegler's pastel depicts such a "young girl," tall and slender, alone and attentive on a street corner. Her purse clutched close, she wears her stylish, fur-trimmed coat short to reveal long legs in dark stockings and high-heeled shoes. Associated with the image, a text verbalizes her thoughts in broadly common Berlin tones: "Early while cocks are still crowing, and stars their twinkling stop, I stand here on my spot, have to get fires glowing."[2] Huddled against the cold of an early springtime morning, she awaits her first customer, one of the corps of night-shift workers from nearby hotels and train stations.

Ziegler's nuanced colors and refined forms lend his depiction a sense of amused sympathy, the fondness of a voyeuristic interest. As he presents her isolated on her street corner in 1927, Ziegler may also be giving unwitting testimony to the official abolition of houses of prostitution that year in Germany. One of the new law's direct but unintended effects was an increase in the number of women, not infrequently homeless, who solicited alone on the streets. Ziegler's well-dressed woman, however, in no way addresses —nor is she intended to address—the problem of prostitution. The image, moreover, ignores the actual situation of Berlin's 6,125 officially registered and significantly more unregistered prostitutes, whether in brothels or not.[3]

Springtime on Tauentzien Street is, instead, a declaration of affection for the Berlin *Mädchen ums Geld*, a creature more imagined than real, humorous and entertaining, attractive and fashionable, but from the *Volk*, speaking the dialect of the city masses and retaining an unspoiled core of naïveté, innocence, and generosity. The type portrayed is not Ziegler's alone, but appears frequently among left-wing intellectuals, writers, and artists. Rejecting the bourgeoisie and bourgeois morality, they praised the prostitute, while also lifting her from her Marxist reality as a symptom of capitalist decadence to a realm of sentimentalized, glorified sexuality and erotic pleasure.

R. H.

1. Fritz Bamberger, as cited by Otto Friedrich, *Before the Deluge: A Portrait of Berlin in the 1920's* (New York: Harper & Row, 1972), 154.
2. "Früh noch die Hähne krähn/wenn die Sternlein ferschwinden/mus ick am trottoir sten/mus Feuer zünden."
3. These statistics are from the 1925 census; see Magnus Hirschfeld, ed., *Sittengeschichte des 20. Jahrhunderts*, vol. 2, *Zwischen zwei Katastrophen*, rev. ed. (Hanau a. M.: Verlag Karl Schustek, 1966), 403.

189 Richard Ziegler
Sylvia von Harden, 1927

Oil pastel, pen and ink on rice paper
39.5 x 29.3 cm (15⁹/₁₆ x 11⁹/₁₆ in.)
Monogrammed and dated l. r. "1927 RZ"; inscribed l. r. "Sylvia von Harden"

Provenance: Galerie Wolfgang Ketterer, Munich.

Exhibitions: West Berlin, Berlinische Galerie, Museum für Moderne Kunst, Photographie und Architektur im Martin-Gropius-Bau, *Ich und die Stadt: Mensch und Grossstadt in der deutschen Kunst des 20. Jahrhunderts* 15 August–22 November 1987, cat. no. 209; Ingelheim am Rhein, Museum-Altes-Rathaus, *Der Traum von einer Neuen Welt: Berlin 1910–1933*, 33 April–4 June 1989, cat. no. 149.

Somewhat like a female version of John Hoexter (see cat. no. 64), but less self-destructive, Sylvia von Harden, née Nehr (1893–1962), was a stalwart of the bohemian group of patrons of the Romanisches Café. She wrote poetry, published cheap novels, and contributed irregularly to various journals, such as Alfred Flechtheim's *Der Querschnitt (The Cross Section)*, and newspapers, such as the *Dresdener Nachrichten (Dresden News)*. Associated with the Dresden Secession Group 1919, she came to know Otto Dix, and his portrait of her seated at a marble café table in 1926[1] established an iconography of androgynous bohemian eccentricity which Richard Ziegler's small pastel echoes in its caricatured features. Both artists show the writer as an awkward, lanky figure in a loosely fitting checkered dress, hair cut short, monocle fixed, and cigarette in hand. Ziegler's subjective distortions, however, provide a more humorous and affectionate view than Dix's hard-edged visual reportage.

Von Harden is seated on cushions, not a chair or sofa, in an informal posture that determines the entire image. At her side, Ziegler renders her purse and an ashtray. Her position forces her gangly legs up, with the result that her already short dress likewise slides upward, and she tugs at it to cover the generous display of undergarments that has appeared. Nonchalance characterizes her attitude, not conventional embarrassment or desperation, and she leans back, one long arm stretched out awkwardly with her cigarette. The trademark monocle does not slip, however, nor does the smile of recognition on her brilliantly red lips.   A. I. S.

1. Musée National d'Art Moderne, Centre Georges Pompidou, Paris, illus. in Fritz Löffler, *Otto Dix: Leben und Werk*, 2d ed. (Wiesbaden: Drei Lilien Verlag, 1989), pl. 88.

190 Richard Ziegler
In the Café (Im Café), c. 1927

Oil pastel, brush and ink on rice paper
32.4 x 21.7 cm (12³/₄ x 8⁹/₁₆ in.)
Signed l. r. "R. Ziegler"

Provenance: Galerie Wolfgang Ketterer, Munich.

Exhibitions: University Art Museum, University of Minnesota, Minneapolis, *Berlin: Art and Metropolis—Works on Paper 1912–1932*, 8 September–11 October 1987; Ingelheim am Rhein, Museum-Altes-Rathaus, *Der Traum von einer neuen Welt: Berlin 1910–1933*, 23 April–4 June 1989, cat. no. 147.

Prosperity, display, and indulgence inform the upper middle-class clientele of Richard Ziegler's café scene. The setting is a familiar one in which patrons sit around a marble-topped table, drinking and smoking, as a uniformed waitress brings their order. Minimal indications of the surroundings are given, just sufficient to identify a curtained interior. The richly saturated colors of the oil pastel medium, the drawing's rubbed surfaces and softened contours, provide a visual analogue of luxury and the tactile pleasures of furs, varieties of cloth, and palpable warmth of the café's atmosphere scented by perfumes, coffee, and smoke. It is a notably sensual and artificial environment, a comfortable alternative reality, a place of escape from the mundane and routine, where drinks do not serve to quench thirst and food is not meant to appease hunger.

Ziegler disrupts his celebration of the café's social pleasures with ribald irony by capping his composition with a sign, immediately above the waitress's shoulder, announcing the café's toilet facilities. Luxury and apparent refinement are undermined by this reference to common needs, and voluptuous curtains simply mask a washroom entrance. Similarly, the trio at the table engage in an ostentatious display that fails to disguise their fundamental vulgarity. In particular, the woman at the right sits unceremoniously, ponderous in her chair, her slip pushing out from under her skirt. She grasps a ludi-crously small purse with her left hand while her right rests claw-like on the table. Her expansive form, constricted in her skirt and luxuriously furred jacket, explodes from the collar into a multiplicity of chins and a face accented by a variety of moles. A fluff of hair escapes her blue cloche hat and deep red lipstick highlights her heavy lips. Ziegler presents her as the smirking, self-satisfied caricature or tragically failed imitation of the young woman seated opposite her, perhaps her daughter—or the mistress of the man accompanying them, presumably the husband, close to the older woman in age and with clothes and demeanor likewise signaling social and financial success.

Like many of the café representations from the Weimar years, Ziegler's pastel records the fixtures of bourgeois society; types, not individuals, are depicted: successful businessman, "pretty young thing," and aging matron desperately wishing to retrieve youth. The artist's distortions join with deftly manipulated colors and nuanced drawing simultaneously to characterize the scene and to serve as antithesis to the commonness of the people depicted.   R. H.

191 Richard Ziegler
Lovers in Armchair (Liebespaar im Sessel), c. 1928

Oil pastel, pen and ink, ink tusche on rag paper
23.5 x 16 cm (9¹/₄ x 6¹/₄ in.)
Signed l. c. "R. Ziegler"

Provenance: Galerie Wolfgang Ketterer, Munich.

Richard Ziegler's small pastel, rendered with a quick and sure hand in which an economy of line and color elegantly defines the scene, depicts a woman draped casually over a man's lap. Her hair cut short, shorter indeed than his, her long legs dangle over the chair arm to reveal a single blue garter. She places one arm casually on his shoulder, the other extends in an ostentatious, mannered display of her cigarette in its silver holder. The man, his arms stretched awkwardly around her, appears as a dark-suited amorphous configuration with broadly splashed outlines, spiky hair, protruding ears, and thick neck. His plump mien contrasts to the tendriled linearity of the female figure, a contrast of bumbling coarseness and sophisticated refinement.

Remarkably, or perhaps perversely, Ziegler arrives at these definitions of his actors' characters and personalities by depicting them from the back. Their faces and other identifying features are not seen, and the broad blue arc of the chair, bending under the weight imposed upon it, hides most of the remainder of their bodies. The pastel, wittily erotic in its implications, is an exceptional display of Ziegler's fluent proficiency as narrative draftsman and social commentator able to render with minimal means the mores of the society he witnesses.   R. H.

192 Richard Ziegler
On the Way to the Office in the Underground (Auf dem Weg ins Kontor in der Untergrund), 1927
From the series *Springtime in Berlin (Frühling in Berlin)*

Oil pastel, brush and ink on rice paper
35.6 x 25.4 cm (14 x 10¹/₁₆ in.)
Monogrammed l. c. of image "RZ"; signed and dated l. r. of image "R Ziegler/27"; inscribed l. c. of sheet "Auf dem Weg ins Kontor/in der Untergrund— '. . . housse-baisse'—'haste Paste Viandal:/lachste machste dir dein Mahl'—'plötzlich stand/er for ir, der Held, fon dem sie so hold geträumt hatte/und daz Blut brannte ihr heiz auf den Wangen'—/'daz rouge der Dame fon Welt'—'Tipfräulein gesucht'—"

Provenance: Neue Münchner Galerie, Munich.

Exhibitions: University Art Museum, University of Minnesota, Minneapolis, *Berlin: Art and Metropolis—Works on Paper 1912–1932*, 8 September–11 October 1987.

The anonymous confrontation of individuals in trains and buses has amused and intrigued artists since the invention of such public conveyances in the nineteenth century. In the late 1920s, the motif of passengers absorbed in their own reality despite the physical closeness of others provided Richard Ziegler with yet another ironic perception of modern women in their urban milieu. Among his series of pastels titled *Springtime in Berlin (Frühling in Berlin)* is this image of a subway car populated by two individuals: a young female office worker sits informally, resting her purse on her lap, lost in the pages of a paperback novel; at her side, but physically separated by a pole, a young man rides with legs crossed, absorbed in the *Berliner Zeitung*, the financial newspaper that identifies him as a bank employee, accountant, or other finance-oriented worker. The two ignore each other, but their reading matter, recorded by Ziegler in the caption, juxtaposes their disparate worlds in an unconsciously flirtatious dialogue of advertisements and narrative fragments rendered in stock market jargon and Berlin dialect: "bullish/bearish"; "if you've got Viandal paste, laugh and you've got it made"; "suddenly he stood before her, the hero she had had such sweet dreams about, and her cheeks burned hot"; "the rouge of the woman of the world"; "typist wanted."

The hero dreamed forth in her book is seated at her side; the secretary he seeks is finding romance next to him between the soft red covers of her book. In Ziegler's world, surely they shall discover each other. The newspaper gently admonishes, "be gentle with her heart."[1] And the advertisements that surround them promise a happy future, beginning with a trip, as one slogan paraphrases Goethe's famous ode to Italy: "Knowest thou the land where the citrons bloom. There too they use Urbin to polish each shoe."[2] As time goes on, she may need to pay attention to another jingle: "Breasts will not get flabby if Hautana you keep handy."[3] And he—as well as she—will be wise to heed the final major commercial adage on the personal relationships of marriage: "If you have a mother-in-law, please her with Karisch coffee, tea, and crackers."[4]   R. H.

1. "Schon ihr Herz."
2. "Kennst du das Land wo die Zitronen blühen. Auch dort putzt man die Schuhe mit Urbin."
3. "Busen breitet sich nicht aus, hast Hautana du im Haus."
4. "Hast du eine Schwiegermutter, Pfleg se mit Karisch-Kaffee, Tee und Keks."

193 Richard Ziegler
Judgment of Paris (Parisurteil), 1928

Oil, ink on canvas
85.3 x 100.4 cm (33¹/₂ x 39¹/₂ in.)
Monogrammed and dated l. r. "R. Z./28"

Provenance: Neue Münchner Galerie, Munich.

Ancient Greek legend tells of the shepherd Paris who was called upon to determine which of three goddesses—Hera, Aphrodite, or Athena—was the most beautiful. A frequent subject in art since antiquity, the judgment of Paris had often been transformed since the nineteenth century into a contemporary scene, usually set in a brothel where a potential customer is presented with a choice among three disrobed prostitutes. In Richard Ziegler's interpretation of the event, a modern office, equipped with telephone, desk, wastebasket, and calendar, becomes the setting for yet another variation on the motif of three young women tendering their bodies for comparative assessment. Their judge in this case is not a naïve shepherd but a prototypical, fat capitalist businessman. Seeking employment as typists or telephone operators, the women are also expected to proffer sexual favors, and it is thus their physical allure more than any secretarial skills that will determine which of the three is to be hired.

By 1925, over one-third of all German women were employed outside the home. This was partly a result of wartime demands, which continued into the postwar era since female labor proved to be cheaper than its male counterpart. Political parties and women's organizations attempted to respond to this new level of women's participation in the public economic life of the nation and the problems which it engendered. Analyzing the conditions under which women gained employment, one commentator has observed:

From the confined and familiar circle of age-old family mores and habits of life, woman here enters the unfamiliar, icy atmosphere of an earnings- and profit-hungry struggle for existence. . . . Her efforts are made more difficult above all by two circumstances: by her own inner uncertainty in this new territory and by the imposed difficulties that arise in her professional relationship with man within this totally new form of interaction among the sexes, and with which man, too, is unfamiliar.

What, then, was often demanded of women as they earned their bread was prostitution. Whoever seeks the specifics should read contemporary reports of the labor and employment courts. . . . Thus the woman employee in workplaces of the kind indicated not only had to supply her working skills, and these at low wages, but often also a piece of her own womanhood, otherwise so avidly protected in the family confines of old.[1]

The situation was one often depicted by Weimar Germany's artists. In a coarsely humorous illustration in the July 1923 issue of *Die Pleite* (*Bankruptcy*), Rudolf Schlichter provided an image of a clerical employee who stands demurely before her boss and asks for a raise only to receive the response, "Why do you need a raise? You have venture capital under your skirt!"[2] In the context of the Communist Party-oriented satirical magazine, Schlichter's drawing is a pointed critique of the capitalist system and its principles of exploitation, made apparent in the contrast of the well-fed boss and undernourished secretary. Ziegler's painting is also concerned with the exploitation of women by employers, but lacks the political context that complemented Schlichter's drawing. The painting now has sexual submission serve as the very condition of employment; its mode of presentation, however, is neutral, without any clear indication of the artist's attitude towards such practices.

As they hike skirts and bare breasts to the consuming male gaze of a prospective employer, Ziegler's women advertise themselves in the conventional poses of contemporary fashion, film, and glamor magazines. One, moreover, stands in a direct quotation of Sandro Botticelli's *Birth of Venus* (c. 1480), transforming the Renaissance goddess's gestures of modesty into a brazen sexual display. With practiced familiarity, the women place themselves in submissive roles and postures through which individuality and personality are denied; they become a class of consumable objects, provocative items of fetishistic spectacle. Stylistically, Ziegler's complex interweaving of highly animated lines, reminiscent of *Jugendstil* but also derived from popular illustration, increases this anonymity of sensual presentation as it distracts the viewer and transforms the scene into a lively linear arabesque. This effect is enhanced by Ziegler's unusual rendering of a large oil painting in the black-and-white linear mode of magazine illustration. The theme of women's metamorphosis into erotically appealing but depersonalized commodities thus applies to the manner of depiction as well. Ziegler clothes the image of a condemnable practice in an alluring, readily acceptable style.   A. I. S. / R. H.

1. "Aus dem beengten und vertrauten Kreise der althergebrachten Familiensitten und Lebensgewohnheiten tritt hier die Frau in die unbekannte, eisige Atmosphäre verdienst- und profithungrigen Daseinskampfes. . . . Erschwert wird ihr dies . . . vor allem durch zwei Umstände: durch die eigene innere Unsicherheit auf dem neuen Boden und die äusseren Schwierigkeiten, die ihr aus ihrem Frauentum im Berufumgang mit dem Manne aus dieser auch für den Mann völlig neuen Form der Beziehungen zwischen den Geschlechtern erwachsen.

"Was da oft von den Frauen verlangt wurde, war Prostitution ums Brot. Wer Information wünscht, lese die Berichte von damaligen Arbeitsgerichtsverhandlungen. . . . So hatte die Angestellte in Arbeitsstellen der genannten Art nicht nur ihre Arbeitskraft und diese für einen niedrigen Lohn, sondern oft auch ein Stück ihres in der alten Familie so gehüteten Weibtums herzugeben." Meta Krauss-Fessel, "Frauenarbeit und Frauenemanzipation in der Nachkriegszeit ab 1919," in Magnus Hirschfeld, ed., *Sittengeschichte des 20. Jahrhunderts*, vol. 2, *Zwischen zwei Katastrophen*, rev. ed. (Hanau a. M.: Verlag Karl Schustek, 1966), 177.
2. Rudolf Schlichter, "Was brauchen Sie Lohnerhöhung, Sie haben ja Kapital unterm Rock!" *Die Pleite* 7 (July 1923), reprinted ibid., 175.

Artists' Biographies

Max Beckmann

1884   Born 12 February in Leipzig, the third child of Antoinette Henriette Bertha Dübler and Carl Christian Heinrich Beckmann, a grain dealer from Brunswick and self-taught experimental chemist.

1890–94   Attends school in Falkenburg in Pomerania.

1894   Father dies; family moves to Brunswick. Schooling continued in Brunswick, Königslutter, and Gandersheim.

1899   Rejected by the Dresden Academy.

1900   Enters Weimar Art School; studies under the painter Carl Frithjof Smith.

1903   Moves to Paris.

1904   Moves to Berlin-Schöneberg.

1906   Exhibits at Third Exhibition of the German Artists' League in Weimar; receives the League's Villa Romana Prize for study in Florence. Exhibits with and joins Berlin Secession. Mother dies of cancer. Marries Minna Tube, and travels via Paris to Florence.

1907   Returns to Berlin; establishes contact with the art dealer Paul Cassirer.

1910   Youngest member of Berlin Secession's governing body.

1911   Berlin art dealer Israel Bar Neumann signs a contract to publish Beckmann's graphics.

1912   Meets Ludwig Meidner and the publisher Reinhard Piper; first one-person exhibitions, Magdeburg and Weimar. *Pan* publishes his dispute with Franz Marc concerning modern art.

1913   Cassirer sponsors first one-person exhibition in Berlin; Hans Kaiser publishes first Beckmann monograph. Among group of artists resigning from the Secession and forming the Berlin New Secession; member of Munich New Secession.

1914   After the outbreak of war, volunteers as nurse in East Prussia, then as medical orderly in Belgium; publishes drawings and letters about his experiences.

1915   Psychological breakdown results in transfer to Strasbourg and then Frankfurt; release from active duty. Except for frequent and extended trips, remains in Frankfurt until 1933.

1916   Paints *Resurrection* and publishes *Briefe im Kriege* (*Letters during the War*).

1917   Exhibits at I. B. Neumann, Berlin.

1919   Publishes the lithograph series *Hell*. Turns down appointment as leader of the nude drawing class at Weimar Art School.

1920   Writes the drama *The Hotel* (unpublished) and the comedy *Ebbi*; exhibits graphics in Frankfurt.

1921   Meets the art critic Wilhelm Hausenstein and the Berlin art dealer Günther Franke.

1924   Publication of monograph by Hausenstein, Curt Glaser, Julius Meier-Graefe, and Wilhelm Fraenger.

1925   Included in the Mannheim exhibition *Neue Sachlichkeit*; divorces Minna Beckmann-Tube and marries Mathilde von Kaulbach; appointed as master at the United Städel Art School–School of Art and Design, Frankfurt.

1926   First exhibition in United States, I. B. Neumann Gallery, New York.

1927   Berlin National Gallery receives Beckmann's *The Barque* (1926) as gift; publishes "Der Künstler im Staat" ("The Artist in the State") in *Europäische Revue*.

1928   Receives the Award of Honor of the City of Düsseldorf.

1929   Receives title of Professor and Award of Honor of the City of Frankfurt.

1933   Moves to Berlin; is dismissed from teaching position at the Städel School after Nazi government is formed.

1935   Paints the triptych *Departure*.

1936   Last exhibitions in Germany before 1946.

1937   Twenty-eight paintings and 562 prints and drawings confiscated from German museums; twenty-two works included in the Munich exhibition *Degenerate Art*; flees to Amsterdam.

1938   Included in *Exhibition of 20th Century German Art*, New Burlington Galleries, London; trips to Zurich, London, and Paris.

1940   Denied U.S.A. visa to teach at the School of the Art Institute of Chicago; burns diaries when German troops invade Holland.

1941   Exhibitions in New York, Cincinnati, St. Louis. Begins *Apocalypse* illustrations.

1942   Exhibition, Art Institute of Chicago.

1943   Stores paintings at home of Helmut Lütjens to avoid confiscation by German occupying forces.

1944   February, suffers from pneumonia and heart complaints. Found to be unfit for military service by Germans.

1945   September, first postwar exhibition, at the Stedelijk Museum, Amsterdam, which purchases *Self-Portrait with Quappi Beckmann* (1941).

1946   Rejects appointments to Munich Academy of Fine Arts and Darmstadt Academy.

1947   Rejects appointment to Berlin College of Fine Arts; trip to Nice and Paris; accepts call to Washington University, St. Louis; sails from Rotterdam to U.S. on 19 August.

1948   "Three Letters to a Woman Painter" delivered as lectures; retrospective exhibition, St. Louis Art Museum and other U.S. cities.

1949   Moves to New York; teaches at Art School of the Brooklyn Museum. Monograph by Benno Reifenberg and Wilhelm Hausenstein published in Germany.

1950   Receives Conte Volpi Prize at Venice Biennale; awarded honorary doctorate by Washington University; teaches at Mills College, Oakland, California, and American Art School, New York. Dies of heart attack on 27 December.

Bibliography

Göpel, Erhard, and Barbara Göpel. *Max Beckmann: Katalog der Gemälde*. 2 vols. Berne: Kornfeld, 1976 (with comprehensive bibliography).

Max Beckmann Retrospective. Ed. Carla Schulz-Hoffmann and Judith C. Weiss. St. Louis: The Saint Louis Art Museum, and Munich: Prestel Verlag, 1984 (with comprehensive bibliography).

Albert Birkle

1900   Born 21 April in Berlin to parents originally from Weislingen near Hechingen in the Swabian area of southwest Germany. Father is an interior decorator and painter with a studio in Berlin.

1912–18   Attends Gymnasium, then trains at the Stuttgart School of Applied Arts.

1918   Briefly serves in the military and designs at least one war poster.

1919   Returns to Berlin. Trains in his father's workshop.

1920   Enters Prussian Academy of Fine Arts, Berlin; studies under Ferdinand Spiegel.

1921   Master student under sponsorship of Arthur Kampf until 1925. Joins Association of Berlin Artists.

1922   Exhibits with the Jury-Free Art Show, Berlin, until 1926.

1923   Joins and exhibits with the Berlin Secession. Active as illustrator in periodicals of the political left and contributes to the IAH portfolio *Eight-Hour Day*.

1926   Rejects professorship at the Academy in Königsberg in order to paint murals in Weislingen, Geislingen, and Sulgen.

1927   Exhibition at Galerie Hinrichsen, Berlin. Accepts invitation to reside for a year at the Hohenlohehütte ironworks in Kattowitz (now Katowice, Poland) in Upper Silesia.

1931   First public-commissioned stained-glass windows, Parish Church of St. Joseph, Herrenberg, Württemberg.

1933   Moves to Salzburg-Larsch, Austria, under patronage of Dr. Max Neumann, who finances construction of Birkle's home and studio.

1936   Exhibits twelve paintings at Venice Biennale.

1937   Biennale paintings shown at the House of German Art, Munich, for inaugural *Great German Art Exhibition*; removed by order of Nazi authorities as degenerate. Not included in the Munich *Degenerate Art* exhibition, but three paintings confiscated from public collections.

1939–45   Serves in the German army.

1946   Obtains Austrian citizenship.

1947   Receives first extensive commissions for stained-glass windows in Austria, Germany, and the United States; travels widely.

1951   Marries Sidonie Weithaler.

1961   Exhibition of stained-glass window designs, Museum of Applied Arts, Vienna, and House of Artists, Graz.

1975   Retrospective exhibition, Mirabell Pavilion, Salzburg, and Galerie Herzog, Vienna.

1977   Retrospective exhibition, Neue Münchner Galerie, Munich.

1980   Retrospective exhibition, Mirabell Pavilion, Salzburg.

1985   Exhibits at Rathaus Galerie Reinickendorf, West Berlin.

1986   Dies in Ostermünchen, near Rosenheim, in Bavaria.

Bibliography

"Arbeiten von A. Birkle." *Monatshefte für Baukunst und Städtebau* 20 (December 1936): 422–423.

B. A. "Christus der Hohepriester, Chorfenster in Herrenberg/Württemberg. St. Michael und Hl. Elisabeth, Glasfenster im Chor zu Weitingen." *Die Christliche Kunst* 31 (March 1935): 161, 183.

Bie, Richard. "Albert Birkle: Der Künstler und sein Werk." *Illustrierte Zeitung* 4799 (1937).

Bornmann, Hans. "Albert Birkle." *Hellweg* [Essen] 7 (1927): 364.

Csokor, Franz Theodor. "Der Glasmaler Albert Birkle: sein graphisches Werk im Wiener Kunstgewerbemuseum." *Das Kunstwerk* 14 (March 1961): 41.

"Glasfenster von Albert Birkle." *Deutsche Kunst und Dekoration* 39, no. 77 (May 1938): 254–256.

Galerie Hinrichsen. *Albert Birkle*. Berlin: Galerie Hinrichsen, 1927.

"Ignóblest Romans: New Stained Glass Window in the Church of the Holy Blood, Graz." *Time* 62 (26 October 1953): 83.

Meissner, C. "Stadt und Land in Birkle's Kunst." *Westermanns illustrierte deutsche Monatshefte* (March 1929): 81–88.

——. "Albert Birkle." *Hellweg* [Essen] 7 (1924): 341.

——. "Albert Birkle." *Die Bergstadt* [Breslau] 19, no. 1 (1931): 522–528.

Neue Münchner Galerie. *Der Maler Albert Birkle: Werke, 1921–1933.* Munich: Neue Münchner Galerie, 1977.

Pfefferkorn, Rudolf. *Albert Birkle: Leben und Werk.* Hamburg: Christians Verlag, 1983.

Rathaus Galerie, Reinickendorf. *Albert Birkle: Bilder—Gouachen—Zeichnungen.* West Berlin: Rathaus Galerie, 1985.

Kulturamt der Stadt Salzburg and Museum Carolino Augusteum. *Albert Birkle.* Salzburg: Kulturamt der Stadt Salzburg and Museum Carolino Augusteum, 1980.

Werner, Bruno E. "Albert Birkle." *Deutsche Allgemeine Zeitung,* 1932.

Wiegrefe, A. W. "Albert Birkle." *Die Kunst für Alle* 43 (January 1928): 127–133.

Volker Böhringer

1912 Born 7 November at Wehneckar Strasse 28 in Esslingen, the youngest of five children of Anna Friederike and Georg David Böhringer. Father a teacher at the Girls' High School.

1914 Family lives in Mettingen.

1929 Enters the Württemberg State School of Arts and Crafts, Stuttgart; studies graphic arts and book design under Ernst Schneidler.

1930–33 Studies draftsmanship at Academy of Fine Arts, Stuttgart.

1931 Wins second prize in a competition of the Academy draftsmanship class, for untitled ink sketch of wrestling workers.

1933 Master student of Hans Spiegel, through 1937. Begins painting industrial motifs using a mixed watercolor and tempera technique.

1935 Receives second prize in competition of Academy composition class.

1937 Spring, breaks off Academy studies after eleven semesters. Does not join the official National Union of Visual Artists of Germany, and thus has no permission to exhibit. Lives with his parents in Mettingen until 1945. Paints in secret and poses as commercial artist.

1940 Begins series of jazz and dance motifs.

1942 Death of father.

1945 Continuous infectious tuberculosis prevents him from working; enters Weinsberg lung hospital.

1946 Mother dies. Resident in Lung Sanatorium Gundelsheim, Schloss Horneck, through 1948. Participates in *All-German Art Exhibition,* Dresden, and sells a painting there. Suffers severe depression due to illness.

1947 First operation to alleviate tuberculosis effects. Participates in Berne exhibition *Modern German Art since 1933.*

1948 Second operation. Released from Gundelsheim sanatorium. Moves to Stuttgart.

1949 Exhibits in *Art in Germany, 1930–1949,* Kunsthaus, Zurich, and at the *Second German Art Exhibition,* Dresden. Friendship with the critic Otto Conzelmann.

1950 Begins work on Christian religious motifs.

1952 Rejects invitation to join Group SW (Southwest German Exhibitors Association). Termination of governmental support payments for his illness results in continuous financial difficulties. Exhibition with Heinrich Wildemann at the temporary rooms of the Württemberg Art Association, Stuttgart.

1953 Rejected for exhibition at the Art Association, Hanover.

1960 First exhibition devoted to his works held at Landolinshof, Esslingen. Exhibits with Otto Dix, Art Association, Heilbronn.

1961 Paints last works with religious motifs. Marries Emmaluise Gommel, a pharmacy student. Severe illness results in heart damage. Dies 9 October of heart failure.

Bibliography

Bartels, D. "Galerie Poll, W. Berlin," *Art and Artists* 12 (November 1977): 4–7.

"Galleria del Levante, Monaco, Germania: mostra," *Casabella* 394, no. 56 (1974).

Röttger, Friedhelm. *Volker Böhringer.* Stuttgart: Clett-Cotta, 1987.

Erich Borchert

1907 Born in Erfurt.

1921–25 Apprenticeship in steam boiler construction department of the firm Topf & Söhne, Erfurt.

1926–29 Student at Workshop for Wall Painting, Bauhaus, Dessau. Takes part in courses for free painting taught by Paul Klee, Vassily Kandinsky, and Lyonel Feininger.

1929 Exhibits with the German Art League, Dessau. Emigrates to Moscow where he works together with Hans Schäfer.

Later he is active in the developing department of the Maljarstroij Architectural Trust in color planning for architecture and city structures. Contacts with Hannes Meyer.

1944 Dies in the Soviet Union.

Armand Bouten

1893 Armand Ferdinand Xavier Bouten born 30 May to a post office clerk and a midwife in Venlo, the Netherlands.

1904–09 Attends Catholic boarding school in Roemond.

1909 Returns to Venlo; begins painting.

1912 Trains in Amsterdam as drawing teacher at Rijksmuseum. Father establishes a stipend which lasts until 1945. Meets sculptors John Raedeker and Hildo Krop; contacts with the Dutch Expressionist painter Herman Kruyder.

1920 Meets the painter Johanna (Hanny) Adriana Korevaar (b. 1893), daughter of a veterinarian. Trip to Hungary and Italy in the company of gypsies.

1921 Returns to Amsterdam; lives in the "Pijp" district.

1923 Briefly in Marseilles.

1923–24 In Berlin, contacts with Hungarian artists associated with *Der Sturm.* Invited by Herwarth Walden to exhibit at *Der Sturm* gallery. Leaves Berlin while arrangements are being made, and exhibition does not take place despite Walden's repeated efforts during the next year to renew exhibition plans.

1924 Exhibits at Galerie National, Venlo.

1925 Lives in Paris, Rue de l'Abbé Grégoire 22. Meets Russian expatriate artists associated with *Der Sturm:* Michail Larianov, Natalia Goncharova, and Marc Chagall. Works on furniture and sculpture. Included in exhibition with Hanny Bouten-Korevaar and Charles Eyck at Kunsthandel Heijstee, Amsterdam, *Works by Limburgian Artists.* Travels extensively during late 1920s.

1935 Moves to Brussels. Virtually ceases painting.

1945 Exhibition at Galerie Apollo, Brussels, 24 March–5 April.

1957 Returns impoverished to Amsterdam.

1965 Dies 20 November in Molenpad, Amsterdam.

Major Posthumous Exhibitions

1981 Amsterdam, Galerie Wending, 25 September–15 November.

1983 Harlingen, Galerie Thom Mercuur, *Armand Bouten 1893–1965: Tekeningen van een peintre maudit/Zeichnungen eines verwünschten Malers/Dessins d'un peintre maudit/Drawings by a Peintre Maudit;* West Berlin, Galerie Michael Haas, *Armand Bouten 1893–1965: Wiederentdeckte Bilder,* October–November.

1984 Kiel, Galerie Michael Neumann, *Armand Bouten 1893–1965: Wiederentdeckte Bilder,* February–March.

1986 Munich, H. G. Brück, *Armand Bouten.*

Bibliography

Juffermans, Jan. *Armand Bouten: Een ontheems talent teruggevonden/A Lost Talent Regained.* Amsterdam: Galerie Wending, 1982.

Venema, Adriaan. *Armand Bouten.* Amsterdam: Art Print Amsterdam, 1982.

Voskuil, Jan. "Hanny Bouten-Korevaar en Armand Bouten," *De Vonk* 1, no. 7 (May 1925).

Eduard Braun

1902 Born 29 July in Wetzlar. After completing studies in agricultural sciences, enters the Academy in Düsseldorf and then the Training Workshops in Munich.

1926 Begins working on woodcuts and as illustrator.

1927 Moves to Berlin. Drawings appear in *Der Querschnitt, Simplizissimus, Jugend,* the Scherl-Verlag's *Der Tag* and *Die Woche,* the Düsseldorf newspapers *Phönix* and *Neue Post, Ulk, Illustrierte Republikanische Zeitung,* and *Velhagen und Klasings Monatshefte.*

1940–45 Serves in military.

1945 Russian prisoner of war.

1946 Returns to Berlin. Under the pseudonym "Urban," becomes regular contributor to the newspapers *Der Telegraf, Kurier,* and *Nacht-Depesche,* as well as the satirical periodicals *Uylenspiegel* and *Insulaner.*

1971 Included in *The Twenties II,* Galerie Nierendorf, Berlin.

1972 *Telegraf* goes bankrupt. Braun, unemployed, works as a doorman at a Berlin student hostel.

1973 Dies in West Berlin.

Major Posthumous Exhibition

1986 Berlin, Galerie Nierendorf, *Eduard Braun.*

Bibliography

Fiedler, W. *Graphik Berliner Künstler.* Vol. 1 of F. A. Herbigs Kunsthefte, 1947.

Neue Gesellschaft für Bildende Kunst. *Wem gehört die Welt?: Kunt und Gesellschaft in der Weimarer Republik.* Berlin: Neue Gesellschaft für Bildende Kunst, 1977, 326.

W. G. O. "Glossen aus der Grossstadt: Karikaturist Eduard Braun 65 Jahre." *Telegraf-Feuilleton* [Berlin], 29 July 1967, 3.

Fritz Burmann

1892 Born 11 August in Wiedenbrueck, Westphalia.

1909 Enters Düsseldorf Academy as student of August Deusser.

1912 Completes studies at Munich Academy under Heinrich Knirr.

1913 Travels to Italy, Belgium, Holland, France, and Dalmatia.

1914 Enlists in military.

1918 Returns to Düsseldorf.

1921 Critical success with painting *Massacre of the Innocents* in exhibition of religious art, Cologne. Begins receiving commissions for church murals and stained-glass window designs.

1923 Ceiling frescoes for parish church, Königswinter am Rhein.

1924 Exhibits six paintings at *Jury-Free Art Show,* Berlin.

1925 Included in the exhibition *Neue Sachlichkeit,* Kunsthalle, Mannheim. Completes *Stations of the Cross* for the Anhaltskirche, Eickelborn near Lippstadt.

1926 Creates stained-glass window designs for Resurrection Chapel, Brauweiler. Appointed professor at the Academy of Art, Königsberg, East Prussia.

1927 Exhibition, City Gallery of Painting, Königsberg.

1928 Included with Otto Herbig, Max Kaus, and Hans Reichel in East Prussian traveling exhibition (Gumbinen, Insterburg, Tilsit) of contemporary realist art organized by Richard Gröning. Designs stained-glass windows for Government Building, Allenstein. Completes altar painting *Madonna* for Roman Catholic church, Königsberg.

1929 Completes murals for Winrich-von-Kniprode School, Marienburg, and a mosaic design for the Schlosskaskaden, Königsberg.

1930 Creates murals for church in Borchersdorf; wall paintings for Officer's Club, Königsberg; and stained-glass windows for Town Hall, Marienburg.

1932 Completes stained-glass windows, Seminary, Braunsberg.

1936   Appointed professor at the College of Visual Arts, Berlin-Charlottenburg. Creates murals for Revenue Board, Elbing, and windows for a church in Burgholzhausen.

1945   Dies in Berlin.

Bibliography

Busch, Harald. "Kurische Bilder: Zu den Bildern von F. Burmann." *Die Kunst* 71 (1935): 348–352.

Ewers, Hanns Heinz. "Fritz Burmann." *Deutsche Kunst und Dekoration* 56 (April 1925): 17–25.

Fischer, E. K. "Ausstellung in Königsberg." *Hartung'sche Zeitung,* 5 May 1927.

Hoelker, Karl. "Wiedenbrucker Maler." *Heimatkalender für den Kreis Wiedenbruck* (1928): 69.

———. "Fritz Burmann." *Heimatblätter aus der roten Erde* 5 (1926): 160.

Klau, Werner. "Der Maler Fritz Burmann." *Deutsche Blätter aus Polen* 8 (January 1931): 31–36.

Kroll, Bruno. "Fritz Burmann: Der Maler der ostpreussischen Haffs." *Die Kunst* 81 (November 1939): 36–40.

Pol Cassel

1892   Born Paul Cassel 17 March in Munich. Family moves to Wehlen shortly after his birth.

1907–09   Attends School of Applied Arts, Erfurt. Meets Otto Griebel.

1909–14   Studies at School of Applied Arts, Dresden.

1914–18   Serves in the military.

1919   Returns to Dresden. Exhibits with Griebel at Kunstsalon Emil Richter, Dresden.

1921–38   Spends summers with his family near Zeichen. Permanent residence in Wehlen.

1925   Participates in final Dresden Secession Group 1919 exhibition. With the artists Eugen Hoffmann, Georg Kind, and Wilhelm Lachnit, and the art collector Dr. Fritz Glaser, founds the Society for the Friends of New Russia.

1926   Studies in France. Hoffmann sculpts portrait bust of Cassel.

1927   Exhibits at Galerie Neue Kunst Fides, Dresden.

1928   Exhibits at Art Association, Erfurt.

1929   Exhibits at Galerie Neue Kunst Fides, Dresden.

1930   Lengthy stay in Algeria.

1932   Founding member of New Dresden Secession 1932.

1933   Work included in the exhibition *Reflections of Decay*, organized by Richard Mueller, Municipal Museum, Dresden.

1937   One work included in the exhibition *Degenerate Art*, Munich.

1944   Drafted into military service and sent to Eastern Front.

1945   Dies as a prisoner of war on 9 July in Kishinev, U. S. S. R.

Bibliography

W. Grohmann. "Maler." *Der Cicerone* 18 (1926): 682.

Paul Citroën

1896   Born 15 December in Berlin of Dutch parents of Jewish ancestry.

1910   Enters the Training Studios for Painting and Sculpture, Berlin-Charlottenburg, as student of Martin Brandenburg. Also receives training as bookstore manager.

1914   Meets Georg Muche.

1915   Through Muche, contacts with Herwarth Walden and *Der Sturm* artists.

1916–17   Sets up the bookstore of *Der Sturm.*

1917–18   Serves as representative of *Der Sturm* gallery and publications in Amsterdam.

1919   Returns to Berlin. Through Walter Mehring, contacts with Berlin Dada group and participation in Dada activities as "Citroën Dada."

1920   Participates in *First International Dada Fair,* Kunstsalon Dr. Burchard, Berlin.

1922   Enters Bauhaus, Weimar, as student, with encouragement of Muche. Participates in Johannes Itten's "Preparatory Course." Works in photomontage and painting.

1923   Included in the Bauhaus student exhibition.

1925   Moves to Berlin.

1925–27   Repeated trips to Amsterdam, Paris, and Basel.

1927   Returns to the Netherlands.

1930–35   Active as a portrait photographer.

1931   Marries Cecile Bendien, sister of the Dutch painter Jakob Bendien. Publishes the book *Palet: Een boek gewijd aan hedendaagsche Nederlansche schilderkunst (Palette: A Book Dedicated to Today's Dutch Painting).*

1933   Founds The New Art School on Bauhaus principles in Amsterdam.

1935–60   Docent at the Royal Academy of Art, The Hague.

1958   Exhibition, Stedelijk Van Abbe Museum, Eindhoven.

1969   Exhibition, *The Portraitist Paul Citroën as Collector,* City Museum at Lakenhal, Leiden.

1978   Exhibition, *Paul Citroën: Retrospective Photography,* Kunsthalle, Bielefeld.

1979   Exhibition, *Paul Citroën, Photographer: Photos from the Years 1929-1935,* Municipal Museum, The Hague.

1983   Dies 13 March in Wassenaar, Holland.

Bibliography

Paul Citroën. *Paul Citroën en het Bauhaus: Herinneringen in woord en beeld.* Comp. Kurt Löb. Utrecht and Antwerp: Bruna, 1974.

Paul Citroën. *Kunsttestament.* The Hague: L. C. J. Boucher, 1952.

Otto Dix

1891   Born 2 December in Gera-Untermhaus, oldest son of the ironworker Franz Dix and Pauline Louise, née Amann.

1899–05   Attends elementary school. Ernst Schunke is his drawing teacher.

1905   Apprenticed to interior decorators/painters in Gera and Pössnick through 1909.

1909   Enters the School of Applied Arts, Dresden, to study under Richard Mebert and Richard Guhr.

1914   Volunteers in fall for military service in Dresden, and initially is trained for Field Artillery.

1915   In Bautzen, undergoes training as machine gunner. In fall, he is at the front in France.

1916   Stationed near Auberive. In June, stationed near Reims. Dix's war drawings included in *Second Exhibition of Dresden Artists on Active Military Service,* Galerie Ernst Arnold, Dresden.

1917   November, transferred to Russia, near Gorodniki.

1918   Returns to France, this time near Langemarck. In fall, volunteers for training as a pilot. Returns to Gera in November or December.

1919   January, returns to Dresden. Enrolls as a student at the Dresden Academy and is a master pupil of Max Feldbauer and Otto Gussmann. Meets Conrad Felixmüller. Founding member of the Dresden Secession Group 1919. Exhibits with it in Dresden and Berlin. Joins November Group.

1920   Exhibits with Dresden Secession Group 1919, Galerie Emil Richter, Dresden. Participates in *First International Dada Fair,* Kunstsalon Dr. Burchard, Berlin. Included in *German Expressionists,* Darmstadt, and November Group, *Great Berlin Art Exhibition.* Felixmüller tries to arrange patronage for Dix through the Düsseldorf art dealer, Johanna Ey ("Mother Ey"), and writes an article about him for *Das Ey.* Works on large collage pictures.

1921   Exhibits with Dresden Secession. Trip to Düsseldorf to meet Ey. Meets his future wife, Martha Koch, and Dr. Hans Koch, a patron. Along with Georg Grosz and Rudolf Schlichter, Dix publicly opposes November Group exhibition policies.

1922   Returns to Dresden with Martha Koch. Exhibits with Dresden Secession and the artists' group Sphere, Magdeburg. Publishes graphic portfolios *Circus, Death and Resurrection, Becoming.* Galerie Nierendorf becomes exclusive agent. In fall, moves to Düsseldorf, and becomes part of the circle of artists at the gallery of "Mother Ey." Joins The Young Rhineland group. Student at the Düsseldorf Academy under Heinrich Nauen and Wilhelm Herberholz.

1923   In February, marries Martha Koch. Acquitted of pornography charges after March-June trial. Daughter, Nelly, born on 14 June. *Trench* purchased by the Wallraf-Richartz-Museum, Cologne. Exhibition at Galerie Nierendorf, Berlin. Participates in spring exhibition, Berlin Academy, and in *German Art 1923,* Darmstadt. *Salon II* is confiscated in Darmstadt. Articles about Dix by Theodor Däubler, Carl Einstein, and Willi Wolfradt appear. In winter, travels to Italy, as far as Palermo.

1924   Joins Berlin Secession. Participates in Berlin Jury-Free and Berlin Academy exhibitions and in *First All-German Art Exhibition,* Moscow, Saratov, and Leningrad. Completes etching portfolio *War.* Works on International Workers' Aid (IAH) *Hunger* portfolio.

1925   Included in *Neue Sachlichkeit* exhibition, Mannheim and Dresden, and in *International Art Exhibition,* Zurich. Fall, moves to Berlin.

1926   Retrospective exhibition, Galerie Neumann-Nierendorf, Berlin, and Galerie Thannhäuser, Munich. Participates in *Workers' Exhibition,* Berlin-Wedding. Rejects invitation from Committee of Revolutionary Artists of the West, State Academy of Sciences, Moscow. Offered a professorship at the Dresden Academy.

1927   Son Ursus born 11 March. Retrospective exhibition, Galerie Neue Kunst Fides, Dresden. Returns to Dresden to teach at Academy.

1928   Founding member of Association of Revolutionary Artists of Germany (ARBKD, or "Asso"). Participates in *International Exhibition of Modern Art,* Brooklyn Museum of Art, New York; 16th Biennale, Venice; *Saxon Art of Our Time,* Art Association, Dresden; *Art and Technology,* Folkwang Museum, Essen. Trips to Danzig and Alsace. Second son, Jan, born 10 October.

1929   Trip to Danzig. Exhibition at Galerie Wolfsberg, Zurich.

1930   Trips to Paris and Vienna. Participates in 17th Biennale, Venice, and in *Socialist Art Today,* Stedelijk Museum, Amsterdam. Exhibition at Galerie Neue Kunst Fides, Dresden.

1931   Becomes a member of the Prussian Academy of Arts, Berlin. Retrospective exhibition, Königsberg, and New Secession, Munich. Participates in exhibitions *German Painting and Sculpture,* Museum of Modern Art, New York, and of German Artists' League, Essen.

1932   Finishes *War* triptych, exhibited at Prussian Academy, Berlin. Wall paintings for Hygiene Museum, Dresden. Retrospective exhibition, Galerie Neue Kunst Fides, Dresden.

1933   Relieved of professorship at Dresden Academy by Nazi Saxon Ministry of the Interior, 6–8 April. Included in Richard Mueller's exhibition *Reflections of Decay,* Municipal Museum, Dresden. Participates in Dresden Secession exhibition. In summer, moves to Randegg Castle, near Singen. In August, expelled from the Prussian Academy.

1934   Declared a "degenerate artist" by the Nazis. Begins making yearly trips to his Dresden studio. Participates in exhibition *New German Painting,* Kunsthaus, Zurich.

1935   Trip to Switzerland. Paints and exhibits at the Galerie Neumann-Nierendorf with Franz Lenk; last exhibition in Germany before the end of World War II. Participates in *International Exhibition of Paintings* at the Carnegie Institute, Pittsburgh, and in *Modern Works of Art,* commemorating the fifth anniversary of the Museum of Modern Art, New York.

1936   Moves into a newly built house in Hemmenhofen on Lake Constance. Participates in exhibition *German Painting and Sculpture,* Art Association, Hamburg.

1937   Eight paintings and additional works included in exhibition *Degenerate Art,* Munich. In July, denounced because of "military sabotage." In Dresden, while standing in front of a Dix painting, Adolf Hitler declares, "It is a disgrace that these people cannot be locked up."

1938   Nazis confiscate, sell, or destroy 260 works by Dix. Fritz Niescher (Chemnitz) secretly supports Dix. Exhibition at

Galerie Wolfsberg, Zurich. Trip to Switzerland.

1939 September, after an assassination attempt on Hitler in Munich, Dix detained for questioning in Dresden for one week.

1940 Trip to Bohemia.

1942 Father dies 27 July.

1945 Recruited for Volkssturm service. Becomes a French prisoner of war, interned at Colmar.

1946 Returns to Hemmenhofen. Exhibits in Tübingen-Reutlingen. Visits Dresden. Participates in *All-German Art Exhibition*, Dresden.

1947 Included in first exhibition of The New Group, Munich.

1949 Included in *Second German Art Exhibition*, Dresden, and in exhibitions in Flensburg and Düsseldorf. Resumes annual visits to Dresden studio.

1950 Exhibition of graphic works, Galerie Franz, Weimar.

1953 Mother dies 26 August.

1955 Daughter, Nelly, dies 11 January. Included in Documenta I exhibition in Kassel. Appointed to Academy of the Arts, West Berlin.

1956 Named corresponding member of German Academy of the Arts, Berlin, GDR.

1959 Awarded Cornelius Prize of Düsseldorf. First comprehensive study of Dix's art published by Otto Conzelmann. Awarded the West German Federal Grand Cross of Merit.

1960 Comissioned to paint a mural in the town hall of Singen.

1962 Travels to Rome as guest of the Villa Massimo Foundation.

1966 Honored in the German Democratic Republic and in the Federal Republic of Germany on the occasion of his seventy-fifth birthday.

1967 Trip to Greece. Suffers a stroke. Receives Hans-Thoma Prize of Baden-Württemberg.

1969 Dies 25 July in Singen.

Major Posthumous Exhibitions

1970 Munich, Galerie Klihm, *Otto Dix: Aquarelle, Zeichnungen, Radierungen 1920–1970*. Paris, Goethe-Institut, *Otto Dix: Aquarelles, Dessins.*

1971 Säckingen, Kunstverein Hochrhein, *Otto Dix: Gemälde.* Freiburg, Augustiner Museum, *Otto Dix.* Stuttgart, Galerie der Stadt, *Otto Dix: Retrospektive anlässlich des 80. Geburtstags.*

1977 Nuremberg, Germanisches Nationalmuseum, Archiv für bildende Kunst, *Otto Dix 1891 bis 1969: Materialien, Dokumente zu Leben und Werk.* Hamburg, Kunstverein, *Otto Dix: Aquarelle, Zeichnungen, Graphik.* West Berlin, Haus am Waldsee, and Hanover, Kunstverein, *Otto Dix: Zwischen den Kriegen, 1912–1939.*

1981 Stuttgart, Galerie der Stadt, *Otto Dix: Menschenbilder.*

1985 Munich, Museum Villa Stuck, *Otto Dix 1891–1969.*

1987 West Berlin, Staatliche Kunsthalle, *Otto Dix.*

Bibliography

Löffler, Fritz. *Otto Dix: Leben und Werk.* 2d ed. Wiesbaden: Drei Lilien Verlag, 1989 (with comprehensive bibliography).

August Wilhelm Dressler

1886 Born 19 December in Bergesgrün, Bohemia.

1900–04 Studies lithography in Chemnitz.

1906–13 Student at the academies in Dresden and Leipzig. Contacts with Otto Dix, Kurt Günther, and Bernhard Kretzschmar.

1914 Works as independent artist in Berlin.

1915 Drafted into military; serves on both eastern and western fronts.

1919 In Leipzig, joins November Group. Moves to Berlin.

1920 Exhibits with November Group, Berlin.

1924–26 Exhibits with Jury-Free Art Show, Berlin. Joins and exhibits with Berlin Secession.

1927 Included in exhibition of the Prussian Academy of Fine Arts, Berlin; awarded Prussian State Prize (Rome Prize). Included in the exhibition *Neue Sachlichkeit*, Galerie Neumann-Nierendorf, Berlin.

1928 Receives Dürer Prize of the City of Nuremberg.

1929 Individual exhibition, Kunsthütte, Chemnitz. Included in *Neue Sachlichkeit* exhibition, Stedelijk Museum, Amsterdam.

1930–31 At Villa Massimo, Rome.

1931 Exhibits at Kunstsalon Gurlitt, Berlin.

1934 Appointed to teach at the United State Schools, Berlin.

1938 Dismissed as "degenerate" from teaching position.

1946 Exhibits at Kunstamt Steglitz and Galerie Franz, Berlin.

1954 Exhibition of graphics, Haus am Lützowplatz, West Berlin.

1955 Retrospective exhibition, Jury-Free Art Show, West Berlin; awarded Art Prize of the City of Berlin.

1956 Teaches at Master School for Applied Arts, West Berlin.

1967 Exhibition, Galerie Nierendorf, West Berlin.

1970 Dies 8 May in West Berlin.

Bibliography

August Wilhelm Dressler. Kunstblätter der Galerie Nierendorf, no. 12. Berlin: Galerie Nierendorf, 1967.

Brattskoven, Otto. "Neue Künstler: A. W. Dressler." *Der Cicerone* 18 (July 1926): 492, 495–6.

———. "A. W. Dressler." *Das Kunstblatt* 9 (1927): 155–156.

Kinkel, Hans. *August Wilhelm Dressler.* Munich: Delp'sche Verlagsbuchhandlung, 1970.

Heinrich Ehmsen

1886 Born 9 August in Kiel, fifth child of a basket weaver.

1892–1901 Attends Volksschule, Kiel.

1901–06 Apprenticeship as interior decorator and painter.

1906–09 Studies under Fritz Ehmcke, Jan Thorn-Prikker, and Peter Behrens at the School of Applied Arts, Düsseldorf.

1909 Exhibits woodcuts in *Düsseldorf Exhibition of Church Art.*

1910–11 In Paris, frequents Café du Dome with Ernesto de Fiori, Jules Pascin, and Alfred Flechtheim. Contacts with Pablo Picasso, Georges Braque, Henri Matisse, André Derain, Maurice Vlaminck, and with F. T. Marinetti and other Italian Futurists. Meets Karl Hofer.

1911–12 In Munich. Obligatory one-year military service.

1913 Visit to Karlsbad. Lives in Munich. Contacts with the *Blaue Reiter* artists. Included in *First German Autumn Salon, Der Sturm* gallery, Berlin. Individual exhibition (as Heinz Ehmke), Municipal Museum, Essen.

1914 Woodcut exhibitions at Galerie Müller, Vienna; Kunstsalon Schmidt-Bertsch, Munich; and Galerie Halm and Goldmann, Vienna.

1914–18 Military service in Flanders, France, and Romania.

1915 Marries Hermine Schneid, 20 November.

1917 Birth of son Horst.

1918–19 Returns to Munich. Witnesses revolution and suppression of the Bavarian Soviet Republic

1920 Exhibition, Galerie Neue Kunst Goltz, Munich.

1921 Birth of daughter Marianna.

1924 Meets Elisabeth Bertram, née Conradi, who becomes his lifelong companion.

1926 Joint exhibition of graphics with Emil Nolde and Frans Masereel, Art Association, Wiesbaden. In May, exhibits at Galerie Goldschmidt, Frankfurt. In July, exhibits at Municipal Painting Gallery, Bochum. Participates in *International Art Exhibition*, Düsseldorf.

1927 January/February, solo exhibition, Kunstkammer Martin Wasservogel, Berlin. In March, lectures at Young Academic Club, Munich; meets Adolf Behne. Publishes print portfolio for Gerhard Hauptmann's *Der Narr in Christo, Emanuel Quint (The Fool in Christ, Emanuel Quint).* Other exhibitions at Galerie Thannhauser, Munich; Galerie Würthle, Vienna; Prussian Academy of Fine Arts, Berlin; New Secession, Munich; Nassau Associations of Art; and Wiesbaden Society for New Art, New Museum, Wiesbaden.

1928 Trip to southern France. Participates in competition/exhibition *Most Beautiful Portrait of a Woman from the Year 1928.* Exhibits with November Group at *Great Berlin Art Exhibition* and with Art Association, Munich. Exhibition, Kunstkammer Wasservogel, Berlin. Included in *New Graphics*, Municipal Museum, Mülheim; *New Acquisitions*, Graphics Collection, Munich; *German Art 1928*, Kunstpalais der Rheinhallen, Düsseldorf.

1929 Moves to Berlin. Separation from Hermine Ehmsen, who moves to Vienna with their children. Participates in exhibitions *Ten Years November Group*, Berlin; *Fall Exhibition*, Academy of Fine Arts, Berlin; Berlin Secession; *Jury-Free Art Show*, Berlin; Association of Berlin Artists.

1930 Member of Task Force of Artists and Brain-Workers in Support of the Communist Party of Germany. Trip to

Italy; resides at German Academy, Villa Massimo, Rome, with Georg Schrimpf and Karl Schmidt-Rottluff. Exhibitions, Kunstkammer Martin Wasservogel, Berlin, and Prinzessinnenschlösschen, Jena. Participates in exhibition *Socialist Art Today*, Stedelijk Museum, Amsterdam.

1931 Participates in exhibitions *Women in Need*, Berlin; *Great Berlin Art Exhibition*, November Group, Berlin; Academy of Arts, Berlin; Association of Berlin Artists. Several paintings purchased by Soviet museums.

1932 Nine-month trip to Russia. Exhibition in Moscow. Receives commission to paint *The Execution of the Sailor Egelhofer.*

1933 In Berlin. Serves as artistic adviser to airplane manufacturer Hugo Junkers, Dessau. 22 September–18 December, placed in "protective custody" by Gestapo as part of successful effort to force Junkers to comply with Nazi demands.

1934 Participates in *Great Berlin Art Exhibition.* Condemned in Nazi newspaper *Westdeutscher Beobachter.* Declared unsuitable for military service.

1935–37 Fulfills commissions for decorative works for Reich Air Traffic Ministry. One hundred and twelve works removed from fifteen German museums in 1937.

1939 Petition to join Reich Chamber of Culture approved.

1940 Drafted into military; stationed with Propaganda Division, Paris.

1942 Classified as unreliable and transferred to a propaganda company on the eastern front.

1944 Dismissed from Corps of Visual Artists. Returns to Berlin.

1945 Studio burns down. After war's end, participates as assistant director in reconstruction of the College of Visual Arts, Berlin-Charlottenburg.

1948 Trip to U. S. S. R.

1949 Dismissed from teaching position after signing the Paris Peace Manifesto. Moves to East Berlin.

1950 Teacher of master class at German Academy of the Arts, East Berlin.

1951 Exhibition, German Academy of the Arts, East Berlin.

1956 Trip to China and Vietnam. Exhibition, German Academy of the Arts, East Berlin.

1957 Exhibition, National Gallery, East Berlin.

1959–60 Trips to Sweden, Italy, France, and Switzerland.

1961 Awarded the GDR National Order of Merit.

1964 Dies 6 May in East Berlin.

Major Posthumous Exhibitions

1977 Dresden, Staatliche Kunstsammlung, *Heinrich Ehmsen: Gemälde, Aquarelle, Zeichnungen.*

1983 Munich, Galerie Michael Hasenclever, *Heinrich Ehmsen: Druckgraphik und Zeichnungen.*

1986 East Berlin, Nationalgalerie, *Heinrich Ehmsen 1886–1964: Gemälde, Aquarelle, Zeichnungen.* West Berlin, Neue Gesellschaft für Bildende Kunst, *Heinrich Ehmsen, Maler: Lebens/Werk/Protokoll* (traveled to Kunstamt Kreuzberg, and Stadtmuseum, Kiel).

Bibliography

Behne, Adolf. *Heinrich Ehmsen*. Kunst der Gegenwart II. Potsdam: Stichnote, 1946.

Cremer, Fritz, Bert Heller, et al. *Heinrich Ehmsen: Gemälde, Aquarelle, Zeichnungen*. Dresden: Staatliche Kunstsammlungen, 1977.

Lang, Lothar. *Heinrich Ehmsen*. Dresden: VEB Verlag der Kunst, 1962.

———. "Heinrich Ehmsen: Zwei Aspekte seines Werkes—Zum 90. Geburtstag des Künstlers." *Bildende Kunst* 24, no. 7 (1976): 338–341.

Nagel, Otto. *Heinrich Ehmsen zum 70. Geburtstag*. East Berlin: Deutscher Akademie Verlag, 1956.

Nationalgalerie, Berlin, GDR. *Heinrich Ehmsen*. East Berlin: Nationalgalerie, 1957.

———. *Heinrich Ehmsen 1886–1964: Gemälde, Aquarelle, Zeichnungen*. East Berlin: Nationalgalerie, 1986.

Neue Gesellschaft für Bildende Kunst, Berlin. *Heinrich Ehmsen, Maler: Lebens/Werk/Protokoll*. West Berlin: Elefanten Press, 1986.

Tietze, Hans. "Heinrich Ehmsens Aquarelle." *Kunstwanderer* 12 (February 1930): 220–221.

Conrad Felixmüller

1897 Born Conrad Felix Müller 21 May in Dresden, the son of Maria Carolina, née Morche, and Ernst Emil Müller, a wagon- and blacksmith.

1903–11 Attends Volksschule in Dresden.

1909 Studies violin at the Royal Conservatory, Dresden.

1911–12 Attends Royal School of Applied Arts, Dresden.

1912 Attends private art school of Ferdinand Dorsch, Dresden. In December, admitted to Dresden Academy as student of Carl Bantzer.

1913 First graphics and oil paintings.

1914 Graphics exhibition, I. B. Neumann, Berlin. Friendship with Peter August Böckstiegel. Contact with Arnold Schoenberg. Joins Dresden Secession.

1915 Ends Academy studies. Trips to Berlin. Meets Ludwig Meidner, Franz Pfemfert, Raoul Hausmann, Walter Rheiner, and Wieland Herzfelde. Contributes to *Der Sturm*. Exhibition, Galerie Arnold, Dresden.

1916 Contributes to *Die Aktion* through 1926.

1917 Cofounder of the periodical *Menschen*. Briefly arrested. Drafted into military as nurse's aid. Founding member of the Expressionist Study Team, Dresden.

1918 Marries Londa, Baroness von Berg. Moves to Wiesbaden, then to Klotzsche near Dresden. Begins to use name "Felixmüller." Birth of son Luca. Death of his mother. Joins Communist Party of Germany. Exhibitions at Galerie Hans Goltz, Munich, and Kunstsalon Ludwig Schames, Frankfurt. Exhibits with Free Secession, Berlin.

1919 Founding member of Dresden Secession Group 1919. Joins November Group. Withdraws from Dresden Secession.

1920 Exhibits with Free Secession, Berlin. Awarded Saxon Great State Prize for Painting (Saxon Rome Prize), Dresden. Trips to southern Germany, the Ruhr, and Westphalia to observe living conditions among workers. Birth of son Titus.

1921 Exhibitions at Galerie I. B. Neumann, Berlin, and Kestner Gesellschaft, Hanover.

1923 Friendship with Carl Sternheim. Meets Frans Masereel. Exhibits studies of miners from the Ruhr, National Gallery, Berlin.

1924 Contributes to the pamphlet *Eight-Hour Day*. National Gallery, Berlin, purchases works. Trips to Helgoland and Czechoslovakia. Included in *First All-German Art Exhibition*, Moscow, Saratov, and Leningrad.

1925 Trips to Belgium, France, and Switzerland. Selected as president of Saxon Union of Visual Artists, and elected secretary of the National Union of Visual Artists in Germany.

1926 Graphics exhibition, Museum of Western Art, Moscow.

1927 Exhibitions in Essen, Elberfeld, Kassel, and Brunswick.

1928 Awarded Grand Prize for Painting, *Jubilee Exhibition of the Saxon Art Association*, Dresden. Visits Switzerland.

1930 Trip to Belgium. Participates in the international exhibition *Socialist Art Today*, Stedelijk Museum, Amsterdam.

1931 Receives Saxon State Prize and Dürer Stipend of the City of Nuremberg. Moves from Klotzsche to Dresden. Travels to Prague.

1933 Forty works included in the Nazi exhibition, *Reflections of Decay*, Municipal Museum, Dresden.

1934 Moves to Berlin-Charlottenburg.

1937 Joins Association of Berlin Artists; participates in spring exhibition of Association; awarded prize, then expelled from Association. Included with seven works in exhibition *Degenerate Art*, Munich. Removal of 151 works from German museum collections.

1938 Trip to Norway.

1939 Trip to England.

1941 Evacuation from Berlin to Damsdorf.

1943 Death of father.

1944 Destruction of Berlin home during bombing raids. Moves to Tautenhain, near Leipzig. In November, drafted into the Volkssturm.

1945 April through fall, Soviet prisoner of war. Exhibition of Hanns-Conon von der Gabelentz Collection, Altenburg, Thuringia.

1949 Appointed professor in design and painting, Martin Luther University, Halle. Exhibition, Staatliche Galerie Moritzburg, Halle.

1957 Graphics exhibition, Art Museum, Düsseldorf; sixtieth birthday exhibition, Lindenau Museum, Altenburg.

1961 Moves to Berlin-Köpenick.

1962 Retirement from teaching at Martin Luther University, Halle.

1965 Exhibition, Galerie Nierendorf, West Berlin.

1967 Moves to Berlin-Zehlendorf.

1973 Retrospective exhibition *Paintings of 1913–1973*, Former National Gallery, and Gallery of the Association of Berlin Artists, West Berlin.

1975 Retrospective exhibition, State Art Collections and Gallery of New Masters, Dresden; Art Museum, Rostock; and State Museums, National Gallery, East Berlin.

1977 Dies 24 March in West Berlin.

Major Posthumous Exhibitions

1978 Wolfenbüttel, Kunstverein, and Göttingen, Kunstverein; Dortmund, Museum am Ostwall; Bergisch-Gladbach, Villa Zanders.

1981 Hamburg, B. A. T. Haus, INTER-VERSA Exhibition, *Conrad Felixmüller: Gemälde, Aquarelle, Zeichnungen, Reliefs und Plastiken* (traveled to Bayreuth, Rathaus, and Moers, Städtische Galerie Peschkenhaus).

1981–82 Nuremberg, Germanisches Nationalmuseum, *Conrad Felixmüller: Werke und Dokumente*.

1987 Düsseldorf, Galerie Remmert und Barth, *Conrad Felixmüller: Die Dresdner Jahre 1913–1933*.

Bibliography

Busch Reisinger Museum, Cambridge, Mass. *Conrad Felixmüller 1897–1977: Prints and Drawings of Dr. Ernst and Anne Fischer*. Cambridge, Mass.: Harvard University, Busch Reisinger Museum, 1979. Catalogue text by Titus Felixmüller, Angelica Schmiegelow Powell, Steven Schuyler.

Conrad Felixmüller: Gemälde, Aquarelle, Zeichnungen, Druckgraphik. Dresden: Staatliche Kunstsammlungen, and East Berlin: Staatliche Museen, 1975.

Felixmüller, Conrad. *Ich sah und schnitt in Holz*. Hamburg: Paul Hartung KG, 1952.

———. *Legenden 1912 bis 1976*. Ed. G. H. Herzog. Tübingen: Wasmuth, 1977.

Galerie Nierendorf, Berlin. *Conrad Felixmüller*. Kunstblätter der Galerie Nierendorf, 47. West Berlin: Galerie Nierendorf, 1985.

Germanisches Nationalmuseum, Nuremberg. *Conrad Felixmüller: Werke und Dokumente*. Nuremberg: Germanisches Nationalmuseum, 1981. Catalogue text by Peter Guenther, Klaus Pese, Gerhart Söhn, Susanne Thesing.

Gleisberg, Dieter. *Conrad Felixmüller: Leben und Werk*. Dresden: VEB Verlag der Kunst, 1982.

Heinz, Hellmuth. *Conrad Felixmüller*. Dresden: VEB Verlag der Kunst, 1979.

Mayer, Alfred. "Conrad Felixmüller." *Die Kunst für Alle* 45 (1930): 302.

Schmidt-Rottluff, Beneeth. *Conrad Felixmüller: Gemälde, Aquarelle, Druckgrafik*. Düsseldorf: Kunstmuseum, 1975.

Söhn, Gerhart. *Conrad Felixmüller: Das graphische Werk 1912 bis 1974*. Düsseldorf: Graphik Salon Gerhart Söhn, 1975.

———. *Conrad Felixmüller: Von ihm—über ihn*. Düsseldorf: Edition GS, 1977.

Sternheim, Carl. "Conrad Felixmüller." *Der Cicerone* 15 (1923): 881 ff.

———. "Conrad Felixmüller." *Jahrbuch der Jungen Kunst* 4 (1923): 299–305.

Von der Gabelentz, Hanns-Conon. *Expressiver Realismus: Zum Werk von Conrad Felixmüller*. Halle, 1949.

Westfälisches Museumsamt, Münster. *Conrad Felixmüller: Gemälde, Aquarelle, Zeichnungen, Druckgrafik*. Münster: Westfälisches Museumsamt, 1982. Catalogue by Hartmut John.

Ernst Fritsch

1892 Born 23 August in Berlin. Attends Realgymnasium at Berlin-Lichterfelde.

1911–13 Studies at the Royal Art School, Berlin; receives diploma as instructor in drawing.

1913–14 Student of Emil Doepler and Emil Orlik at School of the Museum of Applied Arts, Berlin.

1914–18 Military service.

1919 Returns to Berlin. Schoolteacher in Berlin until 1921. Exhibits with Berlin Secession until 1932.

1920 Participates in *Jury-Free Art Show*, Berlin, until 1932.

1922 Exhibits with the November Group, Berlin, until 1924.

1923 Participates in exhibitions of the Prussian Academy of Fine Arts, Berlin, until 1933.

1925 Begins exhibiting regularly with the Munich New Secession.

1927 Receives first post-World War I Great State Prize of the Prussian Academy of Fine Arts (Rome Prize) for residence at Villa Massimo.

1928 Receives silver medal at *Dürer Year Exhibition*, Nuremberg. Exhibits in the *Great Düsseldorf Art Exposition*.

1928–29 Travels to Paris and Rome (Villa Massimo).

1929 Exhibits with November Group. Honorary diploma, Bordeaux.

1931 Exhibits with November Group.

1933 Retrospective exhibition at Berlin Secession. Forbidden to exhibit by Nazi government through 1945.

1937 Eight works are confiscated from German museums as "degenerate." Through Hans Purrmann, is invited to the Villa Romana, Florence.

1939–42 Provisional teacher at Art and Work School, Berlin.

1942 Inducted into the military.

1945 Prisoner of war.

1946 Professor at College of Visual Arts, Berlin-Charlottenburg, where he teaches figure, portrait, composition, and life classes.

1953 Exhibition, Berlin-Zehlendorf, Haus am Waldsee. Heads Department of Art Education at College of Visual Arts until 1958.

1956 Member of Academy of Art, West Berlin.

1960 Guest of honor of Villa Massimo, Rome.

1965 Dies 8 December in West Berlin.

Major Posthumous Exhibition

1978 Munich, Galerie Michael Hasenclever, *Ernst Fritsch: Bilder, Zeichnungen und Druckgraphik*, 28 October–30 November.

Bibliography

Dietrich, Ulrich. "Ernst Fritsch." *Der Kreis* 8 (1931): 563 ff.

Kállai, Ernst. "Ernst Fritsch." *Der Cicerone* 18 (December 1926): 802–805.

Rachlis, M. "Gemälde von Ernst Fritsch." *Deutsche Kunst und Dekoration* 53 (1924): 177–184.

Werner, B. E. "Ernst Fritsch." *Die Kunst für Alle* 4 (May 1929): 259–262.

Fuhrmann

The identity of the artist who signed his or her works "Fuhrmann" is not known. Dating from the time after Hitler's rise to power in 1933, but prior to the beginning of World War II in 1939, the drawings appear to have been in a collection in France. This suggests that they were produced by a member of the German exile community, but no artist named Fuhrmann is known to have been among them. The artist Paul Fuhrmann, active in Berlin during the 1920s and a participant in the anti-Fascist effort of German artists, did not flee Germany, nor is the style of the "Fuhrmann" drawings close to his. The possibility that "Fuhrmann" (German for "coachman") was a pseudonym should not be ruled out.

Otto Gleichmann

1887 Born 20 August in Mainz.

1894–06 Attends Realgymnasium in Strasbourg, Erfurt, and Bielefeld.

1906–10 Studies at the academies of Düsseldorf, Breslau, Weimar, and Warsaw.

1914 Teaches in Erfurt.

1915 Marries the painter Lotte Giese.

1915–16 Serves on Russian and French fronts during World War I.

1916 In military hospital, then further military service until 1917.

1917 Meets the poet and critic Theodor Däubler. Exhibition of drawings and graphics at Kestner Gesellschaft, Hanover. Member of Hanover Secession. Galerie Alfred Flechtheim publishes portfolios of graphic works.

1919 Permanent home in Hanover. Exhibitions in Graphisches Kabinett, Düsseldorf; Art Association, Jena; Kabinett Nierendorf, Cologne; and Galerie Flechtheim, Düsseldorf. Exhibits with The Young Rhineland in Düsseldorf.

1921 Summer vacation in Austria. One-person exhibition at Galerie Nierendorf, Cologne.

1922 Exhibition at Galerie von Garvens, Hanover. Meets Paul Klee.

1923 Exhibition at Galerie Linne, Bremen.

1924 Travels to Italy. Meets Vassily Kandinsky. Exhibition at Galerie Neumann-Nierendorf, Berlin.

1925 Exhibits with Society for the Friends of Recent Art, Brunswick.

1926 Travels to Paris.

1927–28 Exhibition at Art Association, Jena. Travels to Austria, Hungary, Belgium, and Holland.

1931 Exhibits at Galerie Nierendorf, Berlin.

1932 Exhibits at Kestner Gesellschaft, Hanover.

1933 After Nazis come to power, withdraws from public exhibitions.

1943 Destruction of large body of works during bombing raids on Hanover.

1946 Participates in exhibition *Liberated Art*, Brunswick and Celle.

1947 Exhibition at Landesmuseum, Hanover. Exhibitions in Göttingen and Kassel.

1950 Exhibition at Galerie Nebelung, Düsseldorf.

1951 Exhibition in Kunsthaus, Bielefeld.

1953 Exhibition in Rotterdam.

1955 Travels to southern France. Exhibitions in City Museum and in Salve-Hospice-House, Brunswick.

1957 Exhibits at Art Association, Hanover.

1963 Dies in Hanover.

Major Posthumous Exhibition

1987 Hanover, Sprengel Museum, *Otto Gleichmann 1887–1963: Zum 100. Geburtstag* (traveled to Emden, Kunsthalle; Salzburg, Moderne Galerie und Graphische Sammlung Rupertinum; Graz, Kulturhaus der Stadt).

Bibliography

Beil, Ludwig. "Otto Gleichmann." *Der Cicerone* 13 (1921): 297–302.

———. "Otto Gleichmann." *Jahrbuch der Jungen Kunst*, 1921, 169–174.

Däubler, Theodor. "Otto Gleichmann." *Das hohe Ufer*, 1919, 41 ff.

Lange, Rudolf. *Otto Gleichmann*. Göttingen: Musterschmidt-Verlag, 1963.

"Otto Gleichmann." *Das Kunstwerk* 17 (December 1963): 41.

Otto Griebel

1895 Born on 31 March in Meerane, Saxony, the fourth of eight children of wallpaper hanger Bruno Griebel.

1902 Begins school at Bürgerschule, Meerane.

1909 Trains as interior decorator and painter. In fall, enters Royal School of Design, Dresden. Meets Otto Dix.

1911 Attends School of Applied Arts, Dresden; studies stained glass under Josef Goller.

1913 Trip to Switzerland.

1915 Drafted into military service in August. Friendship with writer Rudolf Adrian Dietrich.

1916 Stationed on western front. Participates in Battle of the Somme.

1918 Seriously wounded in late March. Recuperates in military hospital in Karlsruhe. Meets Hans Thoma. Returns to Dresden. Member of revolutionary Soldiers' Council. Friendship with Eric Johansson. Meets Oskar Kokoschka.

1919 Joins the German Communist Party (KPD). Studies at the Dresden Academy under Robert Sterl. Becomes a member of the November Group. Participates in Dresden Dada activities. Exhibition with Pol Cassel at the Galerie Emil Richter, Dresden. Contacts with Berlin Dada group.

1920 Political involvement with the Council for the Unemployed. Visits *First International Dada Fair*, Berlin. Takes part in the struggle against the Kapp Putsch in Dresden.

1921 Courier for KPD during workers' uprisings in central Germany. Active as draftsman for KPD publications. In Berlin, meets George Grosz, Otto Nagel, and Rudolf Schlichter.

1922 Travels to Düsseldorf, Cologne, Hamburg, and Paris. Member of artistic circle around Johanna Ey in Düsseldorf. Joins The Young Rhineland and Dresden Secession Group 1919. Agitational work for Boleslav Strzelewicz's Red Troupe.

1923 Receives unemployment support. Works as street paver. Travels to Hamburg. Marries Elis Franz.

1924 Founding member of Red Group, Dresden. Thirteen works included in the International Workers Aid (IAH) sponsored *First All-German Art Exhibition* in Moscow, Leningrad, and Saratow. Exhibition, Kühl & Kühn, Dresden.

1925 Meets writer Joachim Ringelnatz. Marries second wife, Grete Kliemann. Exhibition, Galerie Hugo Erfurth, Dresden.

1926 Meets art critic and editor of *Das Kunstblatt*, Paul Westheim. Participates in *International Art Exhibition*, Dresden. Exhibits at Galerie Nierendorf, Berlin.

1927 Serves as introductory speaker for the "Red Violinist," Soermus, on a concert tour. Meets Franz Radziwill. Exhibits at Neue Kunst Fides, Dresden.

1929 Founding member of Dresden branch of Association of Revolutionary Artists in Germany (ARBKD or "Asso"). Tried on charges of insulting the German military. Drawings for KPD publications. Participates in exhibition *Neue Sachlichkeit*, Amsterdam.

1930 Participates in agitational puppet show with Otto Kunze. Exhibits at Wertheim Department Store, Berlin, and Galerie Junge Kunst Joseph Sander, Dresden.

1931 Member of organizing committee for exhibition *Women in Need*, Berlin. Drawings for Asso periodical *Stoss von Links*. Founding member of New Dresden Secession 1931.

1933 Arrested by Gestapo; released after protest by Dresden Secession. His house is searched and works are confiscated. Forms the group The Seven Just Men. Represented by four works in the Nazi exhibition *Reflections of Decay*, Municipal Museum, Dresden.

1936 Works as exhibition planner for the Dresden Hygiene Museum, with trips to Berlin and Switzerland through 1938.

1937 All of Griebel's works are removed from German museums; some included in exhibition *Degenerate Art*, Munich.

1939 Drafted into military service; stationed in Poland.

1940 In the fall, obtains release from active military service.

1941–43 With support of Dr. Fritz Löffler, appointed as exhibition organizer in German-occupied Krakow.

1943 Helps twenty Jewish men escape from the Tarnow ghetto.

1944 Drafted into obligatory Civilian Service by German General Government of Poland.

1945 Released from Civilian Service. Drafted into militia but deserts. Studio, apartment, and much of his work are destroyed in the bombing of Dresden on 13 February. In June, returns to Dresden. Employed by Soviet Military Administration.

1946 Begins teaching art at the College of Fine Arts, Dresden. Participates in *All-German Art Exhibition*, Dresden.

1948–52 Art educator at Kreuzschule, Dresden.

1948 Participates in *Exhibition of Social Art*, Dresden and Berlin.

1952 Director of studies and, until 1960, instructor at the Workers' and Farmers' Faculty (ABF) of the College of Fine Arts, Dresden.

1960 Begins work on his autobiography and other writings.

1965 First extensive exhibition, in conjunction with Curt Grosspietsch and Werner Hofmann, Leonhardi Museum, Dresden.

1966–71 Takes part in exhibitions in Berlin, Budapest, Hamburg, Milan, Munich, Nuremberg, Prague, and Sofia. Illness increasingly hampers activity.

1972 Dies 7 March in Dresden-Loschwitz.

Major Posthumous Exhibition

1972 Leipzig, Museum der bildenden Künste, *Otto Griebel: Malerei, Zeichnung und Graphik*.

Bibliography

Griebel, Otto. *Ich war ein Mann der Strasse: Lebenserinnerungen eines Dresdner Malers*. Frankfurt a. M.: Röderberg Verlag, and Leipzig: Mitteldeutscher Verlag Halle, 1986.

Schmidt, Diether, "Ich war ein Mann der Strasse," *Bildende Kunst* 6 (1965): 314–317.

———. *Otto Griebel*. East Berlin: Henschelverlag Kunst und Gesellschaft, 1973.

Rudolf Grossmann

1882 Born 25 January in Freiburg im Breisgau, grandson of the court painter W. Dürr and nephew of Professor Dürr of the Munich Academy. Mother, née Marie Dürr (1852–1889), a portrait painter.

1889 Death of mother.

1902–04 Studies medicine and philosophy in Munich.

1905 Studies briefly at the Düsseldorf Academy, but fails official acceptance tests. Seeks admission to Karlsruhe Academy, but is rejected. Travels to Paris to study under Jean Poulerauce and Lucien Simon. Becomes friendly with the circle of German and Eastern European artists at the Café du Dôme—Hans Purrmann, Jules Pascin, and Lyonel Feininger. Travels to southern France, Vienna, Budapest, and Stockholm.

c. 1910 In Berlin, frequents Romanisches Café. Gains support from the art dealers Paul Cassirer and Alfred Flechtheim.

1915 Three months military service in Engadin.

1918 Returns to Munich. Spends winters in Partenkirchen and summers in Tegernsee until 1921. Becomes friendly with Thomas Theodor Heine, Olaf Gulbransson, Richard von Below, and Kasimir Edschmid. Shares an old farmhouse with Gulbransson and von Below. Meets his future wife in Tegernsee. Illustrations to short stories by Dostoevsky.

1919 Illustrations to Georg Kaiser's *Von Morgen bis Mitternacht* (*From Morning to Midnight*) and Anton Chekhov's *The Cherry Orchard*.

1920 Illustrates stories of E. T. A. Hoffmann.

1921 Travels to Italy with Purrmann. Illustrations to Hans Christian Andersen's *The Tin Soldier*. Completes the portfolios *Boxer* and *A Comedy of Life*.

1922 Participates in exhibition at Galerie Flechtheim. Publishes his illustrated autobiography, *Manege des Lebens* (*The Arena of Life*).

1924 Returns to Berlin. Participates in fall exhibition of the Berlin Secession. Completes graphic portfolios, including *Goethe's Diaries of 1810* and *Cocaine: An Orgy of Modern Life*.

1926 Participates in summer exhibition of Berlin Secession. Publishes the book *Fünfzig Köpfe der Zeit* (*Fifty Personalities of Our Time*).

1929 Accepts a contract to teach at the State School of Art, Berlin. Joins the Berlin Secession, the Free Secession, and the German League of Artists. Develops the graphic technique of "Gelatine etching."

1934 Dismissed by Nazi government from his teaching position. Moves to Freiburg.

1941 Dies 28 November in Freiburg.

Bibliography

Breuer, R. "Köpfe der Zeit von R. Grossmann." *Weltbühne* 21 (1925): 952.

"C. G. Jung diagnostiziert Picasso." *Kunst und Künstler* 32 (January 1933): 28–30.

Edschmid, Kasimir. "Rudolf Grossmann." *Der Cicerone* 11 (1919): 353–362.

Grossmann, Rudolf. "Selbstcharakteristik." *Das Kunstblatt* 5 (1921): 143.

Kolle, H. "Künstlerbildnis." *Das Kunstblatt* 6 (1922): 473–476.

"Rudolf Grossmann: Neue Radierungen." *Kunst und Künstler* 19 (1920): 29.

Rudolf Grossmann: Zeichnungen und Druckgraphik. Karlsruhe: Staatliche Kunsthalle, 1963.

Scheffler, Karl. "Köpfe: Bildniszeichnungen R. Grossmanns." *Kunst und Künstler* 21 (1923): 315.

——. "Rudolf Grossmann." *Kunst und Künstler* 26 (1928): 189–192.

——. "Neue Arbeit R. Grossmanns." *Kunst und Künstler* 27 (1929): 390–393.

George Grosz

1893 Born Georg Ehrenfried Grosz on 26 July in Berlin, Jägerstrasse 63, to Karl Ehrenfried Grosz and Marie Wilhelmine Luise, née Schultze. His sisters are Cläre and Martha.

1898 Family moves to Stolp, Pomerania.

1900 Father dies; family returns to Berlin.

1901 Grosz returns to Stolp. Begins taking private drawing lessons.

1908 Expelled from school.

1909 Passes entrance examination to the Royal Academy in Dresden in September. Initially lives with a family in Dresden.

1910 First drawing published in *Ulk*. Trip to Thorn on the Vistula.

1911 Completes studies at the Academy, graduating with honors. Summer vacation in Thorn.

1913 Visits Paris from August to November. Studies at the Atelier Colarossi. First book jacket appears. In summer, travels to Helgoland, Thorn, and Hamburg.

1914 Wins prize for drawing. Volunteers for military service on 13 November; stationed in Berlin.

1915 Released from military 11 May. Moves in with sister Cläre in Berlin. Moves on 7 July to Stephanstrasse, where he stays until 1918. Meets Wieland Herzfelde in the summer. Publishes a poem and drawing in the periodical *Die Aktion*.

1916 Works on the periodical *Neue Jugend*, and reads his poetry at *Neue Jugend* gatherings in Berlin, Dresden, Munich, and Mannheim. Meets Theodor Däubler in May. Changes name in September from Georg to George.

1917 Inducted into the military 4 January, but hospitalized and eventually transferred to a sanatorium on 23 February. Released from duty 27 April. Returns to Berlin in May. Works with Herzfelde's Malik Verlag. Sells his first oil painting to Sally Falk in Mannheim.

1918 Collaborates with John Heartfield on the animated film *Pierre in St. Nazaire* for The Military Picture Service. Travels to the Baltic with his future wife, Eva Louise Peter. Moves to Nassauischestrasse 4, his residence until 1921. Along with Herzfelde, Heartfield, and Erwin Piscator, joins the German Communist Party (KPD) on 31 December.

1919 Joins Club Dada. Illustrates books and periodicals for Malik Verlag, Sektion Dada, and works on Dada collages with Heartfield.

1920 First solo exhibition at the Hans Goltz Gallery, Munich. Marries Eva Peter on 26 May. Organizes *First International Dada Fair* in Berlin with Heartfield, Rudolf Schlichter, and others. His portfolio *God with Us* is confiscated. Travels to Portofino, Italy, to visit his patron Felix Weil.

1921 Fined 300 marks for slander against the military in a trial that ends on 21 April.

1922 Visits U. S. S. R. (Moscow and Petrograd) and Denmark.

1923 Publishes the portfolio *Ecce Homo*, which is confiscated for obscenity. First exhibition in Berlin. Is represented by the dealer Alfred Flechtheim. Spends August in Baden-Baden and Geneva.

1924 Fined 6,000 marks for obscenity in the portfolio *Ecce Homo*. Begins drawing for the left-wing publication *Der Knüppel*. Completes drawings for the periodical *Der Querschnitt*. Travels to Paris, April through May; exhibits there.

1925 Travels to Paris in June. Travels to Boulogne-sur-Mer in July, and stays at the home of Frans Masereel. Returns to Paris in July. In August, begins travels throughout France. Returns to Berlin on 15 October. Participates in Mannheim exhibition *Neue Sachlichkeit*.

1926 Son Peter Michael is born on 22 May. In July, travels to the Baltic. Contributions to *Simplicissimus*.

1927 Spends much of the summer in France. Returns to Berlin in October. Exhibits twenty-five oil paintings at the Galerie Flechtheim. Stops drawing for *Der Knüppel* in August.

1928 Works on set design for Piscator's production of Jaroslav Hašek's *The Good Soldier Schweik*, which opens on 23 January. Publishes the portfolio *Background*. On 20 December, Grosz is tried and found guilty of blasphemy for publishing a drawing of Christ in a gas mask. Visits London in September.

1929 Wins appeal against blasphemy charges on 10 April. Summers near Lugano. Exhibition at the gallery of Bruno Cassirer in October.

1930 Acquittal of blasphemy charges is overturned on 27 February. Son Martin Oliver is born on 28 February. Spends August and September on the Baltic with Max Pechstein. Participates in Venice Biennale. Acquitted of blasphemy charges a second time in a new trial, 3–4 December.

1931 Returns to the Baltic in August and September. Watson F. Blair Purchase Prize, Art Institute of Chicago.

1932 Arrives in New York 4 June. Teaches there at the Art Students League from June until August. Works for the publication *Americana*, and occasionally contributes to *Vanity Fair* and *The New Yorker*. Visits Philadelphia. Meets James Thurber and George Gershwin. Completes watercolors of New York. Leaves for Germany on 6 October.

1933 Emigrates from Germany on 12 January with Eva. Arrives in New York on 25 January. Teaches at Art Students League and at the Sterne-Grosz School. Exhibits watercolors in New York in March. Applies for American citizenship in April. Moves to Greenwich Village, then to Long Island.

1934 Commissioned by George Macey to illustrate O. Henry stories.

1935 Travels to Denmark, France, and Holland. Returns to New York on 15 September.

1936 Stops teaching at the Art Students League, but continues teaching at his own school. Receives contract for an American book, *Interregnum*.

1937 Wins Guggenheim Fellowship. Closes his art school in spring. Spends the summer in Cape Cod. Walker Gallery begins to represent Grosz in New York. Four paintings and numerous prints included in Munich exhibition *Degenerate Art*.

1938 Begins "Apocalyptic Paintings."

1939 Spends summer in Cape Cod. Herzfelde arrives in New York.

1940 Receives Carol H. Beck Medal from the Pennsylvania Academy of Fine Arts, and the Watson F. Blair Purchase Prize Award from the Art Institute of Chicago. Summer in Cape Cod.

1941 Exhibition in New York of twenty oils, *Paintings of the Nude*. Commissioned to illustrate Ben Hecht's *1001 Afternoons*. Asked to write an autobiography. Lectures at Columbia University, School of Fine Arts. Resumes teaching at Art Students League. Changes dealers, joining the Associated American Artists Galleries. Summer in Cape Cod.

1943 Begins extensive exhibition activity in New York and other American cities. Completes illustrations for Grimm Brothers' fairy tales.

1945 June to October in Cape Cod.

1946 Wins Second Prize, *International Exhibition of Art*, Carnegie Institute, Pittsburgh. Publishes autobiography. Large publication of Grosz's portfolios is issued by Italo Ballo in Italy.

1949 Resumes teaching at the Art Students League in summer terms.

1951 23 May leaves New York to visit France, Holland, Belgium, Italy, Switzerland, and Monte Carlo. Returns to New York 5 December. Teaches at Art Students League.

1952 Exhibition in Dallas, Museum of Fine Arts. Visits Dallas in May and June.

1953 Teaches at Art Students League, and opens up an art school in his home.

1954 Major retrospective mounted from January to March at the Whitney Museum of American Art, New York. Is elected member of the American Academy of Arts and Letters. Leaves for Europe on 12 June. Visits Hamburg and Berlin. In September, leaves Berlin for London. Works on designs for the movie *I Am a Camera*. Returns to Germany; visits Otto Dix at Hemmenhofen.

1955 Returns to U. S. on 2 January. Teaches at Art Students League. Autobiography published in German.

1956 Teaches at the Skowhegan School of Painting and Sculpture in Maine. In November, is guest instructor at the Des Moines Art Center.

1958 Returns to Berlin 2 September. Elected extraordinary member of the Academy of the Arts on 24 November. Returns to New York 3 December.

1959 Awarded Gold Medal at the U. S. National Institute of Arts and Letters on 15 January. Returns to Germany 28 May. Dies 6 July in West Berlin.

Bibliography

Flavell, M. Kay. *George Grosz: A Biography*. New Haven and London: Yale University Press, 1988 (with comprehensive bibliography).

John Heartfield

1891 Born Helmut Franz Josef Herzfelde on 19 June in Berlin-Schmargendorf, the son of socialist writer Franz Herzfelde.

1895 Family moves to Weggis, Switzerland, then to Aigen, near Salzburg, in 1896.

1899 Parents abandon children in Aigen.

1905 Moves with his brother Wieland to Wiesbaden; apprentices as book dealer.

1908–11 Studies at the Munich School of Arts and Crafts.

1912 Active as commercial artist in Mannheim.

1913 Moves to Berlin.

1915 Military service, released after feigned nervous breakdown. Returns to Berlin; civilian service as auxiliary mailman. Friendship with George Grosz.

1916 Changes name to John Heartfield. With Wieland Herzfelde and George Grosz, founds the periodical *Neue Jugend*.

1917 With Herzfelde, founds Malik Verlag publishing house. Works on films for UFA.

1918 Founding member of Berlin's Club Dada. On 31 December, joins newly founded Communist Party of Germany (KPD).

1919–21 Active as "Monteur-Dada" in Berlin Dada movement. With Grosz, forms Grosz-Heartfield Concern.

1920 Among organizers of *First International Dada Fair*, Berlin. Active at the cabaret "Schall und Rauch" (Noise and Smoke). Cofounder of Dada periodicals *Jedermann sein eigener Fussball* and *Die Pleite*.

1920–22 Set designs for Erwin Piscator's Proletarian Theater and for the Max Reinhardt Theater.

1923 Works for the KPD journal *Der Knüppel*.

1924 First political photomontages. Secretary of the Red Group, an association of radical political artists.

1927 Begins work in the Studio for Graphics of the KPD in the Liebknecht-Haus, Berlin. Member of the Working Cooperative of Communist Artists.

1928–29 Set designs for Piscator's theater.

1929 Photographs and photomontages in Kurt Tucholsky's *Deutschland, Deutschland über Alles*.

1930–38 Photomontages for the *Arbeiter Illustrierte Zeitung*.

1931–32 Trip to U. S. S. R.

1933 After Nazis come to power, flees to Prague; continues photomontage and layout work for *Arbeiter Illustrierte Zeitung* and Malik Verlag.

1934 Stripped of German citizenship by Nazi regime. Membership in Oskar Kokoschka League of German exile artists in Prague.

1938 Emigrates to London via Strasbourg. Membership in Artists International Association. In Great Britain is denied permission to engage in political activity.

1939 Membership and participation in exhibition activities of Free German League of Culture (FGLC). Exhibition *One Man's War against Hitler*, Arcade Gallery, London.
    Photomontages for *Reynolds News* and the pamphlet *Freedom Calling!—The Story of the Secret German Radio*. Wieland Herzfelde emigrates to U. S. A. after being denied residence permit in Great Britain.

1940 Internment in three camps for enemy aliens; severe illness results in early release in August.

1941 Exhibition honoring fiftieth birthday, FGLC, London.

1942 Layout and design work for various British publishers through 1950.

1943 In July, receives permission to work as independent cartoonist.

1945 Participates in first international conference of Artists for Peace, London.

1947–48 Health prevents acceptance of appointment to the East Berlin Academy of Art.

1950 On 31 August, returns to Germany via Prague. Settles in Leipzig.

1951 Moves to East Berlin.

1956 Elected member of the GDR Academy of the Arts.

1957 Exhibition *John Heartfield and the Art of Photomontage*, German Academy of the Arts, East Berlin. Trip to China. Awarded National Prize for Art and Literature of the GDR.

1960 Officially awarded title of Professor.

1967 Trip to England to arrange retrospective exhibition and to undertake lecture tour. Exhibition, Moderna Museet, Stockholm. Awarded Order of Karl Marx.

1968 Dies 26 April in East Berlin.

Major Posthumous Exhibitions

1968 East Berlin, German Academy of the Arts, *John Heartfield*.

1969 London, Arts Council of Great Britain, *John Heartfield* (traveled to Newcastle, Birmingham, Lancaster, Brighton, Oxford, Cardiff, Sheffield, Edinburgh, and Durham).

1969–70 West Berlin, Neue Gesellschaft für Bildende Kunst, *John Heartfield*, November 1969–January 1970.

1970 Copenhagen, Charlottenborg, *John Heartfield Fotomontager*.

1971 East Berlin, German Academy of the Arts, June–July.

1972 Moscow, Academy of the Arts, January–February; Oslo, Kunstnernes Hus, June–July.

1977–80 West Berlin, Elefanten Press Galerie, March–April (traveled to cities in West Germany, Italy, Sweden, Great Britain, Switzerland, and France).

Bibliography

Herzfelde, Wieland. *John Heartfield: Leben und Werk*. Dresden: VEB Verlag der Kunst, 1962. Rev. eds., 1971 and 1976.

März, Roland, with Gertrud Heartfield, eds. *John Heartfield: Der Schnitt entlang der Zeit—Selbstzeugnisse, Interpretationen, Erinnerungen*. Dresden: VEB Verlag für Kunst, 1981.

Siepmann, Eckhardt. *Montage John Heartfield: Vom Club Dada zur Arbeiter-Illustrierte-Zeitung*. West Berlin: Elefanten Press, 1977.

Töteberg, Michael. *John Heartfield in Selbstzeugnissen und Bilddokumenten*. Reinbek: Rororo, 1978.

Erich Heckel

1883 Born 31 July in Döbeln, Saxony, the son of a railway construction engineer.

1891–95 Family lives in Olbernhau in the Erzgebirge.

1896 Enters Realgymnasium in Freiberg, Saxony.

1897 Studies at Realgymnasium, Chemnitz, until 1904; member of Vulcan debating club; reads Nietzsche, Dostoevsky, Strindberg, and Ibsen.

1901 Meets Karl Schmidt (later known as Schmidt-Rottluff).

1904 Enrolls at Technical College, Dresden, to study architecture. Meets Ernst Ludwig Kirchner and Fritz Bleyl.

1905 Works in studio of architect Wilhelm Kreis until July 1907. With Kirchner, Bleyl, and Schmidt-Rottluff founds the artists' association *Brücke*.

1906 Establishes contacts with Emil Nolde and Max Pechstein, who join *Brücke*.

1909 In spring, travels to Italy (Verona, Padua, Venice, Ravenna, Rome, Naples). Spends summer at Moritzburg Lakes with Kirchner. During September and October is in Dangast with Schmidt-Rottluff.

1910 Spends spring in Berlin with Pechstein and Kirchner; acquaintance with Otto Mueller. Meets dancer Milda Frieda Georgi (professional name Sidi [or Siddi] Riha). Joins German Artists' League.

1911 Spends summer in Prerow on the Baltic Sea. In August, joins Kirchner at Moritzburg Lakes. Moves to Berlin in fall.

1912 With Kirchner creates wall paintings for the chapel at the Cologne *Sonderbund* exhibition. Meets Walter Kaesbach and Christian Rohlfs. Spends the summer in Stralsund, Hiddensee, and on Fehmarn Island, where he visits Kirchner. In Berlin, during the fall meets Lyonel Feininger, Wilhelm Lehmbruck, Heinrich Nauen, and Ernst Morwitz, who introduces him to the literary circle of Stefan George. Franz Marc and August Macke visit his studio. Reads Dostoevsky again.

1913 In May, *Brücke* is dissolved. Travels to Caputh, near Potsdam, during winter and spring. First individual exhibition, Fritz Gurlitt Gallery, Berlin. Summers in Schiefler's summer house at Mellingstedt, near Hamburg, and at Osterholz on the Flensburg Fjord.

1914 Creates interior of Galerie Feldmann for *Werkbund* exhibition, Cologne. Spends spring in Dillborn with Nauen. Travels in Belgium and Holland; summers in Osterholz. After the outbreak of war, volunteers for military duty, but is rejected. Meets Franz Pfemfert, publisher of *Die Aktion*.

1915 Volunteers as Red Cross orderly. On 19 June, marries Sidi Riha. Stationed as medical orderly in Roselaere and Ostende, Belgium, under command of Walter Kaesbach in a medical unit that also includes painters Max Kaus, Anton Kerschbaumer, and Otto Herbig. Meets James Ensor.

1916 Stationed in Ghent.

1917 Stationed in Ostende.

1918 In November, returns to Berlin. Among founding members of the Work Council for Art. Joins November Group.

1919 Travels to Osterholz in summer; sets up an attic studio to use during subsequent summers through 1944.

1920 through 1944 Travels regularly throughout Germany and other Western European countries each spring and spends summers in Osterholz.

1937 National Socialist Chamber of Art forbids Heckel to exhibit or paint. Seven hundred and twenty-nine works are confiscated from German museums as "degenerate." Included in the Munich exhibition *Degenerate Art*.

1944 His Berlin studio, with most of its contents, destroyed during a bombing raid. Moves to Hemmenhofen on Lake Constance.

1949–55 Teaching appointment at the Karlsruhe Academy of Fine Arts.

1970 Dies 27 January at Radolfzell on Lake Constance.

Bibliography

Brücke Museum. *Erich Heckel: Aquarelle und Zeichnungen aus dem Nachlass*. West Berlin: Brücke Museum, 1976.

——. *Erich Heckel: Der frühe Holzschnitt*. West Berlin: Brücke Museum, 1983.

Dürrson, Werner. "Begegnung mit Erich Heckel." *Brücke-Archiv* 6 (1972–73): 7–10.

Dube, Annemarie and Wolf-Dieter. *Erich Heckel: Das Graphische Werk*. New York: Ernst Rathenau, 1964–65, 1974.

Erich Heckel: Aquarelle. Reutlingen: Hans-Thoma Gesellschaft, and Wiesbaden: Nassauischer Kunstverein, 1988.

Erich Heckel: Zeichnungen. Tübingen: Kunsthalle, 1976. Introduction by Karl-Heinz Gabler.

Gabler, Karl-Heinz, ed. *Erich Heckel: Zeichnungen—Aquarelle*. Stuttgart and Zurich: Belser Verlag, 1983.

——. *Erich Heckel und sein Kreis: Dokumente, Fotos, Briefe, Schriften*. Stuttgart and Zurich: Belser Verlag, 1983.

Heckel, Erich. "Brief über Edvard Munch und Die Brücke." *Die Schanze* 1, no. 1 (1951): 15–16.

Henze, Anton. *Erich Heckel: Leben und Werk*. Stuttgart and Zurich: Belser Verlag, 1983.

Herbig, Otto. "Erinnerungen an Erich Heckel." *Brücke-Archiv* 4 (1970): 38–39.

Kaus, Max. "Mit Erich Heckel im Ersten Weltkrieg." *Brücke-Archiv* 4 (1970): 5–14.

Kerschbaumer, Anton. "Beziehungen zu Erich Heckel." *Brücke-Archiv* 4 (1970): 36–37.

Rathenau, Ernst, comp. *Erich Heckel: Handzeichnungen*. New York: Ernst Rathenau, 1973.

Reidemeister, Leopold. "Erich Heckel: Aquarelle als Vorstudien zu Bildern." *Brücke-Archiv* 5 (1971).

Salter, Ronald. "Erich Heckel und Oscar Wildes 'Ballad of Reading Gaol.'" *Illustrationen 63* 17, no. 2 (1980): 48–50.

Sauerlandt, Max. "Erich Heckels Aquarelle von der Schleswigschen Ostseeküste." *Genius* 3 (1921): 73–77.

Schiefler, Gustav. "Erich Heckels graphisches Werk." *Das Kunstblatt* 2 (1918): 288–292.

Schmidt, Paul Ferdinand. "Erich Heckels Anfänge." *Zeitschrift für bildende Kunst* 21, no. 12 (1912): 257–264.

Sydow, Eckart von. "Erich Heckel als Graphiker." *Der Cicerone* 13 (1921): 1–15.

Thormaelen, Ludwig. *Erich Heckel*. Junge Kunst, vol. 58. Leipzig: Klinkhardt & Biermann, 1931. Rev. eds., 1932, 1953.

Vogt, Paul. *Erich Heckel*. Recklinghausen: Verlag Aurel Bongers, 1963.

Von Börries, Johann Eckardt. *Erich Heckel: Gemälde, Aquarelle und Zeichnungen*. Bildhefte der Staatlichen Kunsthalle Karlsruhe 5. Karlsruhe, 1972.

Wallerstein, Victor. "Eine Madonna von Erich Heckel." *Das Kunstblatt* 1, no. 6 (1917): 162–165.

Zdenek, Felix, ed. *Erich Heckel, 1883–1970: Gemälde, Aquarelle, Zeichnungen und Graphik*. Munich: Prestel Verlag, 1983; reprint, 1984. Essays by Lucius Grisebach, Katharina Hegewisch, Karl-heinz Gabler, Annemarie Dube, et al.

Hein Heckroth

1901 Born 14 April in Giessen. His father, formerly a shepherd, was later employed in a bookstore.

1915–19 Apprenticeship as printer and typesetter, Giessen.

1920 Moves to Frankfurt. Attends the Städel Art School; studies under Ludwig Gies.

1921–22 Attends the Academy of Design, Hanau; studies under Reinhold Ewald. Attends art history lectures of Richard Hamann, Marburg.

1924 Marries the painter Ada Maier. Set designer, Theater of the City of Münster. Works with Kurt Jooss's dance troupe. Meets Leopold von Kalckreuth and Oskar Schlemmer.

1925 Meets Bertholt Brecht.

1926 Daughter Renate (Nandy) is born.

1927 Employed by Civic Theater and Folkwang School, Essen. Belongs to the artists' circle of "Mother Ey" in Düsseldorf.

1932 Receives art prize of the Rhenish Secession. Exhibitions at Galerie Thannhauser, Munich, and Theatermuseum, Munich. Appointed professor of stage design at the Academy of Visual Arts, Dresden.

1933 Forbidden to teach and paint. Wife moves to Paris; lives with art critic Carl Einstein. Heckroth flees to Holland, then Paris. Joins the Jooss Dance Troupe on tour in Holland, Belgium, France, and New York.

1934 Returns to Paris. Contacts with Theodor Werner, Max Ernst, and Jankel Adler.

1935 Moves to London to design *A Kingdom for a Cow* at the Savoy Theater; producer is Kurt Weill. Becomes instructor of stage design and painting at Dorothy Whitney Elmhurst's art school in Dartington Hall, Devon. Meets critics Herbert Read and Roland Penrose. Stage designs for Kurt Jooss.

1937 Travels to Cassis; meets Theodor Werner and Georges Braque.

1938 Included in the exhibition *Twentieth Century German Art*, Burlington Galleries, London.

1939 Dartington Hall closed; moves to London.

1940–41 Internment as enemy alien in Camp Hay, New South Wales, Australia.

1941 Through the intervention of Herbert Read, returns to England. Moves to Dartington Hall, then London. Works for Kurt Jooss and New Russian Ballet.

1943 Befriends Kurt Schwitters and Jankel Adler. Exhibition, *Surrealist Paintings by Hein Heckroth*, Modern Art Gallery, London.

1945 Works regularly for Archer Film Productions with Michael Powell.

1946–47 Works on film *The Red Shoes*.

1948 Travels to Loire Valley and to Mont Saint-Michel. Exhibition, 20 Brook Street Gallery, London, 20 July–15 September.

1949 Receives Oscar for *The Red Shoes*. Stays briefly in Rome.

1950 Works on film *The Tales of Hoffmann*. Travels to Germany and Austria.

1952 Travels to France and Germany.

1956 Chief Stage Designer, Civic Theater, Frankfurt a. M. Exhibition, Frankfurter Kunstkabinett Hanna Becker vom Rath, 25 February–19 March.

1957 Exhibition, Oberhessisches Museum und Gallische Sammlungen der Stadt, Giessen, 3–24 July.

1959 Participates in exhibition at Galleria Montenapoleone, Milan.

1961 Exhibition, Art Association, Frankfurt, 17 November–17 December.

1961–63 Numerous trips to Germany, Holland, Belgium, and England.

1963–65 Works on tapestry designs, decorative paintings, and book illustrations in Germany and Sweden.

1964 Exhibition, Galerie Dorothea Loehr, Frankfurt, 5 May–3 June.

1966 Travels to Greece, London, and Berlin. Exhibits at Downey Museum of Art, Los Angeles, and Museum of Art, Stamford, Connecticut, 11 February–25 March.

1967 Exhibition, Bürgerhaus, Giessen.

1968 Travels to Barcelona and Collioure. In October, collaborates with Bernhard Schultze on the painting of a column in the foyer of the Bürgerhaus, Frankfurt.

1970 Dies 6 July in Alkmaar, Holland.

Major Posthumous Exhibition

1977 Kassel, Staatliche Kunstsammlungen Kassel, *Hein Heckroth, 1901–1970*, 12 February–20 March. Catalogue text by Karl-Heinz Gabler.

Bibliography

Bitsch, H. "Hein Heckroth: Maler und weltbekannter Bühnenbildner." *Hessen Journal* 3, no. 9 (September 1961): 14–16.

Gabler, Karl-Heinz. *Hein Heckroth 1901–1970*. Kassel: Staatliche Kunstsammlungen, 1977.

Otto Herbig

1889 Born 31 December in Dorndorf an der Werra.

1900–09 Attends Gymnasium at Jena. Receives first instruction in drawing from Erich Kuithan, Carl Zeiss School, Jena.

1909–10 Studies under Angelo Jank, Munich Art Academy.

1910 First trip to Italy.

1910–11 Attends Training Studios for Painting and Sculpture, Berlin-Charlottenburg.

1911–13 Studies under Hans Olde and Albin Egger-Lienz, Art School, Weimar. Meets Rudolf Wacker, Otto Pankok, Ernst Penzoldt, and Gert Wollheim.

1913 Travels with Penzoldt to Paris. Moves to Berlin.

1915–18 Serves as Red Cross volunteer in France and Belgium. Works in temporary military hospital, Ostende, with Walter Kaesbach, Erich Heckel, Anton Kerschbaumer, and Max Kaus. Meets James Ensor.

1919 Returns to Berlin; takes over Heckel's studio in Berlin-Steglitz. First marriage. Contacts with Karl Schmidt-Rottluff, Otto Mueller, and Emy Roeder.

1920 Participates in Free Secession exhibition, Berlin. Included in group exhibition with Heckel, Kaus, Schmidt-Rottluff,

Lyonel Feininger, Walter Gramaté, and Bernhard Kretzschmar at the Kunstsalon Heller, Berlin. His lithographs are included in *Die Schaffenden* portfolios until 1929. Participates in exhibitions of the Prussian Academy and in the *Jury-Free Art Show*, Berlin, until 1933.

1921 Birth of son Tyl.

1923 Retrospective exhibition, Galerie Ferdinand Möller, Berlin. Receives financial support from Edvard Munch.

1925 Exhibition at Galerie Dr. Steinbart, Berlin.

1926 Wife dies. Travels to Naples.

1928 Son Tyl dies. Second marriage. Exhibits at Galerie Dr. Steinbart, Berlin. Ludwig Justi purchases painting for National Gallery, Berlin.

1929–30 Rome scholarship to Villa Massimo at the same time as Schmidt-Rottluff and Kerschbaumer. Exhibitions at the galleries of Dr. Steinbart and Ferdinand Möller, Berlin. Receives Dürer Prize of the City of Nuremberg and prize of the German Artists' League.

1931 Travels to Italy.

1937 Visits Florence.

1940 Publishes lithographic portfolio *The World of the Child* with introduction by Helene Voigt-Dieterichs.

1941 Exhibits at Galerie von der Heyde, Berlin.

1943 Drafted into service at armaments factory in Thuringia.

1945–55 Professor at College of Architecture and Visual Arts, Weimar.

1947 Exhibits at Galerie von der Heyde, Berlin.

1948 Exhibits at Municipal Museum in the Moritzburg, Halle.

1951 Included in exhibitions at Landesmuseum, Darmstadt; Municipal Art Collections, Düsseldorf; and Municipal Museum, Wuppertal.

1952 Exhibits at Galerie Commeter, Hamburg.

1953 Exhibits at Art Association, Mannheim.

1954 Exhibits at Galerie Kühl, Dresden.

1955 Moves to Kleinmachnow, near Berlin. Exhibition, Schlossmuseum, Weimar.

1957 Travels to Italy. Exhibition, Art Association, Kassel.

1962 Retrospective at National Gallery, East Berlin. Moves to Weilheim, Bavaria.

1964 Participates in exhibition at Art Association, Erlangen.

1966 Participates in exhibitions at Kunsthalle, Darmstadt, and Haus am Lützowplatz, West Berlin.

1968–69 Exhibition at Galerie Seifert-Binder, Munich.

1970 Exhibition at Otto-Richter-Halle, Würzburg.

1971 Dies 13 June in Weilheim.

Major Posthumous Exhibitions

1973 West Berlin, Brücke Museum, *Otto Herbig*.

1978 West Berlin, Galerie Nierendorf, *Otto Herbig*.

1980 Ravensburg, Galerie Döbele, *Otto Herbig*.

Bibliography

Gerstenberg, Kurt. "Otto Herbig." *Das Kunstwerk* 1, no. 12 (1946–47): 18–20.

[Herbig, Otto]. "Otto Herbig zu seinen Bildern." *Das Innere Reich* 2 (1935): 443.

Müller-Mehl, Reinhard. *Otto Herbig*. Kunstblätter der Galerie Nierendorf no. 42. Berlin: Galerie Nierendorf, 1978.

Roh, Franz. "Der Maler Otto Herbig." *Die Kunst für Alle* 45 (November 1929): 60–62.

Rumer, Eberhard. "Otto Herbig." *Die Kunst und das schöne Heim* 48 (1949): 441 ff.

Scheiben, Wolfgang. "Der Maler Otto Herbig." *Die Sammlung* 12 (1957): 337 ff.

Scheidig, Walther. *Otto Herbig*. Dresden: VEB Verlag der Kunst, 1959.

Von Blankenburg, W. "Kinderbilder von Otto Herbig." *Die Kunst* 81 (March 1940): 139–141.

Wolfradt, Willi. "Maler." *Die Horen* 5 (1929): 701–704.

———. "Der Maler Otto Herbig." *Illustrierte Zeitung* [Berlin] no. 4510, 1931.

Karl Jakob Hirsch

1892 Born 13 November in Hanover, to an Orthodox Jewish family. His great grandfather is Rabbi Samson Raphael Hirsch.

1911–12 Studies at the Debschitz Painting School, Munich.

1912 Resides in artists' colony at Worpswede. Goes to Paris. Studies under Maurice Denis; befriends Amedeo Modigliani.

1914 Returns to Worpswede. Lives there and in Berlin.

1915 Publishes drawings in *Die Aktion* and *Die Schöne Rarität*. Produces eight etchings on the theme of Gustav Mahler's *Kindertotenlieder* (published 1917).

1916 Returns to Worpswede. Father dies. In fall, Hirsch drafted into military, but assigned to office duty following failure to meet physical requirements.

1918 Founding member of the November Group, and member of Work Council for Art and of Society for Proletarian Culture. Becomes chief stage designer and artistic adviser to the Volksbühne, Berlin, until 1922.

1919 Publishes collection of drawings and poems, *Revolutionary Art*. Exhibits with the November Group through 1921.

1921 Publishes lithographic portfolio on the theme of Mahler's symphonies.

1922 Returns to Worpswede.

1926 Exhibition with the November Group, Berlin.

1929 Exhibition with the November Group, Berlin.

1931 Publishes his novel, *Kaiserwetter* (*Weather Fit for Kings*).

1933 Emigrates to the United States via Denmark and Switzerland. Publishes under the pseudonym John Gassner.

1945 Returns to Germany. Lives in Munich.

1946 Publishes autobiography, *Heimkehr zu Gott* (*Return to God*).

1952 Dies 8 July in Munich.

Major Posthumous Exhibition

1967 West Berlin, Akademie der Künste, *Karl Jakob Hirsch 1892–1952*, 5 February– 5 March (traveled to Hanover, Stadtbuch- verein, 2–30 April; Munich, Theater- museum, 14 May–11 June).

Bibliography

Karl Jakob Hirsch 1892–1952. West Berlin: Akademie der Künste; Hanover: Stadt- buchverein; and Munich: Theater- museum, 1967.

Kastein, J. "Karl Jakob Hirsch." *Nieder- deutsche Heimatblätter* 4 (1927): 266 ff.

Hirsch, Karl Jakob. *Acht Radierungen zu Liedern Gustav Mahlers.* Reprint. Lilien- thal: Worpswede Verlag, n. d. [c. 1980].

——. *Heimkehr zu Gott: Briefe an meinen Sohn.* Dresden: Kurt Desch, 1946.

——. *Kaiserwetter.* Frankfurt a. M.: Fischer Verlag, 1931; reprinted 1971, 1981.

——. "Novembertage." *Kunst der Zeit* 3 (1928): 18.

——. *Revolutionäre Kunst.* Der Rote Hahn nos. 31/32. Berlin-Wilmersdorf: Verlag Die Aktion, 1919.

John Hoexter

1884 Born 2 January in Hanover, son of Samuel, a Jewish merchant, and Jenny, née Herzfeld.

1902 About this time, becomes student of Leo von König, School of the Museum of Art and Design, Berlin.

1907 Publishes *Sechs Romantiker Porträts* (*Six Portraits of Romantics*).

1908–10 Writes reviews and poetry; creates drawings for *Deutsche Theater Zeitschrift.* Becomes a well-known figure in Berlin's artistic and literary bohemia, frequenting the Café des Westens (also known as Café Grössenwahn [Café Megalomania]) and the Romanisches Café.

1909–11 Associated with Kurt Hiller's New Club and Neo-Pathetic Cabaret.

1912–13 Regular contributor to Franz Pfemfert's periodical *Die Aktion.*

1916 Drafted into military, 48th Infantry Regiment; released as unfit for service.

1919 Contributor to, and editor and il- lustrator of, first two issues of *Der Blutige Ernst.* Portrays Else Lasker-Schüler for the periodical *Schlemiel: Jüdische Blätter für Humor und Kunst.*

1926–28 Contributes to *Der Querschnitt.*

1928–29 Creates series of anecdotal es- says and drawings titled *So lebten wir: 25 Jahre Berliner Bohème* (*This Was Our Life: 25 Years Berlin-Bohème*), commissioned by Berlin newspaper *Bild-Zeitung am Mittag* to mark the closing of the Café des Wes- tens.

1930 About this time, privately publishes poetry collection *Apropoésies Bohémiennes.*

1933 Persecuted by the Nazis for bohe- mianism, morphine addiction, and Jewishness.

1938 Following *Kristallnacht,* writes let- ter of farewell to Leo von König. Hangs himself 16 November in Grunewald.

Bibliography

Bergmann, Alfred. *John Hoexter: Ein Denkstein.* Jahresgaben der Grabbe Gesellschaft 19. Detmold: Grabbe Gesellschaft, 1971.

Hoexter, John. *So lebten wir: 25 Jahre Ber- liner Bohème—Erinnerungen.* Berlin: Biko Verlag, 1929.

——. *Ich bin noch ein ungeübter Selbstmörder.* Randfiguren der Moderne, ed. Karl Riha and Franz J. Weber. Hanover: Postskrip- tum Verlag, 1988.

Richard Hohly

1902 Born 13 March in Löwenstein, near Heilbronn. Parents are innkeepers and vintners.

1907–14 Attends Volksschule.

1915–22 Attends teachers' college in Kirchheim and Heilbronn.

1922–24 Active as temporary worker in industry and banking. First itinerant studies.

1924–29 Studies at the Stuttgart Art Academy.

1926 Second period of itinerant studies. Master student in painting at the Art Academy, Kassel.

1929 Passes first examination for teach- ing in higher-level schools.

1930 Passes academic examination for teaching in higher-level schools. Trip to Norway. Meets Edvard Munch in Oslo. One-person exhibitions, Art Academy, Kassel; Art Association, Stuttgart; and Art Association, Heilbronn. Marries Annemarie Neumann.

1931–32 Member of Berlin Secession.

1932 Exhibition, Art Museum, Ulm. Museum purchases his painting *Woman with Attendants.*

1936 Placed on list of "degenerate" art- ists. His painting in the collection of the Art Museum, Ulm, is destroyed.

1941 In October, drafted into German military.

1942 Service in the Ukraine and Stalin- grad as war artist.

1943 Transferred to France.

1946 Joins the artists' group Red Rider. Participates in exhibition of German art at Die Palette, Zurich.

1947 Intense studies of Rudolf Steiner's anthroposophy and art theory.

1952 Experiments in stained glass.

1955 Exhibits at Art Assocation, Heil- bronn.

1956 Exhibits at Art Association, Stutt- gart.

1960 Physical and economic collapse.

1965 Joins Art Association, Heilbronn.

1967 Participates in exhibition at Land- ratsamt, Ludwigsburg.

1969 Participates in exhibition at Bietig- heim.

1970 Participates in exhibition at Rudolf- Steiner-Haus, Stuttgart.

1971 Exhibition, Kunsthalle, Heilbronn.

1973 Exhibition, Hornmoldhaus, Bie- tigheim.

1975 Exhibition, Galerie Hohly, Bie- tigheim.

1976 Death of his wife.

1977 Included in exhibitions at Waib- lingen and Galerie Aenigma, Basel. Con- structs own museum at his home.

1978 Awarded the Baden-Württemberg Order of Merit.

1979 Exhibition, Weilheim.

1980 Exhibitions, Landratsamt, Lud- wigsburg; Rudolf-Steiner-Haus, Stutt- gart.

1990 Lives in Bietigheim.

Bibliography

Richard Hohly: Leben und Werk. Stuttgart: Rudolf-Steiner-Haus, 1980.

Karl Holtz

1899 Born 14 January in Berlin, son of a domestic servant. Attends high school in Danzig.

1914–19 Studies at the School of the Museum of Applied Arts, Berlin, under Emil Orlik and Ludwig Sterlin.

1916 First caricature published in *Ulk;* continues to contribute to this magazine as well as creating drawings for *Wieland* and *Lustige Blätter.*

1918 Drafted into the military; serves in Zabern and Strasbourg. Moves to Berlin after World War I. In December, first cari- cature published in the Communist Par- ty's periodical *Die Rote Fahne.*

1919 Participates with Paul Fuhrmann in revolutionary struggles in Berlin. Arrested briefly by Freikorps troops.

1920 Drawings published in *Freiheit* and *Freie Welt,* both organs of the Independent Socialist Party of Germany, as well as in *Syndikalisten* and other periodicals of the political left.

1920–21 Journeys on foot through northern and southern Germany.

1922–23 Travels to Italy, southern France, and Tunisia.

1924 Drawings published in *Der Wahre Jakob* and *Lachen Links.*

1925 Participates in *First All-German Art Exhibition* in Moscow, Saratow, and Leningrad, as well as in the exhibition of the Prussian Academy of Fine Arts, Ber- lin.

1926 Included in exhibition organized by Otto Nagel in Tietz Department Store, Berlin, and in *Great Berlin Art Exhibition.*

1932 Moves to Rehbrücke near Potsdam.

1933 Forbidden by Nazis to practice his profession as a newspaper and periodical illustrator.

1934 Works as a technical draftsman and anonymously as a commercial artist pro- ducing book covers for Auffenberg Ver- lag.

1939–45 Serves as soldier in Warsaw.

1945 In March, deserts from the German army; returns to Rehbrücke. Drawings published in East German periodicals *Uy- lenspiegel, Neue Berliner Illustrierte, Freie Welt, Neue Deutsche Bauernzeitung,* and *Zeit im Bild.* Produces illustrations for books.

1978 Dies 18 April in Potsdam-Reh- brücke.

Major Posthumous Exhibition

1981 Altenburg, Staatliches Lindenau- Museum, *Karl Holtz: Das frühe Werk 1918–1933.*

Bibliography

Arnheim, Rudolf. "Karl Holtz." *Ge- brauchsgrafik* 6 (1931): 2–13.

Kuhirt, Ulrich. *Karl Holtz: Aus der Holtz- kiste.* East Berlin: Malik Verlag, 1971.

Schütte, Wolfgang U. "Der Illustrator Karl Holtz." *Marginalien,* no. 43 (1971), 32–39.

——. "Karl Holtz und die linke Publizistik 1918–1933." *Bildende Kunst,* no. 10 (1980).

——. *Karl Holtz: Klassiker der Karikatur.* East Berlin: Eulenspiegel-Verlag, 1983.

Karl Hubbuch

1891 Born 21 November in Karlsruhe, son of an employee of the German tele- graph system.

1908–12 Studies at Karlsruhe Academy, where he meets Rudolf Schlichter, Willi Müller-Hufschmid, and Georg Scholz.

1912–14 Studies at the School of the Museum of Applied Arts, Berlin, under Emil Orlik. George Grosz is among fel- low students.

1914–18 Volunteers for military service; serves as artilleryman.

1918–19 Suffers from malaria. Re- cuperates in isolation in villages in Baden.

1920–22 Resumes studies at the Karls- ruhe Academy as master student of Walter Conz. Participates in *German Art Exhibi- tion,* Baden-Baden.

1922 Returns to Berlin. Studies under Orlik, Prussian Academy of Fine Arts, Berlin.

1924 Assistant teacher of lithography at the Karlsruhe Academy. Participates in the fall exhibition of the Prussian Academy of Fine Arts, Berlin. Exhibition of lithographs and drawings, Galerie Trittler, Frankfurt a. M.

1925–28 Serves as director of the second drawing class at the Karlsruhe Academy. Participates in the Mannheim *Neue Sach- lichkeit* exhibition and in a group exhibi- tion with Otto Dix, George Grosz, Alex- ander Kanoldt, Carlo Mense, Georg Scholz, and Georg Schrimpf, Galerie Neumann-Nierendorf, Berlin.

1928 Becomes professor at the Karlsruhe Academy. Travels regularly to France. Participates in Berlin Secession summer exhibition.

1929 Participates in exhibition *Twenty Years of the Graphics Collection,* Kunsthalle, Mannheim.

1930 Included in the exhibition *Self-Por- traits of Baden Artists,* Baden Art Associa- tion, Karlsruhe.

1931 Participates in autumn exhibition at Prussian Academy of Fine Arts, Berlin.

1933 Dismissed from Karlsruhe Acad- emy professorship.

1933–45 Forbidden to practice as artist. Earns occasional money by painting ceramics and cuckoo clocks.

1947 Exhibits with the group The Circle at the Kunsthaus Biesel, Karlsruhe.

1948 Renewed appointment as professor at Karlsruhe Academy. Makes study trips to Holland, France, and Italy.

1951 Participates in the first postwar exhibition of the reconstituted German Artists' League, Academy of Fine Arts, West Berlin, and continues to do so annually until 1967.

1952 Exhibition, Art Association, Karlsruhe.

1954 Participates in exhibition celebrating the hundredth anniversary of Karlsruhe Art Association.

1955 Included in *Contemporary German Drawing*, Pergamon Museum, East Berlin.

1957 Retires from professorship.

1958 Included in *Karlsruhe Artists*, Stadthalle, Freiburg.

1959 Wins silver medal in the International Competition for Peace, Leipzig.

1961 Receives Hans Thoma State Prize of Baden-Württemberg. Participates in exhibitions for Hans Thoma Prize in Bernau, Black Forest, and in *Neue Sachlichkeit*, Haus am Waldsee, Berlin.

1962 Included in exhibition *Artists from Baden*, Museum of Fine Arts, Besançon.

1964 Exhibition *Karl Hubbuch: Drawings and Graphics 1913–1963*, German Academy of the Arts, East Berlin.

1965 Guest of honor at Villa Massimo, Rome. Exhibits at Ladengalerie, Berlin.

1967 *The Work of Karl Hubbuch in Two Exhibitions*, Neue Münchner Galerie, Munich.

1969 Exhibits at Stadthalle, Freiburg.

1971 Exhibits at Galleria del Levante, Munich.

1974 Exhibition, Kunsthalle, Bremen.

1979 Exhibition, Galerie Michael Hasenclever, Munich. Dies 26 December in Karlsruhe.

Major Posthumous Exhibitions

1981 Karlsruhe, Kunsthalle, *Karl Hubbuch*.

1984 Paris, Galerie Karl Flinker, *Karl Hubbuch*, August; Munich, Galerie Michael Hasenclever, *Karl Hubbuch: Druckgraphik*.

Bibliography

Hartmann, W. "Kinder, die unter Steinen aufwachsen: Ein Beitrag zu Karl Hubbuchs Tätigkeit und Ikonographie nach 1933." *Jahrbuch der Staatlichen Kunstsammlungen in Baden-Württemberg* 20 (1983): 161–174.

———. "Wissend und blind: Eine Allegorie reelle von Karl Hubbuch." *Zeitschrift des Deutschen Vereins für Kunstwissenschaft* 37, nos. 1–4 (1983): 1–49.

Heusinger von Waldegg, J. "Über einige Motive im Frühwerk von Otto Dix und Karl Hubbuch." *Pantheon* 40 (October–December 1982): 317–320.

Hiepe, Rudolf. *Karl Hubbuch*. Dresden: VEB Verlag der Kunst, 1961.

Schmidt, Diether. *Karl Hubbuch*. Munich: Limes Verlag, 1976.

Wolfradt, Willi. "Karl Hubbuch". *Die Horen* 5 (1928): 158 ff.

Willy Jaeckel

1888 Born 10 February in Breslau, son of civil servant.

1902 Studies painting with Breslau artist.

1904 Breaks off artistic training for health reasons. Apprentices in forestry.

1906 Attends Royal School of Applied Arts, Breslau. Studies under Eduard Kaempffer.

1908–11 Attends Dresden Academy. Studies under Otto Gussmann.

1911 Returns to Breslau. Active as interior decorator and painter.

1913 Marries Charlotte Sommer. Commission for painting Hans Poelzig's Confectionery Pavilion at Breslau Centenary Exposition permits existence as independent artist. Critical success at *Jury-Free Art Show*, Berlin. Moves to Berlin. In October, individual exhibition at Kunstsalon Fritz Gurlitt, Berlin.

1915 Member of Berlin Secession. Lithographic portfolio *Memento 1914/15* is apparently banned for anti-military imagery. Military service as cartographer in Russia.

1916–17 Special leave for the execution of four monumental paintings at Bahlsen Cookie Factory, Hanover.

1917 Lithographs for the *Book of Job*.

1918 Recalled to military service. Serves in Russia. National Gallery, Berlin, purchases painting *Sandpit* (1916).

1919 Moves to Gunzesries in Allgäu region of southwest Germany.

1920 Creates his last lithographs.

1921 Writes autobiographical statement for Fritz Gurlitt's annual *Das graphische Jahr*.

1925 Appointed professor at the State College of Art, Berlin. First of numerous summers spent in Hiddensee.

1928 Awarded Georg Schicht Prize for "the most beautiful German portrait of a woman" with stipend for a semester at Villa Massimo, Rome.

1933 Dismissal from teaching position; reinstated at demand of the students.

1935 Painting *Madonna* removed from *Great Munich Art Exhibition* "at the personal behest of Adolf Hitler."

1937 Works removed from public collections as "degenerate." Graphics destroyed in Düsseldorf, Hamburg, and Mannheim museums.

1938 Renewed efforts to remove Jaeckel from teaching position fail due to personal intervention of Air Force General Milch.

1943 Decides to resign from teaching position. Summer at Hiddensee. On 21 November, studio destroyed during bombing raid on Berlin. Visits Count Schwerin, Zettenin.

1944 Late January, returns to Berlin. Dies 30 January when his house is destroyed during Allied bombing raid and he perishes with others in air raid shelter.

Bibliography

Cohn-Wiener, Ernst. "Willy Jaeckel." *Der Cicerone* 12 (1920): 561–568.

———. "Willy Jaeckel." *Jahrbuch der Jungen Kunst*, 1920, 237–244.

———. *Willy Jaeckel*. Bibliothek der Jungen Kunst, vol. 2. Ed. Karl Schmidt-Rottluff. Leipzig: Klinkhardt & Biermann, 1921.

Landau, L. "Willy Jaeckel." *Der Deutsche Bote* 32 (1926): 465–469.

Liebermann, Max. "Zu den Werken von Willy Jaeckel." *Deutsche Kunst und Dekoration* 45 (February 1920): 261–264.

Mobius, M. R. "Neue Arbeiten von Willy Jaeckel." *Die Kunst für Alle* 45 (October 1929): 36–40.

Plunnecke, Wilhelm. "Willy Jaeckel." *Die Kunst für Alle* 34 (March 1919): 209–216.

Stiljanov-Nedo, Ingrid. *Willy Jaeckel 1888–1944: Das Druckgraphische Werk*. Regensburg: Museum Ostdeutsche Galerie, 1987.

Unus, Wilhelm. "Willy Jaeckel." *Velhagen und Klasings Monatshefte* 38, no. 2 (1924): 169–184.

Willy Jaeckel: Gemälde, Pastelle, Graphik. Regensburg: Museum Ostdeutsche Galerie, 1975.

Zucker, P. „Willy Jaeckel." *Ikarus* 1 (1925): 92–95.

Richard Janthur

1883 Born 12 April in Zerbst.

1908 Moves to Berlin. Studies at Art School, Breslau.

1911 Exhibits with Berlin Secession. Travels to Greece.

1912 Founds artists' group The Ones Filled with Pathos with Ludwig Meidner and Jakob Steinhardt; it exhibits at *Der Sturm* gallery. Publishes drawings in *Die Aktion*.

1918 Founding member of the November Group. Member of Work Council for Art.

1919–24 Produces numerous lithographs for *Gulliver's Travels, Robinson Crusoe, The Golden Ass, The Jungle Book, Gilgamesh*.

1921 Exhibition, I. B. Neumann, Berlin.

1922 I. B. Neumann, Berlin, publishes *Exotic Portfolio: People and Animals* and *Peter Schlemihl*.

1929 Exhibits with the November Group, Berlin.

1956 Dies in Berlin.

Major Posthumous Exhibitions

1961 West Berlin, National Gallery, *Der Sturm*.

1968 Munich, Galleria del Levante, *Die Pathetiker*.

Bibliography

Kliemann, Helga. *Die Novembergruppe*. Berlin: Mann, 1969.

Riess, M. "Richard Janthur." *Schlesische Monatshefte* 3 (1926): 521.

Grethe Jürgens

1899 Born 15 February in Holzhausen near Osnabrück.

1900 Family moves to Wilhelmshaven.

1918 Completes high school and studies architecture at the Technical College in Berlin. College closes due to the outbreak of the revolution.

1919–23 Returns to Wilhelmshaven and studies at the Municipal Craftsmen's and Applied Arts School, Hanover, under Fritz Burger-Mühlfeld.

1923 Active professionally as a commercial artist; draws advertisements for the Hackethal Wire and Cable Plant, Hanover, and for the magazine *Der Manufakturist* through 1927.

1926 Completes first oil paintings.

1928 Included in exhibition at the Art Association, Nordhausen.

1929 Moves to Podbielskistrasse 112 (today 288) in Hanover. Earns a living as a painter with occasional commissions.

1931–32 Contributing editor to *Der Wachsbogen* (twelve issues published). Included in an exhibition at the Herzog Anton Ulrich Museum, Brunswick.

1933 Exhibition at Galerie Abels, Cologne. Travels to Italy with Gustav Schenk, whose article in *Kölnische Zeitung* she is commissioned to illustrate. Spends a few weeks in Positano.

1933–34 Completes watercolors of plants for Gustav Schenk's book *Aron oder das tropische Feuer (Aaron, or The Tropical Fire*; Hanover: Adolf Sponholtz Verlag, 1937). In the following years, she primarily creates book illustrations and jackets.

1951 Retrospective exhibition at the Wilhelm Busch Museum in Hanover.

1962 Exhibits in *The Twenties*, Art Association, Hamburg.

1963 Exhibits at Galerie Zwirner, Cologne.

1967 Exhibits at Galerie Brockstedt, Hamburg, and Art and Museum Association, Hanover.

1968 Included in *Aspects of New Objectivity*, Galleria del Levante, Rome/Munich.

1970 Exhibits at League of Visual Artists, Hanover.

1971 Included in *Realism between Revolution and Seizure of Power 1919–1933*, Württemberg Art Association, Stuttgart, and in *Realism in Germany*, Rotunda di Via Besana, Milan.

1972 Included in *Painters of Reality in Germany, 1920–32*, Art Association, Oldenburg.

1973 Begins to work primarily in colored pencil. Included in *Realism of the Twenties*, Galerie Hasenclever, Munich, and in *Twelve Painters between the Wars*, Art Association, Hanover.

1974 Included in *Realism in Germany 1919–1933*, Musée d'Art et d'Histoire, St. Etienne-Chambery; *Realism and Objectivity: Aspects of German Art 1919–1933*, National Gallery, East Berlin; and *Neue Sachlichkeit in Hanover*, Art Association, Hanover.

1975 Exhibits at Galerie Krokodil, Hamburg.

1976 Exhibits at Stubengalerie-Goslar.

1981 Dies in Hanover.

Major Posthumous Exhibition

1982 Bonn, Art Association, *Grethe Jürgens, Gerta Overbeck*, 27 October–5 December.

Bibliography

Jochimsen, Margarethe, Georg Reinhardt, and Hildegard Reinhardt. *Grethe Jürgens, Gerta Overbeck*. Bonn: Art Association, 1982.

Georg Kinzer

1896 Georg Philippus Maria Kinzer born 1 May to a Catholic family in Ratibor, Upper Silesia.

1920–22 Student of Leo Bartning and Paul Plotke at the School of the Museum of Applied Arts, and the State Art School, Berlin.

1922 Passes examination as art educator; appointed teacher of drawing in Leobschütz.

1920s Marries Stephanie Johanna Wandzik. Has two children.

1933 Arrested and banned from teaching by Nazi government. After release, practices secretly as artist in Berlin until 1945.

1945 Appointed professor of landscape and figure painting at College of Fine Arts, Berlin.

1953–55 Participates in graphics exhibitions, Kestner Gesellschaft, Hanover.

1961 Retires from teaching.

1983 Dies in Munich on 28 September.

Ernst Ludwig Kirchner

1880 Born 6 May in Aschaffenburg, son of an engineer/chemist in the paper industry.

1886 Family moves to Frankfurt a. M.

1887–90 Family moves to Perlen, near Lucerne, Switzerland, where his father is deputy director of the paper factory. Enters school.

1890 Father is appointed Professor of Paper Research at the Industrial Academy, Chemnitz.

1901 Graduates from Realgymnasium, Chemnitz. Studies architecture at Saxon Technical College, Dresden; meets Fritz Bleyl.

1903 In April, awarded preliminary diploma in architecture. In fall, goes to Munich.

1903–04 Studies winter semester at Munich Technical College and at Studio for Teaching and Experimentation in the Applied and Fine Arts of Wilhelm von Debschitz and Hermann Obrist. Visits the *Phalanx* Neo-Impressionist exhibition (includes Georges Seurat, Henri Cross, Paul Signac, and Camille Pissarro) and also sees works by Max Klinger, Théo Van Rysselberghe, Henri de Toulouse-Lautrec, Felix Vallotton, and Vincent van Gogh. In October, travels to Nuremberg, where Renaissance German woodcut blocks are displayed at the Germanisches Nationalmuseum.

1904 In March, creates his first woodcut. In spring, returns to Dresden to continue architectural studies. Meets Erich Heckel. Begins painting in oils.

1905 Meets Karl Schmidt-Rottluff during spring. On 7 June, founds *Brücke* with Bleyl, Heckel, and Schmidt-Rottluff. On 1 July, receives diploma in architecture.

1906 Publishes *Brücke Program*. Liaison with Doris "Dodo" Grosse begins. Contacts with Emil Nolde and Max Pechstein, who join *Brücke*.

1907 Spends summer with Pechstein in Göppeln, near Dresden.

1908 In January, exhibition with Schmidt-Rottluff at Kunstsalon August

Dörbandt, Brunswick. Summer with Emmy Frisch on Baltic Sea island of Fehmarn. Creates painted wall-hangings and furnishings for his studio.

1909 In January, visits Pechstein in Berlin; sees Henri Matisse exhibition at Paul Cassirer's gallery. Visits Berlin in April. Spends summer with Doris Grosse and Heckel at Moritzburg Lakes. Travels to Chemnitz in September. In late October, travels to Moritzburg. In November, sees Schmidt-Rottluff in Berlin, where he visits the Paul Cézanne exhibition at Paul Cassirer's gallery. Joins the German Artists' League. Probably during this year, he develops an interest in works from the Cameroon and the Palau Islands at Dresden Ethnographic Museum. Makes pewter and terra-cotta sculptures and perhaps his first wooden sculptures and carved furnishings.

1910 Spends March in Berlin with Heckel in Pechstein's studio. Attends New Secession exhibition and meets Otto Mueller. Travels to Fehmarn during the spring. Spends the summer at Moritzburg Lakes with Heckel and Pechstein. In September, is in Dresden. With Heckel visits Gustav Schiefler and Rosa Schapire in Hamburg during October. In December, Schiefler visits the *Brücke* studios in Dresden.

1911 Spends January in Berlin; close contacts with Pechstein and Mueller. Travels with Mueller to Mnishek in Bohemia in July; visits Prague; meets Bohumil Kubista. Travels with Heckel to Moritzburg Lakes during August. Moves to Berlin in October; takes over Pechstein's studio at Durlacher Strasse 14 in the Wilmersdorf district of the city. With Pechstein founds MUIM-Institute (Moderner Unterricht in Malerei [Modern Instruction in Painting]). Meets Erna and Gerda ("Gerti") Schilling. Contacts with Herwarth Walden and artists and writers of Neo-Pathetic Cabaret.

1912 Creates wall paintings with Heckel for chapel at the Cologne *Sonderbund* exhibition. Travels to Fehmarn with Erna and Gerda Schilling during the summer; visits by Heckel and Schmidt-Rottluff. Begins work on *Brücke Chronicle*.

1913 In May, dissolution of *Brücke*. Friendship with Alfred Döblin. On Fehmarn with Erna Schilling during summer. In October and November, first exhibitions devoted to his work held at Folkwang Museum, Hagen, and Galerie Fritz Gurlitt, Berlin.

1914 Travels to Jena in mid-February for one-man exhibition at the Art Association, organized by Eberhard Grisebach; contacts with Botho Graef and the circle of intellectuals at the University, Jena. Moves with Erna to a new studio at Körnerstrasse 45 in Berlin-Friedenau during April. Designs "Art in the Tobacco Industry" booth for Cologne *Werkbund* exhibition. Spends summer on Fehmarn with Erna. Returns to Berlin in August; during the trip, briefly arrested on suspicion of espionage. Increasing dependence on absinthe; develops phobia of uniforms.

1915 Begins association with Karl Ernst Osthaus. In the spring, becomes an "involuntary volunteer" serving as a driver in the artillery. Mobilized as a recruit in the Field Artillery Regiment 75 in Halle-an-der-Saale during July. Through the intervention of Professor Hans Fehr, furloughed 12 September because of "lung infection and general weakness." Returns to Berlin; works on the model for a war monument at Hagen titled *The Iron Smith*.

1916 In January, enters the sanatorium of Dr. Kohnstamm in Königstein/Taunus. In Berlin during February and March. Returns in June to the sanatorium, where he is treated for general constitutional weakness and intense nervousness resulting from military service and misuse of sleeping potions. Creates wall paintings in sanatorium stairwell. Meets Carl Sternheim. July through December, stays in Berlin and Jena. First exhibition held in October at Ludwig Schames's gallery, Frankfurt. In December, enters the sanatorium of Dr. Edel in Berlin-Charlottenburg to cure nervous crisis induced by alcohol and narcotics. His parents force him to leave the sanatorium and move to Chemnitz in late December.

1917 Takes his first trip to Davos in Switzerland during January. Resides in Berlin February through April. In May, moves to Davos; contacts Henry Van de Velde. Enters the sanatorium at Kreuzlingen in September. Schiefler begins to work on a catalogue of Kirchner's graphics.

1918 Released from the sanatorium in July; moves to the Stafelalb near Frauenkirch.

1919 Begins to restore, rework, and redate his earlier works. Writes about his works under the pseudonym Louis de Marsalle.

1921 Exhibition of fifty works held at Kronprinzenpalais, Berlin. Death of father. Meets dancer Nina Hard.

1923 Participates in retrospective exhibition at Kunsthalle, Basel. Moves into a large mountaineer's hut at the entrance of Sertig Valley near Frauenkirch.

1925 Swiss artists befriended by Kirchner form Red-Blue group in Basel. Meets Paul Klee.

1926 Travels to Germany.

1931 Appointed a member of the Prussian Academy of Fine Arts, Berlin.

1933 Retrospective exhibition at Kunsthalle, Berne.

1935 Suffers from angina and recurring stomach and intestinal inflammation; resumes consumption of tranquilizing drugs.

1937 In January, W. R. Valentiner organizes first Kirchner exhibition in the U. S. at the Detroit Institute of Arts. In Germany, 639 works are confiscated from museums as "degenerate." Summer exhibition *Degenerate Art* in Munich includes thirty-two works by Kirchner. Prussian Academy of Fine Arts asks for his resignation in July.

1938 Continuing intestinal inflammation and despair about German political developments. Destroys a number of his works. On 15 June, commits suicide.

Bibliography

Ernst Ludwig Kirchner 1880–1938. West Berlin: Nationalgalerie, 1979 (with comprehensive bibliography and exhibition listing).

Immanuel Knayer

1896 Born 19 April in Schöneberg/Enz, son of the teacher Immanuel Knayer and Maria Knayer, née Waidelich.

1902–14 School in Schöneberg. Attends Gymnasium at Ratingen, near Düsseldorf,

while staying with relatives there. Studies at boarding school in Korntal, near Stuttgart.

1914–18 Volunteers for military service and serves on Western Front. Is seriously wounded.

1919–21 Attends the Stuttgart School of Applied Arts.

1921–22 Stay in Düsseldorf.

1922–28 Attends Stuttgart Academy of Fine Arts. Master student of Robert Breyer.

1924–27 Repeated visits to Düsseldorf.

1927 Participates in exhibitions of the Academy graphics class.

1929 Participates in the sixth Stuttgart Secession exhibition.

1931–32 Participates in exhibitions of the Stuttgart New Secession.

1932 Participates in the third Stuttgart jury-free exhibition.

1933 Marries Helene Müller, sister of the artist Rudolf Müller. Participates in the *Württemberg Art Show*, Stuttgart.

1933–45 Active primarily in applied graphics and heraldic design.

1941 Painting *Freight Train Station in Snow* is rejected by jury of Munich *Great German Art Exhibition*. Painting ban imposed by Nazi officials.

1945 Studio in Stuttgart destroyed during bombing raids.

1945–54 Increasingly poor health forces reduction of activity as artist, except in heraldic design.

1955 Participates in the Art Week at Stuttgart's Killesberg.

1962 Dies 7 November in Stuttgart.

Major Posthumous Exhibition

1987 Böblingen, Städtische "galerie contact," *Immanuel Knayer 1896–1962: Gemälde, Aquarelle, Zeichnungen, Druckgraphik.*

D. W. Koeppen

Other than the watercolor included here, no work by this artist is known. For a conjecture as to the artist's true identity, see cat. no. 82.

Bernhard Kretzschmar

1889 Born 29 December in Döbeln (Saxony), son of a tailor.

1896 Attends elementary school in Döbeln.

1898 Begins drawing classes taught by Schieferdecker.

1900 Attends Volksschule.

1904–07 Apprenticeship with an interior decorator and painter.

1906 First visits Dresden.

1907–09 Works as an assistant to an interior decorator, supporting himself by playing the violin.

1908 Second visit to Dresden.

1909 With savings of one thousand marks, attends School of Applied Arts, Dresden, where he studies with E. Donadini. Lives at 11 Dürer Strasse.

1911 Leaves School of Applied Arts. Travels through southern Germany and Switzerland, using his savings and working occasionally as an interior decorator. Accepted at Dresden Academy. Begins studies in lower classes taught by Robert Sterl and Johann Raphael Wehle.

1911–12 Continues at Dresden Academy; meets Conrad Felixmüller and Peter August Böckstiegel. Takes intermediate classes taught by Richard Müller and Osmar Schindler.

1913 With savings of 327 marks, travels to Switzerland, Italy, France, and Spain.

1913–14 Returns to Dresden during fall of 1913; receives monthly stipend of thirty marks to study under Oskar Zwintscher. Paints outdoors in Goppeln. Sells first painting.

1914 Travels to Saarbrücken. Attends painting class of Otto Gussmann in late summer. Becomes master student of Carl Bantzer in the fall.

1916 Becomes a member of Dresden Artists' Association.

1917 Recruited for military service. Stationed in Bautzen as a medical orderly. Marries Susanne Magdalene Charlotte Uhmann (1891–1942) on 31 December.

1918 Released from military duty. Moves to Gostritz, near Dresden, where he sketches local scenes for paintings and etchings.

1919 Exhibition organized by Richard Hamann, University of Marburg.

1920 Destroys many works to begin anew. Is supported and encouraged by the art critic Julius Meier-Graefe. Completes first etching series, *Confessions*, and eight lithographs for Georg Kaiser's *Von Morgen bis Mitternacht (From Morning to Midnight)*. Participates in summer exhibition of Artists' Association, Dresden.

1920–21 Participates in *Lia* (Leipzig Annual International) exhibitions. Completes graphic series *Experiences* and *Six Etchings*.

1922 Completes series of ten etchings, *Little Circus*.

1923 Exhibition of graphic works and watercolors, Kabinett Hugo Erfurth, Dresden. Meets Paul Westheim. Participates in group exhibition of Artists' Association, Dresden.

1924 Exhibits at Euphorion Verlag, Berlin. Travels to Switzerland.

1926 Participates in *The International Exhibition of Art*, Dresden, and in the fall exhibition of the Berlin Secession.

1927 Exhibits at Galerie Neue Kunst Fides, Dresden. Joins Dresden Secession.

1928 Participates in an exhibition with Art League, Dresden.

1929 Participates in Amsterdam exhibition *Neue Sachlichkeit*.

1930 Exhibits graphics at Galerie Arnold, Dresden.

1932 Cofounds Dresden Secession '32.

1934 Participates in exhibition of Dresden Secession.

1936 Exhibits at *International Exhibition of Art*, Carnegie Institute, Pittsburgh.

1937 Forty-seven works confiscated from museums as "degenerate."

1945 Much work destroyed by bombings.

1946 Appointed professor at Dresden College of Art. Participates in *All-German Art Exhibition*, Dresden.

1947 Included in *Exhibition of Dresden Artists*.

1950 Included in *Painting in Dresden since 1925*, Radebeul.

1953 Included in *Third German Art Exhibition*, Dresden.

1954 Visits Peoples Republic of China. Participates in exhibition *China Experienced by German Artists*.

1956 Participates in exhibitions of German Cultural Day, Munich, and of the German Academy of the Arts, East Berlin.

1959 Awarded National Award of the German Democratic Republic. Participates in Moscow exhibition *Landscapes of Socialist Countries*.

1961–72 Participates in exhibitions in West Germany, East Germany, Bulgaria, Romania, and Czechoslovakia.

1969 Becomes honorary member of German Academy of the Arts, East Berlin.

1972 Dies 16 December in Dresden.

Major Posthumous Exhibitions

1971 Köpenick, Köpenicker Pädagogenkreis, *Bernhard Kretzschmar*.

1974 East Berlin, Staatliche Museen, National Gallery, *Bernhard Kretzschmar: Malerei, Graphik*.

Bibliography

Gurlitt, Hildebrand. "Bernhard Kretzschmar." *Das Kunstblatt* 8 (January 1924): 13–16.

Löffler, Fritz. *Bernhard Kretzschmar*. Dresden: VEB Verlag der Kunst, 1985.

———. "Bernhard Kretzschmar als Graphiker." *Bildende Kunst* 7 (1969): 363 ff.

———. "Bernhard Kretzschmar: 75 Jahre." *Bildende Kunst* 4 (1965): 182 ff.

Schmidt, Diether. *Bernhard Kretzschmar*. Dresden: VEB Verlag der Kunst, 1970.

Schmidt, Gudrun, Klaus Werner, and Fritz Löffler. *Bernhard Kretzschmar: Werkverzeichnis der Druckgraphik 1914 bis 1969*. Arkade-Œuvre 2. East Berlin: Arkade, 1981.

Schürer, Oskar. "Das graphische Werk Bernhard Kretzschmars." *Der Cicerone* 15 (1923): 353 ff.

Wilhelm Lachnit

1899 Born 12 November at Gittersee, near Dresden, son of a carpenter.

1914–20 Studies sign painting in Dresden. Takes evening life-drawing courses at Dresden School of Applied Arts; informal studies under Georg Oehme.

1921–23 Master student of Richard Dreher, Dresden Academy. Contacts with Otto Dix, Otto Griebel, Conrad Felixmüller, and other members of Dresden Secession Group 1919.

1924 Member of Red Group. Creates woodcuts for German Communist Party (KPD) publications and posters. Represented in *First All-German Art Exhibition*, Moscow, Leningrad, and Saratow. Member of the Society of Friends of the New Russia.

Creates frescoes for Deaf and Dumb Institution, Leipzig, until 1929.

1925 Joins KPD. With Griebel, Hans Grundig, and Fritz Skade founds New Group. Travels to North Africa, southern France, Switzerland, and Italy through 1928.

1926 Represented in *International Art Exhibition*, Dresden.

1927 With other Dresden artists forms group Action, which in 1932 becomes Dresden Secession '32.

1929 Founding member of Dresden chapter of Association of Revolutionary Artists of Germany (ARBKD or "Asso"). Represented in Amsterdam *Neue Sachlichkeit* exhibition.

1930 Represented in *Socialist Art Today*, Amsterdam.

1931 Dresden delegate to National Congress of ARBKD, Berlin.

1933 Brief arrest by Gestapo. Restrictions placed on his activity as artist. Works as free-lance organizer of exhibitions and trade fairs.

1937 Four works removed from museum collections as "degenerate."

1944–45 Conscription into military service.

1945 Studio and home destroyed 13 February during bombing raids on Dresden.

1946 Represented with seven works at *All-German Art Exhibition*, Dresden.

1947–54 Professor of painting at College of Fine Arts, Dresden.

1956 Travels to Italy with K. Kröner.

1954–62 Heads artists' association Little Academy.

1962 Dies 14 November in Dresden.

Franz Lenk

1898 Born 21 June at Langenbernsdorf in the Vogtland.

1912 Trains as an interior decorator and painter.

1912–15 Trains as a lithographer. In spring 1915, enters Dresden Academy to study under Richard Müller and Ludwig von Hofmann.

1916–18 Serves in the military.

1918 Returns to Dresden and studies at the Academy.

1920–22 Resumes training at the Academy. In 1922, studies under Ferdinand Dorsch. Sets up a studio in Zirkusstrasse.

1924 Switches to master teacher Robert Sterl. Marries Anneliese Hoernecke. Moves to Klotzschke, outside Dresden.

1925 Leaves the Academy after the winter semester; moves to Lausa.

1926 Moves to Berlin to take up an appointment at the College of Fine Arts. Travels to Dresden, the Vogtland, and Thuringia. First exhibition, Kunstsalon Emil Richter, Dresden.

1927–28 Exhibits with Berlin Secession. Begins using oil-tempera technique in 1928. Cofounds The Seven with Champion, Dietrich, von Hugo, Alexander Kanoldt, Franz Radziwill, and Georg Schrimpf. Travels to the Vogtland and Saxony. Member of hanging committee for *Jury-Free Art Show*, Berlin.

1929 Travels to Thuringia, Weida, and Orlamünde. Participates in *100 Years of Berlin Art*. Member of hanging committee for *Jury-Free Art Show*, Berlin. Joins the Association of Berlin Artists.

1931 Trips for landscape painting to Heilbronn, the Neckarbergland, upper Danube Valley, Heuberg, Hegau, Lake Constance, the Wilhelmsdorfer Moors, and Harburg. Exhibition, Neumann-Nierendorf Gallery, Berlin.

1932 Further trips to southern Germany and Schleswig. Establishes a studio at Kaiserdamm 20, Berlin-Charlottenburg. Exhibition, Kunsthütte, Chemnitz.

1933 Appointed professor at United State Schools for Fine and Applied Arts, Berlin. Befriends Georg Schrimpf. Birth of son Thomas.

1934 Joins Otto Dix to paint landscapes in Hegau.

1935 Dix-Lenk exhibition, Galerie Nierendorf, Berlin.

1936 Appointed to board of governors, Berlin Secession.

1937 Accepted into Prussian Academy of the Arts.

1938 Participates in *Great Spring Exhibition*, Hanover. Resigns from teaching position in protest against politicizing of art and persecution of colleagues by Nazi government. Moves to Orlamünde, Thuringia.

1940 Landscape painting trips to Potsdam and Cologne, and to Chiemsee and Fuschl-See in Bavaria through 1943.

1941 Exhibition, Nassau Art League, Wiesbaden.

1944–48 Moves via Wilhelmsdorf, near Ravensburg, and Grossheppach to Fellbach, near Stuttgart.

1949 Exhibits at Art Association, Cologne.

1950 Exhibits at City Museum, Erfurt.

1951 Exhibits at Art Association, Stuttgart.

1955 Exhibits at German Academy of the Arts, East Berlin.

1959 Moves to Schwäbisch-Hall and accepts appointment as the Cultural Officer of the town.

1968 Dies in Schwäbisch-Hall.

Major Posthumous Exhibition

1976 Cologne, Galerie von Abercron, *Franz Lenk 1898–1968: Retrospektive und Dokumentation*.

Bibliography

Hartmann-Zeller, F. "Zum Schaffen Franz Lenks." *Die Kunst* 69 (May 1934): 241–255.

———. "Zum Schaffen Franz Lenks." *Die Kunst für Alle* 49 (1936): 225–228.

Kroll, B. "Franz Lenk." *Kunst und Antiquitäten: Rundschau* 45 (1937): 212–214.

Linde, Franz. "Franz Lenk." *Westermanns Monatshefte*, October 1933, 109–116.

———. "Zum Bild 'Kaktus' von Franz Lenk." *Deutsche Kunst und Jugend: Blätter f. Zeichenkunst* 14 (1934): 248.

Käthe Loewenthal

1877 Born in Berlin, the oldest of five daughters in an Orthodox Jewish family. Father, a noted optometrist and hygienist, accepts position in Berne.

1889 Remains in Berne, although family returns to Berlin. Lives with Protestant minister's family; is baptized and confirmed. Meets Ferdinand Hodler.

1891 Returns to Berlin.

1893 Father dies unexpectedly.

1895 Begins studies under Hodler. Paints landscapes.

1898 In Paris meets painter Leo von König, who becomes director of Prussian Academy of Fine Arts in 1902.

1902 Studies at Prussian Academy of Fine Arts, Berlin. Meets Erna Raabe.

1905 Moves to Munich. Studio in Ohmstrasse 5.

1912 Begins annual summer visits to sister at Vitte on Hiddensee.

1914 Moves to Stuttgart. Works with Adolf Hölzel.

1919 Writes *Dem Vaterland* (*To the Fatherland*), a collection of twelve poems about German heroes, including Charlemagne, Kant, and Beethoven.

1920 During the 1920s, participates in exhibitions at Berlin Secession, Hamburg Art Association, Westphalian Art Association, and in Munich.

1935 Paintings banned in Stuttgart along with those of Oskar Schlemmer and Willi Baumeister. Stores her paintings at Albrecht Kämmerer's warehouse, Stuttgart.

1938 Death of Erna Raabe.

1941 Deported to extermination camp Izbeka in Lithuania.

1942 Murdered at Izbeka.

1943 Paintings stored in Stuttgart warehouse destroyed in bombing raid.

Bibliography

Käthe Loewenthal: Ein Erinnerungsbuch. Munich: Verlag der Neuen Münchner Galerie, 1985.

Elfriede Lohse-Wächtler

1899 Born in Dresden to established middle-class parents.

1916 Enters School of Applied Arts, Dresden. Studies applied graphics, linocut, woodcut, and batik.

1919 Contact with Dresden New Secession Group 1919, as well as with Oskar Kokoschka and Otto Griebel. Adopts pseudonym Nikolaus Wächtler and nickname Laus. Wears male attire, cropped hair. Participates in Spartakusbund.

1921 Marries opera singer and artist Kurt Lohse. Establishes studio with him and Griebel near Wehlen, close to a stone quarry. Bankruptcy apparently brought on by Lohse results in confiscation of her personal property.

1926–27 Moves to Hamburg. Marriage collapses. Works primarily in watercolor.

1929 Nervous breakdown; hospitalized at psychiatric hospital, Friedrichsberg. Exhibition of *Friedrichsberg Portraits*, Galerie Maria Kunde, Hamburg.

1930 Individual exhibition, United City Clubs of the Hamburg Women's Leagues, Hamburg. Included in exhibition, Art Association, Hamburg.

1931 Divorce from Lohse is finalized. Lives with gypsy band.

1932 Returns to Dresden.

1933 Declared mentally "degenerate" by Nazis and interned in the Arnsdorf "clinic" near Dresden. Paints extensively, but all her work is destroyed.

1940 Gassed at Brandenburg/Havel concentration camp in accordance with Nazi "hygiene" programs.

Bibliography

Banaschewski, A. "Friedrichsberger Köpfe: Zeichnungen von Elfriede Lohse-Waechtler." *Der Kreis* 6 (1929): 307–310.

Jeanne Mammen

1890 Gertrud Johanna Louise Mammen born 21 November in Berlin, the youngest daughter of Gustav Oskar Mammen, a merchant, and Ernestine Juliane Karoline, née del Haes, a native of the Netherlands.

1895 Family moves to Paris.

1906 Completes studies at Lycée Molière; enters Académie Julian.

1908–11 Attends Académie des Beaux Arts, Brussels, and Scuola Libra Academica at Villa Medici, Rome.

1912 Organizes exhibition of work in studio. Begins exhibiting with Salon des Indépendants, Paris and Brussels.

1914 On outbreak of World War I, family flees from France to Belgium and Holland.

1916 Moves to Berlin.

1919 In September, moves to studio at Kurfürstendamm 29, where she remains for the rest of her life. Works as fashion and book illustrator. Membership of German Communist Party.

1923 Watercolors and drawings for periodicals *Ulk, Jugend, Simplicissimus,* and *Uhu*, through 1933.

1930 Exhibition at Galerie Gurlitt, Berlin, with catalogue introduction by Hermann Sinsheimer.

1931–32 Color lithograph series for *The Songs of Bilitis*.

1933 Adopts Cubo-Expressionist style in rejection of Third Reich cultural policies; ceases exhibiting or publishing her work.

1946 Resumes exhibition activities.

1947 Exhibition at Galerie Gerd Rosen with catalogue introduction by Carl Linfert.

1949–50 Participates in artists' cabaret "Die Badewanne" (The Bathtub).

1954 Exhibition at Galerie Anja Bremer, Berlin.

1960 Seventieth birthday exhibition, Academy of the Arts, West Berlin.

1969 Trip to Morocco; patient in the clinic at Rabat-Salé.

1970 Exhibition at New Berlin Art Association.

1971 Exhibitions at Galerie Brockstedt, Hamburg; Galerie Valentien, Stuttgart; and Landesmuseum, Oldenburg.

1972 Participates in exhibition at the Gallery La Boëtie, New York.

1974 Participates in exhibition at Galerie G. A. Richter, Stuttgart.

1975 Paints last work; exhibitions at Galerie Schoenbrunn, Frankfurt a. M., and Galerie Valentien, Stuttgart.

1976 Dies 22 April in Berlin.

Bibliography

Akademie der Künste. *Zwischen Widerstand und Anpassung: Kunst in Deutschland 1933–1945*. West Berlin: Akademie der Künste, 1978.

Berlinische Galerie. *Berlinische Galerie: Neuerwerbungen.* West Berlin: Berlinische Galerie, 1976.

Fischer Fine Art. *Jeanne Mammen 1890–1976: Works from 1914–1930.* London: Fischer Fine Art, 1980.

Galerie Brockstedt. *Jeanne Mammen: Aquarelle—Paris, Brüssel vor 1915, Berlin 20er Jahre.* Hamburg: Galerie Brockstedt, 1971.

Galerie Pels Leusden. *Der Anteil der Frau an der Kunst der 20er Jahre.* West Berlin: Galerie Pels Leusden, 1977.

Hellwag, Fritz. "M. L. Folcardy & J. Mammen." *Kunstgewerbeblatt* 27, no. 10 (July 1916): 181, 187–189.

Klunner, Lothar, and Heinz Ohff. *Jeanne Mammen, Hans Thiemann.* West Berlin: Staatliche Kunsthalle, 1979.

Kunstverein, Bonn. *Jeanne Mammen, 1890–1976: Retrospektive.* Bonn: Kunstverein, 1981.

Neuer Berliner Kunstverein. *Jeanne Mammen.* West Berlin: Neuer Berliner Kunstverein, 1971.

Reinhardt, Hildegard. "Jeanne Mammen (1890–1976): Gesellschaftsszenen und Porträtstudien der zwanziger Jahre." *Niederdeutsche Beiträge zur Kunstgeschichte* 21 (1982): 163–182.

Schloss Charlottenburg, Berlin. *Künstlerinnen International 1877–1977.* West Berlin: Neue Gesellschaft für Bildende Kunst, 1977.

Herbert Marxen

1900 Born 27 January in Flensburg.

1901 Father dies.

1915 Graduates from Volksschule. Begins apprenticeship with Flensburg public transit.

1917 Resigns from transit service. Enters Flensburg School of Applied Arts.

1918 Military service.

1919 Returns to Flensburg.

1921 Studies under Willi Titze at Hamburg School of Applied Arts.

1922 First commercial graphics for Flensburg firms. Joins Association of Commercial Graphic Artists.

1924 Studies figure drawing in Munich. Travels to Italy; returns to Flensburg when stepfather dies.

1925 Active as commercial artist; receives support from city of Flensburg.

1926–27 Publishes caricatures in *Flensburger Nachrichten*.

1928 Caricatures in *Kölnische Illustrierte Zeitung*. Begins free-lance work for *Jugend*.

1929 Free-lance association with *Simplicissimus*. Included in exhibition at Artists' Club, Altona.

1930 Moves to Munich; becomes regular staff member of *Jugend*.

1931 During economic difficulties of *Jugend*, seeks contact with Berlin satirical publications. Returns to Flensburg.

1932 Dismissal from *Jugend* along with all other artists.

1936 Participates in Schleswig-Holstein annual exhibition at Kiel chapter of National Chamber of Pictorial Arts.

1938 Works confiscated by Gestapo; Marxen dismissed from National Union of Visual Artists in Germany and prohibited from artistic activity.

1939 Military service as radio operator.

1941 Through efforts of Nazi governor of Romania, readmitted into National Union of Visual Artists in Germany.

1944 Studio requisitioned by SS.

1945 Prisoner of war; returns to Flensburg. Wife, Herta, supports family through her bookstore.

1946 Exhibits woodcuts in Kampen on Sylt. Purchase of woodcuts by Flensburg Museum of Applied Arts.

1947 Participates in exhibition at Kampen on Sylt. Begins efforts to receive compensation for works confiscated by Gestapo. Registers as member of Danish minority of Schleswig-Holstein.

1948 Woodcut exhibition in Flensburg. Contributes to magazine *Dreiklang* (*Tritone*) of Flensburg *Tageblatt* (*Daily Paper*).

1954 Contributes to satirical periodical, *Der Deutsche Michel*. Dies 28 July of heart attack brought on by anxiety during hearings concerning confiscated work. Awarded ten thousand marks posthumously in compensation for the lost works.

Frans Masereel

1889 Born 30 July in Blankenberge, Belgium.

1896–06 Spends youth in Ghent. Travels to Holland, Germany, and England.

1907–08 Studies at the Academy in Ghent.

1909–10 Trip to Paris and, with his wife Pauline, née Imhoff, to Tunisia for a long stay. Completes first painting.

1911–16 Moves to Paris. Begins working in woodcut. Returns to Belgium at the beginning of World War I.

1916 Moves to Geneva. Works for the Red Cross. Completes graphics for the pacifist magazines *Demain* and *Les Tablettes*. Meets Romain Rolland, René Arcos, Pierre-Jean Jouvé, and the pacifist writers' group L'Abbaye.

1917 Meets Stefan Zweig and Andreas Latzko. Publication of the first book illustrated with Masereel's woodcuts, *Quinze Poèmes d'Emile Verhaeren.* Cofounder of the pacifist newspaper *La Feuille,* published until 1920; completes some thousand drawings for the paper. Publication of first woodcut portfolios *Around the Dead* and *The Dead Speak*.

1918 Publishes his first pictorial novel, *25 Images de la Passion d'un Homme* (*25 Images from the Passion of a Man*).

1919 Publishes *Mon Livre d'heures* (*My Book of Hours*). With Arcos founds the publishing house Editions du Sablier in Geneva, which specializes in woodcut illustrations.

1920 Creates first large-format woodcuts. Meets Kurt Wolff, who publishes the German edition of *Mon Livre d'heures*, as well as other works by Masereel.

1922 First exhibition in Germany. Returns to Paris.

1924–25 Buys a house in Equihen, near Boulogne-sur-Mer, where he spends summers.

1925–26 Completes the woodcut portfolio *The City* and illustrations to Romain Rolland's *Jean-Christophe*.

1926 Meets Kurt Tucholsky through George Grosz. Illustrates Charles de Coster's *Till Eulenspiegel*. Exhibition in the gallery of Alfred Flechtheim, Berlin.

1929 Exhibits paintings in Mannheim, Städtische Kunsthalle.

1930 Retrospective exhibitions, Amsterdam, Stedelijk Museum; Munich, Städtische Galerie; Karlsruhe, Art Association; Bochum, Städtisches Museum; Hamburg, Art Association; Cologne, Art Association; Salzburg, Künstlerhaus. Sketches for thirteen mosaics for Georg Reinhart, Winterthur.

1932 Participates in the World Congress against War and Fascism, Amsterdam. Exhibits in Bremen and Ulm.

1933 Publishes the small volume *Geschichte ohne Worte* (*Tale without Words*), the last work of Masereel's to appear in Germany until after World War II. Resumes illustrations for pacifist publications.

1934 Exhibits at Modern Gallery, Zagreb.

1935 Exhibits in Moscow and Tbilisi.

1936 Travels to Moscow. Meets Bertolt Brecht.

1937 Completes a mural for the Belgian pavilion at the World Exhibition in Paris.

1938 Masereel's books censored by the Nazis; his works are removed from German museums.

1939 Sketches for Brecht's *Furcht und Elend des Dritten Reichs* (*The Private Life of the Master Race*). Exhibition at Perls Gallery, New York.

1940–46 Flees Paris for southern France during German occupation. Works in the resistance. Lives in Avignon, then in Lot-et-Garonne. Exhibition in Bogotá in 1941.

1947–51 Teaches painting at the School of Applied Arts in Saarbrücken. Two portfolios published by Saarverlag-Saarbrücken: *Angel* and *Apparitions*. Exhibits at the School of Applied Arts, Saarbrücken.

1948 Exhibits widely in East and West Germany.

1949 Designs mosaics for Haus der Arbeiter Wohlfahrt, Saarländische Kreditbank Saarlouis, and for the porcelain factory of Villeroy & Boch, Mettlach. Completes stage designs for the Stadttheater, Saarbrücken, production of Igor Stravinsky's *L'Histoire du Soldat*. Moves to Nice. Exhibits in New York and in the national museum in Mexico City.

1950 Awarded the Great International Prize for graphics at the Venice Biennale. Exhibits in the Kunsthalle, Hamburg.

1951 Becomes member of the Académie Royale des Sciences, Lettres et Beaux-Arts de Belgique. Leaves Saarbrücken. Exhibits at Kunstmuseum, Berne; Museum für Kunst, Lübeck; Musée des Beaux-Arts de Gand, Ghent; Palais des Beaux-Arts in Liège; Palais des Beaux-Arts in Brussels; and in museums in Rotterdam and Antibes. In the coming years, exhibits also in Paris, Zurich, Berlin, New York, Beijing, Darmstadt, Rotterdam, and Brussels.

1952 Completes stage designs for plays by Federico Garcia Lorca.

1953 Series of drawings *The Apocalypse of Our Time* is purchased by the Hessian government, and is published in facsimile.

1957 Becomes a corresponding member of the German Academy of the Arts, East Berlin.

1958 Travels to China, where he has numerous exhibitions.

1962 Wins the Joost-van-den-Vandel Prize of Wilhelms University, Münster.

1964 Along with Ernst Bloch, wins the Culture Award of the German Association of Labor Unions.

1965 Retrospective exhibition in Nice, with a special section titled "Frans Masereel and German Literature."

1967 Wins the Käthe Kollwitz Medal in East Berlin. Exhibits at the Pfalzgalerie, Kaiserslautern, and at the Art Association, Hamburg.

1968 Earns the title of Honorary Senator of the College of Fine Arts, Dresden. Death of wife.

1969 Marries Laure Malclès. Takes a second apartment in Avignon. Honorary doctorate from Humboldt University, East Berlin. Becomes honorary citizen of his native city, Blankenberge. Retrospective exhibition in the Kunsthalle, Weimar, the German Academy of the Arts, East Berlin, and in Leipzig.

1972 Dies 3 January in Avignon. Buried in Ghent.

Bibliography

Art Gallery of Windsor. *Frans Masereel*. Windsor, Ont.: Art Gallery of Windsor, 1981.

Avermaete, Roger. *Frans Masereel*. Antwerp: Fonds Mercator, 1976; New York: Rizzoli, 1977.

Bazarov, K. "Overlooked Masereel." *Art and Artists* 12 (March 1978): 16–19.

Eckstein, Hermann. "Frans Masereel." *Die Kunst für Alle* 45 (1930): 159.

Edschmied, Kasimir. "Frans Masereel." *Der Cicerone* 12 (1920): 805–813.

Frans Masereel: Danse Macabre. New York: Pantheon Books, 1942.

Galerie Karin Hielscher. *Frans Masereel*. Munich: Galerie Karin Hielscher, 1951.

Galerie St. Etienne. *Georges Rouault and Frans Masereel*. New York: Galerie St. Etienne, 1975.

"Glorious Adventures of Tyl Eulenspiegl by C. T. H. de Coster: Woodcuts by F. Masereel." *American Artist* 8 (September 1944): 40.

Hartlaub, Georg Friedrich. "Frans Masereel." *Deutsche Kunst und Dekoration* 65 (1930): 301.

Heise, Carl Georg. "Ausstellung in der Galerie Victor Hartberg." *Kunst und Künstler* 29 (1931): 49–52.

——. "Mosaiken von F. Masereel." *Die Kunst für Alle* 48 (1932): 81–85.

Hilberseimer, Ludwig. "Frans Masereel." *Sozialistische Monatshefte* (1922): 548.

Hoffmann, Edith. "Matisse und Masereel in London." *Die Kunstwelt* [Prague] 3 (1937): 66.

Jansen, E. "Die Bilderwelt Franz Masereels." *Das Kunstwerk* 13 (October 1959): 33.

Koninklijkie Academie voor schone Kunsten. *Retrospectieve Frans Masereel*. Antwerp: Koninklijkie Academie voor schone Kunsten, 1958.

Kornfeld, H. "Frans Masereel." *Leipziger Vorschau* 31 (1932): 129.

Lehmann, A. "Masereel und Van de Velde in Mannheim." *Deutsch-Französische Rundschau* [Berlin] 2 (1929): 1058.

Meuer, Adolph. "Franz Masereel: Ein positiver Künstler." *Gral* [Munich] 27 (1933): 931–933.

Musée du Dessin et de l'Estampe Originale de Gravelines. *Frans Masereel: Peintres, aquarelles, dessins, gravures*. Gravelines: Musée du Dessin et de l'Estampe Originale de Gravelines, 1984.

Museum Boymans. *Frans Masereel*. Rotterdam: Museum Boymans, 1951.

Perls Galleries. *Masereel*. New York: Perls Galleries, 1939.

Pfalzgalerie. *Frans Masereel: Gemälde und Graphik*. Kaiserslautern: Pfalzgalerie, 1967.

Ritter, Paul. *Die frühen Holzschnittfolgen Frans Masereels*. Darmstadt: Offenbach, 1983.

Rumpel, H. "Frans Masereel: Graphisches Schaffen." *Das Werk* 36 (October 1949): 339–344.

Schneider, Theo. "Moderne Meister des Holzschnittes." *Hamburger Fremdenblatt*. 18 May 1927.

Staatliche Museen, Kupferstichkabinett, Pergamon Museum. *Frans Masereel: Neue Holzschnitte*. East Berlin: Staatliche Museen, 1955.

Städtische Kunsthalle Mannheim. *Frans Masereel: Das Gesammelte Werk*. Mannheim: Städtische Kunsthalle, 1929.

Van de Velde, Henry. "Frans Masereel." *Almanach für Kunst und Dichtung* (1925): 110–153.

Vorms, Pierre. *Masereel: Catalogue Raisonné*. Antwerp: Fonds Mercator, 1976.

Wolfradt, W. "Frans Masereel und die pazifistische 'Karikatur.'" *Freie deutsche Blätter* 2 (1921): 1093–1097.

Ziller, Gerhard. *Frans Masereel*. Dresden: Sachsenverlag, 1949.

Zweig, Stefan, Pierrre Vorms, and Gerhard Pommeranz-Liedtke. *Frans Masereel*. Dresden: VEB Verlag der Kunst, 1959.

Else (Meyer) Meidner

1901 Else Meyer born 2 September in Berlin, daughter of Margaret Fürst and the highly successful physician Dr. Heinrich Meyer.

1908–18 Studies at the Sophien Lyceum, Berlin.

1918 Runs away to Hamburg after father rejects her plans to study art. Receives encouragement from Friedrich Adler of the Hamburg School of Applied Arts, and in Berlin from Käthe Kollwitz, Emil Orlik, and Max Slevogt.

1918–25 Studies under Adolf Meyer at the School of the Museum of Applied Arts and at Lewin-Funke's Training Studios for Painting and Sculpture, Berlin-Charlottenburg, where Ludwig Meidner is her instructor in drawing.

1927 Marries Meidner on 20 February.

1929 Receives Second Prize in Graphics Competition of *Die Schaffenden* for portrait etching of Alfred Döblin. Son David born 10 October.

1932 Exhibition of thirty paintings at the *Jury-Free Art Show*, Berlin.

1933 Banned from exhibiting in Germany by National Socialist government.

1935 Moves to Cologne with her husband and son.

1939 Meidner family flees to London.

1945 David Meidner emigrates to Israel.

1949 Joint exhibition with Ludwig Meidner, Ben Uri Gallery, London.

1953 Does not join Ludwig Meidner on his return to Germany; visits him there irregularly.

1954 Exhibits at Kunstkabinett Hanna Becker vom Rath, Frankfurt a. M.

1956 Exhibition, Matthiesen Gallery, London.

1959 Exhibition, Beaux Arts Gallery, London.

1963 Lengthy stay with Ludwig Meidner in Darmstadt.

1964 Exhibition, Ben Uri Gallery, London.

1966 Death of Ludwig Meidner.

1969 Exhibition, Justus Liebig Haus, Darmstadt.

1972 Exhibition, Ben Uri Gallery, London.

1987 Dies 5 May in London.

Bibliography

Hodin, Josef Paul. *Aus den Erinnerungen von Else Meidner*. Darmstädter Schriften, vol. 42. Darmstadt: Justus von Liebig Verlag, 1979.

——. "Else Meidner." *Art News and Review* 24 (October 1959).

——. "Else Meidner." *Studio* 159, no. 805 (May 1960): 164 ff.

Ludwig Meidner

1884 Ludwig Baruch Meidner born 18 April in Bernstadt, Silesia (today Bierutów, Poland), son of a textile merchant. Attends Volksschule, then Oberrealschule in Breslau and Kattowitz.

1901–02   Apprenticed as a mason in preparation for training as an architect.

1903   Enters Royal Art School, Breslau.

1905   Employed as a fashion illustrator, Atelier Wulf-Schwertfeger, Berlin.

1906   Trip to Paris financed by father's sister, Frau Sachs. Attends Académie Cormon and Académie Julian. Befriends Amedeo Modigliani.

1907   In summer, recalled to Berlin for a military physical examination, which he fails. Lives in poverty.

1911   On the recommendation of Max Beckmann, receives a monthly stipend of 100 marks.

1912   Paints his first "apocalyptic landscapes." With Richard Janthur and Jakob Steinhardt, forms the artists' group The Ones Filled with Pathos; it exhibits at Herwarth Walden's *Der Sturm* gallery. Meets Ernst Ludwig Kirchner, Erich Heckel, and Otto Mueller. Renews contact with Beckmann.

1913   Organizes Wednesday evening meetings of artists and writers in his studio, Wilhelmshöher Strasse 21, Berlin-Friedenau. Contacts with Max Hermann-Neisse, René Schickele, and Raoul Hausmann.

1914   Publishes "Anleitung zum Malen von Grossstadtbildern" ("Instructions for the Painting of Pictures of the Metropolis") in *Kunst und Künstler*. Member of Berlin Free Secession. Moves to Dresden with poet Ernst Wilhelm Lotz to establish a periodical and a lithography studio under the patronage of Franz Kochmann. Frequents Café König. During November or December, returns to Berlin. Association with Franz Pfemfert and his periodical *Die Aktion*.

1915   Frequents Café des Westens. Contacts with Johannes R. Becher, Conrad Felixmüller, George Grosz, Wieland Herzfelde, and Wilhelm Lehmbruck. In *Die Aktion*, publishes "Sehnsüchte des Malers" ("Yearnings of the Painter").

1916   Drafted into infantry, then stationed as a French translator in prisoner-of-war camp Merzdorf, near Kottbus. Begins writing *Im Nacken das Sternemeer* (*At my Back, a Sea of Stars*) and *Septemberschrei: Hymnen/Gebete/Lästerungen* (*September Scream: Hymns/Prayers/Blasphemies*).

1917   Produces drawings in three sketchbooks titled *Psalm Books*.

1918   First individual exhibition, Paul Cassirer Gallery, Berlin. Returns to Berlin. Founding member of November Group and Work Council for Art. Publishes *Im Nacken das Sternemeer*.

1919   Stays with his mother in Bernstadt, then returns to Berlin. Exhibition at I. B. Neumann, Berlin. Publishes manifesto "An alle Künstler, Dichter und Musiker" ("To All Artists, Poets and Musicians") in Paul Westheim's periodical *Das Kunstblatt*. Lothar Brieger publishes first Meidner monograph in the series *Junge Kunst*.

1920   Publishes *Septemberschrei*.

1922   Trips to Bernstadt and to Kampen on the Island of Sylt. Second edition of *Junge Kunst* monograph contains different illustrations from the first and appears as *Eine autobiographische Plauderei* (*Autobiographic Chatter*) which confirms his religious visionary inspiration. Reaffirms his attachment to Judaism. Exhibition, Ferdinand Möller, Berlin.

1923   Designs sets for Karl Grune's film *The Street*.

1924–26   Teaches at Training Studios for Painting and Sculpture, Berlin-Charlottenburg. Meets Else Meyer.

1926   Exhibition, Galerie Emil Richter, Dresden.

1927   Marries Else Meyer.

1928   Travels to Heidelberg and Badenweiler.

1929   Birth of son David. Publishes "Eigenlob stinkt nicht oder lustiger Traktat über Porträtmalerei" ("Self-Praise Doesn't Stink, or Merry Tract about Portrait Painting") in *Das Kunstblatt* and *Gang in die Stille* (*Path into Silence*).

1934   Exhibition, Jewish Museum, Berlin.

1935   In November, moves to Cologne. Teaches drawing at the Jewish school Jawneh.

1937   Two works and a copy of *Septemberschrei* included in the exhibition *Degenerate Art*, Munich. Eighty-four works removed from German public collections.

1939   Flees with family to England.

1940–41   Interned as an enemy alien at Hutchinson Camp, near Liverpool, then at Onchan Internment Camp, Isle of Man.

1941   Exhibition, Onchan Internment Camp. In November, returns to London.

1949   With Else Meidner exhibits at Ben Uri Art Gallery, London.

1952   Travels to Hamburg and Bonn.

1953–55   Lives in Jewish Old Age Home, Frankfurt a. M. Else Meidner remains in England.

1955   Establishes a studio in Marxheim, near Hofheim in the Taunus. Stays there until 1963.

1959   Exhibition, Art Association, Wiesbaden.

1963   Moves to Darmstadt. Traveling exhibition, Kunsthalle, Recklinghausen; Haus am Waldsee, West Berlin; and Kunsthalle, Darmstadt.

1964   Awarded Grand Cross of Merit of German Federal Republic. Membership of Academy of the Arts, West Berlin. Villa Romana Prize. Exhibition, Art Association, Darmstadt.

1966   Meidner monograph by Thomas Grochowiak published. Dies 14 May in Darmstadt.

Bibliography

Eliel, Carol S. *The Apocalyptic Landscapes of Ludwig Meidner*. Los Angeles: Los Angeles County Museum of Art, and Munich: Prestel Verlag, 1989 (with bibliography).

Grochowiak, Thomas. *Ludwig Meidner*. Recklinghausen: Aurel Bongers, 1966 (with bibliography).

Kunstverein Wolfsburg. *Ludwig Meidner 1884–1966*. Wolfsburg: Kunstverein, 1985.

Walter Meyer-Vax (Meyer-Villwock)

1905   Born in Brunswick, the ninth child in a worker's family.

1912–19   Attends elementary school. Premature death of his parents.

1920–23   Apprenticeship as an interior decorator and painter; part-time studies at Brunswick School of Applied Arts.

1923–27   Journeyman stage designer. In Berlin begins to paint "in a garret, without an easel, with colors bought with food-money." Presents his work to Karl Hofer, who in 1927 invites him to the Prussian Academy of Fine Arts, Berlin; appointed master student with stipend. His brothers, Arthur Meyer and Otto Villwock, also enter Academy. Participates in *Das Kunstblatt*'s first *Exhibition of Young Painters*, German Art League, Berlin.

1928   Extended stay in Paris.

1930   Awarded Great State Prize of the Prussian Academy of Fine Arts, Berlin. Travels to Norway. Befriends Felix Nussbaum.

1931   Travels to Italy. Takes part in the exhibition of the Berlin Secession.

1940   Drafted into the military.

1942   Killed 4 November at Stalingrad.

Bibliography

Zimmermann, Rainer. *Die Kunst der verschollenen Generation: Deutsche Malerei des expressiven Realismus von 1925–1975*. Düsseldorf: Econ, 1980.

Ernest Neuschul

1895   Born 17 May in Aussig (today Ústí nad Labem, Czechoslovakia) to Jewish parents.

1913   Studies through 1916 at academies in Prague and Vienna.

1916–17   Leaves Vienna for Krakow, where he is a student at the Academy. Moves to Russian-controlled area of what later became Poland; first political activity for the Soviet Communist Party.

1918   Travels to Lublin, using passport of dead Russian soldier. Moves to Berlin.

1919   Joins German Communist Party; member of November Group.

1920   Creates choreography and costume designs for dancer Takka Takka until 1925.

1922   Marries Takka Takka.

1922–23   Travels to Paris, Spain, Italy, and United States. Exhibitions in Rome, Madrid, New York, and Chicago.

1925   Returns to Berlin. Exhibits with November Group.

1926   Exhibits at Galerie Neumann-Nierendorf, Berlin, through 1933.

1928   Member of Association of Revolutionary Artists of Germany (ARBKD or "Asso"), Berlin.

1931   Meets painter Christine Bell.

1932   Teaching appointment at the College of Fine Arts, Berlin.

1933   Dismissed from teaching position by Nazis because of Jewish ancestry. Fifteen works from exhibition at House of the Association of Berlin Women Artists destroyed by SA.

1934   Emigrates to Aussig and marries Christine Bell.

1935   Travels to Moscow following invitation from Society of Soviet Artists.

1935–36   Exhibition at Museum of Western Art, Moscow. Teaches painting at Academy in Charkov.

1936   Returns to Aussig to escape Stalinist persecutions.

1937   Series of paintings on anti-Fascist resistance is destroyed by group of Sudeten German Nazis.

1938   Emigrates to Prague; membership in anti-Fascist artists' association Oskar Kokoschka League.

1939   In March, flees to London; member of the Free German Culture Group.

1940   Lives in Mumbles, Wales, until 1945.

1944   Exhibition at National Museum of Wales, Cardiff.

1946   Moves to Hampstead, London, and adopts name "Norland."

1949   Exhibits at Galerie Barreio, Paris. Travels to Paris.

1950   Exhibits at Brook Street Gallery, London.

1959   Travels to Israel via France and Spain; exhibition at Bezalel National Museum, Jerusalem.

1966   Travels to Germany; exhibition at Haus am Lützowplatz, West Berlin.

1968   Travels to East Germany. Dies 11 September in Hampstead.

Bibliography

"Ausstellungen in Berlin." *Der Cicerone* 19, no. 3 (1927): 95.

Campbell & Franks Gallery, London. *Ernest Neuschul*. London: Campbell & Franks Gallery, 1978.

Ernest Neuschul. Berlin: Tiergarten, 1966.

Hermann Niehaus

No information on the artist was available.

Felix Nussbaum

1904   Born 11 December in Osnabrück.

1910   Begins attending a Jewish elementary school.

1913   Enters the Ratsgymnasium.

1914   Transfers to the Realgymnasium.

1920   Completes first known artwork. Has contact with local artists.

1922   Completes studies at Realgymnasium. In summer, studies at the State School of Applied Arts, Hamburg, under Fritz Behnke.

1923   In late February, finishes studies at the Hamburg School of Applied Arts. Moves to Berlin.

1924   Studies under Willy Jaeckel at the Lewin-Funke Training Studios for Painting and Sculpture.

1924–25   Accepted for the winter semester at the United State Schools for Fine and Applied Arts, as a student of Cesar Klein and Paul Plontke.

1925–26   Meets Felka Platek. Travels to East Frisian Islands.

1927   First exhibition and critical reviews.

1928   Participates in several exhibitions. Travels to Belgium and southern France. Becomes a master student of Hans Meid.

1929   Completes formal studies. Begins working as independent painter.

1930   Brother Justus (born 1 March 1901) marries Herta Bein from Oberhausen. Befriends Walter Meyer-Vax.

1932   Competes for the Great State Prize of the Prussian Academy of Arts for study in Rome. In August, is awarded a stay as a guest student at the Villa Massimo, Rome. Remains in Rome until 1934.

1932   His Berlin studio burns down, destroying about 150 artworks. Begins contributing to the magazine *Der Querschnitt*. Participates in the Berlin Secession exhibition, his last exhibition.

1933   In March, applies for an extension of his study in Rome, which is granted until 30 June. However, this is revoked at the end of May by the Nazis. Fearing anti-Semitic incidents, leaves Rome for Alassio.

1934   Meets his parents in Rapallo, but they soon return to Germany. Parents move to Cologne, selling their home and store. Nussbaum emigrates to Belgium via Paris. By the end of February, he is living in Ostende.

1935–37   Moves frequently between Ostende and Brussels. After September 1937, his residence is in Brussels.

1937   Brother Justus flees to Amsterdam. Nussbaum marries Felka Platek in Brussels on 6 October.

1938   Moves frequently in Brussels, finally residing with the Billestraet family on the rue Archimede.

1939   Nussbaum's parents intend to emigrate to Brussels, but Felka prevents them coming. Parents decide to go to Amsterdam to live with Justus instead.

1940   After the outbreak of World War II, Nussbaum is taken into custody in Brussels as an enemy alien, and is imprisoned in the Saint-Cypres camp in southern France. Nussbaum's brother pressed into service because of his business in melting down metals for German armaments; Justus Nussbaum and family, as well as other Jewish persons in his firm, are put under protection as "persons vital to the war effort." In September, Nussbaum is transferred from Saint-Cypres to a camp in Bordeaux. From Bordeaux he escapes to Brussels. Lives in hiding, working on ceramics and illustration commissions to support himself and his wife.

1942   Avoids capture in Belgium by frequently changing apartments.

1943   After May, raids in Amsterdam are intensified; Nussbaum's family is arrested and imprisoned in the Dutch concentration camp Westerbork.

1944   Attempting to change his residence, Nussbaum is captured and interned in the villa Quatre Bras in a suburb of Brussels. Nussbaum's parents are deported from Westerbork to Auschwitz 8 February. On 31 July, Felix and Felka are among those on the last deportation train out of Belgium, arriving at Auschwitz on 3 August. On 3 September, Justus also deported to Auschwitz; he is transferred to Stutthof, another concentration camp, where he dies on 7 December.

1946   The name Felix Nussbaum is removed from the registry in Belgium. The date of his death is believed to be 9 August 1944.

Major Posthumous Exhibitions

1971   Osnabrück, Kulturgeschichtliches Museum, *Felix Nussbaum 1904–1944: Gemälde aus dem Nachlass*, 19 February–4 April.

1972   West Berlin, Kunstamt Neukölln, January–March.

1973   Hamm, Gustav Lübke-Museum, May–July.

1981   Hamburg, Galerie Levy, August–October.

1982   Haarlem, Frans Hals Museum, May.

1985   New York, The Jewish Museum, *Art and Exile: Felix Nussbaum, 1904–1944*, 15 April–15 August.

1988   Duisburg, Wilhelm Lehmbruck Museum, *Felix Nussbaum: Gemälde, Zeichnungen und Dokumente*, 17 April–19 June.

1990   Osnabrück, Kulturgeschichtliches Museum, *Felix Nussbaum: Verfemte Kunst—Exilkunst—Widerstandskunst: Die 100 wichtigsten Werke*, 6 May–18 August.

Bibliography

Berger, Eva, et al. *Felix Nussbaum: Verfemte Kunst—Exilkunst—Widerstandskunst: Die 100 wichtigsten Werke*. Bramsche: Rasch Verlag, 1990.

Bilski, Emily D. *Art and Exile: Felix Nussbaum, 1904–1944*. New York: The Jewish Museum, 1985.

Junk, Peter, and Wendelin Zimmer, with Manfred Meinz. *Felix Nussbaum: Leben und Werk*. Cologne: DuMont Buchverlag, and Bramsche: Rasch Verlag, 1982.

Kaster, Karl Georg. *Felix Nussbaum*. Cologne: Vista Point Verlag, 1989.

Steinfeld, Fritz. *Vergast—nicht vergessen: Erinnerungen an den Malerfreund Felix Nussbaum*. Osnabrück: Kulturgeschichtliches Museum, and Bramsche: Rasch Verlag, 1984.

Hermann Max Pechstein

1881   Born 31 December in Eckerbach, near Zwickau, son of a textile worker.

1888–96   Attends Volksschule at Zwickau.

1896–1900   Apprenticeship as an interior decorator and painter, Zwickau.

1900   In October, enters the Dresden School of Applied Arts.

1902   Enters the Royal Academy of Fine Arts, Dresden. Becomes master student of Otto Gussmann.

1905   Awarded Saxon State Prize for Painting (Rome Prize). Produces his first woodcuts.

1906   Meets Erich Heckel. Joins *Brücke*; exhibits with group until 1912.

1907   Travels to Italy and Paris.

1908   In Paris, meets Kees van Dongen and other Fauvists. Exhibits with Société Anonyme. Travels to Berlin during the summer; moves there in winter to carry out commissions for wall paintings. Lives at Kurfürstendamm 152.

1909   Joins and exhibits with Berlin Secession. Visited by Ernst Ludwig Kirchner in January, April, and November. Spends June through September at Nidden.

1910   Works rejected by Berlin Secession; resigns from Secession. In March, Heckel and Kirchner join him in Berlin and work at his studio. Cofounder of New Secession. Spends summer with Heckel and Kirchner at Moritzburg Lakes, then with Heckel and Karl Schmidt-Rottluff at Dangast. Moves studio to Berlin-Wilmersdorf, Durlacher Strasse 14.

1911   In January, visited by Kirchner. Marries Lotte Kaprolat. Travels to Rome. Spends summer in Nidden. In October, Kirchner takes over the Durlacher Strasse studio; Pechstein moves his studio to Offenbacher Strasse 1 in Berlin-Friedenau. With Kirchner founds MUIM Institute (Moderner Unterricht in Malerei [Modern Instruction in Painting]).

1912   Exhibits with Berlin Secession as a guest and is consequently barred from *Brücke*. Summers in Nidden. Graphics exhibition, Gutenberg, Berlin. Exhibition, Kunsthalle, Mannheim, and Galerie Thannhauser, Munich. Included in *Sonderbund* exhibition, Cologne.

1913   Rejoins Berlin Secession. Travels to Ghent, Brussels, Paris, Florence, and Monterosso al Mare. Birth of son Frank. Exhibition, Kunstsalon Fritz Gurlitt, and Graphics Department, A. Wertheim, Berlin.

1914   Exhibits at Kunstsalon Ludwig Schames, Frankfurt a. M. In April, travels to Palau Islands via Suez Canal, India, China, and Philippines. Imprisoned by Japanese at Nagasaki in November.

1915   After his release, goes to Shanghai and Manila. In April, his works are returned through the intervention of the American consul. Travels to New York via San Francisco. In August, works his way across the Atlantic to Holland via London as a mechanic on a Dutch ship. On 12 September, returns to Germany. Drafted into the infantry.

1916   Stationed on western front; participates in the Battle of the Somme. Exhibition, Art Association, Leipzig.

1917   In spring, receives a military discharge; returns to Berlin.

1918   Opening exhibition at the new Fritz Gurlitt Gallery, Berlin. With Georg Tappert and others, founds November Group and the Work Council for Art. Designs a poster in support of the Republic.

1919   Spends summer in Nidden. Included in exhibitions at Galerie Arnold, Dresden, and Fritz Gurlitt Gallery, Berlin (with Rudolf Belling, Renée Sintenis, and Paul Cohen).

1920   Travels to Nidden for the summer.

1921   Spends the summer in Leba in eastern Pomerania. Exhibition in Kronprinzenpalais, Berlin.

1922   Appointed professor and member of the Prussian Academy of Fine Arts. Spends the summer in Leba.

1923   Marries Marta Möller. Travels to Montreux and Monterosso al Mare.

1926   Awarded prize at *International Exhibition*, Carnegie Institute, Pittsburgh. Birth of son Max. Creates a window design for the International Labor Organization, Geneva.

1927   Spends summers in Leba and Rowe, Pomerania, annually through 1944.

1932   Receives State Prize of the German government.

1933   Is forbidden to exhibit in Germany. Dismissed from teaching position.

1934   Exhibition, London.

1935   Exhibition, New York.

1937   Three hundred and twenty-six works confiscated in German museums as "degenerate." Six paintings and numerous graphics included in *Degenerate Art* exhibition, Munich.

1939   Seventh and final trip to Nidden.

1944–45   Drafted into Labor Detail in Pomerania. Brief Russian captivity. Berlin studio destroyed during Allied bombing raid.

1945   Returns to Berlin. Appointed to a teaching position at Berlin College of Fine Arts.

1946   Exhibition, Berlin.

1951   Honorary Senator of College of Fine Arts, West Berlin.

1952   Awarded Grand Cross of Merit of Federal Republic of Germany.

1954   Awarded Art Prize of Senate of City of West Berlin.

1955   Dies 29 June in West Berlin.

Bibliography

Schilling, Jürgen, ed. *Max Pechstein: Zeichnungen und Aquarelle*. Wolfsburg: Kunstverein, 1987 (with comprehensive bibliography and exhibition listing).

Max Radler

1904   Born in Breslau, son of a wheelwright and mill builder.

c. 1914   Apprenticed as a stucco worker, carpenter, and mason.

1919   Apprenticed to an interior decorator, painter, and coffin maker in Zeitz.

1923   Leaves home to live in Munich. Works for an interior decorator and painter.

1927   Enrolls at the Technical School for the Craft of Painting, where he meets Rosa März, a painter. Studies under Georg Schrimpf. Marries März. Befriends the author Oskar Maria Graf.

1930–31   Exhibits at *Jury-Free Art Show*, Munich.

1939   Induction into armed forces.

1945   Most of his work is destroyed during a bombing raid on Munich. After war, returns to Munich; begins to work for revived *Simplicissimus*.

1947   First participation in exhibitions of New Group Munich.

1971   Dies in Munich.

Hans Rilke

1881   Born in Rheydt.

After 1900   Studies at Karlsruhe Academy and at School of Applied Arts, Düsseldorf. Teaches art at Rethel Gymnasium, Düsseldorf.

1919 Joins Activists' League 1919, Düsseldorf.

1920 Contacts circle of Johanna Ey.

1922 Joins The Young Rhineland. Exhibits at Johanna Ey's gallery.

1947 Dies in Düsseldorf.

Marcel Ronay

1910 Born 3 September in Budapest to Jewish parents; his mother is Hungarian, his father Romanian.

1915 Family moves to Berlin after his father volunteers for the German army.

1916 Family moves to Vienna when his father is transferred into the Imperial Austrian Army.

1924 Completes his formal schooling.

1925 Begins a five-year apprenticeship as master carver.

1928 Ends apprenticeship and enrolls in School of Applied Arts, Vienna; studies under Eugene Steinhof.

1931 Nominated for State Prize in Art, but submitted work confiscated by school director as erotic. Exhibits with Vienna Secession.

1931–36 Active in his family business as a designer of porcelain costume jewelry.

1936 Moves to England with family.

1944 Exhibits with Royal Academy of Arts.

1945 Active as commercial artist.

(No further information on the artist was available.)

Christian Schad

1894 Born in Miesbach.

1913 Studies at the Munich Academy under Heinrich von Zügel. Completes Expressionist woodcuts for the periodical *Die Aktion*.

1915 Moves to Zurich to avoid military duty; remains there until 1920, participating in the Dada movement.

1918 Develops a photographic process without a camera, "Schadography."

1920 Moves to Italy; stays there until 1925. Becomes acquainted with the Casa d'arte Bragaglia circle. Begins working almost exclusively on portraits.

1921 First solo exhibition at the Galerie Goldschmidt, Frankfurt a. M. Visits Naples.

1927 Moves to Vienna. Major exhibition at Galerie Würthle, Berlin. Max Osborn publishes a monograph on Schad on the occasion of the Berlin Exhibition.

1928 Moves to Berlin. Participates in exhibitions at the Galerie Neumann-Nierendorf.

1929 Participates in the *Neue Sachlichkeit* exhibitions at the Stedelijk Museum in Amsterdam and at the Galerie Gurlitt, Berlin. Travels to England and Switzerland.

1935–42 Takes over a business venture and works on commissions.

1943–47 After destruction of studio in bombing raid, moves to Keilberg near Aschaffenburg. Commissioned by the city to copy the *Stuppach Madonna* by Matthias Grünewald.

1960 Works with photography/Schadography.

1970 Exhibition in Munich, Galleria del Levante.

1975 Von-der-Heydt Museum in Wuppertal mounts exhibition *Schadographien 1918–1975*.

1980 Exhibition at Staatliche Kunsthalle, West Berlin.

1982 Dies in Keilberg.

Bibliography

Staatliche Kunsthalle. *Christian Schad.* West Berlin: Staatliche Kunsthalle, 1980 (with bibliography).

Josef Scharl

1896 Born 9 December, the second of fourteen children, ten of whom survive. Father employed at Seidlsche Court Bakery, and later in an antique shop.

1910–15 Attends Painting School on Westenriederstrasse, Munich.

1915 Paints first large oil painting, a still life.

1915–16 Serves in military; wounded at Douaumont.

1917–18 Recuperates in various military hospitals. Undergoes successful surgery on paralyzed right arm.

1919–21 Studies at Munich Academy under Angelo Jank and Heinrich von Zügel.

1921 Withdraws from Munich Academy. Studies life drawing at evening school.

1922 Marries Magdalena Gruber. Birth of son, Alois. Establishes studio with Alois Seidl at Maillingerstrasse 15, Munich.

1923 City of Munich purchases oil painting. Makes his first trip to Rome.

1925–28 Exhibits with New Secession, Munich.

1927 Visits Berlin. Meets Albert Einstein; draws his portrait.

1929 Included in *Jury-Free Art Show*, Munich. First individual exhibition. Awarded Dürer Prize by city of Nuremberg. Participates in exhibitions in Kassel and Cologne.

1930 Participates in exhibitions at Gerg and Graphisches Kabinett, Munich, and in Berlin and Vienna. Receives Rome Prize from city of Munich. First trip to Paris.

1931 Receives the Dr. Mond Award, Academy of Fine Arts, Munich. Temporary residence and exhibition at Villa Massimo, Rome.

1932 Visits Paris. Exhibition, Graphisches Kabinett, Munich.

1933 Exhibition, Galerie Nierendorf, Berlin.

1935 Exhibitions, Kunstzaal van Lier, Amsterdam, and Galerie Nierendorf, Berlin.

1935–36 Formation of Circle of Friends of Josef Scharl to provide a minimum of financial support.

1936 Exhibitions at Graphisches Kabinett, Munich, and Art Association, Hamburg. Friendship with Johann David and Wolfgang Sauerländer.

1937 Works removed from collection of Munich City Gallery but not included in the exhibition *Degenerate Art*.

1938 Visits Switzerland twice. On 26 December, leaves Munich with Sauerländer and emigrates to United States.

1939 Spends first weeks with sister, Cilly Nadler, in New York. Moves to small atelier in Amityville, New York, and works again with great intensity. Travels to Florida in fall.

1940 Moves 1 October with Sauerländer to Claremont Avenue in New York. In April, first large individual exhibition at Nierendorf Gallery, New York.

1941 Begins correspondence with Einstein.

1943 Individual exhibitions in Louisville and New York. Works on book illustrations.

1945 Alfred Neumeyer's monograph published by Nierendorf. First of numerous visits to Einstein at Princeton; they continue through 1953.

1946 Resumes exhibiting in Germany.

1950–51 Declines offer of professorship at Munich Academy.

1951–52 Appointed corresponding member of Bavarian Academy of Art, Munich.

1954 Dies 6 December of a heart attack.

Bibliography

Galerie Nierendorf. *Josef Scharl.* Kunstblätter der Galerie Nierendorf, nos. 3, 24, 29. West Berlin: Galerie Nierendorf, 1964, 1971, 1973.

————. *Josef Scharl: Werke aus drei Jahrzehnten—Gemälde, Temperas, Zeichnungen.* West Berlin: Galerie Nierendorf, 1983.

————. *Josef Scharl zum siebzigsten Geburtstag: Ölbilder und Temperablätter.* West Berlin: Galerie Nierendorf, 1967.

Galerie St. Etienne. *Isabel Case Borgatta—Josef Scharl.* New York: Galerie St. Etienne, 1954.

————. *Josef Scharl: Last Paintings and Drawings.* New York: Galerie St. Etienne, 1959.

————. *Josef Scharl: Memorial Exhibition.* New York: Galerie St. Etienne, 1956.

Greither, Aloys. *Josef Scharl: 50 Bibelzeichnungen.* Düsseldorf, 1967.

Josef Scharl Ausstellung. Munich: I. B. Neumann & Gunther Franke, 1931.

Neumeyer, Alfred. *Josef Scharl.* New York: Nierendorf Editions, 1945.

————. "Josef Scharl." *Burlington Magazine* 91 (November 1949): 328.

Nierendorf Gallery. *Josef Scharl.* New York: Nierendorf Gallery, 1941, 1943, 1945.

————. *Josef Scharl: Paintings and Drawings.* New York: Nierendorf Gallery, 1946.

————. *Scharl: Interpretations of the Old and New Testament.* New York: Nierendorf Gallery, n. d.

Städtische Galerie im Lenbachhaus. *Josef Scharl: 1898–1954.* Munich: Prestel Verlag, 1982.

Hugo Scheiber

1873 Born in Budapest, Hungary, to Jewish parents. Father is a sign and scene painter for stores, circuses, and theater groups.

1898–1900 Works during the day as a scene painter; studies in the evenings at the School of Applied Arts, Budapest. Begins to paint independently, in a Neo-Impressionist manner.

1922 Moves to Berlin at invitation of Herwarth Walden.

1924 Exhibition, *Der Sturm* gallery, Berlin.

1925 Exhibition *Scheiber and Moholy-Nagy*, *Der Sturm* gallery, Berlin.

1926 Represented in exhibition of Société Anonyme, New York.

1927 Two individual exhibitions at *Der Sturm* gallery, Berlin.

1930 Included in *Exhibition of the Hagenbund*, Vienna.

1933 At the invitation of F. T. Marinetti, participates in Congress of Futurists, Rome.

1939 Returns to Hungary.

1950 Dies 7 March in Budapest.

Bibliography

Darany, Georges. *Hugo Scheiber: Leben und Werk.* Basel: Edition Inter Art Galerie, 1982.

National Gallery, Budapest. *Hugo Scheiber, 1873–1950.* Budapest: National Gallery, 1964.

Wechselwirkungen: Ungarische Avantgarde in der Weimarer Republik. Ed. Hubertus Gassner. Kassel: Neue Galerie, and Marburg: Jonas Verlag, 1986.

Rudolf Schlichter

1890 Born 6 December in Calw, his parents' sixth child. Death of father, a hired gardener, soon after his birth. Mother, a seamstress, rears four children remaining at home.

1896 Attends Catholic school; later transfers to Volksschule.

1904 Leaves school to apprentice in enamel painting at Pforzheim Factory, where he decorates porcelain and cutlery.

1907 Attends School of Applied Arts, Stuttgart.

1909 Completes preparatory studies to take an acceptance test for Karlsruhe Academy.

1910 Enrolls at Karlsruhe Academy. Studies drawing for two years under Walther Georgi, and painting for two years under Kaspar Ritter. Becomes master student of Ritter and Wilhelm Trübner. Learns techniques of etching and lithography from Walter Conz. Travels to Italy.

1916 Recruited for military service; stationed at western front. After a hunger strike, released from military duty.

1919 Cofounds Group Rih, Karlsruhe. Moves to Berlin. Joins November Group; meets Berlin Dadaists, including George Grosz and John Heartfield. Joins the German Communist Party.

1920 First individual exhibition at Galerie Otto Burchard, Berlin. Participates in *First International Dada Fair*, Kunstsalon Dr. Burchard, Berlin.

1921–23 Completes illustrations for publishers Kiepenheuer Verlag, Orchis Verlag, and O. C. Recht Verlag. Receives financial support from Edvard Munch.

1924 Founding member and secretary of Red Group. Associates with intellectuals of the political left, including Bertolt Brecht, Alfred Döblin, Erich Kästner, and Egon Erwin Kisch. Illustrates Bret Harte's *California Tales* (Potsdam: Kiepenheuer Verlag).

1925 Included in *Neue Sachlichkeit* exhibition, Mannheim.

1927 Exhibits in *The Problem of Portrait Painting in Recent Art*, Galerie Neumann-Nierendorf, Berlin. Meets future wife, Speedy.

1928 Individual exhibition at Galerie Neumann-Nierendorf. Marries Speedy.

1932 Moves to Rottenburg am Neckar. First volume of autobiography, *Das widerspenstige Fleisch* (*Obstinate Flesh*), published by Rowohlt Verlag.

1933 Second volume of autobiography, *Tönerne Füsse* (*Feet of Clay*), appears.

1935 Moves to Stuttgart. Completes the illustration *Goliath Mocks the People of Israel* for Catholic youth publication *Junger Front*, for which he is temporarily dismissed from the National Union of Visual Artists.

1936 Exhibits secretly in home of Hugo Borst, Stuttgart.

1937 Permanently expelled from National Union of Visual Artists for his painting *Blind Power*. Seventeen works confiscated from museums.

1938 Arrested for slander and "un-National Socialist" conduct. Released after three months.

1939 Moves to Munich. Involved with Catholic friends C. Muth, Theodor Haecker, and Hans Scholl who are associated with publication *Hochland*.

1942 Studio destroyed by bombs.

1946 First public viewing of Surrealist works in *All-German Art Exhibition*, Dresden.

1949 Autobiography *Das Abenteuer der Kunst* (*The Adventure of Art*) published by Rowohlt Verlag.

1950–55 Exhibits with New Group in Munich and at *Great Munich Art Exhibition*. Participates in exhibitions in Berlin, Stuttgart, and Kaiserslautern.

1955 Dies 3 May in Munich.

Bibliography

Compagnia del Disegno. *Rudolf Schlichter: Disegni e Acquarelli dal 1920 al 1955*. Milan: Compagnia del Disegno, 1974.

Galleria del Levante. *Rudolf Schlichter: Prima mostra retrospettiva/Erste Retrospektiv-Ausstellung*. Milan and Munich: Galleria del Levante, 1970.

Staatliche Kunsthalle, Berlin. *Rudolf Schlichter*. West Berlin: Frölich & Kaufmann, 1984 (with bibliography).

Georg Scholz

1890 Born 19 October in Wolfenbüttel.

1908 Graduates from the local Gymnasium. Studies at the State Art School of Baden, Karlsruhe, under Ludwig Dill, Hans Thoma, and Wilhelm Trübner.

1914–18 Military service in World War I.

1918 Wounded, he spends time in a military hospital to recuperate.

1919 Moves with his family to Grötzingen, near Karlsruhe. Designs cigarette packages and illustrates books to make a living. Joins November Group and cofounds its local affiliate, Group Rih, along with Karl Hubbuch, Rudolf Schlichter, and Vladimir Zabotin. In April, participates in a controversial exhibition with Group Rih at the Galerie Moos in Karlsruhe. Joins Communist Party of Germany (KPD).

1920 Group Rih dissolves. Participates in *First International Dada Fair*, Kunstsalon Dr. Burchard, Berlin.

1922 Participates in an exhibition at the Munich gallery Goltz, *10 Years of New Art in Munich, Part I*. Around this time, Scholz is commissioned by a Karlsruhe businessman to make pornographic drawings.

1923 On 1 January, begins work as an assistant in the lithography class at the Karlsruhe Academy. Begins regular contributions of drawings to the KPD periodicals *Gegner* and *Der Knüppel*.

1924 On 1 January, becomes Head of the Preparatory Class at the Karlsruhe Academy. Writes an article for *Das Kunstblatt*, in which he explains new artistic theories.

1925 Participates in the Mannheim *Neue Sachlichkeit* exhibition.

1926 Contributes drawings to the periodical *Simplizissimus*.

1927 Probably in response to financial difficulties, founds the Karlsruhe Institute for Applied Art. With his students he prepares ninety-three panels for the exhibition *Bavarian Handicraft*. Scholz increasingly receives, and carries out, industrial commissions. Participates in an exhibition of *Neue Sachlichkeit* at the Galerie Neumann-Nierendorf in Berlin. Joins the Baden Secession, Freiburg.

1928 In September, travels to Paris with a friend, Dr. Kiefer. Friendship with Christoph Voll intensifies, and together they try to redirect the course of the Karlsruhe Academy.

1930 Travels to Berlin to see Henri Matisse exhibition.

1933 On 1 September, is dismissed from his position as a professor at the Karlsruhe Academy and forbidden to paint under the regime of the Third Reich. Scholz continues to paint under a false name. Work includes murals for officers' clubs. In April, his works are included in the first of the Nazi anti-modern art exhibitions, *Government Art from 1918 to 1933*, at the Kunsthalle, Karlsruhe.

1934 Stays at Beuron Monastery on the Danube as a guest, and studies monastic life.

1935 Converts to Catholicism.

1936 Begins work on frescoes for St. Urban's Church in Freiburg-Herdern.

1937 Twenty-three works removed from German museum collections as "degenerate."

1940 Active as portrait painter.

1942 Begins writing a novel, *Anton Bundschuh*.

1945 Is installed by the French military government as mayor of Waldkirch im Breisgau. Dies on 27 November in Waldkirch.

Major Posthumous Exhibitions

1975 Karlsruhe, Staatliche Kunsthalle, *Georg Scholz: Ein Beitrag zur Diskussion realistischer Kunst*.

1982 Karlsruhe, Künstlerhaus-Galerie, *Georg Scholz: Das druckgraphische Werk*.

Bibliography

Badischer Kunstverein. *Georg Scholz: Ein Beitrag zur Diskussion realistischer Kunst*. Karlsruhe: Badischer Kunstverein, 1975.

Curjel, Hans. "Zur Entwicklung des Malers Georg Scholz." *Das Kunstblatt* 5 (1923): 257–264.

Goettl, Helmut. "Ein Künstler der zwanziger Jahre: Zum Schaffen des Malers Georg Scholz." *Bildende Kunst* 3 (1955): 134–137.

Künstlerhaus-Galerie. *Georg Scholz: Das druckgraphische Werk*. Karlsruhe: Künstlerhaus-Galerie, 1982.

Marr, Otto. "Die Grossindustriellen und ihre Maler." *Der Querschnitt* 8/9 (1928): 618ff.

Scholz, Georg. "Die Elemente zur Erzielung der Wirkung im Bilde." *Das Kunstblatt* 6 (1924): 77–80.

——. "Kunst und Kitsch." *Die Pyramide* 11 (1922): 97–98.

Franz Theodor Schütt

1908 Born 15 December in Stettin, son of Franz Friedrich Christian Schütt (1874–1962), a Pomeranian painter and professor at Stettin School of Applied Arts.

1915 Lives in Stettin through 1937.

1925 Studies sculpture under Kurd Schwerdtfeger and painting and graphics under his father at the Stettin School of Applied Arts, through 1929. Begins exhibiting with the group The Stream in Stettin.

1928 Participates in Academy exhibition, Berlin, and the Biennale, Monza.

1929–30 Studies architecture and interior design in Munich and Stettin.

1931 Contact with the artist Mac Zimmermann and Breslau artists' groups through 1937.

1934 Exhibits in Köslin (Koszalin), Pomerania, with Max Pechstein, Willy Jaeckel, Joachim Utech, Willy Robert Huth, and Schwerdtfeger. Exhibition closes for political reasons.

1937–40 Lives in Danzig; is construction worker.

1940 Military service in Prague, Normandy, and Channel Islands until 1945.

1943 Nearly one thousand works of his are destroyed during an air raid on Stettin.

1945–47 Prisoner of war.

1947–50 Lives in Frankfurt a. M. Works in publishing and applied graphic arts.

1948 Marries.

1950 Birth of his daughter. Moves to Wiesbaden; resumes independent artistic activity.

1955 Founding member of the Union of Pictorial Artists, Wiesbaden.

1956 Participates in *Great Munich Art Exhibition*.

1965 Founding member of the artists' group REAL.

1971 Teaches at the Technical College, Darmstadt, through 1978: chair for painting, drawing, and graphics.

1973 Exhibition in Frankfurt and Cologne. Named honorary president of the Union of Pictorial Artists, Wiesbaden.

1974 Exhibitions, Vonderaumuseum, Fulda, and Gemäldegalerie Schloss Rantzaubau, Kiel.

1975 Retrospective exhibition, Galerie Krokodil, Hamburg.

1977 Receives the citizen's silver medal from the city of Wiesbaden.

1979 Retrospective exhibition, Nassau Art Association, Wiesbaden.

1981 Awarded the Cross of Merit of the Federal Republic of Germany.

1985 Awarded the Culture Prize of the city of Wiesbaden.

1989 Exhibition, City Hall, Wiesbaden.

1990 Lives in Wiesbaden.

Karl Schwesig

1898 Born 19 June in Gelsenkirchen, Westphalia, son of a miner and surveyor.

1914–15 After leaving Realschule, works as a gardener's assistant.

1915–18 Drafted into military service; because of physical deformity, serves as a clerk in mine office.

1918–21 Attends Düsseldorf Art Academy with stipend.

1920 Close contact with Johanna Ey.

1921 Joins and exhibits with The Young Rhineland at the Kunsthalle, Düsseldorf.

1922 Included in *First International Art Exhibition*, Düsseldorf. Forms close friendship with Gert Wollheim and Trude Brück.

1924 With Wollheim and Peter Ludwigs publishes the political-satirical periodical *Die Peitsche*. Participates in the exhibition *The Struggle*, Kunsthalle, Düsseldorf, and the *First All-German Art Exhibition*, Moscow, Leningrad, and Saratow.

1925 Otto Dix paints *Karl Schwesig with Model* (whereabouts unknown). Exhibits with Berlin Secession.

1926 Included in exhibition *The Young Rhineland*, Essen.

1927 Self-portrait acquired by City Art Collections, Düsseldorf.

1928 Founding member of Rhenish Secession.

1930 Founding member of Association of Revolutionary Artists in Germany (ARBKD or "Asso"), Düsseldorf chapter. Joins Communist Party of Germany. Six-month trip to Toulon in southern France with Werner Gilles, Josef Pieper, and Heinz Tappeser.

1933 Aids in the creation and distribution of anti-Nazi leaflets. On 10 July, elected first national secretary of National Union of Visual Artists, Düsseldorf. On 11 July, arrested and tortured by Gestapo on suspicion of hiding socialist and Communist friends. Pictures and books confiscated from his studio. Sentenced to sixteen months in prison for high treason.

1934 Released on probation. Begins work on a drawings series titled *The Cellar of Schlegel House* depicting his experiences while detained by the Gestapo.

1935 Illegal emigration to Belgium; political exile in Antwerp.

1935–36 Completes forty-eight drawings for *The Cellar of Schlegel House.*

1936 Exhibition of *The Cellar of Schlegel House.* First European Amnesty Congress, Brussels, and *Olympiad under Dictatorship,* Amsterdam. Creates works for the Belgian Spanish relief organization through 1939.

1937 Exhibition of *The Cellar of Schlegel House,* Museum of Modern West European Art, Moscow. Receives invitation to visit Moscow. Deprived of German citizenship.

1938 Contributes drawings to illegal anti-Nazi paper *Kölner Rosenmontagszeitung.*

1940–43 After German invasion of Belgium, interned as enemy alien by Belgian police in Antwerp. Shipped to southern France internment camps of Saint-Cypres, Gurs, Noé, and Nexon.

1943 Taken by SS to Düsseldorf and imprisoned there.

1944 Performs forced labor in clearing bombed streets, Düsseldorf. Released under police surveillance with orders not to leave city. After major bombing of Düsseldorf, leaves for Mosel Valley.

1945 In February, arrested by the SS and imprisoned at Bernkastel. Released at the approach of U. S. army. Returns to Düsseldorf and resumes profession of artist.

1946 Marriage to Hannelore Müller.

1955 Dies 19 June, his fifty-seventh birthday.

Bibliography

Galerie Remmert und Barth. *Karl Schwesig: Ausgewählte Werke 1920–1955.* Düsseldorf: Galerie Remmert und Barth, 1988.

Goethe-Institute. *Karl Schwesig 1898–1955: Gemälde—Graphik—Dokumente.* Brussels: Goethe-Institute, 1986.

Karl Schwesig: Schlegelkeller, Mit einem Vorwort von Heinrich Mann. Düsseldorf: Frölich & Kaufmann, 1983.

Stadtmuseum, Düsseldorf. *Karl Schwesig: Leben und Werk.* Düsseldorf: Frölich & Kaufmann, 1984.

Martel Schwichtenberg

1896 Born 5 June in Hanover, daughter of a government clerk and his wife, a former druggist.

1900 Death of father.

1913–16 Studies at Kunowsky's private art school, then at the School of Applied Arts, Düsseldorf. Publishes her first woodcut series, *Cinnabar.*

1916 In Hagen, in contact with Carl Ernst Osthaus, Christian Rohlfs, and Milly Steger.

1917 Begins work with Bernhard Hoetger at the Bahlsen Cookie Factory, Hanover, with which she remains associated as a designer through 1932.

1918–19 Spends summers at the artists' colony in Worpswede with Hoetger, Heinrich Vogeler, Karl Jakob Hirsch, and Georg Biermann.

1920 Acquires a studio on Sybelstrasse, Berlin. Forms friendships with Johannes R. Becher, Theodor Däubler, Ernst Oppler, and Wilhelm R. Valentiner. Marries the painter Robert W. Huth. Joins and exhibits with November Group.

1921–22 Spends summers at Jershöft in Pomerania. Associates with Karl Schmidt-Rottluff, Erich Heckel, Hermann Max Pechstein, Anton Kerschbaumer, and Franz Radziwill. Produces lithographic series *From Pomerania.*

1922 Travels in Italy with Valentiner and his wife. In October, exhibits at Galerie Ferdinand Moeller, Berlin. Two works purchased by Katherine Dreyer for the Société Anonyme, New York.

1923 Included in Valentiner's exhibition *A Collection of Modern German Art,* Anderson Gallery, New York.

1924 Studies in Paris under Moïse Kisling.

1927–28 Buys house in Berlin-Grunewald. Associates with Tilla Durieux, Nell Walden, Margot Lion, and F. W. Goldschmidt.

1930 Exhibition, Galerie Flechtheim, Berlin. Participates in Valentiner's exhibition *Modern German Art,* Society for Contemporary Art, Harvard University, Cambridge, Massachusetts.

1931 Exhibition, Galerie Flechtheim, Berlin.

1932 Travels to St. Tropez. Associates with Kurt Wolff, René Schickele, Walter Hasenclever, Collette. Contributes to the periodical *Omnibus.* Sells house in Berlin.

1933 In January, emigrates to Italy; in April, to South Africa. Opens a pottery kiln in Johannesburg. Travels throughout Africa. Forms friendships with Rex Gubb, Everill Hodgson, and Johannes Berninger.

1937 Creates mural for Broadcasting House, Johannesburg.

1938 Fire destroys most of her possessions and her home in Johannesburg.

1939 Visits U. S. at invitation of Valentiner. In April, returns to Africa. In August, travels to Berlin. With outbreak of World War II, unable to leave Germany. Writes *Whiskey and Stars: African Sketches* (unpublished); drinks heavily.

1940 In sanatorium at Glotterbad. Berninger, her close companion, dies.

1941 Spends winter in Badenweiler.

1942 Travels to Meierhof in Laugen with Countess Zeppelin.

1943 Suffers nervous breakdown.

1944 Resumes painting and produces new prints.

1945 Dies 31 July in Sulzburg (Baden).

Bibliography

Frenzel, H. K. "H. Bahlsen, Hannover." *Gebrauchsgraphik* 9 (January 1932): 2–14.

Friedemann, K. "Vier Künstlerinnen: M. Laurencin, M. Schwichtenberg, A. Exter

[sic]." *An der Wende: Zeitschrift für weibliche Bildung* 4 (1931): 48.

Rathke, Christian. "Martel Schwichtenberg." *Die Weltkunst* 52, no. 22 (15 November 1982): 3302–3303.

Turkel-Deri, Flora. "Exhibition, Flechtheim Gallery." *Art News* 29 (27 December 1930): 6.

Richard Seewald

1889 Born 4 May in Arnswalde.

1909 Studies architecture in Munich and teaches himself painting and graphics. Earns a living from drawing caricatures for *Jugend, Lustige Blätter,* and *Meggendorfer Blätter.*

1911 First exhibition at Galerie Thannhauser, Munich. Participates in the Salon d'Automne, Paris.

1912 First etchings and woodcuts. Participates in the Salon d'Automne, Paris.

1913 Exhibits in *First German Autumn Salon* at *Der Sturm* gallery, Berlin. Contributes to the Munich periodical *Revolution.* First individual exhibition in the Neue Kunstsalon, Munich. Member of New Secession and German Art Association. Travels to Ascona, Corsica, and southern France.

1914 Exhibits at New Munich Secession and at Free Secession, Berlin.

1920 Several exhibitions, including a major retrospective of his paintings and graphic work at Galerie Thannhauser, Munich.

1923 Travels to Sicily and Tunis. Purchases property in Ronco sopra Ascona.

1924–31 Professor of painting, stained glass, graphics, and book illustration, Werkschule, Cologne.

1931 Leaves Cologne Werkschule and emigrates to Ronco.

1934 Travels to Greece and Palestine.

1939 Becomes a Swiss citizen.

1939 Exhibition in London at the Staford Gallery, arranged with the help of Aldous Huxley.

1954–58 Teaches at the Academy of Fine Arts, Munich.

1961 Paints the arcades of the Munich Hofgarten.

1976 Dies 29 November in Munich.

Bibliography

"Bemerkungen eines Malers zum Problem der abstrakten Malerei." *Kunst und Künstler* 32 (March 1933): 97–104.

"Bibelillustration heute: Ein neues Werk Richard Seewalds." *Die Neue Saat* 1 (April 1938).

Brues, O. "Richard Seewalds Weg." *Hellweg* 5 (1925): 610.

Grunthal, E. "Richard Seewald." *Das Kunstblatt* 4 (1920): 301–305.

Hausenstein, Wilhelm. "Richard Seewald." *Der Cicerone* 14 (1922): 491–502. (Reprinted in *Jahrbuch der jungen Kunst,* 1922, 133–144.)

Linfert, C. "Der Maler Richard Seewald: Zu seiner Ausstellung im Kölnischen Kunstverein." *Kunst und Künstler* 29 (January 1931): 137–143.

"Das Lob der Dinge von Richard Seewald." *Die Kunst* 77 (June 1938): 286–287.

Mueller-Wulckow, W. "Der Maler Richard Seewald." *Deutsche Kunst und Dekoration* 49 (January 1922): 187–193.

Netzer, R. "Illustrationen von Richard Seewald: Aufs Wasser geschrieben" *Gebrauchsgraphik* 31 (May 1960): 24–29.

Pfister, Kurt. "Richard Seewald." *Deutsche Kunst und Dekoration* 45 (October 1919): 35–41.

Sailer, Anton. *Seewald 1889–1976.* Munich: Thiemig, 1977.

Seewald, Richard. "Über Malerei." *Die Kunst für Alle* 39 (November 1923): 41–51.

Straus-Ernst, Luise. "Neue Arbeiten von Richard Seewald." *Das Kunstblatt* 11 (1927): 353–355.

——. "Richard Seewald." *Deutsche Kunst und Dekoration* 61 (January 1928): 268–276.

"Über die Möglichkeit der religiösen Malerei in unseren Tagen." *Kunst und Künstler* 31 (March 1932): 88–94.

W. A. "Berner Kunsthalle: W. K. Weimken and Richard Seewald." *Das Werk* 29 (February/March 1942): XXXVIII–XL.

W. N. "Richard Seewalds Fresken in der Annunziatakapelle in Ronco am Lago Maggiore." *Das Werk* 29 (August 1942): 195–198.

"Wallfahrt zum Tempel der Aphaia." *Die Kunst* 77 (March 1938): 178–184.

"Wir segelten durch Holland." *Die Neue Saat* 2 (July 1939): 228–234.

With, K. "Richard Seewald." *Deutsche Kunst und Dekoration* 57 (1925): 75.

Friedrich (Fritz) Skade

1898 Born 17 June in Döhlen, near Dresden, into a working-class family.

1912 After attending Volksschule, enters School of Applied Arts, Dresden.

1914 Serves in the army during World War I.

1919–22 Resumes studies at School of Applied Arts, Dresden.

1922 Enters Dresden Academy as master student of Richard Dreher; also studies under Paul Rössler and Otto Gussmann until 1927.

1924 First exhibition in Dresden during summer. Included in *Jury-Free Art Show,* Berlin.

1926 Participates in exhibition *Young Dresden,* organized by Paul Gurlitt in Zwickau. Joins Dresden Artists' Association, Dresden Secession, and German Communist Party.

1927 Receives Saxon State Prize for Figure Painting.

1928 Study trip to Paris.

1929 Receives Saxon State Prize for Mural Painting.

1930 Joins the Dresden chapter of the Association of Revolutionary Artists of Germany (ARBKD or "Asso"). Drawings published in periodical *Arbeiterstimme.*

1937 Two works removed from Dresden Municipal Museum as "degenerate."

1945 Studio bombed; most of his works destroyed.

1945–51 Active in Löwenhain (Erzgebirge), then returns to Dresden.

1968 Awarded National Order of Merit of the GDR.

1971 Dies 4 April in Dresden.

Alice Sommer

1898 Born 13 December in Dresden, daughter of a master baker.

1918 Enters Painting School for Women, Dresden. Studies under Max Feldbauer.

1920 On 18 March, accepted into Dresden Academy in the first year women are admitted as students.

1922–24 Completes Academy studies with honors.

1927 Upon marriage, stops activity as artist.

1982 Dies 1 June in Dresden.

Jakob Steinhardt

1887 Born 23 May of Jewish parents in Zerkow, in the province of Posen.

1906 Sent to Gymnasium in Berlin.

1907 Studies at the School of the Museum of Applied Arts, Berlin. Private study under Lovis Corinth. Studies etching under Hermann Struck.

1909–10 Leaves for Paris in November. Studies briefly at Académie Julian. Enrolls at the school run by Henri Matisse. Meets Rudolf Levy and Hans Purrmann; leaves after one month. Enrolls at Académie Colarossi; studies under Théophile Steinlen. Rents a studio in Cité Falguière. Meets Leo Stein, Pablo Picasso, Henri Rousseau, Paul Durand-Ruel, and Pierre Auguste Renoir.

1910 Returns to Berlin.

1911 Visits Florence and Rome.

1912 Returns to Berlin. Meets Ludwig Meidner. With Meidner and Richard Janthur, founds The Ones Filled with Pathos; the group exhibits at Der Sturm gallery, 2–15 November.

1913 First one-man exhibition, I. B. Neumann Gallery, Berlin.

1914 Participates in group exhibition at I. B. Neumann Graphic Arts Cabinet, Berlin. Drafted into military; serves through 1918. Assigned to garrison duty in Lithuania; draws scenes of Jewish life in Lithuanian *shtetls*.

1917 Sends fifty drawings to exhibition of Berlin Secession; all are sold. Corinth buys two. Invited to join Berlin Secession.

1917–18 Transferred to Macedonian front. During French artillery attack, deserts and returns to Zerkow via Nuremberg. Suffers nervous collapse.

1919 Individual exhibition in October at I. B. Neumann Gallery. Publishes etching portfolios *Dreams I* and *Dreams II*.

1920 One-man exhibition of graphic work at Neue Kunsthandlung, Berlin, 15 September–15 October.

1920–22 Illustrates series from biblical and Yiddish literature with lithographs and woodcuts, commissioned by Fritz Gurlitt of Verlag für Jüdische Kunst und Kultur. Socino Press commissions series of woodcuts illustrating passages by Ben Sira. Marries Minni Gumpert.

1922 From May to September, one-man exhibition at Kunsthütte, Chemnitz.

1925 Visits Palestine; paints Palestinian landscapes.

1933 Three armed Nazis invade apartment and take Steinhardt to headquarters for questioning on charges that his radio was used to jam a speech given by Adolf Hitler. Investigating officer urges Steinhardt to leave Germany and drops charges. Moves to Palestine; settles in Jerusalem. Executes woodcuts. Most of earlier work destroyed or removed from public collections during World War II. Founds art school.

1934 Individual exhibitions at Divan Gallery, 8–28 February, and Bezalel Museum, 6–17 March, Jerusalem.

1936–39 Participates in exhibitions in London, Paris, and New York.

1947 One-man exhibition at Bezalel Museum, Jerusalem, 18 January–1 March.

1949 Art school closes. Becomes director of Bezalel School of Applied Arts.

1950 Exhibition at The Art Institute of Chicago. All work is sold before exhibition opens.

1952 Visits United States. Exhibits graphic work at Kennedy Galleries, New York. Included in exhibition at Museum of Fine Arts, Boston.

1953 Exhibition at Smithsonian Institution, Washington, D. C.

1955 Participates in Bienal de São Paulo.

1956 Exhibitions at California Palace of Legion of Honor, San Francisco, and in Athens and Beograd.

1957 Exhibits at Stedelijk Museum, Amsterdam; included in exhibition at Art Museum, Düsseldorf, 29 October–19 November.

1962 In February, individual exhibition at Bezalel Museum, Jerusalem.

1964 From October to November, one-man exhibition at Beth Dizzengoff Gallery, Tel Aviv.

1966 Exhibits at Haus am Lützowplatz, Berlin.

1967–68 One-man exhibition at Museum of Modern Art, New York, 23 December–20 January.

1968 Exhibits graphic work in Haifa, Israel. Dies in Nahariya, Israel. Memorial exhibition, Kunstamt Wedding, Berlin.

Bibliography

Amishai-Maisels, Ziva. "Jacob Steinhardt's Call for Peace." *Journal of Jewish Art* 3/4 (1977): 90–102.

Artists House. *Jacob Steinhardt: Woodcuts 1912–1951.* Jerusalem: Artists House, 1957.

Bezalel National Museum. *Steinhardt: Retrospective Exhibition.* Jerusalem: Bezalel National Museum, 1962.

Cohen, Arthur A. *The Unknown Steinhardt.* New York: The Jewish Museum, 1987.

Gamzu, Haim. *The Graphic Work of Jacob Steinhardt.* New York: Thomas Yoseloff, 1963.

Haus am Lützowplatz. *Jakob Steinhardt (Jerusalem).* West Berlin: Haus am Lützowplatz, 1966.

Israel Museum. *Jacob Steinhardt: His Graphic Work.* Jerusalem: Israel Museum, 1967.

Kennedy & Co. *Jacob Steinhardt.* New York: Kennedy, 1952.

Kolb, Leon, ed. *The Woodcuts of Jacob Steinhardt Chronologically Arranged and Fully Reproduced.* San Francisco: Genuart, 1959.

Kunstamt Reinickendorf. *Jacob Steinhardts Jerusalem: Holzschnitt, Farbholzschnitt aus den Jahren 1913–1962.* West Berlin: Kunstamt Reinickendorf, 1963

Kunstamt Wedding. *Jakob Steinhardt: Das graphische Werk.* West Berlin: Kunstamt Wedding, 1987.

Kunstmuseum Düsseldorf. *Jacob Steinhardt.* Düsseldorf: Kunstmuseum Düsseldorf, 1957.

Nadel, Arno. *Jacob Steinhardt.* Berlin: Verlag Neue Kunsthandlung, 1920.

———. *"Rot und Glühend ist das Auge des Juden": Gedichte zu 8 Radierungen von Jacob Steinhardt.* Berlin: Verlag für Jüdische Kunst und Kultur, Fritz Gurlitt, 1920.

Pfefferkorn, Rudolf. *Jacob Steinhardt.* Berlin: Stapp, 1967.

Schwarz, K. "Zum 50. Geburtstag." *Jüdische Rundschau* [Berlin] 40 (1937): 11.

———. "Zwei Welten: Die Kunst J. Steinhardt's." *Jüdische Rundschau* [Berlin] 31 (1926): 608.

Stedelijk Museum. *Jacob Steinhardt.* Amsterdam: Stedelijk Museum, 1957.

Steinhardt, Jacob. *Woodcuts.* Jerusalem: Art Publishing Society, 1953.

Tietze, Hans. *Jacob Steinhardt.* Berlin-Frohnau: J. J. Ottens Verlag, n. d.

Weyl, H. "Jacob Steinhardts Graphik." *Jeschurun: Monatsschrift für Lehre und Leben im Judentum* [Berlin] 12, no. 8 (1925): 231.

Georg Tappert

1880 Born 20 October at Friedrichstrasse 10, Berlin, the only child of parents who had recently moved there from Silesia and Pomerania. Father is a tailor. Attends Protestant Volksschule.

1896–98 Apprenticeship as a tailor.

1898–1900 Becomes a tailor in the Gerson workshop, Berlin. Teaches himself to draw.

1900 In December, recommended by Max Liebermann and Paul Schultze-Naumburg for formal artistic training.

1901–03 Attends Karlsruhe Academy. Studies painting under Ludwig Schmid-Reutte and lithography under Karl Langbein.

1903 Visits graphics exhibition of Berlin Secession; impressed by prints of Edvard Munch.

1903–04 Assistant to Schultze-Naumburg at his reformist School Workshops, Saaleck.

1905 Moves to Berlin.

1906 First individual exhibition, Galerie Paul Cassirer, Berlin. Moves to Worpswede. Founds the Art School Worpswede. Associates with Heinrich Vogeler, Otto

Modersohn, and Paula Modersohn-Becker. Joins German Artists' Group and Northwest German Artists' Association. Individual exhibition in Kunsthalle, Bremen.

1907 Exhibition, Kunsthalle, Worpswede.

1908 Exhibitions at Weimar Archducal Museum and Wiesbaden's Kunstsalon Banger. Wilhelm Morgner becomes his student. Exhibits with Berlin Secession. Joins Worpswede artists' group Bee.

1910 With Moritz Melzer, founds the School for Visual and Applied Arts, Berlin. Among twenty-seven artists rejected for exhibition by Berlin Secession. Founding member and first executive officer of New Secession. Participates in exhibitions of New Secession through 1914.

1911 Founding member of *Jury-Free Art Show.*

1912 Included in international *Sonderbund* exhibition, Cologne. Teaches at Professional and Developmental Schools for Manual Skills, Berlin

1913 Participates in international exhibition *New Art*, Vienna. Conflicts with Herwarth Walden. Appointed assistant at Royal School of Art and instructor in graphics and calligraphy at School of the Museum of Applied Arts, Berlin.

1914 Responds to a questionnaire from the periodical *Kunst und Künstler* about a program for new art. Graphics exhibition, Graphisches Kabinett I. B. Neumann, Berlin.

1915 Drafted into the military, Second Reserve Battalion of Infantry Regiment 97. Stationed in Mörchingen, Lorraine.

1916 Transfers to Airborne Troop, Adlersdorf and Berlin. *Die Aktion* publishes special Tappert issue.

1917 Cofounder of the periodical *Die Schöne Rarität.*

1918 Participates in exhibition *New Religious Art*, Municipal Art Building, Mannheim. Individual exhibition, Buchkunst (Axel Juncker), Berlin. Released from military duty in December. Founding member and organizer of November Group. Signs founding manifesto of Work Council for Art.

1919 Appointed to teach at United State Schools for Fine and Applied Arts, Berlin. Marries Worpswede student Kathleen Bagot. Teaches life drawing and composition class at innovative Reimann School, Berlin, through 1924.

1919 Exhibits with November Group, Berlin, through 1929.

1920 Alfred Flechtheim publishes his woodcut portfolio for Theodor Däubler's poem "The Sleepwalker." Begins an intensive effort to champion the work of Morgner.

1921 Member of governing board of *Deutscher Werkbund.* Rejects appointment as director of Hanover School of Applied Arts.

1922 Appointed to the newly formed national Office for Art Examination.

1923 Purchases house at Birkbuchstrasse 64a, Berlin-Steglitz.

1925 Death of his wife.

1926 Marries former student Elisabeth Foerstemann.

1929 Elisabeth Foerstemann dies.

1933   Nazi students at United State Schools interrupt examination administered by Tappert, drag him from class, and demand dismissal. Temporarily dismissed from teaching position, but reinstated through intervention of newly appointed director, Alexander Kanoldt. Dismissed from national Office for Art Examination.

1937   Dismissed from teaching position. Included as example of artistic decay in Wolfgang Willrich's pamphlet *Säuberung des Kunsttempels* (*The Cleansing of the Temple of Art*). Works not included in Munich exhibition *Degenerate Art* but are removed from public collections.

1938   Travels to Switzerland.

1944–45   Approximately one hundred works destroyed in his studio during bombing raids. Decides to stop painting.

1945–53   Appointed by American Military Government of Berlin to rebuild School for Art Education, which is fused with the College of Visual Arts.

1953   Marries Annalise Friedrich. Resigns from teaching position.

1957   Dies 17 November in Berlin.

Bibliography

Akademie der Künste. *Georg Tappert 1880–1957.* West Berlin: Akademie der Künste, 1961.

Altonaer Museum. *Georg Tappert 1880–1957.* Hamburg: Altonaer Museum, 1971.

B. A. T. Cigaretten-Fabriken. *Wiederentdeckung eines Expressionisten: Georg Tappert—Gemälde 1906–1933.* Hamburg: B. A. T. Cigaretten-Fabriken, 1977.

Berlinische Galerie. *Georg Tappert: Ein Berliner Expressionist 1880 bis 1957.* West Berlin: Berlinische Galerie, 1981.

Frieg, Will. *Wilhelm Morgner, mit einem Nachwort über des Künstlers Schaffen von Georg Tappert.* Leipzig: Klinkhardt & Biermann, 1920.

Galerie Michael Neumann. *Georg Tappert 1880–1957: Aquarelle, Pastelle, Zeichnungen.* Kiel: Galerie Michael Neumann, 1982.

Galerie Nierendorf. *Georg Tappert.* Kunstblätter der Galerie Nierendorf, no. 1. West Berlin: Galerie Nierendorf, 1963.

Galerie Rolf Ohse. *Georg Tappert 1880–1957.* Bremen: Galerie Rolf Ohse, 1980.

Galerie Thomas. *Georg Tappert: Bilder—Aquarelle—Zeichnungen.* Munich: Galerie Thomas, 1986.

Hans-Thoma Gesellschaft. *Georg Tappert.* Reutlingen: Hans-Thoma Gesellschaft, 1981.

———. *Georg Tappert 1880–1957: Pastelle, Aquarelle.* Reutlingen: Hans-Thoma Gesellschaft, 1988.

Leinster Fine Art. *Georg Tappert.* London: Leinster Fine Art, 1984.

———. *Georg Tappert and Richard Ziegler: Two Artists of the "Novembergruppe"—Works on Paper.* London: Leinster Fine Art, 1986.

Leonard Hutton Galleries. *A Retrospective Exhibition of Paintings by Georg Tappert 1880–1957.* New York: Leonard Hutton Galleries, 1964.

Ohff, H. "Georg Tappert zum Hundertsten." *Das Kunstwerk* 34, no. 2 (1981): 71–72.

Wietek, Gerhard. *Georg Tappert 1880–1957: Ein Wegbereiter der Deutschen Moderne.* Munich: Karl Thiemig, 1980.

Bruno Voigt

1912   Born 20 September in Gotha, Thuringia. Father a school teacher and drawing instructor. Family active in Social Democratic Party.

1918   Father agitates for revolution, organizing one of the soldiers' and sailors' councils at his home.

1919   Enters primary school.

1922   Enters Oberrealschule, Gotha.

1924   Father dies at age forty-eight. Voigt transfers from Oberrealschule, Gotha, to College of Fine Arts, Weimar. Becomes a student of Walter Klemm.

1931   Joins the political action group Red Unit and the agit-prop section of Red Aid. Works with the political cabaret Red Rockets.

1932   Rents a studio in Weimar. Contracts with Bavaria Verlag, Gauting, to publish caricatures and prints.

1933   In December, Left Cartel of the Workers of the Mind founded in his studio to combat the Third Reich. Group dissolved after fifth meeting. Founding member of Weimar chapter of Association of Revolutionary Artists in Germany (ARBKD or "Asso"); chapter disbands shortly after its founding. His contract with Bavaria Verlag dissolved. Studio searched by police and SA during summer. In fall, ends formal art studies. Marries; returns to Gotha. Begins to copy Old Master paintings.

1936   Moves to village of Ulrichhalben near Weimar. Suspends political activity but continues political art.

1941   Drafted into infantry; serves on eastern front at Leningrad and in Karelia.

1944   Severely wounded in February. Hospitalized in Oldenburg. In September, his company of recuperating soldiers transferred to Holland; deserts after nine days. Hidden by Dutch farmer; surrenders to British. Prisoner of war at Rouen. Acts as translator.

1946   Transferred to French command; employed as a translator and draftsman of anti-mine unit Déminage Cabourg, Calvados, in Normandy.

1947   Released from captivity. Returns to Gotha, now in Soviet Occupation Zone.

1948   Attends School of Socialist Unity Party of Germany (SED). Becomes a city councilman for Culture and Education, Gotha.

1949   Joins the local leadership of SED.

1951   On 1 October, appointed director of State Museums, Gotha.

1954   Appointed division head in Ministry of Culture, Section for Museums and Preservation of Monuments. Becomes director of East Asian Collection, State Museums, East Berlin.

1975   Divorce and remarriage.

1983   Retires from directorship. Resumes painting and drawing.

1983–84   From November to February, exhibits paintings, drawings, and graphics at Neue Münchner Galerie, Munich. Participates in exhibition *On the Evening before the Brown Night*, Satiricum, Creiz. Included in *They Have a World to Gain*, Wittenberg, and *Painters Build Barricades*, Neubrandenburg and Rostock.

1984   Removed from SED membership due to inactivity resulting from age.

1985   Included in exhibition *Art in the Class Struggle*, State Gallery in the Moritzburg, Halle.

1986   August to September, exhibition at Galerie Sachsenplatz, Leipzig. Included in exhibition *German Realist Drawings of the 1920's*, Solomon R. Guggenheim Museum, New York (travels to Busch-Reisinger Museum, Harvard University, Cambridge, Massachusetts, and Graphische Sammlung, Staatsgalerie, Stuttgart). Exhibition *Berlin in the 1920s and 1930s: A City of Decadence, Revolt, and Chaos—Watercolors and Drawings of Bruno Voigt*, Patrick and Beatrice Haggerty Museum of Art, Marquette University, Milwaukee, Wisconsin.

1988   Dies 14 October in East Berlin.

Bibliography

AGO Galerie Wolfgang Thiede. *Bruno Voigt 1912–1988: Widerstandskunst 1933–1944.* West Berlin: AGO Galerie, 1988.

Galerie am Sachsenplatz. *Bruno Voigt: Aquarelle, Zeichnungen und Radierungen.* Leipzig: Staatlicher Kunsthandel der DDR, 1986.

Neue Münchner Galerie. *Bruno Voigt: Gemälde, Zeichnungen, Graphik 1930–1948.* Munich: Neue Münchner Galerie, 1983.

Patrick and Beatrice Haggerty Museum of Art. *Berlin in the 1920s and 1930s: A City of Decadence, Revolt, and Chaos—Watercolors and Drawings of Bruno Voigt.* Milwaukee: Marquette University, 1987.

Christoph Voll

1897   Born 25 April in Munich, son of sculptor Roman Voll. Enters orphanage in Kötzting, Bavaria, upon father's premature death.

1911   Apprentice to a stonemason in Dresden.

1915–18   Serves in the German army.

1919   Returns to Dresden; studies at School of Applied Arts.

1920–22   Studies at Dresden Art Academy under Oskar Kokoschka, Carl Albiker, and Robert Sterl. Contact with Otto Dix. Marries Erna, a Danish Kokoschka student.

1920   Joins and exhibits with Dresden Secession Group 1919.

1922   In April, exhibits at Galerie Emil Richter, Dresden.

1923   Daughter born by this date. In October, joins the faculty of the School of Applied Arts, Saarbrücken.

1926   Appointed professor at Saarbrücken. Travels to Denmark and southern France.

1927   Exhibits at Galerie I. B. Neumann and Galerie Nierendorf, Berlin.

1928   Receives Award for Sculpture, Prussian Academy of Fine Arts exhibition, Berlin. Appointed professor of sculpture, Karlsruhe Art Academy.

1931   Participates in international sculpture exhibition, Zurich.

1933   Dismissed from Karlsruhe Academy by Nazi government.

1937   Five works included in exhibition *Degenerate Art*, Munich. Exhibits at international sculpture exhibition, Zurich.

1938   Sculpture exhibition, Denmark.

1939   Dies 16 June in Karlsruhe.

Bibliography

"Christoph Voll, 1930: Kunsthalle, Mannheim." *Museum der Gegenwart* 2, no. 3 (1931): 117.

Galleria del Levante. *Der Bildhauer Christoph Voll.* Munich: Galleria del Levante, 1975.

———. *Christoph Voll: Radierungen und Holzschnitte.* Munich: Galleria del Levante, 1981.

———. *Christoph Voll: Skulpturen—Aquarelle—Zeichnungen.* Munich: Galleria del Levante, 1981.

Martin, K. "Christoph Voll: Bildhauer." *Der Kunstwart* 44 (May 1931): 532.

Meissner, C. "Holzbildhauer." *Hellweg* 6/7 (1927): 365.

Morschel, J. "Galleria del Levante, München: Ausstellung." *Das Kunstwerk* 29 (March 1976): 76–77.

Schmidt, Paul F. "Christoph Voll." *Die Horen* 5 (1928): 961–968.

Schurer, O. "Christoph Voll." *Deutsche Kunst und Dekoration* 61/62 (1928): 37.

Städtische Kunsthalle Mannheim. *Christoph Voll: 1897–1939.* Mannheim: Städtische Kunsthalle, 1960.

Weber, Wilhelm. *Der Bildhauer Christoph Voll: Leben und Werk.* Milan and Munich: Galleria del Levante, 1975.

Wolfradt, Willi. "Christoph Voll." *Die Weltbühne* 23, no. 2 (1927): 765.

Aloys Wach

1892   Born Aloys Ludwig Wachlmayr 30 April in Lambach, Austria, the second of ten children of innkeeper Anton Wachlmayr and his wife, Anna Grundner.

1904   Death of his father, whose brother Aloys becomes guardian of the family. Boy chorister for three years at the Benedictine Abbey of Lambach. Attends Bürgerschule in Wels. Receives three years' training as merchant's apprentice.

1909–12   Repeatedly rejected by Munich Academy. Rejected by Vienna Academy. Briefly attends two art schools in Vienna, then returns to Lambach.

1912   Travels to Berlin. Receives encouragement from Richard Janthur. Wach establishes contacts with gallery and periodical *Der Sturm*.

1912–13   Studies at the art school of Heinrich Knirr and Sailer, Munich. Deeply impressed by exhibition of *Der Blaue Reiter* at Kunsthaus Goltz.

1913–14   Lives in Paris; studies at the Académie Colarossi. Becomes acquainted with Amedeo Modigliani. Meets the German art historian Ernest Tross.

1914   After leaving Paris, stays briefly on the Ammersee. Studies at Stuttgart Academy under Heinrich Altberr. Moves to Munich. Publishes prints in *Der Sturm*.

1915   Exhibits with Munich Secession. Military service in press company, then in propaganda and exhibitions corps of the Tyrolean Imperial Rifle Corps until 1918.

1917   Prints appear in *Das Kunstblatt* through 1920.

1918   Returns to Munich. Begins correspondence with Egon Schiele. Supports Berlin November Group.

1919   In January, exhibits at Graphisches Kabinett von Bergh & Company, Düsseldorf. Publishes woodcuts supportive of Bavarian Soviet Republic in newspapers *Bayerischer Kurier* and *Münchner Neueste Nachrichten*. Signs name as "Alois Wach." Included in exhibition of recent graphics, Galerie Neue Kunst, Hans Goltz, Munich. Exhibits graphics in Duisburg, Bielefeld, Frankfurt a. M., Mannheim, and Hagen. Contacts with sculptor Berthold Müller and with Jenny Wiegmann, Ricarda Huch, and Georg Schrimpf. Carves woodcuts for Georg Kaiser's *Gas*. Publishes woodcuts in the revolutionary journals *Der Weg* and *Die Freiheit*. Marries. Flees to Lambach to escape arrest for participation in Bavarian Soviet Republic. Jailed nine days at Simbach due to passport irregularities. Isolates himself at a farm in Aufhausen, near Braunau am Inn, Austria. Designs emergency money for the communities of Hochburg and Feldkirchen. Publishes the pamphlet *Aloys Wach: Holzschnitte 1918* (*Aloys Wach: Woodcuts, 1918*).

1919–20   Produces woodcut series *The Prodigal Son*.

1920   Moves to Braunau am Inn. Active as designer of stained-glass windows and graphics.

1922   Publishes cycle of engravings *A Dance of Death from 1914*, designed 1916–17. Encourages founding of the Inn Area Artists' Guild.

1924   Participates in the fall exhibition of the Vienna House of Artists.

1924–25   Produces series of paintings, drawings, and prints with motifs from Upper Austrian Peasant Wars of 1625.

1925   Receives State Award and summer exhibition at House of Artists, Vienna, for Peasant Wars paintings. Makes an extended trip to Rome with Berthold and Jenny Müller.

1926   Participates in *Mission Exhibition*, Vatican City. Awarded Rome Prize (Papal Medal) by Pope Pius XI. Rejects professorship at the Prussian Academy of Fine Arts, Berlin. Paints frescoes at the Kreuzschwesternschule, Linz.

1927   His brother, Dr. Max Wachlmeyr, dies of tuberculosis. Paints flower still lifes on commission.

1931   Dr. Ernest Tross visits Wach's studio in Braunau am Inn.

1933   Creates frescoes for public and private buildings in Braunau through 1939.

1935   Moves family to new housing development on Grenzstrasse.

1938   Repeatedly distances himself from his Expressionist work. After German annexation of Austria, refuses commission for further paintings on the Peasant Wars. Forbidden to practice professionally as artist.

1939   As Aloys Wachlmayr, publishes *Das Christgeburtsbild der frühen Sakralkunst* (*The Image of the Birth of Christ in Early Sacred Art*).

1940   Wills his works of 1913 to 1920 to Tross, then living in Denver, Colorado. Dies 18 April of tuberculosis and malnutrition in Braunau am Inn.

1945   Tross receives Wach's works through intervention of an American Army officer.

Major Posthumous Exhibitions

1956   Los Angeles County Museum of Art, *Aloys Wach: An Exhibition of Prints and Drawings from the Ernest Tross Collection*.

1979   Braunau am Inn, Ausstellungsgruppe Firesü, *Aloys Wach 1892–1940: Gedächtnisausstellung*.

1982   Linz, Neue Galerie der Stadt Linz, Wolfgang Gurlitt Museum, *Klemens Brosch, Carl Anton Reicher, Aloys Wach*, 4 March–10 April, with catalogue entries by Peter Baum.

Bibliography

Kilger, P. L. "Aloys Wach." *Der Getreue Eckart* 7 (1929): 209–218.

Mayr, W. "Ein Kapitel moderner christlicher Kunst." *Die Kirchenkunst* 1 (1929): 110–113.

William Wauer

1866   Born 26 October in Oberwiesenthal (Erzgebirge).

1884–87   Studies at Dresden and Berlin art academies.

1887–88   Attends Munich Art Academy.

1888   Spends two years in U. S.

1890   Studies art history at University of Leipzig.

1896–97   Travels to Rome.

1899   Becomes editor of Berlin magazine *Quickborn*.

1900   Works for magazine *Die Woche*, then as advertising consultant to a number of large firms. Moves to Dresden. Continues in advertising; founds a weekly magazine, *Dresdner Gesellschaft*. Works as a theater critic.

1905   Returns to Berlin; works for a short time for theater director Max Reinhardt. Later joins the Hebbel Theater and, finally, the Kleines Theater.

1906   Serves as director at the Deutsches Theater with Reinhardt until 1914.

1911   Becomes active in the film industry; gains reputation as a director and produces films with actor Albert Bassermann.

1912   Attends Italian Futurist exhibition at Herwarth Walden's *Der Sturm* gallery; decides to dedicate himself to the visual arts.

1918   In March, exhibits paintings at *Der Sturm* gallery; joins the November Group and Work Council for Art. Begins series of monumental portrait busts.

1919   In March, has his only one-person exhibition at *Der Sturm* gallery. Becomes a close associate of Walden. Publishes graphic works in *Der Sturm* periodical, as well as a number of articles about Expressionism.

1920   On 20 October, Wauer's pantomime play *Die vier Toten von Viametta* (*The Four Corpses from Viametta*) is performed with music by Walden in Dresden. The play is performed once more in the Berlin cabaret Überbrettl.

1924   Following the dissolution of Walden's circle and *Der Sturm*, Wauer forms

the International Association of Cubists, Futurists, and Constructivists and is its president through 1933; the group is later called The Abstract.

1933   The Abstract is prohibited. Nazis forbid Wauer to work. Tries to accept Nazi aesthetics, but quickly rejects them.

1937   Condemned as a "degenerate" artist; two of his works are confiscated from German museums.

1948   Exhibition at Kunsthaus, Tempelhof Town Hall, Berlin.

1956   Exhibition honoring his ninetieth birthday, Haus am Lützowplatz, West Berlin.

1962   Dies 3 October in West Berlin.

Bibliography

Laszlo, Carl. *William Wauer*. Basel: Editions Paderma, 1979.

Wauer, William. *Theater als Kunstwerk*. Berlin: Verlag Der Sturm, 1918.

Erich Wegner

1899   Born in Gnoien, Mecklenburg.

1904   Family moves to Rostock.

1917–18   Active as scene painter at Rostock Theater.

1918–19   Serves in the military.

1919–21   Attends School of Applied Arts, Hanover. Studies under Fritz Burger-Mühlfeld.

1921   Itinerant artist in Frankfurt a. M., Dresden, Hamburg, and Hanover, through 1925.

1923   Works as a painter at the Wuehlfehler Steel Works.

1924   Establishes his own studio on Calenberg Strasse, Hanover.

1925   Marries Katharina Engel. Moves to Marienstrasse, Hanover.

1927   Exhibits at Art Association, Hanover.

1929   Included in exhibition *Neue Sachlichkeit*, Stedelijk Museum, Amsterdam.

1933   Does free-lance work with Canzler's Advertising Agency, which takes him to Steinberg near Sarstedt.

1933–45   Exhibits infrequently.

1946   Becomes an instructor at the Volkshochschule, Hanover.

1951   Retrospective exhibition, Wilhelm Busch Museum, Hanover.

1956   Exhibits at Art Association, Hanover.

1961   Exhibits at Haus am Waldsee, West Berlin.

1962   Participates in exhibition *The Twenties in Hanover*, Art Association, Hanover.

1966   Included in exhibition *Neue Sachlichkeit 1920–1933*, Galerie Zwirner, Cologne. Member of Free Group, Hanover.

1968   Exhibits at the Galerie Brockstedt and Art Association, Hamburg, and at the Art Association, Frankfurt.

1968–69   Exhibits at the Galleria del Levante in Munich and Milan.

1970   Retrospective exhibition, Art Association, Hanover.

1971   Becomes Assistant Professor at the Volkshochschule, Hanover.

1972   Award for distinguished service bestowed on him by the city of Hanover.

1973   Exhibits at the Galleria della Rochetta, Parma.

1974   Exhibitions, Musée d'Art et d'Industrie, St. Etienne; Musée d'Art et d'Industrie, Chamberg; *Neue Sachlichkeit*, Art Association, Hanover; and Galerie Krokodil, Hamburg.

1975   Exhibitions *From Art Brut to Neue Sachlichkeit*, Galerie Krokodil, Hamburg, and *Neue Sachlichkeit*, Galerie von Abercron, Cologne.

1976   Exhibits at Galerie Kühl, Hanover.

1977   Exhibition *German Realists 1918–1933*, Piccadilly Gallery, London.

1978   Participates in *Neue Sachlichkeit and German Realism of the Twenties*, Hayward Gallery, London.

1979   Exhibitions at Kubus and Kühl galleries in Hanover in honor of his eightieth birthday. Awarded Distinguished Service Medal of the Lower Saxony Order of Service.

1980   Dies 11 December in Hanover.

Bibliography

Teschemacher, A. T. *Erich Wegner*. Munich: Westermann Verlag, 1987 (with bibliography).

Kurt Weinhold

1896   Born 28 September in Berlin, son of artist Carl Weinhold. Family lives in Essen and Bonn.

1911   Sometime after this date, family moves to Munich. Weinhold is taught by his father.

1922   Marries Margarete Schütz. Moves to Calw.

1924   Daughter Cora born. Befriends Rudolf Schlichter.

1927–33   Participates in annual Prussian Academy of Fine Arts exhibitions, Berlin.

1934   Awarded Rome Prize of Prussian Academy.

1934–36   Travels to Rome and Villa Böcklin, Florence.

1937   Participates in *Great German Art Exhibition*, House of German Art, Munich.

1965   Dies in Calw.

Bibliography

Galerie Krokodil. *Kurt Weinhold*. Hamburg: Galerie Krokodil, 1974.

Galerie Schlichtenmaier. *Kurt Weinhold 1896–1965*. Grafenau bei Sindelfingen: Galerie Schlichtenmaier, 1986.

Golinski, Hans Günter. *Kurt Weinhold: Sinnbildschaffende Malerei des 20. Jahrhunderts in Deutschland*. Kunst, Geschichte und Theorie, vol. 4. Essen: Verlag Die Blaue Eule, 1985 (with comprehensive bibliography).

Gustav Wunderwald

1882 Born 1 January in Cologne-Calk, son of Karl Wunderwald, a gunsmith, and Adelheid Hirtz.

1896–98 Studies in Cologne under master painter Wilhelm Kuhn.

1899–1900 Works as a scene painter with Max Brückner, Gotha.

1900–04 Works as a theater painter for Georg Hartwig & Company, Salzufer 23, Berlin-Charlottenburg.

1904–07 Works as a stage designer for Royal Opera, Stockholm. Meets Louise Dumont and Gustav Lindemann.

1907 Hired by Dumont and Lindemann as a stage designer for Düsseldorf Theater through 1909. Lasting friendship with Rhineland dramatist Wilhelm Schmidt-bonn (1876–1952) begins. Included in small exhibition at Düsseldorf Theater.

1908 On 8 May marries Amalie Minna Gerull (1881–1941).

1908–09 Resides temporarily with Schmidtbonn in Villa Brand, Tegernsee, where August and Elisabeth Macke also briefly live.

1909 Joins the technical personnel of City Theater, Innsbruck.

1910–11 Works as a stage designer in Freiburg. In 1911, participates in exhibition of Freiburg Art Association.

1912–15 Works as a stage designer for German Opera House, Berlin-Charlottenburg. After 1912, lives at Reichstrasse 8, Berlin-Charlottenburg.

1915–18 Joins the military; serves in Macedonia with Reserve Battalion of Infantry Regiment 43.

1918 Returns to Berlin.

1919 Works again as stage designer for the German Opera House, Berlin-Charlottenburg.

1924 First exhibition of paintings, Landsberg Book and Art Gallery, Berlin.

1925–25 Participates in *Great Berlin Art Exhibition*.

1927–31 Work included in exhibitions in numerous German cities.

1927 Paul Westheim writes the first essay on Wunderwald in *Das Kunstblatt*.

1929–31 Produces illustrations for periodicals *Sendung* and *Der Heimatdienst*.

1933 Participates in *Great Berlin Art Exhibition*.

1934 Participates in *Great Berlin Art Exhibition*. Ceases to exhibit.

1936 Works as a colorist of promotional films for Ufa and Mars-Film, Berlin-Ruhleben, through 1943.

1941 Death of his first wife. On 16 December, marries Berta Ludwig.

1945 After several weeks of illness, dies 24 June in Berlin.

Bibliography

Berlinische Galerie. *Gustav Wunderwald: Gemälde, Handzeichnungen, Bühnenbilder—Eine Ausstellung zum 100. Geburtstag des Künstlers*. West Berlin: Berlinische Galerie, 1982 (with bibliography and exhibition listing).

Magnus Zeller

1888 Born 9 August in Biesenrode near Mansfeld, to Reverend Friedrich Samuel Zeller and Erna Ellen, née Breuning.

1901 Father transferred to Magdeburg.

1906 Father transferred to Berlin-Zehlendorf.

1908 With recommendation by Reinhold Lepsius, enters Lovis Corinth's Training Studios for Painting and Sculpture, Berlin-Charlottenburg.

1911 Ends studies with Corinth. Receives state stipend to study at Prussian Academy of Fine Arts, Berlin.

1912 Exhibits in Berlin Secession. Travels to Paris.

1913 Joins Berlin Secession.

1914 Travels to Italy. Exhibits with and joins Free Secession, Berlin.

1915 Marries Marie Zimmermann. Drafted into the military.

1916 Transferred to Supreme High Command East, Kowno (Kaunas) and Wilna (Vilnius). There he meets Karl Schmidt-Rottluff, Richard Dehmel, Herbert Eulenberg, Alfred Brust, and Arnold Zweig. Illegally produces anti-military graphics. Creates drawings for the *Kownoer Zeitung* and *Wilnaer Zeitung*. Participates in exhibition, *Painters in Ob Ost*, Wilna and Kowno. Produces caricatures for the *Almanach der Bösen Buben*, a pamphlet written by Arnold Zweig, printed and distributed in 1917–18 by the Military Press Division, Kowno.

1918 Transferred to Army High Command 8 at Dorpat (Tatu) in Estonia, then in August to Supreme High Command, Berlin. Joins the Soldiers' Council of the SHC. Attends Soldiers' and Sailors' Council meeting on 10 November, Busch Amphitheater, Berlin. Birth of daughter Susanne.

1919 Builds home and studio in Blomberg, Lippe.

1920 Publishes lithographic portfolios *Rapture and Revolt* and *The Time of Revolution*.

1923–24 Teaches at State School of Art, in Dorpat.

1926 Travels to Paris. Death of his wife. Participates in *Great Berlin Art Exhibition*.

1929 Marries Helga Bagge. Travels to Italy. Exhibits at Municipal Art Building, Bielefeld.

1931 Birth of daughter Helga Marianne.

1932 Included in special exhibition of Berlin Secession with Rudolf Grossmann, Erich Klossowski, and Herbert Garbe.

1933 Karl Vollpracht begins regular purchases of Zeller's work.

1935 Awarded Rome Prize.

1936 Resident in the German Academy, Villa Massimo, Rome. Trip to Greece.

1937 Builds studio and house at Caputh, near Potsdam. Nazi authorities refuse to approve purchases of painting materials.

1938 Exhibition, Art Association, Göttingen.

1939 Birth of son, Conrad Magnus.

1945 After the war, joins German Socialist Party (SPD); later joins Socialist Unity Party of Germany (SED).

1946 Shows his anti-Fascist paintings at the *All-German Art Exhibition* of the German Central Government of the Soviet Occupation Zone, Berlin. Exhibitions in Bonn and Detmold.

1948 Wife and son move to Hamburg.

1954–62 Community Representative, Caputh.

1955 Exhibition at Culture League, Potsdam.

1966 Named honorary citizen of Caputh. Becomes seriously ill.

1967 Participates in exhibitions at House of Culture, Potsdam, and Ladengalerie, West Berlin.

1968 Exhibition, Moritzburg, Halle. Awarded the GDR's Silver Service Order of the Nation.

1972 Dies 25 February in East Berlin.

Major Posthumous Exhibitions

1973 Berlin-Pankow, Kleine Galerie des Kreiskulturhauses Erich Weinert, *Magnus Zeller: Späte Bilder* 16 November–21 December.

1978 Potsdam, Galerie Sozialistischer Kunst am Bezirksmuseum, *Magnus Zeller*, August–September, catalogue text by Diether Schmidt.

1988 Halle, Staatliche Galerie Moritzburg, *Magnus Zeller: Gemälde, Aquarelle, Zeichnungen, Druckgrafiken*, August–9 October, catalogue texts by Horst-Jörg Ludwig and Helga Helm.

Bibliography

Bornmann, Hans. "Magnus Zeller." *Hellweg* 7, no. 9 (10 May 1927): 137.

——. "Magnus Zeller." *Monatshefte für Literatur, Kunst und Wissenschaft* 4, no. 8 (February 1928): 469–474.

Fechter, Paul. "Magnus Zeller." *Der Cicerone* 13, nos. 11/12 (12 June 1921): 339–354.

Graumann, Heinz. "Magnus Zeller." *Die Horen* 5 (1928): 976.

Klutmann, Rudolf. "Der Maler Magnus Zeller." *Der Kreis* 7, no. 10 (October 1930): 590–592.

Lang, Lothar. "Magnus Zeller." *Die Weltbühne* 23, no. 25 (18 June 1968): 793–794.

Osborn, Max. "Magnus Zeller." *Velhagen und Klasings Monatshefte* 47, no. 3 (November 1933): 217–224.

Schifner, Kurt. "Über die graphischen Arbeiten von Magnus Zeller." *Bildende Kunst* 11 (1957): 738–741.

Schmidt, Diether, Arnold Zweig, and Lothar Lang. *Magnus Zeller*. Dresden: VEB Verlag der Kunst, 1960.

Richard Ziegler

1891 Born 3 May, son of a teacher, in Pforzheim.

1911 Completes studies at Gymnasium in Reuchlin. Spends one year in England.

1912–19 Studies philology at universities of Geneva, Greifswald, and Heidelberg.

1920 Begins autodidactic training as artist. Works as translator of Old High German for Swiss publisher.

1923 Travels in Italy.

1925 Moves to Berlin. Meets writer Robert Musil and artist Arthur Segal, who introduces him to November Group.

1925 First exhibition, Galerie Caspar, Berlin.

1926–29 Exhibits with November Group.

1927–28 Creates cycle of pastels *Springtime in Berlin*.

1931 Exhibits with November Group. During summer, emigrates with Jewish wife to Dalmation island of Korcula (Yugoslavia).

1933 Participates in exhibition, Bücherstube am Dom, Cologne. Exhibitions in Berlin and Dresden canceled by Nazis.

1933–36 Returns to Korcula. Produces graphic cycles depicting events in Germany, *Blood and Soil*, *Germany Has Awakened! Illustrated Broadside on the Third Reich*, and *Leaders Are Observing You*.

1936 Spends a few months in Paris. Makes a brief trip to Korcula.

1937 Emigrates to Great Britain. Works for London publishing houses.

1940 Under pseudonym Robert Ziller, publishes *We Make History*, thirty-five reproductions of his anti-Fascist drawings. Drawings and caricatures for London German-exile periodicals *Die Zeitung* and *Die Auslese*, as well as British periodicals *Lilliput* and *Picture Post*.

1940–41 Interned as enemy alien.

1943 Formally expelled from German National Chamber of Pictorial Arts.

1946 Publishes *Faces behind the News*, a collection of drawings from *Die Zeitung*. Resumes book illustrations for works by Voltaire, Musil, Heinrich Mann, and Emile Zola.

1958 Participates in exhibition, League for Art and Handicraft, Pforzheim.

1961 Returns to Germany. Moves to Selva, Mallorca (Spain), for health reasons.

1964 Exhibits at Galerie Wolfgang Gurlitt, Munich.

1976 Exhibits at Galerie Schwarzer, Vienna.

1979 Exhibits at Galerie Brinke und Riemenschneider, Hamburg.

1980–81 Participates in exhibitions at Neue Münchner Galerie, Munich.

1981 Participates in exhibitions at Heimatmuseum, Calw, and Leinster Fine Art, London.

1983 Formation of the Richard Ziegler Foundation, Calw.

1983–84 Included in traveling exhibitions in London, Leicester (England), Cairo, and Athens.

1990 Lives in Calw.

Bibliography

Leinster Fine Art. *Georg Tappert and Richard Ziegler: Two Artists of the "Novembergruppe"—Works on Paper*. London: Leinster Fine Art, 1986.

——. *Richard Ziegler: The Berlin Twenties—An Exhibition of Pastels, Drawings and Prints*. London: Leinster Fine Art, 1983.

Richard Ziegler Stiftung. *Die Richard Ziegler Stiftung Calw*. Calw: Richard Ziegler Stiftung, 1983.

——. *Richard Ziegler: Verlorene Bilder 1923–1937*. Calw: Richard Ziegler Stiftung, 1986.

"Ziegler-Ausstellung Köln." *Die Kunst* 67 (April 1933): 7.

Selected Bibliography

Akademie der Künste. *Arbeitsrat für Kunst 1918-1921.* West Berlin: Akademie der Künste, 1980.

————, Nationalgalerie and Orangerie at Schloss Charlottenburg. *Tendenzen der zwanziger Jahre: 15. Europäische Kunstausstellung.* West Berlin: Dietrich Reimer, 1977.

Anklage und Aufruf: Deutsche Kunst zwischen den Kriegen—Malerei, Graphik, Plastik. East Berlin: Staatliche Museen zu Berlin/National-Galerie, 1964.

Badischer Kunstverein. *Kunst in Karlsruhe 1900-1950.* Karlsruhe: Badischer Kunstverein, 1981.

Barron, Stephanie, ed. *German Expressionism 1915-1925: The Second Generation.* Los Angeles: Los Angeles County Museum of Art, and Munich: Prestel Verlag, 1988.

Behne, Adolf. *Die Wiederkehr der Kunst.* Leipzig: Kurt Wolff, 1919.

Berlin Museum. *Stadtbilder: Berlin in der Malerei vom 17. Jahrhundert bis zur Gegenwart.* West Berlin: Museum & Verlag Willmuth Arenhovel and Nicolaische Verlagsbuchhandlung, 1987.

Boberg, Jochen, Tilman Fichter, and Eckart Gillen, eds. *Die Metropole: Industriekultur in Berlin im 20. Jahrhundert.* Munich: Beck, 1986.

Centre National d'Art et de Culture Georges Pompidou. *Paris/Berlin: Rapports et Contrastes—France/Allemagne 1900-1933.* Paris: Centre National d'Art et de Culture Georges Pompidou, 1978.

————. *Les Réalismes: Entre Révolution et Réaction 1919-1939.* Paris: Centre National d'Art et de Culture Georges Pompidou, 1980.

De Paz, Alfredo. *Realismo Tedesco: Critica Sociale—Oggettività Ideologia.* Bologna: Editrice Clueb, 1981.

Frederick S. Wight Gallery. *Realism and Expressionism in Berlin Art.* Los Angeles: University of California, Frederick S. Wight Gallery, 1980.

Frommhold, Erhard. *Kunst im Widerstand: Malerei, Graphik und Plastik 1922 bis 1945.* Dresden: Verlag der Kunst, 1968.

Galerie von Abercron. *Neue Sachlichkeit: Zwölf Maler zwischen den Kriegen.* Cologne: Galerie von Abercron, 1975.

Galerie Rudolf Zwirner. *Neue Sachlichkeit 1920-1933.* Cologne: Galerie Rudolf Zwirner, 1965.

Galleria del Levante. *Aspetti della Nuova oggettività/Aspekte der Neuen Sachlichkeit.* Florence: Centro DI, 1968.

————. *Dresdner Sezession 1919-1925.* Munich: Galleria del Levante, 1977.

German Realist Drawings of the 1920s. Cambridge, Mass.: Harvard University Art Museums, 1986.

Grohmann, Will. *Bildende Kunst und Architektur.* Vol. 3, *Zwischen den beiden Kriegen.* Berlin: Suhrkamp, 1953.

————. *Zehn Jahre Novembergruppe.* Kunst der Zeit I, nos. 1-3. Berlin: J. J. Ottens, 1928.

Haus am Waldsee. *Die Neue Sachlichkeit.* West Berlin: Haus am Waldsee, 1961.

Haus an der Redoute. *Berliner Malerei der zwanziger Jahre.* Bonn: Haus an der Redoute, 1976.

Haus der Kunst. *Die Dreissiger Jahre: Schauplatz Deutschland.* Munich: Haus der Kunst, 1977.

Hayward Gallery. *Neue Sachlichkeit and German Realism of the Twenties.* London: Arts Council, 1978.

Heuer, Alfred. *Ausdruckskunst und neue Sachlichkeit in der bildenden Kunst unserer Zeit.* Paderborn: Schoningh, 1933.

Heusinger von Waldegg, Joachim. *Die Zwanziger Jahre im Porträt.* Cologne: Rheinland Verlag, and Bonn: Rheinisches Landesmuseum, 1976.

High Museum of Art. *Art in Berlin 1815-1989.* Atlanta: High Museum of Art, 1989.

Hirdina, Karin. *Pathos der Sachlichkeit: Tendenzen materialistischer Ästhetik in den zwanziger Jahren.* East Berlin: Verlag Das europäische Buch, 1981.

Hütt, Wolfgang. *Deutsche Malerei und Graphik im 20. Jahrhundert.* Berlin: Henschelverlag, 1969.

Kliemann, Helga. *Die Novembergruppe.* West Berlin: Mann, 1969.

Krempel, Ulrich, ed. *Am Anfang: Das Junge Rheinland.* Düsseldorf: Städtische Kunsthalle Düsseldorf, 1985.

Kunst- und Museumsverein Wuppertal. *Magischer Realismus in Deutschland 1920-1933.* Wuppertal: Kunst- und Museumsverein, 1967.

Kunstgewerbemuseum, Zurich. *Die Zwanziger Jahre: Kontraste eines Jahrzehnts.* Bern: Benteli, 1973.

Kunstverein Frankfurt. *Realismus in der Malerei der zwanziger Jahre.* Frankfurt a. M.: Kunstverein, and Hamburg: Kunstverein, 1968.

Kunstverein Hannover. *Die Zwanziger Jahre in Hannover.* Hanover: Kunstverein Hannover, 1962.

————. *Neue Sachlichkeit in Hannover.* Ed. Helmut R. Leppien. Hanover: Kunstverein Hannover, 1974.

Lang, Lothar. *Expressionist Book Illustration in Germany, 1907-1927.* Trans. Janet Seligman. Greenwich: New York Graphic Society, 1976.

Lethen, Helmut. *Neue Sachlichkeit 1924-1932: Studien zur Literatur des "Weissen Sozialismus."* Stuttgart: Metzler, 1970.

Liska, Pavel. "Die Malerei der Neuen Sachlichkeit in Deutschland." Ph. D. diss., Osnabrück, 1977.

Minneapolis Institute of Arts. *German Realism of the Twenties: The Artist as Social Critic.* Ed. Louise Lincoln. Minneapolis: Minneapolis Institute of Arts, 1980.

Musée d'Art et d'Industrie. *Réalismes en Allemagne 1919-1933.* St. Etienne: Musée d'Art et d'Industrie, and Chambery: Musée d'Art et d'Histoire, 1974.

Museum des 20. Jahrhunderts. *Neue Sachlichkeit und Realismus: Kunst zwischen den Kriegen.* Vienna: Kulturamt der Stadt Wien, 1977.

Neue Gesellschaft für Bildende Kunst. *Wem gehört die Welt: Kunst und Gesellschaft in der Weimarer Republik.* Berlin: Neue Gesellschaft für Bildende Kunst, 1977.

Oellers, Adam C. *Ikonographische Untersuchungen zur Bildnismalerei der Neuen Sachlichkeit.* Mainz: Louis Schreder, 1983.

Prinz, Ursula, and Eberhard Roters. *Berlinische Galerie, 1913-1933: Bestände—Malerei, Skulptur, Graphik.* West Berlin: Berlinische Galerie, 1979.

Raabe, Paul. *Der späte Expressionismus 1918-1922.* Biberach an der Riss: Kleine Galerie, 1966.

————, ed. *The Era of German Expressionism.* Trans. J. M. Ritchie. Woodstock, N. Y.: Overlook Press, 1974.

Riess, Margot. *Der Arbeiter in der Kunst.* Berlin: Neue Gesellschaft, 1925.

Roh, Franz. *Nach-Expressionismus: Probleme der neuesten europäischen Malerei.* Leipzig: Klinkhardt & Biermann, 1925.

Roters, Eberhard, ed. *Berlin, 1910-1933.* New York: Rizzoli, 1982.

————, and Bernhard Schulz, eds. *Ich und die Stadt: Mensch und Grossstadt in der deutschen Kunst des 20. Jahrhunderts.* West Berlin: Nicolaische Verlagsbuchhandlung Beuermann, 1987.

Salander, Gustav Adolf. *Der ideale Realismus in der Malerei der Gegenwart.* Bremen, 1925.

Sauerland, Max. *Die Kunst der letzten 30 Jahre: Eine Vorlesung aus dem Jahre 1933.* Hamburg: H. Laatzen, 1948.

Schmalenbach, Fritz. *Die Malerei der "Neuen Sachlichkeit."* West Berlin: Gebrüder Mann, 1973.

Schmalenbach, Werner. *Die Kunst der Zwanziger Jahre: Wirklichkeit und Utopie.* West Berlin: Presse und Informationsamt des Landes Berlin, 1977.

Schmidt, Diether. *Ich war, ich bin, ich werde sein: Selbstbildnisse deutscher Künstler des 20. Jahrhunderts.* East Berlin: Henschelverlag, 1968.

Schmidt, Diether. *Schriften deutscher Künstler des zwanzigsten Jahrhunderts.* Vol. 1, *Manifeste Manifeste 1905-1933;* Vol. 2, *In letzter Stunde.* Dresden: VEB Verlag der Kunst, 1964.

Schmied, Wieland. *Neue Sachlichkeit und magischer Realismus in Deutschland, 1918-1933.* Hanover: Fackelträger, 1969.

Schnakenburg, Bernhard, and Gerhard Muller Menckens. *Umwelt 1920: Das Bild der städtischen Umwelt in der Kunst der Neuen Sachlichkeit.* Bremen: Hauschild, 1977.

Schneede, Uwe, ed. *Die zwanziger Jahre: Manifeste und Dokumente deutscher Künstler.* Cologne: DuMont Verlag, 1979.

Schrader, Barbel, and Jürgen Schebera. *The Golden Twenties: Art and Culture of the Weimar Republic.* New Haven: Yale University Press, 1988.

Solomon R. Guggenheim Museum. *Expressionism: A German Intuition 1905-1970.* New York: Solomon R. Guggenheim Foundation, 1980.

Staatliche Kunstsammlungen Dresden. *Kunst im Aufbruch: Dresden 1918-1933.* Dresden: Staatliche Kunstsammlungen Dresden, 1980.

Staatliche Museen zu Berlin. *Realismus und Sachlichkeit: Aspekte deutscher Kunst 1919-1933.* East Berlin: Staatliche Museen, 1974.

————. *Revolution und Realismus.* East Berlin: Staatliche Museen, 1979.

Städtische Galerie im Lenbachhaus. *Kunst und Technik in den 20er Jahren: Neue Sachlichkeit und gegenständlicher Konstruktivismus.* Ed. Helmut Friedel. Munich: Städtische Galerie im Lenbachhaus, 1980.

Städtische Kunsthalle Mannheim. *Ausstellung Neue Sachlichkeit: Deutsche Malerei seit dem Expressionismus.* Mannheim: Städtische Kunsthalle, 1925.

Stadtmuseum München. *Die Zwanziger Jahre in München.* Ed. Christoph Stölzl. Munich: Stadtmuseum München, 1979.

Stedelijk Museum. *Neue Sachlichkeit.* Amsterdam: Stedelijk Museum, 1929.

Steingräber, Erich, ed. *Deutsche Kunst der 20er und 30er Jahre.* Munich: F. Bruckmann, 1979.

Weinstein, Joan. *Art and the November Revolution in Germany 1918-1919.* Chicago: University of Chicago Press, 1990 (in press).

Willett, John. *Art and Politics in the Weimar Republic: The New Sobriety 1917-1933.* New York: Pantheon, 1978.

Württembergischer Kunstverein. *Realismus zwischen Revolution und Machtergreifung 1919-1933.* Stuttgart: Württembergischer Kunstverein, 1971.

Zimmermann, Rainer. *Die Kunst der verschollenen Generation: Deutsche Malerei des expressiven Realismus von 1925-1975.* Düsseldorf: Econ, 1980.

Major Exhibitions with Works from the Fishman Collection

Milwaukee, Milwaukee Art Center, *Ludwig Meidner: Apocalyptic German Expressionist (From the Collection of Marvin and Janet Fishman)*, 4 June–18 July 1976.

Bloomington, Indiana University Art Museum, *German and Austrian Expressionism 1900 to 1920*, 23 October–3 December 1977.

Chicago, Museum of Contemporary Art, *Art in a Turbulent Era: German and American Expressionism*, 10 March–30 April 1978.

Ann Arbor, University of Michigan Museum of Art, *Ludwig Meidner: An Expressionist Master—Drawings and Prints from the D. Thomas Bergen Collection, Paintings from the Marvin and Janet Fishman Collection*, 20 October–19 November 1978.

Milwaukee, Fine Arts Galleries, University of Wisconsin-Milwaukee, *German Expressionism from Milwaukee Collections*, 22 January–11 March 1979.

New York, Solomon R. Guggenheim Museum, *Expressionism: A German Intuition 1905–1920*, 14 November 1980–18 January 1981 (traveled to San Francisco Museum of Art, 19 February–26 April 1981).

West Berlin, Berlinische Galerie, *Georg Tappert: Ein Berliner Expressionist 1880 bis 1957*, 28 November 1980–25 January 1981.

Los Angeles County Museum of Art, *German Expressionist Sculpture*, 30 October 1983–22 January 1984 (traveled to Washington, D. C., Hirshhorn Museum and Sculpture Garden, Smithsonian Institution, 4 April–17 June 1984; Cologne, Josef-Haubrich-Kunsthalle, 7 July–26 August 1984).

Washington, D. C., Hirshhorn Museum and Sculpture Garden, Smithsonian Institution, *Utopian Visions in Modern Art: Dreams and Nightmares*, 8 December 1983–12 February 1984.

London, Royal Academy of Arts, *German Art in the 20th Century: Painting and Sculpture 1905–1985*, 11 October–22 December, 1985 (traveled to Stuttgart, Staatsgalerie, 8 February–27 April 1986).

Milwaukee, Patrick and Beatrice Haggerty Museum of Art, Marquette University, *Twentieth Century Art: Loans and Permanent Collection*, 16 April–30 June 1986.

New York, Solomon R. Guggenheim Museum, *German Realist Drawings of the 1920's*, 15 May–6 July 1986 (traveled to Cambridge, Mass., Busch-Reisinger Museum, Harvard University, 26 July–28 September 1986; Stuttgart, Staatsgalerie, 25 October–28 December 1986).

Milwaukee, Patrick and Beatrice Haggerty Museum of Art, Marquette University, *Netherlandish and German Prints Before 1800*, 13 June–27 July 1986.

Milwaukee, UWM Art Museum, University of Wisconsin, *Reactions to the War: European Art, 1914–1925*, 3 November–14 December 1986.

West Berlin, Martin-Gropius-Bau, *Berlin, Berlin: Die Ausstellung zur Geschichte der Stadt*, 1987.

Madison, Elvehjem Museum of Art, University of Wisconsin, *The Modern Print in Germany 1881–1949*, 18 April–7 June 1987.

Milwaukee, Patrick and Beatrice Haggerty Museum of Art, Marquette University, *Berlin in the 1920s and 1930s: A City of Decadence, Revolt, and Chaos—Watercolors and Drawings of Bruno Voigt*, 11 June–2 August 1987.

West Berlin, Berlinische Galerie, Museum für Moderne Kunst, Photographie und Architektur im Martin-Gropius-Bau, *Ich und die Stadt: Mensch und Grossstadt in der deutschen Kunst des 20. Jahrhunderts*, 15 August–22 November 1987.

Minneapolis, University Art Museum, University of Minnesota, *Berlin: Art and Metropolis—Works on Paper*, 8 September–11 October 1987.

Milwaukee, Milwaukee Art Museum, *Hidden Treasures: Wisconsin Collects Paintings and Sculpture*, 11 September–1 November 1987.

West Berlin, Berlin Museum, *Stadtbilder: Berlin in der Malerei vom 17. Jahrhundert bis zur Gegenwart*, 19 September–1 November 1987.

Milwaukee, Patrick and Beatrice Haggerty Museum of Art, Marquette University, *Selected Acquisitions 1985–87*, 21 January–13 March 1988.

Milwaukee, Patrick and Beatrice Haggerty Museum of Art, Marquette University, *Selections from the Permanent Collection and Loans from Private Collections*, 18 April–17 September 1988.

West Berlin, Berlinische Galerie, Museum für Moderne Kunst, Photographie und Architektur im Martin-Gropius-Bau, *Stationen der Moderne: Die bedeutenden Kunstausstellungen des 20. Jahrhunderts in Deutschland*, 25 September 1988–6 January 1989.

Los Angeles County Museum of Art, *German Expressionism 1915–1925: The Second Generation*, 9 October–31 December 1988 (traveled to Fort Worth Art Museum, 2 February–9 April 1989; Düsseldorf, Kunstmuseum, 18 May–9 July 1989; Halle, Staatliche Galerie Moritzburg, 9 August–30 September 1989).

Milwaukee, Milwaukee Art Museum, *The Velvet Line: Drypoint Prints from Milwaukee Collections*, 12 January–12 March 1989.

Ingelheim am Rhein, Museum-Altes-Rathaus, *Der Traum von einer neuen Welt: Berlin 1910–1933*, 22 April–4 June 1989.

Los Angeles County Museum of Art, *The Apocalyptic Landscapes of Ludwig Meidner*, 12 October–17 December 1989 (traveled to West Berlin, Berlinische Galerie, Museum für Moderne Kunst, Photographie und Architektur im Martin-Gropius-Bau, 1 February–8 April 1990).

Atlanta, High Museum of Art, *Art in Berlin 1815–1989*, 14 November 1989–14 January 1990.

Milwaukee, UWM Art Museum, University of Wisconsin, *Face, Figure and Form: Art and the Human Condition*, 19 January–4 March 1990.

Osnabrück, Kulturgeschichtliches Museum, *Felix Nussbaum: Verfemte Kunst—Exilkunst—Widerstandskunst: Die 100 wichtigsten Werke*, 6 May–18 August 1990.